THE **JFC Swing Tutorial**
Second Edition

THE JFC Swing Tutorial

Second Edition

A Guide to Constructing GUIs

Kathy Walrath
Mary Campione
Alison Huml
Sharon Zakhour

✦ Addison-Wesley

Boston • San Francisco • New York • Toronto • Montreal
London • Munich • Paris • Madrid • Capetown
Sydney • Tokyo • Singapore • Mexico City

Library of Congress Cataloging-in-Publication Data
The JFC Swing tutorial : a guide to constructing GUIs / Kathy Walrath ... [et al.].—2nd ed.
    p. cm.—(The Java series)
    Previous ed. cataloged under Walrath.
    Includes index.
    ISBN 0-201-91467-0 (pbk. : alk. paper)
  1. Graphical user interfaces (Computer systems) 2. Java foundation classes.
I. Walrath, Kathy. II. Walrath, Kathy. JFC swing tutorial. III. Series.

    QA76.9.U83W36 2004
    005.13'3—dc22

                              2003063895

ISBN 0-201-91467-0
Text printed on recycled paper
1 2 3 4 5 6 7 8 9 10—CRS—0807060504
First Printing, February 2004

Contents

CONTENTS

Preface

THIS edition of *The Java™ Tutorial* tells you how to write GUIs that use the Java Foundation Classes (JFC) "Swing" components. In this book we cover the most recent release of the Java 2 platform (v1.4.2 as of this printing). We also include information valuable to programmers using earlier releases and discuss Swing enhancements planned for the near future.

The online form of *The Java Tutorial* has covered the Swing components since their first public early-access release—Swing 0.2, which came out in July 1997. Throughout the early releases, the Tutorial kept pace with API changes and additions. Readers and reviewers kept us on our toes, helping us improve each page tremendously. Although this book has its roots in the online version, this edition has been reorganized and rewritten.

Numerous improvements have been made. First, this book uses current API (v1.4.2), has six new introductory chapters, and has an easy-to-use tabbed reference section. It reflects lessons learned by the Swing team in the years since the introduction of Swing components. Second, we cover newer features such as `JFormattedTextField`, `JSpinner`, indeterminate `JProgressBar`, mouse wheel support, the rearchitected focus subsystem, and improved support for drag and drop.

The book and CD contain more than 150 complete, working examples. The authors have worked closely with the Swing team to ensure that the code and discussions reflect recommended usage. The Swing component set has now been out for several years now and has a mature API. That, combined with the years of experience the Swing writers and engineers have had with the API, enables us to create the definitive introduction and guide for both inexperienced and advanced programmers who use Swing components.

Acknowledgments

We would like to thank every member of the Swing project. They're a great team of people who do excellent work and are fun to be around.

For this second edition, we relied on two reviewers above all others. Scott Violet, the Swing project lead, provided not only reviews of individual sections but also gave sound advice and help with overall issues. Shannon Hickey was a great help as well, advising us and reviewing how-to sections such as the technically challenging drag-and-drop section.

Philip Milne was as helpful as ever despite having moved to another company on a different continent. His contributions included providing the SpringLayout examples and reviewing changes to the table section.

Other reviewers and Swing team members that we'd like to thank include Amy Fowler, Josh Outwater, Leif Samuelsson, Mark Davidson, Igor Kushnirskiy, and Roman Poborchy. Jeff Dinkins, the manager of the Swing team, was supportive as always.

Suzie Pelouch helped us at crucial points, doing various tasks such as checking code snippets and verifying our references to API documentation.

Alan Sommerer, our manager, gave invaluable encouragement and support to the ongoing work on this book. Lisa Friendly, technical publications director and series managing editor, gave us the freedom and support necessary to do our work—and enjoy it. Steve Uhlir, director of User Experience, and Jonathan Schwartz, executive vice president of the Software Group, also contributed to an atmosphere that facilitated everyone doing their best.

We'd also like to thank the star team at Addison-Wesley: Ann Sellers, Michael Mullen, and Julie Nahil; and our diligent and patient copyeditors/proofreaders Marilyn Rash and Dianne Wood. They have been a pleasure to work with.

Finally, thank you to our readers.

About the Authors

Kathy Walrath is a senior technical writer on the Swing team at Sun Microsystems. After graduating from UC Berkeley with a B.S. in Electrical Engineering and Computer Science, she wrote extensively about UNIX, Mach, and NEXTSTEP. Since 1993, Kathy has been writing specifications and how-to guides for the Java platform.

Mary Campione used to work as a senior technical writer at Sun Microsystems, where she started writing about the Java platform in 1995. She and Kathy created the original Java Tutorial Web site and co-wrote several books based on it, including the first edition of this book. Mary graduated from Cal Poly, San Luis Obispo, with a B.S. in Computer Science and has worked as both a technical writer and a programmer.

Alison Huml is a technical writer at Sun Microsystems, where she joined The Java Tutorial team in 1997 and also works with the Security team. Alison received her B.A. in English from the University of California, Berkeley, and is currently pursuing her master's degree in Computer Science at Mills College.

Sharon Zakhour is a senior technical writer who supports the Swing and AWT teams at Sun Microsystems, where she has worked since 1999. She graduated from UC Berkeley with a B.A. in Computer Science and has worked as a programmer, developer support engineer, and technical writer for 18 years.

Before You Start

IF you haven't written and run programs using the Java platform, then please close this book and go to the "Getting Started" trail of *The Java Tutorial*. That trail will introduce the Java programming language and platform and lead you through writing and running a basic application and applet. The trail is included on this book's CD at: `JavaTutorial/getStarted/index.html`.

This book is divided into two distinct parts. The first six chapters describe general Swing concepts and introduce you to progressively more difficult code examples. The last four chapters are composed of how-to reference sections.

Our goal was to make it easy to skip around this book, choosing exactly which sections you want to read. That's why the how-to sections in the reference chapters are self-contained and tabbed. The Appendix contains several handy troubleshooting guides. We also provide the following navigational aids:

- The contents (page v) lists all of the chapters in this book, and the major sections within them.

- The beginning of each chapter describes what you can expect to learn and has its own table of contents that lists the sections within it.

- Within each chapter, you can expect to find links to related information whenever appropriate.

- The Index (page 763) is a traditional book index.

At the back of this book, The Java Tutorial CD description lists the contents of the CD-ROM. In particular, it includes *The Java Tutorial* in HTML and all of the source code for the examples in this book. The CD also includes most of the resources referenced in this book, such as the API documentation and the online magazine—*The Swing Connection*.

It's easy to translate the URLs in the book to their locations on the CD-ROM; for example, the URL for JApplet API documentation is:

    http://java.sun.com/j2se/1.4.2/docs/api/javax/swing/JApplet.html

It can be found on the CD at:

    Docs/j2sdk14-api/docs/api/javax/swing/JApplet.html

If you need some information that's not in this book or in the API documentation, we recommend that you consult these resources:

- The JavaDesktop community Web site, especially its articles and forums at: http://javadesktop.org/ and http://javadesktop.org/forums/.
- The online version of The Java Tutorial: http://java.sun.com/docs/books/tutorial/index.html.

In addition, you can find other resources listed on the following page:

    http://java.sun.com/docs/books/tutorial/information/resources.html

1

Getting Started with Swing

THIS chapter gives you a brief introduction to using the Java™ Foundation Classes (JFC) Swing packages. After telling you about JFC and Swing, it helps you get the necessary software and walks you through how to compile and run a program that uses the Swing packages. Next, it shows you how to run programs using Java Web Start.

The next chapter, Learning Swing by Example (page 11), will build on these first steps to help you create several increasingly more complex examples. For now, let's start with the basics.

About the JFC and Swing

JFC is short for Java Foundation Classes, which encompass a group of features for building graphical user interfaces (GUIs[1]) and adding rich graphics functionality and interactivity to Java applications. JFC was first announced at the 1997 JavaOne[SM] developer conference. It is defined as containing the features shown in Table 1.[2]

Table 1: Features of the Java Foundation Classes

Feature	Description
Swing GUI Components	Includes everything from buttons to split panes to tables. See screenshots of all the components in A Visual Index to Swing Components (page 37) in Chapter 3.
Pluggable Look-and-Feel Support	Gives any program that uses Swing components a choice of look and feel. For example, the same program can use either the Java or the Windows look and feel. Many more look-and-feel packages are available from various sources. As of v1.4.2, the Java platform supports the GTK+ look and feel, which makes hundreds of existing look and feels available to Swing programs.
Accessibility API	Enables assistive technologies, such as screen readers and Braille displays, to get information from the user interface.
Java 2D[TM] API	Enables developers to easily incorporate high-quality 2D graphics, text, and images in applications and applets. Java 2D includes extensive APIs for generating and sending high-quality output to printing devices.
Drag-and-Drop Support	Provides the ability to drag and drop between Java applications and native applications.
Internationalization	Allows developers to build applications that can interact with users worldwide in their own languages and cultural conventions. With the input method framework developers can build applications that accept text in languages that use thousands of different characters, such as Japanese, Chinese, or Korean.

This book concentrates on the Swing components. We help you choose the appropriate components for your GUI, tell you how to use them, and give you the background information you need to use them effectively. We also discuss other JFC features as they apply to Swing components.

---

[1] The acronym for graphical user interface, GUI, is pronounced "gooey."

[2] See the JFC home page for more information on JFC features: `http://java.sun.com/products/jfc/index.html`.

Note: "Swing" was the code name of the project that developed the new components. Although unofficial, it's frequently used to refer to the new components and related API. "Swing" is immortalized in the package names for the Swing API, which begin with `javax.swing`.

Which Releases Contain the Swing API?

The short answer is that the Swing API has been included in the Java 2 platform, Standard Edition (J2SE™) since its initial release (1.2). A 1.4.2 release of the Java 2 platform is included on the CD that accompanies this book. You can also download the latest release from the Sun Microsystems Web site at: `http://java.sun.com/j2se/`.

This book concentrates on the Swing API in the Java 2 platform, Standard Edition, v1.4.2. Except where noted, the code in this book works, without change, with earlier J2SE releases.[1] We also include notes about a few important changes expected in 1.5.

Which Swing Packages Should I Use?

The Swing API is powerful, flexible—and immense. In release 1.4 of the Java platform, the Swing API has 17 public packages:

`javax.accessibility`	`javax.swing.plaf`	`javax.swing.text.html`
`javax.swing`	`javax.swing.plaf.basic`	`javax.swing.text.parser`
`javax.swing.border`	`javax.swing.plaf.metal`	`javax.swing.text.rtf`
`javax.swing.colorchooser`	`javax.swing.plaf.multi`	`javax.swing.tree`
`javax.swing.event`	`javax.swing.table`	`javax.swing.undo`
`javax.swing.filechooser`	`javax.swing.text`	

Fortunately, most programs use only a small subset of the API. This book sorts out the API for you, giving you examples of common code and pointing you to methods and classes you're likely to need. Most of the code in this book uses only one or two Swing packages:

- `javax.swing`
- `javax.swing.event` (not always required)

---

[1] We recommend that you use the latest version of the Java 2 platform. However, it is possible to use the Swing components with releases as early as 1.1. We give tips for using earlier releases where necessary.

Compiling and Running Swing Programs

This section explains how to compile and run a Swing application. The compilation instructions work for all Swing programs—applets, as well as applications. The following are the steps you need to follow:

1. Install the latest release of the Java 2 platform, if you haven't already done so.
2. Create a program that uses Swing components.
3. Compile the program.
4. Run the program.

Note: If you're new to writing and compiling programs that use the Java platform, read *The Java Tutorial* trail "Getting Started" first; it's available online and on the CD at: JavaTutorial/ getStarted/index.html. That trail also explains common errors that users may encounter.

Install the Latest Release of the Java 2 Platform

You can download the latest release of the J2SE SDK for free from http://java.sun.com/ j2se. Version 1.4.2 of the J2SE SDK is included on the CD that accompanies this book.

Create a Program That Uses Swing Components

You can use a simple program we provide, called HelloWorldSwing, that brings up the GUI shown in Figure 1. The program is in a single file, HelloWorldSwing.java.[1] When you save this file, you must match the spelling and capitalization of its name exactly. If you prefer to type in the file's code yourself, you can find the full code starting on page 12 in Chapter 2.

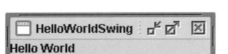

Figure 1   The HelloWorldSwing application.

Compile the Program

Your next step is to compile the program. Here's an example of compiling HelloWorld-Swing.java:

---

[1]   You can find HelloWorldSwing.java here: JavaTutorial/uiswing/14start/example-1dot4/ HelloWorldSwing.java.

```
javac HelloWorldSwing.java
```

If you can't compile, make sure you're using the compiler in a recent release of the Java platform, such as 1.4.2 included on this book's CD. Once you've updated your SDK, you should be able to use the programs in this book without changes. Another common mistake is installing the Java Runtime Environment (JRE) and not the full Software Development Kit (SDK) needed to compile these programs. Refer to the "Getting Started" trail of *The Java Tutorial* to help you solve any compiling problems you encounter.[1] Another installation troubleshooting guide for the Java 2 platform is online at: `http://servlet.java.sun.com/help/installation/`.

Run the Program

After you compile the program successfully, you can run it. Assuming that your program uses a standard look and feel—such as the Java, Windows, or GTK+ look and feel—you can use the interpreter to run the program without adding anything to your class path. For example:

```
java HelloWorldSwing
```

For programs that use a nonstandard look and feel or any other nonstandard code package, you must make sure that the necessary classes are in the class path. For example:

Solaris:
```
java -classpath.:/home/me/lnfdir/newlnf.jar HelloWorldSwing
```

Microsoft Windows:
```
java -classpath .;C:\java\lnfdir\newlnf.jar HelloWorldSwing
```

Alternatively, you can launch your program from a Web browser using Java Web Start.

Running Programs Using Java Web Start

Java Web Start is a technology that simplifies the distribution of applications. With a click on a Web page link, you can launch full-featured applications without a complicated download and installation process. The first time you launch an application, Java Web Start automatically downloads all necessary files. It then caches them on your computer so the application can be quickly relaunched from a desktop shortcut or from a Web browser. Java Web Start checks for updates each time you run a remote application and downloads any updated files automatically.

---

[1] The "Getting Started" trail is available online and on this book's CD at: `JavaTutorial/getStarted/index.html`.

In 1.4.1 and later releases of the Java platform, Java Web Start is shipped as part of the platform. So, if you have J2SE or JRE v1.4.1 or higher, you already have Java Web Start installed. When you install a version of the Java platform with Java Web Start, on most platforms you'll see a Java Web Start shortcut on your desktop. (See Figure 2.)

Figure 2   The Java Web Start desktop shortcut.

To test whether your browser can launch an application using Java Web Start, point it to one of the following places and click the "Launch Java™ Web Start" link:

- `JavaTutorial/tutorial/uiswing/14start/HelloJWS.html` (on this book's CD)
- `http://java.sun.com/docs/books/tutorial/uiswing/14start/HelloJWS.html`

You should see a Java Web Start splash screen. (See Figure 3.)

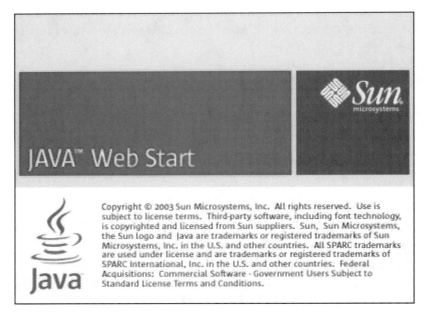

Figure 3   The Java Web Start splash screen.

The application is then downloaded, and you should see what's shown in Figure 4.

You're running an application using Java™ Web Start!

Figure 4   The HelloJWS[1] application launched from a Web browser using Java Web Start.

If you're unable to launch this application, you should check the Java Web Start Trouble-shooting (page 733) guide in the Appendix.

Questions and Exercises

Questions

1. Which package is required for all Swing applications?
2. What is Java Web Start and where can you get it?

Exercises

1. Show how you would set the class path when launching an application.
2. Test if your browser is Java Web Start enabled by following the instructions listed in Running Programs Using Java Web Start (page 7).

Answers

You can find answers to these Questions and Exercises online:

```
http://java.sun.com/docs/books/tutorial/uiswing/QandE/answers.html
```

Example Programs

You can find source files for all the examples from this chapter on the CD and online:

```
JavaTutorial/uiswing/14start/example-1dot4/index.html
```

```
http://java.sun.com/docs/books/tutorial/uiswing/14start/
example-1dot4/index.html
```

---

[1]   You can find the HelloJWS.java source files here: JavaTutorial/uiswing/14start/example-1dot4/index.html#HelloJWS.

The preceding URLs take you to an index that has links to the files required by each example. You can go directly to the entry for a particular example by adding *#ExampleName* to the URL. Most examples have a "Run" link in the example index which executes the example using Java Web Start technology.

Example	Where Described	Notes
HelloWorldSwing	page 6	Demonstrates the basic code in every Swing program.
HelloJWS	page 9	Tests whether you can launch a Java Web Start-enabled application.

Learning Swing by Example

THIS chapter explains the concepts you need to use Swing components in building a user interface. First we examine the simplest Swing application you can write. Then we present several progressively complicated examples of creating user interfaces using components in the java.swing package. We cover several Swing components, such as buttons, labels, and text areas. The handling of events is also discussed, as are layout management and accessibility.

Most of the topics this chapter discusses are covered in depth in later chapters—for example, you can get detailed information on how to use components from Chapter 7, Components Reference—but this chapter gives you the grand tour. This chapter ends with a set of questions and exercises so you can test yourself on what you've learned.

Example One: Your First Swing Program

Figure 1 is a snapshot of the `HelloWorldSwing`[1] program.

Figure 1   The `HelloWorldSwing` application.

And here's the full code for `HelloWorldSwing`:

```
import javax.swing.*;

public class HelloWorldSwing {
    /**
     * Create the GUI and show it.  For thread safety,
     * this method should be invoked from the
     * event-dispatching thread.
     */
    private static void createAndShowGUI() {
        //Make sure we have nice window decorations.
        JFrame.setDefaultLookAndFeelDecorated(true);

        //Create and set up the window.
        JFrame frame = new JFrame("HelloWorldSwing");
        frame.setDefaultCloseOperation(JFrame.EXIT_ON_CLOSE);
```

---

[1] To run `HelloWorldSwing` using Java Web Start, click the `HelloWorldSwing` link on the `RunExamples/start.html` page on the CD. You can find the source files here: `JavaTutorial/uiswing/start/example-1dot4/index.html#HelloWorldSwing`.

```
        //Add the ubiquitous "Hello World" label.
        JLabel label = new JLabel("Hello World");
        frame.getContentPane().add(label);

        //Display the window.
        frame.pack();
        frame.setVisible(true);
    }

    public static void main(String[] args) {
        //Schedule a job for the event-dispatching thread:
        //creating and showing this application's GUI.
        javax.swing.SwingUtilities.invokeLater(new Runnable() {
            public void run() {
                createAndShowGUI();
            }
        });
    }
}
```

This is one of the simplest Swing applications you can write. It doesn't do much, but the code demonstrates the basic code in every Swing program:

- Import the pertinent packages.
- Set up a top-level container.
- Display the container.
- Be thread-safe.

The first line imports the main Swing package:

```
import javax.swing.*;
```

This is the only package that HelloWorldSwing needs. However, most Swing programs also need to import two AWT packages:

```
import java.awt.*;
import java.awt.event.*;
```

These packages are required because Swing components use the AWT infrastructure, including the AWT event model. The event model governs how a component reacts to events such as button clicks and mouse motion. You'll learn more in Handling Events (page 19).

Every program with a Swing GUI must have at least one top-level Swing container. A top-level Swing container provides the support Swing components need for painting and event handling. There are three commonly used top-level Swing containers: JFrame, JDialog, and (for applets) JApplet. Each JFrame object implements a single main window, and each

JDialog implements a secondary window (a window dependent on another window). Each JApplet object implements an applet's display area within a browser window.[1]

The HelloWorldSwing example has only one top-level container, a JFrame. Implemented as an instance of the JFrame class, a frame is a window that, by default, has decorations such as a border, a title, and buttons for iconifying and closing the window. Applications with a GUI typically use at least one frame.

Here's the code that sets up and shows the frame:

```
JFrame.setDefaultLookAndFeelDecorated(true);
JFrame frame = new JFrame("HelloWorldSwing");
...
frame.pack();
frame.setVisible(true);
```

> **Version Note:** The following line of code applies decorative borders and window titles to frames. However, it works only as of v1.4. If you're using an earlier version, you'll need to comment out this code.
>
> ```
> JFrame.setDefaultLookAndFeelDecorated(true);
> ```

With the exception of top-level containers, such as JFrame, all Swing components descend from the JComponent class. HelloWorldSwing uses a JComponent descendant called JLabel, which displays the text "Hello World". These two lines of code construct and then add the JLabel component to the frame:

```
JLabel label = new JLabel("Hello World");
frame.getContentPane().add(label);
```

Note that the label is added to the frame's *content pane* instead of to the frame itself. Every top-level container has a content pane that contains, directly or indirectly, all the visible components (except for menus and window decorations) in the top-level container. More information about content panes is in the Using Top-Level Containers (page 46) section in Chapter 3.

> **Version Note:** We anticipate that in v1.5 invoking add on a top-level container will have the same effect as invoking it on the top-level container's content pane.

To make the program exit when the Close button ⊠ is clicked, we include this code:

```
frame.setDefaultCloseOperation(JFrame.EXIT_ON_CLOSE);
```

---

[1] JApplets are covered in How to Make Applets (page 149) in Chapter 7.

Version Note: In older programs, instead of a call to setDefaultCloseOperation, you might see code like the following:

```
frame.addWindowListener(new WindowAdapter() {
    public void windowClosing(WindowEvent e) {
        System.exit(0);
    }
});
```

It still works, but unnecessarily adds a class, which bloats your program. You can find further information on window events in How to Make Frames (Main Windows) (page 236) in Chapter 7.

The final bit of code in HelloWorldSwing—and in all of our examples—looks like this:

```
javax.swing.SwingUtilities.invokeLater(new Runnable() {
    public void run() {
        /* create and show the GUI */
    }
});
```

You can copy this code and use it as-is. It might look daunting, but we recommend it because it ensures that the GUI won't have a thread-safety problem that could break the UI before it even appears onscreen. For more information, you can read How to Use Threads (page 632) in Chapter 9.

Example Two: SwingApplication

Let's look at another simple program, SwingApplication (see Figure 2).[1] Each time the user clicks the button (JButton), the label (JLabel) is updated.

Figure 2   The simple GUI of SwingApplication presents a JButton and a JLabel.

---

[1] To run SwingApplication using Java Web Start, click the SwingApplication link on the RunExamples/learn.html page on the CD. You can find the source files here: JavaTutorial/ uiswing/learn/example-1dot4/index.html#SwingApplication.

Look and Feel

The screenshots in Figure 3 show the GUI of the SwingApplication, each one with a different look and feel.

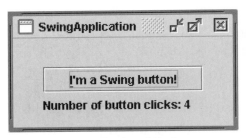
Java Look and Feel

GTK+ Look and Feel

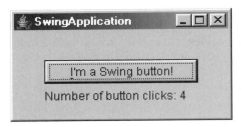
Windows Look and Feel

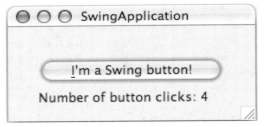
Mac OS Look and Feel

Figure 3   Four different look and feels.

Version Note: The appearance of many look and feels changes from release to release. For example, in v1.5 we expect the Java look and feel to use slightly different colors and decorations, though components will stay the same size as before.

Swing allows you to specify which look and feel your program uses—Java, GTK+, Windows, and so on. The code in boldface type in the following snippet shows you how Swing-Application specifies that it should use the Java look and feel:

```
String lookAndFeel = null;
...
lookAndFeel = UIManager.getCrossPlatformLookAndFeelClassName();
...
```

```
try {
    UIManager.setLookAndFeel(lookAndFeel);
} catch (Exception e) { }
...// Create and show the GUI...
```

This code essentially says, "I don't care what the user has chosen. Use the cross-platform (Java) look and feel." You can learn more in the section How to Set the Look and Feel (page 628) in Chapter 9.

Setting up Buttons and Labels

Like most GUIs, the SwingApplication GUI contains a button and a label. (Unlike most GUIs, that's about all that SwingApplication contains.) Here's the code that initializes the button:

```
JButton button = new JButton("I'm a Swing button!");
button.setMnemonic('i');
button.addActionListener(/*... an action listener...*/);
```

The first line creates the button. The second sets the letter "i" as the mnemonic that the user can use to simulate a button click. For example, in the Java look and feel, typing Alt-i does this. The third line registers an event handler for the button click, as discussed later in this section.

Here's the code that initializes and manipulates the label:

```
...// where instance variables are declared:
private static String labelPrefix = "Number of button clicks: ";
private int numClicks = 0;

...// in GUI initialization code:
final JLabel label = new JLabel(labelPrefix + "0    ");
...
label.setLabelFor(button);

...// in the event handler for button clicks:
label.setText(labelPrefix + numClicks);
```

It's pretty straightforward, except for the line that invokes the setLabelFor method. That code exists solely as a hint to assistive technologies, such as screen readers, that the label describes the button.[1]

---

[1] Assistive technologies enable people with disabilities to use computers. For more information, see How to Support Assistive Technologies (page 519) in Chapter 9.

Now that you know how to set up buttons, you also know much of what's needed to set up check boxes and radio buttons, as they all inherit from the AbstractButton class.

Check boxes are similar to radio buttons, but by convention their selection models are different. Any number of check boxes in a group—none, some, or all—can be selected. On the other hand, by convention only one button can be selected from a group of radio buttons. Figure 4 shows two programs that use check boxes and radio buttons. You'll get a closer look at radio buttons in Example Six: VoteDialog (page 30) later in this chapter.

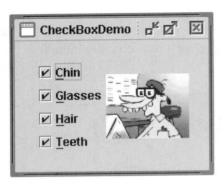

Figure 4   Standard two-state buttons: check boxes and radio buttons.

Adding Components to Containers

SwingApplication groups its label and button in a container (a JPanel) before adding the components to the frame. Here's the code that initializes the container:

```
JPanel panel = new JPanel(new GridLayout 0,1);
panel.add(button);
panel.add(label);
panel.setBorder(BorderFactory.createEmptyBorder(...));
```

The first line creates the container and assigns it a *layout manager*—an object that determines the size and position of each component added to the container. The code new Grid-Layout(0,1) creates a layout manager that forces the container's contents to be displayed in a single column, with every component having the same size.

The next two lines add the button and the label to the container. The last line adds a border to it. We'll discuss the border in the next section.

Layout management concepts are discussed in Chapter 4, Laying Out Components within a Container (page 87). Individual layout managers, such as GridLayout, are covered in Chapter 8, Layout Manager Reference (page 457).

Adding Borders around Components

Figure 5 is another look at the SwingApplication GUI.

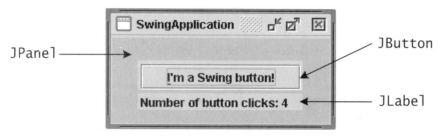

Figure 5   SwingApplication with the JPanel shaded.

Notice that there's extra space surrounding the JPanel on all four edges. Here's the code that adds the padding:

```
panel.setBorder(BorderFactory.createEmptyBorder(
                          30, //top
                          30, //left
                          10, //bottom
                          30) //right
                          );
```

The code creates and sets a border that provides some empty space around the container's contents—30 extra pixels on the top, left, and right and 10 extra pixels on the bottom. Borders are a feature that JPanel inherits from the JComponent class. A Border object isn't a JComponent; instead, it's used by one or more JComponents to paint the component's edges. You can learn more in How to Use Borders (page 535) in Chapter 9.

Handling Events

Every time the user types a character or pushes a mouse button, an event occurs. Any object can be notified of the event. All it has to do is implement the appropriate interface and be registered as an *event listener* on the appropriate *event source.*

SwingApplication class implements an event handler for button clicks (action events). Here's the relevant code:

```
public class SwingApplication implements ActionListener {
    ...
        JButton button = new JButton("I'm a Swing button!");
        button.addActionListener(this);
    ....

    public void actionPerformed(ActionEvent e) {
        numClicks++;
        label.setText(labelPrefix + numClicks);
    }
}
```

Every event handler requires three pieces of code:

1. In the declaration for the event handler class, one line of code specifies that the class either implements a listener interface or extends a class that implements a listener interface. For example:

    ```
    public class MyClass implements ActionListener {
    ```

2. Another line of code registers an instance of the event handler class as a listener on one or more components. For example:

    ```
    someComponent.addActionListener(instanceOfMyClass);
    ```

3. The event handler class has code that implements the methods in the listener interface. For example:

    ```
    public void actionPerformed(ActionEvent e) {
        ...//code that reacts to the action...
    }
    ```

In general, to detect when the user clicks an onscreen button (or does the keyboard equivalent) a program must have an object that implements the ActionListener interface. The program must register this object as an action listener on the button (the event source) using the addActionListener method. When the user clicks the onscreen button, the button fires an action event. This results in the invocation of the action listener's actionPerformed method (the only method in the ActionListener interface). (See Figure 6.) The single argument to the method is an ActionEvent object that gives information about the event and its source.

Figure 6   When the user clicks a button, the button's action listeners are notified.

Swing components can generate many kinds of events. Table 1 lists a few examples.

Table 1: Some Events and Associated Event Listeners

Act that Results in the Event	Listener Type
User clicks a button, presses Enter while typing in a text field, or chooses a menu item	`ActionListener`
User closes a frame (main window)	`WindowListener`
User presses a mouse button while the cursor is over a component	`MouseListener`
User moves the mouse over a component	`MouseMotionListener`
Component becomes visible	`ComponentListener`
Component gets the keyboard focus	`FocusListener`
Table or list selection changes	`ListSelectionListener`
Any property in a component changes such as the text on a label	`PropertyChangeListener`

Note: Event-handling code executes in a single thread, the *event-dispatching thread*. This ensures that each event handler finishes execution before the next one starts. The `actionPerformed` method in the preceding example executes in the event-dispatching thread. Painting code also executes in the event-dispatching thread. Therefore, event-handling code should execute quickly so that the program's GUI stays responsive. If an event takes too long to execute, the GUI will freeze—that is, it won't repaint or respond to mouse clicks. Chapter 5, Writing Event Listeners (page 107), has more information.

Example Three: CelsiusConverter

Our next example, `CelsiusConverter`,[1] is actually useful: It's a simple temperature conversion tool. When the user enters a temperature in degrees Celsius and clicks the **Convert** button, a label displays the equivalent temperature in degrees Fahrenheit (see Figure 7).

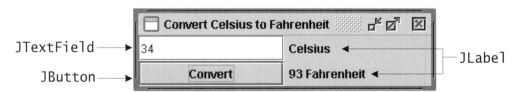

Figure 7   The `CelsiusConverter` GUI.

---

[1] To run `CelsiusConverter` using Java Web Start, click the `CelsiusConverter` link on the `RunExamples/learn.html` page on the CD. You can find the source files here: `JavaTutorial/uiswing/learn/example-1dot4/index.html#CelsiusConverter`.

Let's examine the code to see how `CelsiusConverter` parses the number entered in the `JTextField`. First, here's the code that sets up the `JTextField`:

```
JTextField tempCelsius = null;
...
tempCelsius = new JTextField(5);
```

The integer argument passed in the `JTextField` constructor—5 in the example—indicates the number of columns in the field. This number is used along with metrics provided by the current font to calculate the field's preferred width, which is used by layout managers. This number doesn't limit how many characters the user can enter.

We want to perform the conversion when the user clicks the button or presses Enter in the text field. To do so, we add an action event listener to the `convertTemp` button and `tempCelsius` text field.

```
convertTemp.addActionListener(this);
tempCelsius.addActionListener(this);
...
public void actionPerformed(ActionEvent event) {
    //Parse degrees Celsius as a double and convert to Fahrenheit.
    int tempFahr = (int)((Double.parseDouble(tempCelsius.getText()))
                    * 1.8 + 32);
    fahrenheitLabel.setText(tempFahr + " Fahrenheit");
}
```

The event-handling code goes into the `actionPerformed` method. It calls the `getText` method on the text field, `tempCelsius`, to retrieve the data within it. Next it uses the `parseDouble` method to parse the text as a double-precision floating-point number before converting the temperature and casting the result to an integer. Finally, it calls the `setText` method on the `fahrenheitLabel` to make the label display the converted temperature.

Example Four: An Improved CelsiusConverter

Now that we've examined `CelsiusConverter`, let's improve it. First, we'll spiff it up by adding colored text. Next, we'll improve the button by making it the default button and adding a graphic. Finally, we'll refine the text field so that only numbers are accepted.

Adding HTML

You can specify the appearance of any Swing component's text in a couple of ways. First, you can call the `setFont` method to specify the font and the `setColor` method to set the color. Second, when you want to vary the font or color within the text or insert formatting such as line breaks, you can use HTML tags.

Buttons, labels, and many other Swing components let you use HTML to specify the format of the text displayed by the component. Figure 8 shows `CelsiusConverter2`, which uses HTML to specify multiple text colors on the `fahrenheitLabel`. The code follows the figure.

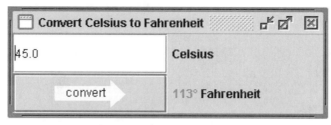

Figure 8   The improved `CelsiusConverter2`[1] application.

```
//Set fahrenheitLabel to new value and
//use font colors based on temperature.
String colorString = "red";
if (tempFahr <= 32) {
    colorString = "blue";
} else if (tempFahr <= 80) {
    colorString = "green";
} //if tempFahr > 80, colorString remains "red"
fahrenheitLabel.setText("<html><font color= " + colorString + ">" +
                        tempFahr + "&#176</font> Fahrenheit </html>");
```

To use HTML in a component's text, simply place the `<HTML>` tag at the beginning of the text string and then use any valid HTML code in the remainder of the string. The preceding code uses the `<font>` tag to specify text color and the HTML code `"&#176"` to display the degree symbol. More information on adding HTML to components is available in Using HTML in Swing Components (page 43) in Chapter 3.

Note: Some older releases don't support HTML text in buttons. In those that don't (such as Swing 1.1) putting HTML in a button results in an ugly-looking button whose label starts with `<HTML>`. You can find out when HTML support was added to each component by consulting the Version Note on page 46.

Adding an Icon

Some Swing components can be decorated with an *icon*—a fixed-size image. In Swing, an icon is an object that adheres to the `Icon` interface. Swing provides a particularly useful

---

[1] To run `CelsiusConverter2` using Java Web Start, click the `CelsiusConverter2` link on the `RunExamples/learn.html` page on the CD. You can find the source files here: `JavaTutorial/uiswing/learn/example-1dot4/index.html#CelsiusConverter2`.

implementation of the Icon interface, ImageIcon, which paints an icon from a GIF, JPEG, or PNG image.[1] Here's the code that adds the arrow graphic to the convertTemp button:

```
ImageIcon convertIcon = createImageIcon("images/convert.gif",
                                        "Convert temperature");
...
convertTemp = new JButton(convertIcon);
```

The createImageIcon method (used in the preceding snippet) is one we use in many of our code samples. The first argument specifies the file to load. The second argument provides a description of the icon that assistive technologies can use. For details, see How to Use Icons (page 603) in Chapter 9.

Setting the Default Button

Only one button in a top-level container can be the default button. The default button typically has a highlighted appearance and acts as though clicked whenever the top-level container has the keyboard focus and the user presses the Enter (or Return) key. The exact implementation depends on the look and feel.

We made the convertTemp button the default button with the following code:

```
//Set the button to be default button in the frame.
converterFrame.getRootPane().setDefaultButton(convertTemp);
```

Invoking getRootPane().setDefaultButton on a top-level container, such as converter-Frame (a JFrame) makes the specified button the default for that container. You might be wondering what a root pane is. Well, every top-level container has one—it works behind the scenes to manage details such as the content pane and the menu bar. You generally don't need to know anything more about root panes to use Swing components.

Creating a Formatted Text Field

In the original CelsiusConverter application, you could enter alphabetic or special characters in the text field. If the **Convert** button was pressed when the text was invalid, a Number-FormatException was thrown and the FahrenheitLabel was not updated.

CelsiusConverter2 prevents the user from entering anything but a number by replacing the JTextField with a JFormattedTextField. Formatted text fields were added in v1.4. They provide a way for developers to easily specify the legal set of characters that can be entered into a text component. In the following code, we use java.text.DecimalFormat to ensure that the text field accepts only numbers.

---

[1] Support for PNG (Portable Network Graphics) images was added to the Java platform in the 1.3 release.

```
//Create the format for the text field and the formatted text field
tempCelsius = new JFormattedTextField(
                              new java.text.DecimalFormat("##0.0#"));
```

Formatted text fields are covered in depth in How to Use Formatted Text Fields (page 221) in Chapter 7.

Example Five: LunarPhases

This section LunarPhases,[1] is a more complicated example of how to use images in your application. As a bonus, you'll also see how to implement combo boxes. Figure 9 shows two pictures of the LunarPhases application.

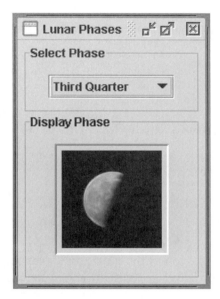 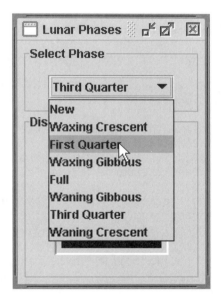

Figure 9   Two screenshots of the LunarPhases application.

In this program, the user chooses the lunar phase from the combo box and the selected phase is shown in the lower panel. This is the first example we've seen that uses multiple panels to group components.

---

[1] To run LunarPhases using Java Web Start, click the LunarPhases link on the RunExamples/ learn.html page on the CD. You can find the source files here: JavaTutorial/uiswing/learn/ example-1dot4/index.html#LunarPhases.

LunarPhases has three panels, as shown in Figure 10.

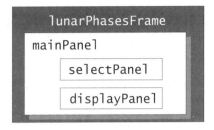

Figure 10   A depiction of the main panel and two subpanels in LunarPhases.

The following code constructs all three panels and adds the two subpanels (selectPanel and displayPanel) to the mainPanel.

```
//Create the phase selection and display panels.
selectPanel = new JPanel();
displayPanel = new JPanel();

//Add various widgets to the subpanels.
addWidgets();

//Create the main panel to contain the two sub panels.
mainPanel = new JPanel();
mainPanel.setLayout(new BoxLayout(mainPanel, BoxLayout.PAGE_AXIS));
mainPanel.setBorder(BorderFactory.createEmptyBorder(5,5,5,5));

//Add the select and display panels to the main panel.
mainPanel.add(selectPanel);
mainPanel.add(displayPanel);
```

When we put the subpanels in the main panel, it is the job of the main panel's layout manager to make sure the subpanels are positioned correctly. The default layout manager for JPanel is FlowLayout, which simply positions components in the container from left to right in the order they're added. In the previous code snippet, we used a layout manager called BoxLayout to position the subpanels more precisely.

Using Layout Managers

The Java platform supplies six commonly used layout managers: BorderLayout, BoxLayout, FlowLayout, GridLayout, GridBagLayout, and SpringLayout.[1]

---

[1]   SpringLayout was added in release 1.4 of the Java platform.

As we mentioned before, all JPanel objects use FlowLayout by default. On the other hand, content panes (the main containers in JApplet, JDialog, and JFrame objects) use Border-Layout by default.

As a rule, the only time you have to think about layout managers is when you create a JPanel or add components to a content pane. If you don't like the default layout manager that a panel or content pane uses, you can use a different one, either by specifying one when creating a panel or by invoking the setLayout method. For example, here's the code for creating a panel that uses BorderLayout:

```
JPanel pane = new JPanel(new BorderLayout());
```

Here's an example of setting the layout manager of the default content pane:

```
Container contentPane = frame.getContentPane();
contentPane.setLayout(new FlowLayout());
```

Version Note: We anticipate that in v1.5 invoking setLayout on a top-level container will have the same effect as invoking it on the top-level container's content pane.

When you add components to a panel or a content pane, the arguments you specify to the add method depend on the layout manager that the panel or content pane is using. Layout is further discussed in Chapter 4, Laying Out Components within a Container (page 87). Be sure to also check the how-to sections for particular layout managers in Chapter 8 for details.

Compound Borders

In previous examples, we added a simple border to create a buffer of space around components. In this example, both subpanels, selectPanel and displayPanel, have a *compound* border, which consists of a titled border (an outlined border with a title) and an empty border (to add extra space), as shown in Figure 11.

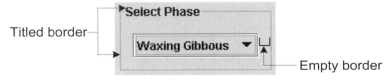

Figure 11   The compound border used in selectPanel.

The code for the selectPanel border follows. The displayPanel sets its own border in the same way.

```
//Add border around the select panel
selectPanel.setBorder(BorderFactory.createCompoundBorder(
                BorderFactory.createTitledBorder("Select Phase"),
                BorderFactory.createEmptyBorder(5,5,5,5)));
```

Combo Boxes

This example uses a combo box to present a group of choices to the user. Combo boxes can be either editable, with a text field that allows the user to enter a choice not in the group, or uneditable (the default), such as the one shown in Figure 12.

Figure 12   An uneditable combo box, before and after the user clicks it.

Combo boxes are useful for displaying one-of-many choices when space is limited. This code in LunarPhases.java creates an uneditable combo box, phaseChoices, and sets it up:

```
JComboBox phaseChoices = null;
...
//Create combo box with lunar phase choices.
String[] phases = { "New", "Waxing Crescent", "First Quarter",
                    "Waxing Gibbous", "Full", "Waning Gibbous",
                    "Third Quarter", "Waning Crescent" };
phaseChoices = new JComboBox(phases);
phaseChoices.setSelectedIndex(START_INDEX);
```

The code initializes the combo box with an array of strings, phases. You can also put an array of icons in a combo box or initialize a combo box with a vector or custom data structure.[1] In the last line of code, the setSelectedIndex method specifies which phase of the moon should be shown when the program starts.

---

[1]   To put other types of objects in a combo box or to customize how the items in a combo box look, you need to write a custom renderer. An editable combo box would also need a custom editor. See How to Use Combo Boxes (page 176) in Chapter 7 for details.

Handling Events on a Combo Box

The combo box fires an action event when the user selects an item from the combo box's drop-down list. The following code from LunarPhases registers and implements an action listener on the combo box:

```
phaseChoices.addActionListener(this);
...
public void actionPerformed(ActionEvent event) {
    if ("comboBoxChanged".equals(event.getActionCommand())) {
        //Update the icon to display the new phase
        phaseIconLabel.setIcon(images[phaseChoices.getSelectedIndex()]);
    }
}
```

This action listener gets the newly selected item from the combo box, uses that item to find the image to display, and updates a label to display the image.

Multiple Images

In the CelsiusConverter program, we saw how to add a single ImageIcon to a button. The LunarPhases program uses eight images. Only one image is used at a time, so we have a choice as to whether we load all of them up front or load them as needed (known as "lazy image loading"). In this example, all of the images are loaded up front when the class is constructed.

```
final static int NUM_IMAGES = 8;
final static int START_INDEX = 3;

ImageIcon[] images = new ImageIcon[NUM_IMAGES];
...

//Get the images and put them into an array of ImageIcon.
for (int i = 0; i < NUM_IMAGES; i++) {
    String imageName = "images/image" + i + ".jpg";
    System.out.println("getting image: " + imageName);
    URL iconURL = LunarPhases.class.getResource(imageName);
    ImageIcon icon = new ImageIcon(iconURL);
    images[i] = icon;
}
```

Note the use of getResource, a method that searches the class path to find the image files. Loading image files is discussed in detail in How to Use Icons (page 603) in Chapter 9.

Example Six: VoteDialog

The last example in this chapter is VoteDialog.[1] It illustrates the use of dialogs and radio buttons, as shown in Figure 13.

In VoteDialog, the user casts a vote by selecting a radio button and clicking the Vote button. After the button is clicked, a dialog appears with an informational message or a follow-up question.

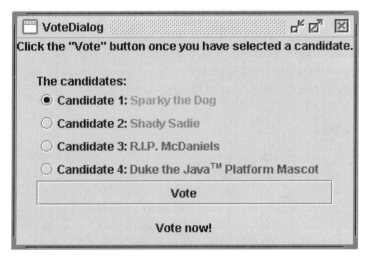

Figure 13   The VoteDialog application.

Radio Buttons

The VoteDialog application has one action listener that listens to clicks on the top-level container's button. Each time the action listener receives an event, the application determines which radio button was selected and displays the appropriate dialog.

For each group of radio buttons, you need to create a ButtonGroup instance and add each radio button to it. ButtonGroup takes care of unselecting the previously selected button when the user selects another one in the group. You should generally initialize a group of radio buttons so that one is selected. However, the API doesn't enforce this rule: A group of

---

[1] To run VoteDialog using Java Web Start, click the VoteDialog link on the RunExamples/ learn.html page on the CD. You can find the source files here: JavaTutorial/uiswing/learn/ example-1dot4/index.html#VoteDialog.

radio buttons can have no initial selection. Once the user has made a selection, exactly one button is selected from then on.

Here's the code from `VoteDialog.java` that creates the radio buttons and the `ButtonGroup` instance that controls them. The `setActionCommand` method associates a specific dialog with each radio button item. We use the `setSelected` method to specify the default selected radio button.

```
final int numButtons = 4;
JRadioButton[] radioButtons = new JRadioButton[numButtons];

final ButtonGroup group = new ButtonGroup();
...

final String defaultMessageCommand = "default";
final String yesNoCommand = "yesno";
final String yeahNahCommand = "yeahnah";
final String yncCommand = "ync";

radioButtons[0] = new JRadioButton("<html>Candidate 1:
    <font color=red>Sparky the Dog</font></html>");
radioButtons[0].setActionCommand(defaultMessageCommand);

radioButtons[1] = new JRadioButton("<html>Candidate 2:
    <font color=green>Shady Sadie</font></html>");
radioButtons[1].setActionCommand(yesNoCommand);

radioButtons[2] = new JRadioButton("<html>Candidate 3:
    <font color=blue>R.I.P. McDaniels</font></html>");
radioButtons[2].setActionCommand(yeahNahCommand);

radioButtons[3] = new JRadioButton("<html>Candidate 4:
    <font color=maroon>Duke the Java<font size=-2><sup>TM</sup>
    </font size> Platform Mascot</font></html>");
radioButtons[3].setActionCommand(yncCommand);

for (int i = 0; i < numButtons; i++) {
    group.add(radioButtons[i]);
}

//Select the first button by default.
radioButtons[0].setSelected(true);
```

Note the use of HTML code on the radio buttons, which lets us specify multiple text colors within each button.

Dialogs

In previous examples, our top-level container was always a JFrame. Another kind of top-level container is a *dialog*—a window that is more limited than a frame. To create simple, standard dialogs, you use the JOptionPane class. The dialogs that JOptionPane provides are *modal*. When a modal dialog is visible, it blocks user input to all other windows in the program.

The code for simple dialogs can be minimal. For example, Figure 14 shows an informational dialog. Here's the code that creates and shows it:

```
JOptionPane.showMessageDialog(frame, "There's no \"there\" there.");
```

Figure 14   A simple dialog.

Every dialog is dependent on a frame. When that frame is destroyed, so are its dependent dialogs. When the frame is iconified, its dependent dialogs disappear from the screen. When the frame is deiconified, its dependent dialogs return to the screen. The AWT automatically provides this behavior. You can get more information on dialogs in the section How to Make Dialogs (page 187) in Chapter 7.

Summary

This chapter glossed over many details and left some things unexplained, but now you should have an understanding of what you can build with Swing components. Also, you should have a general understanding of the following:

- How to set up the containment hierarchy of each Swing component. To add a component to a container, you use some form of the add method.
- How to use many standard GUI components, such as buttons, labels, combo boxes, and radio buttons, which you combine to create your program's GUI.

- How to change the layout of components by using layout managers.
- How events are used in Swing programs. Recall that the event-handling mechanism is based on the AWT event-handling model, in which you register event listeners on objects such as components that generate events.

Questions and Exercises

Questions

1. On what thread should GUIs be created, to guarantee thread safety?
2. Why should you be careful to minimize the time spent in event-handler code?
3. What is the purpose of the `setLabelFor` method?
4. What is the content pane?
5. Describe the three code segments that must be implemented for an event handler.
6. Which text component is best suited for controlling the format of a single line of user-entered text?
7. What is lazy image loading and why would you use it?

Exercises

1. Write the code that creates a label displaying the following text, with the italics and font size as shown in this screenshot:

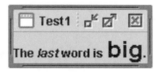

2. Convert the `LunarPhases`[1] example to use radio buttons instead of a combo box.
3. Add a **Show Dialog** check box to the `VoteDialog`[2] example so that the dialogs are shown only if this check box is selected.

---

[1] You can find the LunarPhases source files here: `JavaTutorial/uiswing/learn/example-1dot4/index.html#LunarPhases`.

[2] You can find the VoteDialog source files here: `JavaTutorial/uiswing/learn/example-1dot4/index.html#VoteDialog`.

Answers

You can find answers to the Questions and Exercises online:

    http://java.sun.com/docs/books/tutorial/uiswing/QandE/answers.html

Example Programs

You can find source files for all of the examples from this chapter on the CD and online:

    JavaTutorial/uiswing/learn/example-1dot4/index.html

    http://java.sun.com/docs/books/tutorial/uiswing/learn/
    example-1dot4/index.html

The preceding URLs take you to an index that has links to the files required by each example. You can go directly to the entry for a particular example by adding *#ExampleName* to the URL. Most examples have a "Run" link in the index which executes the example using Java Web Start technology.

Example	Where Described	Notes
HelloWorldSwing	page 12	Demonstrates the basic code in every Swing program.
SwingApplication	page 15	Demonstrates setting up buttons and labels, adding components to a container, adding borders, and event handling.
CelsiusConverter	page 21	Shows event handling and the use of text fields in a simple temperature conversion tool.
CelsiusConverter2	page 22	Adds color and boldface fonts to an improved temperature conversion tool. Also adds a graphic to the button and sets it as the default button.
LunarPhases	page 25	Shows how to use images in your application and how to implement combo boxes.
VoteDialog	page 30	Illustrates the use of dialogs and radio buttons.

Using Swing Components

THIS chapter gives you the background information you need to use Swing components. It assumes that you've successfully compiled and run programs that use Swing components and that you're familiar with basic Swing concepts. These prerequisites were covered in the previous two chapters.

This chapter doesn't tell you how to use a particular Swing components. Once you're ready to start using Swing components in your own programs, you should read the relevant how-to sections in Chapter 7, Individual Components Reference (page 147). For example, if your program needs a frame, a label, a button, and a color chooser, you should read How to Make Frames (Main Windows), How to Use Labels, How to Use Buttons, and How to Use Color Choosers. We recommend that you at least skim this chapter first. Here's a quick overview:

- A Visual Index to Swing Components pictures all the standard Swing components, from top-level containers to scroll panes to buttons.

- Using HTML in Swing Components describes how to vary the font, color, or formatting of text displayed by Swing components by using HTML tags.

- Using Top-Level Containers discusses how to use the features shared by the `JFrame`, `JDialog`, and `JApplet` classes: content panes, menu bars, and root panes. It also discusses the containment hierarchy, which refers to the tree of components in a top-level container.

- Using Models tells you about the Swing model architecture. This variation on Model-View-Controller (MVC) means that you can specify how the data and state of a Swing component are stored and retrieved. The benefits are the ability to share data and state between components and the ability to greatly improve the performance of components, such as tables, that display large amounts of data.

- The JComponent Class tells you about the features `JComponent` provides to its sub-classes—which include almost all Swing components—and gives tips on how to take advantage of these features. The section ends with API tables describing the commonly used API defined by `JComponent` and its superclasses, `Container` and `Component`.

- Using Text Components describes the features and API shared by all components that descend from `JTextComponent`. You probably don't need to read this section if you're just using text fields (formatted or not) or text areas.

- At the end of this chapter is the Summary, followed by Questions and Exercises. Finally, Example Programs lists all the examples in this chapter and indicates where you can find them on the CD and online.

A Visual Index to Swing Components

Top-level containers are the components at the top of any Swing containment hierarchy. They're shown in Figure 1.

Applet (page 149)

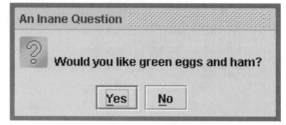

Dialog (page 187)

Frame (page 236)

Figure 1   Top-level containers.

General-purpose containers, shown in Figure 2, are intermediate containers that can be used under many different circumstances.

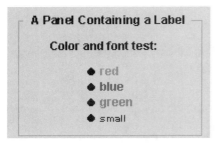

Panel (page 292)

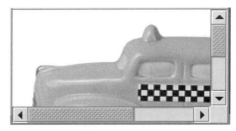

Scroll Pane (page 325)

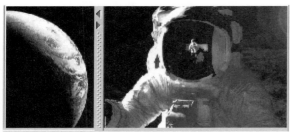

Split Pane (page 369)

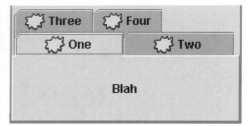

Tabbed Pane (page 382)

Tool Bar (page 427)

Figure 2   General-purpose containers.

Special containers, shown in Figure 3, are intermediate containers that play specific roles in the UI.

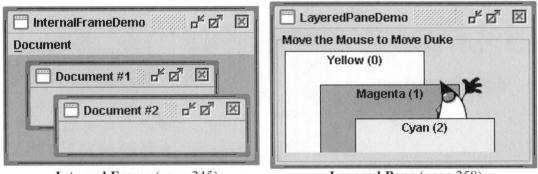

Internal Frame (page 245)   **Layered Pane** (page 258)

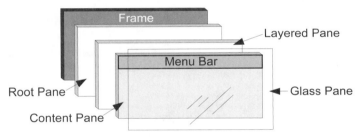

Root Pane (representation) (page 316)

Figure 3   Special-purpose containers.

Basic controls, shown in Figure 4, are atomic components that exist primarily to get input from the user; they generally also show simple state.

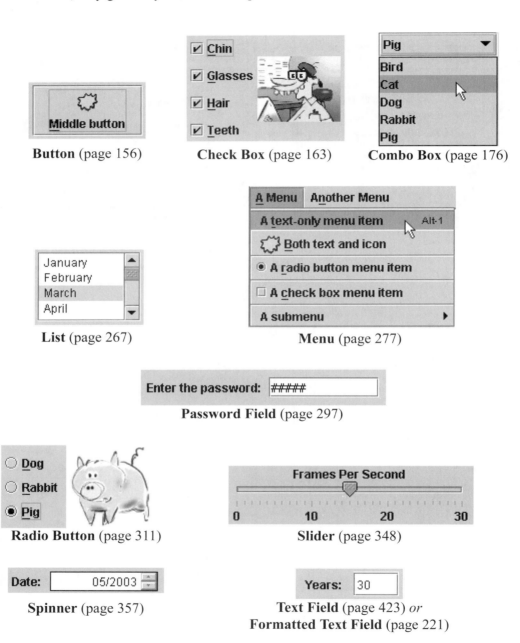

Button (page 156)   **Check Box** (page 163)   **Combo Box** (page 176)

List (page 267)   **Menu** (page 277)

Password Field (page 297)

Radio Button (page 311)   **Slider** (page 348)

Spinner (page 357)   **Text Field** (page 423) *or*
Formatted Text Field (page 221)

Figure 4   Basic controls.

Uneditable information displays, shown in Figure 5, are atomic components that exist solely to give the user information.

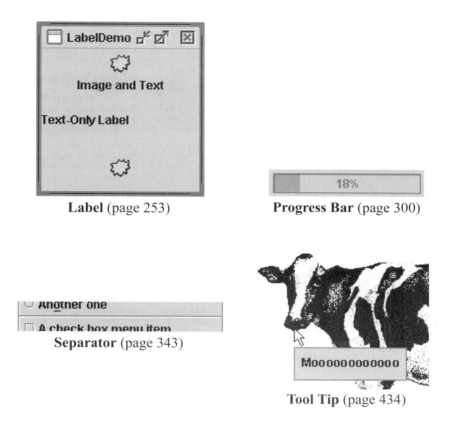

Label (page 253)

Progress Bar (page 300)

Separator (page 343)

Tool Tip (page 434)

Figure 5   Uneditable information displays.

Editable displays of formatted information, shown in Figure 6, are atomic components that display highly formatted information that (if you choose) can be edited by the user.

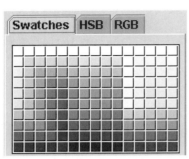

Color Chooser (page 167)

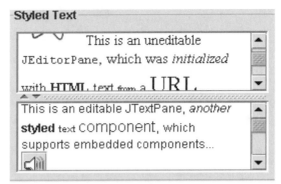

Editor Pane *or* **Text Pane** (page 200)

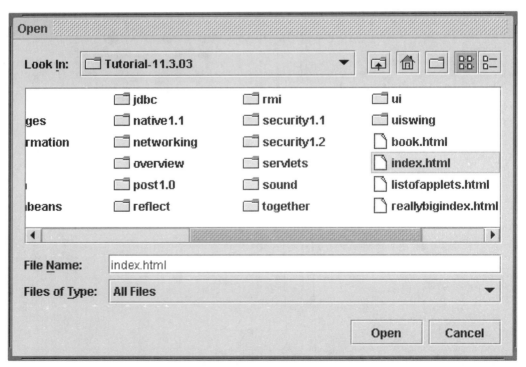

File Chooser (page 206)

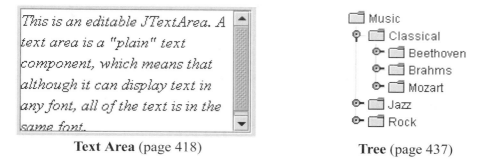

Table (page 388)

Text Area (page 418)   **Tree** (page 437)

Figure 6   Editable displays of formatted information.

Using HTML in Swing Components

Many Swing components display a text string as part of their GUI. By default, that text is displayed in a single font and color, all on one line. You can determine the font and color of a component's text by invoking the component's `setFont` and `setForeground` methods, respectively. For example, the following code creates a label and then sets its font and color:

```
label = new JLabel("A label");
label.setFont(new Font("Serif", Font.PLAIN, 14));
label.setForeground(new Color(0xffffdd));
```

If you want to mix fonts or colors within the text or have formatting, such as multiple lines, you can use HTML. HTML formatting can be used in all Swing buttons, menu items, labels, tool tips, and tabbed panes, as well as in components such as trees and tables that use labels as renderers. To specify that a component's text has HTML formatting, just put the `<html>` tag at the beginning of the text; then use any valid HTML in the remainder. Here's an example of using HTML in a button's text:

```
button = new JButton("<html><b><u>T</u>wo</b><br>lines</html>");
```

Figure 7 shows the resulting button.

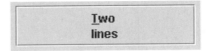

Figure 7   A button with HTML formatting

Performance Note: Because Swing's HTML rendering support uses many classes, users on older systems might notice a delay the first time a component with HTML formatting is shown. One way to avoid this delay is not to show the HTML-formatted component immediately and to create it (or another component that uses HTML) on a background thread.

Example One: HtmlDemo

The snapshot in Figure 8 shows an application called `HtmlDemo` that lets you play with HTML formatting by setting the text on a label.

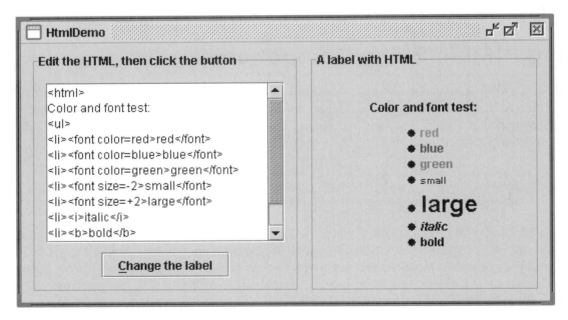

Figure 8   The `HTMLDemo` application.

Try This:

1. Run HtmlDemo using Java Web Start or compile and run the example yourself.[1]

2. Edit the HTML in the text area at the left and click the **Change the label** button. The label at the right shows the result.

3. Remove <html> from the text area on the left. The label's text is no longer parsed as HTML.

Example Two: ButtonHtmlDemo

Let's look at another example that uses HTML (Figure 9). ButtonHtmlDemo adds font, color, and other text formatting to three buttons.[2]

Figure 9   The ButtonHtmlDemo application.

The left and right buttons have multiple lines and text styles and are implemented using HTML. The middle button, on the other hand, uses just one line, font, and color, so it doesn't require HTML. Here's the code that specifies the text formatting for these three buttons:

```
b1 = new JButton("<html><center><b><u>D</u>isable</b><br>"
                + "<font color=#ffffdd>middle button</font>",
                leftButtonIcon);
Font font = b1.getFont().deriveFont(Font.PLAIN);
b1.setFont(font);
...
b2 = new JButton("middle button", middleButtonIcon);
b2.setFont(font);
b2.setForeground(new Color(0xffffdd));
```

---

[1] To run HtmlDemo using Java Web Start, click the HtmlDemo link on the RunExamples/components.html page on the CD. You can find the source files here: JavaTutorial/uiswing/components/example-1dot4/index.html#HTMLDemo.

[2] To run ButtonHtmlDemo using Java Web Start, click the ButtonHtmlDemo link on the RunExamples/components.html page on the CD. You can find the source files here: JavaTutorial/uiswing/components/example-1dot4/index.html#ButtonHTMLDemo.

```
...
b3 = new JButton("<html><center><b><u>E</u>nable</b><br>"
                 + "<font color=#ffffdd>middle button</font>",
                 rightButtonIcon);
b3.setFont(font);
```

Note that we had to use a <u> tag to cause the mnemonic characters D and E to be underlined in the HTML-using buttons. Note also that when a button is disabled its HTML text unfortunately remains black instead of becoming gray.[1]

This section discusses how to use HTML in ordinary, nontext components. For information on components whose primary purpose is formatting text, see Using Text Components (page 60) in this chapter.

Version Note: HTML rendering in ordinary Swing components was first added in v1.2.2 and completed in v1.3. The components that supported HTML in v1.2.2 were JButton, JLabel, JMenuItem, JMenu, JRadioButtonMenuItem, JCheckBoxMenuItem, JTabbedPane, and JToolTip. HTML support was added in v1.3 to JToggleButton, JCheckBox, and JRadioButton.

Using Top-Level Containers

As we mentioned before, Swing provides three generally useful top-level container classes: JFrame, JDialog, and JApplet. When you use these classes, keep these facts in mind:

- To appear onscreen, every GUI component must be part of a *containment hierarchy*. A containment hierarchy is a tree of components that has a top-level container as its root. We'll show you one in a bit.

- Each GUI component can be contained only once. If a component is already in a container and you try to add it to another container, the component will be removed from the first container and added to the second.

- Each top-level container has a content pane that generally contains (directly or indirectly) the visible components in that top-level container's GUI.

- You can optionally add a menu bar to a top-level container. The menu bar is by convention positioned within the top-level container but outside the content pane. Some look and feels, such as Mac OS, give you the option of placing the menu bar in another place more appropriate for the look and feel, such as at the top of the screen.

---

[1] Bug #4783068 requests that HTML text on disabled components be grayed out. You can track the bug status online at: http://developer.java.sun.com/developer/bugParade/bugs/4783068.html.

Note: Although JInternalFrame mimics JFrame, internal frames aren't top-level containers.

Figure 10 shows a snapshot and a diagram of a frame. The frame contains a menu bar (with no menus) and, in the frame's content pane, a large blank label.

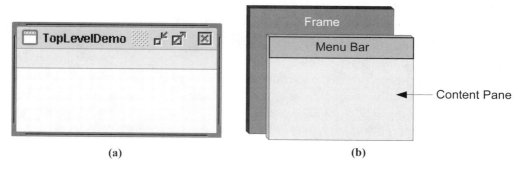

(a)   (b)

Figure 10   (a) A simple application with a frame that contains a menu bar and a content pane; (b) diagram of the frame's major parts.

You can find the entire source for this example in TopLevelDemo.java.[1] Although the example uses a JFrame in a standalone application, the same concepts apply to JApplets and JDialogs.

The containment hierarchy for this example's GUI appears in Figure 11.

Figure 11   Containment hierarchy for the TopLevelDemo example's GUI.

As the ellipses imply, we left some details. We'll reveal them a bit later.

---

[1] You can find the source files for TopLevelDemo on the CD at: JavaTutorial/uiswing/components/ example-1dot4/index.html#TopLevelDemo.

Top-Level Containers and Containment Hierarchies

As we mentioned in the previous chapter, each program that uses Swing components has at least one top-level container. This top-level container is the root of a containment hierarchy that contains all of the Swing components that appear inside it.

As a rule, a standalone application with a Swing-based GUI has at least one containment hierarchy with a `JFrame` as its root. For example, if an application has one main window and two dialogs, it has three containment hierarchies and thus three top-level containers. One containment hierarchy has a `JFrame` as its root, and each of the other two has a `JDialog` object as its root.

A Swing-based applet has at least one containment hierarchy, exactly one of which is rooted by a `JApplet` object. For example, an applet that brings up a dialog has two containment hierarchies. The components in the browser window are in a containment hierarchy rooted by a `JApplet` object. The dialog has a containment hierarchy rooted by a `JDialog` object.

Note: To view the containment hierarchy for any frame or dialog, click its border to select it and then press Control-Shift-F1. The containment hierarchy will be written to the standard output stream.

Adding Components to the Content Pane

Here's the code that the preceding example uses to get a frame's content pane and to add the label to it:

```
frame.getContentPane().add(yellowLabel, BorderLayout.CENTER);
```

As shown, you find the content pane of a top-level container by calling the `getContentPane` method. The default content pane is a simple intermediate container that inherits from `JComponent` and uses a `BorderLayout` as its layout manager.

It's easy to customize the content pane—setting the layout manager or adding a border, for example. However, there's one tiny hitch. The `getContentPane` method returns a `Container` object, not a `JComponent` object. This means that if you want to take advantage of the content pane's `JComponent` features you need to either typecast the return value or create your own component to be the content pane. Our examples generally take the second approach since it's a little cleaner. Another approach we sometimes take is to simply add a customized component to the content pane that covers it completely.

If you create your own content pane, make sure it's opaque. An opaque `JPanel` object makes a good content pane. Note that the default layout manager for `JPanel` is `FlowLayout`; you'll probably want to change it.

To make a component the content pane, use the top-level container's `setContentPane` method. For example:

```
//Create a panel and add components to it.
JPanel contentPane = new JPanel(new BorderLayout());
contentPane.setBorder(someBorder);
contentPane.add(someComponent, BorderLayout.CENTER);
contentPane.add(anotherComponent, BorderLayout.PAGE_END);

//Make it the content pane.
contentPane.setOpaque(true);
topLevelContainer.setContentPane(contentPane);
```

Note: Don't use nonopaque containers such as `JScrollPane`, `JSplitPane`, and `JTabbedPane` as content panes. A nonopaque content pane results in messy repaints. Although you can make any Swing component opaque by invoking `setOpaque(true)` on it, some components don't look right that way. For example, tabbed panes generally let part of the underlying container show through so that the tabs look nonrectangular. An opaque tabbed pane just tends to look bad. In most look and feels, `JPanel`s are opaque by default. However, `JPanel`s in the GTK+ look and feel, which was introduced in v1.4.2, are not initially opaque. To be safe, we invoke `setOpaque` on all `JPanel`s used as content panes.

Adding a Menu Bar

All top-level containers can, in theory, have a menu bar. In practice, however, menu bars usually appear only in frames and perhaps in applets. To add a menu bar to a top-level container, you create a `JMenuBar` object, populate it with menus, and call `setJMenuBar`. The `TopLevelDemo` adds a menu bar to its frame with this code:

```
frame.setJMenuBar(cyanMenuBar);
```

For more information about implementing menus and menu bars, see How to Use Menus (page 277) in Chapter 7.

The Root Pane (The Missing Details)

Each top-level container relies on a reclusive intermediate container called the *root pane*. The root pane manages the content pane and the menu bar, along with a couple of other containers. You generally don't need to know about root panes to use Swing components. However you should get acquainted with root panes if you ever need to intercept mouse clicks or paint over multiple components.

Figure 12 is a glimpse at the components that a root pane provides to a frame (and to every other top-level container).

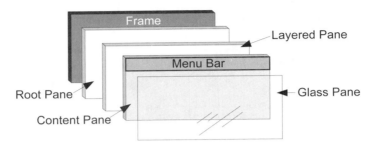

Figure 12   A representation of the components that a root pane provides.

We've already told you about the content pane and the optional menu bar. The two other components that a root pane adds are a layered pane and a glass pane. The layered pane directly contains the menu bar and content pane, and enables Z-ordering of other components you might add. The glass pane is often used to intercept input events occurring over the top-level container and can also be used to paint over multiple components.

For more information about the intricacies of root panes, see How to Use Root Panes (page 316) in Chapter 7.

Using Models

Most noncontainer Swing components have models. A button (JButton) has a model (a ButtonModel object) that stores the button's state—for example, what its keyboard mnemonic is and whether it's enabled, selected, or pressed. Some components have multiple models. A list (JList) uses a ListModel to hold the list's contents and a ListSelection-Model to track the list's current selection.

You often don't need to know about the models that a component uses. For example, programs that use buttons usually deal directly with the JButton object and don't deal at all with the ButtonModel object.

Why do models exist then? The primary reason is that they give you flexibility in determining how data is stored and retrieved. For example, if you're designing a spreadsheet application that displays data in a sparsely populated table, you can create your own table model that is optimized for such use.

Models have other benefits, too. They mean that data isn't copied between a program's data structures and those of the Swing components. Also, they automatically propagate changes to all interested listeners, making it easy for the GUI to stay in sync with the data. For example, to add items to a list you can invoke methods on the list model. When the model's data changes, the model fires events to the JList and any other registered listeners and the GUI is updated accordingly.

Although Swing's model architecture is sometimes referred to as a Model-View-Controller (MVC) design, it really isn't. Swing components are generally implemented so that the view and controller are indivisible, implemented by a single UI object provided by the look and feel. The Swing model architecture is more accurately described as a *separable model architecture*. If you're interested in learning more about it, see the "A Swing Architecture Overview" article[1] in *The Swing Connection*.

An Example: Converter

This section features an example called Converter, an application that continuously converts distance measurements between metric and U.S. units.[2] As Figure 13 shows, Converter has two sliders, each tied to a text field. The sliders and text fields all display the same data—a distance—using two different units of measure.

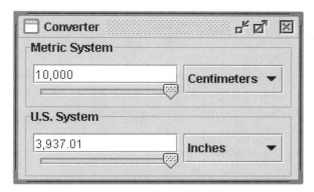

Figure 13   The Converter application.

The important thing for this program is ensuring that only one model controls the value of the data. There are various ways to achieve this; we did it by deferring to the top slider's model. The bottom slider's model (an instance of a custom class called FollowerRange-Model) forwards all data queries to the top slider's model (an instance of a custom class

---

[1] This *Swing Connection* article is online at: http://java.sun.com/products/jfc/tsc/articles/ architecture/index.html.

[2] To run Converter using Java Web Start, click the Converter link on the RunExamples/compo-nents.html page on the CD. You can find the source files here: JavaTutorial/uiswing/components/ example-1dot4/index.html#Converter.

called `ConverterRangeModel`). Each text field is kept in sync with its slider, and vice versa, by event handlers that listen for changes in value. Care is taken to ensure that the top slider's model has the final say about what distance is displayed.

When we started implementing the custom slider models, we first looked at the API section in How to Use Sliders (page 348) in Chapter 7. It informed us that all slider data models must implement the `BoundedRangeModel` interface. The `BoundedRangeModel` API documentation[1] tells us that the interface has an implementing class named `DefaultBoundedRange-Model`.[2] The API documentation for `DefaultBoundedRangeModel` shows that it's a general-purpose implementation of `BoundedRangeModel`.

We didn't use `DefaultBoundedRangeModel` directly because it stores data as integers whereas `Converter` uses floating-point data. Thus, we implemented `ConverterRangeModel` as a subclass of `Object`. We then implemented `FollowerRangeModel` as a subclass of `ConverterRangeModel`.

For More Information

To find out about the models for individual components, see the how-to sections in Chapter 7 and the API documentation for individual components. Here are some of our examples that use models directly:

- All but the simplest of the table examples implement custom table data models.
- The color chooser demos have change listeners on the color chooser's selection model so they can be notified when the user selects a new color. In `ColorChooserDemo2`, the `CrayonPanel` class directly uses the color selection model to set the current color.
- The `DynamicTreeDemo` example sets the tree model (to an instance of `DefaultTree-Model`), interacts directly with it, and listens for changes to it.
- `ListDemo` sets the list data model (to an instance of `DefaultListModel`) and interacts directly with it.
- `SharedModelDemo` defines a `SharedDataModel` class that extends `DefaultListModel` and implements `TableModel`. A `JList` and a `JTable` share an instance of `SharedData-Model`, providing different views of the model's data.
- In the event listener examples, `ListDataEventDemo` creates and uses a `DefaultList-Model`.
- Our spinner examples create spinner models.
- As you've already seen, the `Converter` example defines two custom slider models.

---

[1] BoundedRangeModel API documentation: `http://java.sun.com/j2se/1.4.2/docs/api/javax/swing/BoundedRangeModel.html`.

[2] DefaultBoundedRangeModel API documentation: `http://java.sun.com/j2se/1.4.2/docs/api/javax/swing/DefaultBoundedRangeModel.html`.

The JComponent Class

With the exception of top-level containers, all Swing components whose names begin with "J" descend from the JComponent[1] class. For example, JPanel, JScrollPane, JButton, and JTable all inherit from JComponent. However, JFrame and JDialog don't because they implement top-level containers.

The JComponent class extends the Container[2] class, which itself extends Component.[3] The Component class includes everything from layout hints to painting and event support. The Container class supports adding components to the container and laying them out. This section's API tables summarize the most often used methods of Component and Container, as well as of JComponent.

JComponent Features

The JComponent class gives its descendants many features:

- Tool tips
- Borders
- Application-wide pluggable look and feel
- Custom properties
- Support for layout
- Support for accessibility
- Support for drag and drop
- Double buffering
- Key bindings

Tool Tips

By specifying a string with the setToolTipText method, you can provide help to users of a component. When the cursor pauses over the component, the specified string is displayed in a small window that appears near the component. See How to Use Tool Tips (page 403) in Chapter 7.

---

[1] JComponent API documentation: http://java.sun.com/j2se/1.4.2/docs/api/javax/swing/JComponent.html.
[2] Container API documentation: http://java.sun.com/j2se/1.4.2/docs/api/java/awt/Container.html.
[3] Component API documentation: http://java.sun.com/j2se/1.4.2/docs/api/java/awt/Component.html.

Borders

The `setBorder` method allows you to specify the border that a component displays around its edges. To paint the inside of a component, override the `paintComponent` method. See How to Use Borders (page 535) in Chapter 9 and Performing Custom Painting (page 129) in Chapter 6 for details.

Application-Wide Pluggable Look and Feel

Behind the scenes, each `JComponent` object has a corresponding `ComponentUI` object that performs all the drawing, event handling, size determination, and so on, for that `JComponent`. Exactly which `ComponentUI` object is used depends on the current look and feel, which you can set using the `UIManager.setLookAndFeel` method. See How to Set the Look and Feel (page 628) in Chapter 9.

Custom Properties

You can associate one or more properties (name/object pairs) with any `JComponent`. For example, a layout manager might use properties to associate a constraints object with each `JComponent` it manages. You put and get properties using the `putClientProperty` and `getClientProperty` methods. For general information about properties, see How to Write a Property- Change Listener (page 704) in Chapter 10.

Support for Layout

Although the `Component` class provides layout hint methods such as `getPreferredSize` and `getAlignmentX`, it doesn't provide any way to set these layout hints, short of creating a subclass and overriding the methods. To give you another way to set layout hints, the `JComponent` class adds setter methods—`setPreferredSize`, `setMinimumSize`, `setMaximumSize`, `setAlignmentX`, and `setAlignmentY`. See Chapter 4, Laying Out Components within a Container (page 87), for more information.

Support for Accessibility

The `JComponent` class provides API and basic functionality to help assistive technologies, such as screen readers, get information from Swing components. See How to Support Assistive Technologies (page 519) in Chapter 9.

Support for Drag and Drop

The `JComponent` class provides API to set a component's transfer handler, which is the basis for Swing's drag-and-drop support. See How to Use Drag and Drop and Data Transfer (page 545) in Chapter 9.

Double Buffering

Double buffering smooths onscreen painting. See Chapter 6, Performing Custom Painting (page 129).

Key Bindings

This feature makes components react when the user presses a key on the keyboard. For example, in many look and feels, when a button has the focus, pressing the Space key is equivalent to a mouse click on the button. The look and feel automatically sets up the bindings between pressing and releasing the Space key and the resulting effects on the button. See How to Use Key Bindings (page 623) in Chapter 9 for more information.

The JComponent API

The JComponent class provides many new methods and inherits many methods from Component and Container. Tables 1 through 8 summarize the methods we use the most. You can find the Component, Container, and JComponent API documentation online at:

```
http://java.sun.com/j2se/1.4.2/docs/api/java/awt/Component.html
http://java.sun.com/j2se/1.4.2/docs/api/java/awt/Container.html
http://java.sun.com/j2se/1.4.2/docs/api/javax/swing/JComponent.html
```

Table 1: Customizing Component Appearance

Method	Purpose
void setBorder(Border) Border getBorder() (*in* JComponent)	Set or get the border of the component. See How to Use Borders (page 535) in Chapter 9 for details.
void setForeground(Color) void setBackground(Color) (*in* Component)	Set the foreground or background color for the component. The foreground is generally the color used to draw the text. The background is the color of the background areas of the component, assuming that the component is opaque.
Color getForeground() Color getBackground() (*in* Component)	Get the foreground or background color for the component.
void setOpaque(boolean) (*in* JComponent) boolean isOpaque() (*in* Component)	Set or get whether the component is opaque. An opaque component fills its background with its background color.
void setFont(Font) Font getFont() (*in* Component)	Set or get the component's font. If a font hasn't been set for the component, the font of its parent is returned.
FontMetrics getFontMetrics(Font) (*in* Component)	Get the font metrics for the specified font.

Table 2: Setting and Getting Component State

Method	Purpose
void setToolTipText(String) (*in* JComponent)	Set the text to display in a tool tip. See How to Use Tool Tips (page 434) in Chapter 7 for more information.
void setName(String) String getName() (*in* Component)	Set or get the name of the component. This can be useful when you need to associate text with a component that doesn't display text.
boolean isShowing() (*in* Component)	Determine whether the component is showing onscreen. This means that the component must be visible and must be in a container that's visible and showing.
void setEnabled(boolean) boolean isEnabled() (*in* Component)	Set or get whether the component is enabled. An enabled component can respond to user input and generate events.
void setVisible(boolean) boolean isVisible() (*in* Component)	Set or get whether the component is visible. Components are initially visible, with the exception of top-level components and internal frames.

Table 3: Handling Events
See Writing Event Listeners (page 107).

Method	Purpose
void addMouseListener(MouseListener) void removeMouseListener(MouseListener) (*in* Component)	Add or remove a mouse listener to or from the component. Mouse listeners are notified when the user uses the mouse to interact with the listened-to component.
void addMouseMotionListener(MouseMotionListener) void removeMouseMotionListener(MouseMotionListener) (*in* Component)	Add or remove a mouse motion listener to or from the component. Mouse motion listeners are notified when the user moves the mouse within the listened-to component's bounds.
void addKeyListener(KeyListener) void removeKeyListener(KeyListener) (*in* Component)	Add or remove a key listener to or from the component. Key listeners are notified when the user types at the keyboard and the listened-to component has the keyboard focus.
void addComponentListener(ComponentListener) void removeComponentListener(ComponentListener) (*in* Component)	Add or remove a component listener to or from the component. Component listeners are notified when the listened-to component is hidden, shown, moved, or resized.

Table 3: Handling Events *(continued)*

See Writing Event Listeners (page 107).

Method	Purpose

`void setTransferHandler(`
`        TransferHandler)`
`TransferHandler getTransferHandler()`
(*in* Component)
	Set or remove the `transferHandler` property. The `TransferHandler` supports exchanging data via cut, copy, or paste to/from a clipboard as well as drag and drop. See How to Use Drag and Drop and Data Transfer (page 545) in Chapter 9 for more details. Introduced in 1.4.

`boolean contains(int, int)`
`boolean contains(Point)`
(*in* Component)
	Determine whether the specified point is within the component. The argument should be specified in terms of the component's coordinate system. The two `int` arguments specify *x* and *y* coordinates, respectively.

`Component getComponentAt(int, int)`
`boolean getComponentAt(Point)`
(*in* Component)
	Return the component that contains the specified *x, y* position. The topmost child component is returned in the case where components overlap. This is determined by finding the component closest to the index 0 that claims to contain the given point via `Component.contains()`.

Table 4: Painting Components

See Performing Custom Painting (page 129).

Method	Purpose

`void repaint()`
`void repaint(int, int, int, int)`
(*in* Component)
	Request that all or part of the component be repainted. The four `int` arguments specify the bounds (*x, y*, width, height, in that order) of the rectangle to be painted.

`void repaint(Rectangle)` (*in* JComponent)	Request that the specified area within the component be repainted.
`void revalidate()` (*in* JComponent)	Request that the component and its affected containers be laid out again. Generally you shouldn't have to invoke this method unless you explicitly change a component's size/alignment hints after it's visible or change a containment hierarchy after it's visible. You might need to invoke `repaint` after `revalidate`.
`void paintComponent(Graphics)` (*in* JComponent)	Paint the component. Override this method to implement painting for custom components.

Table 5: Dealing with the Containment Hierarchy

See Top-Level Containers and Containment Hierarchies (page 48).

Method	Purpose

`Component add(Component)`
`Component add(Component, int)`
`void add(Component, Object)`
(*in* Component)
	Add the specified component to this container. The one-argument version of this method adds the component to the end of the container. When present, the `int` argument indicates the new component's position within the container. When present, the `Object` argument provides layout constraints to the current layout manager.

`void remove(int)`
`void remove(Component)`
`void removeAll()`
(*in* Component)
	Removes one of or all of the components from this container. When present, the `int` argument indicates the position within the container of the component to remove.

`JRootPane getRootPane()` (*in* JComponent)	Get the root pane that contains the component.
`Container getTopLevelAncestor()` (*in* JComponent)	Get the topmost container for the component—`Window`, `Applet`, or null if the component hasn't been added to any container.
`Container getParent()` (*in* Component)	Get the component's immediate container.
`int getComponentCount()` (*in* JComponent)	Get the number of components in this container.

`Component getComponent(int)`
`Component[] getComponents()`
(*in* Component)
	Get one or all of the components in this container. The `int` argument indicates the position of the component to get.

Table 6: Laying out Components

See Doing without a Layout Manager (Absolute Positioning) (page 100).

Method	Purpose

`void setPreferredSize(Dimension)`
`void setMaximumSize(Dimension)`
`void setMinimumSize(Dimension)`
(*in* JComponent)
	Set the component's preferred, maximum, or minimum size, measured in pixels. The preferred size indicates the best size for the component. The component should be no larger than its maximum size and no smaller than its minimum size. These are hints only and might be ignored by certain layout managers.

`Dimension getPreferredSize()`
`Dimension getMaximumSize()`
`Dimension getMinimumSize()`
(*in* Component)
	Get the preferred, maximum, or minimum size of the component, measured in pixels. For non-`JComponent` subclasses, which don't have the corresponding setter methods, you can set a component's preferred, maximum, or minimum size by creating a subclass and overriding these methods.

Table 6: Laying out Components *(continued)*

See Doing without a Layout Manager (Absolute Positioning) (page 100).

Method	Purpose
void setAlignmentX(float) void setAlignmentY(float) (*in* JComponent)	Set the alignment along the x or y axis. These values indicate how the component should be aligned relative to other components. The value should be a number between 0 and 1, where 0 represents alignment along the origin, 1 is aligned the furthest away from the origin, and 0.5 is centered, and so on. Be aware that these are hints only and might be ignored by certain layout managers.
float getAlignmentX() float getAlignmentY() (*in* Component)	Get the alignment of the component along the x or y axis. For non-JComponent subclasses, which don't have the corresponding setter methods, you can set a component's alignment by creating a subclass and overriding these methods.
void setLayout(LayoutManager) LayoutManager getLayout() (*in* Component)	Set or get the component's layout manager. The layout manager is responsible for sizing and positioning the components within a container.
void applyComponentOrientation(ComponentOrientation) (*in* Component)	Set the ComponentOrientation property of this container and all the components within it. Introduced in 1.4.

Table 7: Getting Size and Position Information

Method	Purpose
int getWidth() int getHeight() (*in* JComponent)	Get the current width or height of the component, measured in pixels.
Dimension getSize() Dimension getSize(Dimension) (*in* Component)	Get the component's current size, measured in pixels. When using the one-argument version of this method, the caller is responsible for creating the Dimension instance in which the result is returned.
int getX() int getY() (*in* Component)	Get the current x or y coordinate of the component's origin relative to the parent's upper left corner, measured in pixels.
Rectangle getBounds() Rectangle getBounds(Rectangle) (*in* Component)	Get the bounds of the component, measured in pixels. The bounds specify the component's width, height, and origin relative to its parent. When using the one-argument version of this method, the caller is responsible for creating the Rectangle instance in which the result is returned.

Table 7: Getting Size and Position Information *(continued)*

Method	Purpose

`Point getLocation()`
`Point getLocation(Point)`
`Point getLocationOnScreen()`
(*in* Component)
	Get the current location of the component relative to the parent's upper left corner, measured in pixels. When using the one-argument version of the `getLocation` method, the caller is responsible for creating the `Point` instance in which the result is returned. The `getLocationOnScreen` method returns the position relative to the upper left corner of the screen.

`Insets getInsets()` (*in* Component)	Get the size of the component's border.

Table 8: Specifying Absolute Size and Position

Method	Purpose

`void setLocation(int, int)`
`void setLocation(Point)`
(*in* Component)
	Set the location of the component, in pixels, relative to the parent's upper left corner. The two `int` arguments specify *x* and *y*, in that order. Use these methods to position a component when you aren't using a layout manager.

`void setSize(int, int)`
`void setSize(Dimension)`
(*in* Component)
	Set the size of the component, measured in pixels. The two `int` arguments specify width and height, in that order. Use these methods to size a component when you aren't using a layout manager.

`void setBounds(int, int, int, int)`
`void setBounds(Rectangle)`
(*in* Component)
	Set the size and location relative to the parent's upper left corner, in pixels. The four `int` arguments specify *x*, *y*, width, and height, in that order. Use these methods to position and size a component when you aren't using a layout manager.

Using Text Components

This section gives background information you might need when using Swing's text components. If you intend to use an unstyled text component—a text field, password field, formatted text field, or text area—we recommend that you go to its how-to section in Chapter 7 and return here only if necessary. If you intend to use a styled text component, then you're welcome to go to Chapter 7's How to Use Editor Panes and Text Panes (page 200), but you'll probably need to read this section as well. If you don't know which component you need, read on.

Swing's text components display text and optionally allow the user to edit the text. Programs need text components for tasks ranging from the straightforward (enter a word and press Enter) to the complex (display and edit styled text with embedded images in an Asian language).

Swing provides six text components, along with supporting classes and interfaces, that meet even the most complex text requirements. In spite of their different uses and capabilities, all of Swing's text components inherit from the same superclass, JTextComponent,[1] which provides a highly configurable and powerful foundation for text manipulation.

Figure 14 shows the JTextComponent hierarchy.

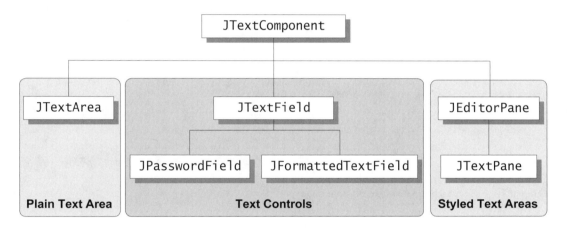

Figure 14   The JTextComponent hierarchy.

Figure 15 shows an application called TextSamplerDemo that uses one of each of Swing's text components.

---

[1] JTextComponent API documentation: `http://java.sun.com/j2se/1.4.2/docs/api/javax/swing/text/JTextComponent.html`.

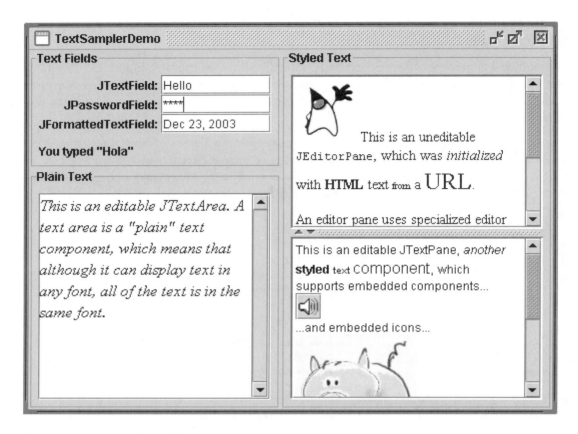

Figure 15   A screenshot of the TextSamplerDemo.

Try This:

1. Run TextSamplerDemo using Java Web Start or compile and run the example your-self.[1]

2. Type some text into the text field and press Enter. Do the same with the password field. The label beneath the fields is updated when you press Enter.

3. Try entering valid and invalid dates into the formatted text field. Note that when you press Enter the label beneath is updated only if the date is valid.

4. Select and edit text in the text area and the text pane. Use special keyboard keys to cut, copy, and paste text.

---

[1]   To run TextSamplerDemo using Java Web Start, click the TextSamplerDemo link on the RunExamples/ components.html page on the CD. You can find the source files here: JavaTutorial/uiswing/com-ponents/example-1dot4/index.html#TextSamplerDemo.

5. Try to edit the text in the editor pane, which has been made uneditable with a call to `setEditable`.

6. Look in the text pane to find an example of an embedded component and an embedded icon.

`TextSamplerDemo` uses the text components in very basic ways. Table 9 tells you a bit more about what you can do with each kind of text component.

Table 9: Kinds of Text Components

Group	Description	Swing Classes
Text Controls	Also known simply as text fields, text controls can display and edit only one line of text. Like buttons, they generate action events. Use them to get a small amount of textual information from the user and take some action after the text entry is complete.	`JTextField` and its subclasses `JPassword-Field` and `JFormatted-TextField`
Plain Text Areas	`JTextArea` can display and edit multiple lines of text. Although a text area can display text in any font, all of the text is in the same font. Use a text area to allow the user to enter unformatted text of any length or to display unformatted help information.	`JTextArea`
Styled Text Areas	A styled text component can display and edit text using more than one font. Some styled text components allow embedded images and even embedded components. Styled text components are powerful and multi-faceted components suitable for high-end needs, and offer more avenues for customization than the other text components. Because they are so powerful and flexible, styled text components typically require more up-front programming to set up and use. One exception is that editor panes can be easily loaded with formatted text from a URL, which makes them useful for displaying uneditable help information.	`JEditorPane` and its subclass `JTextPane`

Note: This book gives you information about the foundation laid by `JTextComponent` and tells you how to accomplish some common text-related tasks. Because `JTextComponent` and its subclasses have too many features to be completely described here, please periodically search the online newsletter, *The Swing Connection*, for pointers to more information: http://java.sun.com/products/jfc/tsc/index.html. We've also included *The Swing Connection* on the CD at: Docs/swingConnect/swingconnection.pdf.

Text Component Features

JTextComponent is the foundation for Swing's text components, and provides these customizable features for all of its descendants:

- A model, known as a *document*, to manage the component's content.
- A view, which is in charge of displaying the component on screen.
- A controller, known as an *editor kit*, that can read and write text and that implements editing capabilitie.
- Support for infinite undo and redo.
- Pluggable caret and support for caret change listeners and navigation filters.

This section uses the application shown in Figure 16 to explore these capabilities. Although the demo application contains a customized instance of JTextPane, the capabilities discussed in this section are inherited by all of JTextComponent's subclasses.

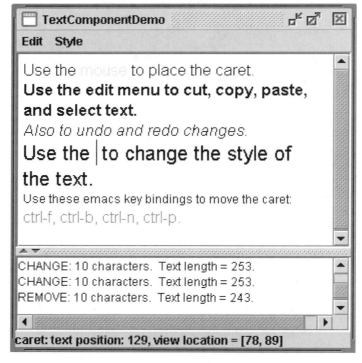

Figure 16   The TextComponentDemo application.

The upper text component is the customized text pane. The lower text component is an instance of JTextArea, which serves as a log that reports all changes made to the contents of the text pane. The status line at the bottom of the window reports either the location of the selection or the position of the caret, depending on whether text is selected.

Try This:

1. Run TextComponentDemo using Java Web Start or compile and run the example yourself.[1]

2. Use the mouse to select text and place the cursor in the text pane. Information about the selection and cursor is displayed at the bottom of the window.

3. Enter text by typing at the keyboard. You can move the caret around using four emacs key bindings: CTRL-B (backward one character), CTRL-F (forward one character), CTRL-N (down one line), and CTRL-P (up one line).

4. Bring up the **Edit** menu, and use its various menu items to perform editing on the text in the text pane. Make a selection in the text area at the bottom of the window. Because the text area is uneditable, only some of the **Edit** menu's commands, such as **copy-to-clipboard**, work. It's important to note, though, that the menu operates on both text components.

5. Use the items in the **Style** menu to apply different styles to the text in the text pane.

Associating Text Actions with Menus and Buttons

All Swing text components support standard editing commands such as cut, copy, paste, and inserting characters. Each editing command is represented and implemented by an Action object. (You can learn about actions by reading How to Use Actions (page 513) in Chapter 9.) Actions make it easy for you to associate a command with a GUI component, such as a menu item or button, and therefore build a GUI around a text component.

You can invoke the getActions method on any text component to get an array containing all of the actions it supports. Often it's convenient to load the array of actions into a HashMap so that your program can retrieve an action by name. Here's the code from TextComponentDemo that gets the actions from the text pane and loads them into a HashMap:

```
private void createActionTable(JTextComponent textComponent) {
    actions = new HashMap();
    Action[] actionsArray = textComponent.getActions();
```

---

[1] To run TextComponentDemo using Java Web Start, click the TextSamplerDemo link on the RunExamples/components.html page on the CD. You can find the source files here: JavaTutorial/ uiswing/components/example-1dot4/index.html#TextComponentDemo.

65

```
        for (int i = 0; i < actionsArray.length; i++) {
            Action a = actionsArray[i];
            actions.put(a.getValue(Action.NAME), a);
        }
    }
```

Here's a convenient method for retrieving an action by its name from the HashMap:

```
    private Action getActionByName(String name) {
        return (Action)(actions.get(name));
    }
```

You can use both methods verbatim in your programs.

Now let's look at how the **Cut** menu item is created and associated with the action of removing text from the text component:

```
    protected JMenu createEditMenu() {
        JMenu menu = new JMenu("Edit");
        ...
        menu.add(getActionByName(DefaultEditorKit.cutAction));
        ...
```

This code gets the action by name using the handy method shown previously. It then adds the action to the menu. That's all you need to do. The menu and the action take care of everything else. You'll note that the name of the action comes from DefaultEditorKit.[1] This kit provides actions for basic text editing and is the superclass for all of the editor kits provided by Swing. So its capabilities are available to all text components unless overridden by a customization.

For efficiency, text components share actions. The Action object returned by getAction-ByName(DefaultEditorKit.cutAction) is shared by the uneditable JTextArea at the bottom of the window. This has two important ramifications:

- Generally speaking, you shouldn't modify Action objects you get from editor kits. If you do, the changes affect all text components in your program.
- Action objects can operate on other text components in the program, perhaps more than you intended. In this example, even though it's uneditable, the JTextArea shares actions with the JTextPane. (Select some text in the text area, then choose the cut-to-clipboard menu item. You'll hear a beep because the text area is uneditable.) If you don't want to share, consider instantiating the Action object yourself. DefaultEditorKit defines a number of useful Action subclasses.

---

[1] DefaultEditorKit API documentation: http://java.sun.com/j2se/1.4.2/docs/api/javax/swing/text/DefaultEditorKit.html.

Here's the code that creates the **Style** menu and puts the **Bold** menu item in it:

```
protected JMenu createStyleMenu() {
    JMenu menu = new JMenu("Style");

    Action action = new StyledEditorKit.BoldAction();
    action.putValue(Action.NAME, "Bold");
    menu.add(action);
    ...
```

The `StyledEditorKit` provides `Action` subclasses to implement editing commands for styled text. You'll note that instead of getting the action from the editor kit, this code creates an instance of the `BoldAction` class. Thus, this action is not shared with any other text component, and changing its name won't affect any other text component.

Associating Text Actions with Keystrokes

In addition to associating an action with a GUI component, you can also associate an action with a keystroke, using a text component's input map. Input maps are described in How to Use Key Bindings (page 623) in Chapter 9.

The text pane in the `TextComponentDemo` supports four key bindings not provided by default.

- CTRL-B for moving the caret backward one character
- CTRL-F for moving the caret forward one character
- CTRL-N for moving the caret down one line
- CTRL-P for moving the caret up one line

The following code adds the CTRL-B key binding to the text pane. The code for adding the other three is similar.

```
InputMap inputMap = textPane.getInputMap();

KeyStroke key = KeyStroke.getKeyStroke(KeyEvent.VK_B, Event.CTRL_MASK);
inputMap.put(key, DefaultEditorKit.backwardAction);
```

The code starts off by getting the text component's input map. Next, it gets a KeyStroke[1] object representing the CTRL-B key sequence. Finally, the code binds the keystroke to the Action that moves the cursor backward.

Version Note: Before v1.3, you needed to use a JTextComponent feature called a *keymap* to associate keystrokes with actions. The keymap API still exists and works, but it is now implemented in terms of the key binding infrastructure added in v1.3. Here's the pre-v1.3 equivalent of the preceding code:

```
//PRE-1.3 CODE
Keymap keymap = textPane.addKeymap("MyEmacsBindings", textPane.getKeymap());
Action action = getActionByName(DefaultEditorKit.backwardAction);
KeyStroke key = KeyStroke.getKeyStroke(KeyEvent.VK_B, Event.CTRL_MASK);
keymap.addActionForKeyStroke(key, action);
...
textPane.setKeymap(keymap);
```

Implementing Undo and Redo

Implementing undo and redo has two parts:

- Remembering undoable edits.
- Implementing the undo and redo commands and providing a user interface for them.

Part 1: Remembering Undoable Edits

To support undo and redo, a text component must remember each edit that occurs, the order of edits, and what it takes to undo each edit. The example program uses an instance of the UndoManager[2] class to manage its list of undoable edits. The undo manager is created where the member variables are declared:

```
protected UndoManager undo = new UndoManager();
```

Now, let's look at how the program finds out about undoable edits and adds them to the undo manager.

A document notifies interested listeners whenever an undoable edit occurs on its content. An important step in implementing undo and redo is to register an undoable edit listener on the

---

[1] KeyStroke API documentation: http://java.sun.com/j2se/1.4.2/docs/api/javax/swing/ KeyStroke.html.
[2] UndoManager API documentation: http://java.sun.com/j2se/1.4.2/docs/api/javax/swing/ undo/UndoManager.html.

document of the text component. The following code adds an instance of MyUndoableEditListener to the text pane's document:

```
lsd.addUndoableEditListener(new MyUndoableEditListener());
```

The undoable edit listener used in our example adds the edit to the undo manager's list:

```
protected class MyUndoableEditListener implements UndoableEditListener {
    public void undoableEditHappened(UndoableEditEvent e) {
        //Remember the edit and update the menus
        undo.addEdit(e.getEdit());
        undoAction.updateUndoState();
        redoAction.updateRedoState();
    }
}
```

Note that this method updates two objects: undoAction and redoAction. These are the action objects attached to the **Undo** and **Redo** menu items, respectively. The next step shows you how the menu items are created and the implementation of the two actions. For general information about undoable edit listeners and undoable edit events, see How to Write an Undoable Edit Listener (page 721) in Chapter 10.

Note: By default, undoable edits can be as fine-grained as single key presses. It is possible, with some effort, to group edits so that (for example) a series of key presses is combined into one undoable edit. The implementation would require defining a class that intercepts undoable edit events from the document, combining them if appropriate and forwarding the results to your undoable edit listener.

Part 2: Implementing the Undo and Redo Commands

The first step in this part of implementing undo and redo is to create the actions to put in the **Edit** menu.

```
JMenu menu = new JMenu("Edit");

//Undo and redo are actions of our own creation
undoAction = new UndoAction();
menu.add(undoAction);

redoAction = new RedoAction();
menu.add(redoAction);
...
```

The undo and redo actions are implemented by custom AbstractAction subclasses: Undo-Action and RedoAction, respectively. These classes are inner classes of the example's primary class.

When the user invokes the **Undo** command, UndoAction's actionPerformed method, shown here, gets called:

```
public void actionPerformed(ActionEvent e) {
    try {
        undo.undo();
    } catch (CannotUndoException ex) {
        System.out.println("Unable to undo: " + ex);
        ex.printStackTrace();
    }
    updateUndoState();
    redoAction.updateRedoState();
}
```

This method calls the undo manager's undo method and updates the menu items to reflect the new undo/redo state. Similarly, when the user invokes the **Redo** command, the action-Performed method in RedoAction gets called:

```
public void actionPerformed(ActionEvent e) {
    try {
        undo.redo();
    } catch (CannotRedoException ex) {
        System.out.println("Unable to redo: " + ex);
        ex.printStackTrace();
    }
    updateRedoState();
    undoAction.updateUndoState();
}
```

This method is similar except that it calls the undo manager's redo method.

Much of the code in the UndoAction and RedoAction classes is dedicated to enabling and disabling the actions as appropriate for the current state, and changing the names of the menu items to reflect the edit to be undone or redone.

Note: The implementation of undo and redo in TextComponentDemo was taken from the Note-Pad demo that comes with the Java 2 SDK. Many programmers will also be able to copy this implementation of undo/redo without modification.

Concepts: About Documents

Like other Swing components, a text component separates its data (known as the *model*) from its view of the data. If you are not yet familiar with the model-view split used by Swing components, refer to Using Models (page 50).

A text component's model is known as a *document* and is an instance of a class that implements the Document[1] interface. A document provides these services for a text component:

- Contains the text. A document stores the textual content in Element objects, which can represent any logical text structure, such as paragraphs, text runs that share styles, and so on. We do not cover Elements; however, the newsletter *The Swing Connection* has at least one article on the subject: http://java.sun.com/products/jfc/tsc/index.html.

- Provides support for editing the text through the remove and insertString methods.

- Notifies document listeners and undoable edit listeners of changes to the text.

- Manages Position objects, which track a particular location within the text even as the text is modified.

- Allows you to get information about the text, such as its length, and segments of the text as a string.

The Swing text package contains a subinterface of Document, StyledDocument,[2] that adds support for marking up the text with styles. One JTextComponent subclass, JTextPane, requires that its document be a StyledDocument rather than merely a Document.

The javax.swing.text package provides the following hierarchy of document classes, which implement specialized documents for the various JTextComponent subclasses.

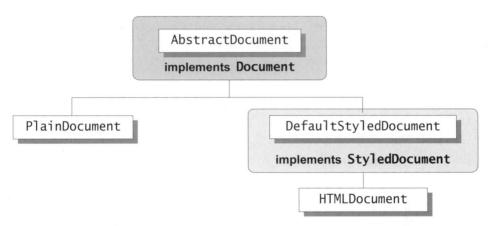

Figure 17   The hierarchy of document classes that javax.swing.text provides.

---

[1] Document API documentation: http://java.sun.com/j2se/1.4.2/docs/api/javax/swing/text/Document.html.

[2] StyledDocument API documentation: http://java.sun.com/j2se/1.4.2/docs/api/javax/swing/text/StyledDocument.html.

A PlainDocument[1] is the default document for text fields, password fields, and text areas. PlainDocument provides a basic container for text where all the text is displayed in the same font. Even though an editor pane is a styled text component, it uses an instance of PlainDocument by default. The default document for a standard JTextPane is an instance of DefaultStyledDocument—a container for styled text in no particular format. However, the document instance used by any particular editor pane or text pane depends on the type of content bound to it. If you use setPage to load text into an editor pane or text pane, the document instance used by the pane might change. Refer to How to Use Editor Panes and Text Panes (page 200) in Chapter 7 for details.

Although you can set the document of a text component, it's usually easier to let it be set automatically, and use a *document filter* if necessary to change how the text component's data is set. You can implement certain customizations either by installing a document filter or by replacing a text component's document with one of your own, For example, the text pane in TextComponentDemo has a document filter that limits the number of characters the text pane can contain.

Implementing a Document Filter

To implement a document filter, you create a subclass of DocumentFilter[2] and then attach it to a document using the setFilter method defined in AbstractDocument.[3] Although it's possible to have documents that don't descend from AbstractDocument, by default Swing text components use AbstractDocument subclasses for their documents.

The TextComponentDemo application has a document filter, DocumentSizeFilter, which limits the number of characters that the text pane can contain. Here's the code that creates the filter and attaches it to the text pane's document:

```
...//Where member variables are declared:
JTextPane textPane;
AbstractDocument doc;
static final int MAX_CHARACTERS = 300;
...
textPane = new JTextPane();
...
StyledDocument styledDoc = textPane.getStyledDocument();
if (styledDoc instanceof AbstractDocument) {
    doc = (AbstractDocument)styledDoc;
    doc.setDocumentFilter(new DocumentSizeFilter(MAX_CHARACTERS));
}
```

---

[1] PlainDocument API documentation: http://java.sun.com/j2se/1.4.2/docs/api/javax/swing/text/PlainDocument.html.

[2] DocumentFilter API documentation: http://java.sun.com/j2se/1.4.2/docs/api/javax/swing/text/DocumentFilter.html.

[3] AbstractDocument API documentation: http://java.sun.com/j2se/1.4.2/docs/api/javax/swing/text/AbstractDocument.html.

To limit the characters allowed in the document, DocumentSizeFilter overrides Document-Filter's insertString method, which is called each time text is inserted into the document. It also overrides the replace method, which is most likely to be called when the user changes text by pasting it in. In general, text insertion can be the result of the user typing or pasting text in, or because of a call to setText. Here's DocumentSizeFilter's implementation of insertString:

```
public void insertString(FilterBypass fb, int offs,
                         String str, AttributeSet a)
    throws BadLocationException {

    if ((fb.getDocument().getLength() + str.length()) <= maxCharacters)
        super.insertString(fb, offs, str, a);
    else
        Toolkit.getDefaultToolkit().beep();
}
```

The code for replace is similar. The FilterBypass[1] parameter to the methods defined by DocumentFilter is simply an object that enables updating the document in a thread-safe way.

Because the preceding document filter is only concerned about additions to the document's data, it only overrides the insertString and replace methods. Most document filters would override DocumentFilter's remove method, as well.

Listening for Changes on a Document

You can register two different types of listeners on a document: document listeners and undoable edit listeners. This subsection covers document listeners. For information about undoable edit listeners, refer to Implementing Undo and Redo (page 68).

A document notifies registered document listeners of changes to the document. Use a document listener to react when text is inserted or removed from a document, or when the style of some of the text changes.

The TextComponentDemo program uses a document listener to update the change log whenever a change is made to the text pane. The line of code that follows registers an instance of MyDocumentListener as a listener on the text pane's document:

```
doc.addDocumentListener(new MyDocumentListener());
```

---

[1] FilterBypass API documentation: http://java.sun.com/j2se/1.4.2/docs/api/javax/swing/text/DocumentFilter.FilterBypass.html.

Here's the implementation of MyDocumentListener:

```
protected class MyDocumentListener implements DocumentListener {
    public void insertUpdate(DocumentEvent e) {
        displayEditInfo(e);
    }
    public void removeUpdate(DocumentEvent e) {
        displayEditInfo(e);
    }
    public void changedUpdate(DocumentEvent e) {
        displayEditInfo(e);
    }
    private void displayEditInfo(DocumentEvent e) {
            Document document = (Document)e.getDocument();
            int changeLength = e.getLength();
            changeLog.append(e.getType().toString() + ": "
                + changeLength + " character"
                + ((changeLength == 1) ? ". " : "s. ")
                + " Text length = " + document.getLength()
                + "." + newline);
    }
}
```

The listener implements three methods for handling three different types of document events: insertion, removal, and style changes. StyledDocuments can fire all three types of events. PlainDocuments fire events only for insertion and removal. For general information about document listeners and document events, see How to Write a Document Listener (page 661) in Chapter 10.

Remember that the document filter for this text pane limits the number of characters allowed in the document. If you try to add more text than the document filter allows, the document filter blocks the change and the listener's insertUpdate method is not called. Document listeners are notified of changes only if the change has already occurred.

Sometimes, you might be tempted to change the document's text from within a document listener. **However, you should never modify the contents of a text component from within a document listener.** In fact, if you do, your program will likely deadlock! Instead, you can use a formatted text field or provide a document filter.

Listening for Caret and Selection Changes

The TextComponentDemo program uses a caret listener to display the current position of the caret or, if text is selected, the extent of the selection.

The caret listener class in this example is a JLabel subclass. Here's the code that creates the caret listener label and makes it a caret listener of the text pane:

```
    //Create the status area
    CaretListenerLabel caretListenerLabel = new CaretListenerLabel(
                                            "Caret Status");
    ...
    textPane.addCaretListener(caretListenerLabel);
```

A caret listener must implement one method, `caretUpdate`, which is called each time the caret moves or the selection changes. Here's the `CaretListenerLabel` implementation of `caretUpdate`:

```
    public void caretUpdate(CaretEvent e) {
        //Get the location in the text
        int dot = e.getDot();
        int mark = e.getMark();
        if (dot == mark) {  // no selection
            try {
                Rectangle caretCoords = textPane.modelToView(dot);
                //Convert it to view coordinates
                setText("caret: text position: " + dot +
                        ", view location = [" + caretCoords.x +
                        ", " + caretCoords.y + "]" + newline);
            } catch (BadLocationException ble) {
                setText("caret: text position: " + dot + newline);
            }
        } else if (dot < mark) {
            setText("selection from: " + dot + " to " + mark + newline);
        } else {
            setText("selection from: " + mark + " to " + dot + newline);
        }
    }
```

As you can see, this listener updates its text label to reflect the current state of the caret or selection. The listener gets the information to display from the caret event object. For general information about caret listeners and caret events, see How to Write a Caret Listener (page 649) in Chapter 10.

As with document listeners, a caret listener is passive. It reacts to changes in the caret or in the selection but does not change the caret or the selection. If you want to change the caret or selection, then you should use a *navigation filter* or a custom caret instead.

Implementing a navigation filter is similar to implementing a document filter. First, you write a subclass of `NavigationFilter`.[1] You then attach an instance of it to a text component with the `setNavigationFilter` method.

---

[1] `NavigationFilter` API documentation: `http://java.sun.com/j2se/1.4.2/docs/api/javax/` `swing/text/NavigationFilter.html`.

You might create a custom caret to customize the appearance of a caret. To create a caret, write a class that implements the `Caret`[1] interface—perhaps by extending the `Default-Caret`[2] class. Then provide an instance of your class as an argument to `setCaret` on a text component.

Concepts: About Editor Kits

Under the hood, text components use an `EditorKit` to tie the various pieces of the text component together. It provides the view factory, document, caret, and actions. An editor kit also reads and writes documents of a particular format. Although all text components use editor kits, some components hide theirs. You can't set or get the editor kit used by a text field or text area. Editor panes and text panes provide the `getEditorKit` method to get the current editor kit and the `setEditorKit` method to change it.

For all components, `JTextComponent` provides an API for you to indirectly invoke or customize some editor kit capabilities. For example, `JTextComponent` provides `read` and `write` methods, which invoke the editor kit's `read` and `write` methods. `JTextComponent` also provides a method, `getActions`, which returns all of the actions supported by a component.

The Swing text package provides the following editor kits:

`DefaultEditorKit`[3]
   Reads and writes plain text, and provides a basic set of editing commands. Details of how the text system treats new lines are in the `DefaultEditorKit` API documentation. (To summarize: The "\n" character is used internally, but the document or platform line separators are used when writing files.) All of the other editor kits are descendants of `DefaultEditorKit`.

`StyledEditorKit`[4]
   Reads and writes styled text, and provides a minimal set of actions for styled text. This class is a subclass of `DefaultEditorKit` and is the editor kit used by `JTextPane` by default.

---

[1] Caret API documentation: `http://java.sun.com/j2se/1.4.2/docs/api/javax/swing/text/Caret.html`.

[2] DefaultCaret API documentation: `http://java.sun.com/j2se/1.4.2/docs/api/javax/swing/text/DefaultCaret.html`.

[3] DefaultEditorKit API documentation: `http://java.sun.com/j2se/1.4.2/docs/api/javax/swing/text/DefaultEditorKit.html`.

[4] StyledEditorKit API documentation: `http://java.sun.com/j2se/1.4.2/docs/api/javax/swing/text/StyledEditorKit.html`.

HTMLEditorKit[1]
Reads, writes, and edits HTML. This is a subclass of StyledEditorKit.

RTFEditorKit
Reads, writes, and edits RTF. This is a subclass of StyledEditorKit.

Each of the editor kits above has been registered with the JEditorPane class and associated with the text format that the kit reads, writes, and edits. When a file is loaded into an editor pane, the pane checks the format of the file against its registered kits. If a registered kit is found that supports that file format, the pane uses the kit to read the file, display, and edit it. Thus, the editor pane effectively transforms itself into an editor for that text format. You can extend JEditorPane to support your own text format by creating an editor kit for it, and then using JEditorPane's registerEditorKitForContentType to associate your kit with your text format.

The Text Component API

This section lists commonly used parts of the API shared by text components, much of it defined by the JTextComponent[2] class. The section Text Component Features (page 64) discussed how to use some of this API.

Also see the section The JComponent Class (page 53), which describes the API that text components inherit from JComponent. For information about the API for specific text components, see the relevant how-to section for the component.

For a complete listing of and further details about the text API, see the API documentation for JTextComponent and for the various classes and interfaces in the text package online at the following URL: http://java.sun.com/j2se/1.4.2/docs/api/javax/swing/text/package-summary.html.

---

[1] HTMLEditorKit API documentation: http://java.sun.com/j2se/1.4.2/docs/api/javax/swing/text/html/HTMLEditorKit.html.

[2] JTextComponent API documentation: http://java.sun.com/j2se/1.4.2/docs/api/javax/swing/text/JTextComponent.html.

Table 10: Setting Attributes

These methods are in the JTextComponent *class.*

Method	Description
`void setDisabledTextColor(Color)` `Color getDisabledTextColor()`	Set or get the color used to display text when the text component is disabled.
`void setMargin(Insets)` `Insets getMargin()`	Set or get the margin between the text and the text component's border.
`void setEditable(boolean)` `boolean isEditable()`	Set or get whether the user can edit the text in the text component.
`void setDragEnabled(boolean)` `boolean getDragEnabled()`	Set or get the `dragEnabled` property, which must be true to enable drag handling on this component. The default value is false. See How to Use Drag and Drop and Data Transfer (page 545) in Chapter 9 for more details. Introduced in 1.4.

Table 11: Manipulating the Selection

These methods are in the JTextComponent *class.*

Method	Description
`String getSelectedText()`	Get the currently selected text.
`void selectAll()` `void select(int, int)`	Select all text or select text within a start and end range.

`void setSelectionStart(int)`
`void setSelectionEnd(int)`
`int getSelectionStart()`
`int getSelectionEnd()`
	Set or get extent of the current selection by index.

`void setSelectedTextColor(Color)` `Color getSelectedTextColor()`	Set or get the color of selected text.
`void setSelectionColor(Color)` `Color getSelectionColor()`	Set or get the background color of selected text.

Table 12: Converting Positions between the Model and the View

These methods are in the JTextComponent *class.*

Method	Description
`int viewToModel(Point)`	Convert the specified point in the view coordinate system to a position within the text.
`Rectangle modelToView(int)`	Convert the specified position within the text to a rectangle in the view coordinate system.

Table 13: Text Editing Commands

Class or Method	Description

`void cut()`
`void copy()`
`void paste()`
`void replaceSelection(String)`
(*in* JTextComponent)
	Cut, copy, and paste text using the system clipboard.

`EditorKit`	Provides a text component's view factory, document, caret, and actions, as well as reading and writing documents of a particular format.
`DefaultEditorKit`	A concrete subclass of `EditorKit` that provides the basic text editing capabilities.
`StyledEditorKit`	A subclass of `Default EditorKit` that provides additional editing capabilities for styled text.
`String xxxxAction` (*in* DefaultEditorKit)	The names of all the actions supported by the default editor kit. See Associating Text Actions with Keystrokes (page 67).

`BeepAction`
`CopyAction`
`CutAction`
`DefaultKeyTypedAction`
`InsertBreakAction`
`InsertContentAction`
`InsertTabAction`
`PasteAction`
(*in* DefaultEditorKit)
	Inner classes that implement various text editing commands.

Table 13: Text Editing Commands *(continued)*

Class or Method	Description

`AlignmentAction`
`BoldAction`
`FontFamilyAction`
`FontSizeAction`
`ForegroundAction`
`ItalicAction`
`StyledTextAction`
`UnderlineAction`
(*in* `StyledEditorKit`)
	Inner classes that implement various editing commands for styled text.

`Action[] getActions()` (*in* `JTextComponent`)	Get the actions supported by this component. This method gets the array of actions from the editor kit if one is used by the component.
`InputMap getInputMap()` (*in* `JComponent`)	Gets the input map that binds keystrokes to actions. See Associating Text Actions with Keystrokes (page 67).
`void put(KeyStroke, Object)` (*in* `InputMap`)	Binds the specified key to the specified action. You generally specify the action by its name, which for standard editing actions is represented by a string constant such as `DefaultEditor-Kit.backwardAction`.

Table 14: Classes and Interfaces That Represent Documents

Interface or Class	Description
`Document`	An interface that defines the API that must be implemented by all documents.
`AbstractDocument`	An abstract superclass implementation of the `Document` interface. This is the superclass for all documents provided by the Swing text package.
`PlainDocument`	A class that implements the `Document` interface. This is the default document for the plain text components (text field, password field, and text area). Additionally used by editor pane and text pane when loading plain text or text of an unknown format.
`StyledDocument`	A `Document` subinterface. Defines the API that must be implemented by documents that support styled text. `JTextPane` requires that its document be of this type.
`DefaultStyledDocument`	A class that implements the `StyledDocument` interface. The default document for `JTextPane`.

Table 15: Working with Documents

Class or Method	Description
`DocumentFilter`	The superclass of all document filters. You can use a document filter to change what gets inserted or removed from a document, without having to implement a document yourself. See Implementing a Document Filter (page 72).
`void setDocumentFilter(DocumentFilter)` (*in* `AbstractDocument`)	Set the document filter.

`void setDocument(Document)`
`Document getDocument()`
(*in* `JTextComponent`)
	Set or get the document for a text component.

`Document createDefaultModel()` (*in* `JTextField`)	Override this method to create a custom document instead of the default `PlainDocument`.

`void addDocumentListener(`
`        DocumentListener)`
`void removeDocumentListener(`
`        DocumentListener)`
(*in* `Document`)
	Add or remove a document listener to a document. See Listening for Changes on a Document (page 73).

`void addUndoableEditListener(`
`        UndoableEditListener)`
`void removeUndoableEditListener(`
`        UndoableEditlistener)`
(*in* `Document`)
	Add or remove an undoable edit listener to a document. Undoable edit listeners are used in Implementing Undo and Redo (page 68).

`int getLength()`
`Position getStartPosition()`
`Position getEndPosition()`
`String getText(int, int)`
(*in* `Document`)
	Document methods that return useful information about the document.

`Object getProperty(Object)`
`void putProperty(Object, Object)`
(*in* `Document`)
`void setDocumentProperties(Dictionary)`
`Dictionary getDocumentProperties()`
(*in* `AbstractDocument`)
	A Document maintains a set of properties that you can manipulate with these methods. The example described in How to Use Text Fields (page 423) uses a property to name text components so that a shared document listener can identify the document that generated the event.

Table 16: Manipulating Carets and Selection Highlighters

The methods in this table are defined in the JTextComponent *class.*

Interface, Class, or Method	Description
Caret	An interface that defines the API for objects that represent an insertion point within documents.
DefaultCaret	The default caret used by all text components.
void setCaret(Caret) Caret getCaret()	Set or get the caret object used by a text component.
void setCaretColor(Color) Color getCaretColor()	Set or get the color of the caret.
void setCaretPosition(int) void moveCaretPosition(int) int getCaretPosition()	Set or get the current position of the caret within the document.

void addCaretListener(
       CaretListener)
void removeCaretListener(
       CaretListener)
	Add or remove a caret listener to a text component.

NavigationFilter	The superclass for all navigation filters. A navigation filter lets you modify caret changes that are about to occur for a text component.
void setNavigationFilter(NavigationFilter)	Attach a navigation filter to a text component.
Highlighter	An interface that defines the API for objects used to highlight the current selection.
DefaultHighlighter	The default highlighter used by all text components.
void setHighlighter(Highlighter) Highlighter getHighlighter()	Set or get the highlighter used by a text component.

Table 17: Reading and Writing Text

Method	Description
void read(Reader, Object) void write(Writer) (*in* JTextComponent)	Read or write text.
void read(Reader, Document, int) void read(InputStream, Document, int) (*in* EditorKit)	Read text from a stream into a document.
void write(Writer, Document, int, int) void write(OutputStream, Document, int, int) (*in* EditorKit)	Write text from a document to a stream.

Summary

You should now have the knowledge you need to start writing programs that use Swing components. The previous chapters gave you a general understanding of Swing components; this chapter showed you the components and discussed the API they have in common.

As you write programs, you'll probably need to look at the how-to sections for the components and layout managers to use. You're also likely to need the how-to sections for other Swing features, such as icons and data transfer. If you want to continue reading or if you find the how-to sections hard to understand, look at the next two chapters, for general information about using layout managers and writing event listeners. If you need to perform custom painting in your program, also read Chapter 6, Performing Custom Painting (page 129).

If you encounter any problems using Swing components, refer to Solving Common Component Problems (page 735) in the Appendix.

Questions and Exercises

Use the information in this chapter and, if necessary, the component how-to sections in Chapter 7 to help you complete these exercises.

Questions

1. Find the component that best fits each of the following needs. Write down both the component's common name (such as "frame") and the page its how-to discussion begins on (such as page 236). [*Hint: You can use the visual index, which begins on page 37, to help you answer this question.*]

   a. A component that lets the user pick a color.

   b. A component that displays an icon, but that doesn't react to user clicks.

   c. A component that looks like a button and that, when pressed, brings up a menu of items for the user to choose from.

   d. A container that looks like a frame, but that appears (usually with other, similar containers) within a real frame.

   e. A container that lets the user determine how two components share a limited amount of space.

2. Which method do you use to add a menu bar to a top-level container such as a `JFrame`?

3. Which method do you use to specify the default button for a top-level container such as a `JFrame` or `JDialog`?

4. Which method do you use to enable and disable components such as JButtons? What class is it defined in?

5. a. Which Swing components use ListSelectionModels?[1] [*Hint: The "Use" link at the top of the specification for each interface and class takes you to a page showing where in the API that interface or class is referenced.*]

    b. Do those components use any other models to handle other aspects of the components' state? If so, list the other models' types.

6. Which type of model holds a text component's content?

Exercises

Use the information in this chapter and, if necessary, the component how-to sections in Chapter 7 to help you complete these exercises.

1. Implement a program with a GUI that looks like the one shown in Question 1. Put the main method in a class named MyDemo1.

2. Make a copy of MyDemo1.java named MyDemo2.java. Add a menu bar to MyDemo2. (The menu bar can be empty.)

3. Copy MyDemo1.java to MyDemo3.java. Add a button (JButton) to MyDemo3.java. Make it the default button.

Answers

You can find answers to the Questions and Exercises online:

    http://java.sun.com/docs/books/tutorial/uiswing/QandE/answers.html

Example Programs

You can find source files for all of the examples from this chapter on the CD and online:

    JavaTutorial/uiswing/components/example-1dot4/index.html

    http://java.sun.com/docs/books/tutorial/uiswing/components/
    example-1dot4/index.html

---

[1] ListSelectionModel API documentation: http://java.sun.com/j2se/1.4.2/docs/api/javax/swing/ListSelectionModel.html.

The preceding URLs take you to an index that has links to the files required by each example. You can go directly to the entry for a particular example by adding *#ExampleName* to the URL. Most examples have a "Run" link in the example index which executes the example using Java Web Start technology

Example	Where Described	Notes
HtmlDemo	page 44	Lets you experiment with HTML formatting by setting the text on a label.
ButtonHtmlDemo	page 45	Adds font, color, and other text formatting to three buttons.
TopLevelDemo	page 47	Demonstrates the use of a top-level container. The frame contains a menu bar and a large blank label in the frame's content pane.
Converter	page 51	Has two sliders, each tied to a text field to convert metric measurements.
TextSamplerDemo	page 62	Uses one of each of Swing's text components.
TextComponentDemo	page 64	Contains a customized instance of JTextPane.

4

Laying Out Components within a Container

THIS chapter tells you how to use layout managers, which are objects that control the size and position of components in a container. It also tells you how to use absolute positioning (no layout manager) and presents an example of how to write a custom layout manager. How-to information for each of the commonly used layout managers is in Chapter 8, Layout Manager Reference (page 457).

The chapter contains the following sections:

- A Visual Guide to Layout Managers shows examples of the standard layout managers and points to each one's how-to section.
- Using Layout Managers includes how to set the layout manager, add components to a container, provide size and alignment hints, put space between components, and set the orientation of the container's layout so that it's appropriate for the locale in which the program is running. The section also has some tips for choosing the right layout manager.
- How Layout Management Works goes through a typical layout sequence and then describes what happens when a component's size changes.
- Creating a Custom Layout Manager tells you how to write your own layout manager.
- Doing without a Layout Manager (Absolute Positioning) discusses setting the size and position of components directly.

Solving Common Layout Problems (page 738) in the Appendix tells you how to fix common layout glitches.

A Visual Guide to Layout Managers

Several AWT and Swing classes provide layout managers for general use:

- `BorderLayout`
- `BoxLayout`
- `CardLayout`
- `FlowLayout`
- `GridBagLayout`
- `GridLayout`
- `SpringLayout`

This section shows example GUIs that use these layout managers and tells you where to find the how-to section for each one. You can run each example using Java Web Start by following the instructions in the how-to sections.

BorderLayout

Every content pane is initialized to use `BorderLayout`.[1] `BorderLayout` places components in up to five areas: top, bottom, left, right, and center. All extra space is placed in the center area (see Figure 1). For further details, see How to Use BorderLayout (page 459) in Chapter 8.

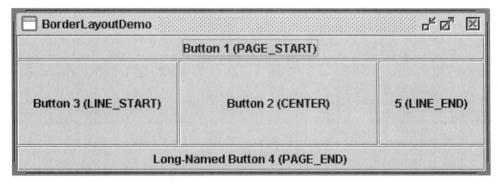

Figure 1   BorderLayoutDemo is an example that uses `BorderLayout`.

BoxLayout

The `BoxLayout` class puts components in a single row or column (see Figure 2). It respects the components' requested maximum sizes and also lets you align components. For further details, see How to Use BoxLayout (page 462) in Chapter 8.

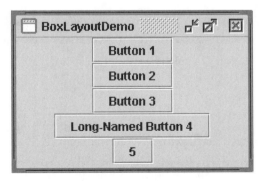

Figure 2   BoxLayoutDemo is an example that uses `BoxLayout`.

---

[1]   As Using Top-Level Containers (page 46) in Chapter 3 explains, the content pane is the main container in all frames, applets, and dialogs.

CardLayout

The CardLayout class lets you implement an area that contains different components at different times (see Figure 3). CardLayout is often controlled by a combo box, the state of which determines which panel (group of components) CardLayout displays. An alternative to CardLayout is a tabbed pane, which provides similar functionality but with a predefined GUI. For further details, see How to Use CardLayout (page 476) in Chapter 8.

Figure 3   CardLayoutDemo is an example that uses CardLayout.

FlowLayout

FlowLayout is the default layout manager for every JPanel (see Figure 4). It simply lays out components in a single row, starting a new row if its container isn't sufficiently wide. Both panels in CardLayoutDemo, shown in Figure 3, use FlowLayout. For further details, see How to Use FlowLayout (page 479) in Chapter 8.

Figure 4   FlowLayoutDemo is an example that uses FlowLayout.

GridBagLayout

GridBagLayout is a sophisticated, flexible layout manager. It aligns components by placing them within a grid of cells, allowing some components to span more than one cell (see Figure 5). The rows in the grid can have different heights, and the columns can have different widths. For further details, see How to Use GridBagLayout (page 481) in Chapter 8.

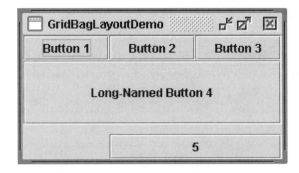

Figure 5   GridBagLayoutDemo is an example that uses GridBagLayout.

GridLayout

GridLayout simply makes components equal in size and displays them in the requested number of rows and columns (see Figure 6). For further details, see How to Use GridLayout (page 490) in Chapter 8.

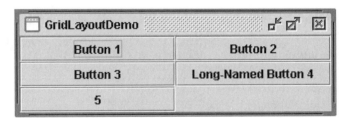

Figure 6   GridLayoutDemo is an example that uses GridLayout.

SpringLayout

SpringLayout is a flexible layout manager designed for GUI builders (see Figure 7). It lets you specify precise relationships between the edges of components under its control. For example, you might define the left edge of one component as a certain distance (which can be dynamically calculated) from the right edge of a second component. For further details, see How to Use SpringLayout (page 492) in Chapter 8.

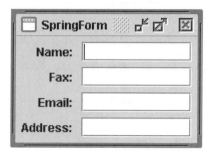

Figure 7   Both SpringBox and SpringForm are examples that use SpringLayout.

Using Layout Managers

A layout manager is an object that implements the LayoutManager interface[1] and deter-mines the size and position of the components within a container.[2] Although components can provide size and alignment hints, a container's layout manager has the final say.

This section discusses some of the common layout tasks:

- Setting the layout manager
- Adding components to a container
- Providing size and alignment hints
- Putting space between components
- Setting the container's orientation

It ends with some tips on choosing a layout manager.

---

[1] LayoutManager API documentation: http://java.sun.com/j2se/1.4.2/docs/api/java/awt/LayoutManager.html.

[2] Way back in JDK 1.1 (an early release of the Java platform) a second interface, LayoutManager2, was in-troduced. LayoutManager2 extends LayoutManager, providing support for maximum size and alignment. Many layout managers don't use those features, however.

Setting the Layout Manager

As a rule, the only containers whose layout managers you need to worry about are JPanels and content panes. Each JPanel object is initialized to use FlowLayout, unless you specify differently when creating it. Content panes use BorderLayout by default. If you don't like the default layout manager that a panel or content pane uses, you're free to change it to a different one.

You can set a panel's layout manager using the JPanel constructor. For example:

```
JPanel panel = new JPanel(new BorderLayout());
```

After a container has been created, you can set its layout manager using the setLayout method. For example:

```
Container contentPane = frame.getContentPane();
contentPane.setLayout(new FlowLayout());
```

Although we recommend that you use layout managers, you can do without them. If you set a container's layout property to null, the container uses no layout manager. With this strategy, called *absolute positioning*, you must specify the size and position of every component within that container. One drawback of absolute positioning is that it doesn't adjust well when the top-level container is resized. It also doesn't adjust well to differences between users and systems, such as different font sizes and locales.

Adding Components to a Container

When you add components to a panel or content pane, the arguments you specify to the add method depend on the layout manager that the panel or content pane is using. For example, BorderLayout requires that you specify the area to which the component should be added using code like this:

```
pane.add(aComponent, BorderLayout.PAGE_START);
```

The how-to section for each layout manager has details on the arguments, if any, you need to specify to the add method. Some layout managers, such as GridBagLayout and Spring-Layout, require elaborate setup procedures. Many, however, simply place components based on the order in which they were added to their container.

Except for JPanels and content panes, Swing containers and content panes generally provide an API that you should use instead of the add method. For example, instead of adding a component directly to a scroll pane (actually to its viewport), you either specify it in the JScrollPane constructor or use setViewportView. Because of specialized API like this, you don't need to know which layout manager (if any) many Swing containers use. (For the curious, scroll panes happen to use ScrollPaneLayout.)

For information about adding components to a specific container, see the container's how-to section. You can find the how-to sections using A Visual Index to Swing Components (page 37) in Chapter 3.

Providing Size and Alignment Hints

Sometimes you need to customize the size hints a component provides to its container's layout manager so that the component will be laid out well. You do this by specifying one or more of the minimum, preferred, and maximum component sizes. You can invoke the component's methods for setting size hints—setMinimumSize, setPreferredSize, and set-MaximumSize. Or you can create a subclass of the component that overrides the appropriate getter methods—getMinimumSize, getPreferredSize, and getMaximumSize. Here's an example of making a component's maximum size unlimited:

```
component.setMaximumSize(new Dimension(Integer.MAX_VALUE,
                                       Integer.MAX_VALUE));
```

Many layout managers don't pay attention to a component's requested maximum size; however, BoxLayout and SpringLayout do.

Besides size hints, you can also provide alignment hints—for example, that the top edges of two components be aligned. You set alignment hints either by invoking the component's setAlignmentX and setAlignmentY methods or by overriding its getAlignmentX and getAlignmentY methods. Although most layout managers ignore alignment hints, Box-Layout honors them. You can find examples of setting the alignment in How to Use Box-Layout (page 462) in Chapter 8.

Putting Space between Components

Three factors influence the amount of space between visible components in a container:

The layout manager

Some layout managers automatically put space between components; others don't. Some also let you specify the amount of space between components. See the how-to section for each layout manager for information about spacing support.

Invisible components

You can create lightweight components that perform no painting but that can take up space in the GUI. Often you use invisible components in containers controlled by Box-Layout. See How to Use BoxLayout (page 462) in Chapter 8 for examples of using invisible components.

Empty borders

No matter which layout manager, you can affect the apparent amount of space between components by adding empty borders to them. The best candidates for empty borders are components that typically have no default border, such as panels and labels. Some other components might not work well with borders in some look-and-feel implementations because of the way their painting code is implemented. For information about borders, see How to Use Borders (page 535) in Chapter 9.

Setting the Container's Orientation

This book is written in English, with text that runs from left to right and then top to bottom. However, many other languages have different orientations, and the property component-Orientation provides a way of indicating that a particular component should use one of them (see Figure 8). In a component such as a radio button, the orientation might hint that the look and feel should switch the locations of the icon and the text in the button. In a container, it's a hint to the layout manager.

To set a container's orientation, you can use either the Component-defined setComponent-Orientation method or, to set the orientation on the container's children as well, the applyComponentOrientation method. The argument to either one can be a constant, such as ComponentOrientation.RIGHT_TO_LEFT, or it can be a call to the ComponentOrientation method getOrientation(Locale). The following code causes all JComponents to be initialized with an Arabic-language locale and then sets the orientation of the content pane and all components inside it accordingly:

```
JComponent.setDefaultLocale(new Locale("ar"));
JFrame frame = new JFrame();
...
Container contentPane = frame.getContentPane();
contentPane.applyComponentOrientation(
            ComponentOrientation.getOrientation(
                    contentPane.getLocale()));
```

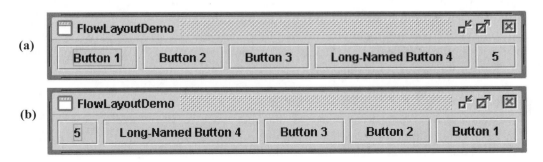

Figure 8 FlowLayoutDemo: (a) left-to-right orientation (default); (b) right-to-left orientation.

The standard layout managers that support component orientation are FlowLayout, Border-Layout, BoxLayout, GridBagLayout, and GridLayout.

Choosing a Layout Manager

Layout managers have different strengths and weaknesses. This section discusses some common layout scenarios and which layout managers might work for each one. If none of the layout managers is right for your situation, feel free to use others that you write or find. Also keep in mind that flexible layout managers, such as GridBagLayout and SpringLayout, can fulfill many needs.

Scenario: You need to display a component in as much space as it can get.
If it's the only component in its container, use GridLayout or BorderLayout. Otherwise, BorderLayout or GridBagLayout might be a good match. If you use BorderLayout, you'll need to put the space-hungry component in the center. With GridBagLayout, you'll need to set the constraints for the component fill=GridBagConstraints.BOTH. Another possibility is to use BoxLayout and have the component specify very large preferred and maximum sizes.

Scenario: You need to display a few components in a compact row at their natural size.
Consider using a JPanel to group the components and using either JPanel's default FlowLayout manager or the BoxLayout manager. SpringLayout is also good for this.

Scenario: You need to display a few components of the same size in rows and columns.
GridLayout is perfect for this.

Scenario: You need to display a few components in a row or column, possibly with varying amounts of space between them, custom alignment, or custom component sizes.
BoxLayout is perfect for this.

Scenario: You need to display aligned columns, as in a form-like interface where a column of labels is used to describe text fields in an adjacent column.
SpringLayout is a natural choice for this. The SpringUtilities class used by several of our examples defines a makeCompactGrid method that lets you easily align multiple rows and columns of components.

Scenario: You have a complex layout with many components.
Consider either a very flexible layout manager, such as GridBagLayout or Spring-Layout, or grouping the components into one or more JPanels to simplify layout. If you take the latter approach, each JPanel might use a different type of layout manager.

How Layout Management Works

Here's an example of a layout management sequence for a frame (JFrame).

1. After the GUI is constructed, the pack method is invoked on the JFrame. This specifies that the frame should be at its preferred size.

2. To find the frame's preferred size, the frame's layout manager adds the size of the frame's edges to the preferred size of the component directly contained by the frame. This is the sum of the preferred size of the frame's content pane plus the size of the frame's menu bar, if any.

3. The content pane's layout manager is responsible for figuring out the content pane's preferred size, and by default, it is a BorderLayout object. However, let's assume that we replace it with a GridLayout object that's set up to create two columns. The interesting thing about grid layout is that it forces all components to be the same size and tries to make them as wide as the widest component's preferred width and as high as the highest one's preferred height. First, the grid layout manager queries the content pane for its insets—the size of the content pane's border, if any. Next, it queries each component in the content pane for its preferred size, noting the largest preferred width and largest preferred height. Then it calculates the content pane's preferred size.

4. When a component in the content pane is asked for its preferred size, the default implementation (used by most components) first checks whether the user specified a preferred size. If so, it reports that; if not, it queries its look and feel for the preferred size.

The end result is that the system determines the best size for the frame by determining the sizes of the components at the bottom of the containment hierarchy. These sizes then percolate up the hierarchy, eventually determining the frame's size as a whole.

If you change the size of a component even indirectly—by changing its font, for example—the component automatically resizes and repaints itself. With a custom component, you can force this to occur by invoking revalidate and then repaint. Both methods are thread-safe—you needn't invoke them from the event-dispatching thread.

When you invoke revalidate on a component, a request is passed up the containment hierarchy until it encounters a container, such as a scroll pane or top-level container, that shouldn't be affected by the component's resizing. (This is determined by calling the container's isValidateRoot method.) The container is then laid out, which has the effect of adjusting the revalidated component's size and the size of all affected components.

Creating a Custom Layout Manager

Note: Before you start creating a custom layout manager, make sure that no existing one will work. Layout managers such as GridBagLayout, SpringLayout, and BoxLayout in particular, are flexible enough to work in many cases. You can also find layout managers from other sources, such as the Internet. Finally, you can simplify layout by grouping components into containers such as invisible panels.

To create a custom layout manager, you must create a class that implements the LayoutManager interface. You can either implement it directly or implement its subinterface, LayoutManager2. Every layout manager must implement at least the following five methods, which are required by the LayoutManager interface:

void addLayoutComponent(String, Component)
> Called by the Container add methods. Layout managers that don't associate strings with their components generally do nothing in this method.

void removeLayoutComponent(Component)
> Called by the Container remove and removeAll methods. Many layout managers do nothing in this method, relying instead on querying the container for its components via the Container method getComponents.

Dimension preferredLayoutSize(Container)
> Called by the Container getPreferredSize method, which is itself called under a variety of circumstances. This method should calculate and return the ideal size of the container, assuming that the components it contains will be at or above their preferred sizes. This method must take into account the container's internal borders, which are returned by the getInsets method.

Dimension minimumLayoutSize(Container)
> Called by the Container getMinimumSize method, which is itself called under a variety of circumstances. This method should calculate and return the minimum size of the container, assuming that the components it contains will be at or above their minimum sizes. It has to take into account the container's internal borders, which are returned by the getInsets method.

void layoutContainer(Container)
> Called when the container is first displayed and each time its size changes. A layout manager's layoutContainer method doesn't actually draw components. It simply invokes each component's setSize, setLocation, and setBounds methods to set the component's size and position. This method must take into account the container's inter-

nal borders, which are returned by the getInsets method. If appropriate, it should also consider the container's orientation (returned by the getComponentOrientation method). You can't assume that the preferredLayoutSize or minimumLayoutSize method will be called before layoutContainer is called.

Besides the preceding five methods, layout managers generally implement at least one public constructor and the toString method.

If you want to support component constraints, maximum sizes, or alignment, your layout manager should implement the LayoutManager2 interface, which adds five methods to those required by LayoutManager:

- addLayoutComponent(Component, Object)
- getLayoutAlignmentX(Container)
- getLayoutAlignmentY(Container)
- invalidateLayout(Container)
- maximumLayoutSize(Container)

For more information about these methods, see the LayoutManager2 API documentation.[1]

When implementing a layout manager, you might want to use SizeRequirements[2] objects to help you determine the size and position of components. For an example of using Size-Requirements, see the source code for BoxLayout.

The example CustomLayoutDemo uses a custom layout manager called DiagonalLayout, which lays out components diagonally, from left to right, one per row (see Figure 9).

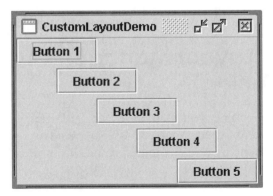

Figure 9   CustomLayoutDemo using DialogalLayout to lay out five buttons.

---

[1] LayoutManager2 API documentation: http://java.sun.com/j2se/1.4.2/docs/api/java/awt/ LayoutManager2.html.

[2] SizeRequirements API documentation: http://java.sun.com/j2se/1.4.2/docs/api/javax/ swing/SizeRequirements.html.

You can run `CustomLayoutDemo` using Java Web Start or compile and run the example yourself.[1]

Another example of a custom layout manager is `GraphPaperLayout`, which implements
`LayoutManager2` and lays out components in a grid (see Figure 10).

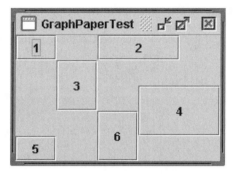

Figure 10   A rough demo called `GraphPaperTest` that uses `GraphPaperLayout`.

You can run `GraphPaperTest` using Java Web Start or compile and run the example yourself.[2]

When a container uses `GraphPaperLayout`, the size and location of its child components are
specified (using grid units rather than absolute locations) as they're added to it. You can set
the relative grid size, the horizontal space between components, and the vertical space
between components when initializing the layout manager. You can also change component
locations and the grid size dynamically.

Doing without a Layout Manager (Absolute Positioning)

Although you can do without one, you should use a layout manager if at all possible. A layout manager makes it easier to adjust to look-and-feel-dependent component appearances, to
different font sizes, to a container's changing size, and to different locales. It can also be
reused easily by other containers as well as other programs.

---

[1]   To run `CustomLayoutDemo` using Java Web Start, click the `CustomLayoutDemo` link on the `RunExam-
ples/layout.html` page on the CD. You can find the source files here: `JavaTutorial/uiswing/lay-
out/example-1dot4/index.html#CustomLayoutDemo`.

[2]   To run `GraphPaperTest` using Java Web Start, click the `GraphPaperTest` link on the `RunExamples/
layout.html` page on the CD. You can find the source files here: `JavaTutorial/uiswing/layout/ex-
ample-1dot4/index.html#GraphPaperTest`.

Still, if a container holds components whose size isn't affected by the container's size or by font and look-and-feel and language changes, absolute positioning might make sense. Desktop panes, which contain internal frames, are in this category. The size and position of the frames don't depend directly on the pane's size. Instead, the programmer determines their initial size and placement, and then the user can move or resize them. A layout manager is unnecessary in this situation. Absolute positioning might also make sense for a custom container that performs size and position calculations that are particular to it and that perhaps require knowledge of its specialized state. This is the situation with split panes. Figure 11 is an example of absolute positioning.

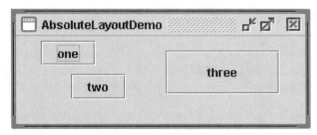

Figure 11   A frame whose content pane uses absolute positioning.

You can run AbsoluteLayoutDemo using Java Web Start or compile and run the example yourself.[1]

The code snippet that follows shows how the components in the content pane are created and laid out:

```
pane.setLayout(null);

JButton b1 = new JButton("one");
JButton b2 = new JButton("two");
JButton b3 = new JButton("three");

pane.add(b1);
pane.add(b2);
pane.add(b3);

Insets insets = pane.getInsets();
Dimension size = b1.getPreferredSize();
b1.setBounds(25 + insets.left, 5 + insets.top,
             size.width, size.height);
```

---

[1]   To run AbsoluteLayoutDemo using Java Web Start, click the AbsoluteLayoutDemo link on the RunExamples/layout.html page on the CD. You can find the source files here: JavaTutorial/uiswing/layout/example-1dot4/index.html#AbsoluteLayoutDemo.

```
size = b2.getPreferredSize();
b2.setBounds(55 + insets.left, 40 + insets.top,
             size.width, size.height);
size = b3.getPreferredSize();
b3.setBounds(150 + insets.left, 15 + insets.top,
             size.width + 50, size.height + 20);

...//In the main method:
Insets insets = frame.getInsets();
frame.setSize(300 + insets.left + insets.right,
              125 + insets.top + insets.bottom);
```

Summary

This chapter gave you the information you need to choose a layout manager and to work with layout managers, in general. It also told you how to lay out components without using a layout manager (not that we recommend that!) and introduced you to how you would create your own layout manager.

Whenever you're considering using layout managers supplied by the Java platform, you can use A Visual Guide to Layout Managers (page 88) and Using Layout Managers (page 92) sections to get an idea of which layout managers are best for which tasks.

Details about how to use individual layout managers are in Chapter 8, Layout Manager Reference (page 457).

If you encounter problems with layout, refer to Solving Common Layout Problems (page 738) in the Appendix.

Questions and Exercises

Questions

In each of the following questions, choose the layout manager(s) most naturally suited for the described layout. Assume that the container controlled by the layout manager is a JPanel. [*Hint: Two sections that might help are A Visual Index to Swing Components (page 37) in Chapter 3 and Choosing a Layout Manager (page 96) in this chapter.*]

1. The container has one component that should take up as much space as possible.

 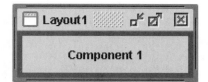

   a. BorderLayout

   b. GridLayout

   c. GridBagLayout

   d. a and b

   e. b and c

2. The container has a row of components that should all be displayed at the same size, filling the container's entire area.

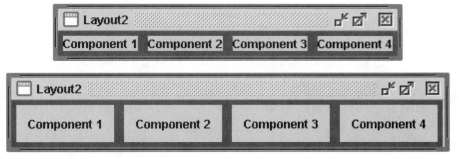

   a. FlowLayout

   b. GridLayout

   c. BoxLayout

   d. a and b

3. The container displays a number of components in a column, with any extra space going between the first two components.

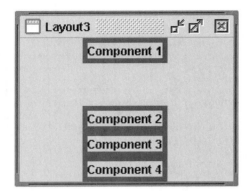

a. FlowLayout

b. BoxLayout

c. GridLayout

d. BorderLayout

4. The container can display three completely different components at different times, depending perhaps on user input or program state. Even if the components' sizes differ, switching from one component to the next shouldn't change the amount of space devoted to the component.

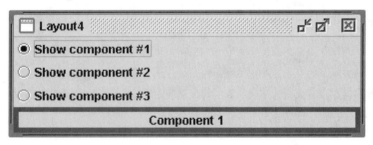

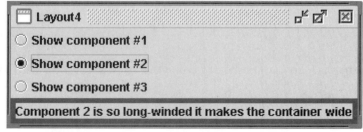

a. SpringLayout

b. BoxLayout

c. CardLayout

d. GridBagLayout

Exercises

1. Implement the layout described and shown in question 1.
2. Implement the layout described and shown in question 2.
3. Implement the layout described and shown in question 3.
4. Implement the layout described and shown in question 4.
5. By adding a single line of code, make the program you wrote for Exercise 2 display the component from right-to-left, instead of from left-to-right.

Answers

You can find answers to the Questions and Exercises online:

```
http://java.sun.com/docs/books/tutorial/uiswing/QandE/answers.html
```

Example Programs

You can find source files for all the examples from this chapter on the CD and online:

```
JavaTutorial/uiswing/layout/example-1dot4/index.html
```

```
http://java.sun.com/docs/books/tutorial/uiswing/layout/
example-1dot4/index.html
```

The preceding URLs take you to an index that has links to the files required by each example. You can go directly to the entry for a particular example by adding *#ExampleName* to the URL. Most examples have a "Run" link in the example index which executes the example using Java Web Start technology.

Code Example	Where Described	Notes
CustomLayoutDemo	page 100	Uses a custom layout manager called `DiagonalLayout`.
GraphPaperTest	page 100	Uses a custom layout manager to lay out components in a grid. This example also implements `LayoutManager2`.
AbsoluteLayoutDemo	page 101	Demonstrates absolute positioning.

5

Writing Event Listeners

THIS chapter gives you details about writing event listeners. It assumes you've already read Handling Events (page 19) in Chapter 2, which gives an overview of the event model.

You might not need to read this section, at all. Your first source of information for event information should be the how-to section for the component in question. You can find the appropriate section using A Visual Index to Swing Components (page 37) in Chapter 3. Each component's section shows code for handling the events most commonly needed when implementing the component. For example, How to Use Check Boxes (page 163) in Chapter 7 shows you how to handle mouse clicks on check boxes using an item listener.

This chapter contains the following sections:

- Some Event-Handling Examples includes programs which illustrate events and event handling.

- General Information about Writing Event Listeners provides information that's useful for handling all types of events. One of the topics covers the use of adapters and inner classes to implement event handlers.

- Listeners Supported by Swing Components is *the* place to find out which Swing components can fire which kinds of events. This section includes a handy quick-reference table.

- Listener API Table features a comprehensive reference table that shows each listener, its adapter class, and its methods.

- At the end of this chapter, the Summary reviews what we've covered and Questions and Exercises tests what you've learned in this chapter. Finally, Example Programs lists all the examples in this chapter and indicates where you can find them on the CD and online.

If you're having some hard-to-debug problems related to handling events, you may find the solutions in Solving Common Event-Handling Problems (page 739) in the Appendix.

Some Event-Handling Examples

If you've read Handling Events (page 19) in Chapter 2, or any of the component how-to pages, you probably already know the basics of event listeners.

Let's look at one of the simplest event-handling examples possible. It's called Beeper, and it features a button that beeps when you click it. You can run Beeper using Java Web Start or compile and run the example yourself.[1] (See Figure 1.)

---

[1] To run Beeper using Java Web Start, click the Beeper link on the RunExamples/events.html page on the CD. You can find the source files here: JavaTutorial/uiswing/events/example-1dot4/ index.html#Beeper.

Figure 1   The Beeper application.

Here's the code that implements the event handling for the button:

```
public class Beeper ... implements ActionListener {
    ...

    //where initialization occurs:
        button.addActionListener(this);
    ...

    public void actionPerformed(ActionEvent e) {
        ...//Make a beep sound...
    }
}
```

The Beeper class implements the ActionListener interface,[1] which contains one method: actionPerformed. Since Beeper implements ActionListener, a Beeper object can register as a listener for the action events that buttons fire. Once the Beeper has been registered using the Button addActionListener method, the Beeper's actionPerformed method is called every time the button is clicked.

Multiple Listeners Example

The event model, which you saw at its simplest in the preceding example, is quite powerful and flexible. Any number of event listener objects can listen for all kinds of events from any number of event source objects. For example, a program might create one listener per event source. Or a program might have a single listener for all events from all sources. A program

---

[1]   For more details on ActionListener, see How to Write an Action Listener (page 646) in Chapter 10.

can even have more than one listener for a single kind of event from a single event source. (See Figure 2.)

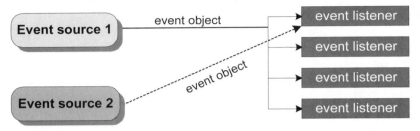

Figure 2   Multiple listeners can register to be notified of events of a particular type from a particular source. Also, the same listener can listen to notifications from different objects.

Each event is represented by an object that gives information about the event and identifies the event source. Event sources are often components or models, but other kinds of objects can also be event sources.

The following example demonstrates that event listeners can be registered on multiple objects and that the same event can be sent to multiple listeners. The example contains two event sources (JButton instances) and two event listeners. One of the event listeners (an instance of a class called MultiListener) listens for events from both buttons. When it receives an event, it adds the event's "action command" (which is set to the text on the button's label) to the top text area. The second event listener (an instance of a class called Eavesdropper) listens for events on only one of the buttons. When it receives an event, it adds the action command to the bottom text area.

```
┌─────────────────────────────────────────────────┐
│ What MultiListener hears:                      ▲  │
│ You don't say!                                    │
│ Blah blah blah                                    │
│ Blah blah blah                                 ▓  │
│ Blah blah blah                                 ▓  │
│ Blah blah blah                                    │
│ You don't say!                                 ▼  │
├─────────────────────────────────────────────────┤
│ What Eavesdropper hears:                          │
│ You don't say!                                    │
│ You don't say!                                    │
│ You don't say!                                    │
│                                                   │
│                                                   │
│                                                   │
│                                                   │
├─────────────────────────┬───────────────────────┤
│      Blah blah blah      │     You don't say!    │
└─────────────────────────┴───────────────────────┘
```

Figure 3   The MultiListener applet.

Try This:

1. Run MultiListener using Java Web Start or compile and run the example yourself.[1]
2. Click the **Blah blah blah** button. Only the MultiListener object is registered to listen to this button.
3. Click the **You don't say!** button. Both the MultiListener object and the Eavesdropper object are registered to listen to this button.

You can find the entire program in MultiListener.java. Here's the code that implements the event handling for the button:

```
public class MultiListener ... implements ActionListener {
    ...
    //where initialization occurs:
        button1.addActionListener(this);
        button2.addActionListener(this);

        button2.addActionListener(new Eavesdropper(bottomTextArea));
    }
```

---

[1] To run MultiListener using Java Web Start, click the MultiListener link on the RunExamples/
    events.html page on the CD. You can find the source files here: JavaTutorial/uiswing/events/
    example-1dot4/index.html#MultiListener.

```
        public void actionPerformed(ActionEvent e) {
            topTextArea.append(e.getActionCommand() + newline);
        }
    }

    class Eavesdropper implements ActionListener {
        ...
        public void actionPerformed(ActionEvent e) {
            myTextArea.append(e.getActionCommand() + newline);
        }
    }
```

In the above code, both MultiListener and Eavesdropper implement the ActionListener interface and register as action listeners using the JButton addActionListener method. Both classes' implementations of the actionPerformed method are similar: They simply add the event's action command to a text area.

General Information about Writing Event Listeners

This section discusses several design considerations to keep in mind when implementing event handlers in your application. We then introduce you to event objects—small objects that describe each event. In particular, we talk about EventObject, the superclass for all AWT and Swing events. Next, we introduce the concepts of low-level events and semantic events, recommending that you choose semantic events when possible. The remainder of this section discusses implementation techniques you might use in some event listeners or see in event listeners created by other people or by GUI builders.

Design Considerations

The most important rule to keep in mind about event listeners is that they should execute very quickly. Because all drawing and event-listening methods are executed in the same thread, a slow event-listener method can make the program seem unresponsive and slow to repaint itself. If you need to perform some lengthy operation as the result of an event, do it by starting up another thread (or somehow sending a request to another thread) to perform the operation. For help on using threads, see How to Use Threads (page 632).

You have many choices on how to implement an event listener. We can't recommend a specific approach because one solution won't suit all situations. However, we can give you some hints and show you some techniques that you might see, even if you don't use the same solution in your program.

For example, you might choose to implement separate classes for different kinds of event listeners. This can be an easy architecture to maintain, but many classes can also mean reduced performance.

When designing your program, you might want to implement your event listeners in a class that is not public, but somewhere more hidden. A private implementation is a more secure implementation.

If you have a very specific kind of simple event listener, you might be able to avoid creating a class at all by using the EventHandler class, as described on page 117.

Getting Event Information: Event Objects

Every event-listener method has a single argument—an object that inherits from the EventObject class.[1] Although the argument always descends from EventObject, its type is generally specified more precisely. For example, the argument for methods that handle mouse events is an instance of MouseEvent, where MouseEvent is an indirect subclass of EventObject.

The EventObject class defines one very useful method:

- **Object getSource()**: Returns the object that fired the event.

Note that the getSource method returns an Object. Event classes sometimes define methods similar to getSource, but having more restricted return types. For example, the ComponentEvent class defines a getComponent method that—just like getSource—returns the object that fired the event. The difference is that getComponent always returns a Component. Each event how-to section in Chapter 10 describes whether you should use getSource or another method to get the event source.

Often, an event class defines methods that return information about the event. For example, you can query a MouseEvent object for information about where the event occurred, how many clicks the user made, which modifier keys were pressed, and so on.

Concepts: Low-Level Events and Semantic Events

Events can be divided into two groups: *low-level* events and *semantic* events. Low-level events represent window-system occurrences or low-level input. Everything else is a semantic event.

Examples of low-level events include mouse and key events—both of which result directly from user input. Examples of semantic events include action and item events. A semantic

---

[1] The API documentation for EventObject is online at: http://java.sun.com/j2se/1.4.2/docs/api/java/util/EventObject.html.

event might be triggered by user input; for example, a button customarily fires an action event when the user clicks it, and a text field fires an action event when the user presses Enter. However, some semantic events aren't triggered by low-level events, at all. For example, a table-model event may be fired when a table model receives new data from a database.

Whenever possible, you should listen for semantic events rather than low-level events. That way, you can make your code as robust and portable as possible. For example, listening for action events on buttons, rather than mouse events, means that the button will react appropriately when the user tries to activate the button using a keyboard alternative or a look-and-feel-specific gesture. When dealing with a compound component such as a combo box, it's imperative that you stick to semantic events, since you have no reliable way of registering listeners on all the look-and-feel-specific components that might be used to form the compound component.

Event Adapters

Some listener interfaces contain more than one method. For example, the `MouseListener` interface contains five methods: `mousePressed`, `mouseReleased`, `mouseEntered`, `mouseExited`, and `mouseClicked`. Even if you care only about mouse clicks, if your class directly implements `MouseListener`, then you must implement all five `MouseListener` methods. Methods for those events you don't care about can have empty bodies. Here's an example:

```
//An example that implements a listener interface directly.
public class MyClass implements MouseListener {
    ...
        someObject.addMouseListener(this);
    ...
    /* Empty method definition. */
    public void mousePressed(MouseEvent e) {
    }

    /* Empty method definition. */
    public void mouseReleased(MouseEvent e) {
    }

    /* Empty method definition. */
    public void mouseEntered(MouseEvent e) {
    }

    /* Empty method definition. */
    public void mouseExited(MouseEvent e) {
    }

    public void mouseClicked(MouseEvent e) {
        ...//Event listener implementation goes here...
    }
}
```

The resulting collection of empty method bodies can make code harder to read and maintain. To help you avoid implementing empty method bodies, the API generally includes an *adapter* class for each listener interface with more than one method. For example, the `MouseAdapter` class implements the `MouseListener` interface. An adapter class implements empty versions of all its interface's methods.

To use an adapter, you create a subclass of it and override only the methods of interest, rather than directly implementing all methods of the listener interface. Here's an example of modifying the preceding code to extend `MouseAdapter`. By extending `MouseAdapter`, it inherits empty definitions of all five of the methods that `MouseListener` contains.

```
/*
 * An example of extending an adapter class instead of
 * directly implementing a listener interface.
 */
public class MyClass extends MouseAdapter {
    ...
        someObject.addMouseListener(this);
    ...
    public void mouseClicked(MouseEvent e) {
        ...//Event listener implementation goes here...
    }
}
```

Inner Classes and Anonymous Inner Classes

What if you want to use an adapter class, but don't want your public class to inherit from an adapter class? For example, suppose you write an applet, and you want your `Applet` subclass to contain some code to handle mouse events. Since the Java platform doesn't permit multiple inheritance, your class can't extend both the `Applet` and `MouseAdapter` classes. A solution is to define an *inner class*—a class inside of your `Applet` subclass—that extends the `MouseAdapter` class.

Inner classes can also be useful for event listeners that implement one or more interfaces directly.

```
//An example of using an inner class.
public class MyClass extends Applet {
    ...
        someObject.addMouseListener(new MyAdapter());
    ...
    class MyAdapter extends MouseAdapter {
        public void mouseClicked(MouseEvent e) {
            ...//Event listener implementation goes here...
        }
    }
}
```

Performance Note: When considering whether to use an inner class, keep in mind that application startup time and memory footprint are typically directly proportional to the number of classes you load. The more classes you create, the longer your program takes to start up and the more memory it will take. As an application developer you have to balance this with other design constraints you may have. We are not suggesting you turn your application into a single monolithic class in hopes of cutting down startup time and memory footprint—this would lead to unnecessary headaches and maintenance burdens.

You can create an inner class without specifying a name—this is known as an *anonymous inner class*. While they might look strange at first glance, anonymous inner classes can make your code easier to read because the class is defined where it is referenced. However, you need to weigh the convenience against possible performance implications of increasing the number of classes.

Here's an example of using an anonymous inner class:

```
//An example of using an anonymous inner class.
public class MyClass extends Applet {
    ...
        someObject.addMouseListener(new MouseAdapter() {
            public void mouseClicked(MouseEvent e) {
                ...//Event listener implementation goes here...
            }
        });
    ...
    }
}
```

Note: One drawback of anonymous inner classes is that they can't be seen by the long-term persistence mechanism. For more information see the API documentation for the JavaBeans package[1] and the "Bean Persistence" lesson in *The Java Tutorial*'s JavaBeans trail.[2]

Inner classes work even if your event listener needs access to private instance variables from the enclosing class. As long as you don't declare an inner class to be `static`, an inner class can refer to instance variables and methods just as if its code were in the containing class. To

---

[1] JavaBeans package API documentation is available on the CD and online at: `http://java.sun.com/ j2se/1.4.2/docs/api/java/beans/package-summary.html#package_description`.

[2] The JavaBeans trail is available on the CD and online at: `http://java.sun.com/docs/books/tutorial/javabeans/index.html`.

make a local variable available to an inner class, just save a copy of the variable as a `final` local variable.

To refer to the enclosing instance, you can use *EnclosingClass*.`this`. For more information about inner classes, see "Implementing Nested Classes," a lesson in *The Java Tutorial* that's available on the CD and online at: `http://java.sun.com/docs/books/tutorial/java/java00/nested.html`.

The EventHandler Class

Release 1.4 introduced an `EventHandler`[1] class that supports dynamically generating simple, one-statement event listeners. Although `EventHandler` is only useful for a certain class of extremely simple event listeners, it's worth mentioning for two reasons. It is useful for:

- Making an event listener that persistence can see and yet doesn't clog up your own classes with event listener interfaces and methods.
- Not adding to the number of classes defined in an application—this can help performance.

Creating an `EventHandler` by hand is difficult. An `EventHandler` must be carefully constructed. If you make a mistake, you won't be notified at compile time—your program will throw an obscure exception at runtime. For this reason, `EventHandler`s are best created by a GUI builder. `EventHandler`s should also be carefully documented. Otherwise, you run the risk of producing hard-to-read code.

An `EventHandler` can only be used in a situation where you need to set a property on an object (any `Object` will work) that has a `set` method for the property, as specified by the JavaBeans component architecture. The value that you set the property to has to be reachable, using a `get`/`is` method, from the event that the `EventHandler` handles. For example, all events have the event source (available via `getSource`). If the event source is the only object you can get to from the event, then whatever value you're getting has to be reachable from the event source. Also, you can't do any "if"s or any other kind of checking in the event listener. It directly assigns a value to a property and nothing more.

The `ColorChooserDemo` example in How to Use Color Choosers (page 167) in Chapter 7 can be modified to use an event listener to dynamically create a `ChangeListener`. The change listener class defines only one method—`stateChanged`. If it had more than one method and handled those methods differently, the method name would need to be specified as one of the parameters. For example, a `MouseListener` would probably want to treat mouse click and mouse down events differently.

---

[1] The API documentation for `EventHandler` is online at: `http://java.sun.com/j2se/1.4.2/docs/api/java/beans/EventHandler.html`.

Here's how ColorChooserDemo would look if it used an EventHandler:

```
import java.beans.EventHandler;
...

//Note that the class no longer implements the
//ChangeListener interface.
public class ColorChooserDemo extends JPanel {
    ...

    //The following replaces the line:
    //tcc.getSelectionModel().addChangeListener(this);
    tcc.getSelectionModel().addChangeListener(
        (ChangeListener)EventHandler.create(
            ChangeListener.class,
            //banner.
            banner,
            //          setForeground(
            "foreground",
            //                      e.getSource().getSelectedColor());
            "source.selectedColor"));
    )

    ...

    //This method is no longer necessary.
    //public void stateChanged(ChangeEvent e) {
    //    Color newColor = tcc.getColor();
    //    banner.setForeground(newColor);
    //}

    ...
}
```

Listeners Supported by Swing Components

You can tell what kinds of events a component can fire by looking at the kinds of event listeners you can register on it. For example, the JComboBox class defines these listener registration methods:

- addActionListener
- addItemListener
- addPopupMenuListener

Thus, a combo box supports action, item, and popup menu listeners in addition to the listener type support it inherits from `JComponent`.

A component fires only those events for which listeners have registered on it. For example, if an action listener is registered on a particular combo box, but the combo box has no other listeners, then the combo box will fire only action events—no item or popup menu events.

Listeners supported by Swing components fall into two categories:

- Listeners that all Swing components support
- Other listeners that Swing components support

Listeners That All Swing Components Support

Because all Swing components descend from the AWT `Component` class, you can register the following listeners on any Swing component:

component listener
> Listens for changes in the component's size, position, or visibility.

focus listener
> Listens for whether the component gained or lost the ability to receive keyboard input.

key listener
> Listens for key presses; key events are fired only by the component that has the current keyboard focus.

mouse listener
> Listens for mouse clicks and mouse movement into or out of the component's drawing area.

mouse-motion listener
> Listens for changes in the cursor's position over the component.

mouse-wheel listener *(introduced in 1.4)*
> Listens for mouse wheel movement over the component.

property-change listener
> Listens for changes to various component properties, such as the component's displayed value.

Two listener types introduced in release 1.3, HierarchyListener and HierarchyBounds-Listener, listen to changes to a component's containment hierarchy. These listener types aren't useful to most programs and can generally be ignored.

All Swing components descend from the AWT Container class, but many of them aren't used as containers. So, technically speaking, any Swing component can fire container events, which notify listeners that a component has been added to or removed from the container. Realistically speaking, however, only containers (such as panels and frames) and compound components (such as combo boxes) fire container events.

JComponent provides support for three more listener types. You can register an ancestor listener[1] to be notified when a component's containment ancestors are added to or removed from a container, hidden, made visible, or moved. This listener type is an implementation detail which predated hierarchy listeners and can generally be ignored.

Swing components conform to the JavaBeans component architecture. Among other things, this means that Swing components support bound and constrained properties and notify listeners of changes to the properties. We've already mentioned property change listeners. Swing components also support vetoable change listeners,[2] which listen for changes to constrained properties.

Other Listeners That Swing Components Support

Table 1 lists Swing components and the listeners that they support, not including listeners supported by all Components, Containers, or JComponents. In many cases, the events are fired directly from the component. In other cases, the events are fired from the component's data or selection model. To find out the details for the particular component and listener you're interested in, go first to the component how-to section and then, if necessary, to the listener how-to section (using the page number in parentheses).

---

[1] API documentation for AncestorListener is online at: http://java.sun.com/j2se/1.4.2/docs/api/javax/swing/event/AncestorListener.html.

[2] API documentation for VetoableChangeListener is online at: http://java.sun.com/j2se/1.4.2/docs/api/java/beans/VetoableChangeListener.html.

Table 1: Swing Components and Listeners They Support

Component	Listener							
	action (page 646)	caret (page 649)	change (page 652)	document (page 661), undoable edit (page 721)	item (page 674)	list selection (page 685)	window (page 723)	other
button (page 156)	●		●		●			
check box (page 163)	●		●		●			
color chooser (page 167)			●					
combo box (page 176)	●				●			
dialog (page 187)							●	
editor pane (page 200)		●		●				hyperlink
file chooser (page 206)	●							
formatted text field (page 221)	●	●		●				
frame (page 236)							●	
internal frame (page 245)								internal frame (page 245)
list (page 267)						●		list data (page 682)
menu (page 277)								menu
menu item (page 277)	●		●		●			menu key, menu drag mouse
option pane (page 187)								
password field (page 423)	●	●		●				
popup menu (page 277)								popup menu
progress bar (page 300)			●					
radio button (page 311)	●		●		●			
slider (page 348)			●					
spinner (page 357)			●					
tabbed pane (page 382)			●					

Table 1: Swing Components and Listeners They Support *(continued)*

Component	Listener							
	action (page 646)	caret (page 649)	change (page 652)	document (page 661), undoable edit (page 721)	item (page 674)	list selection (page 685)	window (page 723)	other
table (page 388)						●		table model (page 388), table column model, cell editor
text area (page 418)		●		●				
text field (page 423)	●	●		●				
text pane (page 60)		●		●				hyperlink
toggle button (page 156)	●		●		●			
tree (page 437)								tree expansion (page 710), tree will expand (page 718), tree model (page 713), tree selection (page 715)
viewport *used by scrollpane* (page 325)			●					

Listener API Table

In Table 2, the first column gives the name of the listener interface. The second column names the corresponding adapter class, if any. For a discussion of how to use adapters, see Event Adapters (page 114). The third column lists the methods that the listener interface contains and shows the type of the event object passed into the method. Typically, the listener, the adapter, and the event type have the same name prefix, but this is not always the case.

Table 2: Listener API Summary

Listener Interface	Adapter Class	Listener Methods
`ActionListener`	*none*	`actionPerformed(ActionEvent)`

`AncestorListener`	*none*	`ancestorAdded(AncestorEvent)`
		`ancestorMoved(AncestorEvent)`
		`ancestorRemoved(AncestorEvent)`

`CaretListener`	*none*	`caretUpdate(CaretEvent)`
`CellEditorListener`	*none*	`editingStopped(ChangeEvent)` `editingCanceled(ChangeEvent)`
`ChangeListener`	*none*	`stateChanged(ChangeEvent)`

`ComponentListener`	`ComponentAdapter`	`componentHidden(ComponentEvent)`
		`componentMoved(ComponentEvent)`
		`componentResized(ComponentEvent)`
		`componentShown(ComponentEvent)`

`ContainerListener`	`ContainerAdapter`	`componentAdded(ContainerEvent)` `componentRemoved(ContainerEvent)`

`DocumentListener`	*none*	`changedUpdate(DocumentEvent)`
		`insertUpdate(DocumentEvent)`
		`removeUpdate(DocumentEvent)`

`ExceptionListener` (*introduced in 1.4*)	*none*	`exceptionThrown(Exception)`
`FocusListener`	`FocusAdapter`	`focusGained(FocusEvent)` `focusLost(FocusEvent)`

`HierarchyBounds-`
`Listener`
(*introduced in 1.3*)
	`HierarchyBounds-`
	`Adapter`
		`ancestorMoved(HierarchyEvent)`
		`ancestorResized(HierarchyEvent)`

`HierarchyListener` (*introduced in 1.3*)	*none*	`hierarchyChanged(HierarchyEvent)`
`HyperlinkListener`	*none*	`hyperlinkUpdate(HyperlinkEvent)`
`InputMethodListener`	*none*	`caretPositionChanged(InputMethodEvent)` `inputMethodTextChanged(InputMethodEvent)`

`InternalFrameListener`	`InternalFrame-`
	`Adapter`
		`internalFrameActivated(InternalFrameEvent)`
		`internalFrameClosed(InternalFrameEvent)`
		`internalFrameClosing(InternalFrameEvent)`
		`internalFrameDeactivated(`
		`        InternalFrameEvent)`
		`internalFrameDeiconified(`
		`        InternalFrameEvent)`
		`internalFrameIconified(InternalFrameEvent)`
		`internalFrameOpened(InternalFrameEvent)`

`ItemListener`	*none*	`itemStateChanged(ItemEvent)`

Table 2: Listener API Summary *(continued)*

Listener Interface	Adapter Class	Listener Methods
KeyListener	KeyAdapter	keyPressed(KeyEvent) keyReleased(KeyEvent) keyTyped(KeyEvent)
ListDataListener	*none*	contentsChanged(ListDataEvent) intervalAdded(ListDataEvent) intervalRemoved(ListDataEvent)
ListSelectionListener	*none*	valueChanged(ListSelectionEvent)
MenuDragMouseListener	*none*	menuDragMouseDragged(MenuDragMouseEvent) menuDragMouseEntered(MenuDragMouseEvent) menuDragMouseExited(MenuDragMouseEvent) menuDragMouseReleased(MenuDragMouseEvent)
MenuKeyListener	*none*	menuKeyPressed(MenuKeyEvent) menuKeyReleased(MenuKeyEvent) menuKeyTyped(MenuKeyEvent)
MenuListener	*none*	menuCanceled(MenuEvent) menuDeselected(MenuEvent) menuSelected(MenuEvent)
MouseInputListener (extends MouseListener and MouseMotionListener)	MouseInput- Adapter	mouseClicked(MouseEvent) mouseEntered(MouseEvent) mouseExited(MouseEvent) mousePressed(MouseEvent) mouseReleased(MouseEvent) mouseDragged(MouseEvent) mouseMoved(MouseEvent)
MouseListener	MouseAdapter, MouseInput- Adapter	mouseClicked(MouseEvent) mouseEntered(MouseEvent) mouseExited(MouseEvent) mousePressed(MouseEvent) mouseReleased(MouseEvent)
MouseMotionListener	MouseMotion- Adapter, MouseInput- Adapter	mouseDragged(MouseEvent) mouseMoved(MouseEvent)
MouseWheelListener (*introduced in 1.4*)	*none*	mouseWheelMoved(MouseWheelEvent)
PopupMenuListener	*none*	popupMenuCanceled(PopupMenuEvent) popupMenuWillBecomeInvisible(Popup- MenuEvent) popupMenuWillBecomeVisible(PopupMenuEvent)
PropertyChangeLis- tener	*none*	propertyChange(PropertyChangeEvent)

Table 2: Listener API Summary *(continued)*

Listener Interface	Adapter Class	Listener Methods
TableColumnModel- Listener	*none*	columnAdded(TableColumnModelEvent) columnMoved(TableColumnModelEvent) columnRemoved(TableColumnModelEvent) columnMarginChanged(ChangeEvent) columnSelectionChanged(ListSelectionEvent)
TableModelListener	*none*	tableChanged(TableModelEvent)
TreeExpansionListener	*none*	treeCollapsed(TreeExpansionEvent) treeExpanded(TreeExpansionEvent)
TreeModelListener	*none*	treeNodesChanged(TreeModelEvent) treeNodesInserted(TreeModelEvent) treeNodesRemoved(TreeModelEvent) treeStructureChanged(TreeModelEvent)
TreeSelectionListener	*none*	valueChanged(TreeSelectionEvent)
TreeWillExpand- Listener	*none*	treeWillCollapse(TreeExpansionEvent) treeWillExpand(TreeExpansionEvent)
UndoableEditListener	*none*	undoableEditHappened(UndoableEditEvent)
VetoableChange- Listener	*none*	vetoableChange(PropertyChangeEvent)
WindowFocusListener (*introduced in 1.4*)	WindowAdapter	windowGainedFocus(WindowEvent) windowLostFocus(WindowEvent)
WindowListener	WindowAdapter	windowActivated(WindowEvent) windowClosed(WindowEvent) windowClosing(WindowEvent) windowDeactivated(WindowEvent) windowDeiconified(WindowEvent) windowIconified(WindowEvent) windowOpened(WindowEvent)
WindowStateListener (*introduced in 1.4*)	WindowAdapter	windowStateChanged(WindowEvent)

Summary

This chapter discussed the event-handling mechanism, the Event object, and how to write event listeners. Event adapters were also discussed, as well as the recommendation to avoid creating more classes in your program than are strictly necessary.

The "Listener API Summary" table (page 123) shows the methods defined in each listener interface.You might find the information in Listeners Supported by Swing Components (page 118) particularly useful—it shows the listeners supported by all Swing components and is followed by a table showing the unique listeners supported by each component.

When writing an event listener, you should first check the how-to section for the particular component—for example, How to Use Check Boxes (page 163) shows you how to handle mouse clicks on check boxes using an item listener. If you still have questions, you should refer to the particular how-to section in Chapter 10, Event Listeners Reference (page 643)—for example, How to Write an Item Listener (page 674) or How to Write Window Listeners (page 723).

The Solving Common Event-Handling Problems (page 739) section in the Appendix may help with any particular problems you encounter.

Questions and Exercises

Use this chapter's tables, the how-to sections for components (Chapter 7), and if necessary the how-to sections for event listeners (Chapter 10) to complete these questions and exercises.

Questions

1. What listener would you implement to be notified when a particular component has appeared on screen? What method tells you this information?
2. What listener would you implement to be notified when the user has finished editing a text field by pressing Enter? What listener would you implement to be notified as each character is typed into a text field? Note that you should not implement a general-purpose key listener, but a listener specific to text.
3. What listener would you implement to be notified when a spinner's value has changed? How would you get the spinner's new value?
4. The default behavior for the focus subsystem is to consume the focus traversal keys, such as Tab and Shift Tab. Say you want to prevent this from happening in one of your application's components. How would you accomplish this?

Exercises

1. Take the Beeper example (discussed on page 108) and add a text field. Implement it so that when the user has finishing entering data, the system beeps.
2. Take the Beeper example and add a selectable component that allows the user to enter a number from 1 to 10. For example, you can use a combo box, a set of radio buttons,

or a spinner. Implement it so that when the user has selected the number, the system beeps that many times.

Answers

You can find answers to the Questions and Exercises online:

    http://java.sun.com/docs/books/tutorial/uiswing/QandE/answers.html

Example Programs

You can find source files for all the examples from this chapter on the CD and online:

    JavaTutorial/uiswing/events/example-1dot4/index.html

    http://java.sun.com/docs/books/tutorial/uiswing/events/
    example-1dot4/index.html

The preceding URLs take you to an index that has links to the files required by each example. You can go directly to the entry for a particular example by adding *#ExampleName* to the URL. Most examples have a "Run" link in the index which executes the example using Java Web Start technology.

Example	Where Described	Notes
Beeper	page 109	Illustrates simple event handling.
MultiListener	page 110	Uses multiple listeners per object. The applet contains two event sources (JButton instances) and two event listeners.
MouseEventDemo	page 111	Shows mouse event handling.

Performing Custom Painting

YOU might not need to read this chapter at all. Many programs get by with no custom painting. If they display images, they do so using icons in standard Swing components such as labels and buttons. To display styled text, perhaps with embedded images and components, they use text components. To customize the edges of components, they use borders. To change the look of all components, they use a customizable look and feel, such as the GTK+ look and feel.

If you can't find a way to make a component look the way you want it to, then read on. This chapter introduces painting concepts, as they apply to Swing components, and then refers you elsewhere so you can write painting code that makes your custom components look great.

This chapter contains the following sections:

- How Swing Components Are Displayed describes how painting happens, with special attention to the framework provided by `JComponent`.

- Introduction to Painting Concepts gives an overview of the coordinate system, including how borders affect it, and discusses the `Graphics` and `Graphics2D` classes.

- Implementing a Custom Component tells how to implement painting code within a Swing component using the `paintComponent` method.

- At the end of this chapter, the Summary summarizes this chapter and points to where you can find out more. Questions and Exercises tests what you've learned in this chapter. Finally, Example Programs lists all the examples in this chapter and indicates where you can find them on the CD and online.

If you run into any problems, you should consult the section Solving Common Painting Problems (page 740) in the Appendix.

How Swing Components Are Displayed

If you plan to create custom painting code for a component, this section is required reading. Understanding the concepts in this section might also help you troubleshoot if Swing components don't seem to be displayed correctly.

How Painting Happens

When a Swing GUI needs to paint itself—whether for the first time, or in response to being uncovered, or because it needs to reflect a change in the program's state—it starts with the highest component that needs to be repainted and works its way down the containment hierarchy. This process is orchestrated by the AWT painting system, and made more efficient and smooth by the Swing repaint manager and double-buffering code.

Swing components generally repaint themselves whenever necessary. When you invoke the setText method on a component, for example, the component automatically repaints itself and, if appropriate, resizes itself. Behind the scenes, when a visible property changes the repaint method is invoked on the component to request that it be scheduled for painting. If the component's size or position also needs to change, a call to revalidate precedes the one to repaint. The repaint and revalidate methods are thread safe—they can be invoked from any thread.

Note: Like event-handling code, painting code executes on the event-dispatching thread. While an event is being handled, no painting will occur. Similarly, if a painting operation takes a long time, no events will be handled during that time.

Programs should paint only when the painting system tells them to because each occurrence of a component painting itself must execute without interruption. Otherwise, unpredictable results could occur, such as a button being painted as half pressed and half unpressed.

For smoothness, Swing painting is *double-buffered* by default—performed to an offscreen buffer and then flushed to the screen once finished. You can improve painting performance by making components opaque when possible, so that the Swing painting system doesn't waste time trying to paint behind these components. To make a Swing component opaque, invoke `setOpaque(true)` on the component.

Although the painting area available to Swing components is always rectangular, non-opaque Swing components can appear to be any shape. A button, for instance, might display itself by painting a filled octagon. The component behind the button (its container, most likely) would then be visible, showing through at the corners of the button's bounds. The button would have to include special hit detection code to avoid acting pressed if the user happens to click its corners.

The Swing Painting Methods

The painting method you're most likely to override is `paintComponent`. It's one of three methods that `JComponent` objects use to paint themselves. The three methods are invoked in this order:

1. `paintComponent`—The main method for painting. By convention, it first paints the background if the component is opaque. Then it performs any custom painting.
2. `paintBorder`—Tells the component's border (if any) to paint. *Do not invoke or override this method.*
3. `paintChildren`—Tells any components contained by this component to paint themselves. *Do not invoke or override this method.*

Note: We recommend that you don't override or invoke the `paint` method, which is the method that calls the `paintXxx` methods. Although overriding `paint` is legitimate in non-Swing components, it's generally not a good thing to do in components that descend from `JComponent`. Overriding `paint` can confuse the painting system, which relies on the `JComponent` implementation of the `paint` method for correct painting, performance enhancements, and features such as double buffering.

Figure 1 illustrates the order in which each component that inherits from `JComponent` paints itself. Steps 1 and 2—painting the background and performing custom painting—are performed by the `paintComponent` method. Step 3 is performed by `paintBorder`, and step 4 is performed by `paintChildren`.

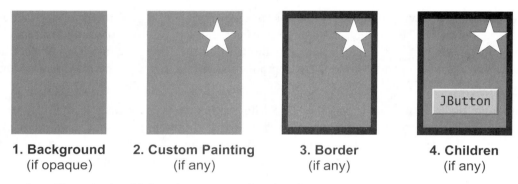

1. Background
(if opaque)

2. Custom Painting
(if any)

3. Border
(if any)

4. Children
(if any)

Figure 1   The order in which each component is painted.

The standard Swing components delegate their look-and-feel-specific painting to an object called a *UI delegate*. When such a component's `paintComponent` method is called, the method asks the UI delegate to paint the component. Generally, the UI delegate first checks whether the component is opaque and, if so, paints the entire background of the component. Then the UI delegate performs any look-and-feel-specific painting. The `JComponent` class doesn't set up a UI delegate—only its subclasses do. This means that if you extend `JComponent`, your component needs to paint its own background if it's opaque.

If you need more information about painting, see *The Swing Connection* article "Painting in AWT and Swing." It discusses in depth the intricacies of painting, and you can find it online at `http://java.sun.com/products/jfc/tsc/articles/painting/index.html`.

An Example of Painting

To illustrate painting, we'll use the `SwingApplication` program. Figure 2 shows its GUI.

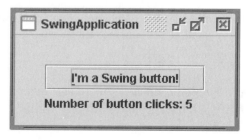

Figure 2   `SwingApplication`'s GUI.

Figure 3 shows its containment hierarchy:

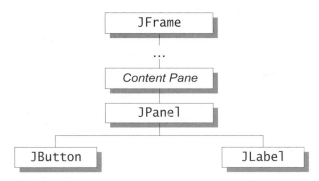

Figure 3   The JFrame hierarchy.

When the GUI for SwingApplication is painted, here's what happens:

1. The top-level container, JFrame, paints itself.
2. The content pane first paints its background, which is a solid gray rectangle. It then tells the JPanel to paint itself. In most look and feels, the JPanel is opaque by default and the content pane's background rectangle doesn't actually appear in the finished GUI, being completely obscured by the JPanel.

Note: It's important that the content pane be opaque. Otherwise, messy repaints will result. SwingApplication could invoke setOpaque(true) on the JPanel and then make it the content pane. This would slightly simplify the containment hierarchy and painting by removing an unnecessary container.

---

3. In most look and feels, the JPanel is opaque and the first painting it does fills its background. Next, it paints its border. In this case, the border is an EmptyBorder, which has no effect except for increasing the JPanel's size by reserving some space at the edge of the panel. Finally, the panel asks its children to paint themselves.
4. To paint itself, the JButton paints its background rectangle, if necessary, then the text that the button contains, and then its border. If the button has the keyboard focus, meaning that any typing goes directly to the button for processing, the button does some look-and-feel-specific painting to make clear that it has the focus.
5. To paint itself, the JLabel paints its text.

In this way, each component paints itself before any of the components it contains. This ensures that the background of a JPanel, for example, is visible only where it isn't covered by painting performed by its contained components.

Repainting Transparent Components

When a transparent (nonopaque) component gets a request to repaint itself, one or more components underneath the transparent component must also repaint themselves. For example, assume you set the text on an ordinary label that's already visible. In most look and feels, the *opaque* property of labels is `false`, so that labels are transparent. When a transparent label's text changes, the label must not only paint itself, but all components that can be seen behind the label must also paint themselves. This painting frenzy is kicked off when the label's `setText` method invokes `repaint`.

Here's the sequence of painting when `repaint` is invoked on a `JComponent` such as a label that is both visible and nonopaque.

1. Code inherited from `JComponent` causes the nonopaque component to look through its containment hierarchy to find the closest containing component that's completely opaque. For example, if the transparent component is a label in a transparent panel in a content pane, then the label's closest opaque container is the content pane.
2. The opaque container paints itself.
3. The children of the opaque container are asked to paint themselves. Eventually, the transparent component is painted.

You can see from this sequence that painting transparent components is more costly than painting opaque components. That's why we encourage you to set components' *opaque* property to `true` whenever practical.

Introduction to Painting Concepts

This section gives an overview of what you need to know before you write code that paints Swing components. It concentrates on the coordinate system, including how borders restrict the coordinates available for painting, and on the `Graphics` object passed into paint methods. Although most of the API discussed isn't specific to Swing components, we concentrate on what `JComponents` need. For information on actually painting, you should refer to the API documentation for the `Graphics` class[1] and to *The Java Tutorial*'s 2D Graphics trail.[2]

---

[1] Graphics API documentation: `http://java.sun.com/j2se/1.4.2/docs/api/java/awt/Graphics.html`.

[2] The 2D Graphics trail is included on this book's CD and is also available online at: `http://java.sun.com/docs/books/tutorial/2d/index.html`

The Coordinate System

Each component has its own integer coordinate system, ranging from (0, 0) to (*width* - 1, *height* - 1), where *width* and *height* are the size of the component in pixels. As Figure 4 shows, the upper left corner of a component's painting area is (0, 0). The *x* coordinate increases to the right, and the *y* coordinate increases downward.

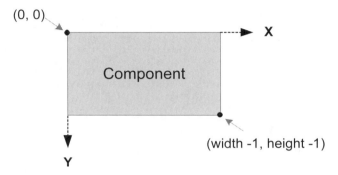

Figure 4   A component's coordinate system.

When painting, you must take into account not only the component's size but also the size of the component's border, if any. For example, a border that paints a 1-pixel line around a component effectively changes the top leftmost corner of the component's nonbackground painting area from (0,0) to (1,1) and reduces the width and the height of the painting area by 2 pixels each (1 pixel per side). Figure 5 demonstrates this:

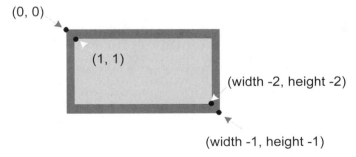

Figure 5   If the component has a border, remember to account for it.

You can get the width and height of any `JComponent` using its `getWidth` and `getHeight` methods. The `getSize` method is another option that works for all `Components`. To determine the border size, use the `getInsets` method. Here's some code that a component might use to determine the width and height available for custom painting:

```
protected void paintComponent(Graphics g) {
    ...
    Insets insets = getInsets();
    int currentWidth = getWidth() - insets.left - insets.right;
    int currentHeight = getHeight() - insets.top - insets.bottom;
    ...
    .../* First painting occurs at (x,y), where x is at least
       insets.left, and y is at least insets.top. */...
}
```

To familiarize yourself with the coordinate system, you can play with the `CoordinatesDemo` application, which features a component implemented using an inner class named `CoordinateArea`. The `CoordinateArea` has a preferred size of 400x75 and a solid red border that occupies 5 pixels at the left and bottom, and 1 pixel at the top and right. Like any good component, it starts painting its innards (a 20x20-pixel gray grid) where the border ends—in this case, at (5,1). The `CoordinateArea` also paints a dot where the user clicks. As you can see from Figure 6, a label at the bottom of the GUI displays information about the cursor and click location.

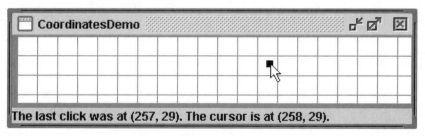

Figure 6   The `CoordinatesDemo` application.

Try This:

1. Run `CoordinatesDemo` using Java Web Start or compile and run the example yourself.[1]

2. Move the cursor over the `CoordinateArea`, including its border. Note the location of the cursor, as displayed at the bottom of the window. (Until bug #4931628 is fixed,

---

[1] To run `CoordinatesDemo` using Java Web Start, click the `CoordinatesDemo` link on the `RunExamples/14painting.html` page on the CD. You can find the source files here: `JavaTutorial/uiswing/14painting/example-1dot4/index.html#CoordinatesDemo`.

when you run `CoordinatesDemo` using Java Web Start the size of the main component won't be 400x75—it'll be taller.[1])

3. Move the cursor to the center of the `CoordinateArea` and click.
   A 7x7 dot appears, and the label at the bottom of the window displays its location, as well as the cursor's current location.

4. Move the cursor to be near or barely within the red border on the left or bottom and click.
   The dot that appears looks smaller than 7x7 because it's obscured by the border. The component's painting code paints it fully, but because the `paintBorder` method is called after `paintComponent`, the border is painted on top of the dot. If the border didn't completely paint over its area in an opaque color, you would be able to see more of the dot.

The `SelectionDemo` example shown in Figure 7 is another that can give you a feeling for coordinates. It paints a continuously updating rectangle, which the user sets by dragging the mouse. To avoid unnecessary painting, the component's mouse-dragged and mouse-released event handler uses a version of the `repaint` method that specifies which area of the component needs to be repainted.

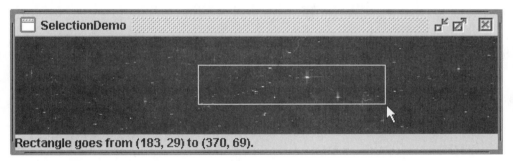

Rectangle goes from (183, 29) to (370, 69).

Figure 7 The `SelectionDemo` application.

You can run `SelectionDemo` using Java Web Start or compile and run the example yourself.[2]

The following code from `SelectionDemo.java` shows how `repaint` is invoked by the event handler for mouse-dragged and mouse-released events. The handler gets the current cursor location, updates the selection rectangle, calculates the total area to be repainted, and then

---

[1] You can track the status of bug #4931628 online at: `http://developer.java.sun.com/developer/bugParade/bugs/4931628.html`.

[2] To run `SelectionDemo` using Java Web Start, click the `SelectionDemo` link on the `RunExamples/14painting.html` page on the CD. You can find the source files here: `JavaTutorial/uiswing/14painting/example-1dot4/index.html#SelectionDemo`.

specifies that area to the `repaint` method. Note that the total area to be repainted is equal to the previously painted area plus the newly selected area. This way, it cleans up the previous painting, avoiding the faux pas of leaving behind ghost images of the selection rectangle.

```
void updateSize(MouseEvent e) {
    int x = e.getX();
    int y = e.getY();
    ...//save previous selection rectangle (rectToDraw)
        //in previousRectDrawn...
        //calculate new values for rectToDraw...
    Rectangle totalRepaint = rectToDraw.union(previousRectDrawn);
    repaint(totalRepaint.x, totalRepaint.y,
            totalRepaint.width, totalRepaint.height);
}
```

Here's the code that paints the selection rectangle on top of the image:

```
g.drawRect(rectToDraw.x, rectToDraw.y,
           rectToDraw.width - 1, rectToDraw.height - 1)
```

Note: The last two arguments to `drawRect` have -1 because the painting system draws lines just below the specified rectangle, instead of within the specified rectangle. The same rule of specifying one less than the desired width and height applies to other drawXxx methods. For `fillXxx` methods, on the other hand, you specify exactly the desired width and height in pixels. Here are examples of painting two rectangles of the same size, one filled and one not:

```
g.fillRect(x, y, rectWidth, rectHeight);
g.drawRect(x, y, rectWidth - 1, rectHeight - 1);
```

The Graphics Object and Graphics2D

The `Graphics` object passed into the `paintComponent` method provides both a context and some methods for simple painting.[1] In almost every case, `Graphics` objects are actually `Graphics2D` objects.[2] The `Graphics2D` class extends `Graphics` to provide more sophisticated control over geometry, coordinate transformations, color management, and text layout. You can cast any `Graphics` parameter into a `Graphics2D` object as long as your program uses the Java 2 platform (1.2 or later) and doesn't use the old printing API.

---

[1] Graphics API documentation: `http://java.sun.com/j2se/1.4.2/docs/api/java/awt/Graphics.html`.

[2] Graphics2D API documentation: `http://java.sun.com/j2se/1.4.2/docs/api/java/awt/Graphics2D.html`.

Version Note: The old printing API is centered around the java.awt.PrintJob class. A newer printing API centered around java.awt.print.PrinterJob was introduced in 1.2; it uses Graphics2D. In 1.4.2, Java Plug-in printing was updated to use the newer printing API. You can learn more about this newer API in the "Printing" section of The Java Tutorial's 2D Graphics trail; this trail is included on the CD and is online at: http://java.sun.com/docs/books/tutorial/2d/printing/index.html.

The painting methods defined by Graphics include such standbys as drawRect, fillRect, and drawLine. The Graphics2D class adds more flexible methods such as draw(Shape) and fill(Shape).

The graphics context provided by a Graphics object consists of state such as the current painting color, the current font, and the current painting area. The Graphics2D class adds more state, such as the alpha compositing mode, stroke, rendering hints, and color patterns such as textures and gradients.

In JComponents, the Graphics object is initialized just before it's passed to paintComponent, so that its color and font are set to the foreground color and font of the component. The same Graphics object is then passed to the paintBorder and paintChildren methods. This reuse is efficient but can lead to trouble if painting code permanently changes the Graphics object's state. For example, permanently changing the alpha compositing mode of a Graphics2D object could cause the component's border or children to be painted incorrectly. To avoid problems, remember this rule:

> **The Graphics object should have the same state when you're finished painting as it had when you started.**

You can take two approaches to avoid permanently changing the Graphics object: Either restore the Graphics object's original state, or use a copy of the original object. If you take the first approach, you don't need to bother restoring the font and color, since those properties are usually set before painting. Here's an example of the first approach:

```
//Example of restoring the Graphics object's state
Graphics2D g2d = (Graphics2D)g;
g2d.translate(x, y);   //set the transform
...
g2d.translate(-x, -y); //go back to the original transform
```

Here's an example of the second approach:

```
//Example of copying the Graphics object
Graphics2D g2d = (Graphics2D)g.create(); //copy g
```

```
g2d.translate(x, y);
...
g2d.dispose(); //release the copy's resources
```

The advantage of the first approach is that it doesn't create extra objects. The advantage of the second is that it's easy and guaranteed to succeed, no matter how much state you change.

When writing your painting code, keep in mind that you can't depend on any graphics context except what's provided by the `Graphics` object. For example, if you specify a painting area to `repaint`, you can't rely on the same painting area being specified in the next call to `paintComponent`. For one thing, multiple repaint requests can be coalesced into a single `paintComponent` call. For another, the painting system occasionally calls `paintComponent` on its own, without any repaint request from your program—for example, in response to first being shown or to a window that obscured it from being moved.

Implementing a Custom Component

Before you implement a component that performs custom painting, first make sure that you really need to do so. You might be able to use the text and image capabilities of labels, buttons, or text components instead. And remember, you can sometimes use borders to customize the outside edges of a component and icons to paint an area that perhaps varies by component state. If you need to make changes to many standard components, you should consider doing it by customizing a look and feel, such as the GTK+ look and feel.

If you really need to perform custom painting, then you need to decide which superclass to use. Your component can extend `JComponent`, `JPanel`, or a more specialized Swing component class.

For example, if you're creating a custom button class, you should probably implement it by extending a button class such as `JButton` or `JToggleButton`. That way you'll inherit the state management provided by those classes. If you're creating a component that paints on top of an image, you might want to create a `JLabel` subclass. A component that's a specialized container should probably extend `JPanel`. On the other hand, if you're implementing a component that generates and displays a graph, for example—with or without providing user interaction—then you might want to use a `JComponent` subclass.

When implementing custom painting code for a component, keep these rules in mind:

- Your custom painting code should be in a method with the signature `protected void paintComponent(Graphics)`.
- You can—and probably should—use a border to paint the outside edges of your component.

- Except when painting the background of the component, you should avoid painting over the border area of the component. You can determine this area using the `getInsets` method.

- Your component must honor the *opaque* property. If your component is opaque, it must paint its complete area using an opaque color or colors. If its *opaque* property is false, then you have the option of not painting over the entire component.

- Make sure that when the `paintComponent` method exits, the `Graphics` object that was passed into it has the same state that it had at the start of the method.

- To gain access to the power of the 2D graphics API, you can cast the `Graphics` parameter into a `Graphics2D` object.

Besides those painting-related considerations, here are a few more rules to keep in mind:

- Your component should return reasonable size information. Specifically, you should either override the `getMinimumSize`, `getPreferredSize`, and `getMaximumSize` methods or make sure that your component's superclass supplies values that are appropriate.

- Your component should be as accessible as possible. For details, see Making Custom Components Accessible (page 529) in Chapter 9.

- You should separate out strings and resources such as images so that your component can be easily localized. More information is in *The Java Tutorial* trail "Internationalization."[1]

An Example of Custom Painting

The application shown in Figure 8 gives an example of custom painting. It features a custom component called `IconDisplayer` that paints an icon multiple times, with all but the rightmost icon transparent.

Figure 8   The `IconDisplayer` application.

---

[1] This trail is included on the CD and is available online at: `http://java.sun.com/docs/books/ tutorial/i18n/index.html`.

You can run `IconDisplayer` using Java Web Start or compile and run the example yourself.[1]

Here are the main painting-related parts in `IconDisplayer.java`:

```java
public class IconDisplayer extends JComponent {
    ...
    protected void paintComponent(Graphics g) {
        if (isOpaque()) { //paint background
            g.setColor(getBackground());
            g.fillRect(0, 0, getWidth(), getHeight());
        }

        if (icon != null) {
            ...
            Graphics2D g2d = (Graphics2D)g.create();

            while (/* we're not done */) {
                /* Paint an icon. */
            }
            g2d.dispose(); //clean up
        }
    }
    ...
}
```

The first thing the `paintComponent` method does is check whether the `IconDisplayer` needs to be opaque and, if so, paint its background. If `IconDisplayer` were a subclass of something other than `JComponent`, we might omit this code and just call `super.paint-Component`.

The second part of the `paintComponent` method paints the main part of the component. It creates a copy of the `Graphics` object it was handed and casts it into a `Graphics2D` object. The typecast lets `paintComponent` use 2D features such as alpha compositing; the copy lets it avoid making changes to the passed-in `Graphics` object, which would have to be undone before returning.

Here's a complete listing of the code that paints the icon repeatedly:

```java
if (icon != null) {
    Insets insets = getInsets();
    int iconWidth = icon.getIconWidth();
    int iconX = getWidth() - insets.right - iconWidth;
    int iconY = insets.top;
    boolean faded = false;
```

---

[1] To run `IconDisplayer` using Java Web Start, click the `IconDisplayer` link on the `RunExamples/14painting.html` page on the CD. You can find the source files here: `JavaTutorial/uiswing/14painting/example-1dot4/index.html#IconDisplayer`.

```
Graphics2D g2d = (Graphics2D)g.create();
g.getClipBounds(clipRect);

while (iconX >= insets.left) {
    iconRect.setBounds(iconX, iconY, iconWidth,
                       icon.getIconHeight());
    if (iconRect.intersects(clipRect)) {
        icon.paintIcon(this, g2d, iconX, iconY);
    }
    iconX -= (iconWidth + pad);
    if (!faded) {
        g2d.setComposite(AlphaComposite.getInstance(
            AlphaComposite.SRC_OVER, 0.1f));
        faded = true;
    }
}
g2d.dispose(); //clean up
}
```

The first thing the code does is prepare for painting icons. It gets its border size, using the getInsets method. It then uses the insets, along with the component and icon sizes, when calculating where the first icon—the rightmost one—should be painted. The icon is an ImageIcon, so it's easy to get its size using methods such as getIconWidth, and it can paint itself using the Icon-defined method paintIcon. The code next gets a Graphics2D object so that it can use alpha compositing when painting some of the icons.

Next comes a bit of performance tuning. The code gets the *clipping area*, using the Graphics method getClipBounds. The clipping area is the part of the component that needs to be repainted. For example, if a window covering the right half of the component goes away, then only the right half of the component needs to be repainted. After getting the clipping area, the code checks whether this clipping area intersects with the icon's current painting area. If so, it paints the icon. If not, it saves a little time by not painting the icon.

After dealing with the first (rightmost) occurrence of the icon, the code invokes setComposite on the Graphics2D object, specifying parameters that make the subsequently painted icons appear to be only 10% opaque. You can find information on using alpha compositing in "Compositing Graphics," a section in the *The Java Tutorial*'s 2D Graphics trail.[1]

After the paintComponent method paints all the icons, there's nothing for it to do but clean up. In this case, the cleanup is as simple as disposing of the Graphics2D object the method created.

---

[1] This section is included on the CD and is online at: http://java.sun.com/docs/books/tutorial/2d/display/compositing.html.

Summary

This chapter introduced you to the concepts and rules that will enable you to create Swing components that perform custom painting. Although the chapter doesn't explicitly talk about implementing an icon or border, the rules are similar. An icon or border is just an object that knows how to paint itself; it needs a component to provide the graphics context. An example of implementing a custom icon is in Creating a Custom Icon Implementation (page 618) in Chapter 9.

For information on painting, see the *The Java Tutorial*'s 2D Graphics trail.[1] Another great resource is the online newsletter *The Swing Connection*, which has articles such as "Painting in AWT and Swing"[2] and "Unleash Your Creativity with Swing and the Java 2D API!"[3]

If you run into any problems, you should consult the section Solving Common Painting Problems (page 740) in the Appendix.

Questions and Exercises

Questions

1. What method defined by `JComponent` paints the inside of a component?
2. Which of the following code snippets paint a rectangle (filled or not) that is 100x100 pixels?
    a. `g.fillRect(x, y, 100, 100)`
    b. `g.fillRect(x, y,  99,  99)`
    c. `g.drawRect(x, y, 100, 100)`
    d. b and c
    e. a and c
3. What code would you use to make a component perform the next painting operation using the background color at 50% transparency?

---

[1] The 2D Graphics trail is included on this book's CD and is also available online at: `http://java.sun.com/docs/books/tutorial/2d/index.html`.
[2] This article is online at: `http://java.sun.com/products/jfc/tsc/articles/painting/`.
[3] This article is online at: `http://java.sun.com/products/jfc/tsc/articles/swing2d/`.

Exercises

1. Using a standard border and custom component painting, implement a component that has a preferred size of 250x100, is opaque by default, has a 5-pixel black border, and paints an "X" (using 5-pixel-thick lines) in the foreground color, as shown in the following figure.

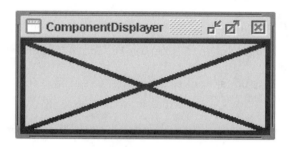

2. Implement an icon that's 10x10 pixels and paints a solid rectangle that fills the 10x10 area. If the icon's component is enabled, the rectangle should be red; if disabled, gray. Make a copy of ButtonDemo.java that uses your custom Icon for the middle button, instead of displaying middle.gif. The following pictures show what the icon should look like.

3. Implement a border that paints a red 15-pixel-tall stripe all the way across the top of its component. Test this border by substituting it for the border on the component you created in exercise 1. The result should look like the following figure.

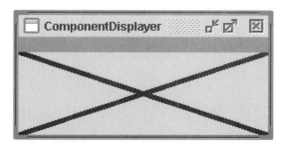

Answers

You can find answers to the Questions and Exercises online:

`http://java.sun.com/docs/books/tutorial/uiswing/QandE/answers.html`

Example Programs

You can find source files for all the examples from this chapter on the CD and online:

`JavaTutorial/uiswing/14painting/example-1dot4/index.html`

`http://java.sun.com/docs/books/tutorial/uiswing/14painting/`
`example-1dot4/index.html`

The preceding URLs take you to an index that has links to the files required by each example. You can go directly to the entry for a particular example by adding *#ExampleName* to the URL. Most examples have a "Run" link in the index which executes the example using Java Web Start technology.

Example	Where Described	Notes
CoordinatesDemo	page 136	Lets you familiarize yourself with the coordinate system.
SelectionDemo	page 137	Gives you a feeling for coordinates. To avoid unnecessary painting, the `repaint` method specifies which area of the component needs to be repainted.
IconDisplayer	page 141	Demonstrates custom painting. The application features a custom component that paints an icon multiple times with all but the rightmost icon transparent.

Components Reference

EACH of the following sections describes how to use a particular Swing component. These sections are organized alphabetically for quick reference. For an easy-to-use visual reference, refer to A Visual Index to Swing Components (page 37) in Chapter 3.

All of these sections assume that you've successfully compiled and run a program that uses Swing components and that you're familiar with Swing concepts. These prerequisites are covered in Chapter 1, Getting Started with Swing (page 3), and Chapter 2, Learning Swing by Example (page 11). For an overview of Swing components and the Swing component hierarchy, be sure to read Chapter 3, Using Swing Components (page 35).

You can find source files for all the examples from this chapter on the CD and online:

```
JavaTutorial/uiswing/components/example-1dot4/index.html
```

```
http://java.sun.com/docs/books/tutorial/uiswing/components/
example-1dot4/index.html
```

The preceding URLs take you to an index that has links to the files required by each example. You can go directly to the entry for a particular example by adding *#ExampleName* to the URL. Most examples have a "Run" link in the example index which executes the example using Java Web Start technology.

How to Make Applets

This section covers JApplet,[1] a class that enables applets to use Swing components. JApplet is a subclass of java.applet.Applet, which is covered in the "Writing Applets" trail in *The Java Tutorial*.[2] If you've never written a regular applet before, we urge you to read that trail before proceeding with this section. The information provided there applies to all applets, including Swing applets, with a few exceptions that this section explains.

Any applet that contains Swing components must be implemented with a subclass of JApplet. Here's a Swing version of one of the applets that helped make the Java technology famous. Figure 1, an animation applet (in its best-known configuration), shows our mascot Duke doing cartwheels.

Figure 1 To run this applet using Java Web Start, click the TumbleItem link on the RunExamples/ components.html page on the CD. You can also run it inside your browser by visiting: http://java.sun.com/docs/books/tutorial/uiswing/components/applet.html.

Note: To view this applet in your browser, you need to install Java Plug-in software. For more information, refer to the Java Plug-In home page: http://java.sun.com/products/plugin/ index.html.

Features Provided by JApplet

Because JApplet is a top-level Swing container, each Swing applet has a root pane. The most noticeable effects of the root pane's presence are support for adding a menu bar and the need to use a content pane.

As described in Using Top-Level Containers (page 46) in Chapter 3, each top-level container such as a JApplet has a single content pane. The content pane makes Swing applets different from regular applets in the following ways:

---

[1] JApplet API documentation: http://java.sun.com/j2se/1.4.2/docs/api/javax/swing/ JApplet.html.
[2] *The Java Tutorial*'s "Writing Applets" trail is available on this book's CD and online at: http:// java.sun.com/docs/books/tutorial/applets/index.html.

- You add components to a Swing applet's content pane, not directly to the applet. Adding Components to the Content Pane (page 48) in Chapter 3 shows you how.

- You set the layout manager on a Swing applet's content pane, not directly on the applet.

- The default layout manager for a Swing applet's content pane is BorderLayout. This differs from the default layout manager for Applet, which is FlowLayout.

- You don't put painting code directly in a JApplet object. See Chapter 6, Performing Custom Painting (page 129), for examples of how to perform custom painting in applets.

Version Note: In release 1.5, we expect that invoking add or setLayout on a top-level container will be equivalent to invoking it on the content pane.

Threads in Applets

Swing components should be created, queried, and manipulated on the event-dispatching thread, but browsers don't invoke applet "milestone" methods from that thread. For this reason, the milestone methods—init, start, stop, and destroy—should use the SwingUtilities method invokeAndWait (or, if appropriate, invokeLater) so that code that refers to the Swing components is executed on the event-dispatching thread. More information about these methods and the event-dispatching thread is in How to Use Threads (page 632) in Chapter 9.

Here's an example of an init method:

```
public void init() {
    //Execute a job on the event-dispatching thread:
    //creating this applet's GUI.
    try {
        javax.swing.SwingUtilities.invokeAndWait(new Runnable() {
            public void run() {
                createGUI();
            }
        });
    } catch (Exception e) {
        System.err.println("createGUI didn't successfully complete");
    }
}

private void createGUI() {
    JLabel label = new JLabel(
                    "You are successfully running a Swing applet!");
```

```
        label.setHorizontalAlignment(JLabel.CENTER);
        label.setBorder(BorderFactory.createMatteBorder(1,1,1,1,
                                                Color.black));
        getContentPane().add(label, BorderLayout.CENTER);
    }
```

The `invokeLater` method is not appropriate for this implementation because it allows `init` to return before initialization is complete, which can cause applet problems that are difficult to debug.

The `init` method in `TumbleItem` is more complex, as the following code shows.[1] As in the first example, this `init` method implementation uses `SwingUtilities.invokeAndWait` to execute the GUI creation code on the event-dispatching thread. This `init` method also sets up two background threads to perform GUI-related tasks. First, it uses a Swing timer (which uses a shared thread) to fire action events whenever the animation needs to be updated. Second, it uses a `SwingWorker` object to create a background thread that loads the animation image files, letting the applet present a GUI before all of its resources are available.

```
    private void createGUI() {
        ...
        animator = new Animator();
        animator.setOpaque(true);
        animator.setBackground(Color.white);
        setContentPane(animator);
        ...
    }

    public void init() {
        loadAppletParameters();

        try {
            javax.swing.SwingUtilities.invokeAndWait(new Runnable() {
                public void run() {
                    createGUI();
                }
            });
        } catch (Exception e) {
            System.err.println("createGUI didn't successfully complete");
        }

        //Set up the timer that will perform the animation.
        timer = new javax.swing.Timer(speed, this);
        timer.setInitialDelay(pause);
        timer.setCoalesce(false);
        timer.start(); //Start the animation.
```

---

[1] You can find the source files for `TumbleItem` here: `JavaTutorial/uiswing/components/example-1dot4/index.html#TumbleItem`.

```
    //Loading the images can take quite a while, so to
    //avoid staying in init() (and thus not being able
    //to show the "Loading Images..." label) we'll
    //load the images in a SwingWorker thread.
    imgs = new ImageIcon[nimgs];
    final SwingWorker worker = new SwingWorker() {
        public Object construct() {
            ...//Load all the images...
            finishedLoading = true;
            return imgs;
        }

        //Executes in the event-dispatching thread.
        public void finished() {
            //Remove the "Loading images" label.
            animator.removeAll();
            loopslot = -1;
        }
    };
    worker.start();
}
```

Using Images in a Swing Applet

The `Applet` class provides the `getImage` method for loading images into an applet. This method creates and returns an `Image` object that represents the loaded image. Because Swing components use `Icon`s rather than `Image`s to refer to pictures, Swing applets tend not to use `getImage` but instead create instances of `ImageIcon`—an icon loaded from an image file. `ImageIcon` comes with a code-saving benefit: It handles image tracking automatically. Refer to How to Use Icons (page 603) in Chapter 9 for more information.

The animation of Duke doing cartwheels requires 17 different pictures. The applet uses one `ImageIcon` per picture and loads them all in its `init` method. Because images can take a long time to load, the icons are loaded in a separate thread implemented by a `SwingWorker` object. Here's the code:

```
public void init() {
    ...
    imgs = new ImageIcon[nimgs];
    ...
    final SwingWorker worker = new SwingWorker() {
        public Object construct() {
            //Images are numbered 1 to nimgs,
            //but fill array from 0 to nimgs-1.
            for (int i = 0; i < nimgs; i++) {
                imgs[i] = loadImage(i+1);
            }
```

```
                    finishedLoading = true;
                    return imgs;
                }
                ...
            };
        worker.start();
    }
    ...
    protected ImageIcon loadImage(int imageNum) {
        String path = dir + "/T" + imageNum + ".gif";
        int MAX_IMAGE_SIZE = 2400;   //Change this to the size of
                                     //your biggest image, in bytes.

        int count = 0;
        BufferedInputStream imgStream = new BufferedInputStream(
            this.getClass().getResourceAsStream(path));
        if (imgStream != null) {
            byte buf[] = new byte[MAX_IMAGE_SIZE];
            try {
                count = imgStream.read(buf);
                imgStream.close();
            } catch (java.io.IOException ioe) {
              System.err.println("Couldn't read stream from file: " + path);
                return null;
            }
            if (count <= 0) {
                System.err.println("Empty file: " + path);
                return null;
            }
            return new ImageIcon(Toolkit.getDefaultToolkit().
                                         createImage(buf));
        } else {
            System.err.println("Couldn't find file: " + path);
            return null;
        }
    }
}
```

Embedding an Applet in an HTML Page

The recommended way to include an applet in an HTML page is with the APPLET tag. The following is the APPLET tag for the cartwheeling Duke applet:

```
<APPLET code="TumbleItem.class"
        codebase="example-1dot4/"
        archive="tumbleClasses.jar tumbleImages.jar"
        width="600" height="95">
```

```
<param name="maxwidth" value="120">
<param name="nimgs" value="17">
<param name="offset" value="-57">
<param name="img" value="images/tumble">

Your browser is completely ignoring the &lt;APPLET&gt; tag!
</APPLET>
```

Version Note: Before J2SE v1.3.1_01a, Java Plug-in required the OBJECT or EMBED tag instead of the APPLET tag. Details are available through the Java Plug-in home page.[1]

To find out about the various APPLET tag parameters, refer to "Using the APPLET Tag" in *The Java Tutorial*.

The JApplet API

Table 1 lists the interesting methods that JApplet adds to the applet API. These methods give you access to features provided by the root pane. Other methods you might use are defined by the Component and Applet classes. See The JComponent API (page 55) in Chapter 3 for a list of commonly used Component methods and "Taking Advantage of the Applet API" in *The Java Tutorial* for help in using Applet methods.[2]

Table 1: JApplet Methods

Method	Purpose
void setContentPane(Container) Container getContentPane()	Set or get the applet's content pane. The content pane contains the applet's visible GUI components and should be opaque.
JRootPane createRootPane() void setRootPane(JRootPane) JRootPane getRootPane()	Create, set, or get the applet's root pane. The root pane manages the interior of the applet, including the content pane, the glass pane, and so on.
void setJMenuBar(JMenuBar) JMenuBar getJMenuBar()	Set or get the applet's menu bar to manage a set of menus for the frame.
void setGlassPane(Component) Component getGlassPane()	Set or get the applet's glass pane. You can use the glass pane to intercept mouse events.
void setLayeredPane(JLayeredPane) JLayeredPane getLayeredPane()	Set or get the applet's layered pane. You can use the frame's layered pane to put components on top of or behind other components.

---

[1] http://java.sun.com/products/plugin/.

[2] You can find the "Taking Advantage of the Applet API" section in *The Java Tutorial* on the CD or online at http://java.sun.com/docs/books/tutorial/applet/appletsonly/.

Applet Examples

The following table shows examples of Swing applets and where they're described.

Example	Where Described	Notes
TumbleItem	This section (page 150)	An animation applet.
HelloSwingApplet	Compiling and Running Swing Programs (page 6)	The simplest of all Swing applets—it contains only a label.
IconDemoApplet	How to Use Icons (page 603)	An applet for showing photos.

Components

How to Use Buttons

To create a button, you can instantiate one of the many classes that descend from the AbstractButton[1] class. Table 2 shows the Swing-defined AbstractButton subclasses that you might want to use.

Table 2: Swing-Defined AbstractButton Subclasses

Class	Summary	Where Described
JButton	A common button.	How to Use the Common Button API (page 157) and How to Use JButton Features (page 159)
JCheckBox	A check box button.	How to Use Check Boxes (page 163)
JRadioButton	One of a group of radio buttons.	How to Use Radio Buttons (page 311)
JMenuItem	An item in a menu.	How to Use Menus (page 277)
JCheckBoxMenuItem	A menu item that has a check box.	How to Use Menus (page 277) and How to Use Check Boxes (page 163)
JRadioButtonMenuItem	A menu item that has a radio button.	How to Use Menus (page 277) and How to Use Radio Buttons (page 311)
JToggleButton	Implements toggle functionality inherited by JCheckBox and JRadioButton. Can be instantiated or subclassed to create two-state buttons.	Used in some examples listed in Examples That Use Buttons (page 162)

Note: If you want to collect a group of buttons into a row or column, then you should check out tool bars. You can read about them in How to Use Tool Bars (page 427) later in this chapter.

First, this section explains the basic button API that AbstractButton defines—and thus what all Swing buttons have in common. Next, it describes the small amount of API that JButton adds to AbstractButton. After that, this section shows you how to use specialized API to implement check boxes and radio buttons.

---

[1] AbstractButton API documentation: http://java.sun.com/j2se/1.4.2/docs/api/javax/swing/AbstractButton.html.

How to Use the Common Button API

Figure 2 shows a picture of an application that displays three buttons.

Figure 2   The ButtonDemo application.

Try This:

1. Run ButtonDemo using Java Web Start or compile and run the example yourself.[1]
2. Click the left button. It disables the middle button (and itself since it's no longer useful) and enables the right button.
3. Click the right button. It enables the middle button and the left button, and disables itself.

As the ButtonDemo example shows, a Swing button can display both text and an image. In ButtonDemo, each button has its text in a different place, relative to its image. The underlined letter in each button's text shows the button's *mnemonic*—the keyboard alternative. In most look and feels, the user can click a button by pressing the Alt key and the mnemonic. For example, Alt-M clicks the middle button in ButtonDemo.

When a button is disabled, the look and feel automatically generates the button's disabled appearance. However, you could provide an image to substitute for the normal image—for example, gray versions of the images used in the left and right buttons.

How you implement event handling depends on the type of button you use and how you use it. Generally, you implement an action listener, which is notified every time the user clicks the button.

The code that follows is from ButtonDemo.java. It creates the buttons in the previous example and reacts to button clicks. The bold code is what would remain if the buttons had no images.

---

[1] To run ButtonDemo using Java Web Start, click the ButtonDemo link on the RunExamples/ components.html page on the CD. You can find the source files here: JavaTutorial/uiswing/ components/example-1dot4/index.html#ButtonDemo.

```
//In initialization code:
    ImageIcon leftButtonIcon = createImageIcon("images/right.gif");
    ImageIcon middleButtonIcon = createImageIcon("images/middle.gif");
    ImageIcon rightButtonIcon = createImageIcon("images/left.gif");

    b1 = new JButton("Disable middle button", leftButtonIcon);
    b1.setVerticalTextPosition(AbstractButton.CENTER);
    b1.setHorizontalTextPosition(AbstractButton.LEADING);
    //aka LEFT, for left-to-right locales

    b1.setMnemonic(KeyEvent.VK_D);
    b1.setActionCommand("disable");

    b2 = new JButton("Middle button", middleButtonIcon);
    b2.setVerticalTextPosition(AbstractButton.BOTTOM);
    b2.setHorizontalTextPosition(AbstractButton.CENTER);
    b2.setMnemonic(KeyEvent.VK_M);

    b3 = new JButton("Enable middle button", rightButtonIcon);
    //Use the default text position of CENTER, TRAILING (RIGHT).
    b3.setMnemonic(KeyEvent.VK_E);
    b3.setActionCommand("enable");
    b3.setEnabled(false);

    //Listen for actions on buttons 1 and 3.
    b1.addActionListener(this);
    b3.addActionListener(this);

    b1.setToolTipText("Click this button to disable "
                    + "the middle button.");
    b2.setToolTipText("This middle button does nothing "
                    + "when you click it.");
    b3.setToolTipText("Click this button to enable the "
                    + "middle button.");
    ...
}

public void actionPerformed(ActionEvent e) {
    if ("disable".equals(e.getActionCommand())) {
        b2.setEnabled(false);
        b1.setEnabled(false);
        b3.setEnabled(true);
    } else {
        b2.setEnabled(true);
        b1.setEnabled(true);
        b3.setEnabled(false);
    }
}
```

```
protected static ImageIcon createImageIcon(String path) {
    java.net.URL imgURL = ButtonDemo.class.getResource(path);
    ...//error handling omitted for clarity...
    return new ImageIcon(imgURL);
}
```

How to Use JButton Features

Ordinary buttons—JButton[1] objects—have just a bit more functionality than the Abstract-Button class provides: You can make a JButton the default button.

At most one button in a top-level container can be the default button. The default button typically has a highlighted appearance and acts clicked whenever the top-level container has the keyboard focus and the user presses the Enter key. Figure 3 is a picture of a dialog in which the **Set** button is the default button.

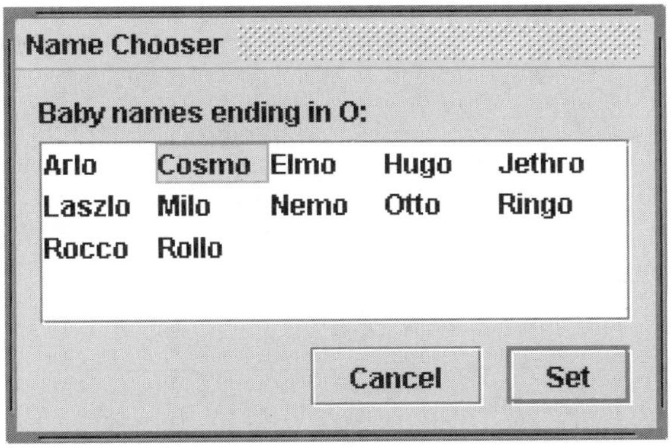

Figure 3   The ListDialog component.

You set the default button by invoking the setDefaultButton method on a top-level container's root pane. Here's the code that sets up the default button for the ListDialog example:

```
//In the constructor for a JDialog subclass:
getRootPane().setDefaultButton(setButton);
```

The exact implementation of the default button feature depends on the look and feel. For example, in the Windows look and feel, the default button changes to whichever button has

---

[1] JButton API documentation: http://java.sun.com/j2se/1.4.2/docs/api/javax/swing/JButton.html.

the focus so that pressing Enter clicks the focused button. When no button has the focus, the button you originally specified as the default button becomes the default button again.

The Button API

Tables 3 through 5 list the commonly used button-related API. With the exception of the JButton constructors, all of the listed API is defined by the AbstractButton class. Other methods you might call, such as setFont and setForeground, are listed in the API tables in the section The JComponent Class (page 53) in Chapter 3. You should also refer to the API documentation for AbstractButton[1] and JButton.[2]

Table 3: Setting or Getting the Button's Contents

Method or Constructor	Purpose
JButton(Action) JButton(String, Icon) JButton(String) JButton(Icon) JButton()	Create a JButton instance, initializing it to have the specified text/image/action. The JButton(Action) constructor was added to JButton in 1.3.
void setAction(Action) Action getAction()	Set or get the button's properties according to values from the Action instance. Introduced in 1.3.
void setText(String) String getText()	Set or get the text displayed by the button.
void setIcon(Icon) Icon getIcon()	Set or get the image displayed by the button when the button isn't selected or pressed.
void setDisabledIcon(Icon) Icon getDisabledIcon()	Set or get the image displayed by the button when it's disabled. If you don't specify a disabled image, the look and feel creates one by manipulating the default image.
void setPressedIcon(Icon) Icon getPressedIcon()	Set or get the image displayed by the button when it's being pressed.
void setSelectedIcon(Icon) Icon getSelectedIcon() void setDisabledSelectedIcon(Icon) Icon getDisabledSelectedIcon()	Set or get the image displayed by the button when it's selected. If you don't specify a disabled selected image, the look and feel creates one by manipulating the selected image.
setRolloverEnabled(boolean) boolean isRolloverEnabled() void setRolloverIcon(Icon) Icon getRolloverIcon() void setRolloverSelectedIcon(Icon) Icon getRolloverSelectedIcon()	Use setRolloverIcon(someIcon) to make the button display the specified icon when the cursor passes over it. The setRolloverSelectedIcon method lets you specify the rollover icon when the button is selected—this is useful for two-state buttons such as toggle buttons. Setting the rollover icon automatically calls setRollover(true), enabling rollover.

Table 4: Fine-Tuning the Button's Appearance

Method or Constructor	Purpose

`void setHorizontalAlignment(int)`
`void setVerticalAlignment(int)`
`int getHorizontalAlignment()`
`int getVerticalAlignment()`
	Set or get where in the button its contents should be placed. The `AbstractButton` class allows any one of the following values for horizontal alignment: RIGHT, LEFT, CENTER (the default), LEADING, and TRAILING. For vertical alignment: TOP, CENTER (the default), and BOTTOM.

`void setHorizontalText-`
`      Position(int)`
`void setVerticalText-`
`      Position(int)`
`int getHorizontalTextPosition()`
`int getVerticalTextPosition()`
	Set or get where the button's text should be placed, relative to the button's image. The `AbstractButton` class allows any one of the following values for horizontal alignment: RIGHT, LEFT, CENTER, LEADING, and TRAILING (the default). For vertical alignment: TOP, CENTER (the default), and BOTTOM.

`void setMargin(Insets)` `Insets getMargin()`	Set or get the number of pixels between the button's border and its contents.
`void setFocusPainted(boolean)` `boolean isFocusPainted()`	Set or get whether the button should look different when it has the focus.
`void setBorderPainted(boolean)` `boolean isBorderPainted()`	Set or get whether the border of the button should be painted.
`void setIconTextGap(int)` `int getIconTextGap()`	Set or get the amount of space between the text and the icon displayed in this button. Introduced in 1.4.

Table 5: Implementing the Button's Functionality

Method or Constructor	Purpose
`void setMnemonic(int)` `char getMnemonic()`	Set or get the keyboard alternative to clicking the button. One form of the `setMnemonic` method accepts a character argument; however, it's recommended that you use an `int` argument instead, specifying a `KeyEvent.VK_X` constant.
`void setDisplayedMnemonicIndex(int)` `int getDisplayedMnemonicIndex()`	Set or get a hint as to which character in the text should be decorated to represent the mnemonic. Not all look and feels support this. Introduced in 1.4.
`void setActionCommand(String)` `String getActionCommand()`	Set or get the name of the action performed by the button.

---

[1] `AbstractButton` API documentation: `http://java.sun.com/j2se/1.4.2/docs/api/javax/swing/AbstractButton.html`.

[2] `JButton` API documentation: `http://java.sun.com/j2se/1.4.2/docs/api/javax/swing/JButton.html`.

B

Components

Table 5: Implementing the Button's Functionality *(continued)*

Method or Constructor	Purpose
void addActionListener(ActionListener) ActionListener removeActionListener()	Add or remove an object that listens for action events fired by the button.
void addItemListener(ItemListener) ItemListener removeItemListener()	Add or remove an object that listens for item events fired by the button.
void setSelected(boolean) boolean isSelected()	Set or get whether the button is selected. Makes sense only for buttons that have on/off state, such as check boxes.
void doClick() void doClick(int)	Programmatically perform a "click." The optional argument specifies the amount of time (in milliseconds) that the button should look pressed.
void setMultiClickThreshhold(long) long getMultiClickThreshhold()	Set or get the amount of time (in milliseconds) required between mouse press events for the button to generate corresponding action events. Introduced in 1.4.

Examples That Use Buttons

The following table lists some of the many examples that use buttons. Also see Examples That Use Tool Bars (page 433), which lists programs that add `JButton` objects to `JToolBars`, Examples That Use Check Boxes (page 166), and Examples That Use Radio Buttons (page 315).

Example	Where Described	Notes
ButtonDemo	How to Use the Common Button API (page 157)	Uses mnemonics and icons. Specifies the button text position, relative to the button icon. Uses action commands.
ListDialog	How to Use JButton Features (page 159)	Implements a dialog with two buttons, one of which is the default button.
ProgressBarDemo	How to Use Progress Bars (page 300)	Implements a button's action listener with a named inner class.

How to Use Check Boxes

The JCheckBox[1] class provides support for check box buttons. You can also put check boxes in menus using the JCheckBoxMenuItem[2] class. Because JCheckBox and JCheckBoxMenuItem inherit from AbstractButton, Swing check boxes have all of the usual button characteristics, as discussed in How to Use Buttons (page 156). For example, you can specify images to be used in them.

Check boxes are similar to radio buttons, but their selection model is different, by convention. Any number of check boxes in a group—none, some, or all—can be selected. A group of radio buttons, on the other hand, can have only one button selected. See How to Use Radio Buttons (page 311) later in this chapter.

Figure 4 is a picture of an application that uses four check boxes to customize a cartoon.

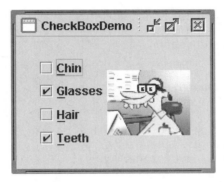

Figure 4   The CheckBoxDemo application.

Try This:

1. Run CheckBoxDemo using Java Web Start, or compile and run the example yourself.[3]
2. Click the **Chin** button or press Alt-c. The **Chin** check box becomes unselected, and the chin disappears from the picture; the other check boxes remain selected. This applica-

---

[1] JCheckbox API documentation: http://java.sun.com/j2se/1.4.2/docs/api/javax/swing/ JCheckBox.html.

[2] JCheckboxMenuItem API documentation: http://java.sun.com/j2se/1.4.2/docs/api/javax/ swing/JCheckBoxMenuItem.html.

[3] To run CheckBoxDemo using Java Web Start, click the CheckBoxDemo link on the RunExamples/ components.html page on the CD. You can find the source files here: JavaTutorial/uiswing/ components/example-1dot4/index.html#CheckBoxDemo.

tion has one item listener that listens to all of the check boxes. Each time it receives an event, the application loads a new picture that reflects the current state of the check boxes.

A check box generates one item event and one action event per click. Usually, you listen only for item events since they let you determine whether the click selected or deselected the check box. Below is the code from CheckBoxDemo.java that creates the check boxes and reacts to clicks.

```
//In initialization code:
    chinButton = new JCheckBox("Chin");
    chinButton.setMnemonic(KeyEvent.VK_C);
    chinButton.setSelected(true);

    glassesButton = new JCheckBox("Glasses");
    glassesButton.setMnemonic(KeyEvent.VK_G);
    glassesButton.setSelected(true);

    hairButton = new JCheckBox("Hair");
    hairButton.setMnemonic(KeyEvent.VK_H);
    hairButton.setSelected(true);

    teethButton = new JCheckBox("Teeth");
    teethButton.setMnemonic(KeyEvent.VK_T);
    teethButton.setSelected(true);

    //Register a listener for the check boxes.
    chinButton.addItemListener(this);
    glassesButton.addItemListener(this);
    hairButton.addItemListener(this);
    teethButton.addItemListener(this);
..
public void itemStateChanged(ItemEvent e) {
    ...
    Object source = e.getItemSelectable();

    if (source == chinButton) {
        //...make a note of it...
    } else if (source == glassesButton) {
        //...make a note of it...
    } else if (source == hairButton) {
        //...make a note of it...
    } else if (source == teethButton) {
        //...make a note of it...
    }
```

```
    if (e.getStateChange() == ItemEvent.DESELECTED)
        //...make a note of it...
    ...
    updatePicture();
}
```

The Check Box API

Table 6 lists the commonly used check box-related API. Check boxes also use the common button API, which is listed in the tables in The Button API (page 160). Other methods you might call, such as `setFont` and `setForeground`, are listed in the API tables in The JComponent Class (page 53) in Chapter 3. Also refer to the API documentation for `JCheckBox`[1] and `JCheckBoxMenuItem`.[2]

Table 6: Check Box Constructors

Constructor	Purpose
JCheckBox(Action) JCheckBox(String) JCheckBox(String, boolean) JCheckBox(Icon) JCheckBox(Icon, boolean) JCheckBox(String, Icon) JCheckBox(String, Icon, boolean) JCheckBox()	Create a JCheckBox instance. The string argument specifies the text, if any, that the check box should display. Similarly, the Icon argument specifies the image that should be used instead of the look and feel's default check box image. Specifying the boolean argument as true initializes the check box to be selected. If the boolean argument is absent or false, then the check box is initially unselected. The JCheckBox(Action) constructor was introduced in 1.3.
JCheckBoxMenuItem(Action) JCheckBoxMenuItem(String) JCheckBoxMenuItem(String, boolean) JCheckBoxMenuItem(Icon) JCheckBoxMenuItem(String, Icon) JCheckBoxMenuItem(String, Icon, boolean) JCheckBoxMenuItem()	Create a JCheckBoxMenuItem instance. The arguments are interpreted in the same way as the arguments to the JCheckBox constructors, except that any specified icon is shown in addition to the normal check box icon. The JCheckBoxMenu-Item(Action) constructor was introduced in 1.3.

---

[1] JCheckbox API documentation: http://java.sun.com/j2se/1.4.2/docs/api/javax/swing/JCheckBox.html.

[2] JCheckboxMenuItem API documentation: http://java.sun.com/j2se/1.4.2/docs/api/javax/swing/JCheckBoxMenuItem.html.

Examples That Use Check Boxes

The following table lists two examples that use check boxes.

Example	Where Described	Notes
CheckBoxDemo	How to Use Check Boxes (page 163)	Uses check box buttons to determine which of 16 images it should display.
ActionDemo	How to Use Actions (page 513)	Uses check box menu items to set the state of the program.

How to Use Color Choosers

Use the JColorChooser[1] class to provide users with a palette of colors to select from. A color chooser is a component that you can place anywhere within your program's GUI. The JColorChooser API also makes it easy to bring up a dialog (modal or not) that contains a color chooser. Figure 5 shows an application that uses a color chooser to set the text color in a banner.

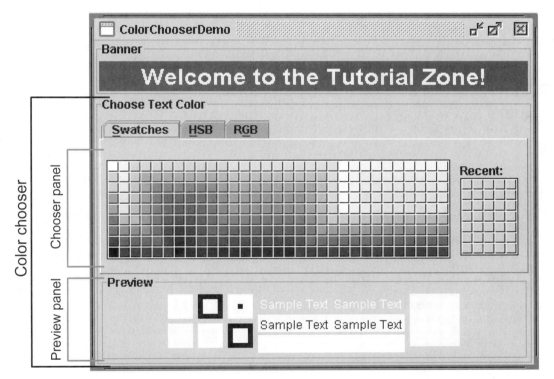

Figure 5   The ColorChooserDemo application with callouts added to identify the color chooser and the chooser and preview panels.

You can run ColorChooserDemo using Java Web Start or compile the source code yourself.[2]

---

[1] JColorChooser   API   documentation: http://java.sun.com/j2se/1.4.2/docs/api/javax/ swing/JColorChooser.html.

[2] To run ColorChooserDemo using Java Web Start, click the ColorChooserDemo link on the RunExamples/components.html page on the CD. You can find the source files here: JavaTutorial/ uiswing/components/example-1dot4/index.html#ColorChooserDemo.

C

Components

The color chooser consists of everything within the box labeled **Choose Text Color**. This is what a standard color chooser looks like in the Java look and feel. It contains two parts: a tabbed pane and a preview panel. The three tabs in the tabbed pane select chooser panels. The preview panel below the tabbed pane displays the currently selected color.

Here's the code from the example that creates a JColorChooser instance and adds it to the demo's window:

```
public class ColorChooserDemo extends JPanel ... {
    public ColorChooserDemo() {
        . . .
        banner = new JLabel("Welcome to the Tutorial Zone!",
                            JLabel.CENTER);
        banner.setForeground(Color.yellow);
        . . .
        tcc = new JColorChooser(banner.getForeground());
        . . .
        add(tcc, BorderLayout.PAGE_END);
    }
    . . .
    frame.setContentPane(new ColorChooserDemo());
```

The JColorChooser constructor in the code snippet takes a Color argument, which specifies the chooser's initially selected color. If you don't specify the initial color, then the color chooser displays Color.white. See the Color[1] API for a list of color constants you can use.

A color chooser uses an instance of ColorSelectionModel to contain and manage the current selection. The color selection model fires a change event whenever the user changes the color in the color chooser. The example program registers a change listener with the color selection model so that it can update the banner at the top of the window. The following code registers and implements the change listener:

```
tcc.getSelectionModel().addChangeListener(this);
. . .
public void stateChanged(ChangeEvent e) {
    Color newColor = tcc.getColor();
    banner.setForeground(newColor);
}
```

See How to Write a Change Listener (page 652) in Chapter 10 for general information about change listeners and change events.

A basic color chooser, like the one used in the example program, is sufficient for many programs. However, the color chooser API allows you to customize a color chooser by provid-

---

[1] Color API documentation: http://java.sun.com/j2se/1.4.2/docs/api/java/awt/Color.html.

ing it with a preview panel of your own design, by adding your own chooser panels to it, or by removing existing chooser panels. Additionally, the JColorChooser class provides two methods that make it easy to use a color chooser within a dialog.

Another Example: ColorChooserDemo2

Now let's turn our attention to ColorChooserDemo2, a modified version of the previous demo program that uses more of the JColorChooser API. You can run ColorChooserDemo2 using Java Web Start.[1] Figure 6 shows a picture of ColorChooserDemo2.

Figure 6   The ColorChooserDemo2 application.

---

[1] To run ColorChooserDemo2 using Java Web Start, click the ColorChooserDemo2 link on the RunExamples/components.html page on the CD. You can find the source files here: JavaTutorial/uiswing/components/example-1dot4/index.html#ColorChooserDemo2.

This program customizes the banner's text color chooser in these ways:

- Removes the preview panel
- Removes all of the default chooser panels
- Adds a custom chooser panel

Removing or Replacing the Preview Panel (page 171) covers the first customization. Creating a Custom Chooser Panel (page 171) discusses the last two.

The program also adds a button that brings up a color chooser in a dialog, which you can use to set the banner's background color.

Showing a Color Chooser in a Dialog

The JColorChooser class provides two class methods to make it easy to use a color chooser in a dialog. ColorChooserDemo2 uses one of these methods, showDialog, to display the background color chooser when the user clicks the **Show Color Chooser...** button. Here's the single line of code from the example that brings up the background color chooser in a dialog:

```
Color newColor = JColorChooser.showDialog(ColorChooserDemo2.this,
                                          "Choose Background Color",
                                          banner.getBackground());
```

The first argument is the parent for the dialog, the second is the dialog's title, and the third is the initially selected color.

The dialog disappears under three conditions: (1) the user chooses a color and clicks the **OK** button, (2) the user cancels the operation with the **Cancel** button, or (3) the user dismisses the dialog with a frame control. If the user chooses a color, the showDialog method returns the new color. If the user cancels the operation or dismisses the window, the method returns null. Here's the code from the example that updates the banner's background color according to the value returned by showDialog:

```
if (newColor != null) {
    banner.setBackground(newColor);
}
```

The dialog created by showDialog is modal. If you want a nonmodal dialog, you can use JColorChooser's createDialog method to create one. This method also lets you specify action listeners for the **OK** and **Cancel** buttons in the dialog window. Use JDialog's show method to display the dialog created by this method. For an example that uses this method, see Using Other Editors (page 402) in the How to Use Tables (page 388) section later in this chapter.

Removing or Replacing the Preview Panel

By default, the color chooser displays a preview panel. `ColorChooserDemo2` removes the text color chooser's preview panel with this line of code:

```
tcc.setPreviewPanel(new JPanel());
```

This effectively removes the preview panel because a plain `JPanel` has no size and no default view. To set the preview panel back to the default, use `null` as the argument to `set-PreviewPanel`.

To provide a custom preview panel, you also use `setPreviewPanel`. The component you pass into the method should inherit from `JComponent`, specify a reasonable size, and provide a customized view of the current color. To be notified when the user changes the color in the color chooser, the preview panel must register as a change listener on the color chooser's color selection model as described previously.

Version Note: In some releases, you either couldn't replace the preview panel or couldn't remove it properly (the titled border would remain). We believe that both problems have been fixed as of v1.4.2. If your program depends on removing or replacing the preview panel, you should test it against all releases that it supports.

Creating a Custom Chooser Panel

The default color chooser provides three chooser panels:

- Swatches—for choosing a color from a collection of swatches
- HSB—for choosing a color using the hue-saturation-brightness color model
- RGB—for choosing a color using the red-green-blue color model

You can extend the default color chooser by adding chooser panels of your own design with `addChooserPanel`, or you can limit it by removing chooser panels with `removeChooser-Panel`.

If you want to remove all of the default chooser panels and add one or more of your own, you can do so with a single call to `setChooserPanels`. `ColorChooserDemo2` uses this method to replace the default chooser panels with an instance of `CrayonPanel`, a custom chooser panel. Here's the call to `setChooserPanels` from that example:

```
//Override the chooser panels with our own.
AbstractColorChooserPanel panels[] = { new CrayonPanel() };
tcc.setChooserPanels(panels);
```

The code is straightforward: It creates an array containing the CrayonPanel; next it calls setChooserPanels to set the contents of the array as the color chooser's chooser panels. CrayonPanel is a subclass of AbstractColorChooserPanel and overrides the following five abstract methods defined in its superclass:

void buildChooser()

Creates the GUI that comprises the chooser panel. The example creates one toggle buttons for each of the four crayons and adds them to the chooser panel.

void updateChooser()

This method is called whenever the chooser panel is displayed. The example's implementation of this method selects the toggle button that represents the currently selected color.

```
public void updateChooser() {
    Color color = getColorFromModel();
    if (Color.red.equals(color)) {
        redCrayon.setSelected(true);
    } else if (Color.yellow.equals(color)) {
        yellowCrayon.setSelected(true);
    } else if (Color.green.equals(color)) {
        greenCrayon.setSelected(true);
    } else if (Color.blue.equals(color)) {
        blueCrayon.setSelected(true);
    }
}
```

String getDisplayName()

Returns the display name of the chooser panel, which is used on the tab for the chooser panel. Here's the example's getDisplayName method:

```
public String getDisplayName() {
    return "Crayons";
}
```

Icon getSmallDisplayIcon()

Returns a small icon to represent this chooser panel. It's currently unused. Future versions of the color chooser might use this icon or the large one to represent this chooser panel in the display. The example's implementation of this method returns null.

```
Icon getLargeDisplayIcon()
```
Returns a large icon to represent this chooser panel. It, too, is currently unused. Future versions of the color chooser might use this icon or the small one to represent this chooser panel in the display. The example's implementation of this method returns null.

The Color Chooser API

Tables 7 through 9 list the commonly used JColorChooser constructors and methods. Other methods you might call are listed in the API tables in The JComponent Class (page 53) in Chapter 3. Refer to the JColorChooser API documentation at: http://java.sun.com/j2se/1.4.2/docs/api/javax/swing/JColorChooser.html.

Table 7: Creating and Displaying the Color Chooser

Method or Constructor	Purpose
JColorChooser() JColorChooser(Color) JColorChooser(ColorSelectionModel)	Create a color chooser. The default constructor creates a color chooser with an initial color of Color.white. Use the second constructor to specify a different initial color. The ColorSelectionModel argument, when present, provides the color chooser with a color selection model.

Color showDialog(Component,
                 String,
                 Color)
	Create and show a color chooser in a modal dialog. The Component argument is the dialog's parent, the String argument specifies the dialog's title, and the Color argument specifies the chooser's initial color.

JDialog createDialog(Component,
                 String,
                 boolean,
                 JColorChooser,
                 ActionListener,
                 ActionListener)
	Create a dialog for the specified color chooser. As with showDialog, the Component argument is the dialog's parent and the String argument specifies the dialog's title. The other arguments are as follows: the boolean specifies whether the dialog is modal, the JColorChooser is the color chooser to display in the dialog, the first ActionListener is for the **OK** button, and the second is for the **Cancel** button.

C

Components

173

Table 8: Customizing the Color Chooser's GUI

Method	Purpose
`void setPreviewPanel(JComponent)` `JComponent getPreviewPanel()`	Set or get the component used to preview the color selection. To remove the preview panel, use `new JPanel()` as an argument. To specify the default preview panel, use null.

`void setChooserPanel(`
`        AbstractColorChooserPanel)`
`AbstractColorChooserPanel[]`
`        getChooserPanels()`
	Set or get the chooser panels in the color chooser.

`void addChooserPanel(`
`        AbstractColorChooserPanel)`
`AbstractColorChooserPanel removeChooserPanel(`
`        AbstractColorChooserPanel)`
	Add a chooser panel to the color chooser or remove a chooser panel from it.

`void setDragEnabled(boolean)` `boolean getDragEnabled()`	Set or get the *dragEnabled* property, which must be true to enable drag handling on this component. The default value is false. See How to Use Drag and Drop and Data Transfer (page 545) in Chapter 9 for more details. Introduced in 1.4.

Table 9: Setting or Getting the Current Color

Method	Purpose

`void setColor(Color)`
`void setColor(int, int, int)`
`void setColor(int)`
`Color getColor()`
	Set or get the currently selected color. The three-integer version interprets the three integers together as an RGB color. The single-integer version divides the integer into four 8-bit bytes and interprets the integer as an RGB color.

`void setSelectionModel(`
`        ColorSelectionModel)`
`ColorSelectionModel getSelectionModel()`
	Set or get the selection model for the color chooser. This object contains the current selection and fires change events to registered listeners whenever the selection changes.

Examples That Use Color Choosers

The following table shows examples that use JColorChooser and where those examples are described.

Example	Where Described	Notes
ColorChooserDemo	This section	Uses a standard color chooser.
ColorChooserDemo2	This section	Uses one customized color chooser and one standard color chooser in a dialog created with showDialog.
TableDialogEditDemo	How to Use Tables (page 388)	Shows how to use a color chooser as a custom cell editor in a table. The color chooser used by this example is created with createDialog.

C

Components

How to Use Combo Boxes

A JComboBox,[1] which lets the user choose one of several choices, can have two very different forms. The default form is the uneditable combo box, which features a button and a drop-down list of values. The second form is the editable combo box, which features a text field with a small button next to it. The user can type a value in the text field or click the button to display a drop-down list. Figure 7 shows what the two forms of combo box look like in the Java look and feel.

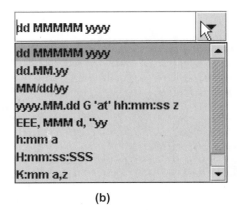

(a)   (b)

Figure 7   (a) Uneditable combo box, before (*top*) and after the button is clicked; (b) editable combo box, before (*top*) and after the arrow button is clicked.

Combo boxes require little screen space, and their editable (text field) form is useful for letting the user quickly choose a value without limiting her to the displayed values. Other components that can display one-of-many choices are groups of radio buttons and lists. Groups of radio buttons are generally the easiest for users to understand, but combo boxes can be more appropriate when space is limited or more than a few choices are available. Lists aren't terribly attractive, but they're more appropriate than combo boxes when the number of items is large (say, more than 20) or when selecting multiple items might be valid.

---

[1]   JComboBox API documentation: `http://java.sun.com/j2se/1.4.2/docs/api/javax/swing/` `JComboBox.html`.

Using an Uneditable Combo Box

The application shown in Figure 8 uses an uneditable combo box for choosing a pet picture.

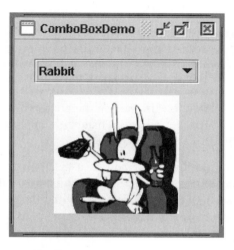

Figure 8   The ComboBoxDemo application.

Try This:

1. Run ComboBoxDemo using Java Web Start or compile and run the source code your-self.[1]

2. Choose an animal name from the combo box to view its picture.

3. Compare the operation and GUI of this program to one that uses radio buttons; run RadioButtonDemo.[2]

The following code, taken from ComboBoxDemo.java, creates an uneditable combo box and sets it up:

```
String[] petStrings = { "Bird", "Cat", "Dog", "Rabbit", "Pig" };
```

---

[1] To run ComboBoxDemo using Java Web Start, click the ComboBoxDemo link on the RunExamples/ components.html page on the CD. You can find the source files here: JavaTutorial/uiswing/ components/example-1dot4/index.html#ComboBoxDemo.

[2] To run RadioButtonDemo using Java Web Start, click the RadioButtonDemo link on the RunExamples/ components.html page on the CD. You can find the source files here: JavaTutorial/uiswing/ components/example-1dot4/index.html#RadioButtonDemo.

C

Components

```
//Create the combo box, select item at index 4.
//Indices start at 0, so 4 specifies the pig.
JComboBox petList = new JComboBox(petStrings);
petList.setSelectedIndex(4);
petList.addActionListener(this);
```

This combo box contains an array of strings, but you could just as easily use icons instead. To put anything else into a combo box or to customize how the items in it look, you need to write a custom renderer. An editable combo box also needs a custom editor. See Providing a Custom Renderer (page 181) for information and an example.

The preceding code registers an action listener on the combo box. To see the action listener implementation and learn about other types of listeners supported by JComboBox, refer to Handling Events on a Combo Box (page 178).

No matter which constructor you use, a combo box uses a combo box model to contain and manage the items in its menu. When you initialize a combo box with an array or a vector, the combo box creates a default model object for you. As with other Swing components, you can customize a combo box in part by implementing a custom model—an object that implements the ComboBoxModel interface.

Note: Be careful when implementing a custom model for a combo box. The JComboBox methods that change the items in the combo box's menu, such as insertItemAt, work only if the data model implements the MutableComboBoxModel[1] interface (a subinterface of ComboBoxModel). Refer to the API tables to see which methods are affected (page 184).

Something else to watch out for—even for uneditable combo boxes—is ensuring that your custom model fires list data events when the combo box's data or state changes. Even immutable combo box models, whose data never changes, must fire a list data event (a CONTENTS_CHANGED event) when the selection changes. One way to get the list data event firing code for free is to make your combo box model a subclass of AbstractListModel.

Handling Events on a Combo Box

Here's the code from ComboBoxDemo.java that registers and implements an action listener on the combo box:

---

[1] MutableComboBoxModel API documentation: http://java.sun.com/j2se/1.4.2/docs/api/javax/swing/MutableComboBoxModel.html.

```java
public class ComboBoxDemo ... implements ActionListener {
    . . .
        petList.addActionListener(this) {
    . . .
    public void actionPerformed(ActionEvent e) {
        JComboBox cb = (JComboBox)e.getSource();
        String petName = (String)cb.getSelectedItem();
        updateLabel(petName);
    }
    . . .
}
```

This action listener gets the newly selected item from the combo box, uses it to compute the name of an image file, and updates a label to display the image. The combo box fires an action event when the user selects an item from the combo box's menu. See How to Write an Action Listener (page 646) in Chapter 10 for general information about implementing action listeners.

Combo boxes also generate item events, which are fired when the selection state of any item changes. Only one item at a time can be selected in a combo box, so when the user makes a new selection the previously selected item becomes unselected. Thus, two item events are fired each time the user selects a different item from the menu. If the user chooses the same item, no item events are fired. Use addItemListener to register an item listener on a combo box. How to Write an Item Listener (page 674) in Chapter 10 gives general information about implementing item listeners.

Although JComboBox inherits methods to register listeners for low-level events—focus, key, and mouse events, for example—we recommend that you don't listen for low-level events on a combo box. Here's why: A combo box is a *compound component*, comprising two or more other components. The combo box itself fires high-level events such as actions. Its subcomponents fire low-level events such as mouse, key, and focus events. The low-level events and the subcomponent that fires them are look-and-feel-dependent. To avoid writing look-and-feel-dependent code, you should listen only for high-level events on a compound component such as a combo box.

For information about events, including a discussion of high- and low-level events, see Chapter 5, Writing Event Listeners (page 107).

C

Components

Using an Editable Combo Box

Figure 9 is a picture of a demo application that uses an editable combo box to enter a pattern with which to format dates.

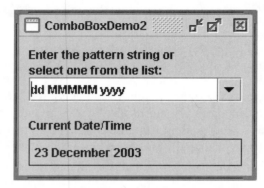

Figure 9   ComboBoxDemo2, an application that demonstrates the use of editable combo boxes.

Try This:

1. Run ComboBoxDemo2 using Java Web Start or compile and run the source code your- self.[1]

2. Enter a new pattern by choosing one from the combo box's menu. The program reformats the current date and time.

3. Enter a new pattern by typing one in and pressing Enter. Again the program reformats the current date and time.

The following code, taken from ComboBoxDemo2.java, creates and sets up the combo box:

```
String[] patternExamples = {
        "dd MMMMM yyyy",
        "dd.MM.yy",
        "MM/dd/yy",
        "yyyy.MM.dd G 'at' hh:mm:ss z",
        "EEE, MMM d, ''yy",
        "h:mm a",
        "H:mm:ss:SSS",
        "K:mm a,z",
        "yyyy.MMMMM.dd GGG hh:mm aaa"
};
```

---

[1] To run ComboBoxDemo2 using Java Web Start, click the ComboBoxDemo2 link on the RunExamples/ components.html page on the CD. You can find the source files here: JavaTutorial/uiswing/ components/example-1dot4/index.html#ComboBoxDemo2.

```
    . . .
    JComboBox patternList = new JComboBox(patternExamples);
    patternList.setEditable(true);
    patternList.addActionListener(this);
```

It's very similar to the previous example, but warrants a few words of explanation. The bold line explicitly turns on editing to allow the user to type in values. This is necessary because, by default, a combo box is not editable. This particular example allows editing on the combo box because its menu doesn't provide all possible date-formatting patterns but just shortcuts to frequently used patterns.

An editable combo box fires an action event when the user chooses an item from the menu and when the user presses Enter. Note that the menu remains unchanged when the user enters a value into the combo box. If you want, you can easily write an action listener that adds a new item to the combo box's menu each time the user types in a unique value.

See *The Java Tutorial*'s "Internationalization" trail to learn more about formatting dates and other types of data.[1]

Providing a Custom Renderer

A combo box uses a *renderer* to display each item in its menu. If the combo box is uneditable, it also uses the renderer to display the currently selected item. An editable combo box, on the other hand, uses an *editor* to display the selected item. A renderer for a combo box must implement the `ListCellRenderer`[2] interface; a combo box's editor must implement `ComboBoxEditor`.[3] This section shows how to provide a custom renderer for an uneditable combo box.

The default renderer knows how to render strings and icons. If you put other objects in a combo box, the default renderer calls the `toString` method to provide a string to display. You can customize the way a combo box renders itself and its items by implementing your own `ListCellRenderer`.

---

[1] The "Internationalization" trail is available in *The Java Tutorial* on this book's CD and online at: `http://java.sun.com/docs/books/tutorial/i18n/index.html`.

[2] `ListCellRenderer` API documentation: `http://java.sun.com/j2se/1.4.2/docs/api/javax/swing/ListCellRenderer.html`.

[3] `ComboBoxEditor` API documentation: `http://java.sun.com/j2se/1.4.2/docs/api/javax/swing/ComboBoxEditor.html`.

Components

Figure 10 is a picture of an application that uses a combo box with a custom renderer.

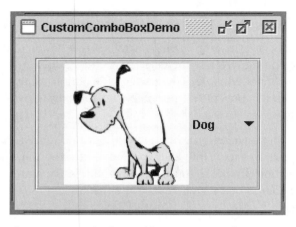

Figure 10   This application uses a combo box with a custom renderer.

You can run `CustomComboBoxDemo` using Java Web Start or compile and run the source code yourself.[1]

The following statements from the example create an instance of `ComboBoxRenderer` (a custom class) and set it up as the combo box's renderer:

```
JComboBox petList = new JComboBox(intArray);
. . .
ComboBoxRenderer renderer = new ComboBoxRenderer();
renderer.setPreferredSize(new Dimension(200, 130));
petList.setRenderer(renderer);
petList.setMaximumRowCount(3);
```

The last line sets the combo box's maximum row count, which determines the number of items visible when the menu is displayed. If the number of items in the combo box is larger than its maximum row count, the menu has a scroll bar. The icons are pretty big for a menu, so our code limits the number of rows to three. Here's the implementation of `ComboBox-Renderer`, which puts an icon and text side by side:

---

[1]   To run `CustomComboBoxDemo` using Java Web Start, click the `CustomComboBoxDemo` link on the `RunExamples/components.html` page on the CD. You can find the source files here: `JavaTutorial/uiswing/components/example-1dot4/index.html#CustomComboBoxDemo`.

```
class ComboBoxRenderer extends JLabel
                      implements ListCellRenderer {
    . . .
    public ComboBoxRenderer() {
        setOpaque(true);
        setHorizontalAlignment(CENTER);
        setVerticalAlignment(CENTER);
    }

    /*
     * This method finds the image and text corresponding
     * to the selected value and returns the label, set up
     * to display the text and image.
     */
    public Component getListCellRendererComponent(
                                    JList list,
                                    Object value,
                                    int index,
                                    boolean isSelected,
                                    boolean cellHasFocus) {
        //Get the selected index. (The index param isn't
        //always valid, so just use the value.)
        int selectedIndex = ((Integer)value).intValue();

        if (isSelected) {
            setBackground(list.getSelectionBackground());
            setForeground(list.getSelectionForeground());
        } else {
            setBackground(list.getBackground());
            setForeground(list.getForeground());
        }

        //Set the icon and text.  If icon was null, say so.
        ImageIcon icon = images[selectedIndex];
        String pet = petStrings[selectedIndex];
        setIcon(icon);
        if (icon != null) {
            setText(pet);
            setFont(list.getFont());
        } else {
            setUhOhText(pet + " (no image available)", list.getFont());
        }

        return this;
    }
    . . .
}
```

As a `ListCellRenderer`, `ComboBoxRenderer` implements a method called `getListCell-RendererComponent`, which returns a component whose `paintComponent` method is used to display the combo box and each of its items. The easiest way to display an image and an icon is to use a label, so `ComboBoxRenderer` is a subclass of label and returns itself. The implementation of `getListCellRendererComponent` configures the renderer to display the currently selected icon and its description.

These arguments are passed to `getListCellRendererComponent`:

- `JList list`—a list object used behind the scenes to display the items. The example uses this object's colors to set up foreground and background colors.
- `Object value`—the object to render, an `Integer` in this example.
- `int index`—the index of the object to render.
- `boolean isSelected`—indicates whether the object to render is selected. It's used by the example to determine which colors to use.
- `boolean cellHasFocus`—indicates whether the object to render has the focus.

Note that combo boxes and lists[1] both use `ListCellRenderer`. You can save yourself some time by sharing renderers between combo boxes and lists if it makes sense for your program.

The Combo Box API

Tables 10 and 11 list the commonly used `JComboBox` constructors and methods. Other methods you're most likely to invoke on a `JComboBox` object are those the object inherits from its superclasses, such as `setPreferredSize`. See The JComponent Class (page 53) in Chapter 3 for tables of commonly used inherited methods. You can also refer to the API documentation for `JComboBox`.[2]

---

[1] See How to Use Lists (page 267).

[2] `JComboBox` API documentation: `http://java.sun.com/j2se/1.4.2/docs/api/javax/swing/JComboBox.html`.

Table 10: Setting or Getting the Items in the Combo Box Menu

Method	Purpose

`JComboBox()`
`JComboBox(ComboBoxModel)`
`JComboBox(Object[])`
`JComboBox(Vector)`
	Create a combo box with the specified items in its menu. A combo box created with the default constructor has no items in the menu initially. Each of the other constructors initializes the menu from its argument: a model object, an array of objects, or a `Vector` of objects.

`void addItem(Object)` `void insertItemAt(Object, int)`	Add or insert the specified object in the combo box menu. The `insert` method places the specified object *at* the specified index, thus inserting it before the object currently at that index. These methods require that the combo box data model be an instance of `MutableComboBoxModel`.
`Object getItemAt(int)` `Object getSelectedItem()`	Get an item from the combo box menu.

`void removeAllItems()`
`void removeItemAt(int)`
`void removeItem(Object)`
	Remove one or more items from the combo box menu. These methods require that the combo box data model be an instance of `MutableComboBoxModel`.

`int getItemCount()`	Get the number of items in the combo box menu.
`void setModel(ComboBoxModel)` `ComboBoxModel getModel()`	Set or get the data model that provides the items in the combo box menu.
`void setAction(Action)` `Action getAction()`	Set or get the `Action` associated with the combo box. For further information, see How to Use Actions (page 513) in Chapter 9. Introduced in 1.3.

Table 11: Customizing the Combo Box's Operation

Method or Constructor	Purpose
`void addActionListener(ActionListener)`	Add an action listener to the combo box. The listener's `actionPerformed` method is called when the user selects an item from the combo box menu or, in an editable combo box, when the user presses Enter.
`void addItemListener(ItemListener)`	Add an item listener to the combo box. The listener's `itemStateChanged` method is called when the selection state of any combo box item changes.

C

Components

Table 11: Customizing the Combo Box's Operation *(continued)*

Method or Constructor	Purpose
`void setEditable(boolean)` `boolean isEditable()`	Set or get whether the user can type in the combo box.
`void setRenderer(ListCellRenderer)` `ListCellRenderer getRenderer()`	Set or get the object responsible for painting the selected item in the combo box. The renderer is used only when the combo box is uneditable. If the combo box is editable, the editor is used to paint the selected item instead.
`void setEditor(ComboBoxEditor)` `ComboBoxEditor getEditor()`	Set or get the object responsible for painting and editing the selected item in the combo box. The editor is used only when the combo box is editable. If the combo box is uneditable, the renderer is used to paint the selected item instead.

Examples That Use Combo Boxes

The following table shows examples that use `JComboBox` and where those examples are described.

Example	Where Described	Notes
`ComboBoxDemo`	This section	Uses an uneditable combo box.
`ComboBoxDemo2`	This section	Uses an editable combo box.
`CustomComboBoxDemo`	This section	Provides a custom renderer for a combo box.
`LunarPhases`	Example Five: LunarPhases (page 25)	Uses an uneditable combo box.
`TableRenderDemo`	How to Use Tables (page 388)	Shows how to use a combo box as a table cell editor.

How to Make Dialogs

Several classes support *dialogs*—windows that are more limited than frames. To create simple, standard dialogs, you use the JOptionPane class.[1] The ProgressMonitor class can put up a dialog that shows the progress of an operation.[2] Two other classes, JColorChooser and JFileChooser, also supply standard dialogs.[3] To bring up a print dialog, you use the Printing API.[4] To create custom dialogs, use the JDialog[5] class directly.

The code for simple dialogs can be minimal. Figure 11, for example, shows an informational dialog.

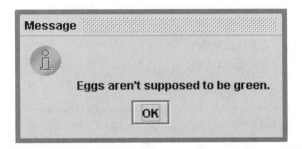

Figure 11   A simple dialog.

Here's the code that creates and shows the dialog:

```
JOptionPane.showMessageDialog(frame,
                    "Eggs aren't supposed to be green.");
```

An Overview of Dialogs

Every dialog is dependent on a frame. When the frame is destroyed, so are its dialogs. When the frame is iconified, its dialogs disappear from the screen. When the frame is deiconified, its dialogs return to the screen. The AWT automatically provides this behavior.

---

[1] JOptionPane API documentation: http://java.sun.com/j2se/1.4.2/docs/api/javax/swing/JOptionPane.html.

[2] See How to Use Progress Bars (page 300).

[3] See How to Use Color Choosers (page 167) and How to Use File Choosers (page 206).

[4] You can learn more about printing in the "2D" trail in *The Java Tutorial* on this book's CD and online at: http://java.sun.com/docs/books/tutorial/2d.

[5] JDialog API documentation: http://java.sun.com/j2se/1.4.2/docs/api/javax/swing/JDialog.html.

A dialog can be *modal*. When a modal dialog is visible, it blocks user input to all other windows in the program. The dialogs that JOptionPane provides are modal. To create a nonmodal dialog, you must use the JDialog class directly.

The JDialog class is a subclass of the AWT java.awt.Dialog class. It adds to Dialog a root pane and support for a default close operation. These are the same features that JFrame has, and using JDialog directly is very similar to using JFrame directly. If you're going to use JDialog directly, then you should understand the material in Using Top-Level Containers (page 46) in Chapter 3 and How to Make Frames (Main Windows) (page 236) later in this chapter, especially Responding to Window-Closing Events (page 240).

Even when you use JOptionPane to implement a dialog, you're still using a JDialog behind the scenes. The reason is that JOptionPane is simply a container that can automatically create a JDialog and add itself to the JDialog's content pane.

The DialogDemo Example

Figure 12 is a picture of an application that displays dialogs.

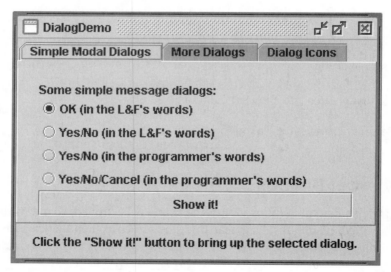

Figure 12 The DialogDemo application.

Try This:

1. Run DialogDemo using Java Web Start or compile and run the source code yourself.[1]

---

[1] To run DialogDemo using Java Web Start, click the DialogDemo link on the RunExamples/ components.html page on the CD. You can find the source files here: JavaTutorial/uiswing/ components/example-1dot4/index.html#DialogDemo.

2. Click the Show it! button. A modal dialog will appear. Until you close it, the application will be unresponsive, although it will repaint itself if necessary. You can close the dialog by clicking a button in the dialog or you can close it explicitly, such as by using the dialog's window decorations.

3. Iconify the `DialogDemo` window while a dialog is showing. The dialog will disappear from the screen until you deiconify the `DialogDemo` window.

4. In the More Dialogs pane, click the bottom radio button and then the Show it! button. A nonmodal dialog will appear. Note that the `DialogDemo` window remains fully functional while the nonmodal dialog is up.

JOptionPane Features

Using `JOptionPane`, you can create and customize several different kinds of dialogs. `JOptionPane` provides support for laying out standard dialogs, providing icons, specifying the dialog's title and text, and customizing the button text. Other features allow you to customize the components the dialog displays and specify where the dialog should appear onscreen. You can even specify that an option pane put itself into an internal frame (`JInternalFrame`) instead of a `JDialog`.

Note: The internal frames that `JOptionPane` creates currently behave differently from modal dialogs. They don't behave modally and in general seem more like frames than like dialogs. For this reason, we don't currently recommend their use.

When you create a `JOptionPane`, look-and-feel-specific code adds components to it and determines their layout.

`JOptionPane`'s icon support lets you easily specify which icon the dialog displays. You can use a custom icon, no icon at all, or any one of four standard `JOptionPane` icons (question, information, warning, and error). Each look and feel has its own versions of the four standard icons. Figure 13 shows the icons used in the Java look and feel.

| question | information | warning | error |

Figure 13   Icons provided by `JOptionPane` (Java look and feel shown).

D

Components

Creating and Showing Simple Dialogs

Most simple modal dialogs you create and show using one of JOptionPane's show*Xxx*-Dialog methods. If your dialog should be an internal frame, add Internal after show—for example, showMessageDialog changes to showInternalMessageDialog. If you need to control the dialog's window-closing behavior or if the dialog isn't modal, you should directly instantiate JOptionPane and add it to a JDialog instance. Then invoke setVisible(true) on the JDialog to make it appear.

The two most useful show*Xxx*Dialog methods are showMessageDialog and showOption-Dialog. The showMessageDialog method displays a simple, one-button dialog. The show-OptionDialog method displays a customized dialog that can display a variety of buttons with customized button text and can contain a standard text message or a collection of components.

The other two show*Xxx*Dialog methods are used less often. The showConfirmDialog method asks the user to confirm something, but has the disadvantage of having standard button text (Yes/No or the localized equivalent, for example) rather than button text customized to the user's situation (Start/Cancel, for example). A fourth method, showInputDialog, is designed to display a modal dialog that gets a string from the user, using either a text field or an uneditable combo box.

The following are some examples, taken from DialogDemo.java, of using showMessageDialog, showOptionDialog, and the JOptionPane constructor. For more example code, see DialogDemo.java and the other programs listed in Examples That Use Dialogs (page 199) later in this chapter.

showMessageDialog

Displays a modal dialog with one button, which is labeled OK (or the localized equivalent). You can easily specify the message, icon, and title the dialog displays. Table 12 shows some examples.

Table 12: Examples Using showMessageDialog

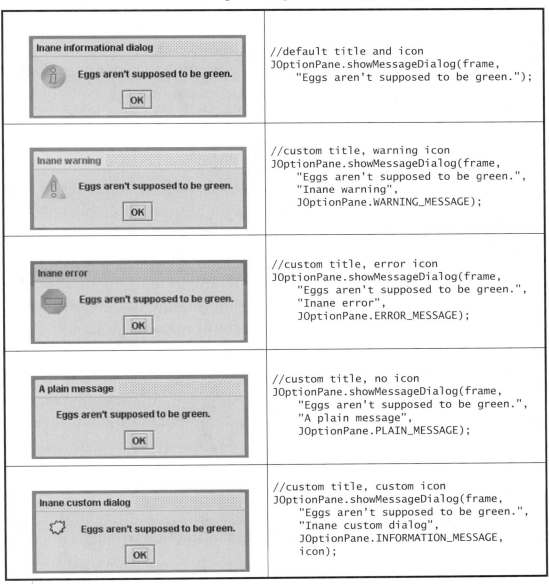

Inane informational dialog — Eggs aren't supposed to be green. OK	`//default title and icon`
	`JOptionPane.showMessageDialog(frame,`
	`    "Eggs aren't supposed to be green.");`

Inane warning — Eggs aren't supposed to be green. OK	`//custom title, warning icon`
	`JOptionPane.showMessageDialog(frame,`
	`    "Eggs aren't supposed to be green.",`
	`    "Inane warning",`
	`    JOptionPane.WARNING_MESSAGE);`

Inane error — Eggs aren't supposed to be green. OK	`//custom title, error icon`
	`JOptionPane.showMessageDialog(frame,`
	`    "Eggs aren't supposed to be green.",`
	`    "Inane error",`
	`    JOptionPane.ERROR_MESSAGE);`

A plain message — Eggs aren't supposed to be green. OK	`//custom title, no icon`
	`JOptionPane.showMessageDialog(frame,`
	`    "Eggs aren't supposed to be green.",`
	`    "A plain message",`
	`    JOptionPane.PLAIN_MESSAGE);`

Inane custom dialog — Eggs aren't supposed to be green. OK	`//custom title, custom icon`
	`JOptionPane.showMessageDialog(frame,`
	`    "Eggs aren't supposed to be green.",`
	`    "Inane custom dialog",`
	`    JOptionPane.INFORMATION_MESSAGE,`
	`    icon);`

D

Components

191

showOptionDialog

Displays a modal dialog with the specified buttons, icons, message, title, and so on. With this method, you can change the text that appears on the buttons of standard dialogs and perform many other kinds of customization. (See Table 13.)

Table 13: An Example Using showOptionDialog

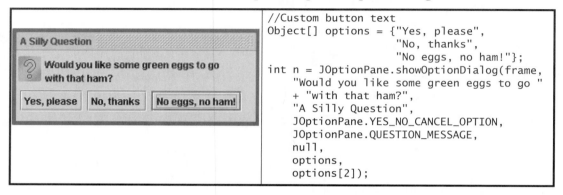

```
//Custom button text
Object[] options = {"Yes, please",
                    "No, thanks",
                    "No eggs, no ham!"};
int n = JOptionPane.showOptionDialog(frame,
    "Would you like some green eggs to go "
    + "with that ham?",
    "A Silly Question",
    JOptionPane.YES_NO_CANCEL_OPTION,
    JOptionPane.QUESTION_MESSAGE,
    null,
    options,
    options[2]);
```

JOptionPane (constructor)

Creates a JOptionPane with the specified buttons, icons, message, title, and so on. You then have to add the option pane to a JDialog, register a property-change listener on the option pane, and show the dialog. (See Table 14.) See Stopping Automatic Dialog Closing (page 195) for details.

Table 14: An Example Using JOptionPane

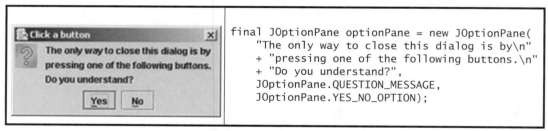

```
final JOptionPane optionPane = new JOptionPane(
    "The only way to close this dialog is by\n"
    + "pressing one of the following buttons.\n"
    + "Do you understand?",
    JOptionPane.QUESTION_MESSAGE,
    JOptionPane.YES_NO_OPTION);
```

The arguments to all of the show*Xxx*Dialog methods and JOptionPane constructors are standardized, though the number of arguments for each method and constructor varies. The following list describes each argument. To look at the complete list of arguments for a particular method, see The Dialog API (page 196).

Component parentComponent

Always the first argument to each show*Xxx*Dialog method, it must be a frame, a component inside a frame, or null. If you specify a frame, the dialog will appear over its center and depend on it. If you specify a component inside a frame, the dialog will appear over the center of that component and depend on that component's frame. If you specify null, the look and feel picks an appropriate position for the dialog—generally the center of the screen—and the dialog doesn't depend on any visible frame.

The JOptionPane constructors don't include this argument. Instead, you specify the parent frame when you create the JDialog that contains the JOptionPane and use the JDialog setLocationRelativeTo method to set the dialog's position.

Object message

A required argument, this specifies what the dialog should display in its main area. Generally, you specify a string, which results in the dialog displaying a label with the specified text. You can split the message over several lines by putting newline (\n) characters inside the message string. For example:

`"Complete the sentence:\n \"Green eggs and...\""`

String title

Specifies the title of the dialog.

int optionType

Specifies the buttons that appear at the bottom of the dialog. Choose from one of the following standard sets:

DEFAULT_OPTION, YES_NO_OPTION, YES_NO_CANCEL_OPTION, OK_CANCEL_OPTION.

int messageType

Determines the icon displayed in the dialog. Choose from the following values:

PLAIN_MESSAGE (no icon), ERROR_MESSAGE, INFORMATION_MESSAGE, WARNING_MESSAGE, QUESTION_MESSAGE.

Icon icon

The icon to display in the dialog.

Object[] options

Further specifies the option buttons to appear at the bottom of the dialog. Generally, you specify an array of strings for the buttons. See Customizing Button Text (page 194) for more information.

`Object initialValue`

> Specifies the default value to be selected. You can either let the default icon be used or specify the icon using the message type or icon argument. By default, a dialog created with `showMessageDialog` displays the information icon, and a dialog created with `showConfirmDialog` or `showInputDialog` displays the question icon. An option pane created with a `JOptionPane` constructor displays no icon by default. To specify that the dialog display a standard icon or no icon, specify the message type. To specify a custom icon, use the icon argument. The icon argument takes precedence over the message type; as long as the icon argument has a non-null value, the dialog displays the specified icon.

Customizing Button Text

When you use `JOptionPane` to create a dialog, you can choose either to use the standard button text (which might vary by look and feel) or to specify different text.

The code shown in Table 15, taken from `DialogDemo.java`, creates two Yes/No dialogs. The first is implemented with `showConfirmDialog`, which uses the look-and-feel wording for the two buttons. The second uses `showOptionDialog` so that it can customize the wording. With the exception of wording changes, the dialogs are identical.

Table 15: Two Yes/No Dialog Examples

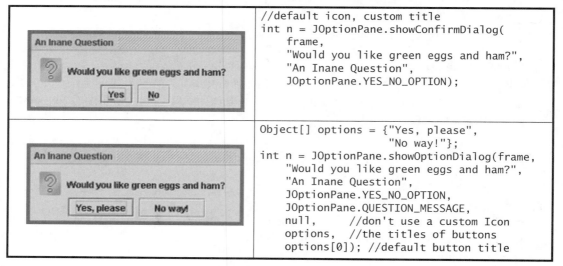

An Inane Question / Would you like green eggs and ham? / Yes No	`//default icon, custom title`
	`int n = JOptionPane.showConfirmDialog(`
	`    frame,`
	`    "Would you like green eggs and ham?",`
	`    "An Inane Question",`
	`    JOptionPane.YES_NO_OPTION);`

An Inane Question / Would you like green eggs and ham? / Yes, please No way!	`Object[] options = {"Yes, please",`
	`                    "No way!"};`
	`int n = JOptionPane.showOptionDialog(frame,`
	`    "Would you like green eggs and ham?",`
	`    "An Inane Question",`
	`    JOptionPane.YES_NO_OPTION,`
	`    JOptionPane.QUESTION_MESSAGE,`
	`    null,     //don't use a custom Icon`
	`    options,  //the titles of buttons`
	`    options[0]); //default button title`

Getting the User's Input from a Dialog

As the previous code snippets in Table 15 show, the showMessageDialog, showConfirm-Dialog, and showOptionDialog methods return an integer indicating the user's choice. The values for this integer are YES_OPTION, NO_OPTION, CANCEL_OPTION, OK_OPTION, and CLOSED_OPTION. Except for CLOSED_OPTION, each option corresponds to the button the user presses. CLOSED_OPTION indicates that the user is closing the dialog window explicitly rather than by choosing a button inside the option pane.

Even if you change the strings that the standard dialog buttons display, the return value is still one of the predefined integers. For example, a YES_NO_OPTION dialog always returns one of the following values: YES_OPTION, NO_OPTION, or CLOSED_OPTION.

If you're designing a custom dialog, on the other hand, you need to design its API so that you can query the dialog about what the user chose. For example, the dialog implemented in CustomDialog.java[1] has a getValidatedText method that returns the text the user entered.

Stopping Automatic Dialog Closing

By default, when the user clicks a JOptionPane-created button, the dialog closes. But what if you want to check the user's answer before closing the dialog? In this case, you must implement your own property-change listener so that when the user clicks a button the dialog doesn't automatically close.

DialogDemo contains two dialogs that implement a property-change listener. One of these is a custom modal dialog, implemented in CustomDialog, that uses JOptionPane both to get the standard icon and to get layout assistance. The other dialog, whose code is below, uses a standard Yes/No JOptionPane. Though this dialog is useless as written, its code is simple enough that you can use it as a template for more complex dialogs.

Besides setting the property-change listener, the following code also calls JDialog's set-DefaultCloseOperation method and implements a window listener that handles the window close attempt properly. If you don't care to be notified when the user closes the window explicitly, ignore the bold code.

```
final JOptionPane optionPane = new JOptionPane(
            "The only way to close this dialog is by\n"
            + "pressing one of the following buttons.\n"
            + "Do you understand?",
            JOptionPane.QUESTION_MESSAGE,
            JOptionPane.YES_NO_OPTION);
```

---

[1] You can find CustomDialog.java here: JavaTutorial/uiswing/components/example-1dot4/ CustomDialog.java.

```
final JDialog dialog = new JDialog(frame, "Click a button", true);
dialog.setContentPane(optionPane);
dialog.setDefaultCloseOperation(
    JDialog.DO_NOTHING_ON_CLOSE);
dialog.addWindowListener(new WindowAdapter() {
    public void windowClosing(WindowEvent we) {
        setLabel("Thwarted user attempt to close window.");
    }
});

optionPane.addPropertyChangeListener(
    new PropertyChangeListener() {
        public void propertyChange(PropertyChangeEvent e) {
            String prop = e.getPropertyName();

            if (dialog.isVisible()
             && (e.getSource() == optionPane)
             && (prop.equals(JOptionPane.VALUE_PROPERTY) ||
                 prop.equals(JOptionPane.INPUT_VALUE_PROPERTY)))
            {
                //If you were going to check something
                //before closing the window, you'd do
                //it here.
                dialog.setVisible(false);
            }
        }
    });
dialog.pack();
dialog.setVisible(true);

int value = ((Integer)optionPane.getValue()).intValue();
if (value == JOptionPane.YES_OPTION) {
    setLabel("Good.");
} else if (value == JOptionPane.NO_OPTION) {
    setLabel("Try using the window decorations "
            + "to close the non-auto-closing dialog. "
            + "You can't!");
}
```

The Dialog API

Tables 16 through 18 list the commonly used JOptionPane[1] and JDialog[2] constructors and methods. Other methods you're likely to call are defined by the Dialog, Window, and Component classes and include pack, setSize, and setVisible.

---

[1] JOptionPane API documentation: http://java.sun.com/j2se/1.4.2/docs/api/javax/swing/ JOptionPane.html.

[2] JDialog API documentation: http://java.sun.com/j2se/1.4.2/docs/api/javax/swing/ JDialog.html.

Table 16: Showing Standard Modal Dialogs
(Using JOptionPane Class Methods)

Method	Purpose

`static void showMessageDialog(Component,`
`                 Object)`
`static void showMessageDialog(Component,`
`                 Object,`
`                 String, int)`
`static void showMessageDialog(Component,`
`                 Object,`
`                 String,`
`                 int, Icon)`
	Show a one-button, modal dialog that gives the user some information. The arguments specify (in order) parent component, message, title, message type, and icon for the dialog. See Creating and Showing Simple Dialogs (page 190) for a discussion of the arguments and their effects.

`static int showOptionDialog(Component, Object,`
`                 String, int, int,`
`                 Icon, Object[],`
`                 Object)`
	Show a customized modal dialog. The arguments specify (in order) parent component, message, title, option type, message type, icon, options, and initial value for the dialog. See also Creating and Showing Simple Dialogs (page 190).

`static int showConfirmDialog(Component, Object)`
`static int showConfirmDialog(Component, Object,`
`                 String, int)`
`static int showConfirmDialog(Component, Object,`
`                 String, int, int)`
`static int showConfirmDialog(Component, Object,`
`                 String,`
`                 int, int, Icon)`
	Show a modal dialog that asks the user a question. The arguments specify (in order) parent component, message, title, option type, message type, and icon for the dialog. See also Creating and Showing Simple Dialogs (page 190).

`static String showInputDialog(Object)`
`static String showInputDialog(Component,`
`                 Object)`
`static String showInputDialog(Component,`
`                 Object,`
`                 String, int)`
`static String showInputDialog(Component,`
`                 Object,`
`                 String,`
`                 int,`
`                 Icon,`
`                 Object[],`
`                 Object)`
	Show a modal dialog that prompts the user for input. The single-argument version specifies just the message, with the parent component assumed to be null. The arguments for the other versions specify (in order) parent component, message, title, message type, icon, options, and initial value for the dialog. See also Creating and Showing Simple Dialogs (page 190).

`static void showInternalMessageDialog(...)`
`static void showInternalOptionDialog(...)`
`static void showInternalConfirmDialog(...)`
`static String showInternalInputDialog(...)`
	Implement a standard dialog as an internal frame. See Table 17 (page 198) for the exact list of arguments.

D

Components

Table 17: Methods for Using JOptionPanes Directly

Method or Constructor	Purpose
JOptionPane() JOptionPane(Object) JOptionPane(Object, int) JOptionPane(Object, int, int) JOptionPane(Object, int, int, Icon) JOptionPane(Object, int, int, Icon, Object[]) JOptionPane(Object, int, int, Icon, Object[], Object)	Creates a JOptionPane instance. See Creating and Showing Simple Dialogs (page 190) for a discussion of the arguments and their effects.
static Frame getFrameForComponent(Component) static JDesktopPane getDesktopPaneForComponent(Component)	Handy JOptionPane class methods that find the frame or desktop pane, respectively, that the specified component is in.

Table 18: Frequently Used JDialog Constructors and Methods

Method or Constructor	Purpose

JDialog()
JDialog(Dialog)
JDialog(Dialog, boolean)
JDialog(Dialog, String)
JDialog(Dialog, String, boolean)
JDialog(Dialog, String, boolean,
    GraphicsConfiguration)
JDialog(Frame)
JDialog(Frame, boolean)
JDialog(Frame, String)
JDialog(Frame, String, boolean)
JDialog(Frame, String, boolean,
    GraphicsConfiguration)
	Create a JDialog instance. The Frame argument, if any, is the frame (usually a JFrame object) that the dialog depends on. Make the boolean argument true to specify a modal dialog, false or absent to specify a nonmodal dialog. You can also specify the title of the dialog using a string argument. The constructors taking the java.awt.GraphicsConfiguration argument were introduced in 1.4.

void setContentPane(Container) Container getContentPane()	Get and set the content pane, which is usually the container of all the dialog's components. See Using Top-Level Containers (page 46) for more information.

Table 18: Frequently Used JDialog Constructors and Methods *(continued)*

Method or Constructor	Purpose
`void setDefaultCloseOperation(int)` `int getDefaultCloseOperation()`	Get and set what happens when the user tries to close the dialog. Possible values: `DISPOSE_ON_CLOSE`, `DO_NOTHING_ON_CLOSE`, `HIDE_ON_CLOSE` (the default). See Responding to Window-Closing Events (page 240) for more information.
`void setLocationRelativeTo(Component)`	Center the dialog over the specified component.

`static void`
`  setDefaultLookAndFeelDecorated(boolean)`
 	
`static boolean`
`  isDefaultLookAndFeelDecorated()`
	Set or get a hint as to whether the dialog's window decorations (such as borders or widgets to close the window) should be provided by the current look and feel. Otherwise the dialog's decorations are provided by the current window manager. Note that this is only a hint, as some look and feels do not support this feature. Introduced in 1.4.

Examples That Use Dialogs

The following table lists examples that use `JOptionPane` or `JDialog`. To find other examples that use dialogs, see these sections: Examples That Monitor Progress (page 310), Examples That Use Color Choosers (page 175), and Examples That Use File Choosers (page 220).

Example	Where Described	Notes
`DialogDemo`, `CustomDialog`	This section	Creates many kinds of dialogs using `JOptionPane` and `JDialog`.
`Framework`	—	Brings up a confirmation dialog when the user selects the Quit menu item.
`ListDialog`	How to Use BoxLayout (page 462)	Implements a modal dialog containing a scrolling list and two buttons. Doesn't use `JOptionPane`, except for the utility method `getFrameForComponent`.
`TableDialogEditDemo`	How to Use Tables (page 388)	Implements a table with a dialog that indirectly serves as a cell editor.

D

Components

How to Use Editor Panes and Text Panes

Two Swing classes support styled text: `JEditorPane` and its subclass `JTextPane`. `JEditor-Pane` is the foundation for Swing's styled text components and provides the mechanism through which you can add support for custom text formats. If you want unstyled text, consider using a text area instead. See also How to Use Text Areas (page 418).

Figure 14 shows `TextSamplerDemo`, which uses many text components, including an editor pane and text demo.

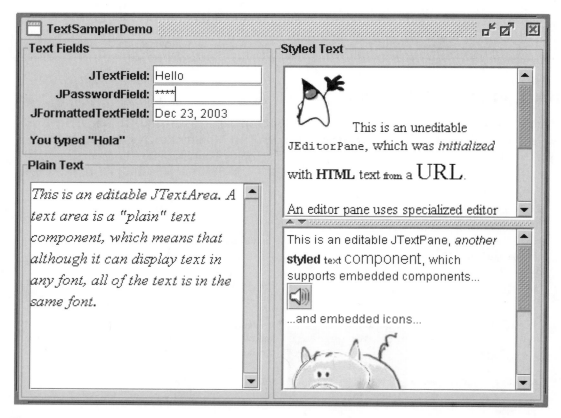

Figure 14   `TextSamplerDemo` demonstrates the use of each Swing text component in a single application.

You can run `TextSamplerDemo` using Java Web Start or compile and run the example yourself.[1]

`TextSamplerDemo` hardly begins to exercise the capabilities of editor and text panes. However, the editor pane at its top right does illustrate a very handy, easy-to-use feature: displaying uneditable help information loaded from a URL. The text pane at the lower right demonstrates that you can easily embed images and even components directly into text panes.

Note: If you need a full-fledged help system, take a look at the JavaHelp™ system: `http://java.sun.com/products/javahelp/`.

The Swing text API is powerful and immense, and we could devote an entire book just to using editor panes and text panes. This section introduces their capabilities, offers hints on which one you might want to use, and points to other sources of information.

Using an Editor Pane to Display Text from a URL

One task that you can accomplish without knowing anything about the Swing text system is displaying text from a URL. Here's the code from `TextSamplerDemo.java` that creates an uneditable editor pane that displays text formatted with HTML tags:

```
JEditorPane editorPane = new JEditorPane();
editorPane.setEditable(false);
java.net.URL helpURL = TextSamplerDemo.class.getResource(
                            "TextSamplerDemoHelp.html");
if (helpURL != null) {
    try {
        editorPane.setPage(helpURL);
    } catch (IOException e) {
        System.err.println("Attempted to read a bad URL: " + helpURL);
    }
} else {
    System.err.println("Couldn't find file: TextSampleDemoHelp.html");
}

//Put the editor pane in a scroll pane.
JScrollPane editorScrollPane = new JScrollPane(editorPane);
```

---

[1]   To run `TextSamplerDemo` using Java Web Start, click the `TextSamplerDemo` link on the `RunExamples/components.html` page on the CD. You can find the source files here: `JavaTutorial/uiswing/components/example-1dot4/index.html#TextSamplerDemo`.

```
editorScrollPane.setVerticalScrollBarPolicy(
                JScrollPane.VERTICAL_SCROLLBAR_ALWAYS);
editorScrollPane.setPreferredSize(new Dimension(250, 145));
editorScrollPane.setMinimumSize(new Dimension(10, 10));
```

The code uses the default constructor to create the editor pane, then calls `set-Editable(false)` so that the user cannot edit the text. Next, the code creates the URL object and calls the `setPage` method with it.

The `setPage` method opens the resource pointed to by the URL and figures out the format of the text (which in the example is HTML). If the text format is known, the editor pane initializes itself with the text found at the URL. A standard editor pane can understand plain text, HTML, and RTF. Note that the page might be loaded asynchronously, which keeps the GUI responsive but means that you shouldn't count on the data being completely loaded after the call to `setPage` returns.

Editor Panes versus Text Panes

For most uses of editor panes and text panes, you need to understand the text system, which is described in Text Component Features (page 64) in Chapter 3. Several facts about editor panes and text panes are sprinkled throughout that section. Here we list the facts again, to collect them in one place and to provide a bit more detail. The information here should help you understand the differences between editor panes and text panes and when to use which.

- An editor pane or a text pane can easily be loaded with text from a URL using the `set-Page` method. The `JEditorPane` class also provides constructors that let you initialize an editor pane from a URL. `JTextPane` has no such constructors. See Using an Editor Pane to Display Text from a URL (page 201) for an example of using this feature to load an uneditable editor pane with HTML-formatted text.

  Be aware that the document and editor kit might change when using the `setPage` method. For example, if an editor pane contains plain text (the default) and you load it with HTML, the document will change to an `HTMLDocument` instance and the editor kit will change to an `HTMLEditorKit` instance. If your program uses the `setPage` method, make sure that the code adjusts for possible changes to the pane's document and editor kit instances (reregister document listeners on the new document, and so on).

- Editor panes, by default, know how to read, write, and edit plain, HTML, and RTF text. Text panes inherit this capability but impose certain limitations. A text pane insists that its document implement the `StyledDocument` interface. `HTMLDocument` and `RTFDocument` are both `StyledDocuments` so HTML and RTF work as expected within a text pane. If you load a text pane with plain text though, the text pane's document is not a `PlainDocument` as you might expect, but a `DefaultStyledDocument`.

- To support a custom text format, implement an editor kit that can read, write, and edit text of that format. Then call the registerEditorKitForContentType method to register your kit with the JEditorPane class. By registering an editor kit in this way, all editor panes and text panes in your program will be able to read, write, and edit the new format. However, if the new editor kit is not a StyledEditorKit, text panes will not support the new format.

- As mentioned previously, a text pane requires its document to implement the Styled-Document interface. The Swing text package provides a default implementation of this interface, DefaultStyledDocument, which is the document text panes use by default. A text pane also requires that its editor kit be an instance of a StyledEditorKit (or a subclass). Be aware that the read and write methods for StyledEditorKit write plain text.

- Through its styled document and styled editor kit, text panes provide support for named styles and logical styles. The JTextPane class itself contains many methods for working with styles that simply call methods in its document or editor kit.

- Through the API provided in the JTextPane class, you can embed images and components in a text pane. You can embed images in an editor pane, too, but only by including the images in an HTML or RTF file.

An Example of Using a Text Pane

Here's the code from TextSamplerDemo that creates and initializes the text pane.

```
String[] initString =
        { /* ...  fill array with initial text  ... */ };

String[] initStyles =
        { /* ...  fill array with names of styles  ... */ };

JTextPane textPane = new JTextPane();
StyledDocument doc = textPane.getStyledDocument();
addStylesToDocument(doc);

//Load the text pane with styled text.
try {
    for (int i=0; i < initString.length; i++) {
        doc.insertString(doc.getLength(), initString[i],
                    doc.getStyle(initStyles[i]));
    }
} catch (BadLocationException ble) {
    System.err.println("Couldn't insert initial text into text pane.");
}
```

E

Components

Briefly, this code hard-codes the initial text into an array and creates and hard-codes several *styles*—objects that represent different paragraph and character formats—into another array. Next, the code loops over the arrays, inserts the text into the text pane, and specifies the style to use for the inserted text.

Although this makes for an interesting example and concisely shows off several features of JTextPane, "real-world" programs aren't likely to initialize a text pane this way. Instead, the program would use a text pane to save out a document, which would then be used to initialize the text pane.

The Editor Pane and Text Pane API

Tables 19 and 20 list a bit of the API related to text and editor panes. Many of the most useful methods for JEditorPane and its subclass JTextPane are inherited from JTextComponent. You can find the API tables for JTextComponent in The Text Component API (page 77) in Chapter 3. Also see The JComponent Class (page 53), which describes the API inherited from JComponent. You can also refer to the API documentation for JEditorPane and JTextPane:

```
http://java.sun.com/j2se/1.4.2/docs/api/javax/swing/JEditorPane.html
http://java.sun.com/j2se/1.4.2/docs/api/javax/swing/JTextPane.html
```

Table 19: JEditorPane API for Displaying Text from a URL

Method or Constructor	Description
JEditorPane(URL) JEditorPane(String)	Create an editor pane loaded with the text at the specified URL.
setPage(URL) setPage(String)	Load an editor pane (or text pane) with the text at the specified URL.
URL getPage()	Get the URL for the editor pane's (or text pane's) current page.

Table 20: JTextPane API

Method or Constructor	Description
JTextPane() JTextPane(StyledDocument)	Create a text pane. The optional argument specifies the text pane's model.
StyledDocument getStyledDocument setStyledDocument(StyledDocument)	Get or set the text pane's model.

Examples That Use Editor Panes and Text Panes

To get started with text, you might want to run these programs and examine their code to find something similar to what you want to do.

Example	Where Described	Notes
TextSamplerDemo	Using Text Components (page 60)	Uses one of each of Swing's text components.
TextComponentDemo	Text Component Features (page 64)	Provides a customized text pane. Illustrates many text component features, such as undo and redo, document filters, document listeners, caret change listeners, and associates editing actions with menus and keystrokes.
TreeDemo	How to Use Trees (page 437)	Uses an editor pane to display help loaded from an HTML file.

E

Components

How to Use File Choosers

File choosers provide a GUI for navigating the file system and then either choosing a file or directory from a list or entering the name of a file or directory. To display a file chooser, you usually use the JFileChooser API[1] to show a modal dialog that contains it. Another way to present a file chooser is to add an instance of JFileChooser to a container.

Note: If you intend to distribute your program as an unsigned Java Web Start application, instead of using the JFileChooser API you should use the file services provided by the JNLP API. These services—FileOpenService and FileSaveService—not only provide support for choosing files in a restricted environment but also take care of actually opening and saving them. An example of using these services is in JWSFileChooserDemo.[2] Documentation for using the JNLP API is in the Java Web Start Developer's Guide at http://java.sun.com/products/javawebstart/developers.html.

The rest of this section discusses how to use the JFileChooser API. A JFileChooser object only presents the GUI for choosing files. Your program is responsible for doing something with the chosen file, such as opening or saving it. Refer to *The Java Tutorial* trail "I/O: Reading and Writing (but no 'rithmetic)" online for information on how to read and write files.[3]

Example One: FileChooserDemo

The JFileChooser API makes it easy to bring up open and save dialogs. The look and feel determines what these standard dialogs look like and how they differ. In the Java look and

---

[1] JFileChooser API documentation: http://java.sun.com/j2se/1.4.2/docs/api/javax/swing/JFileChooser.html.

[2] To run JWSFileChooserDemo using Java Web Start, click the JWSFileChooserDemo link on the RunExamples/components.html page on the CD. You can find the source files here: JavaTutorial/uiswing/components/example-1dot4/index.html#JWSFileChooserDemo.

[3] The "I/O" trail is available in the *The Java Tutorial* on this book's CD and online at: http://java.sun.com/docs/books/tutorial/essential/io/index.html.

feel (see Figure 15), the save dialog looks the same as the open dialog except for the title on the dialog's window and the text on the button that approves the operation (see Figure 16).

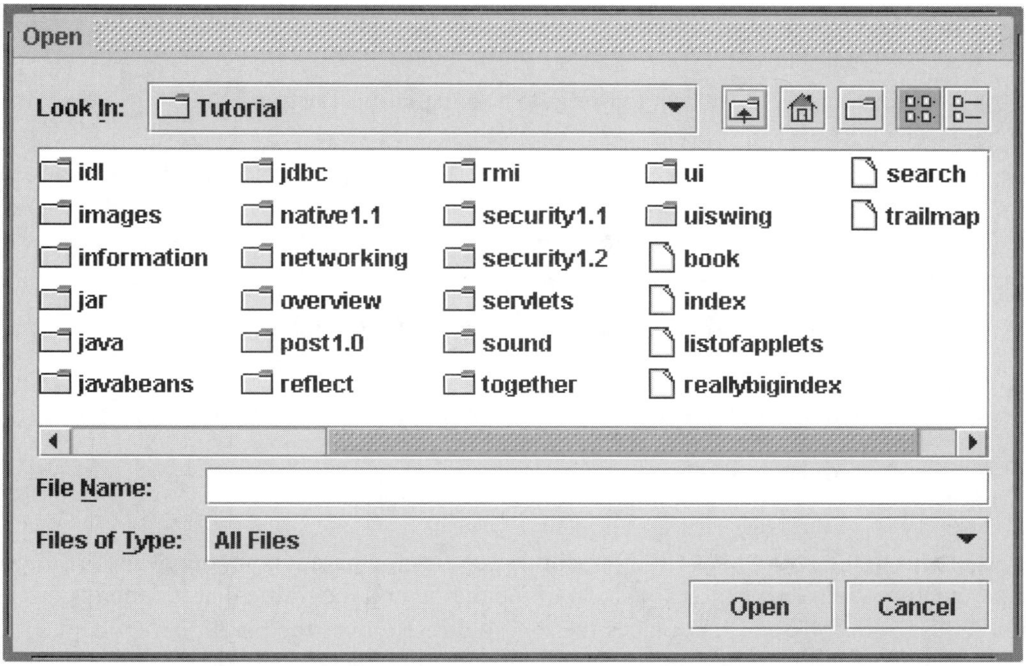

Figure 15   The Java look and feel's standard open dialog.

Figure 16   The FileChooserDemo, an application that brings up an open dialog and a save dialog.

Try This:

1. Run `FileChooserDemo` using Java Web Start, or compile and run the example yourself.[1]

2. Click the Open a File... button. Navigate the file chooser, choose a file, and click the dialog's Open button.

3. Use the Save a File... button to bring up a save dialog. Try to use all of the controls on the file chooser.

4. In the source file `FileChooserDemo.java`, change the file selection mode to directories-only mode. (Search for `DIRECTORIES_ONLY` and uncomment the line that contains it.) Then compile and run the example again. You'll be able to see and select only directories, not ordinary files.

Bringing up a standard open dialog requires only two lines of code:

```
//Create a file chooser
final JFileChooser fc = new JFileChooser();
..
//In response to a button click:
int returnVal = fc.showOpenDialog(aComponent);
```

The argument to the `showOpenDialog` method specifies the parent component for the dialog. The parent component affects the position of the dialog and the frame that it depends on. For example, the Java look and feel places the dialog directly over the parent component. If the parent component is in a frame, the dialog is dependent on that frame, disappearing when the frame is iconified and reappearing when it's deiconified.

By default, a file chooser that hasn't been shown previously displays all files in the user's home directory. You can specify the file chooser's initial directory using one of `JFileChooser`'s other constructors, or you can set the directory with the `setCurrentDirectory` method.

The call to `showOpenDialog` appears in the `actionPerformed` method of the **Open a File...** button's action listener:

```
public void actionPerformed(ActionEvent e) {
    //Handle open button action.
    if (e.getSource() == openButton) {
        int returnVal = fc.showOpenDialog(FileChooserDemo.this);
```

---

[1] To run `FileChooserDemo` using Java Web Start, click the `FileChooserDemo` link on the `RunExamples/ components.html` page on the CD. You can find the source files here: `JavaTutorial/uiswing/ components/example-1dot4/index.html#FileChooserDemo`.

```
        if (returnVal == JFileChooser.APPROVE_OPTION) {
            File file = fc.getSelectedFile();
            //This is where a real application would open the file.
            log.append("Opening: " + file.getName() + "." + newline);
        } else {
            log.append("Open command canceled by user." + newline);
        }
    } ...
}
```

The show*Xxx*Dialog methods return an integer that indicates whether the user selected a file. Depending on how you use a file chooser, it's often sufficient to check whether the return value is APPROVE_OPTION and to do nothing for any other value. To get the chosen file, call getSelectedFile on the file chooser. This method returns an instance of File.[1]

The example gets the name of the file and uses it in the log message. You can call other methods on the File object, such as getPath, isDirectory, or exists, to get information about the file. You can also call other methods, such as delete and rename, to change the file in some way. Of course, you might also want to open or save the file using one of the reader or writer classes provided by the Java platform. See *The Java Tutorial* trail "I/O: Reading and Writing (but no 'rithmetic)" for information on using readers and writers to read and write data to and from the file system.[2]

The example program uses the same instance of JFileChooser to display a standard save dialog. This time the program calls showSaveDialog:

```
int returnVal = fc.showSaveDialog(FileChooserDemo.this);
```

By using the same file chooser instance to display its open and save dialogs, the program reaps these benefits:

- The chooser remembers the current directory between uses, so the open and save versions automatically share the same current directory.
- You have to customize only one file chooser, and the customizations apply to both its open and save versions.

The example program has commented-out lines of code that let you change the file selection mode. For example, the following line of code makes the file chooser select only directories, and not files:

```
fc.setFileSelectionMode(JFileChooser.DIRECTORIES_ONLY);
```

---

[1] File API documentation is on the CD and online at: http://java.sun.com/j2se/1.4.2/docs/api/java/io/File.html.

[2] The "I/O" trail is available in the *The Java Tutorial* on this book's CD and online at: http://java.sun.com/docs/books/tutorial/essential/io/index.html.

Another possible selection mode is FILES_AND_DIRECTORIES. The default is FILES_ONLY. Figure 17 shows an open dialog with the file-selection mode set to DIRECTORIES_ONLY.

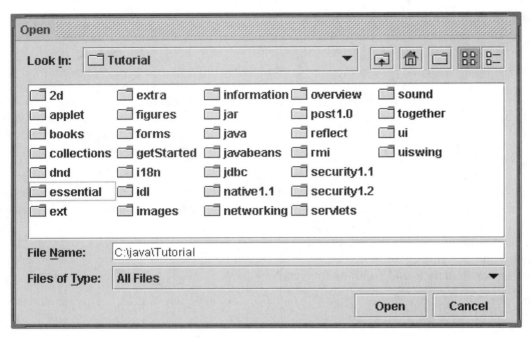

Figure 17   An open dialog in DIRECTORIES_ONLY mode in the Java look and feel.

If you want to create a file chooser for a task other than opening or saving, or if you want to customize the file chooser, keep reading.

Example Two: FileChooserDemo2

Let's look at FileChooserDemo2,[1] a modified version of the previous demo program that uses more of the JFileChooser API. The example in Figure 18 uses a file chooser that has been customized in several ways. As in the original example, the user invokes a file chooser with the push of a button.

---

[1]   To run FileChooserDemo2 using Java Web Start, click the FileChooserDemo2 link on the RunExamples/components.html page on the CD. You can find the source files here: JavaTutorial/ uiswing/components/example-1dot4/index.html#FileChooserDemo2.

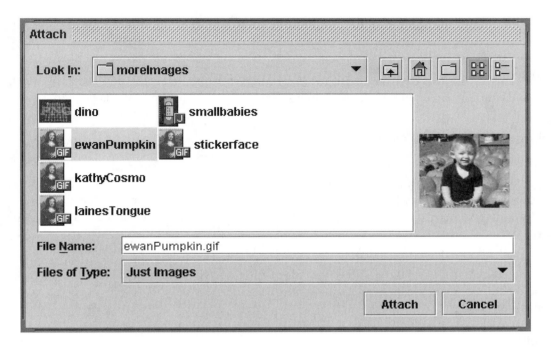

Figure 18   The `FileChooserDemo2` application permits the preview of image files.

The figure shows that this file chooser has been customized for a special task (**Attach**), provides a user-choosable file filter (**Just Images**), uses a special file view for image files (PNG/GIF/JPEG symbols), and has an accessory component that displays a thumbnail sketch of the currently selected image file.

Using a File Chooser for a Custom Task

As you've seen, `JFileChooser` provides the `showOpenDialog` method for displaying an open dialog and the `showSaveDialog` method for displaying a save dialog.

The class has another method, `showDialog`, for displaying a file chooser for a custom task in a dialog. In the Java look and feel, the only difference between this dialog and the other file chooser dialogs is the title on the dialog window and the label on the Approve button. The following is the code from `FileChooserDemo2` that brings up the file chooser dialog for the **Attach** task:

```
JFileChooser fc = new JFileChooser();
int returnVal = fc.showDialog(FileChooserDemo2.this, "Attach");
```

The first argument to the showDialog method is the parent component for the dialog. The second argument is a String that provides both the title for the dialog window and the label for the Approve button.

Once again, the file chooser doesn't do anything with the selected file. The program is responsible for implementing the custom task for which the file chooser was created.

Filtering the List of Files

By default, a file chooser displays all of the files and directories, except hidden files, that it detects. A program can apply one or more *file filters* to a file chooser so that the chooser shows only some files. The file chooser calls the filter's accept method for each file to determine whether it should be displayed. A file filter accepts or rejects a file based on some criteria such as file type, size, ownership, and so on. Filters affect the list of files displayed by the file chooser. The user can enter the name of any file even if it's not displayed.

JFileChooser supports three different kinds of filtering. The filters are checked in the order listed here. For example, an application-controlled filter sees only those files accepted by the built-in filtering.

Built-in Filtering

Filtering is set up through specific method calls on a file chooser. Currently the only built-in filter available is for hidden files, such as those that begin with a period (.) on UNIX systems. By default, hidden files are not shown. Call setFileHiding-Enabled(false) to show hidden files.

Application-Controlled Filtering

The application determines which files are shown. Create a custom subclass of File-Filter,[1] instantiate it, and use the instance as an argument to setFileFilter. The file chooser shows only those files that the filter accepts.

User-Choosable Filtering

The file chooser GUI provides a list of filters that the user can choose from. When the user selects a filter, the file chooser shows only those files that the filter accepts. FileChooserDemo2 adds a custom file filter to the list of user-choosable filters:

```
fc.addChoosableFileFilter(new ImageFilter());
```

---

[1] FileFilter API documentation is on the CD and online at: http://java.sun.com/j2se/1.4.2/docs/api/java/io/FileFilter.html.

By default, the list of user-choosable filters includes the **Accept All** filter, which lets the user see all nonhidden files. This example uses the following code to disable the **Accept All** filter:

```
fc.setAcceptAllFileFilterUsed(false);
```

Our custom file filter is implemented in `ImageFilter.java` and is a subclass of `File-Filter`.[1] The `ImageFilter` class implements the `getDescription` method to return `"Just Images"`—a string to put in the list of user-choosable filters. `ImageFilter` also implements the `accept` method so that it can accept all directories and any file that has a `.png`, `.jpg`, `.jpeg`, `.gif`, `.tif`, or `.tiff` filename extension.

```
public boolean accept(File f) {
    if (f.isDirectory()) {
        return true;
    }

    String extension = Utils.getExtension(f);
    if (extension != null) {
        if (extension.equals(Utils.tiff) ||
            extension.equals(Utils.tif) ||
            extension.equals(Utils.gif) ||
            extension.equals(Utils.jpeg) ||
            extension.equals(Utils.jpg) ||
            extension.equals(Utils.png)) {
                return true;
        } else {
            return false;
        }
    }

    return false;
}
```

By accepting all directories, this filter allows the user to navigate the file system. If the bold lines were omitted from this method, the user would be limited to the directory with which the chooser was initialized.

The preceding code sample used the `getExtension` method and several string constants from `Utils.java`,[2] shown next:

---

[1] `ImageFilter.java` is included on the CD and is available online. You can find it here: `JavaTutorial/uiswing/components/example-1dot4/ImageFilter.java`.

[2] `Utils.java` is included on the CD and is available online. You can also find it here: `JavaTutorial/uiswing/components/example-1dot4/Utils.java`.

```
public class Utils {
    public final static String jpeg = "jpeg";
    public final static String jpg = "jpg";
    public final static String gif = "gif";
    public final static String tiff = "tiff";
    public final static String tif = "tif";
    public final static String png = "png";

    /*
     * Get the extension of a file.
     */
    public static String getExtension(File f) {
        String ext = null;
        String s = f.getName();
        int i = s.lastIndexOf('.');

        if (i > 0 &&  i < s.length() - 1) {
            ext = s.substring(i+1).toLowerCase();
        }
        return ext;
    }
}
```

Customizing the File View

In the Java look and feel, the chooser's list shows each file's name and displays a small icon that represents whether the file is a true file or a directory. You can customize this *file view* by creating a custom subclass of FileView[1] and using an instance of the class as an argument to setFileView. The example uses an instance of a custom class, implemented in ImageFileView.java,[2] as the file chooser's file view.

```
fc.setFileView(new ImageFileView());
```

ImageFileView shows a different icon for each type of image accepted by the image filter described previously.

The ImageFileView class overrides the five abstract methods defined in FileView as follows:

---

[1] FileView API documentation: http://java.sun.com/j2se/1.4.2/docs/api/javax/swing/filechooser/FileView.html.

[2] ImageFileView.java is included on the CD and is available online. You can find it here: JavaTutorial/uiswing/components/example-1dot4/ImageFileView.java.

String getTypeDescription(File f)

Returns a description of the file type. This is not yet used by any look and feel. Here's ImageFileView's implementation of this method:

```
public String getTypeDescription(File f) {
    String extension = Utils.getExtension(f);
    String type = null;

    if (extension != null) {
        if (extension.equals(Utils.jpeg) ||
            extension.equals(Utils.jpg)) {
            type = "JPEG Image";
        } else if (extension.equals(Utils.gif)){
            type = "GIF Image";
        } else if (extension.equals(Utils.tiff) ||
                    extension.equals(Utils.tif)) {
            type = "TIFF Image";
        } else if (extension.equals(Utils.png)){
            type = "PNG Image";
        }
    }
    return type;
}
```

Icon getIcon(File f)

Returns an icon representing the file or its type. Here's ImageFileView's implementation of this method:

```
public Icon getIcon(File f) {
    String extension = Utils.getExtension(f);
    Icon icon = null;

    if (extension != null) {
        if (extension.equals(Utils.jpeg) ||
            extension.equals(Utils.jpg)) {
            icon = jpgIcon;
        } else if (extension.equals(Utils.gif)) {
            icon = gifIcon;
        } else if (extension.equals(Utils.tiff) ||
                    extension.equals(Utils.tif)) {
            icon = tiffIcon;
        } else if (extension.equals(Utils.png)) {
            icon = pngIcon;
        }
    }
    return icon;
}
```

F

Components

215

String getName(File f)
> Returns the name of the file. Most implementations of this method return `null` to indicate that the look and feel should figure it out. Another common implementation returns `f.getName()`.

String getDescription(File f)
> Returns a description of the file. This isn't used by any look and feel yet. The intent is to describe individual files more specifically. A common implementation of this method returns `null` to indicate that the look and feel should figure it out.

Boolean isTraversable(File f)
> Returns whether a directory is traversable. Most implementations return `null` to indicate that the look and feel should figure it out. Some applications might want to prevent users from descending into a certain type of directory that represents a compound document. The `isTraversable` method should never return `true` for a nondirectory.

Providing an Accessory Component

The customized file chooser in `FileChooserDemo2` has an accessory component. If the currently selected item is a PNG, JPEG, TIFF, or GIF image, the accessory component displays a thumbnail sketch of the image. Otherwise, the accessory component is empty. Aside from a previewer, probably the most common use for the accessory component is a panel with more controls on it—say, check boxes that toggle some features.

The example calls the `setAccessory` method to establish an instance of the `ImagePreview` class, implemented in the file `ImagePreview.java`,[1] as the chooser's accessory component:

```
fc.setAccessory(new ImagePreview(fc));
```

Any object that inherits from `JComponent` can be an accessory component. The component should have a preferred size that looks good in the file chooser.

The file chooser fires a property change event when the user selects an item in the list. A program with an accessory component must register to receive these events to update the accessory component whenever the selection changes. In the example, the `ImagePreview` object itself registers for these events. This keeps all of the code related to the accessory component together in one class.

---

[1] `ImagePreview.java` is included on the CD and is available online. You can find it here: `JavaTutorial/uiswing/components/example-1dot4/ImagePreview.java`.

Here's the example's implementation of the propertyChange method, which is called when a property change event is fired:

```
//where member variables are declared
File file = null;
..
public void propertyChange(PropertyChangeEvent e) {
    boolean update = false;
    String prop = e.getPropertyName();

    //If the directory changed, don't show an image.
    if (JFileChooser.DIRECTORY_CHANGED_PROPERTY.equals(prop)) {
        file = null;
        update = true;

    //If a file became selected, find out which one.
    } else if (JFileChooser.SELECTED_FILE_CHANGED_PROPERTY.
                                                equals(prop)){
        file = (File) e.getNewValue();
        update = true;
    }

    //Update the preview accordingly.
    if (update) {
        thumbnail = null;
        if (isShowing()) {
            loadImage();
            repaint();
        }
    }
}
```

If SELECTED_FILE_CHANGED_PROPERTY is the property that changed, this method gets a File object from the file chooser. The loadImage and repaint methods use the File object to load the image and repaint the accessory component.

The File Chooser API

The API for using file choosers falls into four categories, as shown in Tables 21 through 24. You should also refer to the `JFileChooser` API documentation.[1]

Table 21: Creating and Showing the File Chooser

Method or Constructor	Purpose

`JFileChooser()`
`JFileChooser(File)`
`JFileChooser(String)`
	Create a file chooser instance. The `File` and `String` arguments, when present, provide the initial directory.

`int showOpenDialog(Component)`
`int showSaveDialog(Component)`
`int showDialog(Component, String)`
	Show a modal dialog containing the file chooser. These methods return `APPROVE_OPTION` if the user approved the operation and `CANCEL_OPTION` if the user canceled it. Another possible return value is `ERROR_OPTION`, which means that an unanticipated error occurred.

Table 22: Selecting Files and Directories

Method	Purpose
`void setSelectedFile(File)` `File getSelectedFile()`	Set or get the currently selected file.
`void setSelectedFiles(File[])` `File[] getSelectedFiles()`	Set or get the currently selected files.

`void setFileSelectionMode(int)`
`void getFileSelectionMode()`
`boolean isDirectorySelectionEnabled()`
`boolean isFileSelectionEnabled()`
	Set the file selection mode. Acceptable values are `FILES_ONLY` (the default), `DIRECTORIES_ONLY`, and `FILES_AND_DIRECTORIES`.

`void setMultiSelectionEnabled(boolean)` `void isMultiSelectionEnabled()`	Set or get whether multiple files can be selected at once. By default, a user can choose only one file.
`void setAcceptAllFileFilterUsed(boolean)` `boolean isAcceptAllFileFilterUsed()`	Set or get whether the `AcceptAll` file filter is used as an allowable choice in the choosable filter list; the default value is true. Introduced in 1.3.
`Dialog createDialog(Component)`	Given a parent component, create and return a new dialog that contains this file chooser, is dependent on the parent's frame, and is centered over the parent. Introduced in 1.4.

---

[1] JFileChooser API documentation: `http://java.sun.com/j2se/1.4.2/docs/api/javax/swing/JFileChooser.html`.

Table 23: Navigating the File Chooser's List

Method	Purpose
`void ensureFileIsVisible(File)`	Scroll the file chooser's list such that the indicated file is visible.
`void setCurrentDirectory(File)` `File getCurrentDirectory()`	Set or get the directory whose files are displayed in the file chooser's list.
`void changeToParentDirectory()`	Change the list to display the current directory's parent.
`void rescanCurrentDirectory()`	Check the file system and update the chooser's list.
`void setDragEnabled(boolean)` `boolean getDragEnabled()`	Set or get the property that determines whether automatic drag handling is enabled. See How to Use Drag and Drop and Data Transfer (page 545) for more details. Introduced in 1.4.

Table 24: Customizing the File Chooser

Method	Purpose
`void setAccessory(javax.swing.JComponent)` `JComponent getAccessory()`	Set or get the file chooser's accessory component.
`void setFileFilter(FileFilter)` `FileFilter getFileFilter()`	Set or get the file chooser's primary file filter.
`void setFileView(FileView)` `FileView getFileView()`	Set or get the chooser's file view.

`FileFilter[] getChoosableFileFilters()`
`void addChoosableFileFilter(FileFilter)`
`boolean removeChoosableFileFilter(FileFilter)`
`void resetChoosableFileFilters()`
`FileFilter getAcceptAllFileFilter()`
	Set, get, or modify the list of user-choosable file filters.

`void setFileHidingEnabled(boolean)` `boolean isFileHidingEnabled()`	Set or get whether hidden files are displayed.
`void setControlButtonsAreShown(boolean)` `boolean getControlButtonsAreShown()`	Set or get the property that indicates whether the Approve and Cancel buttons are shown in the file chooser. This property is true by default. Introduced in 1.3.

F

Components

Examples That Use File Choosers

The following table shows examples that use `JFileChooser` and where those examples are described.

Example	Where Described	Notes
FileChooserDemo	This section	Displays an open dialog and a save dialog.
FileChooserDemo2	This section	Uses a file chooser with custom filtering, a custom file view, and an accessory component.
JWSFileChooserDemo	This section	Uses the JNLP API to open and save files.
DragFileDemo	Importing a New Flavor: Files (page 566)	Uses a file chooser inside a frame to demonstrates exporting filenames, so that the user can drag a file displayed by a file chooser into another component.

How to Use Formatted Text Fields

Release 1.4 introduced a subclass of `JTextField` called `JFormattedTextField`.[1] Formatted text fields provide a way for developers to specify the legal set of characters that can be entered into a text field. Specifically, `JFormattedTextField` adds a *formatter* and an object *value* to the features inherited from `JTextField`. The formatter performs the translation from the field's value into the text it displays, and vice versa.

Using the formatters Swing provides, you can set up formatted text fields for easy input of dates and numbers in localized formats. Another kind of formatter lets you use a character mask to specify the set of characters that can be entered at each position in the field. For example, you can specify a mask for entering phone numbers in a particular format, such as (XX) X-XX-XX-XX-XX.

Version Note: Before v1.4, text field formatting required more effort. You could check the field's value when the user pressed Enter by putting format-checking code in your action listener, but you couldn't do any checking before the action event was generated unless you implemented a custom model (`Document`) for the text field. Version 1.3 introduced input verification, but that isn't specialized for text fields and is tied to focus changes. For details, see Validating Input (page 587) in Chapter 9.

If the possible values of a formatted text field have an obvious order, consider using a spinner instead. A spinner uses a formatted text field, by default, but adds two buttons that let the user step through a sequence of values.

Another alternative or adjunct to using a formatted text field is installing an input verifier on the field. A component's input verifier is called when the component is about to lose the keyboard focus. It lets you check whether the value of the component is legal and, optionally, change it or stop the focus from being transferred.

F

Components

---

[1] `JFormattedTextField` API documentation: `http://java.sun.com/j2se/1.4.2/docs/api/ javax/swing/JFormattedTextField.html`.

Figure 19 shows a picture of a GUI that uses formatted text fields to display numbers in four different formats.

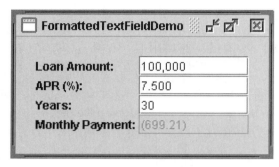

Figure 19   The FormattedTextFieldDemo application.

Try This:

1. Run FormattedTextFieldDemo using Java Web Start or compile and run the example 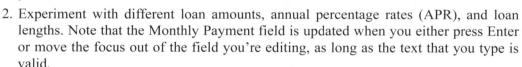 yourself.[1]

2. Experiment with different loan amounts, annual percentage rates (APR), and loan lengths. Note that the Monthly Payment field is updated when you either press Enter or move the focus out of the field you're editing, as long as the text that you type is valid.

3. Enter invalid text such as "abcd" in the Loan Amount field and then press Enter. See, nothing happens. When you move the focus from the field, the text reverts to the field's last valid value.

4. Enter marginally valid text such as "2000abcd" in the Loan Amount field and press Enter. The Monthly Payment field is updated, though the Loan Amount field still looks strange. When you move the focus from the Loan Amount field, the text it displays is updated to be a nicely formatted version of its value—for example, "2,000" (see Figure 20).

---

[1] To run FormattedTextFieldDemo using Java Web Start, click the FormattedTextFieldDemo link on the RunExamples/components.html page on the CD. You can find the source files here: JavaTutorial/uiswing/components/example-1dot4/index.html#FormattedTextFieldDemo.

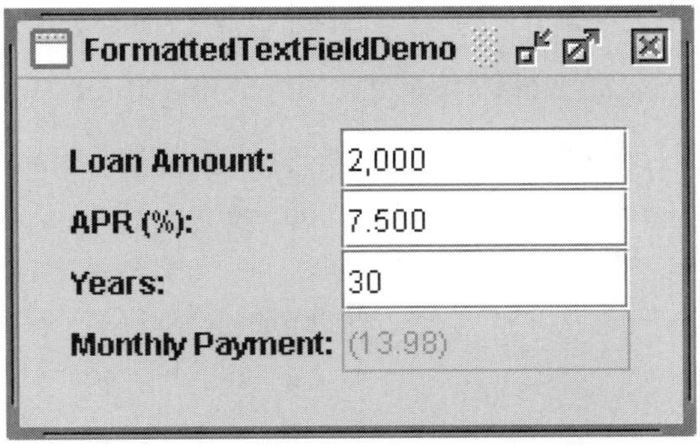

Figure 20 The Loan Amount field automatically reformats the value "2000abcd" to "2,000."

Here's the code that creates the first field in `FormattedTextFieldDemo`:

```
amountField = new JFormattedTextField(amountFormat);
amountField.setValue(new Double(amount));
amountField.setColumns(10);
amountField.addPropertyChangeListener("value", this);
...
amountFormat = NumberFormat.getNumberInstance();
```

The constructor used to create `amountField` takes a `java.text.Format` argument. The `Format` object is used by the field's formatter to translate between the field's text and value.

The rest of the code sets up `amountField`. The `setValue` method sets the field's value property to a floating-point number represented as a `Double` object. The `setColumns` method, inherited from `JTextField`, provides a hint as to the preferred size of the field. Finally, the call to `addPropertyChangeListener` registers a listener for the value property of the field so that the program can update the Monthly Payment field whenever the user changes the Loan Amount field.

Note: This section doesn't explain the API inherited from `JTextField`; that API is described in How to Use Text Fields (page 423).

Creating and Initializing Formatted Text Fields

The following code creates and initializes the remaining three fields in `FormattedText-FieldDemo`.

```
rateField = new JFormattedTextField(percentFormat);
rateField.setValue(new Double(rate));
rateField.setColumns(10);
rateField.addPropertyChangeListener("value", this);

numPeriodsField = new JFormattedTextField();
numPeriodsField.setValue(new Integer(numPeriods));
numPeriodsField.setColumns(10);
numPeriodsField.addPropertyChangeListener("value", this);

paymentField = new JFormattedTextField(paymentFormat);
paymentField.setValue(new Double(payment));
paymentField.setColumns(10);
paymentField.setEditable(false);
paymentField.setForeground(Color.red);

...
percentFormat = NumberFormat.getNumberInstance();
percentFormat.setMinimumFractionDigits(2);

paymentFormat = NumberFormat.getCurrencyInstance();
```

The code for setting up `numPeriodsField` is almost identical to the code you saw before. The only difference is that the format is slightly different, thanks to the code `percent-Format.setMinimumFractionDigits(2)`.

The code that creates the `numPeriodsField` doesn't explicitly set a format or formatter. Instead, it sets the value to an `Integer` and lets the field use the default formatter for `Integers`. We couldn't do this in the previous two fields because we didn't want to use the default formatter for `Doubles`; the result didn't look exactly like we wanted it to. We'll discuss how to specify formats and formatters a little later.

The payment field is different from the other fields because it's uneditable, uses a different color for its text, and doesn't happen to have a property-change listener. However, it's otherwise the same as the other fields. We could have chosen to use a text field or label instead. Whatever the component, we could still use `paymentFormat` to parse the payment amount into the text to be displayed.

Setting and Getting the Field's Value

Keep this in mind when using a formatted text field:

> **A formatted text field's *text* and its *value* are two different properties, and the value often lags behind the text.**

The *text* property is defined by JTextField; it always reflects what the field displays. The *value* property, defined by JFormattedTextField, might not reflect the latest text displayed in the field. While the user is typing, the text property changes, but the value property doesn't until the changes are *committed*.

To be more precise, the value of a formatted text field can be set using either the setValue method or the commitEdit method. The setValue method sets the value to the specified argument. Although the argument can technically be any Object, it needs to be something that the formatter can convert into a string. Otherwise, the text field won't display anything useful.

The commitEdit method sets the value to whatever object the formatter determines is represented by the field's text. The commitEdit method is automatically called when either of the following happens:

- When the user presses Enter while the field has the focus.
- By default, when the field loses the focus—for example, the user presses the Tab key to change the focus to another component. You can use the setFocusLostBehavior method to specify that something different should happen when the field loses the focus.

Note: Some formatters might update the value constantly, making the focus-lost behavior moot since the value will always be the same as what the text specifies.

When you set the value of a formatted text field, the field's text is updated to reflect the value. Exactly how the value is represented as text depends on the field's formatter.

Note that although JFormattedTextField inherits the setText method from JTextField, you don't usually invoke setText on a formatted text field. If you do, the field's display will change accordingly but the value will not be updated (unless the field's formatter updates it constantly).

To get a formatted text field's current value, use the getValue method. If necessary, you can ensure that the value reflects the text by calling commitEdit before getValue. Because getValue returns an Object, you need to cast it to the type used for your field's value. For example, see the following:

```
Date enteredDate = (Date)dateField.getValue();
```

To detect changes in a formatted text field's value, you can register a property change listener on the formatted text field to listen for changes to the *value* property. Here's the property change listener from `FormattedTextFieldDemo`:

```
//The property change listener is registered on each
//field using code like this:
//    someField.addPropertyChangeListener("value", this);

/** Called when a field's "value" property changes. */
public void propertyChange(PropertyChangeEvent e) {
    Object source = e.getSource();
    if (source == amountField) {
        amount = ((Number)amountField.getValue()).doubleValue();
    } else if (source == rateField) {
        rate = ((Number)rateField.getValue()).doubleValue();
    } else if (source == numPeriodsField) {
        numPeriods = ((Number)numPeriodsField.getValue()).intValue();
    }

    double payment = computePayment(amount, rate, numPeriods);
    paymentField.setValue(new Double(payment));
}
```

Specifying Formats

The `Format`[1] class provides a way to format locale-sensitive information such as dates and numbers. Formatters that descend from `InternationalFormatter`,[2] such as `DateFormatter` and `NumberFormatter`, use `Format` objects to translate between the field's text and value. You can get a `Format` object by invoking one of the factory methods in `DateFormat` or `NumberFormat`, or by using one of the `SimpleDateFormat` constructors.

Note: A third commonly used formatter class, known as `MaskFormatter`, does not descend from `InternationalFormatter` and does not use formats. It's discussed in Using MaskFormatter (page 227).

---

[1] Format API documentation: http://java.sun.com/j2se/1.4.2/docs/api/java/text/Format.html.

[2] InternationalFormatter.html API documentation: http://java.sun.com/j2se/1.4.2/docs/api/javax/swing/text/InternationalFormatter.html.

You can customize certain format aspects when you create the Format, and others through a format-specific API. For example, DecimalFormat objects, which inherit from Number-Format and are often returned by its factory methods, can be customized using the methods setMaximumFractionDigits and setNegativePrefix. For information about using Formats, see the "Formatting" lesson of *The Java Tutorial*'s "Internationalization" trail available on the CD and online at: http://java.sun.com/docs/books/tutorial/i18n/index.html.

The easiest way to associate a customized format with a formatted text field is to create the field using the JFormattedTextField constructor that takes a Format as an argument. You can see this in the preceding code snippets that create amountField and rateField.

Using MaskFormatter

The MaskFormatter[1] class implements a formatter that specifies exactly which characters are legal in each position of the field's text. For example, the following code creates a Mask-Formatter that lets the user enter a 5-digit zip code:

```
zipField = new JFormattedTextField(
                createFormatter("#####"));
...
protected MaskFormatter createFormatter(String s) {
    MaskFormatter formatter = null;
    try {
        formatter = new MaskFormatter(s);
    } catch (java.text.ParseException exc) {
        System.err.println("formatter is bad: " + exc.getMessage());
        System.exit(-1);
    }
    return formatter;
}
```

---

[1] MaskFormatter API documentation: http://java.sun.com/j2se/1.4.2/docs/api/javax/swing/text/MaskFormatter.html.

You can try out the results of the preceding code by running `TextInputDemo`. Figure 21 shows the program's GUI. Table 25 shows the characters you can use in the formatting mask.

Figure 21   The `TextInputDemo` GUI.

Table 25: Characters to Use in the Formatting Mask

Character	Description
#	Any valid number (`Character.isDigit`).
' *(single quote)*	Escape character, used to escape any of the special formatting characters.
U	Any character (`Character.isLetter`). All lowercase letters are mapped to uppercase.
L	Any character (`Character.isLetter`). All uppercase letters are mapped to lowercase.
A	Any character or number (`Character.isLetter` or `Character.isDigit`).
?	Any character (`Character.isLetter`).
*	Anything.
H	Any hex character (0-9, a-f or A-F).

Specifying Formatters and Using Formatter Factories

When specifying formatters, keep in mind that each formatter object can be used by at most one formatted text field at a time. Each field should have at least one formatter associated with it, of which exactly one is used at any time.

You can specify the formatters to be used by a formatted text field in several ways:

Use the `JFormattedTextField` constructor that takes a `Format` argument.

A formatter for the field that uses the specified format is automatically created.

Use the `JFormattedTextField` constructor that takes a `JFormattedTextField.AbstractFormatter` argument.

The specified formatter is used for the field.

Set the value of a formatted text field that has no format, formatter, or formatter factory specified.

A formatter is assigned to the field by the default formatter factory, using the type of the field's value as a guide. If the value is a `Date`, the formatter is a `DateFormatter`. If the value is a `Number`, the formatter is a `NumberFormatter`. Other types result in an instance of `DefaultFormatter`.

Make the formatted text field use a formatter factory that returns customized formatter objects.

This is the most flexible approach. It's useful when you want to associate more than one formatter with a field or add a new kind of formatter to be used for multiple fields. As an example of the former use, you might have a field that should interpret user typing in a certain way but display the value (when the user isn't typing) another way. As an example of the latter use, you might have several fields that have values of a custom class— say, `PhoneNumber`. You could set up the fields to use a formatter factory that can return specialized formatters for phone numbers.

You can set a field's formatter factory either by creating the field using a constructor that takes a formatter factory argument or by invoking the `setFormatterFactory` method on the field. To create a formatter factory, you can often use an instance of `DefaultFormatter-Factory`.[1] A `DefaultFormatterFactory` object lets you specify the formatters returned when a value is being edited, not being edited, or has a null value.

The pictures in Figure 22 show an application based on `FormattedTextFieldDemo` that uses formatter factories to set multiple editors for the Loan Amount and APR fields. While the user is editing the Loan Amount, the $ character is not used so that the user isn't forced to enter it. Similarly, while the user is editing the APR field, the % sign is not required.

---

[1] `DefaultFormatterFactory` API documentation: `http://java.sun.com/j2se/1.4.2/docs/api/javax/swing/text/DefaultFormatterFactory.html`.

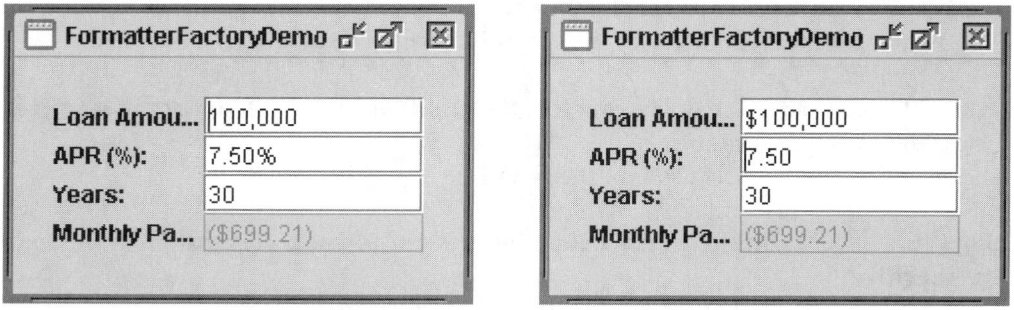

Figure 22   In the first FormatterFactoryDemo GUI, the percent symbol (%) is required in the APR field. In the second GUI, the dollar sign ($) is required in the Loan Amount field.

You can run FormatterFactoryDemo using Java Web Start or compile and run the example yourself.[1]

Here's the code that creates the formatters and sets them up using instances of Default-FormatterFactory:

```
private double rate = .075;   //7.5 %
...
amountField = new JFormattedTextField(
                    new DefaultFormatterFactory(
                        new NumberFormatter(amountDisplayFormat),
                        new NumberFormatter(amountDisplayFormat),
                        new NumberFormatter(amountEditFormat)));
...
NumberFormatter percentEditFormatter =
        new NumberFormatter(percentEditFormat) {
    public String valueToString(Object o)
          throws ParseException {
        Number number = (Number)o;
        if (number != null) {
            double d = number.doubleValue() * 100.0;
            number = new Double(d);
        }
        return super.valueToString(number);
    }

    public Object stringToValue(String s)
          throws ParseException {
        Number number = (Number)super.stringToValue(s);
```

---

[1] To run FormatterFactoryDemo using Java Web Start, click the FormatterFactoryDemo link on the RunExamples/components.html page on the CD. You can find the source files here: JavaTutorial/ uiswing/components/example-1dot4/index.html#FormatterFactoryDemo.

```
        if (number != null) {
            double d = number.doubleValue() / 100.0;
            number = new Double(d);
        }
        return number;
    }
};

rateField = new JFormattedTextField(
                new DefaultFormatterFactory(
                    new NumberFormatter(percentDisplayFormat),
                    new NumberFormatter(percentDisplayFormat),
                    percentEditFormatter));
...
amountDisplayFormat = NumberFormat.getCurrencyInstance();
amountDisplayFormat.setMinimumFractionDigits(0);
amountEditFormat = NumberFormat.getNumberInstance();

percentDisplayFormat = NumberFormat.getPercentInstance();
percentDisplayFormat.setMinimumFractionDigits(2);
percentEditFormat = NumberFormat.getNumberInstance();
percentEditFormat.setMinimumFractionDigits(2);
```

The boldface code highlights the calls to DefaultFormatterFactory constructors. The first argument to the constructor specifies the default formatter to use for the formatted text field. The second specifies the display formatter, which is used when the field doesn't have the focus. The third specifies the edit formatter, used when the field has the focus. The code doesn't use a fourth argument, but if it did it would specify the null formatter, which is used when the field's value is null. Because no null formatter is specified, the default formatter is used when the value is null.

The code customizes the formatter that uses percentEditFormat by creating a subclass of NumberFormatter. This subclass overrides the valueToString and stringToValue methods of NumberFormatter so that they convert the displayed number to the value actually used in calculations, and vice versa. Specifically, the displayed number is 100 times the actual value. The reason is that the percent format used by the display formatter automatically displays the text as 100 times the value, so the corresponding editor formatter must do so as well. The first demo, FormattedTextFieldDemo, doesn't need to worry about this conversion because it uses only one format for both display and editing.

The Formatted Text Field API

Tables 26 through 28 list some of the commonly used API for using formatted text fields. You can find the relevant API doc at:

F

Components

231

```
http://java.sun.com/j2se/1.4.2/docs/api/javax/swing/
     JFormattedTextField.html
http://java.sun.com/j2se/1.4.2/docs/api/javax/swing/
     JFormattedTextField.AbstractFormatter.html
http://java.sun.com/j2se/1.4.2/docs/api/javax/swing/
     JFormattedTextField.AbstractFormatterFactory.html
http://java.sun.com/j2se/1.4.2/docs/api/javax/swing/text/
     DefaultFormatterFactory.html
http://java.sun.com/j2se/1.4.2/docs/api/javax/swing/text/
     DefaultFormatter.html
http://java.sun.com/j2se/1.4.2/docs/api/javax/swing/text/
     MaskFormatter.html
http://java.sun.com/j2se/1.4.2/docs/api/javax/swing/text/
     InternationalFormatter.html
http://java.sun.com/j2se/1.4.2/docs/api/javax/swing/text/
     NumberFormatter.html
http://java.sun.com/j2se/1.4.2/docs/api/javax/swing/text/
     DateFormatter.html
```

Table 26: Classes Related to Formatted Text Fields

Class	Purpose
`JFormattedTextField`	Subclass of `JTextField` that supports formatting arbitrary values.
`JFormattedTextField.Abstract-Formatter`	The superclass of all formatters for `JFormattedTextField`. A formatter enforces editing policies and navigation policies, handles string-to-object conversions, and manipulates the `JFormatted-TextField` as necessary to enforce the desired policy.
`JFormattedTextField.Abstract-FormatterFactory`	The superclass of all formatter factories. Each `JFormattedText-Field` uses a formatter factory to obtain the formatter that best corresponds to the text field's state.
`DefaultFormatterFactory`	The formatter factory normally used. Dishes out formatters based on details such as passed-in parameters and focus state.
`DefaultFormatter`	Subclass of `JFormattedTextField.AbstractFormatter` that formats arbitrary objects using the `toString` method.
`MaskFormatter`	Subclass of `DefaultFormatter` that formats and edits strings using a specified character mask. For example, 7-digit phone numbers can be specified using "`###-####`".
`InternationalFormatter`	Subclass of `DefaultFormatter` that uses an instance of `java.text.Format` to handle conversion to and from a `String`.
`NumberFormatter`	Subclass of `InternationalFormatter` that supports number formats using an instance of `NumberFormat`.
`DateFormatter`	Subclass of `InternationalFormatter` that supports date formats using an instance of `DateFormat`.

Table 27: JFormattedTextField Methods

Method or Constructor	Purpose

`JFormattedTextField()`
`JFormattedTextField(Object)`
`JFormattedTextField(Format)`
`JFormattedTextField(AbstractFormatter)`
`JFormattedTextField(`
`        AbstractFormatterFactory)`
`JFormattedTextField(`
`        AbstractFormatterFactory,`
`        Object)`
	Create a new formatted text field. The `Object` argument, if present, specifies the initial value of the field and causes an appropriate formatter factory to be created. The `Format` or `AbstractFormatter` argument specifies the format or formatter to be used for the field, causing an appropriate formatter factory to be created. The `AbstractFormatterFactory` argument specifies the formatter factory to be used, which determines which formatters are used for the field.

`void setValue(Object)` `Object getValue()`	Set or get the value of the formatted text field. You must cast the return type based on how the `JFormattedText-Field` has been configured. If the formatter hasn't been set yet, invoking `setValue` sets the formatter to one returned by the field's formatter factory.
`void setFormatterFactory(` `        AbstractFormatterFactory)`	Set the object that determines the formatters used for the formatted text field. It is often an instance of `Default-FormatterFactory`.
`AbstractFormatter getFormatter()`	Get the formatter of the formatted text field. It is often an instance of `DefaultFormatter`.
`void setFocusLostBehavior(int)`	Specifies what should happen when the field loses the focus. Possible values are defined in `JFormattedText-Field` as COMMIT_OR_REVERT (the default), COMMIT (commit if valid, otherwise leave everything the same), PERSIST (do nothing), and REVERT (change the text to reflect the value).
`void commitEdit()`	Sets the value to the object represented by the field's text (as determined by the field's formatter). If the text is invalid, the value remains the same and a `Parse-Exception` is thrown.
`boolean isEditValid()`	Returns true if the formatter considers the current text to be valid (as determined by the field's formatter).

F

Components

Table 28: DefaultFormatter Options

Method	Purpose
`void setCommitsOnValidEdit(boolean)` `boolean getCommitsOnValidEdit()`	Set or get when edits are pushed back to the `JFormattedTextField`. If true, `commitEdit` is invoked after every valid edit. This property is false by default.
`void setOverwriteMode(boolean)` `boolean getOverwriteMode()`	Set or get the behavior when inserting characters. If true, new characters overwrite existing characters in the model as they are inserted. The default value of this property is true in `DefaultFormatter` (and thus in `MaskFormatter`) and false in `InternationalFormatter` (and thus in `DateFormatter` and `NumberFormatter`).
`void setAllowsInvalid(boolean)` `boolean getAllowsInvalid()`	Set or get whether the value being edited is allowed to be invalid for a length of time. It is often convenient to allow the user to enter invalid values until a commit is attempted. `DefaultFormatter` initializes this property to true. Of the standard Swing formatters, only `MaskFormatter` sets it to false.

Examples That Use Formatted Text Fields

A few of our examples use formatted text fields.

Example	Where Described	Notes
FormattedTextFieldDemo	This section	Uses four formatted text fields.
SpinnerDemo	How to Use Spinners (page 357)	Customizes the appearance of the formatted text fields used by two spinners.
SliderDemo3	How to Use Sliders (page 348)	Pairs a formatted text field with a slider to allow editing of an integer value.
Converter	Using Models (page 50)	Each `ConversionPanel` pairs a formatted text field with a slider.
CelsiusConverter2	Example Four: An Improved CelsiusConverter (page 22)	Uses a formatted text field to let the user enter a decimal number.

Example	Where Described	Notes
TextInputDemo	This section	Shows how to use text fields, spinners, and formatted text fields together, and demonstrates how to use MaskFormatter. Includes code for selecting the text of the field that has just gotten the focus.
FormatterFactoryDemo	This section	A variation on FormattedText-FieldDemo that uses formatter factories to specify multiple formatters for two formatted text fields.
RegexFormatter	"Regular Expression Based AbstractFormatter," a *Swing Connection* article online at: http://java.sun.com/ products/jfc/tsc/ articles/reftf/	A regular expression formatter that you can use. Includes source code and information on how it was implemented.

F

Components

235

How to Make Frames (Main Windows)

A frame, implemented as an instance of the JFrame class,[1] is a window that typically has decorations such as a border, a title, and buttons for closing and iconifying itself. Applications with a GUI typically use at least one frame. Applets sometimes use frames as well.

To make a window that's dependent on another window—disappearing when the other window is iconified, for example—use a dialog[2] instead of a frame.[3] To make a window that appears within another window, use an internal frame.

Creating and Showing Frames

Figure 23 is a picture of an extremely plain window created by an example called Frame-Demo. You can run FrameDemo using Java Web Start or compile and run the example yourself.[4]

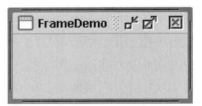

Figure 23   The FrameDemo application.

The following code, taken from FrameDemo, is a typical example of the code used to create and set up a frame.

```
//1. Optional: Specify who draws the window decorations.
JFrame.setDefaultLookAndFeelDecorated(true);
```

---

[1] JFrame API documentation is on the CD and online at: http://java.sun.com/j2se/1.4.2/docs/api/javax/swing/JFrame.html.
[2] See How to Make Dialogs (page 187).
[3] See How to Use Internal Frames (page 245).
[4] To run FrameDemo using Java Web Start, click the FrameDemo link on the RunExamples/components.html page on the CD. You can find the source files here: JavaTutorial/uiswing/components/example-1dot4/index.html#FrameDemo.

```
//2. Create the frame.
JFrame frame = new JFrame("FrameDemo");

//3. Optional: What happens when the frame closes?
frame.setDefaultCloseOperation(JFrame.EXIT_ON_CLOSE);

//4. Create components and put them in the frame.
//...create emptyLabel...
frame.getContentPane().add(emptyLabel, BorderLayout.CENTER);

//5. Size the frame.
frame.pack();

//6. Show it.
frame.setVisible(true);
```

Calling `setDefaultLookAndFeelDecorated(true)` requests that any subsequently created frames have window decorations provided by the look and feel, not by the window system. For details, see the next section, Specifying Window Decorations (page 238).

The next line of code creates a frame using a constructor that lets you set the frame's title. The other frequently used `JFrame` constructor is the no-argument constructor.

Next the code specifies what should happen when the user closes the frame. The `EXIT_ON_CLOSE` operation, not surprisingly, makes the program exit when the user closes the frame. This behavior is appropriate because it has only one frame and closing it makes the program useless. See Responding to Window-Closing Events (page 240) for details.

The next bit of code adds a blank label to the frame's content pane. If you're not already familiar with content panes and how to add components to them, please read Adding Components to the Content Pane (page 48) in Chapter 3.

For frames that have menus, you typically add the menu bar to the frame, here using the `setJMenuBar` method. See How to Use Menus (page 277) for details.

The `pack` method sizes the frame so that all of its contents are at or above their preferred sizes. An alternative to `pack` is to establish a frame's size explicitly by calling `setSize` or `setBounds` (which also sets the frame's location). In general, `pack` is preferable to calling `setSize`, since it leaves the frame's layout manager in charge of the frame's size, and layout managers are good at adjusting to platform dependencies and other factors that affect component size.

F

Components

This example doesn't set the frame's location, but it's easy to do so using either the `set-LocationRelativeTo` or the `setLocation` method. For example, the following code centers a frame onscreen:

```
frame.setLocationRelativeTo(null);
```

Calling `setVisible(true)` makes the frame appear onscreen. Sometimes you might see the `show` method used instead. The two methods are equivalent, but we use `setVisible(true)` for consistency's sake.

Specifying Window Decorations

By default, window decorations are supplied by the native window system. However, you can request that the look and feel provide the decorations for a frame. You can even specify that the frame have no window decorations at all, a feature typically used with full-screen exclusive mode.[1] (If you want a smaller-than-full-screen window without decorations, you should use the `JWindow` or `Window` class instead.)

Besides specifying how the window decorations are provided, you can also specify which icon is used the represent the window. Exactly how this icon is used depends on the window system or look and feel that provides the window decorations. If the window system supports minimization, the icon is used to represent the minimized window. Most window systems or look and feels also display the icon in the window decorations. A typical icon size is 16x16 pixels, but some window systems use other sizes.

Figure 24 shows three frames that are identical except for their window decorations. As you can tell by the appearance of the button in each frame, all three use the Java look and feel. However, only the first and third frames use window decorations provided by the Java look and feel. The second uses decorations provided by the window system, which happens to be Microsoft Windows but could as easily have been any other system running the 1.4 version of the Java platform. The third frame uses Java look-and-feel window decorations, but has a custom icon.

---

[1] Refer to the "Full-Screen Exclusive Mode" trail in *The Java Tutorial* on the CD and online at: `http://java.sun.com/docs/books/tutorial/extra/fullscreen/index.html`.

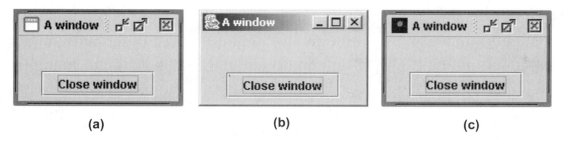

Figure 24 (a) Window decorations provided by the look and feel; (b) window decorations provided by the window system; and (c) custom icon with window decorations provided by the look and feel.

Here's an example of creating a frame with a custom icon and with window decorations provided by the look and feel:

```
//Ask for window decorations provided by the look and feel.
JFrame.setDefaultLookAndFeelDecorated(true);

//Create the frame.
JFrame frame = new JFrame("A window");

//Set the frame's icon to an image loaded from a file.
frame.setIconImage(new ImageIcon(imgURL).getImage());
```

As the code snippet here implies, you must invoke the setDefaultLookAndFeelDecorated method *before* creating the frame whose decorations you want to affect. The value you set with setDefaultLookAndFeelDecorated is used for all subsequently created JFrames. You can switch back to window system decorations by invoking JFrame.setDefaultLookAndFeelDecorated(false). Some look and feels might not support window decorations; in this case, the window system decorations are used.

Version Note: The setDefaultLookAndFeelDecorated method was added in v1.4. Previously, the decorations on a frame were always provided by the window system.

The full source code for the application that creates the frames pictured in Figure 24 is in FrameDemo2.java.[1] Besides showing how to choose window decorations, FrameDemo2 also shows how to disable all window decorations and gives an example of positioning windows.

---

[1] FrameDemo2.java is included on the CD and is available online. You can find it here: JavaTutorial/uiswing/components/example-1dot4/FrameDemo2.java.

F

Components

It includes two methods that create the `Image` objects used as icons—one is loaded from a file and the other is painted from scratch.

Try This:

1. Run `FrameDemo2` using Java Web Start or compile and run the example yourself.[1]
2. Bring up two windows, both with look-and-feel-provided decorations but with different icons. The Java look and feel displays the icons in its window decorations. Depending on your window system, the icons may be used elsewhere to represent the window, especially when the window is minimized.
3. Bring up one or more windows with window system decorations. See if your window system treats these icons differently.
4. Bring up one or more windows with no window decorations. Play with the various windows types to see how the window decorations, window system, and frame icons interact.

Responding to Window-Closing Events

By default, when the user closes a frame onscreen the frame is hidden. Although invisible, the frame still exists and the program can make it visible again. If you want different behavior, you need to either register a window listener that handles window-closing events or specify default close behavior using the `setDefaultCloseOperation` method. You can even do both.

The argument to `setDefaultCloseOperation` must be one of the following values, the first three of which are defined in the `WindowConstants` interface (implemented by `JFrame`, `JInternalPane`, and `JDialog`):

DO_NOTHING_ON_CLOSE
Do nothing when the user requests that the window close. Instead, the program should probably use a window listener that performs some other action in its `windowClosing` method.

HIDE_ON_CLOSE (the default for `JDialog` and `JFrame`)
Hide the window when the user closes it. This removes the window from the screen but leaves it displayable.

---

[1] To run `FrameDemo2` using Java Web Start, click the `FrameDemo2` link on the `RunExamples/components.html` page on the CD. You can find the source files here: `JavaTutorial/uiswing/components/example-1dot4/index.html#FrameDemo2`.

DISPOSE_ON_CLOSE (the default for `JInternalFrame`)

Hide and dispose of the window when the user closes it. This removes the window from the screen and frees up any resources used by it.

EXIT_ON_CLOSE (defined in the `JFrame` class)

Exit the application, using `System.exit(0)`. This is recommended for applications only. If it's used within an applet, a `SecurityException` may be thrown. Introduced in version 1.3.

Version Note: As of v1.4, `DISPOSE_ON_CLOSE` can have results similar to those of `EXIT_ON_CLOSE` if only one window is onscreen. More precisely, when the last displayable window within the Java Virtual Machine (VM) is disposed of, the VM may terminate if it is 1.4 or a compatible version. In earlier versions such as 1.3, the VM remains running even when all windows have been disposed of. For details, see "AWT Threading Issues" in the API documentation: `http://java.sun.com/j2se/1.4.2/jcp/beta/apidiffs/java/awt/doc-files/AWTThreadIssues.html`.

The default close operation is executed after any window listeners handle the window-closing event. So, for example, if you specify that the default close operation is to dispose of a frame, you can also implement a window listener that tests whether the frame is the last one visible and, if so, saves some data and exits the application. Under these conditions, when the user closes a frame the window listener will be called first. If it doesn't exit the application, the default close operation—disposing of the frame—will execute.

For more information about handling window-closing events, see the section How to Write Window Listeners (page 723) in Chapter 10. Besides handling window-closing events, window listeners can also react to other window state changes, such as iconification and activation.

The Frame API

Tables 29 through 31 list the commonly used `JFrame` constructors and methods. Other methods you might want to call are defined by the `java.awt.Frame`,[1] `java.awt.Window`,[2] and `java.awt.Component`[3] classes, from which `JFrame`[4] descends.

---

[1] Frame API documentation: `http://java.sun.com/j2se/1.4.2/docs/api/java/awt/Frame.html`.

[2] Window API documentation: `http://java.sun.com/j2se/1.4.2/docs/api/java/awt/Window.html`.

[3] Component API documentation: `http://java.sun.com/j2se/1.4.2/docs/api/java/awt/Component.html`.

[4] JFrame API documentation: `http://java.sun.com/j2se/1.4.2/docs/api/javax/swing/JFrame.html`.

Because each `JFrame` object has a root pane, frames support interposing input and painting behavior in front of the frame's children, placing children on different "layers," and Swing menu bars. These topics were introduced in Using Top-Level Containers (page 46) in Chapter 3 and are explained in detail in How to Use Root Panes (page 316) later in this chapter.

Table 29: Creating and Setting up a Frame

Method or Constructor	Purpose
`JFrame()` `JFrame(String)`	Create a frame that is initially invisible. The `String` argument provides a title for the frame. You can also use `setTitle` to set a frame's title. To make the frame visible, invoke `setVisible(true)` on it.
`void setDefaultCloseOperation(int)` `int getDefaultCloseOperation()`	Set or get the operation that occurs when the user pushes the Close button on this frame. Possible choices are: `DO_NOTHING_ON_CLOSE`, `HIDE_ON_CLOSE`, `DISPOSE_ON_CLOSE`, and `EXIT_ON_CLOSE`. The first three constants are defined in the `WindowConstants` interface, which `JFrame` implements. The constant `EXIT_ON_CLOSE` is defined in the `JFrame` class, and was introduced in 1.3.

`void setIconImage(Image)`
`Image getIconImage()`
(*in* Frame)
	Set or get the icon that represents the frame. Note that the argument is a `java.awt.Image` object, not a `javax.swing.ImageIcon` (or any other `javax.swing.Icon` implementation).

`void setUndecorated(boolean)`
`boolean isUndecorated()`
(*in* Frame)
	Set or get whether the window system should provide decorations for this frame. Works only if the frame is not yet displayable (hasn't been packed or shown). Typically used with full-screen exclusive mode or to enable custom window decorations.[a] Introduced in 1.4.

`static void setDefaultLookAndFeel-Decorated(boolean)`
 	
`static boolean isDefaultLookAndFeel-Decorated()`
	Determine whether subsequently created `JFrames` should have their window decorations (such as borders, widgets for closing the window, title) provided by the current look and feel. This is only a hint, as some look and feels may not support this feature. Introduced in 1.4.

a. Refer to the "Full-Screen Exclusive Mode" trail in *The Java Tutorial* on this book's CD and online at: `http://java.sun.com/docs/books/tutorial/extra/fullscreen/index.html`.

Table 30: Setting the Window Size and Location

Method	Purpose
void pack() *(in* Window*)*	Size the window so that all of its contents are at or above their preferred sizes.
void setSize(int, int) void setSize(Dimension) Dimension getSize() *(in* Component*)*	Set or get the total size of the window. The integer arguments to setSize specify the width and height, respectively.
void setBounds(int, int, int, int) void setBounds(Rectangle) Rectangle getBounds() *(in* Component*)*	Set or get the size and position of the window. For the integer version of setBounds, the window's upper left corner is at the *x, y* location specified by the first two arguments, and has the width and height specified by the last two arguments.
void setLocation(int, int) Point getLocation() *(in* Component*)*	Set or get the location of the upper left corner of the window. The parameters are the *x* and *y* values, respectively.
void setLocationRelativeTo(Component) *(in* Window*)*	Position the window so that it's centered over the specified component. If the argument is null, the window is centered onscreen. To properly center the window, invoke this method after the window's size has been set.

Table 31: JFrame Methods Related to the Root Pane

Method	Purpose
void setContentPane(Container) Container getContentPane()	Set or get the frame's content pane. The content pane contains the frame's visible GUI components and should be opaque.
JRootPane createRootPane() void setRootPane(JRootPane) JRootPane getRootPane()	Create, set, or get the frame's root pane. The root pane manages the interior of the frame, including the content pane, the glass pane, and so on.
void setJMenuBar(JMenuBar) JMenuBar getJMenuBar()	Set or get the frame's menu bar to manage a set of menus for the frame.
void setGlassPane(Component) Component getGlassPane()	Set or get the frame's glass pane. Use the glass pane to intercept mouse events or paint on top of your program's GUI.
void setLayeredPane(JLayeredPane) JLayeredPane getLayeredPane()	Set or get the frame's layered pane. Use the frame's layered pane to put components on top of or behind other components.

F

Components

243

Examples That Use Frames

Every standalone application in this chapter uses JFrame. The following table lists a few and tells you where each is discussed.

Example	Where Described	Notes
FrameDemo	Creating and Showing Frames (page 236)	Displays a basic frame with one component.
FrameDemo2	Specifying Window Decorations (page 238)	Lets you create frames with various window decorations.
Framework	—	Creates and destroys windows, implements a menu bar, and exits an application.
ColorChooserDemo	How to Use Color Choosers (page 167)	A subclass of JFrame that adds components to the default content pane.
TableDemo	How to Use Tables (page 388)	A subclass of JFrame that sets the frame's content pane.
LayeredPaneDemo	How to Use Layered Panes (page 258)	Illustrates how to use a layered pane (but not the frame's layered pane).
GlassPaneDemo	The Glass Pane (page 317)	Illustrates the use of a frame's glass pane.
MenuDemo	How to Use Menus (page 277)	Shows how to put a JMenuBar in a JFrame.

How to Use Internal Frames

With the `JInternalFrame`[1] class, you can display a `JFrame`-like window within another window. Usually, you add internal frames to a desktop pane, which in turn might be used as the content pane of a `JFrame`. The desktop pane is an instance of `JDesktopPane`,[2] which is a subclass of `JLayeredPane`[3] that has added API for managing multiple overlapping internal frames.

Consider carefully whether to base your program's GUI around frames or internal frames. Switching from internal frames to frames or vice versa isn't necessarily a simple task. By experimenting, you can get an idea of the tradeoffs involved in choosing one over the other.

Figure 25 shows an application that has two internal frames (one of which is iconified) inside a regular frame.

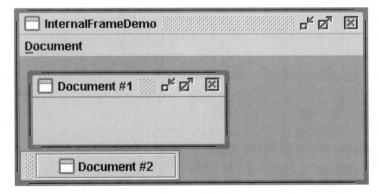

Figure 25   The `InternalFrameDemo` application.

Try This:

1. Run `InternalFrameDemo` using Java Web Start or compile and run the example your-self.[4]

---

[1] `InternalFrame` API documentation: `http://java.sun.com/j2se/1.4.2/docs/api/javax/swing/JInternalFrame.html`.

[2] `JDesktopPane` API documentation is on the CD and online at: `http://java.sun.com/j2se/1.4.2/docs/api/javax/swing/JDesktopPane.html`.

[3] Layered panes are discussed in How to Use Layered Panes (page 258).

[4] To run `InternalFrameDemo` using Java Web Start, click the `InternalFrameDemo` link on the `RunExamples/components.html` page on the CD. You can find the source files here: `JavaTutorial/uiswing/components/example-1dot4/index.html#InternalFrameDemo`.

Components

2. Create new internal frames using the Create item in the Document menu. Each internal frame comes up 30 pixels lower and to the right of where the previous internal frame first appeared. This functionality is implemented in the `MyInternalFrame` class, which is the custom subclass of `JInternalFrame`.

The following code, taken from `InternalFrameDemo.java`, creates the desktop and internal frames in the previous example.

```
.../In the constructor of InternalFrameDemo, a JFrame subclass:
    desktop = new JDesktopPane();
    createFrame(); //Create first window
    setContentPane(desktop);
    ...
    //Make dragging faster:
    //desktop.putClientProperty("JDesktopPane.dragMode", //pre-1.3 code
                                "outline");
    desktop.setDragMode(JDesktopPane.OUTLINE_DRAG_MODE); //1.3+ code
...
protected void createFrame() {
    MyInternalFrame frame = new MyInternalFrame();
    frame.setVisible(true); //necessary as of 1.3
    desktop.add(frame);
    try {
        frame.setSelected(true);
    } catch (java.beans.PropertyVetoException e) {}
}

.../In the constructor of MyInternalFrame, a JInternalFrame subclass:
static int openFrameCount = 0;
static final int xOffset = 30, yOffset = 30;

public MyInternalFrame() {
    super("Document #" + (++openFrameCount),
            true, //resizable
            true, //closable
            true, //maximizable
            true);//iconifiable
    //...Create the GUI and put it in the window...
    //...Then set the window size or call pack...
    ...
    //Set the window's location.
    setLocation(xOffset*openFrameCount, yOffset*openFrameCount);
}
```

Internal Frames versus Regular Frames

The code for using internal frames is similar in many ways to that for using regular Swing frames. Because internal frames have root panes, setting up the GUI for a JInternalFrame is very similar to setting up the GUI for a JFrame. JInternalFrame also provides other API, such as pack, that makes it similar to JFrame.

Note: Just as for a regular frame, you must invoke setVisible(true) or show() on an internal frame to display it. In early versions of the Java 2 platform (such as 1.2.2), this code has no effect because the internal frame is visible by default. However, starting in the v1.3 release, the internal frame doesn't appear until you explicitly make it visible.

That internal frames aren't windows or top-level containers makes them different from frames. For example, you must add an internal frame to a container (usually a JDesktop-Pane); an internal frame can't be the root of a containment hierarchy. Also, internal frames don't generate window events. Instead, the user actions that cause a frame to fire window events cause an internal frame to fire internal frame events.

Because internal frames are implemented with platform-independent code, they add functionality that frames can't give you. For example, internal frames give you more control over their state and capabilities than frames do. You can programatically iconify or maximize an internal frame. You can also specify what icon goes in the internal frame's title bar. You can even specify whether the internal frame has the window decorations to support resizing, iconifying, closing, and maximizing.

Another feature is that internal frames are designed to work within desktop panes. The JInternalFrame API contains methods, such as moveToFront, that work only if the internal frame's container is a layered pane such as a JDesktopPane.

Rules of Using Internal Frames

If you've built any programs using JFrame and the other Swing components, you already know a lot about how to use them. The following list summarizes the rules for using internal frames. For additional information, see How to Make Frames (Main Windows) (page 236) earlier in this chapter and The JComponent Class (page 53) in Chapter 3.

You must set the size of the internal frame.
> If you don't, it will have zero size and thus never be visible. You can set the size using setSize, pack, or setBounds.

As a rule, you should set the location of the internal frame.

If you don't, it will come up at 0,0 (the upper left of its container). You can use `set-Location` or `setBounds` to specify the upper left point of the internal frame, relative to its container.

To add components to an internal frame, add them to its content pane.

This is exactly like the `JFrame` situation. See Adding Components to the Content Pane (page 48) in Chapter 3 for details.

Dialogs that are internal frames should be implemented using `JOptionPane` or `JInternalFrame`, not `JDialog`.

To create a simple dialog, you can use the `JOptionPane showInternalXxxDialog` methods, as described in How to Make Dialogs (page 187).

You must add an internal frame to a container.

If you don't add the internal frame to a container (usually a `JDesktopPane`), the internal frame won't appear.

You need to call `show` or `setVisible` on internal frames.

Beginning with the v1.3 release, internal frames are invisible by default. You must invoke `setVisible(true)` or `show()` to make them visible.

Internal frames fire internal frame events, not window events.

Handling internal frame events is almost identical to handling window events. See How to Write an Internal Frame Listener (page 670) in Chapter 10 for more information.

Performance Tip: Because dragging internal frames can be slow, Swing 1.1.1 and the Java 2 platform, v1.2.2, added a way to make it zippy: outline dragging. With outline dragging, only the outline of the internal frame is painted at the current mouse position while the window is being dragged. The internal frame's innards are not repainted at a new position until the dragging stops. The default, slow behavior is to reposition and repaint the entire internal frame continuously while it's being moved.

In releases before v1.3, you can specify outline dragging by setting a client property of the desktop pane, like this:

```
desktop.putClientProperty("JDesktopPane.dragMode", "outline");
```

The code has no effect in JFC implementations before Swing 1.1.1 Beta 1. As of version 1.3, use the new JDesktopPane method—setDragMode—to specify outline dragging. For example:

```
desktop.setDragMode(JDesktopPane.OUTLINE_DRAG_MODE);
```

The Internal Frame API

Tables 32 through 37 list the commonly used JInternalFrame constructors and methods, as well as a few methods that JDesktopPane provides. Besides the API listed in this section, JInternalFrame inherits useful API from its superclasses: JComponent, Component, and Container. See The JComponent Class (page 53) in Chapter 3 for lists of methods from those classes.

Like JInternalFrame, JDesktopPane descends from JComponent and thus provides the methods described in The JComponent Class (page 53) in Chapter 3. Because JDesktop-Pane extends JLayeredPane, it also supports the methods described in The Layered Pane API (page 264) later in this chapter. Also consult the API documentation for JInternal-Frame and JDesktopPane at:

```
http://java.sun.com/j2se/1.4.2/docs/api/javax/swing/JInternalFrame.html
http://java.sun.com/j2se/1.4.2/docs/api/javax/swing/JDesktopPane.html
```

Table 32: Creating the Internal Frame

Constructor or Method	Purpose

JInternalFrame()
JInternalFrame(String)
JInternalFrame(String, boolean)
JInternalFrame(String, boolean,
        boolean)
JInternalFrame(String, boolean,
        boolean, boolean)
JInternalFrame(String, boolean,
        boolean, boolean,
        boolean)
	Create a JInternalFrame instance. The first argument specifies the title (if any) to be displayed by the internal frame. The rest of the arguments specify whether the internal frame should contain decorations that allow the user to resize, close, maximize, and iconify the internal frame (specified in that order). The default value for each boolean argument is false, which means that the operation is not allowed.

static int showInternalConfirmDialog(
        Component, Object)
static String showInternalInputDialog(
        Component, Object)
static Object showInternalMessageDialog(
        Component, Object)
static int showInternalOptionDialog(
        Component, Object,
        String, int, int,
        Icon, Object[], Object)
	Create a JInternalFrame that simulates a dialog. See How to Make Dialogs (page 187) for details.

Components

249

Table 33: Adding Components to the Internal Frame

Method	Purpose
`void setContentPane(Container)` `Container getContentPane()`	Set or get the internal frame's content pane, which generally contains all of the internal frame's GUI, with the exception of the menu bar and window decorations.
`void setJMenuBar(JMenuBar)` `JMenuBar getJMenuBar()`	Set or get the internal frame's menu bar. (Some very early Swing releases do not include this method.)

Table 34: Specifying the Internal Frame's Visibility, Size, and Location

Method	Purpose
`void setVisible(boolean)` (*in* Component)	Make the internal frame visible (if true) or invisible (if false). Invoke `setVisible(true)` on each `JInternalFrame` before adding it to its container.
`void pack()` (*in* JInternalFrame)	Size the internal frame so that its components are at their preferred sizes.
`void setLocation(Point)` `void setLocation(int, int)` (*in* Component)	Set the position of the internal frame.
`void setBounds(Rectangle)` `void setBounds(int, int, int, int)` (*in* Component)	Explicitly set the size and location of the internal frame.
`void setSize(Dimension)` `void setSize(int, int)` (*in* Component)	Explicitly set the size of the internal frame.

Table 35: Performing Window Operations on the Internal Frame

Method	Purpose
`void setDefaultCloseOperation(int)` `int getDefaultCloseOperation()`	Set or get what the internal frame does when the user attempts to "close" the internal frame. The default value is `HIDE_ON_CLOSE`. Other possible values are `DO_NOTHING_ON_CLOSE` and `DISPOSE_ON_CLOSE`. See Responding to Window-Closing Events (page 240) for details.
`void addInternalFrameListener(` `InternalFrameListener)` `void removeInternalFrameListener(` `InternalFrameListener)`	Add or remove an internal frame listener (`JInternalFrame`'s equivalent of a window listener). See How to Use Internal Frames (page 245) for more information.

Table 35: Performing Window Operations on the Internal Frame *(continued)*

Method	Purpose
`void moveToFront()` `void moveToBack()`	If the internal frame's parent is a layered pane such as a desktop pane, move the internal frame to the front or back (respectively) of its layer.
`void setClosed(boolean)` `boolean isClosed()`	Set or get whether the internal frame is currently closed.
`void setIcon(boolean)` `boolean isIcon()`	Iconify or deiconify the internal frame, or determine whether it's currently iconified.
`void setMaximum(boolean)` `boolean isMaximum()`	Maximize or restore the internal frame, or determine whether it's maximized.
`void setSelected(boolean)` `boolean isSelected()`	Set or get whether the internal frame is the currently "selected" (activated) internal frame.

Table 36: Controlling Window Decorations and Capabilities

Method	Purpose
`void setFrameIcon(Icon)` `Icon getFrameIcon()`	Set or get the icon displayed in the title bar of the internal frame (usually in the top left corner).
`void setClosable(boolean)` `boolean isClosable()`	Set or get whether the user can close the internal frame.
`void setIconifiable(boolean)` `boolean isIconifiable()`	Set or get whether the internal frame can be iconified.
`void setMaximizable(boolean)` `boolean isMaximizable()`	Set or get whether the user can maximize this internal frame.
`void setResizable(boolean)` `boolean isResizable()`	Set or get whether the internal frame can be resized.
`void setTitle(String)` `String getTitle()`	Set or get the window title.

Table 37: Using the JDesktopPane API

Constructor or Method	Purpose
`JDesktopPane()`	Create a new instance of `JDesktopPane`.
`JInternalFrame[]` `  getAllFrames()`	Return all `JInternalFrame` objects that the desktop contains.
`JInternalFrame[]` `    getAllFramesInLayer(int)`	Return all `JInternalFrame` objects that the desktop contains that are in the specified layer. See How to Use Layered Panes (page 258) for information about layers.
`void setDragMode(int)` `int getDragMode()`	Set or get the drag mode used for internal frames in this desktop. The integer can be either `JDesktopPane.LIVE_DRAG_MODE` or `JDesktopPane.OUTLINE_DRAG_MODE`. The default for the Java look and feel is live-drag mode.

Examples That Use Internal Frames

The following examples use internal frames. Because internal frames are similar to regular frames, you should also look at Examples That Use Frames (page 244) earlier in this chapter.

Example	Where Described	Notes
`MyInternalFrame`	This section.	Implements an internal frame that appears at an offset to the previously created internal frame.
`InternalFrameDemo`	This section.	Lets you create internal frames (instances of `MyInternalFrame`) that go into the application's `JDesktopPane`.
`InternalFrameEvent-Demo`	How to Write an Internal Frame Listener (page 670)	Demonstrates listening for internal frame events. Also demonstrates positioning internal frames within a desktop pane.

How to Use Labels

With the `JLabel`[1] class, you can display unselectable text and images. If you need to create a component that displays a string or an image (or both), you can do so by using or extending `JLabel`. If the component is interactive and has state, consider using a button instead of a label.

By specifying HTML codes in a label's text, you can make the label have multiple lines, multiple fonts, multiple colors, and so on. If the label uses just a single color or font, you can avoid the overhead of HTML processing by using the `setForeground` or `setFont` method instead. See Using HTML in Swing Components (page 43) for details.

Figure 26 is a picture of an application that displays three labels. The window is divided into three rows of equal height; the label in each row is as wide as possible.

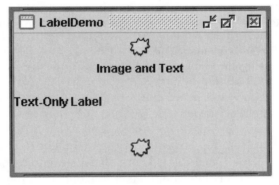

Figure 26   A screenshot of the `LabelDemo`, which displays three labels.

Try This:

1. Run `LabelDemo` using Java Web Start or compile and run the example yourself.[2]
2. Resize the window so you can see how the labels' contents are placed within the labels' drawing area. All the label contents have the default vertical alignment—the label contents are centered vertically in the label's drawing area. The top label, which contains both image and text, is specified to have horizontal center alignment. The second label,

---

[1] `JLabel` API documentation: `http://java.sun.com/j2se/1.4.2/docs/api/javax/swing/JLabel.html`.
[2] To run `LabelDemo` using Java Web Start, click the `LabelDemo` link on the `RunExamples/components.html` page on the CD. You can find the source files here: `JavaTutorial/uiswing/components/example-1dot4/index.html#LabelDemo`.

which contains just text, has the left (leading) alignment that is the default for text-only labels in left-to-right languages. The third label, which contains just an image, has horizontal center alignment, which is the default for image-only labels.

Below is the code from LabelDemo.java that creates the labels in the previous example.

```
ImageIcon icon = createImageIcon("images/middle.gif");
. . .
label1 = new JLabel("Image and Text",
                    icon,
                    JLabel.CENTER);
//Set the position of the text, relative to the icon:
label1.setVerticalTextPosition(JLabel.BOTTOM);
label1.setHorizontalTextPosition(JLabel.CENTER);

label2 = new JLabel("Text-Only Label");
label3 = new JLabel(icon);
```

The code for the createImageIcon method is similar to that used throughout this tutorial. You can find it explained in How to Use Icons (page 603) in Chapter 9.

Often, a label describes another component. When this is true, you can improve your program's accessibility by using the setLabelFor method to identify the component the label describes. For example:

```
amountLabel.setLabelFor(amountField);
```

The preceding code, taken from the FormattedTextFieldDemo example discussed in How to Use Formatted Text Fields (page 221), lets assistive technologies know that the label (amountLabel) provides information about the formatted text field (amountField). For more information about assistive technologies, see How to Support Assistive Technologies (page 519) in Chapter 9.

The Label API

Tables 38 through 40 list the commonly used JLabel constructors and methods. Other methods you're likely to call are defined by the Component and JComponent classes. They include setFont, setForeground, setBorder, setOpaque, and setBackground. See The JComponent Class (page 53) for details. You should also refer to the JLabel API documentation at: http://java.sun.com/j2se/1.4.2/docs/api/javax/swing/JLabel.html.

Note: In the following API, don't confuse label alignment with *x* and *y* alignment, which are used by layout managers and can affect the way any component—not just a label—is sized or positioned. Label alignment, on the other hand, has no effect on a label's size or position. It simply determines where, inside the label's painting area, the label's contents are positioned. In the usual case, the label's painting area is exactly the size needed to paint the label, and thus label alignment is irrelevant. For more information about *x* and *y* alignment, see How to Use Box-Layout (page 462) in Chapter 8.

Table 38: Setting or Getting the Label's Contents

Method or Constructor	Purpose

`JLabel(Icon)`
`JLabel(Icon, int)`
`JLabel(String)`
`JLabel(String, Icon, int)`
`JLabel(String, int)`
`JLabel()`
	Create a `JLabel` instance, initializing it to have the specified text/image/alignment. The `int` argument specifies the horizontal alignment of the label's contents within its drawing area. The horizontal alignment must be one of the following constants defined in the `SwingConstants` interface (which `JLabel` implements): LEFT, CENTER, RIGHT, LEADING, or TRAILING. For ease of localization, we strongly encourage you to use LEADING and TRAILING, rather than LEFT and RIGHT.

`void setText(String)` `String getText()`	Set or get the text displayed by the label. You can use HTML tags to format the text, as described in Using HTML in Swing Components (page 43) in Chapter 3.
`void setIcon(Icon)` `Icon getIcon()`	Set or get the image displayed by the label.
`void setDisplayedMnemonic(char)` `char getDisplayedMnemonic()`	Set or get the letter that should look like a keyboard alternative. This is handy when a label describes a component (such as a text field) that has a keyboard alternative but can't display it. If the *labelFor* property is also set (using `setLabelFor`), then when the user activates the mnemonic, the keyboard focus is transferred to the component specified by the *labelFor* property.
`void setDisplayedMnemonicIndex(int)` `int getDisplayedMnemonicIndex()`	Set or get a hint as to which character in the text should be decorated to represent the mnemonic. This is handy when you have two instances of the same character and wish to decorate the second instance. For example, `setDisplayed-MnemonicIndex(5)` decorates the character that's at position 5 (that is, the 6th character in the text). Not all look and feels may support this feature. Introduced in 1.4.
`void setDisabledIcon(Icon)` `Icon getDisabledIcon()`	Set or get the image displayed by the label when it's disabled. If you don't specify a disabled image, then the look and feel creates one by manipulating the default image.

Table 39: Fine Tuning the Label's Appearance

Method	Purpose

`void setHorizontalAlignment(int)`
`void setVerticalAlignment(int)`
`int getHorizontalAlignment()`
`int getVerticalAlignment()`
	Set or get where in the label its contents should be placed. The `SwingConstants` interface defines five possible values for horizontal alignment: LEFT, CENTER (the default for image-only labels), RIGHT, LEADING (the default for text-only labels), TRAILING. For vertical alignment: TOP, CENTER (the default), and BOTTOM.

`void setHorizontalTextPosition(int)`
`void setVerticalTextPosition(int)`
`int getHorizontalTextPosition()`
`int getVerticalTextPosition()`
	Set or get where the button's text should be placed, relative to the button's image. The `SwingConstants` interface defines five possible values for horizontal position: LEADING, LEFT, CENTER, RIGHT, and TRAILING (the default). For vertical position: TOP, CENTER (the default), and BOTTOM.

`void setIconTextGap(int)` `int getIconTextGap()`	Set or get the number of pixels between the label's text and its image.

Table 40: Supporting Accessibility

Method	Purpose
`void setLabelFor(Component)` `Component getLabelFor()`	Set or get which component the label describes.

Examples That Use Labels

The following table lists some of the many examples that use labels.

Example	Where Described	Notes
`LabelDemo`	This section	Shows how to specify horizontal and vertical alignment, as well as aligning a label's text and image.
`HtmlDemo`	Using HTML in Swing Components (page 43)	Lets you experiment with specifying HTML text for a label.
`AlignmentDemo`	Providing Size and Alignment Hints (page 94)	Demonstrates a possible alignment problem when using a label in a vertical box layout. Shows how to solve the problem.

	Where	
Example	**Described**	**Notes**
DialogDemo	How to Make Dialogs (page 187)	Uses a changeable label to display instructions and provide feedback.
SplitPaneDemo	How to Use Split Panes (page 369) and How to Use Lists (page 267)	Displays an image using a label inside of a scroll pane.
SliderDemo2	How to Use Sliders (page 348)	Uses JLabel to provide labels for a slider.
TableDialogEditDemo	How to Use Tables (page 388)	Implements a label subclass, ColorRenderer, to display colors in table cells.
FormattedTextField-Demo	How to Use Formatted Text Fields (page 221)	Has four rows, each containing a label and the formatted text field it describes.
TextComponentDemo	Using Text Components (page 60)	TextComponentDemo has an inner class (CaretListenerLabel) that extends JLabel to provide a label that listens for events, updating itself based on the events.
ColorChooserDemo	How to Use Color Choosers (page 167)	Uses an opaque label to display the currently chosen color against a fixed-color background.

L

Components

How to Use Layered Panes

A layered pane is a Swing container that provides a third dimension for positioning components: *depth*, also known as *Z order*. When adding a component to a layered pane, you specify its depth as an integer. The higher the number, the higher the depth. If components overlap, components at a higher depth are drawn on top of components at a lower depth. The relationship between components at the same depth is determined by their positions within the depth.

Version Note: In 1.5, we expect that API will be added to allow direct manipulation of a component's Z order within a container. When this is available, you won't need to use a `JLayered-Pane` to assign a Z order to a lightweight component.

Every Swing container that has a root pane—such as `JFrame`, `JApplet`, `JDialog`, or `JInternalFrame`—automatically has a layered pane. Most programs don't explicitly use the root pane's layered pane, so we don't discuss it in this section. You can find information about it in How to Use Root Panes (page 316), which provides an overview, and in The Layered Pane (page 320), which has further details. This section concentrates on telling you how to create your own layered pane and use it anywhere you might use a regular Swing container.

Swing provides two layered pane classes. The first, `JLayeredPane`,[1] is the class that root panes use and is the class used by the example in this section. The second, `JDesktopPane`, is a `JLayeredPane` subclass that's specialized for the task of holding internal frames. For examples of using `JDesktopPane`, see How to Use Internal Frames (page 245).

The `LayeredPaneDemo` application creates a layered pane and places overlapping, colored labels at different depths, as shown in Figure 27.

---

[1] JLayeredPane API documentation: `http://java.sun.com/j2se/1.4.2/docs/api/javax/swing/JLayeredPane.html`.

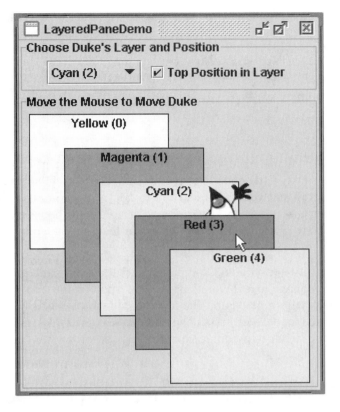

Figure 27   The LayeredPaneDemo application.

Try This:

1. Run LayeredPaneDemo using Java Web Start or compile and run the example your-self.[1]

2. Move the mouse around in the lower part of the window. The image of Duke drags behind the green and red labels but in front of the other three labels.

3. Use the combo box at the top of the window to change Duke's depth. Use the check box to set whether Duke is in the top position—position 0—within the current depth.

---

[1]   To run LayeredPaneDemo using Java Web Start, click the LayeredPaneDemo link on the RunExamples/ components.html page on the CD. You can find the source files here: JavaTutorial/uiswing/ components/example-1dot4/index.html#LayeredPaneDemo.

Here's the code from `LayeredPaneDemo.java` that creates the layered pane:

```
layeredPane = new JLayeredPane();
layeredPane.setPreferredSize(new Dimension(300, 310));
layeredPane.setBorder(BorderFactory.createTitledBorder(
                                    "Move the Mouse to Move Duke"));
layeredPane.addMouseMotionListener(new MouseMotionAdapter() {
    ...
});
```

The code uses `JLayeredPane`'s only constructor—the no-argument constructor—to create the layered pane. The rest of the code uses methods inherited from superclasses to give the layered pane a preferred size and a border, and to add a mouse-motion listener to it. The mouse-motion listener just moves the Duke image around in response to mouse movement. Although we don't show the code here, the example adds the layered pane to the frame's content pane.

As we'll show you a bit later, you add components to a layered pane using an add method. When adding a component to a layered pane, you specify the component's depth and, optionally, its position within its depth. The layered pane in the demo program contains six labels—the five colored labels and a sixth one that displays the Duke image. As the program demonstrates, both the depth of a component and its position within that depth can change dynamically.

Adding Components and Setting Component Depth

Here's the code from the sample program that adds the colored labels to the layered pane:

```
for (int i = 0; i < ...number of labels...; i++) {
    JLabel label = createColoredLabel(...);
    layeredPane.add(label, new Integer(i))
    ...
}
```

You can find the implementation of the `createColoredLabel` method in the source code for the program. It just creates an opaque `JLabel` initialized with a background color, a border, some text, and a size.

The example program uses a two-argument version of the add method. The first argument is the component to add, the second is an `Integer` object, specifying the depth. This program uses the `for` loop's iteration variable to specify depths. The actual values don't matter much. What matters is the relative value of the depths and that you are consistent within your program in how you use each depth.

Note: If you use the root pane's layered pane, be sure to use its depth conventions. Refer to The Layered Pane (page 320) for details. That section shows you how to modify Layered-PaneDemo to use the root pane's layered pane. With the modifications, you can see how the dragging Duke image relates to the combo box in the control panel.

As you can see from the example program, if components overlap, components at a higher depth are on top of components at a lower depth. To change a component's depth dynamically, use the setLayer method. In the example, the user can change Duke's layer by making a selection from the combo box. Here's the actionPerformed method of the action listener registered on the combo box:

```
public void actionPerformed(ActionEvent e) {
    int position = onTop.isSelected() ? 0 : 1;
    layeredPane.setLayer(dukeLabel,
                         layerList.getSelectedIndex(),
                         position);
}
```

The setLayer method used here takes three arguments: the component whose depth is to be set, the new depth, and the position within the depth. JLayeredPane has a two-argument version of setLayer that takes only the component and the new depth. That method puts the component at the bottom position in its depth.

Note: When adding a component to a layered pane you specify the layer with an Integer. When using setLayer to change a component's layer, you use an int. You might think that if you use an int instead of an Integer with the add method, the compiler would complain or your program would throw an illegal argument exception. But the compiler says nothing, which results in a common layered pane problem. You can use the API tables at the end of this section to check the types of the arguments and return values for methods that deal with layers.

Setting a Component's Position within Its Depth

The following code creates the label that displays Duke's image and then adds the label to the layered pane.

```
final ImageIcon icon = createImageIcon("images/dukeWaveRed.gif");
...
dukeLabel = new JLabel(icon);
...
```

```
dukeLabel.setBounds(15, 225,
                    icon.getIconWidth(),
                    icon.getIconHeight());
...
layeredPane.add(dukeLabel, new Integer(2), 0);
```

This code uses the three-argument version of the add method. The third argument specifies the Duke label's position within its depth, which determines the component's relationship with other components at the same depth.

Positions are specified with an int between -1 and (n - 1), where n is the number of components at the depth. Unlike layer numbers, the smaller the position number, the higher the component within its depth. (See Figure 28.) Using -1 is the same as using n - 1; it indicates the bottom-most position. Using 0 specifies that the component should be in the topmost position within its depth.

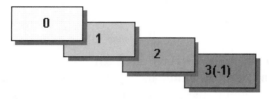

Figure 28   With the exception of -1, a lower position number indicates a higher position within a depth.

A component's position within its layer can change dynamically. In the example, you can use the check box to determine whether the Duke label is in the top position at its depth. Here's the actionPerformed method for the action listener registered on the check box:

```
public void actionPerformed(ActionEvent e) {
    if (onTop.isSelected())
        layeredPane.moveToFront(dukeLabel);
    else
        layeredPane.moveToBack(dukeLabel);
}
```

When the user selects the check box, the moveToFront method moves Duke to the front (position 0). And when the user deselects the check box, Duke gets moved to the back with the moveToBack method. You can also use the setPosition method or the three-argument version of setLayer to change a component's position.

Laying Out Components in a Layered Pane

By default a layered pane has no layout manager. This means that you typically have to write the code that positions and sizes the components you put in it.

The example uses the `setBounds` method to set the size and position of each of the labels:

```
dukeLabel.setBounds(15, 225,
                    icon.getIconWidth(),
                    icon.getIconHeight());
...
label.setBounds(origin.x, origin.y, 140, 140);
```

When the user moves the mouse around, the program calls `setPosition` to change Duke's position:

```
dukeLabel.setLocation(e.getX()-XFUDGE, e.getY()-YFUDGE);
```

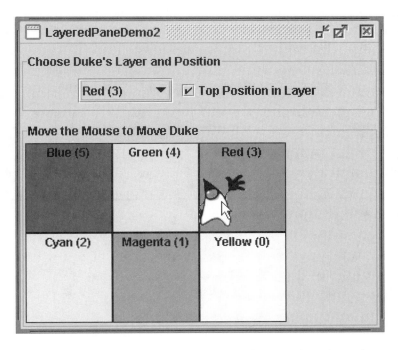

Figure 29 A screenshot of `LayeredPaneDemo2`, a version of the previous demo that sets the layered pane's layout manager to an instance of `GridLayout`, using that layout manager to lay out six colored labels.

Although a layered pane has no layout manager by default, you can still assign a layout manager to it. All of the layout managers provided by the Java platform arrange the components as if they were all on one layer.

Figure 29 shows a demo called `LayeredPaneDemo2` that assigns a layout manager to a layered pane. You can run `LayeredPaneDemo2` using Java Web Start or compile and run the example yourself.[1]

Many programs use intermediate containers (such as panels) and their layout managers to lay out components on the same layer, but use absolute positioning to lay out components on different layers. For more information about absolute positioning, see Doing without a Layout Manager (Absolute Positioning) (page 100).

The Layered Pane API

Tables 41 through 43 list the commonly used `JLayeredPane` constructors and methods. Other methods you are most likely to invoke on a `JLayeredPane` object are those it inherits from its superclasses, such as `setBorder`, `setPreferredSize`, and so on. See The JComponent API (page 55) for tables of commonly used inherited methods. You should also refer to the `JLayeredPane` API documentation: `http://java.sun.com/j2se/1.4.2/docs/api/ javax/swing/JLayeredPane.html`.

Table 41: Creating or Getting a Layered Pane

Method or Constructor	Purpose
`JLayeredPane()`	Create a layered pane.
`JLayeredPane getLayeredPane()` (*in* `JApplet`, `JDialog`, `JFrame`, *and* `JInternal-Frame`)	Get the automatic layered pane in an applet, dialog, frame, or internal frame.

---

[1] To run `LayeredPaneDemo2` using Java Web Start, click the `LayeredPaneDemo2` link on the `RunExamples/components.html` page on the CD. You can find the source files here: `JavaTutorial/ uiswing/components/example-1dot4/index.html#LayeredPaneDemo2`.

Table 42: Layering Components

Method	Purpose

`void add(Component)`
`void add(Component, Object)`
`void add(Component, Object, int)`
	Add the specified component to the layered pane. The second argument, when present, is an `Integer` that indicates the layer. The third argument, when present, indicates the component's position within its layer. If you use the one-argument version of this method, the component is added to layer 0. If you use the one- or two-argument version of this method, the component is placed underneath all other components currently in the same layer.

`void setLayer(Component, int)` `void setLayer(Component, int, int)`	Change the component's layer. The second argument indicates the layer. The third argument, when present, indicates the component's position within its layer.
`int getLayer(Component)` `int getLayer(JComponent)`	Get the layer for the specified component.
`int getComponentCountInLayer(int)`	Get the number of components in the specified layer. The value returned by this method can be useful for computing position values.
`Component[] getComponentsInLayer(int)`	Get an array of all the components in the specified layer.
`int highestLayer()` `int lowestLayer()`	Compute the highest or lowest layer currently in use.

Table 43: Setting Components' Intra-Layer Positions

Method	Purpose
`void setPosition(Component, int)` `int getPosition(Component)`	Set or get the position for the specified component within its layer.
`void moveToFront(Component)` `void moveToBack(Component)`	Move the specified component to the front or back of its layer.

L

Components

265

Examples That Use Layered Panes

This table shows examples that use `JLayeredPane` and where those examples are described.

Example	Where Described	Notes
LayeredPaneDemo	This section	Illustrates layers and intra-layer positions of a `JLayeredPane`.
LayeredPaneDemo2	This section	Uses a layout manager to help lay out the components in a layered pane.
RootLayeredPaneDemo	The Layered Pane (page 320)	A version of how to change `LayeredPaneDemo` modified to use the root pane's layered pane.
InternalFrameDemo	How to Use Internal Frames (page 245)	Uses a `JDesktopFrame` to manage internal frames.

How to Use Lists

A JList[1] presents the user with a group of items, displayed in one or more columns, to choose from. Lists can have many items, so they are often put in scroll panes.

In addition to lists, the following Swing components present multiple selectable items to the user: combo boxes, menus, tables, and groups of check boxes or radio buttons. To display hierarchical data, use a tree.

Figure 30 shows two GUIs that use lists. This section uses these examples as a basis for the discussions that follow.

          ListDialog   ListDemo

Figure 30   Screenshots of ListDialog (used by ListDialogRunner) and ListDemo.

Try This:

1. Run ListDialogRunner and ListDemo using Java Web Start or compile and run the examples yourself.[2]

2. To bring up the ListDialog, click the **Pick a new name...** button in the window titled "Name That Baby." The resulting dialog is a ListDialog instance that's been customized to have the title "Name Chooser."

3. In ListDemo, try adding (hiring) and removing (firing) a few items.

---

[1] JList API documentation: `http://java.sun.com/j2se/1.4.2/docs/api/javax/swing/JList.html`.

[2] To run ListDialogRunner and ListDemo using Java Web Start, click the ListDialogRunner and ListDemo links on the RunExamples/components.html page on the CD. You can find the source files here: JavaTutorial/uiswing/components/example-1dot4/index.html#ListDialogRunner.

Components

Initializing a List

Here's the code from `ListDialog.java` that creates and sets up its list:

```
list = new JList(data); //data has type Object[]
list.setSelectionMode(ListSelectionModel.SINGLE_INTERVAL_SELECTION);
list.setLayoutOrientation(JList.HORIZONTAL_WRAP);
list.setVisibleRowCount(-1);
...
JScrollPane listScroller = new JScrollPane(list);
listScroller.setPreferredSize(new Dimension(250, 80));
```

The code passes an array to the list's constructor. The array is filled with strings that were passed in from another object. In our example, the strings happen to be boys' names.

Other `JList` constructors let you initialize a list from a `Vector` or from an object that adheres to the `ListModel`[1] interface. If you initialize a list with an array or vector, the constructor implicitly creates a default list model. The default list model is immutable—you cannot add, remove, or replace items in the list. To create a list whose items can be changed individually, set the list's model to an instance of a mutable list model class, such as an instance of `DefaultListModel`.[2] You can set a list's model when you create the list or by calling the `setModel` method. See Adding Items to and Removing Items from a List (page 270) for an example.

The call to `setSelectionMode` specifies how many items the user can select and whether they must be contiguous. The next section tells you more about selection modes.

The call to `setLayoutOrientation` lets the list display its data in multiple columns. The value `JList.HORIZONTAL_WRAP` specifies that the list should display its items from left to right before wrapping to a new row. Another possible value is `JList.VERTICAL_WRAP`, which specifies that the data be displayed from top to bottom (as usual) before wrapping to a new column. The following figures show these two wrapping possibilities, together with the default, `JList.VERTICAL`.

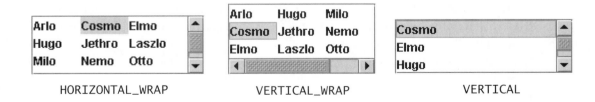

HORIZONTAL_WRAP   VERTICAL_WRAP   VERTICAL

---

[1] `ListModel` API documentation: http://java.sun.com/j2se/1.4.2/docs/api/javax/swing/ListModel.html.

[2] `DefaultListModel` API documentation: http://java.sun.com/j2se/1.4.2/docs/api/javax/swing/DefaultListModel.html.

In combination with the call to `setLayoutOrientation`, invoking the method `setVisible-RowCount(-1)` makes the list display the maximum number of items possible in the available space onscreen. Another common use of `setVisibleRowCount` is to specify to the lists's scroll pane how many rows the list prefers to display.

Selecting Items in a List

A list uses an instance of `ListSelectionModel`[1] to manage its selection. By default, a list selection model allows any combination of items to be selected at a time. You can specify a different selection mode by calling the `setSelectionMode` method on the list. For example, both `ListDialog` and `ListDemo` set the selection mode to `SINGLE_SELECTION` (a constant defined by `ListSelectionModel`) so that only one item in the list can be selected. The following table describes the three list selection modes.

SINGLE_SELECTION one two three four five	Only one item can be selected at a time. When the user selects an item, any previously selected item is deselected first.
SINGLE_INTERVAL_SELECTION one two three four five	Multiple, contiguous items can be selected. When the user begins a new selection range, any previously selected items are deselected first.
MULTIPLE_INTERVAL_SELECTION one two three four five	The default. Any combination of items can be selected. The user must explicitly deselect items.

---

[1] `ListSelectionModel` API documentation: `http://java.sun.com/j2se/1.4.2/docs/api/javax/swing/ListSelectionModel.html`.

L

Components

No matter which selection mode your list uses, the list fires list selection events whenever the selection changes. You can process these events by adding a list selection listener[1] to the list with the addListSelectionListener method. A list selection listener must implement one method: valueChanged. Here's the valueChanged method for the listener in ListDemo:

```
public void valueChanged(ListSelectionEvent e) {
    if (e.getValueIsAdjusting() == false) {

        if (list.getSelectedIndex() == -1){
        //No selection, disable fire button.
            fireButton.setEnabled(false);

        } else {
        //Selection, enable the fire button.
            fireButton.setEnabled(true);
        }
    }
}
```

Many list selection events can be generated from a single user action such as a mouse click. The getValueIsAdjusting method returns true if the user is still manipulating the selection. This particular program is interested only in the final result of the user's action, so the valueChanged method does something only if getValueIsAdjusting returns false.

Because the list is in single-selection mode, this code can use getSelectedIndex to get the index of the just-selected item. JList provides other methods for setting or getting the selection when the selection mode allows more than one item to be selected. If you want, you can listen for events on the list's list selection model rather than on the list itself. ListSelectionDemo[2] is an example that shows how to listen for list selection events on the list selection model and lets you change the selection mode of a list dynamically.

Adding Items to and Removing Items from a List

The ListDemo example that we showed previously features a list whose contents can change. Here's the ListDemo code that creates a mutable list model object, puts the initial items in it, and uses the list model to create a list:

```
listModel = new DefaultListModel();
listModel.addElement("Alison Huml");
listModel.addElement("Kathy Walrath");
```

---

[1] See How to Write a List Selection Listener (page 685).
[2] ListSelectionDemo is featured in How to Write a List Selection Listener (page 685) in Chapter 10.

```
listModel.addElement("Lisa Friendly");
listModel.addElement("Mary Campione");
listModel.addElement("Sharon Zakhour");
listModel.addElement("Alan Sommerer");

list = new JList(listModel);
```

This particular program uses an instance of DefaultListModel, a class provided by Swing. In spite of the class name, a list does not have a DefaultListModel unless your program explicitly makes it so. If DefaultListModel doesn't suit your needs, you can write a custom list model, which must adhere to the ListModel interface.

The following code snippet shows the actionPerformed method for the action listener registered on the **Fire** button. The bold line of code removes the selected item in the list. The remaining lines in the method disable the **Fire** button if the list is now empty, and make another selection if it's not.

```
public void actionPerformed(ActionEvent e) {
    int index = list.getSelectedIndex();
    listModel.remove(index);

    int size = listModel.getSize();

    if (size == 0) { //Nobody's left, disable firing.
        fireButton.setEnabled(false);

    } else { //Select an index.
        if (index == listModel.getSize()) {
            //removed item in last position
            index--;
        }

        list.setSelectedIndex(index);
        list.ensureIndexIsVisible(index);
    }
}
```

Here's the actionPerformed method for the action listener shared by the **Hire** button and the text field:

Components

```
public void actionPerformed(ActionEvent e) {
    String name = employeeName.getText();

    //User didn't type in a unique name...
    if (name.equals("") || alreadyInList(name)) {
        Toolkit.getDefaultToolkit().beep();
        employeeName.requestFocusInWindow();
        employeeName.selectAll();
        return;
    }

    int index = list.getSelectedIndex(); //get selected index
    if (index == -1) { //no selection, so insert at beginning
        index = 0;
    } else {            //add after the selected item
        index++;
    }

    listModel.insertElementAt(employeeName.getText(), index);

    //Reset the text field.
    employeeName.requestFocusInWindow();
    employeeName.setText("");

    //Select the new item and make it visible.
    list.setSelectedIndex(index);
    list.ensureIndexIsVisible(index);
}
```

This bold line of code uses the list model's `insertElementAt` method to insert the new name after the current selection or, if no selection exists, at the beginning of the list. If you just want to add to the end of the list, you can use `DefaultListModel`'s `addElement` method instead.

Whenever items are added to, removed from, or modified in a list, the list model fires list data events. Refer to How to Write a List Data Listener (page 682) for information about listening for these events. That section contains an example that is similar to `ListDemo` but adds buttons that move items up or down in the list.

Writing a Custom Cell Renderer

A list uses an object called a cell renderer to display each of its items. The default cell renderer knows how to display strings and icons. If you want to put any other `Object` in a list or if you want to change the way the default renderer displays icons or strings, you can implement a custom cell renderer. Take these steps to provide a custom cell renderer for a list:

- Write a class that implements the `ListCellRenderer` interface.[1]
- Create an instance of your class and call the list's `setCellRenderer` method using the instance as an argument.

We don't provide an example of a list with a custom cell renderer, but we do have an example of a combo box with a custom renderer—and combo boxes use the same type of renderer as lists. See the example described in Providing a Custom Renderer (page 181).

The List API

Tables 44 through 47 list the commonly used `JList` constructors and methods. Other methods you are most likely to invoke on a `JList` object are those such as `setPreferredSize` that its superclasses provide. See The JComponent API (page 55) for tables of commonly used inherited methods. Also refer to the `JList` API documentation: `http://java.sun.com/j2se/1.4.2/docs/api/javax/swing/JList.html`.

Much of the operation of a list is managed by other objects. The items in the list are managed by a list model object, the selection is managed by a list selection model object, and most programs put a list in a scroll pane to handle scrolling. For the most part, you don't need to worry about the models because `JList` creates them as necessary and you interact with them implicitly with `JList`'s convenience methods.

Table 44: Initializing List Data

Method or Constructor	Purpose

`JList(ListModel)`
`JList(Object[])`
`JList(Vector)`
`JList()`
	Create a list with the initial list items specified. The second and third constructors implicitly create an immutable `ListModel`; you should not subsequently modify the passed-in array or `Vector`.

`void setModel(ListModel)` `ListModel getModel()`	Set or get the model that contains the contents of the list.
`void setListData(Object[])` `void setListData(Vector)`	Set the items in the list. These methods implicitly create an immutable `ListModel`.

---

[1] `ListCellRenderer` API documentation: `http://java.sun.com/j2se/1.4.2/docs/api/javax/swing/ListCellRenderer.html`.

Table 45: Displaying the List

Method	Purpose
`void setVisibleRowCount(int)` `int getVisibleRowCount()`	Set or get how many rows of the list should be visible.
`void setLayoutOrientation(int)` `int getLayoutOrientation()`	Set or get the way list cells are laid out. The possible layout formats are specified by the `JList`-defined values `VERTICAL` (a single column of cells; the default), `HORIZONTAL_WRAP` ("newspaper" style with the content flowing horizontally then vertically), and `VERTICAL_WRAP` ("newspaper" style with the content flowing vertically then horizontally). Introduced in 1.4.
`int getFirstVisibleIndex()` `int getLastVisibleIndex()`	Get the index of the first or last visible item.
`void ensureIndexIsVisible(int)`	Scroll so that the specified index is visible within the viewport that this list is in.

Table 46: Managing the List's Selection

Method	Purpose
`void addListSelectionListener(` `        ListSelectionListener)`	Register to receive notification of selection changes.

`void setSelectedIndex(int)`
`void setSelectedIndices(int[])`
`void setSelectedValue(Object, boolean)`
`void setSelectionInterval(int, int)`
	Set the current selection as indicated. Use `setSelectionMode` to set what ranges of selections are acceptable. The boolean argument specifies whether the list should attempt to scroll itself so that the selected item is visible.

`int getSelectedIndex()`
`int getMinSelectionIndex()`
`int getMaxSelectionIndex()`
`int[] getSelectedIndices()`
`Object getSelectedValue()`
`Object[] getSelectedValues()`
	Get information about the current selection as indicated.

`void setSelectionMode(int)` `int getSelectionMode()`	Set or get the selection mode. Acceptable values are: `SINGLE_SELECTION`, `SINGLE_INTERVAL_SELECTION`, or `MULTIPLE_INTERVAL_SELECTION` (the default), which are defined in `ListSelectionModel`.
`void clearSelection()` `boolean isSelectionEmpty()`	Set or get whether any items are selected.
`boolean isSelectedIndex(int)`	Determine whether the specified index is selected.

Table 47: Managing List Data

Class or Method	Purpose

`int getNextMatch(`
`        String,`
`        int,`
`        javax.swing.text.Position.Bias)`
	Given the starting index, search through the list for an item that starts with the specified string and return that index (or -1 if the string isn't found). The third argument, which specifies the search direction, can be either `Position.Bias.Forward` or `Position.Bias.Backward`. For example, if you have a 6-item list, `getNextMatch("Matisse", 5, javax.swing.text.Position.Bias.Forward)` searches for the string "Matisse" in the item at index 5, then (if necessary) at index 0, index 1, and so on. Introduced in 1.4.

`void setDragEnabled(boolean)` `boolean getDragEnabled()`	Set or get the property that determines whether automatic drag handling is enabled. See How to Use Drag and Drop and Data Transfer (page 545) for more details. Introduced in 1.4.

Examples That Use Lists

This table shows the examples that use `JList` and where those examples are described.

Example	Where Described	Notes
SplitPaneDemo	How to Use Split Panes (page 369)	Contains a single-selection, immutable list.
ListDemo	This section	Demonstrates how to add and remove items from a list at runtime.
ListDialog	This section and How to Use BoxLayout (page 462)	Implements a modal dialog with a single-selection list.
ListDataEventDemo	How to Write a List Data Listener (page 682)	Demonstrates listening for list data events on a list model.
ListSelectionDemo	How to Write a List Selection Listener (page 685)	Contains a list and a table that share the same selection model. You can dynamically choose the selection mode.

L

Components

275

Example	Where Described	Notes
`SharedModelDemo`	Using Models (page 50)	Modifies `ListSelectionDemo` so that the list and table share the same data model.
`CustomComboBox-Demo`	Providing a Custom Renderer (page 181)	Shows how to provide a custom renderer for a combo box. Because lists and combo boxes use the same type of renderer, you can use what you learn there and apply it to lists. In fact, a list and a combo box can share a renderer.

How to Use Menus

A menu provides a space-saving way to let the user choose one of several options. Other components with which the user can make a one-of-many choice include combo boxes, lists, radio buttons, spinners, and tool bars. If any of your menu items performs an action that is duplicated by another menu item or by a tool-bar button, then in addition to this section you should read How to Use Actions (page 513) in Chapter 9.

Menus are unique in that, by convention, they aren't placed with the other components in the UI. Instead, a menu usually appears either in a *menu bar* or as a *popup menu*. A menu bar contains one or more menus and has a customary, platform-dependent location—usually along the top of a window. A popup menu is a menu that is invisible until the user performs a platform-specific mouse action, such as pressing the right mouse button, over a popup-enabled component. The popup menu then appears under the cursor.

Figure 31 shows many of Swing's menu-related components: a menu bar, menus, menu items, radio button menu items, check box menu items, and separators. As you can see, a menu item can have either an image or text, or both. You can also specify other properties, such as font and color.

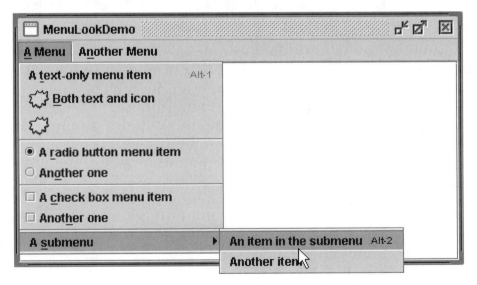

Figure 31 The MenuLookDemo example shows many menu-related components.

The Menu Component Hierarchy

As Figure 32 shows, menu items (including menus) are simply buttons.[1] You might be wondering how a menu, if it's only a button, shows its menu items. The answer is that when a menu is activated, it automatically brings up a popup menu that displays the menu items.

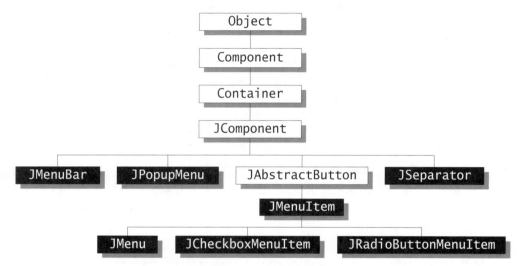

Figure 32 The inheritance hierarchy for the menu-related classes.

Creating Menus

The following code creates the menus shown in Figure 31. The bold lines of code create and connect the menu objects; the other code sets up or customizes the menu objects. You can find the entire program in MenuLookDemo.java. You can run MenuLookDemo using Java Web Start or compile and run the example yourself.[2]

Note: Because this code has no event handling, the menus do nothing useful except look like they should. If you run the example, you'll notice that despite the lack of custom event handling, menus and submenus appear when they should, and the check boxes and radio buttons respond appropriately when the user chooses them.

---

[1] All the menu-related classes in Figure 32 are in the javax.swing package. You can find their API documentation using a URL such as: http://java.sun.com/j2se/1.4.2/docs/api/javax/swing/ JMenu.html.

[2] To run MenuLookDemo using Java Web Start, click the MenuLookDemo link on the RunExamples/ components.html page on the CD. You can find the source files here: JavaTutorial/uiswing/ components/example-1dot4/index.html#MenuLookDemo.

```
//Where the GUI is created:
JMenuBar menuBar;
JMenu menu, submenu;
JMenuItem menuItem;
JCheckBoxMenuItem cbMenuItem;
JRadioButtonMenuItem rbMenuItem;
...
//Create the menu bar.
menuBar = new JMenuBar();
setJMenuBar(menuBar);

//Build the first menu.
menu = new JMenu("A Menu");
menu.setMnemonic(KeyEvent.VK_A);
menu.getAccessibleContext().setAccessibleDescription(
        "The only menu in this program that has menu items");
menuBar.add(menu);

//a group of JMenuItems
menuItem = new JMenuItem("A text-only menu item",
                        KeyEvent.VK_T);
menuItem.setAccelerator(KeyStroke.getKeyStroke(
        KeyEvent.VK_1, ActionEvent.ALT_MASK));
menuItem.getAccessibleContext().setAccessibleDescription(
        "This doesn't really do anything");
menu.add(menuItem);

menuItem = new JMenuItem("Both text and icon",
                        new ImageIcon("images/middle.gif"));
menuItem.setMnemonic(KeyEvent.VK_B);
menu.add(menuItem);

menuItem = new JMenuItem(new ImageIcon("images/middle.gif"));
menuItem.setMnemonic(KeyEvent.VK_D);
menu.add(menuItem);

//a group of radio button menu items
menu.addSeparator();
ButtonGroup group = new ButtonGroup();
rbMenuItem = new JRadioButtonMenuItem("A radio button menu item");
rbMenuItem.setSelected(true);
rbMenuItem.setMnemonic(KeyEvent.VK_R);
group.add(rbMenuItem);
menu.add(rbMenuItem);

rbMenuItem = new JRadioButtonMenuItem("Another one");
rbMenuItem.setMnemonic(KeyEvent.VK_O);
group.add(rbMenuItem);
menu.add(rbMenuItem);
```

M

Components

```
//a group of check box menu items
menu.addSeparator();
cbMenuItem = new JCheckBoxMenuItem("A check box menu item");
cbMenuItem.setMnemonic(KeyEvent.VK_C);
menu.add(cbMenuItem);

cbMenuItem = new JCheckBoxMenuItem("Another one");
cbMenuItem.setMnemonic(KeyEvent.VK_H);
menu.add(cbMenuItem);

//a submenu
menu.addSeparator();
submenu = new JMenu("A submenu");
submenu.setMnemonic(KeyEvent.VK_S);

menuItem = new JMenuItem("An item in the submenu");
menuItem.setAccelerator(KeyStroke.getKeyStroke(
        KeyEvent.VK_2, ActionEvent.ALT_MASK));
submenu.add(menuItem);

menuItem = new JMenuItem("Another item");
submenu.add(menuItem);
menu.add(submenu);

//Build second menu in the menu bar.
menu = new JMenu("Another Menu");
menu.setMnemonic(KeyEvent.VK_N);
menu.getAccessibleContext().setAccessibleDescription(
        "This menu does nothing");
menuBar.add(menu);
```

As the code shows, to set the menu bar for a JFrame, you use the setJMenuBar method. To add a JMenu to a JMenuBar, you use the add(JMenu) method. To add menu items and submenus to a JMenu, you use the add(JMenuItem) method.

Note: Menu items, like other components, can be in at most one container. If you try to add a menu item to a second menu, it will be removed from the first menu before being added to the second. For a way of implementing multiple components that do the same thing, see How to Use Actions (page 513) in Chapter 9.

Other methods in the preceding code include setAccelerator and setMnemonic, which are discussed next in Enabling Keyboard Operation (page 282). The setAccessible-Description method is discussed in How to Support Assistive Technologies (page 519) in Chapter 9.

Handling Events from Menu Items

To detect when the user selects a JMenuItem,[1] you can listen for action events (just as you would for a JButton). To detect when the user selects a JRadioButtonMenuItem,[2] you can listen for either action events or item events, as described in How to Use Radio Buttons (page 311). For JCheckBoxMenuItems,[3] you generally listen for item events, as described in How to Use Check Boxes (page 163).

Figure 33 shows the GUI for a program called MenuDemo. It looks just like MenuLookDemo, but it reacts when the user chooses a menu item. You can run MenuDemo using Java Web Start or compile and run the example yourself.[4]

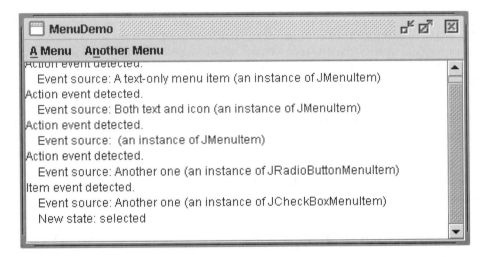

Figure 33   MenuDemo adds event listeners to MenuLookDemo.

---

1 JMenuItem API documentation: `http://java.sun.com/j2se/1.4.2/docs/api/javax/swing/JMenuItem.html`.

2 JRadioButtonMenuItem API documentation: `http://java.sun.com/j2se/1.4.2/docs/api/javax/swing/JRadioButtonMenuItem.html`.

3 JCheckBoxMenuItem API documentation: `http://java.sun.com/j2se/1.4.2/docs/api/javax/swing/JCheckBoxMenuItem.html`.

4 To run MenuDemo using Java Web Start, click the MenuDemo link on the RunExamples/components.html page on the CD. You can find the source files here: JavaTutorial/uiswing/components/example-1dot4/index.html#MenuDemo.

M

Components

Here's the code that implements the event handling in MenuDemo:

```
public class MenuDemo ... implements ActionListener,
                                     ItemListener {
    ...
        //...Where the menu bar's contents are constructed:
        //for each JMenuItem instance:
        menuItem.addActionListener(this);
        ...
        //for each JRadioButtonMenuItem:
        rbMenuItem.addActionListener(this);
        ...
        //for each JCheckBoxMenuItem:
        cbMenuItem.addItemListener(this);
        ...

    public void actionPerformed(ActionEvent e) {
        //...Get information from the action event...
        //...Display it in the text area...
    }

    public void itemStateChanged(ItemEvent e) {
        //...Get information from the item event...
        //...Display it in the text area...
    }
```

For examples of handling action and item events, see the button, radio button, and check box sections, as well as the Examples That Use Menus (page 290) section.

Enabling Keyboard Operation

Menus support two kinds of keyboard alternatives: mnemonics and accelerators. *Mnemonics* offer a way to use the keyboard to navigate the menu hierarchy, increasing the accessibility of programs. *Accelerators*, on the other hand, offer keyboard shortcuts to *bypass* navigating the menu hierarchy. Mnemonics are for all users; accelerators are for power users.

A mnemonic is a key that makes an already visible menu item be chosen. For example, in MenuDemo the first menu has the mnemonic A, and its second menu item has the mnemonic B. This means that, when you run MenuDemo with the Java look and feel, pressing the Alt and A keys makes the first menu appear. While the first menu is visible, pressing the B key (with or without Alt) makes the second menu item be chosen. A menu item generally displays its mnemonic by underlining the first occurrence of the mnemonic character in the menu item's text, as the snapshot in Figure 34 shows.

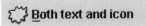

Figure 34   A menu item with the mnemonic character "B."

An accelerator is a key combination that causes a menu item to be chosen, whether or not it's visible. For example, pressing the Alt and 2 keys in MenuDemo makes the first item in the first menu's submenu be chosen, without bringing up any menus. Only leaf menu items—menus that don't bring up other menus—can have accelerators. The snapshot in Figure 35 shows how the Java look and feel displays a menu item that has an accelerator.

Figure 35   A menu item with the accelerator "Alt+2."

You can specify a mnemonic either when constructing the menu item or with the setMnemonic method. To specify an accelerator, use the setAccelerator method. Here are examples of setting mnemonics and accelerators:

```
//Setting the mnemonic when constructing a menu item:
menuItem = new JMenuItem("A text-only menu item",
                    KeyEvent.VK_T);

//Setting the mnemonic after creation time:
menuItem.setMnemonic(KeyEvent.VK_T);

//Setting the accelerator:
menuItem.setAccelerator(KeyStroke.getKeyStroke(
        KeyEvent.VK_T, ActionEvent.ALT_MASK));
```

As you can see, you set a mnemonic by specifying the KeyEvent[1] constant corresponding to the key the user should press. To specify an accelerator you must use a KeyStroke[2] object, which combines a key (specified by a KeyEvent constant) and a modifier-key mask (specified by an ActionEvent constant).

---

[1] KeyEvent API documentation: http://java.sun.com/j2se/1.4.2/docs/api/java/awt/event/
    KeyEvent.html.
[2] KeyStroke API documentation: http://java.sun.com/j2se/1.4.2/docs/api/javax/swing/
    KeyStroke.html.

M

Components

Note: Because popup menus, unlike regular menus, aren't always contained by a component, accelerators in popup menu items don't work unless the popup menu is visible.

Bringing up a Popup Menu

To bring up a popup menu (JPopupMenu), you must register a mouse listener on each component that the popup menu should be associated with. The mouse listener must detect user requests the popup menu to be brought up.

The exact gesture that should bring up a popup menu varies by look and feel. In Microsoft Windows, the user by convention brings up a popup menu by releasing the right mouse button while the cursor is over a component that is popup-enabled. In the Java look and feel, the customary trigger is either pressing the right mouse button (for a popup that goes away when the button is released) or clicking it (for a popup that stays up).[1]

The mouse listener brings up the popup menu by invoking the show method on the appropriate JPopupMenu instance. The following code, taken from PopupMenuDemo.java, shows how to create and show popup menus. You can run PopupMenuDemo using Java Web Start or compile and run the example yourself.[2]

```
//...where instance variables are declared:
JPopupMenu popup;

    //...where the GUI is constructed:
    //Create the popup menu.
    popup = new JPopupMenu();
    menuItem = new JMenuItem("A popup menu item");
    menuItem.addActionListener(this);
    popup.add(menuItem);
    menuItem = new JMenuItem("Another popup menu item");
    menuItem.addActionListener(this);
    popup.add(menuItem);

    //Add listener to components that can bring up popup menus.
    MouseListener popupListener = new PopupListener();
    output.addMouseListener(popupListener);
    menuBar.addMouseListener(popupListener);
...
```

---

[1] In a future release, a new mechanism for automatically triggering popup menus in the appropriate way for the look and feel might be added. You can follow bug #4634626 online at: http://developer.java.sun.com/developer/bugParade/bugs/4634626.html.

[2] To run PopupMenuDemo using Java Web Start, click the PopupMenuDemo link on the RunExamples/components.html page on the CD. You can find the source files here: JavaTutorial/uiswing/components/example-1dot4/index.html#PopupMenuDemo.

```
class PopupListener extends MouseAdapter {
    public void mousePressed(MouseEvent e) {
        maybeShowPopup(e);
    }

    public void mouseReleased(MouseEvent e) {
        maybeShowPopup(e);
    }

    private void maybeShowPopup(MouseEvent e) {
        if (e.isPopupTrigger()) {
            popup.show(e.getComponent(),
                        e.getX(), e.getY());
        }
    }
}
```

Popup menus have a few interesting implementation details. One is that every menu has an associated popup menu. When the menu is activated, it uses its associated popup menu to show its menu items.

Another detail is that a popup menu itself uses another component to implement the window containing the menu items. Depending on the circumstances under which the popup menu is displayed, the popup menu might implement its "window" using a lightweight component (such as a JPanel), a "mediumweight" component (such as a Panel), or a heavyweight window (something that inherits from Window).

Lightweight popup windows are more efficient than heavyweight windows, but they don't work well if you have any heavyweight components inside your GUI. Specifically, when the lightweight popup's display area intersects the heavyweight component's display area, the heavyweight component is drawn on top. This is one of the reasons we recommend against mixing heavyweight and lightweight components. If you absolutely need to use a heavyweight component in your GUI, then you can invoke JPopupMenu.setLightWeightPopup-Enabled(false) to disable lightweight popup windows.[1]

Customizing Menu Layout

Because menus are made up of ordinary Swing components, you can easily customize them. For example, you can add any lightweight component to a JMenu or JMenuBar. And because JMenuBar uses BoxLayout, you can customize a menu bar's layout just by adding invisible components to it. Here's an example of adding a glue component to a menu bar so that the last menu is at the right edge of the menu bar:

---

[1] For details, see *The Swing Connection* article "Mixing Heavy and Light Components" online at: http://java.sun.com/products/jfc/tsc/articles/mixing/index.html.

```
//...create and add some menus...
menuBar.add(Box.createHorizontalGlue());
//...create the rightmost menu...
menuBar.add(rightMenu);
```

Figure 36 shows the result. You can run `MenuGlueDemo` using Java Web Start or compile and  run the example yourself.[1]

Figure 36 A screenshot of the `MenuGlueDemo` example in which Menu 3 is "glued" to the right side of the menu bar.

Another way of changing the look of menus is to change the layout managers used to control them. For example, you can change a menu bar's layout manager from the default left-to-right `BoxLayout` to something such as `GridLayout`. You can also change how an activated menu or other popup menu lays out its items, as `MenuLayoutDemo.java` demonstrates. (See Figure 37.) You can run `MenuLayoutDemo` using Java Web Start or compile and run the example yourself.[2]

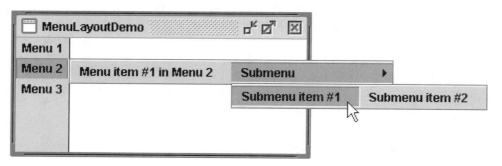

Figure 37 A picture of the menu layout that `MenuLayoutDemo` creates.

---

[1] To run `MenuGlueDemo` using Java Web Start, click the `MenuGlueDemo` link on the `RunExamples/components.html` page on the CD. You can find the source files here: `JavaTutorial/uiswing/components/example-1dot4/index.html#MenuGlueDemo`.

[2] To run `MenuLayoutDemo` using Java Web Start, click the `MenuLayoutDemo` link on the `RunExamples/components.html` page on the CD. You can find the source files here: `JavaTutorial/uiswing/components/example-1dot4/index.html#MenuLayoutDemo`.

The Menu API

Tables 48 through 51 list the commonly used menu constructors and methods.

Table 48: Creating and Setting up Menu Bars

Constructor or Method	Purpose
`JMenuBar()`	Create a menu bar.
`JMenu add(JMenu)`	Create a menu bar.

`void setJMenuBar(JMenuBar)`
`JMenuBar getJMenuBar()`
(*in* `JApplet, JDialog, JFrame,`
`    JInternalFrame, JRootPane`)
	Set or get the menu bar of an applet, dialog, frame, internal frame, or root pane.

Table 49: Creating and Populating Menus

Constructor or Method	Purpose

`JMenu()`
`JMenu(String)`
`JMenu(Action)`
	Create a menu. The string specifies the text to display for the menu. The `Action` specifies the text and other properties of the menu. See How to Use Actions (page 513). The constructor taking the `Action` parameter was introduced in 1.3.

`JMenuItem add(JMenuItem)` `JMenuItem add(String)`	Add a menu item to the current end of the menu. If the argument is a string, then the menu automatically creates a `JMenuItem` object that displays the specified text. **Version Note:** Before 1.3, the only way to associate an `Action` with a menu item was to use menu's `add(Action)` method to create the menu item and add it to the menu. As of 1.3, that method is no longer recommended. You can instead associate a menu item with an `Action` using the `setAction` method.
`void addSeparator()`	Add a separator to the current end of the menu.

`JMenuItem insert(`
`        JMenuItem, int)`
`void insert(String, int)`
`void insertSeparator(int)`
	Insert a menu item or separator into the menu at the specified position. The first menu item is at position 0, the second at position 1, and so on. The `JMenuItem` and `String` arguments are treated the same as in the corresponding add methods.

`void remove(JMenuItem)`
`void remove(int)`
`void removeAll()`
	Remove the specified item(s) from the menu. If the argument is an integer, then it specifies the position of the menu item to be removed.

M

Components

Table 50: Creating, Populating, and Controlling Popup Menus

Constructor or Method	Purpose
`JPopupMenu()` `JPopupMenu(String)`	Create a popup menu. The optional string argument specifies the title that a look and feel might display as part of the popup window.
`JMenuItem add(JMenuItem)` `JMenuItem add(String)`	Add a menu item to the current end of the popup menu. If the argument is a string, then the menu automatically creates a `JMenuItem` object that displays the specified text. **Version Note:** Before 1.3, the only way to associate an `Action` with an item in a popup menu was to use the popup menu's `add(Action)` method to create the menu item and add it to the popup menu. As of 1.3, that method is no longer recommended. You can instead associate a menu item with an `Action` using the `setAction` method.
`void addSeparator()`	Add a separator to the current end of the popup menu.
`void insert(Component, int)`	Insert a menu item into the menu at the specified position. The first menu item is at position 0, the second at position 1, and so on. The `Component` argument specifies the menu item to add.
`void remove(int)` `void removeAll()`	Remove the specified item(s) from the menu. If the argument is an integer, then it specifies the position of the menu item to be removed.
`static void` `    setLightWeightPopupEnabled(boolean)`	By default, Swing implements a menu's window using a lightweight component. This can cause problems if you use any heavyweight components in your Swing program, as described in Bringing up a Popup Menu (page 284). (This is one of several reasons to avoid using heavyweight components.) As a workaround, invoke `JPopupMenu.setLightWeightPopupEnabled(false)`.

`void show(Component,`
`        int,`
`        int)`
	Display the popup menu at the specified x,y position (specified in that order by the integer arguments) in the coordinate system of the specified component.

Table 51: Implementing Menu Items[a]

Constructor or Method	Purpose

`JMenuItem()`
`JMenuItem(String)`
`JMenuItem(Icon)`
`JMenuItem(String, Icon)`
`JMenuItem(String, int)`
`JMenuItem(Action)`
	Create an ordinary menu item. The icon argument, if present, specifies the icon that the menu item should display. Similarly, the string argument specifies the text that the menu item should display. The integer argument specifies the keyboard mnemonic to use. You can specify any of the relevant VK constants defined in the KeyEvent class. For example, to specify the A key, use KeyEvent.VK_A.
	
	The constructor with the Action parameter, which was introduced in 1.3, sets the menu item's Action, causing the menu item's properties to be initialized from the Action. See How to Use Actions (page 513) for details.

`JCheckBoxMenuItem()`
`JCheckBoxMenuItem(String)`
`JCheckBoxMenuItem(Icon)`
`JCheckBoxMenuItem(String, Icon)`
`JCheckBoxMenuItem(String, boolean)`
`JCheckBoxMenuItem(String,`
`                  Icon,`
`                  boolean)`
	Create a menu item that looks and acts like a check box. The string argument, if any, specifies the text that the menu item should display. If you specify true for the boolean argument, then the menu item is initially selected (checked). Otherwise, the menu item is initially unselected.

`JRadioButtonMenuItem()`
`JRadioButtonMenuItem(String)`
`JRadioButtonMenuItem(Icon)`
`JRadioButtonMenuItem(String,`
`                     Icon)`
`JRadioButtonMenuItem(String,`
`                     boolean)`
`JRadioButtonMenuItem(Icon,`
`                     boolean)`
`JRadioButtonMenuItem(String,`
`                     Icon,`
`                     boolean)`
	Create a menu item that looks and acts like a radio button. The string argument, if any, specifies the text that the menu item should display. If you specify true for the boolean argument, then the menu item is initially selected. Otherwise, the menu item is initially unselected.

`void setState(boolean)`
`boolean getState()`
(*in* `JCheckBoxMenuItem`)
	Set or get the selection state of a check box menu item.

`void setEnabled(boolean)`	If the argument is true, enable the menu item. Otherwise, disable the menu item.
`void setMnemonic(int)`	Set the mnemonic that enables keyboard navigation to the menu or menu item. Use one of the VK constants defined in the KeyEvent class.
`void setAccelerator(KeyStroke)`	Set the accelerator that activates the menu item.

M

Components

Table 51: Implementing Menu Items[a] *(continued)*

Constructor or Method	Purpose
void setActionCommand(String)	Set the name of the action performed by the menu item.
void addActionListener(ActionListener) void addItemListener(ItemListener)	Add an event listener to the menu item. See Handling Events from Menu Items (page 281) for details.
void setAction(Action)	Set the Action associated with the menu item. See How to Use Actions (page 513) for details.

a. These methods are inherited from AbstractButton. See The Button API (page 160) for information about other useful methods that AbstractButton provides.

Examples That Use Menus

The following examples use menus.

Example	Where Described	Notes
MenuLookDemo	This section	A simple example that creates all kinds of menus except popup menus, but doesn't handle events from the menu items.
MenuDemo	This section	Adds event handling to MenuLookDemo.
PopupMenuDemo	This section	Adds popup menus to MenuDemo.
MenuGlueDemo	This section	Demonstrates affecting menu layout by adding an invisible components to the menu bar.
MenuLayoutDemo	This section	Implements sideways-opening menus arranged in a vertical menu bar.
ActionDemo	How to Use Actions (page 513)	Uses Action objects to implement menu items that duplicate functionality provided by tool bar buttons.
Framework	—	Brings up multiple identical frames, each with a menu in its menu bar.
InternalFrameDemo	How to Use Internal Frames (page 245)	Uses a menu item to create windows.

Example	Where Described	Notes
`DragColorTextField-Demo`	How to Use Drag and Drop and Data Transfer (page 545)	Sets up menu items for cut/copy/paste.
`DragPictureDemo`	How to Use Drag and Drop and Data Transfer (page 545)	Sets up menu items for cut/copy/paste with a non-text component.

M

Components

How to Use Panels

The JPanel[1] class provides general-purpose containers for lightweight components. By default, panels don't paint anything except their background; however, you can easily add borders to them. Borders are covered in How to Use Borders (page 535) in Chapter 9.

In many look and feels (but not GTK+), panels are opaque by default. Opaque panels work well as content panes and can help painting efficiency, as described in Chapter 6. You can toggle a panel's transparency by invoking setOpaque. A transparent panel draws no background, so any components underneath show through.

An Example

Figure 38 shows a shaded version of the Converter application, which is discussed in more detail in Using Models (page 50).

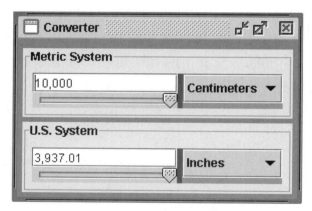

Figure 38   A screenshot of the Converter applications with several of its JPanels shaded.

Converter uses panels in several ways (as shown in Figure 39):

- One JPanel instance (shaded black) serves as a content pane for the application's frame. This content pane uses a top-to-bottom BoxLayout to lay out its contents, and an empty border to put 5 pixels of space around them. See Using Top-Level Containers (page 46) for information about content panes.

---

[1] JPanel API documentation: http://java.sun.com/j2se/1.4.2/docs/api/javax/swing/JPanel.html.

- Two instances of a custom `JPanel` subclass named `ConversionPanel` are used to both contain components and coordinate communication between components. The panels also have titled borders, which describe their contents and paint a line around them. Each panel uses a left-to-right `BoxLayout` object to lay out its contents.

- In each `ConversionPanel`, a `JPanel` instance is used to ensure that a combo box is at the right size and position. Each panel uses a top-to-bottom `BoxLayout` object (helped by an invisible space-filling component) to lay out the combo box.

- In each `ConversionPanel`, an instance of an unnamed `JPanel` subclass groups two components (a text field and a slider) and restricts their size. Each panel uses a top-to-bottom `BoxLayout` object to lay out its contents.

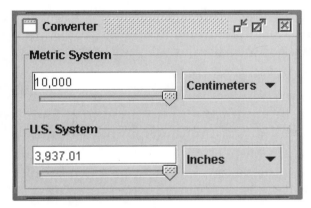

Figure 39   A screenshot of what `Converter` normally looks like (without shading).

As `Converter` demonstrates, panels are useful for grouping components, simplifying component layout, and putting borders around groups of components. The rest of this section gives hints on grouping and laying out components. For information about using borders, see How to Use Borders (page 535) in Chapter 9.

Setting the Layout Manager

Like other containers, a panel uses a layout manager to position and size its components. By default, a panel's layout manager is an instance of `FlowLayout`, which places the panel's contents in a row. You can easily make a panel use any other layout manager by invoking the `setLayout` method or specifying a layout manager when creating the panel. The latter approach is preferable for performance reasons, since it avoids the unnecessary creation of a `FlowLayout` object.

Here's an example of setting the layout manager when creating the panel:

```
JPanel p = new JPanel(new BorderLayout()); //PREFERRED!
```

This approach doesn't work with BoxLayout, since the BoxLayout constructor requires a pre-existing container. Here's an example that uses BoxLayout:

```
JPanel p = new JPanel();
p.setLayout(new BoxLayout(p, BoxLayout.PAGE_AXIS));
```

Adding Components

When you add components to a panel, you use the add method. Exactly which arguments you specify to the add method depend on which layout manager the panel uses. When the layout manager is FlowLayout, BoxLayout, GridLayout, or SpringLayout, you'll typically use the one-argument add method, like this:

```
aFlowPanel.add(aComponent);
aFlowPanel.add(anotherComponent);
```

When the layout manager is BorderLayout, you need to provide an argument specifying the added component's position within the panel. For example:

```
aBorderPanel.add(aComponent, BorderLayout.CENTER);
aBorderPanel.add(anotherComponent, BorderLayout.PAGE_END);
```

With GridBagLayout you can use either add method, but you must somehow specify grid bag constraints for each component.

For information about using the standard layout managers, see Chapter 4, Laying Out Components within a Container (page 87).

The Panel API

The API in the JPanel class itself is minimal. The methods you are most likely to invoke on a JPanel object are those it inherits from its superclasses—JComponent, Container, and Component. Tables 52 through 54 list the API you're most likely to use, with the exception of methods related to borders and layout hints.

For more information about the API all JComponents can use, see The JComponent Class (page 53). Also refer to the JPanel API documentation at: `http://java.sun.com/j2se/1.4.2/docs/api/javax/swing/JPanel.html`.

Table 52: Creating a JPanel

Constructor	Purpose
JPanel() JPanel(LayoutManager)	Create a panel. The LayoutManager parameter provides a layout manager for the new panel. By default, a panel uses a FlowLayout to lay out its components.

Table 53: Managing a Container's Components

Method	Purpose
void add(Component) void add(Component, int) void add(Component, Object) void add(Component, Object, int) void add(String, Component)	Add the specified component to the panel. When present, the int parameter is the index of the component within the container. By default, the first component added is at index 0, the second is at index 1, and so on. The Object parameter is layout manager dependent and typically provides information to the layout manager regarding positioning and other layout constraints for the added component. The String parameter is similar to the Object parameter.
int getComponentCount()	Get the number of components in this panel.
Component getComponent(int) Component getComponentAt(int, int) Component getComponentAt(Point) Component[] getComponents()	Get the specified component or components. You can get a component based on its index or *x, y* position.
void remove(Component) void remove(int) void removeAll()	Remove the specified component(s).

Table 54: Setting/Getting the Layout Manager

Method	Purpose
void setLayout(LayoutManager) LayoutManager getLayout()	Set or get the layout manager for this panel. The layout manager is responsible for positioning the panel's components within the panel's bounds according to some philosophy.

P

Components

295

Examples That Use Panels

Many examples in this book use `JPanel` objects. The following table lists a few.

Example	Where Described	Notes
Converter	This section and An Example: Converter (page 51)	Uses five panels, four of which use `BoxLayout` and one of which uses `GridLayout`. The panels use borders and, as necessary, size and alignment hints to affect layout.
ListDemo	How to Use Lists (page 267)	Uses a panel, with its default `FlowLayout` manager, to center three components in a row.
ToolBarDemo	How to Use Tool Bars (page 427)	Uses a panel as a content pane. The panel contains three components, laid out by `BorderLayout`.
BorderDemo	How to Use Borders (page 535)	Contains many panels that have various kinds of borders. Several panels use `BoxLayout`.
BoxLayoutDemo	How to Use BoxLayout (page 462)	Illustrates the use of a panel with Swing's `BoxLayout` manager.

How to Use Password Fields

The JPasswordField[1] class, a subclass of JTextField, provides text fields specialized for password entry. (See Figure 40.) For security reasons, a password field doesn't show the characters the user types. Instead, the field displays another character such as an asterisk (*). As another security precaution, a password field stores its value as an array of characters, rather than as a string. Like an ordinary text field, a password field fires an action event when the user indicates that text entry is complete, such as by pressing the Enter key.

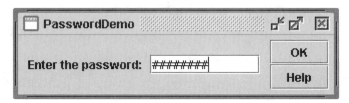

Figure 40   PasswordDemo brings up a small window and prompts the user to type in a password.

You can run PasswordDemo using Java Web Start or compile and run the example yourself.[2] Here's the code that creates and sets up the password field:

```
passwordField = new JPasswordField(10);
passwordField.setEchoChar('#');
passwordField.setActionCommand(OK);
passwordField.addActionListener(this);
```

The argument passed into the JPasswordField constructor indicates the preferred size of the field—at least 10 columns wide in this case. By default a password field displays an asterisk (*) for each character typed. The call to setEchoChar changes it to a pound sign (#). Finally, the code adds an action listener to the password field, which checks the value typed in by the user. Here's the implementation of the action listener's actionPerformed method:

```
public void actionPerformed(ActionEvent e) {
    String cmd = e.getActionCommand();
```

---

[1] JPasswordField API documentation: http://java.sun.com/j2se/1.4.2/docs/api/javax/ swing/JPasswordField.html.

[2] To run PasswordDemo using Java Web Start, click the PasswordDemo link on the RunExamples/ components.html page on the CD. You can find the source files here: JavaTutorial/uiswing/ components/example-1dot4/index.html#PasswordDemo.

```
  if (OK.equals(cmd)) { //Process the password.
      char[] input = passwordField.getPassword();
      if (isPasswordCorrect(input)) {
          JOptionPane.showMessageDialog(controllingFrame,
              "Success! You typed the right password.");
      } else {
          JOptionPane.showMessageDialog(controllingFrame,
              "Invalid password. Try again.",
              "Error Message",
              JOptionPane.ERROR_MESSAGE);
      }

      //Zero out the possible password, for security.
      for (int i = 0; i < input.length; i++) {
          input[i] = 0;
      }

      passwordField.selectAll();
      resetFocus();
  } else ...//handle the Help button...
}
```

Security Note: Although the JPasswordField class inherits the getText method, you should use the getPassword method instead. Not only is getText less secure, but in the future it might return the visible string instead of the typed-in string. To further enhance security, once you are finished with the character array returned by getPassword, you should set each of its elements to zero. The preceding code snippet shows how to do this.

A program using a password field typically validates the password before completing any actions requiring the password. This program calls a private method, isPasswordCorrect, that compares the value returned by getPassword to a value stored in a character array. Here's its code:

```
private static boolean isPasswordCorrect(char[] input) {
    boolean isCorrect = true;
    char[] correctPassword = { 'b', 'u', 'g', 'a', 'b', 'o', 'o' };

    if (input.length != correctPassword.length) {
        isCorrect = false;
    } else {
        for (int i = 0; i < input.length; i++) {
            if (input[i] != correctPassword[i]) {
                isCorrect = false;
            }
        }
    }
```

```
    //Zero out the password.
    for (int i = 0; i < correctPassword.length; i++) {
        correctPassword[i] = 0;
    }

    return isCorrect;
}
```

The Password Field API

Table 55 lists the commonly used JPasswordField constructors and methods. For information on the API that password fields inherit, see How to Use Text Fields (page 423).

Table 55: Commonly Used JPasswordField Constructors and Methods

Constructor or Method	Purpose
JPasswordField() JPasswordField(String) JPasswordField(String, int) JPasswordField(int) JPasswordField(Document, String, int)	Create a password field. When present, the int argument specifies the desired width in columns. The String argument contains the field's initial text. The Document argument provides a custom model for the field.
char[] getPassword()	Set or get the text displayed by the password field.
void setEchoChar(char) char getEchoChar()	Set or get the echo character—the character displayed instead of the actual characters typed by the user.
void addActionListener(ActionListener) void removeActionListener(ActionListener) *(defined in* JTextField*)*	Add or remove an action listener.
void selectAll() *(defined in* JTextComponent*)*	Select all characters in the password field.

Examples That Use Password Fields

The following examples use password fields. Also see Examples That Use Text Fields (page 426) for examples that use the API that password fields inherit.

Example	Where Described	Notes
PasswordDemo	This section	Implements a specialized panel that asks for a password and has OK and Help buttons.
TextSamplerDemo	Using Text Components (page 60)	Shows each kind of text component.

How to Use Progress Bars

Sometimes a task running within a program might take a while to complete. A user-friendly program provides some indication to the user that the task is occurring, how long the task might take, and how much work has already been done. One way of indicating work, and perhaps the amount of progress, is to use an animated image.

Another way of indicating work is to set the wait cursor, using the Cursor class and the Component-defined setCursor method. For example, the following code causes the wait cursor to be displayed when the cursor is over container (including any components it contains that have no cursor specified):

```
container.setCursor(Cursor.getPredefinedCursor(Cursor.WAIT_CURSOR));
```

To convey how complete a task is, you can use a progress bar like the one in Figure 41.

Figure 41   Standard progress bar.

Sometimes you can't immediately determine the length of a long-running task, or the task might stay stuck at the same state of completion for a long time. As of 1.4, you can show work without measurable progress by putting the progress bar in *indeterminate mode.* A progress bar in indeterminate mode displays animation to indicate that work is occurring. As soon as the progress bar can display more meaningful information, you should switch it back into its default, determinate mode. In the Java look and feel, indeterminate progress bars look like Figure 42.

Figure 42   Indeterminate progress bar.

Swing provides three classes to help you use progress bars:

JProgressBar
A visible component to graphically display how much of a total task has completed. The next section has information and an example of using a typical progress bar. The section after that, Using Indeterminate Mode (page 303), tells you how to animate a progress bar to show activity before the task's scope is known.

ProgressMonitor

> *Not* a visible component. Instead, an instance of this class monitors the progress of a task and pops up a dialog if necessary. See Using Progress Monitors (page 305) for details and an example of using a progress monitor.

ProgressMonitorInputStream

> An input stream with an attached progress monitor, which monitors reading from the stream. You use an instance of this stream like any of the other input streams described in *The Java Tutorial* trail, "I/O: Reading and Writing (but no 'rithmetic)."[1] You can get the stream's progress monitor with a call to getProgressMonitor and configure it as described in Using Progress Monitors (page 305).

> After you see a progress bar and a progress monitor in action, Deciding Whether to Use a Progress Bar or a Progress Monitor (page 307) can help you figure out which is appropriate for your application.

Using Determinate Progress Bars

Figure 43 is a picture of a small demo application that uses a progress bar to measure the progress of a task that runs in its own thread.

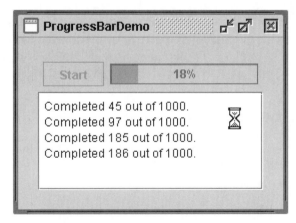

Figure 43   A screenshot of the ProgressBarDemo example. Note the use of the wait cursor (the hourglass).

---

[1]   This trail is on the CD at: JavaTutorial/essentials/index.html and on this book's CD.

P

Components

Try This:

1. Run `ProgressBarDemo` using Java Web Start or compile and run the example your-self.[1]

2. Push the **Start** button. The demo puts up a wait cursor and starts updating the progress bar. The task displays its output in the text area at the bottom of the window.

Below is the code from `ProgressBarDemo.java` that creates and sets up the progress bar:

```
//Where member variables are declared:
JProgressBar progressBar;
    //...where the GUI is created:
    progressBar = new JProgressBar(0, task.getLengthOfTask());
    progressBar.setValue(0);
    progressBar.setStringPainted(true);
```

The constructor that creates the progress bar sets the progress bar's minimum and maximum values. You can also set these values with `setMinimum` and `setMaximum`. The minimum and maximum values used in this program are 0 and the length of the task, which is typical of many programs and tasks. However, a progress bar's minimum and maximum values can be any value, even negative. The code snippet also sets the progress bar's current value to 0.

The call to `setStringPainted` causes the progress bar to display, within its bounds, a textual indication of the percentage of the task that has completed. By default, the progress bar displays the value returned by its `getPercentComplete` method formatted as a percent, such as 33%. Alternatively, you can replace the default with a different string by calling `set-String`. For example,

```
if (/*...half way done...*/)
    progressBar.setString("Half way there!");
```

You start `ProgressBarDemo`'s task by clicking the **Start** button. Once the task has begun, a timer (an instance of the `javax.swing.Timer` class) fires an action event every second. Here's the `actionPerformed` method of the timer's action listener:

```
public void actionPerformed(ActionEvent evt) {
    progressBar.setValue(task.getCurrent());
    String s = task.getMessage();
    if (s != null) {
        taskOutput.append(s + newline);
```

---

[1] To run `ProgressBarDemo` using Java Web Start, click the `ProgressBarDemo` link on the `RunExamples/components.html` page on the CD. You can find the source files here: `JavaTutorial/uiswing/components/example-1dot4/index.html#ProgressBarDemo`.

```
        taskOutput.setCaretPosition(
                taskOutput.getDocument().getLength());
    }
    if (task.isDone()) {
        Toolkit.getDefaultToolkit().beep();
        timer.stop();
        startButton.setEnabled(true);
        setCursor(null); //turn off the wait cursor
        progressBar.setValue(progressBar.getMinimum());
    }
}
```

The boldface line of code gets the amount of work completed by the task and updates the progress bar with that value. Thus, this example's progress bar measures the progress made by the task each second, *not* the elapsed time. The rest of the code appends a message to the output log (a text area named `taskOutput`) and, if the task is done, turns the timer off and resets the other controls and the cursor.

As mentioned, the long-running task in this program executes in a separate thread. Generally, it's a good idea to isolate a potentially long-running task in its own thread so that the task doesn't block the rest of the program. The long-running task is implemented by `Long-Task.java`, which uses a `SwingWorker` to ensure that the thread runs safely.[1] See Using the SwingWorker Class (page 636) in Chapter 9 for information about the `SwingWorker` class.

Using Indeterminate Mode

Adding indeterminate mode to `ProgressBarDemo` requires just a few lines of code (shown in bold):

```
//Where the progress bar is created:
progressBar.setStringPainted(true); //get space for the string
progressBar.setString("");          //but don't paint it
. . .
//In the actionPerformed method of the timer's action listener:
progressBar.setValue(task.getCurrent());
String s = task.getMessage();
if (s != null) {
    if (progressBar.isIndeterminate()) {
        progressBar.setIndeterminate(false);
        progressBar.setString(null); //display % string
    }
```

---

[1] You can find the source files here: `JavaTutorial/uiswing/components/example-1dot4/index.html#LongTask`.

```
            taskOutput.append(s + newline);
            taskOutput.setCaretPosition(
                    taskOutput.getDocument().getLength());
        }
        if (task.isDone()) {
            ...
            progressBar.setString(""); //hide % string
        }
        . . .
        //In the event handler that handles Start button clicks:
        progressBar.setIndeterminate(true);
```

The most important code additions are calls to the `setIndeterminate` method. When the user clicks the **Start** button, `setIndeterminate(true)` is invoked so that the user can tell that the task has started, even before any meaningful information about the task's progress can be conveyed. Once the progress bar has some concrete status to display, a call to `setIndeterminate(false)` switches the progress bar back into its normal mode. The `isIndeterminate` method is used to test the progress bar's current state.

The other changes in the code are related to string display. A progress bar that displays a string is likely to be taller than one that doesn't, and, as the demo designers, we've arbitrarily decided that this progress bar should display a string only when it's in the default, determinate mode. However, we want to avoid the layout ugliness that might result if the progress bar changed height when it changed modes. Thus, the code leaves in the call to `setStringPainted(true)` but adds a call to `setString("")` so that no text will be displayed. Later, when the progress bar switches from indeterminate to determinate mode, invoking `setString(null)` makes the progress bar display its default string.

One change we did *not* make was removing the call to `progressBar.setValue` from the timer's action handler. The call doesn't do any harm because an indeterminate progress bar doesn't use its *value* property, except perhaps to display it in the status string. In fact, keeping the progress bar's data as up to date as possible is a good practice, since some look and feels might not support indeterminate mode.

Try This:

1. Run `ProgressBarDemo2` using Java Web Start or compile and run the example yourself.[1]

2. Push the **Start** button. Note that the progress bar starts animating as soon as the button is pressed and then switches back into determinate mode (like `ProgressBarDemo`).

---

[1] To run `ProgressBarDemo2` using Java Web Start, click the `ProgressBarDemo2` link on the RunExamples/components.html page on the CD. You can find the source files here: `JavaTutorial/uiswing/components/example-1dot4/index.html#ProgressBarDemo2`.

Using Progress Monitors

Now let's rewrite `ProgressBarDemo` to use a progress monitor instead of a progress bar. (See Figure 44.)

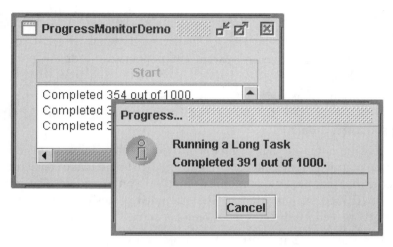

Figure 44   A screenshot of the new demo program, `ProgressMonitorDemo`.

Try This:

1. Run `ProgressMonitorDemo` using Java Web Start or compile and run the example yourself.[1]
2. Push the **Start** button. After a certain amount of time, the program displays a progress dialog.
3. Click the **OK** button. Note that the task continues even though the dialog is gone.
4. Start another task. After the dialog pops up, click the **Cancel** button. The dialog goes away and the task stops.

A progress monitor cannot be used again, so a new one must be created each time a new task is started. This program creates a progress monitor each time the user starts a new task with the **Start** button.

---

[1] To run `ProgressMonitorDemo` using Java Web Start, click the `ProgressMonitorDemo` link on the `RunExamples/components.html` page on the CD. You can find the source files here: `JavaTutorial/uiswing/components/example-1dot4/index.html#ProgressMonitorDemo`.

Here's the statement that creates the progress monitor:

```
progressMonitor = new ProgressMonitor(ProgressMonitorDemo.this,
                                      "Running a Long Task",
                                      "", 0, task.getLengthOfTask());
```

This code uses `ProgressMonitor`'s only constructor to create the monitor and initialize several arguments:

- The first argument provides the parent component to the dialog popped up by the progress monitor.

- The second argument is a string that describes the nature of the task being monitored. This string is displayed on the dialog. See The Progress Monitoring API (page 308) for details about this argument.

- The third argument is another string that provides a changeable status note. The example uses an empty string to indicate that the dialog should make space for a changeable status note, but that the note is initially empty. If you provide `null` for this argument, the note is omitted from the dialog. The example updates the note each time the timer fires an action event. It updates the monitor's current value at the same time:

```
progressMonitor.setNote(task.getMessage());
progressMonitor.setProgress(task.getCurrent());
```

- The last two arguments provide the minimum and maximum values, respectively, for the progress bar displayed in the dialog.

After the example creates the progress monitor, it configures the monitor further:

```
progressMonitor.setProgress(0);
progressMonitor.setMillisToDecideToPopup(2 * ONE_SECOND);
```

The first line sets the current position of the progress bar on the dialog. The second tells the progress monitor to wait two seconds before deciding whether to bring up a dialog. If, after two seconds, the progress monitor's progress is less than its maximum, the monitor will bring up the dialog.

By the simple fact that this example uses a progress monitor, it adds a feature that wasn't present in the version of the program that uses a progress bar: The user can cancel the task by clicking the **Cancel** button on the dialog. Here's the code in the example that checks to see if the user canceled the task or if the task exited normally:

```
if (progressMonitor.isCanceled() || task.done()) {
    progressMonitor.close();
    task.stop();
    Toolkit.getDefaultToolkit().beep();
```

```
        timer.stop();
        startButton.setEnabled(true);
    }
```

Note that the progress monitor doesn't itself cancel the task. It provides the GUI and API to allow the program to do so easily.

Deciding Whether to Use a Progress Bar or a Progress Monitor

Use a *progress bar* if:

- You want more control over the configuration of the progress bar. If you are working directly with a progress bar, you can set it to be indeterminate, make it display vertically, provide a string for it to display, register change listeners on it, and provide it with a bounded range model to control its minimum, maximum, and current values.
- The program needs to display other components along with the progress bar.
- You need more than one progress bar. With some tasks, you need to monitor more than one parameter. For example, an installation program might monitor disk space usage in addition to how many files have been successfully installed.
- You need to reuse the progress bar. A progress bar can be reused; a progress monitor cannot. Once the progress monitor has decided to display a dialog (or not), it cannot do it again.

Use a *progress monitor* if:

- You want an easy way to display progress in a dialog.
- The running task is secondary and the user might not be interested in the progress of the task. A progress monitor provides a way for the user to dismiss the dialog while the task is still running.
- You want an easy way for the task to be cancelled. A progress monitor provides a GUI for the user to cancel the task. All you have to do is call the progress monitor's `isCanceled` method to find out if the user pressed the **Cancel** button.
- Your task displays a short message periodically while running. The progress monitor dialog provides the `setNote` method so that the task can provide further information about what it's doing. For example, an installation task might report the name of each file as it's installed.
- The task might not take a long time to complete. You decide at what point a running task is taking long enough to warrant letting the user know about it. A progress monitor won't pop up a dialog if the task completes within the timeframe you set.
- If you decide to use a progress monitor *and* the task you are monitoring is reading from an input stream, use the `ProgressMonitorInputStream` class.

The Progress Monitoring API

Tables 56 through 61 list the commonly used API for progress bars and progress monitors. Because JProgressBar is a subclass of JComponent, other methods you are likely to call on a JProgressBar are listed in The JComponent Class (page 53). Note that ProgressMonitor is a subclass of Object and is not a visual component. Also see the API documentation for the JProgressBar and ProgressMonitor classes at:

```
http://java.sun.com/j2se/1.4.2/docs/api/javax/swing/JProgressBar.html
http://java.sun.com/j2se/1.4.2/docs/api/javax/swing/
       ProgressMonitor.html
```

Table 56: Creating the Progress Bar

Constructor	Purpose
JProgressBar() JProgressBar(int, int)	Create a horizontal progress bar. The no-argument constructor initializes the progress bar with a minimum and initial value of 0 and a maximum of 100. The constructor with two integer arguments specifies the minimum and maximum values.
JProgressBar(int) JProgressBar(int, int, int)	Create a progress bar with the specified orientation, which can be either JProgressBar.HORIZONTAL or JProgress-Bar.VERTICAL. The optional second and third arguments specify minimum and maximum values.
JProgressBar(BoundedRangeModel)	Create a horizontal progress bar with the specified range model.

Table 57: Setting or Getting the Progress Bar's Constraints/Values

Method	Purpose
void setValue(int) int getValue()	Set or get the current value of the progress bar. The value is constrained by the minimum and maximum values.
double getPercentComplete()	Get the percent complete for the progress bar.
void setMinimum(int) int getMinimum()	Set or get the minimum value of the progress bar.
void setMaximum(int) int getMaximum()	Set or get the maximum value of the progress bar.
void setModel(BoundedRangeModel) BoundedRangeModel getModel()	Set or get the model used by the progress bar. The model establishes the progress bar's constraints and values, so you can use it directly as an alternative to using the individual set/get methods listed above.

Table 58: Controlling the Progress Bar's Appearance

Method	Purpose
`void setIndeterminate(boolean)`	By specifying true, put the progress bar into indeterminate mode. Specifying false puts the progress bar back into its default, determinate mode. Introduced in 1.4.
`void setOrientation(int)` `int getOrientation()`	Set or get whether the progress bar is vertical or horizontal. Acceptable values are `JProgressBar.VERTICAL` or `JProgress-Bar.HORIZONTAL`.
`void setBorderPainted(boolean)` `boolean isBorderPainted()`	Set or get whether the progress bar has a border.
`void setStringPainted(boolean)` `boolean isStringPainted()`	Set or get whether the progress bar displays a percent string. By default, the value of the percent string is the value returned by `get-PercentComplete` formatted as a percent. You can set the string to be displayed with `setString`.
`void setString(String)` `String getString()`	Set or get the percent string.

Table 59: Creating the Progress Monitor

Method or Constructor	Purpose
`ProgressMonitor(Component, Object, String, int, int)`	Create a progress monitor. The `Component` argument is the parent for the monitor's dialog. The `Object` argument is a message to put on the option pane within the dialog. The value of this object is typically a `String`. The `String` argument is a changeable status note. The final two `int` arguments set the minimum and maximum values, respectively, for the progress bar used in the dialog.
`ProgressMonitor getProgressMonitor()` *(in* `ProgressMonitorInputStream`*)*	Get a progress monitor that monitors reading from an input stream.

P

Components

Table 60: Configuring the Progress Monitor

Method	Purpose
`void setMinimum(int)` `int getMinimum()`	Set or get the minimum value of the progress monitor. This value is used by the monitor to set up the progress bar in the dialog.
`void setMaximum(int)` `int getMaximum()`	Set or get the maximum value of the progress monitor. This value is used by the monitor to set up the progress bar in the dialog.
`void setProgress(int)`	Update the monitor's progress.
`void setNote(String)` `String getNote()`	Set or get the status note. This note is displayed on the dialog. To omit the status note from the dialog, provide null as the third argument to the monitor's constructor.
`void setMillisToDecideToPopup(int)` `int getMillisToDecideToPopup()`	Set or get the time after which the monitor should decide whether to pop up a dialog.

Table 61: Terminating the Progress Monitor

Method	Purpose
`void close()`	Close the progress monitor. This disposes of the dialog.
`boolean isCanceled()`	Determine whether the user pressed the **Cancel** button.

Examples That Monitor Progress

The following examples use `JProgressBar` or `ProgressMonitor`.

Example	Where Described	Notes
ProgressBarDemo	This section and How to Use Timers (page 639)	Uses a basic progress bar to show progress on a task running in a separate thread.
ProgressBarDemo2	This section	Uses a basic progress bar to show progress on a task running in a separate thread.
ProgressMonitorDemo	This section	Modification of the previous example that uses a progress monitor instead of a progress bar.

How to Use Radio Buttons

Radio buttons are groups of buttons in which, by convention, only one button at a time can be selected. The Swing release supports radio buttons with the JRadioButton[1] and Button-Group[2] classes. To put a radio button in a menu, use the JRadioButtonMenuItem[3] class. Other ways of displaying one-of-many choices are combo boxes and lists. Radio buttons look similar to check boxes, but, by convention, check boxes place no limits on how many items can be selected at a time.

Because JRadioButton inherits from AbstractButton, Swing radio buttons have all the usual button characteristics, as discussed earlier in How to Use Buttons (page 156). For example, you can specify the image displayed in a radio button.

Figure 45 is a picture of an application that uses five radio buttons to let you choose which kind of pet is displayed.

Figure 45   The RadioButtonDemo application.

---

[1] JRadioButton API documentation: http://java.sun.com/j2se/1.4.2/docs/api/javax/swing/JRadioButton.html.

[2] ButtonGroup API documentation: http://java.sun.com/j2se/1.4.2/docs/api/javax/swing/ButtonGroup.html.

[3] JRadioButtonMenuItem API documentation: http://java.sun.com/j2se/1.4.2/docs/api/javax/swing/JRadioButtonMenuItem.html.

Try This:

1. Run RadioButtonDemo using Java Web Start or compile and run the example yourself.[1]

2. Click the **Dog** button or press Alt-D. The **Dog** button becomes selected, which makes the **Bird** button become unselected. The picture switches from a bird to a dog. This application has one action listener that listens to all the radio buttons. Each time the action listener receives an event, the application displays the picture for the radio button that was just clicked.

Each time the user clicks a radio button (even if it was already selected), the button fires an action event. One or two item events also occur—one from the button that was just selected and another from the button that lost the selection (if any). Usually, you handle radio button clicks using an action listener.

Below is the code from RadioButtonDemo.java that creates the radio buttons in the previous example and reacts to clicks.

```
//In initialization code:
    //Create the radio buttons.
    JRadioButton birdButton = new JRadioButton(birdString);
    birdButton.setMnemonic(KeyEvent.VK_B);
    birdButton.setActionCommand(birdString);
    birdButton.setSelected(true);

    JRadioButton catButton = new JRadioButton(catString);
    catButton.setMnemonic(KeyEvent.VK_C);
    catButton.setActionCommand(catString);

    JRadioButton dogButton = new JRadioButton(dogString);
    dogButton.setMnemonic(KeyEvent.VK_D);
    dogButton.setActionCommand(dogString);

    JRadioButton rabbitButton = new JRadioButton(rabbitString);
    rabbitButton.setMnemonic(KeyEvent.VK_R);
    rabbitButton.setActionCommand(rabbitString);

    JRadioButton pigButton = new JRadioButton(pigString);
    pigButton.setMnemonic(KeyEvent.VK_P);
    pigButton.setActionCommand(pigString);
```

---

[1] To run RadioButtonDemo using Java Web Start, click the RadioButtonDemo link on the RunExamples/components.html page on the CD. You can find the source files here: JavaTutorial/uiswing/components/example-1dot4/index.html#RadioButtonDemo.

```
    //Group the radio buttons.
    ButtonGroup group = new ButtonGroup();
    group.add(birdButton);
    group.add(catButton);
    group.add(dogButton);
    group.add(rabbitButton);
    group.add(pigButton);

    //Register a listener for the radio buttons.
    birdButton.addActionListener(this);
    catButton.addActionListener(this);
    dogButton.addActionListener(this);
    rabbitButton.addActionListener(this);
    pigButton.addActionListener(this);
..
public void actionPerformed(ActionEvent e) {
    picture.setIcon(new ImageIcon("images/"
                    + e.getActionCommand() + ".gif"));
}
```

For each group of radio buttons, you need to create a `ButtonGroup` instance and add each radio button to it. The `ButtonGroup` takes care of unselecting the previously selected button when the user selects another button in the group.

You should generally initialize a group of radio buttons so that one is selected. However, the API doesn't enforce this rule—a group of radio buttons can have no initial selection. Once the user has made a selection, exactly one button is selected from then on. There's no supported API for unselecting all the buttons.

Version Note: In versions prior to 1.4, invoking `setSelected(null, true)` on the `ButtonGroup` happened to deselect all the buttons. It no longer does so.

The Radio Button API

Tables 62 and 63 list the commonly used radio button-related API. Also consult the tables in The Button API (page 160) for methods inherited from `AbstractButton`. Other methods you might call, such as `setFont` and `setForeground`, are listed in the API tables in The JComponent Class (page 53). Also refer to the API documentation for `JRadioButton` and `JRadioButtonMenuItem` at:

```
http://java.sun.com/j2se/1.4.2/docs/api/javax/swing/
        JRadioButton.html
```

```
http://java.sun.com/j2se/1.4.2/docs/api/javax/swing/
        JRadioButtonMenuItem.html
```

Table 62: Radio Button Constructors

Constructor	Purpose

JRadioButton(Action)
JRadioButton(String)
JRadioButton(String,
        boolean)
JRadioButton(Icon)
JRadioButton(Icon, boolean)
JRadioButton(String, Icon)
JRadioButton(String, Icon,
        boolean)
JRadioButton()
	Create a JRadioButton instance. The string argument specifies the text, if any, that the radio button should display. Similarly, the Icon argument specifies the image that should be used instead of the look and feel's default radio button image. Specifying the boolean argument as true initializes the radio button to be selected, subject to the approval of the ButtonGroup object. If the boolean argument is absent or false, then the radio button is initially unselected. The JRadioButton(Action) constructor was introduced in 1.3.

JRadioButtonMenuItem(Action) JRadioButtonMenuItem(String) JRadioButtonMenuItem(Icon) JRadioButtonMenuItem(String, Icon) JRadioButtonMenuItem()	Create a JRadioButtonMenuItem instance. The arguments are interpreted in the same way as the arguments to the JRadioButton constructors, except that any specified icon is shown in addition to the normal radio button icon. The JRadioButtonMenuItem(Action) constructor was introduced in 1.3.

Table 63: Commonly Used Button Group Constructors and Methods

Constructor or Method	Purpose
ButtonGroup()	Create a ButtonGroup instance.
void add(AbstractButton) void remove(AbstractButton)	Add a button to the group, or remove a button from the group.

public ButtonGroup getGroup()
(in DefaultButtonModel*)*
	Get the ButtonGroup, if any, that controls a button. For example:
	  ButtonGroup group =
	        ((DefaultButtonModel)
	           button.getModel())).getGroup();
	Introduced in 1.3.

Examples That Use Radio Buttons

The following examples use radio buttons.

Example	Where Described	Notes
DialogDemo	How to Make Dialogs (page 187)	Has **Show it** buttons whose behavior is tied to the state of radio buttons. Uses sizable, though anonymous, inner classes to implement the action listeners.
RadioButtonDemo	This section	Uses radio buttons to determine which of five images it should display.
MenuDemo	How to Use Menus (page 277)	Contains radio button menu items and check box menu items.

R

Components

How to Use Root Panes

In general, you don't directly create a JRootPane[1] object. Instead, you get a JRootPane (whether you want it or not!) when you instantiate JInternalFrame[2] or one of the top-level Swing containers, such as JApplet, JDialog, and JFrame.

Using Top-Level Containers (page 46) tells you the basics of using root panes—getting the content pane, setting its layout manager, and adding Swing components to it. This section tells you more about root panes, including the components that make up a root pane and how you can use them.[3]

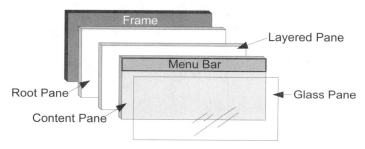

Figure 46   A root pane manages four other panes: a glass pane, a layered pane, a content pane, and a menu bar.

As Figure 46 shows, a root pane has four parts.

The Glass Pane

Hidden, by default. If you make the glass pane visible, then it's like a sheet of glass over all the other parts of the root pane. It's completely transparent unless you implement the glass pane's paintComponent method so that it does something, and it intercepts input events for the root pane. In the next section, you'll see an example of using a glass pane.

---

[1] JRootPane API documentation: http://java.sun.com/j2se/1.4.2/docs/api/javax/swing/ JRootPane.html.

[2] JInternalFrame API documentation: http://java.sun.com/j2se/1.4.2/docs/api/javax/ swing/JInternalFrame.html.

[3] Another source for root pane information is *The Swing Connection* article "Understanding Containers," online at: http://java.sun.com/products/jfc/tsc/articles/containers/index.html.

The Layered Pane

Serves to position its contents, which consist of the content pane and the optional menu bar. Can also hold other components in a specified Z order. For information, see The Layered Pane (page 320).

The Content Pane

The container of the root pane's visible components, excluding the menu bar. For details on using the content pane, see Using Top-Level Containers (page 46) in Chapter 3.

The Optional Menu Bar

The home for the root pane's container's menus. If the container has a menu bar, you generally use the container's setJMenuBar method to put the menu bar in the appropriate place. For more information on using menus and menu bars, see How to Use Menus (page 277).

The Glass Pane

The glass pane is useful when you want to be able to catch events or paint over an area that already contains one or more components. For example, you can deactivate mouse events for a multi-component region by having the glass pane intercept them. Or you can display an image over multiple components using the glass pane.

Figure 47 shows an application that demonstrates glass pane features. It contains a check box that lets you set whether the glass pane is "visible"—whether it can get events and paint itself onscreen. When the glass pane is visible, it blocks all input events from reaching the components in the content pane. It also paints a red dot in the place where it last detected a mouse-pressed event.

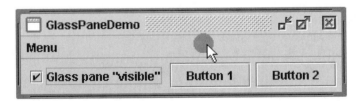

Figure 47   The GlassPaneDemo example.

Try This:

1. Run GlassPaneDemo using Java Web Start or compile and run the example yourself.[1]

---

[1]   To run GlassPaneDemo using Java Web Start, click the GlassPaneDemo link on the RunExamples/ components.html page on the CD. You can find the source files here: JavaTutorial/uiswing/ components/example-1dot4/index.html#GlassPaneDemo.

2. Click **Button 1**. The button's appearance changes to show that it's been clicked.

3. Click the check box so that the glass pane becomes "visible," and then click **Button 1** again. The button does not act clicked because the glass pane intercepts all the mouse events. The glass pane paints a red circle where you release the mouse.

4. Click the check box again so that the glass pane is hidden. When the glass pane detects an event over the check box, it forwards it to the check box. Otherwise, the check box does not respond to clicks.

The following code from GlassPaneDemo.java shows and hides the glass pane. This program happens to create its own glass pane. However, if a glass pane doesn't do any painting, the program might simply attach listeners to the default glass pane, as returned by get-GlassPane.

```
myGlassPane = new MyGlassPane(...);
changeButton.addItemListener(myGlassPane);
frame.setGlassPane(myGlassPane);
...
class MyGlassPane extends JComponent
                implements ItemListener {
    ...
    //React to change button clicks.
    public void itemStateChanged(ItemEvent e) {
        setVisible(e.getStateChange() == ItemEvent.SELECTED);
    }
...
}
```

The next code snippet implements the mouse-event handling for the glass pane. If a mouse event occurs over the check box, then the glass pane redispatches the event so that the check box receives it.

```
...//In the implementation of the glass pane's mouse listener:
public void mouseMoved(MouseEvent e) {
    redispatchMouseEvent(e, false);
}

.../* The mouseDragged, mouseClicked, mouseEntered,
 * mouseExited, and mousePressed methods have the
 * same implementation as mouseMoved. */...

public void mouseReleased(MouseEvent e) {
    redispatchMouseEvent(e, true);
}

private void redispatchMouseEvent(MouseEvent e,
                                 boolean repaint) {
    Point glassPanePoint = e.getPoint();
```

```
    Container container = contentPane;
    Point containerPoint = SwingUtilities.convertPoint(glassPane,
                                               glassPanePoint,
                                               contentPane);
    if (containerPoint.y < 0) { //we're not in the content pane
        //Could have special code to handle mouse events over
        //the menu bar or non-system window decorations, such as
        //the ones provided by the Java look and feel.
    } else {
        //The mouse event is probably over the content pane.
        //Find out exactly which component it's over.
        Component component =
            SwingUtilities.getDeepestComponentAt(container,
                                                 containerPoint.x,
                                                 containerPoint.y);

        if ((component != null)
            && (component.equals(liveButton))) {
            //Forward events over the check box.
            Point componentPoint = SwingUtilities.convertPoint(
                                        glassPane,
                                        glassPanePoint,
                                        component);
            component.dispatchEvent(new MouseEvent(component,
                                        e.getID(),
                                        e.getWhen(),
                                        e.getModifiers(),
                                        componentPoint.x,
                                        componentPoint.y,
                                        e.getClickCount(),
                                        e.isPopupTrigger()));
        }
    }

    //Update the glass pane if requested.
    if (repaint) {
        glassPane.setPoint(glassPanePoint);
        glassPane.repaint();
    }
}
```

Here's the code in MyGlassPane that implements the painting.

```
protected void paintComponent(Graphics g) {
    if (point != null) {
        g.setColor(Color.red);
        g.fillOval(point.x - 10, point.y - 10, 20, 20);
    }
}
```

The Layered Pane

A layered pane is a container with depth such that overlapping components can appear one on top of the other. General information about layered panes is in How to Use Layered Panes (page 258). This section discusses the particulars of how root panes use layered panes.

Each root pane places its menu bar and content pane in an instance of JLayeredPane. The Z ordering that the layered pane provides enables behavior such as displaying popup menus above other components.

You can choose to put components in the root pane's layered pane. If you do, then you should be aware that certain depths are defined to be used for specific functions (see Figure 48), and you should use the depths as intended. Otherwise, your components might not play well with the others.

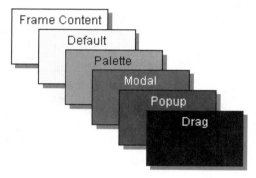

Figure 48   This diagram shows the functional layers and their relationship.

Table 64 describes the intended use for each layer and lists the JLayeredPane constant that corresponds to each layer.

Table 64: Standard Layers

Layer Name	Value	Description
FRAME_CONTENT_LAYER	new Integer(-30000)	The root pane adds the menu bar and content pane to its layered pane at this depth.
DEFAULT_LAYER	new Integer(0)	If you don't specify a component's depth when adding it to a layered pane, the layered pane puts it at this depth.
PALETTE_LAYER	new Integer(100)	This layer is useful for floating tool bars and palettes.

Table 64: Standard Layers *(continued)*

Layer Name	Value	Description
MODAL_LAYER	new Integer(200)	Modal internal-frame dialogs would belong in this layer.
POPUP_LAYER	new Integer(300)	Popups go in this layer because they need to appear above just about everything.
DRAG_LAYER	new Integer(400)	Intended to be used when a component is being dragged. The component should return to its regular layer when dropped. For information on the built-in drag-and-drop support, see How to Use Drag and Drop and Data Transfer (page 545).

Figure 49 shows RootLayeredPaneDemo, which is a version of LayeredPaneDemo[1] that uses the root pane's layered pane, rather than creating a new layered pane.

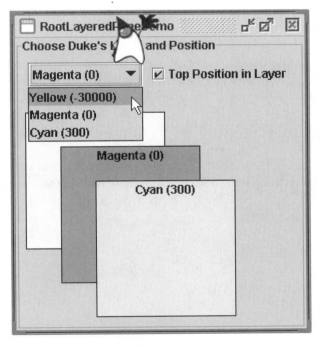

Figure 49   The RootLayeredPaneDemo example.

---

[1]   LayeredPaneDemo is discussed in How to Use Layered Panes (page 258).

Try This:

1. Run `RootLayeredPaneDemo` using Java Web Start or compile and run the example yourself.[1]

2. Move the cursor around in the window so that Duke moves on top of the other components. When the cursor is on top of a nonlabel component—whether it's in the content pane or in the Java-look-and-feel-provided title bar—Duke's movement is temporarily stopped. This is because mouse-motion events go to the component that's deepest in the containment hierarchy and is interested in mouse events. The mouse-motion listener that moves Duke is registered on the layered pane, and most of the components in that pane (with the exception of the labels) happen to have mouse-motion listeners. When the mouse moves over an interested component in the layered pane, the layered pane doesn't get the event and the interested component does.

3. Making sure that the **Top Position in Layer** check box is selected, change Duke's layer to Yellow (-30000). As before, he appears on top of other components, except for the Magenta (0) and Cyan (301) rectangles.

4. Keeping Duke in the Yellow layer, click the check box to send Duke to the back of layer -30000. Duke disappears because the content pane and all the components in it are now above him.

5. Change Duke's layer to Cyan (301), move Duke down a bit so he's standing on the top edge of the Yellow rectangle, and then press the Space bar to bring up the combo box's drop-down list. If the look and feel implements the drop-down list as a lightweight popup, Duke appears on top of the drop-down list.

The Root Pane API

Tables 65 and 66 list the API for using root panes, glass panes, and content panes. For more information on using content panes, refer to Using Top-Level Containers (page 46). Also see the JRootPane API documentation: `http://java.sun.com/j2se/1.4.2/docs/api/javax/swing/JRootPane.html`.

---

[1] To run `RootLayeredPaneDemo` using Java Web Start, click the `RootLayeredPaneDemo` link on the `RunExamples/components.html` page on the CD. You can find the source files here: `JavaTutorial/uiswing/components/example-1dot4/index.html#RootLayeredPaneDemo`.

Table 65: Using a Root Pane

Method	Purpose
JRootPane getRootPane() *(in* JApplet, JDialog, JFrame, JInternalFrame, *and* JWindow*)*	Get the root pane of the applet, dialog, frame, internal frame, or window.
static JRootPane getRootPane(Component) *(in* SwingUtilities*)*	If the component contains a root pane, return that root pane. Otherwise, return the root pane (if any) that contains the component.
JRootPane getRootPane() *(in* JComponent*)*	Invoke the SwingUtilities getRootPane method for the JComponent.
void setDefaultButton(JButton) JButton getDefaultButton()	Set or get which button (if any) is the default button in the root pane. A look-and-feel-specific action, such as pressing Enter, causes the button's action to be performed.

Table 66: Setting or Getting the Root Pane's Contents[a]

Method	Purpose
void setGlassPane(Component) Component getGlassPane()	Set or get the glass pane.
void setLayeredPane(JLayeredPane) Container getLayeredPane()	Set or get the layered pane.
void setContentPane(Container) Container getContentPane()	Set or get the content pane.
void setJMenuBar(JMenuBar) JMenuBar getJMenuBar() *(not defined in* JWindow*)*	Set or get the menu bar.

a. These methods are defined in JApplet, JDialog, JFrame, JInternalFrame, JRootPane, and JWindow, unless noted otherwise.

Examples That Use Root Panes

Every Swing program has a root pane, but few reference it directly. The examples in the following list illustrate how to use features of JRootPane or the glass pane. Also see these lists: Examples That Use Layered Panes (page 266), Examples That Use Menus (page 290), and (for examples of using content panes) Examples That Use Frames (page 244).

R

Components

323

Example	Where Described	Notes
GlassPaneDemo	This section	Uses a glass pane that paints a bit and redispatches events.
RootLayered-PaneDemo	This section	Adapts LayeredPaneDemo to use the root pane's layered pane.
ListDialog	How to Use Lists (page 267)	Sets the default button for a JDialog.
FrameDemo2	How to Make Frames (Main Windows) (page 236)	Sets the default button for a JFrame.
DragFileDemo	How to Use Drag and Drop and Data Transfer (page 545)	Sets the default button for whatever root pane contains an instance of a particular JPanel subclass. Uses the getRootPane method inherited from JComponent.

How to Use Scroll Panes

A `JScrollPane`[1] provides a scrollable view of a component. When screen real estate is limited, use a scroll pane to display a component that is large or one whose size can change dynamically. (See Figure 50.) Other containers used to save screen space include split panes and tabbed panes.

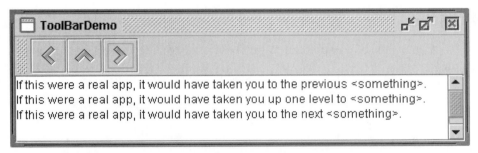

Figure 50 A screenshot of a demo program that puts a text area in a scroll pane because the text area's size grows dynamically as text is appended to it.

The code to create a scroll pane can be minimal. For example, here's the code from Tool-BarDemo that creates the text area, makes it the scroll pane's client, and adds the scroll pane to a container:

```
//In a container that uses a BorderLayout:
textArea = new JTextArea(5, 30);
...
JScrollPane scrollPane = new JScrollPane(textArea);
...
setPreferredSize(new Dimension(450, 110));
...
add(scrollPane, BorderLayout.CENTER);
```

The boldface line of code creates the `JScrollPane`, specifying the text area as the scroll pane's client. The program doesn't invoke any methods on the `JScrollPane` object, since the scroll pane handles everything automatically: creating the scroll bars when necessary, redrawing the client when the user moves the scroll knobs, and so on.

---

[1] JScrollPane API documentation: http://java.sun.com/j2se/1.4.2/docs/api/javax/swing/JScrollPane.html.

You might have noticed that the preceding code sets the preferred size of the scroll pane's container. In the Java look and feel, this preferred size happens to be a bit less tall than required for the text area to display the 5 rows that we requested when creating it, so the scroll bar initially displays a vertical scroll bar. If we didn't restrict the size of the scroll pane's container, the scroll pane would be big enough for the text area to display the full 5 rows and 30 columns specified with the JTextArea constructor. Refer to Sizing a Scroll Pane (page 336) for information about techniques for making a scroll pane the size you want.

How a Scroll Pane Works

Figure 51 is a snapshot of an application that uses a customized scroll pane to view a large photograph.

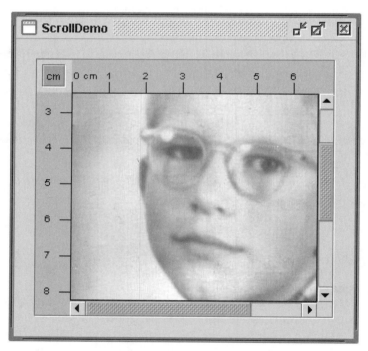

Figure 51 A screenshot of the ScrollDemo example, which uses scroll panes.

The scroll pane in this application looks very different from the one in the previous demo program. Rather than displaying text, this scroll pane contains a large image. The scroll pane also has two scroll bars, a row header, a column header, and four corners, three of which have been customized.

Try This:

1. Run ScrollDemo using Java Web Start or compile and run the example yourself.[1]

2. Move the knobs on the scroll bars. Watch the image scroll and the horizontal and vertical rulers scroll along.

3. If you have a mouse with a wheel (which is generally between the mouse buttons) use the mouse wheel to scroll the image vertically. Support for mouse-wheel scrolling was added in 1.4.

4. Click the **cm** toggle in the upper left corner of the scroll pane. The units on the row and column headers change to inches (or back to centimeters).

5. Click the arrow buttons on the scroll bars. Also, try clicking on the track above or below the knob on the vertical scroll bar or to the left or right of the horizontal one.

6. Move the cursor over the image and press the cursor. Continuing to press the cursor, drag to a point outside the image and pause. The visible area of the image moves toward the cursor. This scroll-by-dragging functionality is enabled by the scroll pane and by the JComponent API, but implemented by the custom component that displays the image.

7. Resize the window. Notice that the scroll bars disappear when the scroll pane is large enough to display the entire image and reappear when the scroll pane is too small to show the entire image.

The ScrollDemo program establishes the scroll pane's client when creating the scroll pane:

```
//Where the member variables are declared:
private ScrollablePicture picture;
...
//Where the GUI is created:
picture = new ScrollablePicture( ... );
JScrollPane pictureScrollPane = new JScrollPane(picture);
```

The scroll pane's client is also known as the *view* or *viewport view*. You can change the client dynamically by calling the setViewportView method. Note that JScrollPane has no corresponding getViewportView method. If you need to refer to the client object again, you can either cache it in a variable or invoke getViewport().getViewportView() on the scroll pane. (See Figure 52.)

---

[1] To run ScrollDemo using Java Web Start, click the ScrollDemo link on the RunExamples/ components.html page on the CD. You can find the source files here: JavaTutorial/uiswing/ components/example-1dot4/index.html#ScrollDemo.

S

Components

When the user manipulates the scroll bars in a scroll pane, the area of the client that is visible changes accordingly.

Client

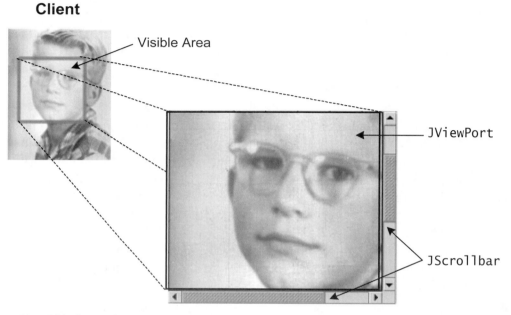

Figure 52   This figure shows the relationship between the scroll pane and its client and indicates the classes that the scroll pane commissions to help.

A scroll pane uses a JViewport[1] instance to manage the visible area of the client. The viewport is responsible for computing the bounds of the current visible area, based on the positions of the scroll bars, and displaying it.

A scroll pane uses two separate instances of JScrollBar[2] for the scroll bars. The scroll bars provide the interface for the user to manipulate the visible area.

[1] JViewport   API documentation: http://java.sun.com/j2se/1.4.2/docs/api/javax/swing/JViewport.html.
[2] JScrollBar   API documentation: http://java.sun.com/j2se/1.4.2/docs/api/javax/swing/JScrollBar.html.

Figure 53 shows the three areas of a scroll bar.

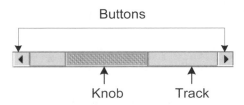

Buttons

Knob   Track

Figure 53   Scrollbar areas: the knob (sometimes called the *thumb*), the buttons, and the track.

When the user moves the knob on the vertical scroll bar up and down, the visible area of the client moves up and down. (See Figure 53.) Similarly, when the user moves the knob on the horizontal scroll bar to the right and left, the visible area of the client moves back and forth accordingly. The position of the knob relative to its track is proportionally equal to the position of the visible area relative to the client. In the Java look and feel and some others, the size of the knob gives a visual clue as to how much of the client is visible.

By clicking a button, the user can scroll by a *unit increment*. By clicking within the track, the user can scroll by a *block increment*. If the user has a mouse with a wheel, then the user can scroll vertically using the mouse wheel. The amount that the mouse wheel scrolls is platform dependent. For example, by default on Windows XP, the mouse wheel scrolls three unit increments; the Mouse control panel allows you to specify a different number of unit increments or to use a block increment instead. More information about unit and block increments is in Implementing a Scrolling-Savvy Client (page 333).

Typical programs don't directly instantiate or call methods on a viewport or scroll bar. Instead, programs achieve their scrolling behavior using the JScrollPane API and the API discussed in Implementing a Scrolling-Savvy Client (page 333). Some scrolling-savvy components such as JList, JTable, and JTree also provide additional API to help you affect their scrolling behavior.

Setting the Scroll Bar Policy

On startup, the scroll pane in the ScrollDemo application has two scroll bars. If you make the window very large, both scroll bars disappear because they are no longer needed. If you then shrink the height of the window without changing its width, the vertical scroll bar reappears. Further experimentation will show that in this application both scroll bars disappear and reappear as needed. This behavior is controlled by the scroll pane's *scroll bar policy*. Actually, it's two policies: Each scroll bar has its own.

S

Components

329

`ScrollDemo` doesn't explicitly set the scroll pane's scroll bar policies—it uses the default. You can set the policies when you create the scroll pane or change them dynamically.

Of the constructors provided by `JScrollPane`, these two let you set the scroll bar policies when you create the scroll pane:

```
JScrollPane(Component, int, int)
JScrollPane(int, int)
```

The first `int` specifies the policy for the vertical scroll bar; the second specifies the policy for the horizontal scroll bar. You can also set the policies dynamically with the `setHorizontalScrollBarPolicy` and `setVerticalScrollBarPolicy` methods. With both the constructors and the methods, use one of the following constants defined in the `ScrollPaneConstants`[1] interface (which is implemented by `JScrollPane`):

Policy	Description
VERTICAL_SCROLLBAR_AS_NEEDED HORIZONTAL_SCROLLBAR_AS_NEEDED	The default. The scroll bar appears when the viewport is smaller than the client and disappears when the viewport is larger than the client.
VERTICAL_SCROLLBAR_ALWAYS HORIZONTAL_SCROLLBAR_ALWAYS	Always display the scroll bar. The knob disappears if the viewport is large enough to show the whole client.
VERTICAL_SCROLLBAR_NEVER HORIZONTAL_SCROLLBAR_NEVER	Never display the scroll bar. Use this option if you don't want the user to directly control what part of the client is shown, or if you want them to use only non-scroll-bar techniques (such as dragging).

Providing Custom Decorations

The area drawn by a scroll pane consists of up to nine parts: the center, four sides, and four corners. The center is the only component that is always present in all scroll panes. Besides scroll bars, the sides can contain column and row headers. A corner component is visible only if both sides that intersect at that corner contain visible components.

---

[1] ScrollPaneConstants API documentation: `http://java.sun.com/j2se/1.4.2/docs/api/ javax/swing/ScrollPaneConstants.html`.

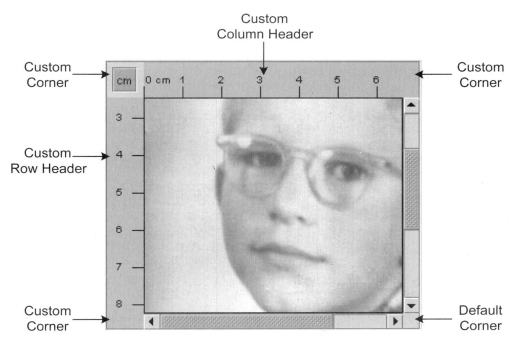

Figure 54   The custom row and column headers in ScrollDemo.

As shown in Figure 54, the scroll pane in ScrollDemo has custom row and column headers. Additionally, because all four sides are populated, all four corners are present. The program customizes three of the corners—two just fill their area with the same color as the Rules, and the other contains a toggle button. The fourth corner, the lower right corner, is the default provided by the scroll pane. Notice that because the row and column headers are always present in this example, the toggle button is also always present.

If a corner contains a control that the user needs access to all the time, make sure the sides that intersect at the corner are always present. For example, if this application placed the toggle in the lower right corner where the scroll bars intersect, then the toggle would disappear if the user resized the window and even one of the scroll bars disappeared.

The scroll pane's row and column headers are provided by a custom JComponent subclass, Rule, that draws a ruler in centimeters or inches. Here's the code that creates and sets the scroll pane's row and column headers:

```
//Where the member variables are defined:
private Rule columnView;
private Rule rowView;
...
```

```
//Where the GUI is initialized:
ImageIcon david = createImageIcon("images/youngdad.jpeg");
...
//Create the row and column headers.
columnView = new Rule(Rule.HORIZONTAL, true);
rowView = new Rule(Rule.VERTICAL, true);

if (david != null) {
    columnView.setPreferredWidth(david.getIconWidth());
    rowView.setPreferredHeight(david.getIconHeight());
}
...
pictureScrollPane.setColumnHeaderView(columnView);
pictureScrollPane.setRowHeaderView(rowView);
```

You can use any component for a scroll pane's row and column headers. The scroll pane puts the row and column headers in JViewPorts of their own. Thus, when scrolling horizontally, the column header follows along, and when scrolling vertically, the row header follows along.

As a JComponent subclass, our custom Rule class puts its rendering code in its paintComponent method. The Rule rendering code takes care to draw only within the current clipping bounds to ensure speedy scrolling. Your custom row and column headers should do the same.

You can also use any component for the corners of a scroll pane. ScrollDemo illustrates this by putting a toggle button in the upper left corner and custom Corner objects in the upper right and lower left corners. Here's the code that creates the Corner objects and calls set-Corner to place them:

```
//Create the corners.
JPanel buttonCorner = new JPanel(); //use FlowLayout
isMetric = new JToggleButton("cm", true);
isMetric.setFont(new Font("SansSerif", Font.PLAIN, 11));
isMetric.setMargin(new Insets(2,2,2,2));
isMetric.addItemListener(this);
buttonCorner.add(isMetric);
...
//Set the corners.
pictureScrollPane.setCorner(JScrollPane.UPPER_LEFT_CORNER,
                           buttonCorner);
pictureScrollPane.setCorner(JScrollPane.LOWER_LEFT_CORNER,
                           new Corner());
pictureScrollPane.setCorner(JScrollPane.UPPER_RIGHT_CORNER,
                           new Corner());
```

Remember that the size of each corner is determined by the size of the sides intersecting there. For some components you must take care that the specific instance of the component fits in its corner. For example, the program sets the font and margins on the toggle button so that it fits within the space established by the headers. It's not an issue with the Corner class because that class colors its entire bounds, whatever they happen to be, with a solid color.

As you can see from the code, constants indicate the corner positions (see Figure 55).

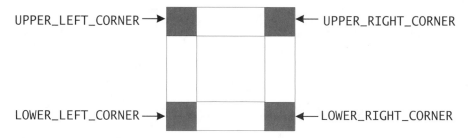

Figure 55   This figure shows the constant for each corner position.

The constants are defined in the ScrollPaneConstants interface, which JScrollPane implements.

Implementing a Scrolling-Savvy Client

To customize the way that a client component interacts with its scroll pane, you can make the component implement the Scrollable[1] interface. By implementing Scrollable, a client can specify both the size of the viewport used to view it and the amount to scroll for clicks on the different controls on a scroll bar.

Note: If you can't or don't want to implement a scrollable client, you can specify the unit and block increments using the setUnitIncrement and setBlockIncrement methods of JScrollBar. For example, the following code sets the unit increment for vertical scrolling to 10 pixels:

```
scrollPane.getVerticalScrollBar().setUnitIncrement(10);
```

Figure 56 shows, again, the three control areas of a scroll bar: the knob, the buttons, and the track.

---

[1]   Scrollable API documentation: http://java.sun.com/j2se/1.4.2/docs/api/javax/swing/Scrollable.html.

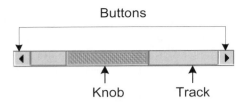

Figure 56   The control areas of a scroll bar.

You might have noticed when manipulating the scroll bars in ScrollDemo that clicking the buttons scrolls the image to a tick boundary. You might also have noticed that clicking in the track scrolls the picture by a "screenful." More generally, the button scrolls the visible area by a unit increment and the track scrolls the visible area by a block increment. The behavior you see in the example is not the scroll pane's default behavior, but is specified by the client in its implementation of the Scrollable interface.

The client for the ScrollDemo program is ScrollablePicture. ScrollablePicture is a subclass of JLabel that provides implementations of all five Scrollable methods:

- getScrollableBlockIncrement
- getScrollableUnitIncrement
- getPreferredScrollableViewportSize
- getScrollableTracksViewportHeight
- getScrollableTracksViewportWidth

ScrollablePicture implements the Scrollable interface primarily to affect the unit and block increments. However, it must provide implementations for all five methods. Thus, it provides reasonable defaults for the other three methods that you might want to copy for your scrolling-savvy classes.

The scroll pane calls the client's getScrollableUnitIncrement method whenever the user clicks one of the buttons on the scroll bar. This method returns the number of pixels to scroll. An obvious implementation of this method returns the number of pixels between tick marks on the header rulers. ScrollablePicture, however, does something different: It returns the value required to position the image on a tick mark boundary. Here's the implementation:

```
public int getScrollableUnitIncrement(Rectangle visibleRect,
                                      int orientation,
                                      int direction) {
    //Get the current position.
    int currentPosition = 0;
```

```
    if (orientation == SwingConstants.HORIZONTAL) {
        currentPosition = visibleRect.x;
    } else {
        currentPosition = visibleRect.y;
    }

    //Return the number of pixels between currentPosition
    //and the nearest tick mark in the indicated direction.
    if (direction < 0) {
        int newPosition = currentPosition -
                       (currentPosition / maxUnitIncrement)
                       * maxUnitIncrement;
        return (newPosition == 0) ? maxUnitIncrement : newPosition;
    } else {
        return ((currentPosition / maxUnitIncrement) + 1)
               * maxUnitIncrement
               - currentPosition;
    }
}
```

If the image is already on a tick mark boundary, this method returns the number of pixels between ticks. Otherwise, it returns the number of pixels from the current location to the nearest tick.

Likewise, the scroll pane calls the client's `getScrollableBlockIncrement` method each time the user clicks on the track. Here's `ScrollablePicture`'s implementation of this method:

```
public int getScrollableBlockIncrement(Rectangle visibleRect,
                                       int orientation,
                                       int direction) {
    if (orientation == SwingConstants.HORIZONTAL)
        return visibleRect.width - maxUnitIncrement;
    else
        return visibleRect.height - maxUnitIncrement;
}
```

This method returns the height of the visible rectangle minus a tick mark. This behavior is typical. A block increment should be slightly smaller than the viewport to leave a little of the previous visible area for context. For example, a text area might leave one or two lines of text for context and a table might leave a row or column (depending on the scroll direction).

`ScrollablePicture.java` has one more bit of code that's not required by the `Scrollable` interface but is common in scrollable components: a mouse-motion listener that lets the user scroll the picture by dragging from it. The boldface code in the following snippet implements scrolling by dragging:

```
public class ScrollablePicture extends JLabel
                          implements Scrollable,
                                     MouseMotionListener {
    ...
    public ScrollablePicture(...) {
        ...
        setAutoscrolls(true); //enable synthetic drag events
        addMouseMotionListener(this); //handle mouse drags
    }
    ...
    public void mouseDragged(MouseEvent e) {
        //The user is dragging us, so scroll!
        Rectangle r = new Rectangle(e.getX(), e.getY(), 1, 1);
        scrollRectToVisible(r);
    }
    ...
}
```

This snippet scrolls the picture whenever the user drags from the picture to a location outside the picture and pauses. The setAutoscrolls method is defined by JComponent for the purpose of assisting—but not implementing—scrolling by dragging. Setting the *autoscrolls* property to true makes the component fire synthetic mouse-dragged events even when the mouse isn't moving (because it stopped, mid-drag, outside the component). It's up to the component's mouse motion listener to listen for these events and react accordingly.

Sizing a Scroll Pane

Unless you explicitly set a scroll pane's preferred size, the scroll pane computes it based on the preferred size of its nine components (the viewport and, if present, the two scroll bars, the row and column headers, and the four corners). The largest factor, and the one most programmers care about, is the size of the viewport used to display the client.

If the client is not scrolling-savvy, then the scroll pane sizes itself so that the client displays at its preferred size. For typical unsavvy clients, this makes the scroll pane redundant. That is, the scroll pane has no scroll bars because the client's preferred size is big enough to display the entire client. In this case, if the client doesn't change size dynamically, you should probably limit the size of the scroll pane by setting its preferred size or the preferred size of its container.

If the client is scrolling-savvy, then the scroll pane uses the value returned by the client's getPreferredScrollableViewportSize method to compute the size of its viewport. Implementations of this method generally report a preferred size for scrolling that's smaller than the component's standard preferred size. For example, by default the value returned by

JList's implementation of getPreferredScrollableViewportSize is just big enough to display eight rows.

Scrolling-savvy classes, like lists, tables, text components, and trees, often provide one or more methods that let programmers affect the size returned from getPreferredScrollableViewportSize. For example, you can set the number of visible rows in a list or a tree by calling the setVisibleRowCount method. The list or tree takes care of figuring out the size needed to display that number of rows.

Refer to Table 70 (page 340) for information about scrolling-related methods provided by classes other than JScrollPane. And remember—if you don't like the value that getPreferredScrollableViewportSize returns, you can always set the preferred size of the scroll pane or its container.

Dynamically Changing the Client's Size

Changing the size of a scroll pane's client is a two-step process. First set the client's preferred size. Then, call revalidate on the client to let the scroll pane know that it should update itself and its scroll bars. Let's look at an example.

Figure 57 is a picture of an application that changes the client's size whenever the user places a circle whose bounds fall outside of the client's current bounds. The program also changes the client's size when the user clears the drawing area.

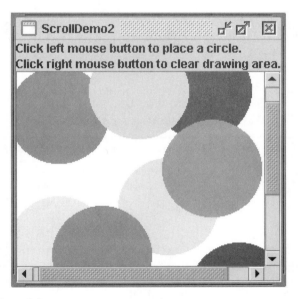

Figure 57   A screenshot of the ScrollDemo2 example.

S

Components

337

You can run `ScrollDemo2` using Java Web Start or compile and run the example yourself.[1]

```
if (changed) {
    //Update client's preferred size because
    //the area taken up by the graphics has
    //gotten larger or smaller (if cleared).
    drawingArea.setPreferredSize(/* the new size */);

    //Let the scroll pane know to update itself
    //and its scroll bars.
    drawingArea.revalidate();
}
```

When the client changes size, the scroll bars adjust. The scroll pane doesn't resize, nor does the viewport. Refer to `SplitPaneDemo` in How to Use Split Panes (page 369) for another example in which the client object changes size.

The Scroll Pane API

Tables 67 through 70 list the commonly used scroll-related constructors and methods. Other methods you are most likely to invoke on a `JScrollPane` object are those such as `setPreferredSize` that its superclasses provide. See The JComponent API (page 55) for tables of commonly used inherited methods. See also the API documentation for `JScrollPane`, `ScrollPaneConstants`, and `Scrollable`:

```
http://java.sun.com/j2se/1.4.2/docs/api/javax/swing/JScrollPane.html
http://java.sun.com/j2se/1.4.2/docs/api/javax/swing/
        ScrollPaneConstants.html
http://java.sun.com/j2se/1.4.2/docs/api/javax/swing/Scrollable.html
```

Table 67: Setting up the Scroll Pane

(`JScrollPane` *constructors and methods*)

Method or Constructor	Purpose
`JScrollPane()` `JScrollPane(Component)` `JScrollPane(int, int)` `JScrollPane(Component,int, int)`	Create a scroll pane. The Component parameter, when present, sets the scroll pane's client. The two int parameters, when present, set the vertical and horizontal scroll bar policies (respectively).
`void setViewportView(Component)`	Set the scroll pane's client.

---

[1] To run `ScrollDemo2` using Java Web Start, click the `ScrollDemo2` link on the `RunExamples/` `components.html` page on the CD. You can find the source files here: `JavaTutorial/uiswing/` `components/example-1dot4/index.html#ScrollDemo2`.

Table 67: Setting up the Scroll Pane *(continued)*

(`JScrollPane` *constructors and methods*)

Method or Constructor	Purpose
`void setVerticalScrollBarPolicy(int)` `int getVerticalScrollBarPolicy()`	Set or get the vertical scroll policy. `ScrollPane-Constants` defines three values for specifying this policy: `VERTICAL_SCROLLBAR_AS_NEEDED` (the default), `VERTICAL_SCROLLBAR_ALWAYS`, and `VERTICAL_SCROLLBAR_NEVER`.
`void setHorizontalScrollBarPolicy(int)` `int getHorizontalScrollBarPolicy()`	Set or get the horizontal scroll policy. `ScrollPane-Constants` defines three values for specifying this policy: `HORIZONTAL_SCROLLBAR_AS_NEEDED` (the default), `HORIZONTAL_SCROLLBAR_ALWAYS`, and `HORIZONTAL_SCROLLBAR_NEVER`.
`void setViewportBorder(Border)` `Border getViewportBorder()`	Set or get the border around the viewport.
`void setWheelScrollingEnabled(boolean)` `boolean isWheelScrollingEnabled()`	Set or get whether scrolling occurs in response to the mouse wheel. Mouse-wheel scrolling is enabled by default. Introduced in 1.4.

Table 68: Decorating the Scroll Pane

(`JScrollPane` *methods*)

Method	Purpose
`void setColumnHeaderView(Component)` `void setRowHeaderView(Component)`	Set the column or row header for the scroll pane.
`void setCorner(String, Component)` `Component getCorner(String)`	Set or get the corner specified. The `int` parameter specifies which corner and must be one of the following constants defined in `ScrollPaneConstants`: `UPPER_LEFT_CORNER`, `UPPER_RIGHT_CORNER`, `LOWER_LEFT_CORNER`, `LOWER_RIGHT_CORNER`, `LOWER_LEADING_CORNER`, `LOWER_TRAILING_CORNER`, `UPPER_LEADING_CORNER`, and `UPPER_TRAILING_CORNER`. The last four constants (LEADING/TRAILING) were introduced in 1.3, but aren't usable as late as 1.4.2 due to bug #4467063. Track this bug online at: `http://developer.java.sun.com/developer/bugParade/bugs/4467063.html`.

S

Components

Table 69: Implementing a Scrolling-Savvy Client

Method	Purpose

`int getScrollableUnitIncrement(`
`                Rectangle, int, int)`
`int getScrollableBlockIncrement(`
`                Rectangle, int, int)`
(required by the `Scrollable` *interface)*
	Get the unit or block increment in pixels. The `Rectangle` parameter is the bounds of the currently visible rectangle. The first `int` parameter is either `SwingConstants.HOR-IZONTAL` or `SwingConstants.VERTICAL` depending on what scroll bar the user clicked on. The second `int` parameter indicates which direction to scroll. A value less than 0 indicates up or left. A value greater than 0 indicates down or right.

`Dimension getPreferredScrollableViewportSize()` *(required by the* `Scrollable` *interface)*	Get the preferred size of the viewport. This allows the client to influence the size of the viewport in which it is displayed. If the viewport size is unimportant, implement this method to return `getPreferredSize`.

`boolean getScrollableTracksViewportWidth()`
`boolean getScrollableTracksViewportHeight()`
(required by the `Scrollable` *interface)*
	Get whether the scroll pane should force the client to be the same width or height as the viewport. A return value of true from either of these methods effectively disallows horizontal or vertical scrolling (respectively).

`void setAutoscrolls(boolean)` *(in* `JComponent`*)*	Set whether synthetic mouse-dragged events should be generated when the user drags the mouse outside of the component and stops; these events are necessary for scrolling by dragging. By default, the value is false, but many scrollable components such as `JTable` and custom components set the value to true.

Table 70: Methods in Other Classes Related to Scrolling

Method	Purpose
`void scrollRectToVisible(Rectangle)` *(in* `JComponent`*)*	If the component is in a container that supports scrolling, such as a scroll pane, then calling this method scrolls the scroll pane such that the specified rectangle is visible.

`void setVisibleRowCount(int)`
`int getVisibleRowCount()`
(in `JList`*)*
	Set or get how many rows of the list are visible. The `getPreferredScrollableViewportSize` method uses the visible row count to compute its return value.

Table 70: Methods in Other Classes Related to Scrolling *(continued)*

Method	Purpose
void ensureIndexIsVisible(int) *(in* JList*)*	Scroll so that the row at the specified index is visible. This method calls scrollRectToVisible and works only if the list is in a container, such as a scroll pane, that supports scrolling.
void setVisibleRowCount(int) int getVisibleRowCount() *(in* JTree*)*	Set or get how many rows of the tree are visible. The getPreferredScrollableViewportSize method uses the visible row count to compute its return value.
void scrollPathToVisible(TreePath) void scrollRowToVisible(int) *(in* JTree*)*	Scroll so that the specified tree path or row at the specified index is visible. These methods call scrollRectToVisible and work only if the tree is in a container, such as a scroll pane, that supports scrolling.
void setScrollsOnExpand(boolean) boolean getScrollsOnExpand() *(in* JTree*)*	Set or get whether scrolling occurs automatically when the user expands a node. True by default. This feature works only when the tree is in a container, such as a scroll pane, that supports scrolling.
void setPreferredScrollableViewportSize(Dimension) *(in* JTable*)*	Set the value to be returned by getPreferred-ScrollableViewportSize.

Examples That Use Scroll Panes

This table shows some examples that use JScrollPane and where those examples are described.

Example	Where Described	Notes
ToolBarDemo	This section, How to Use Tool Bars (page 427)	Shows a simple, yet typical, use of a scroll pane.
ScrollDemo	This section	Uses many of scroll pane's bells and whistles.
ScrollDemo2	This section	Shows how to change the client's size.

S

Components

341

Example	Where Described	Notes
SplitPaneDemo	How to Use Split Panes (page 369), How to Use Lists (page 267)	Puts a list and a label in a scroll pane. Also, shows how to handle the case when a scroll pane's client changes size.
TableDemo	How to Use Tables (page 388)	Puts a table in a scroll pane.
TextSamplerDemo	Using Text Components (page 60)	Puts a text area, an editor pane, and a text pane in scroll panes.
TreeDemo	How to Use Trees (page 437)	Puts a tree in a scroll pane.

How to Use Separators

The JSeparator[1] class provides a horizontal or vertical dividing line or empty space. It's most commonly used in menus and tool bars. In fact, you can use separators without even knowing that a JSeparator class exists, since menus and tool bars provide convenience methods that create and add separators customized for their containers. Separators are somewhat similar to borders, except that they are genuine components and, as such, are painted inside a container rather than around the edges of a particular component.

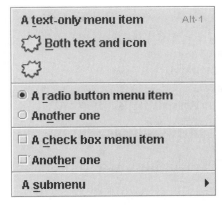

Figure 58 A picture of a menu that has three separators, used to divide the menu into four groups of items.

The code to add the menu items and separators to a menu such as the one in Figure 58 is extremely simple, boiling down to something like this:

```
menu.add(menuItem1);
menu.add(menuItem2);
menu.add(menuItem3);
menu.addSeparator();
menu.add(rbMenuItem1);
menu.add(rbMenuItem2);
menu.addSeparator();
menu.add(cbMenuItem1);
menu.add(cbMenuItem2);
menu.addSeparator();
menu.add(submenu);
```

---

[1] JSeparator API documentation: http://java.sun.com/j2se/1.4.2/docs/api/javax/swing/JSeparator.html.

Adding separators to a tool bar is similar. You can find the full code explained in the how-to sections for menus and tool bars. If you want more control over separators in menus and tool bars, you can directly use the `JSeparator` subclasses that implement them: `JPopup-Menu.Separator`[1] and `JToolBar.Separator`.[2] In particular, `JToolBar.Separator` has API for specifying the separator's size.

Using JSeparator

You can use the `JSeparator` class directly to provide a dividing line in any container (see Figure 59).

Figure 59   This GUI has a separator to the right of the **Fire** button.

Separators have almost no API and are extremely easy to use as long as you keep one thing in mind: In most implementations, a vertical separator has a preferred height of 0, and a horizontal separator has a preferred width of 0. This means that a separator *is not visible* unless you either set its preferred size or put it in under the control of a layout manager such as `BorderLayout` or `BoxLayout` that stretches it to fill its available display area.

The vertical separator does have a bit of width (and the horizontal a bit of height), so you should see some space where the separator is. However, the actual dividing line isn't drawn unless the width and height are both nonzero.

---

[1] `JPopupMenu.Separator` API documentation: `http://java.sun.com/j2se/1.4.2/docs/api/javax/swing/JPopupMenu.Separator.html`.

[2] `JToolBar.Separator` API documentation: `http://java.sun.com/j2se/1.4.2/docs/api/javax/swing/JToolBar.Separator.html`.

The following code snippet shows how ListDemo[1] puts together the panel that contains the vertical separator.

```
JPanel buttonPane = new JPanel();
buttonPane.setLayout(new BoxLayout(buttonPane, BoxLayout.LINE_AXIS));
buttonPane.add(fireButton);
buttonPane.add(Box.createHorizontalStrut(5));
buttonPane.add(new JSeparator(SwingConstants.VERTICAL));
buttonPane.add(Box.createHorizontalStrut(5));
buttonPane.add(employeeName);
buttonPane.add(hireButton);
buttonPane.setBorder(BorderFactory.createEmptyBorder(5,5,5,5));
```

As the code shows, the buttons, separator, and text field all share a single container—a JPanel instance that uses a left-to-right box layout. Thanks to the layout manager (and to the fact that separators have unlimited maximum sizes), the separator is automatically made as tall as its available display area.

In the preceding code, the horizontal struts are invisible components used to provide space around the separator. A 5-pixel empty border provides a cushion around the panel and also serves to prevent the separator from extending all the way to the component above it and the window's edge below it.

Figure 60 shows another GUI that uses a separator, this time to put a dividing line between a group of controls and a display area.

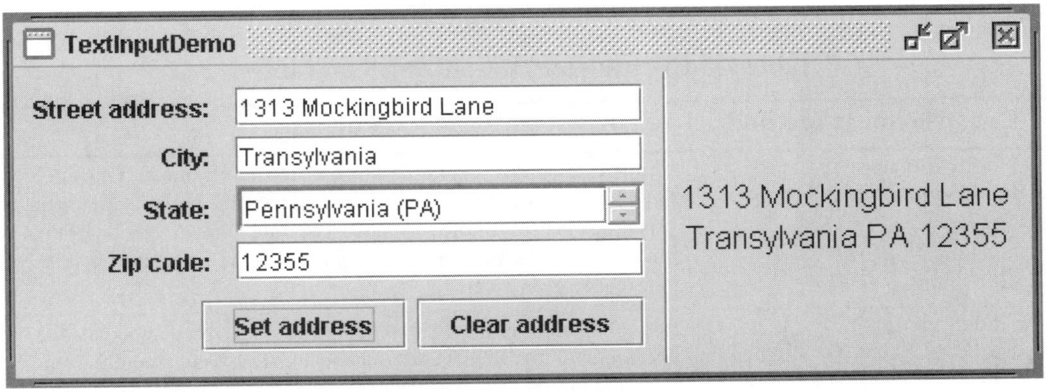

Figure 60 TextInputDemo uses a separator to divide two areas.

---

[1] To run ListDemo using Java Web Start, click the ListDemo link on the RunExamples/components.html page on the CD. You can find the source files here: JavaTutorial/uiswing/components/example-1dot4/index.html#ListDemo.

Here's the code that sets up the separator's container in `TextInputDemo`:[1]

```
JPanel panel = new JPanel(new BorderLayout());
...
panel.setBorder(BorderFactory.createEmptyBorder(
                        GAP/2, //top
                        0,     //left
                        GAP/2, //bottom
                        0));   //right
panel.add(new JSeparator(JSeparator.VERTICAL),
        BorderLayout.LINE_START);
panel.add(addressDisplay,
        BorderLayout.CENTER);
```

As in the last example, the panel uses an empty border so that the separator doesn't extend all the way to the edges of its container. Placing the separator in the leftmost area of the BorderLayout-controlled container makes the separator as tall as the address-display component that's in the center of the container. See How to Use BorderLayout (page 459) in Chapter 8 for details on how border layouts work.

The Separator API

The API for using separators (see Table 71) is minimal, since separators have no contents and don't respond to user input. See The JComponent API (page 55) for tables of commonly used inherited methods. See also the API documentation for `JSeparator` at: `http://java.sun.com/j2se/1.4.2/docs/api/javax/swing/JSeparator.html`.

Table 71: Creating and Initializing Separators

Constructor or Method	Purpose
void addSeparator() void addSeparator(Dimension) *(in* JToolBar*)*	Append a tool bar separator (which is invisible in most, if not all, look and feels) to the current end of the tool bar. The optional argument specifies the size of the separator. The no-argument version of this method uses a separator with a default size, as determined by the current look and feel.
void addSeparator() void insertSeparator(int) *(in* JMenu*)*	Put a separator in the menu. The addSeparator method puts the separator at the current end of the menu. The insertSeparator method inserts the separator into the menu at the specified position.
void addSeparator() *(in* JPopupMenu*)*	Put a separator at the current end of the popup menu.

---

[1] TextInputDemo is described in How to Use Formatted Text Fields (page 329).

Table 71: Creating and Initializing Separators *(continued)*

Constructor or Method	Purpose
`JSeparator()` `JSeparator(int)`	Create a separator. If you don't specify an argument, the separator is horizontal. The argument can be either `SwingConstants.HORIZON-TAL` or `SwingConstants.VERTICAL`.

`void setOrientation(int)`
`int getOrientation()`
(in `JSeparator`*)*
	Get or set the separator's orientation, which can be either `SwingConstants.HORIZONTAL` or `SwingConstants.VERTICAL`.

`JToolBar.Separator()` `JToolBar.Separator(Dimension)`	Create a separator for use in a tool bar. The optional argument specifies the separator's size.
`setSeparatorSize(Dimension)` *(in* `JToolBar.Separator`*)*	Specify the separator's size. More specifically, the specified `Dimension` is used as the separator's minimum, preferred, and maximum sizes.
`JPopupMenu.Separator()`	Create a separator for use in a menu.

Examples That Use Separators

Several of this chapter's examples use separators, usually in menus. Here's a list of some of the more interesting examples.

Example	Where Described	Notes
`ListDemo`	This section and How to Use Lists (page 267)	Uses a vertical separator in a panel controlled by a horizontal box layout.
`TextInputDemo`	This section and How to Use Formatted Text Fields (page 221)	Uses a vertical separator at the left of a panel controlled by a border layout.
`MenuDemo`	This section and How to Use Menus (page 277)	Uses the `JMenu` method `addSeparator` to put separators in a menu.
`ToolBarDemo2`	How to Use Tool Bars (page 427)	Uses the `JToolBar` method `addSeparator` to put space between two kinds of buttons.

S

Components

How to Use Sliders

Use a JSlider[1] to let the user easily enter a numeric value bounded by a minimum and maximum value. If the ability to specify precise numbers is important, a slider can be coupled with a formatted text field. If space is limited, a spinner is a possible alternative to a slider.

Figure 61   A picture of an application that uses a slider to control animation speed.

Try This:

1. Run SliderDemo using Java Web Start or compile and run the example yourself.[2]
2. Use the slider to adjust the animation speed.
3. Push the slider to 0 to stop the animation.

The following code from SliderDemo.java creates the slider in Figure 61.

---

[1]   JSlider   API   documentation: http://java.sun.com/j2se/1.4.2/docs/api/javax/swing/ JSlider.html.

[2]   To run SliderDemo using Java Web Start, click the SliderDemo link on the RunExamples/ components.html page on the CD. You can find the source files here: JavaTutorial/uiswing/ components/example-1dot4/index.html#SliderDemo.

```
static final int FPS_MIN = 0;
static final int FPS_MAX = 30;
static final int FPS_INIT = 15;     //initial frames per second
. . .
JSlider framesPerSecond = new JSlider(JSlider.HORIZONTAL,
                                    FPS_MIN, FPS_MAX, FPS_INIT);
framesPerSecond.addChangeListener(this);

//Turn on labels at major tick marks.
framesPerSecond.setMajorTickSpacing(10);
framesPerSecond.setMinorTickSpacing(1);
framesPerSecond.setPaintTicks(true);

framesPerSecond.setPaintLabels(true);
```

By default, spacing for major and minor tick marks is zero. To see tick marks, you must explicitly set the spacing for either major or minor tick marks (or both) to a nonzero value and call setPaintTicks(true). Just calling setPaintTicks(true) is not enough. To display standard, numeric labels at major tick mark locations, set the major tick spacing, then call setPaintLabels(true). The example program provides labels for its slider this way. But you don't have to settle for these labels. The next section, Customizing Labels on a Slider, shows you how to customize slider labels.

When you move the slider's knob, the stateChanged method of the slider's ChangeListener is called. For information about change listeners, refer to How to Write a Change Listener (page 652). Here's the change listener code that reacts to slider value changes:

```
public void stateChanged(ChangeEvent e) {
    JSlider source = (JSlider)e.getSource();
    if (!source.getValueIsAdjusting()) {
        int fps = (int)source.getValue();
        if (fps == 0) {
            if (!frozen) stopAnimation();
        } else {
            delay = 1000 / fps;
            timer.setDelay(delay);
            timer.setInitialDelay(delay * 10);
            if (frozen) startAnimation();
        }
    }
}
```

Notice that our stateChanged method changes the animation speed only if getValueIs-Adjusting returns false. Many change events are fired as the user moves the slider knob. This program is interested only in the final result of the user's action.

Customizing Labels on a Slider

Figure 62 shows a modified version of the previous program that uses a slider with custom labels.

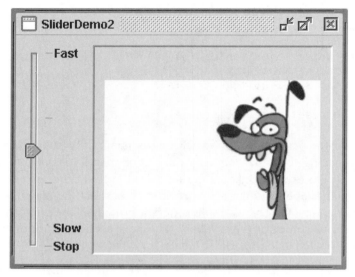

Figure 62 The SliderDemo2 example, which uses three custom labels: **Fast**, **Slow**, and **Stop**.

You can run SliderDemo2 using Java Web Start or compile and run the example yourself.[1]
The following code creates the slider and customizes its labels:

```
//Create the slider
JSlider framesPerSecond = new JSlider(JSlider.VERTICAL,
                                      FPS_MIN, FPS_MAX, FPS_INIT);
framesPerSecond.addChangeListener(this);
framesPerSecond.setMajorTickSpacing(10);
framesPerSecond.setPaintTicks(true);

//Create the label table
Hashtable labelTable = new Hashtable();
labelTable.put( new Integer( 0 ), new JLabel("Stop") );
labelTable.put( new Integer( FPS_MAX/10 ), new JLabel("Slow") );
labelTable.put( new Integer( FPS_MAX ), new JLabel("Fast") );
```

---

[1] To run SliderDemo2 using Java Web Start, click the SliderDemo2 link on the RunExamples/ components.html page on the CD. You can find the source files here: JavaTutorial/uiswing/ components/example-1dot4/index.html#SliderDemo2.

```
framesPerSecond.setLabelTable( labelTable );
framesPerSecond.setPaintLabels(true);
```

Each key-value pair in the hashtable specified with setLabelTable gives the position and the value of one label. The hashtable key must be an Integer and a value within the slider's range at which to place the label. The hashtable value associated with each key must be a Component. This program uses JLabel instances with text only. An interesting variation would be to use JLabel instances with icons, or perhaps buttons that move the knob to the label's position.

If you want a set of numeric labels positioned at a specific interval, you can use JSlider's createStandardLabels method to create the Hashtable for you. You can also modify the table returned by createStandardLabels to then customize it.

Using a Formatted Text Field with a Slider

Often, a slider is paired with a text field so that the user can enter a precise value. SliderDemo3 (see Figure 63) adds a formatted text field to SliderDemo, tying the text field's value to that of the slider.

Figure 63   A screenshot of SliderDemo3, which uses a formatted text field that lets the user enter the number of frames per second.

You can run SliderDemo3 using Java Web Start or compile and run the example yourself.[1]

The next few code snippets show the code in SliderDemo3.java that supports the formatted text field. If you find it hard to understand, you might want to refer to How to Use Formatted Text Fields (page 221).

The following snippet creates the text field and its formatter. The formatter is created using an integer NumberFormat, and the number formatter's minimum and maximum are set to the same values used for the slider.

```
JFormattedTextField textField;
...
//Where the components are created:
java.text.NumberFormat numberFormat =
    java.text.NumberFormat.getIntegerInstance();
NumberFormatter formatter = new NumberFormatter(numberFormat);
formatter.setMinimum(new Integer(FPS_MIN));
formatter.setMaximum(new Integer(FPS_MAX));
textField = new JFormattedTextField(formatter);
textField.setValue(new Integer(FPS_INIT));
textField.setColumns(5); //get some space
```

The rest of the code we'll show you sets up the event handling for the text field. But first you need to know that changing a formatted text field's *text* property (which always holds data of type String) doesn't directly change the formatted text field's *value* property (which, in this example, is a Number). The value property is set only after a method called commitEdit is invoked on the text field, which typically happens when the text field contains valid text and either the user presses Enter or the text field loses focus.

The following code creates a key binding for the Enter key so that whenever the user puts valid text in the text field and presses Enter, the text field's *value* (a Number) is set accordingly. (If the text is invalid, the system beeps and selects all the text.) The key binding is created by adding entries to the text field's input and action maps. More information on input and action maps is in How to Use Key Bindings (page 623).

```
textField.getInputMap().put(KeyStroke.getKeyStroke(
                            KeyEvent.VK_ENTER, 0),
                            "check");
textField.getActionMap().put("check", anAction);
...
```

---

[1] To run SliderDemo3 using Java Web Start, click the SliderDemo3 link on the RunExamples/ components.html page on the CD. You can find the source files here: JavaTutorial/uiswing/ components/example-1dot4/index.html#SliderDemo3.

```
//Where anAction is implemented (as a subclass of AbstractAction):
public void actionPerformed(ActionEvent e) {
    if (!textField.isEditValid()) { //The text is invalid.
        Toolkit.getDefaultToolkit().beep();
        textField.selectAll();
    } else try {                       //The text is valid,
        textField.commitEdit();     //so use it.
    } catch (java.text.ParseException exc) { }
}
```

The next snippet shows how we make the slider's value change whenever the text field's value changes. Recall that framesPerSecond is the variable that refers to the JSlider.

```
textField.addPropertyChangeListener(this);
...
public void propertyChange(PropertyChangeEvent e) {
    if ("value".equals(e.getPropertyName())) {
        Number value = (Number)e.getNewValue();
        if (framesPerSecond != null && value != null) {
            framesPerSecond.setValue(value.intValue());
        }
    }
}
```

Finally, adding bit of code to the slider's change listener updates the formatted text field whenever the slider's value changes. While the user is dragging the slider, we update the text field's *text*—not its *value*—to prevent the text field's property-change listener from trying to update the slider (which might then try to update the text field, which would try to update the slider, and so on, in an unnecessary and perhaps unending cycle). Once the user has finished dragging the slider, we update the text field's *value*.

```
public void stateChanged(ChangeEvent e) {
    JSlider source = (JSlider)e.getSource();
    int fps = (int)source.getValue();
    if (!source.getValueIsAdjusting()) { //done adjusting
        textField.setValue(new Integer(fps)); //update ftf value
        ...
    } else { //value is adjusting; just set the text
        textField.setText(String.valueOf(fps));
    }
}
```

You have seen one possible way of implementing a text field tied to a slider. Other ways are possible, but keep the following rules in mind:

- Only one component (or, more precisely, only one data model) should have the final say on the value. In SliderDemo3, only the slider controls how fast the animation goes. The text field just displays the slider's value and allows the user a second way of setting the slider's value.

- The *value* and *text* properties of a formatted text field can have different types, and the *value* property generally lags behind the *text* property (until commitEdit is invoked).

- You can detect when the text field's *value* property changes (so you can update the slider's value, for example) by registering a property-change listener on the text field.

- You can display the slider's current value in a text field (or other component, such as a label) by adding a line to the slider's change-event handler that invokes setText on the text field. Once the slider's value has settled, you should update the formatted text field's value using setValue.

For more information, see How to Use Formatted Text Fields (page 221).

The Slider API

Tables 72 through 75 list the commonly used JSlider constructors and methods. See The JComponent Class (page 53) for tables of commonly used inherited methods. Also refer to the JSlider API documentation at: http://java.sun.com/j2se/1.4.2/docs/api/ javax/swing/JSlider.html.

Table 72: Creating the Slider

Constructor	Purpose
JSlider()	Create a horizontal slider with the range 0 to 100 and an initial value of 50.

JSlider(int min,
  int max)
JSlider(int min,
  int max,
  int value)
	Create a horizontal slider with the specified minimum and maximum values. The third int argument, when present, specifies the slider's initial value.

JSlider(int orientation)
JSlider(int orientation,
  int min,
  int max,
  int value)
	Create a slider with the specified orientation, which must be either SwingConstants.HORIZONTAL or SwingConstants.VERTICAL. The last three int arguments, when present, specify the slider's minimum, maximum, and initial values, respectively.

JSlider(BoundedRangeModel)	Create a horizontal slider with the specified model, which manages the slider's minimum, maximum, and current values and their relationship.

Table 73: Fine-Tuning the Slider's Appearance

Method	Purpose
`void setValue(int)` `int getValue()`	Set or get the slider's current value. This method also positions the slider's knob.
`void setOrientation(int)` `int getOrientation()`	Set or get the orientation of the slider. Possible values are `SwingConstants.HORIZONTAL` or `SwingConstants.VERTICAL`.
`void setInverted(boolean)` `boolean getInverted()`	Set or get whether the maximum is shown at the left of a horizontal slider or at the bottom of a vertical one, thereby inverting the slider's range.

`void setMinimum(int)`
`void getMinimum()`
`void setMaximum(int)`
`void getMaximum()`
	Set or get the minimum or maximum values of the slider. Together, these methods set or get the slider's range.

`void setMajorTickSpacing(int)`
`int getMajorTickSpacing()`
`void setMinorTickSpacing(int)`
`int getMinorTickSpacing()`
	Set or get the range between major and minor ticks. You must call `setPaintTicks(true)` for the tick marks to appear.

`void setPaintTicks(boolean)` `boolean getPaintTicks()`	Set or get whether tick marks are painted on the slider.
`void setPaintLabels(boolean)` `boolean getPaintLabels()`	Set or get whether labels are painted on the slider. You can provide custom labels with `setLabelTable` or get automatic labels by setting the major tick spacing to a nonzero value.
`void setLabelTable(Dictionary)` `Dictionary getLabelTable()`	Set or get the labels for the slider. You must call `setPaintLabels(true)` for the labels to appear.
`Hashtable createStandardLabels(int)` `Hashtable createStandardLabels(int, int)`	Create a standard set of numeric labels. The first `int` argument specifies the increment; the second `int` argument specifies the starting point. When left unspecified, the slider's minimum is used as the starting point.

Table 74: Watching the Slider Operate

Method	Purpose
`void addChangeListener(ChangeListener)`	Register a change listener with the slider.
`boolean getValueIsAdjusting()`	Determine whether the user gesture to move the slider's knob is complete.

S

Components

Table 75: Working Directly with the Data Model

Class, Interface, or Method	Purpose
`BoundedRangeModel`	The interface required for the slider's data model.
`DefaultBoundedRangeModel`	An implementation of the `BoundedRangeModel` interface.

`boolean setModel()`
`boolean getModel()`
(*in* `JSlider`)
	Set or get the data model used by the slider. You can also set the model using the constructor that takes a single argument of type `BoundedRangeModel`.

Examples That Use Sliders

This table shows examples that use `JSlider` and where those examples are described.

Example	Where Described	Notes
`SliderDemo`	This section	Shows a slider with labels at major tick marks.
`SliderDemo2`	Customizing Labels on a Slider (page 350)	Shows a vertical slider with custom labels.
`SliderDemo3`	Using a Formatted Text Field with a Slider (page 351)	Demonstrates using a formatted text field with a slider to set and display a single value.
`Converter`	Using Models (page 50) and How to Use Panels (page 292)	A measurement conversion application featuring two sliders that share data and have custom `BoundedRangeModel`s.

How to Use Spinners

Release 1.4 introduced a new component called JSpinner.[1] Spinners are similar to combo boxes and lists in that they let the user choose from a range of values. Like editable combo boxes, spinners generally allow the user to type in a value. Unlike combo boxes, spinners don't have a drop-down list that can cover up other components. Because spinners don't display possible values—only the current value is visible—spinners are often used instead of combo boxes or lists when the set of possible values is extremely large. However, spinners should only be used when the possible values and their sequence are obvious.

A spinner is a compound component with three subcomponents: two small buttons and an *editor*. The editor can be any JComponent, but by default is implemented as a panel that contains a formatted text field. The spinner's possible and current values are managed by its *model*.

Figure 1 shows an application named SpinnerDemo that has three spinners.

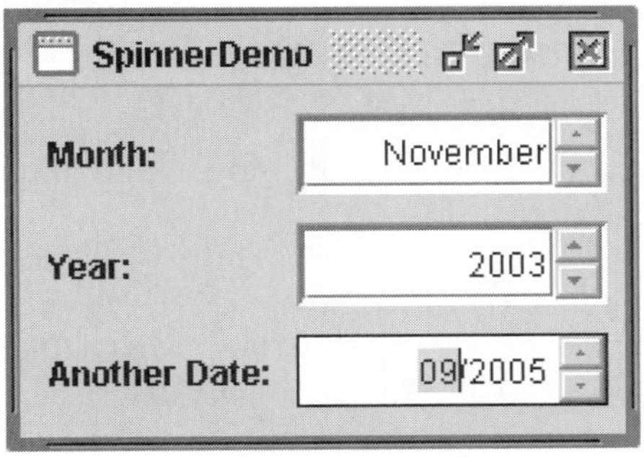

Figure 64 SpinnerDemo has three spinners used to specify dates.

The demo's Month spinner initially displays the name of the first month in the user's locale. The possible values for this spinner are specified using an array of strings. The Year spinner displays one of a range of integers, initialized to the current year. The Another Date spinner displays one in a range of dates (initially the current date) in a custom format that shows just the month and year. You might notice that the edges of the Another Date spinner look different from those of the spinners above it. This is because the example customizes the border of both that spinner and the formatted text field inside it.

---

[1] JSpinner API documentation: `http://java.sun.com/j2se/1.4.2/docs/api/javax/swing/JSpinner.html`.

Try This:

1. Run SpinnerDemo using Java Web Start or compile and run the example yourself.[1]

2. With the Month spinner, use the arrow buttons or keys to cycle forward and backward through the possible values. Note that the lowest value is the first month of the year (for example, January) and the highest is the last (for example, December). The exact values depend on your locale. Also note that the values do not cycle—you can't use the up-arrow button or key to go from December directly to January. This is because the standard spinner models don't support cycling.

3. Type in a valid month name for your locale—for example, July. The spinner automatically completes the month name.

4. Moving on to the Year spinner, try typing a year over 100 years ago—for example, 1800—and then click or tab to move the focus out of the spinner. Because this program restricts the spinner's model to numbers within 100 years of the current year, 1800 is invalid. When the focus moves out of the spinner, the displayed text changes back to the last valid value.

5. Moving to the Another Date spinner, use the arrow buttons or keys to change the date. By default, the first part of the date—in this case, the month number—changes. You can change which part changes by clicking or using the arrow keys to move to another part of the date.

To create a spinner, you generally create its model and then pass the model into the JSpinner constructor. For example:

```
String[] monthStrings = getMonthStrings(); //get month names
SpinnerListModel monthModel = new SpinnerListModel(monthStrings);
JSpinner spinner = new JSpinner(monthModel);
```

Using Standard Spinner Models and Editors

The Swing API provides three spinner models:

SpinnerListModel[2]

A spinner model whose values are defined by an array of objects or a List. Spinner-Demo's Month spinner uses this model, initialized with an array derived from the value

---

[1] To run SpinnerDemo using Java Web Start, click the SpinnerDemo link on the RunExamples/components.html page on the CD. You can find the source files here: JavaTutorial/uiswing/components/example-1dot4/index.html#SpinnerDemo.

[2] SpinnerListModel API documentation: http://java.sun.com/j2se/1.4.2/docs/api/javax/swing/SpinnerListModel.html.

returned by the getMonths method of java.text.DateFormatSymbols. See Spinner-Demo.java for details.

SpinnerNumberModel[1]

Supports sequences of numbers, which can be expressed as doubles, ints, or Numbers. You can specify the minimum and maximum allowable values, as well as the *step size*—the amount of each increment or decrement. The Year spinner uses this model, created with the following code:

```
SpinnerModel model =
        new SpinnerNumberModel(currentYear, //initial value
                               currentYear - 100, //min
                               currentYear + 100, //max
                               1);                 //step
```

SpinnerDateModel[2]

Supports sequences of Date objects. You can specify the minimum and maximum dates, as well as the field (such as Calendar.YEAR) to increment or decrement. Note, however, that some look and feels ignore the specified field and instead change the field that appears selected. The Another Date spinner uses this model, created with the following code:

```
Date initDate = calendar.getTime();
calendar.add(Calendar.YEAR, -100);
Date earliestDate = calendar.getTime();
calendar.add(Calendar.YEAR, 200);
Date latestDate = calendar.getTime();
model = new SpinnerDateModel(initDate,
                            earliestDate,
                            latestDate,
                            Calendar.YEAR);
```

When you set the spinner's model, the spinner's editor is automatically set. The Swing API provides an editor class corresponding to each of the three model classes listed above. These classes—JSpinner.ListEditor,[3] JSpinner.NumberEditor,[4] and JSpinner.Date-

---

[1] SpinnerNumberModel API documentation: http://java.sun.com/j2se/1.4.2/docs/api/javax/swing/SpinnerNumberModel.html.

[2] SpinnerDateModel API documentation: http://java.sun.com/j2se/1.4.2/docs/api/javax/swing/SpinnerDateModel.html.

[3] JSpinner.ListEditor API documentation: http://java.sun.com/j2se/1.4.2/docs/api/javax/swing/JSpinner.ListEditor.html.

[4] JSpinner.NumberEditor API documentation: http://java.sun.com/j2se/1.4.2/docs/api/javax/swing/JSpinner.NumberEditor.html.

S

Components

Editor[1]—are all subclasses of JSpinner.DefaultEditor[2] that feature editable formatted text fields. If you use a model that doesn't have an editor associated with it, the editor is by default a JSpinner.DefaultEditor instance with an uneditable formatted text field.

Specifying Spinner Formatting

To change the formatting used in a standard spinner editor, you can create and set the editor yourself. Another approach, which requires a little more code but gives you more options when using a default editor, is to get the editor's formatted text field and invoke methods on it.

The JSpinner.NumberEditor and JSpinner.DateEditor classes have constructors that allow you to create an editor that formats its data a particular way. For example, the following code sets up the Another Date spinner so that instead of using the default date format, which is long and includes the time, it shows just the month and year in a compact way.

```
spinner.setEditor(new JSpinner.DateEditor(spinner, "MM/yyyy"));
```

Note: You can play with date formats by running ComboBoxDemo2 using Java Web Start. For information about format strings, see the "Formatting" lesson of the Internationalization trail: JavaTutorial/i18n/format/index.html. Tables of number format characters are in the section "Number Format Pattern Syntax."

If you wish to invoke methods directly on the spinner's formatted text field—to set its horizontal alignment, for example—you can get it using the getTextField method defined in JSpinner.DefaultEditor. Note that the Swing-provided editors aren't themselves formatted text fields. Instead, they're JPanels that contain a formatted text field. Here's an example of getting and invoking methods on the editor's formatted text field:

```
//Tweak the spinner's formatted text field.
ftf = getTextField(spinner);
if (ftf != null ) {
    ftf.setColumns(8); //specify more width than we need
    ftf.setHorizontalAlignment(JTextField.RIGHT);
}
...
```

[1] JSpinner.DateEditor API documentation: http://java.sun.com/j2se/1.4.2/docs/api/javax/swing/JSpinner.DateEditor.html.
[2] JSpinner.DefaultEditor API documentation: http://java.sun.com/j2se/1.4.2/docs/api/javax/swing/JSpinner.DefaultEditor.html.

```
public JFormattedTextField getTextField(JSpinner spinner) {
    JComponent editor = spinner.getEditor();
    if (editor instanceof JSpinner.DefaultEditor) {
        return ((JSpinner.DefaultEditor)editor).getTextField();
    } else {
        System.err.println("Unexpected editor type: "
                            + spinner.getEditor().getClass()
                            + " isn't a descendant of DefaultEditor");
        return null;
    }
}
```

Creating Custom Spinner Models and Editors

If the existing spinner models or editors don't meet your needs, you can create your own. The easiest route to creating a custom spinner model is to create a subclass of an existing AbstractSpinnerModel[1] subclass that already does most of what you need. An alternative is to implement your own class by extending AbstractSpinnerModel, which implements the event notifications required for all spinner models.

The following subclass of SpinnerListModel implements a spinner model that cycles through an array of objects. It also lets you specify a second spinner's model to be updated whenever the cycle begins again. For example, if the array of objects is a list of months, the linked model could be for a spinner that displays the year. When the month flips over from December to January the year is incremented. Similarly, when the month flips back from January to December the year is decremented.

```
public class CyclingSpinnerListModel extends SpinnerListModel {
    Object firstValue, lastValue;
    SpinnerModel linkedModel = null;

    public CyclingSpinnerListModel(Object[] values) {
        super(values);
        firstValue = values[0];
        lastValue = values[values.length - 1];
    }

    public void setLinkedModel(SpinnerModel linkedModel) {
        this.linkedModel = linkedModel;
    }
```

---

[1] AbstractSpinnerModel API documentation: http://java.sun.com/j2se/1.4.2/docs/api/javax/swing/AbstractSpinnerModel.html.

```
    public Object getNextValue() {
        Object value = super.getNextValue();
        if (value == null) {
            value = firstValue;
            if (linkedModel != null) {
                linkedModel.setValue(linkedModel.getNextValue());
            }
        }
        return value;
    }

    public Object getPreviousValue() {
        Object value = super.getPreviousValue();
        if (value == null) {
            value = lastValue;
            if (linkedModel != null) {
                linkedModel.setValue(linkedModel.getPreviousValue());
            }
        }
        return value;
    }
}
```

A `CyclingSpinnerListModel` object is used as the model for the Month spinner in SpinnerDemo2, an example that is almost identical to SpinnerDemo. You can run SpinnerDemo2 using Java Web Start or compile and run the example yourself.[1]

As we mentioned before, if you implement a spinner model that does not descend from `SpinnerListModel`, `SpinnerNumberModel`, or `SpinnerDateModel`, then the spinner's default editor is an uneditable instance of `JSpinner.DefaultEditor`. As you've already seen, you can set the editor of a spinner by invoking the `setEditor` method on the spinner after the spinner's model property has been set. An alternative to using `setEditor` is to create a subclass of `JSpinner` and override its `createEditor` method so that it returns a particular kind of editor whenever the spinner model is of a certain type.

In theory at least, you can use any `JComponent` as an editor. Possibilities include using a subclass of a standard component such as `JLabel`, or a component you've implemented from scratch, or a subclass of `JSpinner.DefaultEditor`. The only requirements are that the editor must be updated to reflect changes in the spinner's value, and it must have a reasonable preferred size. The editor should generally also set its tool tip text to whatever tool tip text has been specified for the spinner. An example of implementing an editor is in the next section.

---

[1] To run SpinnerDemo2 using Java Web Start, click the SpinnerDemo2 link on the `RunExamples/ components.html` page on the CD. You can find the source files here: `JavaTutorial/uiswing/ components/example-1dot4/index.html#SpinnerDemo2`.

Detecting Spinner Value Changes

You can detect that a spinner's value has changed by registering a change listener on either the spinner or its model. Here's an example of implementing such a change listener. It's from SpinnerDemo3, which is based on SpinnerDemo and uses a change listener to change the color of some text to match the value of the Another Date spinner.

You can run SpinnerDemo3 using Java Web Start or compile and run the example yourself.[1]

Here's the implementation of SpinnerDemo3:

```java
public class SpinnerDemo3 extends JPanel
                          implements ChangeListener {
    protected Calendar calendar;
    protected JSpinner dateSpinner;
    ...
    public SpinnerDemo3() {
        ...
        SpinnerDateModel dateModel = ...;
        ...
        setSeasonalColor(dateModel.getDate()); //initialize color

        //Listen for changes on the date spinner.
        dateSpinner.addChangeListener(this);
        ...
    }

    public void stateChanged(ChangeEvent e) {
        SpinnerModel dateModel = dateSpinner.getModel();
        if (dateModel instanceof SpinnerDateModel) {
            setSeasonalColor(((SpinnerDateModel)dateModel).getDate());
        }
    }

    protected void setSeasonalColor(Date date) {
        calendar.setTime(date);
        int month = calendar.get(Calendar.MONTH);
        JFormattedTextField ftf = getTextField(dateSpinner);
        if (ftf == null) return;

        //Set the color to match northern hemisphere seasonal conventions.
        switch (month) {
            case 2:  //March
            case 3:  //April
```

S

Components

```
            case 4:  //May
                    ftf.setForeground(SPRING_COLOR);
                    break;

            ...
            default: //December, January, February
                    ftf.setForeground(WINTER_COLOR);
        }
    }
    ...
}
```

The following example implements an editor, which has a change listener so that it can reflect the spinner's current value. This particular editor displays a solid color of gray, ranging anywhere from white to black. You can try it out by running SpinnerDemo4.[1]

```
.../Where the components are created:
JSpinner spinner = new JSpinner(new GrayModel(170));
spinner.setEditor(new GrayEditor(spinner));

class GrayModel extends SpinnerNumberModel {
    ...
}

class GrayEditor extends JLabel
                implements ChangeListener {
    public GrayEditor(JSpinner spinner) {
        setOpaque(true);
        ...
        //Get info from the model.
        GrayModel myModel = (GrayModel)(spinner.getModel());
        setBackground(myModel.getColor());
        spinner.addChangeListener(this);
        ...
        updateToolTipText(spinner);
    }

    protected void updateToolTipText(JSpinner spinner) {
        String toolTipText = spinner.getToolTipText();
        if (toolTipText != null) {
            //JSpinner has tool tip text.  Use it.
            if (!toolTipText.equals(getToolTipText())) {
                setToolTipText(toolTipText);
            }
```

---

[1] To run SpinnerDemo4 using Java Web Start, click the SpinnerDemo4 link on the RunExamples/ components.html page on the CD. You can find the source files here: JavaTutorial/uiswing/ components/example-1dot4/index.html#SpinnerDemo4.

```
        } else {
            //Define our own tool tip text.
            GrayModel myModel = (GrayModel)(spinner.getModel());
            int rgb = myModel.getIntValue();
            setToolTipText("(" + rgb + "," + rgb + "," + rgb + ")");
        }
    }

    public void stateChanged(ChangeEvent e) {
            JSpinner mySpinner = (JSpinner)(e.getSource());
            GrayModel myModel = (GrayModel)(mySpinner.getModel());
            setBackground(myModel.getColor());
            updateToolTipText(mySpinner);
    }
}
```

The Spinner API

Tables 76 through 81 list some of the commonly used API for spinners. If you need to deal
directly with the editor's formatted text field, you should also see The Formatted Text Field
API (page 231). Other methods you might use are listed in the API tables in The JComponent Class (page 53). Also see the JSpinner API documentation at: http://java.sun.com/
j2se/1.4.2/docs/api/javax/swing/JSpinner.html.

Table 76: Classes Related to Spinners

Class or Interface	Purpose
JSpinner	A single-line input field that allows the user to select a number or object value from an ordered sequence.
SpinnerModel	The interface implemented by all spinner models.
AbstractSpinnerModel	The usual superclass for spinner model implementations.
SpinnerListModel	A subclass of AbstractSpinnerModel whose values are defined by an array or a List.
SpinnerDateModel	A subclass of AbstractSpinnerModel that supports sequences of Dates.
SpinnerNumberModel	A subclass of AbstractSpinnerModel that supports sequences of numbers.
JSpinner.DefaultEditor	Implements an uneditable component that displays the spinner's value. Subclasses of this class are generally more specialized (and editable).
JSpinner.ListEditor	A subclass of JSpinner.DefaultEditor whose values are defined by an array or a List.
JSpinner.DateEditor	A subclass of JSpinner.DefaultEditor that supports sequences of Dates.
JSpinner.NumberEditor	A subclass of JSpinner.DefaultEditor that supports sequences of numbers.

S

Components

365

Table 77: Useful JSpinner Constructors and Methods

Constructor or Method	Purpose
`JSpinner()` `JSpinner(SpinnerModel)`	Create a new `JSpinner`. The no-argument constructor creates a spinner with an integer `SpinnerNumberModel` with an initial value of 0 and no minimum or maximum limits. The optional parameter on the second constructor allows you to specify your own `SpinnerModel`.

`void set-`
`Value(java.lang.Object)`
`Object getValue()`
	Set or get the currently displayed element of the sequence.

`Object getNextValue()` `Object getPreviousValue()`	Get the object in the sequence that comes after or before the object returned by `getValue`.
`SpinnerModel getModel()` `void setModel(SpinnerModel)`	Get or set the spinner's model.
`JComponent getEditor()` `void setEditor(JComponent)`	Get or set the spinner's editor, which is often an object of type `JSpinner.DefaultEditor`.
`protected JComponent` `    createEditor(SpinnerModel)`	Called by the `JSpinner` constructors to create the spinner's editor. Override this method to associate an editor with a particular type of model.

Table 78: Useful Editor Constructors and Methods

Constructor or Method	Purpose
`JSpinner.NumberEditor(JSpinner,` `                String)`	Create a `JSpinner.NumberEditor` instance that displays and allows editing of the number value of the specified spinner. The string argument specifies the format to use to display the number. See the API documentation for `DecimalFormat` for information about decimal format strings.
`JSpinner.DateEditor(JSpinner,` `                String)`	Create a `JSpinner.DateEditor` instance that displays and allows editing of the `Date` value of the specified spinner. The string argument specifies the format to use to display the date. See the API documentation for `SimpleDateFormat` for information about date format strings.
`JFormattedTextField getTextField()` (*defined in* `JSpinner.DefaultEditor`)	Get the formatted text field that provides the main GUI for this editor.

Table 79: SpinnerListModel Methods

Method	Purpose
`void setList(List)` `List getList()`	Set or get the `List` that defines the sequence for this model.

Table 80: SpinnerDateModel Methods

Method	Purpose

`void setValue(Object)`
`Date getDate()`
`Object getValue()`
	Set or get the current `Date` for this sequence.

`void setStart(Comparable)` `Comparable getStart()`	Set or get the first `Date` in this sequence. Use null to specify that the spinner has no lower limit.
`void setEnd(Comparable)` `Comparable getEnd()`	Set or get the last `Date` in this sequence. Use null to specify that the spinner has no upper limit.
`void setCalendarField(int)` `int getCalendarField()`	Set or get the size of the date value increment used by the `getNext-Value` and `getPreviousValue` methods. This property is *not* used when the user explicitly increases or decreases the value; instead, the selected part of the formatted text field is incremented or decremented. The specified parameter must be one of the following constants, defined in `Calendar`: ERA, YEAR, MONTH, WEEK_OF_YEAR, WEEK_OF_MONTH, DAY_OF_MONTH, DAY_OF_YEAR, DAY_OF_WEEK, DAY_OF_WEEK_IN_MONTH, AM_PM, HOUR_OF_DAY, MINUTE, SECOND, MILLISECOND.

Table 81: SpinnerNumberModel Methods

Method	Purpose
`void setValue(Object)` `Number getNumber()`	Set or get the current value for this sequence.
`void setMaximum(Comparable)` `Comparable getMaximum()`	Set or get the upper bound for numbers in this sequence. If the maximum is null, there is no upper bound.
`void setMinimum(Comparable)` `Comparable getMinimum()`	Set or get the lower bound for numbers in this sequence. If the minimum is null, there is no lower bound.
`void setStepSize(Number)` `Number getStepSize()`	Set or get the increment used by `getNextValue` and `getPrevi-ousValue` methods.

S

Components

Examples That Use Spinners

The following examples use spinners.

Example	Where Described	Notes
SpinnerDemo	This section	Uses all three standard spinner model classes. Contains the code to use a custom spinner model, but the code is turned off by default.
SpinnerDemo2	This section	A SpinnerDemo subclass that uses the custom spinner model for its Month spinner.
SpinnerDemo3	This section	Based on SpinnerDemo, this application shows how to listen for changes in a spinner's value.
SpinnerDemo4	This section	Implements a custom model and a custom editor for a spinner that displays shades of gray.

How to Use Split Panes

A JSplitPane[1] displays two components, either side by side or one on top of the other. (See Figure 65.) By dragging the divider that appears between the components, the user can specify how much of the split pane's total area goes to each component. You can divide screen space among three or more components by putting split panes inside of split panes, as described in Nesting Split Panes (page 377).

Instead of adding the components of interest directly to a split pane, you often put each component into a scroll pane. You then put the scroll panes into the split pane. This allows the user to view any part of a component of interest, without requiring the component to take up a lot of screen space or adapt to displaying itself in varying amounts of screen space.

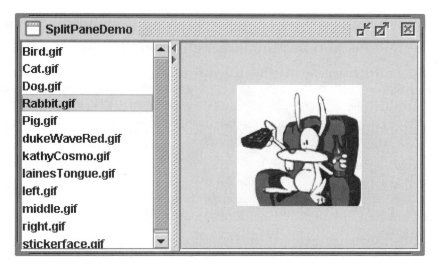

Figure 65   An application that uses a split pane to display a list and an image side by side.

Try This:

1. Run SplitPaneDemo using Java Web Start or compile and run the example yourself.[2]

---

[1]   JSplitPane API documentation: http://java.sun.com/j2se/1.4.2/docs/api/javax/swing/JSplitPane.html.

[2]   To run SplitPaneDemo using Java Web Start, click the SplitPaneDemo link on the RunExamples/components.html page on the CD. You can find the source files here: JavaTutorial/uiswing/components/example-1dot4/index.html#SplitPaneDemo.

S

Components

2. Drag the line that divides the list and the image to the left or right. Try to drag the divider all the way to the window's edge.

3. Click the tiny arrows on the divider to hide/expand the left or right component.

Below is the code from SplitPaneDemo.java that creates and sets up the split pane:

```
//Create a split pane with the two scroll panes in it.
splitPane = new JSplitPane(JSplitPane.HORIZONTAL_SPLIT,
                           listScrollPane, pictureScrollPane);
splitPane.setOneTouchExpandable(true);
splitPane.setDividerLocation(150);

//Provide minimum sizes for the two components in the split pane
Dimension minimumSize = new Dimension(100, 50);
listScrollPane.setMinimumSize(minimumSize);
pictureScrollPane.setMinimumSize(minimumSize);
```

The constructor used by this example takes three arguments. The first indicates the split direction. The other arguments are the two components to put in the split pane.

The split pane in this example is split horizontally—the two components appear side by side—as specified by the JSplitPane.HORIZONTAL_SPLIT argument to the constructor. Split panes provide one other option, specified with JSplitPane.VERTICAL_SPLIT, that places one component above the other. You can change the split direction after the split pane has been created with the setOrientation method.

Two small arrows appear at the top of the divider in the example's split pane. These arrows let the user collapse (and then expand) either of the components with a single click. The current look and feel determines whether these controls appear by default. In the Java look and feel, they are turned off by default. The example turned them on using the setOneTouch-Expandable method.

The range of a split pane's divider is determined in part by the minimum sizes of the components within the split pane. See Positioning the Divider and Restricting Its Range (page 371) for details.

Setting the Components in a Split Pane

A program can set a split pane's two components dynamically with these four methods:

- setLeftComponent
- setRightComponent
- setTopComponent
- setBottomComponent

You can use any of these methods at any time regardless of the split pane's current split direction. Calls to `setLeftComponent` and `setTopComponent` are equivalent and set the specified component in the top or left position, depending on the split pane's current split orientation. Similarly, calls to `setRightComponent` and `setBottomComponent` are equivalent. These methods replace whatever component is already in that position with the new one.

Like other containers, `JSplitPane` supports the add method. Split panes put the first component added into the left or top position. The danger of using add is that you can inadvertently call it too many times, in which case the split pane's layout manager will throw a rather esoteric-looking exception. If you are using the add method and a split pane is already populated, you first need to remove the existing components with `remove`.

If you put only one component in a split pane, then the divider will be stuck at the right side or the bottom of the split pane, depending on its split direction.

Positioning the Divider and Restricting Its Range

To make your split pane work well, you often need to set the minimum sizes of components in the split pane, as well as the preferred size of either the split pane or its contained components. Choosing which sizes you should set is an art that requires understanding how a split pane's preferred size and divider location are determined. Before we get into details, let's take another look at `SplitPaneDemo`.

Try This:

1. Run `SplitPaneDemo` using Java Web Start or compile and run the example yourself.[1] Because the size of the demo's frame is set using the `pack` method, the split pane is at its preferred size, which `SplitPaneDemo` happens to set explicitly. The divider is automatically placed so that the left component is at its preferred width and all remaining space goes to the right component.

2. Make the window wider. The divider stays where it is, and the extra space goes to the component at the right.

3. Make the window noticeably narrower than when it first came up—perhaps twice as wide as the left component. Again, the left component's size and the divider position stay the same. Only the size of the right component changes.

4. Make the window as narrow as possible. Assuming the window uses the Java look and feel-provided decorations, you can't size the window smaller than the split pane's min-

---

[1] To run `SplitPaneDemo` using Java Web Start, click the `SplitPaneDemo` link on the `RunExamples/components.html` page on the CD. You can find the source files here: `JavaTutorial/uiswing/components/example-1dot4/index.html#SplitPaneDemo`.

imum size, which is determined by the minimum size of the components contained by the split pane. SplitPaneDemo sets the minimum size of these contained components explicitly.

5. Make the window wider, and then drag the divider as far as it will go to the right. The divider goes only as far as the right component's minimum size allows. If you drag the divider to the left, you'll see that it also respects the left component's minimum size.

Now that you've seen the default behavior of split panes, we can tell you what's happening behind the scenes and how you can affect it. In this discussion, when we refer to a component's preferred or minimum size, we often mean the preferred or minimum width of the component if the split pane is horizontal, or its preferred or minimum height if the split pane is vertical.

By default, a split pane's preferred size and divider location are initialized so that the two components in the split pane are at their preferred sizes. If the split pane isn't displayed at this preferred size and the program hasn't set the divider's location explicitly, then the initial position of the divider (and thus the sizes of the two components) depends on a split pane property called the *resize weight*. If the split pane is initially at its preferred size or bigger, then the contained components start out at their preferred sizes, before adjusting for the resize weight. If the split pane is initially too small to display both components at their preferred sizes, then they start out at their *minimum* sizes, before adjusting for the resize weight.

A split pane's resize weight has a value between 0.0 and 1.0 and determines how space is distributed between the two contained components when the split pane's size is set—whether programmatically or by the user resizing the split pane (enlarging its containing window, for example). The resize weight of a split pane is 0.0 by default, indicating that the left or top component's size is fixed, and the right or bottom component adjusts its size to fit the remaining space. Setting the resize weight to 0.5 splits any extra or missing space evenly between the two components. Setting the resize weight to 1.0 makes the right or bottom component's size remain fixed. The resize weight has no effect, however, when the user drags the divider.

The user can drag the divider to any position *as long as* neither contained component goes below its minimum size. If the divider has one-touch buttons, the user can use them to make the divider move completely to one side or the other—no matter what the minimum sizes of the components are.

Now that you know the factors that affect a split pane's size and divider location, here are some rules for making them work well:

- To ensure that the divider can be dragged when the split pane is at its preferred size, make sure the minimum size of one or both contained components is smaller than the contained component's preferred size. You can set the minimum size of a component either by invoking `setMinimumSize` on it or by overriding its `getMinimumSize` method. For example, if you want the user to be able to drag the divider all the way to both sides:

```
Dimension minimumSize = new Dimension(0, 0);
leftComponent.setMinimumSize(minimumSize);
rightComponent.setMinimumSize(minimumSize);
```

- To guarantee that both contained components appear, make sure either that the split pane is initially at or above its preferred size or that the minimum sizes of the contained components are greater than zero.

- If you want the bottom or right component to stay the same size and the top or left component to be flexible when the split pane gets bigger, set the resize weight to 1.0. You can do this by invoking `setResizeWeight`:

```
splitPane.setResizeWeight(1.0);
```

- If you want both halves of the split pane to share in the split pane's extra or removed space, set the resize weight to 0.5:

```
splitPane.setResizeWeight(0.5);
```

- Make sure each component contained by a split pane has a reasonable preferred size. If the component is a panel that uses a layout manager, you can generally just use the value it returns. If the component is a scroll pane, you have a few choices. You can invoke the `setPreferredSize` method on the scroll pane, invoke the appropriate method on the component in the scroll pane (such as the `setVisibleRowCount` method for `JList` or `JTree`), or just set the split pane's preferred size and the divider's location.

- Make sure each component contained by a split pane can display itself reasonably in varying amounts of space. For example, panels that contain multiple components should use layout managers that use extra space in a reasonable way.

- If you want to set the size of contained components to something other than their preferred sizes, use the `setDividerLocation` method. For example, to make the left component 150 pixels wide:

```
splitPane.setDividerLocation(150 + splitPane.getInsets().left);
```

To make the right component 150 pixels wide:

```
splitPane.setDividerLocation(splitPane.getSize().width
                        - splitPane.getInsets().right
                        - splitPane.getDividerSize()
                        - 150);
```

S

Components

373

If the split pane is already visible, you can set the divider location as a percentage of the split pane. For example, to make 25% of the space go to left/top:

```
splitPane.setDividerLocation(0.25);
```

- To lay out the split pane as if it just came up, likely repositioning the divider in the process, invoke `resetToPreferredSizes()` on the split pane. Note that just changing the contained components' preferred sizes—even if you invoke `revalidate` afterwards—is not enough to cause the split pane to lay itself out again. You must invoke `resetToPreferredSizes` as well.

Figure 66 shows an example named `SplitPaneDividerDemo`.

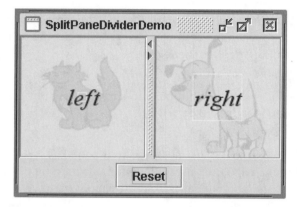

Figure 66   `SplitPaneDividerDemo` demonstrates split pane component sizes and divider placement.

Like `SplitPaneDemo`, `SplitPaneDividerDemo` features a horizontal split pane with one-touch buttons. `SplitPaneDividerDemo` has the following additional features:

- The split pane's *resize weight* is explicitly set (to 0.5).
- The split pane is displayed at its default preferred size.
- A **Reset** button at the bottom of the window invokes `resetToPreferredSizes` on the split pane.
- The components in the split pane are instances of a custom `JComponent` subclass called `SizeDisplayer`. A `SizeDisplayer` displays optional text against the background of a faded (and also optional) image. More importantly, it has rectangles that show its preferred and minimum sizes.
- `SplitPaneDividerDemo` sets up its `SizeDisplayer`s to have equal preferred sizes (because of the equally large images they show) but unequal minimum sizes.

Try This:

1. Run `SplitPaneDividerDemo` using Java Web Start or compile and run the example yourself.[1] Because the size of the demo's frame is set using the pack method, the split pane is at its preferred size, which by default is just big enough for the `SizeDisplay-ers` to be at their preferred sizes. The preferred size of each `SizeDisplayer` is indicated by a red rectangle. The divider is automatically placed so that both components are at their preferred widths.

Note: If you're running the example in Java Web Start, the `SizeDisplayer` components might be taller than their preferred sizes. This is due to bug #4931628. The preferred size for look-and-feel-decorated windows is calculated incorrectly. You can follow the status of this bug online: `http://developer.java.sun.com/developer/bugParade/bugs/4931628.html`.

---

2. Make the window wider. Because the split pane's resize weight is 0.5, the extra space is divided evenly between the left and right components. The divider moves accordingly.

3. Make the window as narrow as possible. Assuming it uses the Java look-and-feel-provided decorations, it will not let you size the window smaller than the split pane's minimum size, which is determined by the minimum size of the `SizeDisplayers` it contains. The minimum size of each `SizeDisplayer` is indicated by a bright blue rectangle.

4. Make the window a bit wider, and then drag the divider as far as it will go to the right. The divider goes only as far as the right component's minimum size allows.

5. After making sure the split pane is smaller than its preferred size, click the **Reset** button. The two `SizeDisplayers` are displayed at the different sizes, even though when the application came up they had equal sizes. The reason is that although their preferred sizes are equal, their minimum sizes are not. Because the split pane can't display them at their preferred sizes or larger, it lays them out using their minimum sizes. The leftover space is divided equally between the components, since the split pane's resize weight is 0.5.

6. Widen the split pane so that it's large enough for both `SizeDisplayers` to be shown at their preferred sizes, and then click the **Reset** button. The divider is placed in the middle again, so that both components are the same size.

---

[1] To run `SplitPaneDividerDemo` using Java Web Start, click the `SplitPaneDividerDemo` link on the `RunExamples/components.html` page on the CD. You can find the source files here: `JavaTutorial/uiswing/components/example-1dot4/index.html#SplitPaneDividerDemo`.

Here's the code that creates the GUI for SplitPaneDividerDemo:

```
public class SplitPaneDividerDemo extends JPanel ... {

    private JSplitPane splitPane;

    public SplitPaneDividerDemo() {
        super(new BorderLayout());

        Font font = new Font("Serif", Font.ITALIC, 24);

        ImageIcon icon = createImageIcon("images/Cat.gif");
        SizeDisplayer sd1 = new SizeDisplayer("left", icon);
        sd1.setMinimumSize(new Dimension(30,30));
        sd1.setFont(font);

        icon = createImageIcon("images/Dog.gif");
        SizeDisplayer sd2 = new SizeDisplayer("right", icon);
        sd2.setMinimumSize(new Dimension(60,60));
        sd2.setFont(font);

        splitPane = new JSplitPane(JSplitPane.HORIZONTAL_SPLIT,
                                   sd1, sd2);
        splitPane.setResizeWeight(0.5);
        splitPane.setOneTouchExpandable(true);
        splitPane.setContinuousLayout(true);

        add(splitPane, BorderLayout.CENTER);
        add(createControlPanel(), BorderLayout.PAGE_END);
    }
    ...
}
```

The code is fairly self-explanatory, except perhaps for the call to setContinuousLayout. Setting the *continuousLayout* property to true makes the split pane's contents be painted continuously while the user is moving the divider. Continuous layout is not on, by default, because it can have a negative performance impact. However, it makes sense to use it in this demo, when having the split pane's components as up to date as possible can improve the user experience.

Nesting Split Panes

Figure 67 shows a picture of a program that achieves a three-way split by nesting one split pane inside of another.

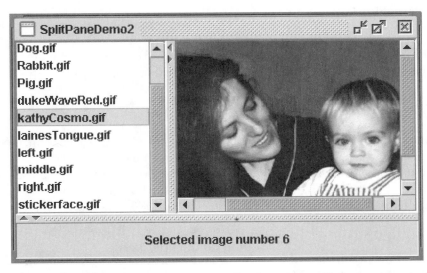

Figure 67   A screenshot of SplitPaneDemo2, an application with a split pane nesting inside another split pane.

If the top portion of the split pane looks familiar to you, it's because the program puts the split pane created by SplitPaneDemo inside a second split pane. A simple JLabel is the other component in the second split pane. This is not the most practical use of a nested split pane, but it gets the point across.

You can run SplitPaneDemo2 using Java Web Start or compile and run the example yourself.[1] Here's the interesting part of the code, which you can find in SplitPaneDemo2.java:

```
//Create an instance of SplitPaneDemo
SplitPaneDemo splitPaneDemo = new SplitPaneDemo();
JSplitPane top = splitPaneDemo.getSplitPane();

...
```

---

[1]   To run SplitPaneDemo2 using Java Web Start, click the SplitPaneDemo2 link on the RunExamples/ components.html page on the CD. You can find the source files here: JavaTutorial/uiswing/ components/example-1dot4/index.html#SplitPaneDemo2.

```
//Create a regular old label
label = new JLabel("Click on an image name in the list.",
                   JLabel.CENTER);

//Create a split pane and put "top" (a split pane)
//and JLabel instance in it.
JSplitPane splitPane = new JSplitPane(JSplitPane.VERTICAL_SPLIT,
                                      top, label);
```

Refer to Solving Common Component Problems (page 735) in the Appendix for information about fixing a border problem that can appear when nesting split panes.

The Split Pane API

Tables 82 through 87 list the commonly used `JSplitPane` constructors and methods. Other methods you are most likely to invoke on a `JSplitPane` object are those such as `setPreferredSize` that its superclasses provide. See The JComponent API (page 55) in Chapter 3 for tables of commonly used inherited methods. Also see the `JSplitPane` API documentation at: `http://java.sun.com/j2se/1.4.2/docs/api/javax/swing/JSplitPane.html`.

Table 82: Setting up the Split Pane

Method or Constructor	Purpose

`JSplitPane()`
`JSplitPane(int)`
`JSplitPane(int, boolean)`
`JSplitPane(int, Component, Component)`
`JSplitPane(int, boolean, Component, Component)`
	Create a split pane. When present, the `int` parameter indicates the split pane's orientation, either `HORIZONTAL_SPLIT` (the default) or `VERTICAL_SPLIT`. The boolean parameter, when present, sets whether the components continually repaint as the user drags the split pane. If left unspecified, this option (called *continuous layout*) is turned off. The `Component` parameters set the initial left and right or top and bottom components, respectively.

`void setOrientation(int)` `int getOrientation()`	Set or get the split pane's orientation. Use either `HORIZONTAL_SPLIT` or `VERTICAL_SPLIT` defined in `JSplitPane`. If left unspecified, the split pane will be horizontally split.
`void setDividerSize(int)` `int getDividerSize()`	Set or get the size of the divider in pixels.

Table 82: Setting up the Split Pane *(continued)*

Method or Constructor	Purpose
`void setContinuousLayout(boolean)` `boolean isContinuousLayout()`	Set or get whether the split pane's components are continually laid out and painted while the user is dragging the divider. By default, continuous layout is turned off.
`void setOneTouchExpandable(boolean)` `boolean isOneTouchExpandable()`	Set or get whether the split pane displays a control on the divider to expand/collapse the divider. The default depends on the look and feel. In the Java look and feel, it's off by default.

Table 83: Managing the Split Pane's Contents

Method	Purpose

`void setTopComponent(Component)`
`void setBottomComponent(Component)`
`void setLeftComponent(Component)`
`void setRightComponent(Component)`
`Component getTopComponent()`
`Component getBottomComponent()`
`Component getLeftComponent()`
`Component getRightComponent()`
	Set or get the indicated component. Each method works regardless of the split pane's orientation. Top and left are equivalent, and bottom and right are equivalent.

`void remove(Component)` `void removeAll()`	Remove the indicated component(s) from the split pane.
`void add(Component)`	Add the component to the split pane. You can add only two components to a split pane. The first component added is the top/left component. The second component added is the bottom/right component. Any attempt to add more components results in an exception.

Table 84: Positioning the Divider

Method	Purpose

`void setDividerLocation(double)`
`void setDividerLocation(int)`
`int getDividerLocation()`
	Set or get the current divider location. When setting the divider location, you can specify the new location as a percentage (`double`) or a pixel location (`int`).

`void resetToPreferredSizes()`	Move the divider such that both components are at their preferred sizes. This is how a split pane divides itself at startup, unless specified otherwise.

S

Components

Table 84: Positioning the Divider *(continued)*

Method	Purpose
`void setLastDividerLocation(int)` `int getLastDividerLocation()`	Set or get the previous position of the divider.
`int getMaximumDividerLocation()` `int getMinimumDividerLocation()`	Get the minimum and maximum locations for the divider. These are set implicitly by setting the minimum sizes of the split pane's two components.
`void setResizeWeight(float)` `float getResizeWeight()`	Set or get the resize weight for the split pane, a value between 0.0 (the default) and 1.0. See Positioning the Divider and Restricting Its Range (page 371) for an explanation of and examples of using the resize weight.

Examples That Use Split Panes

This table shows some examples that use `JSplitPane` and where those examples are described.

Example	Where Described	Notes
SplitPaneDemo	This section and How to Use Lists (page 267)	Shows a split pane with a horizontal split.
SplitPaneDividerDemo	This section	Demonstrates how component size information and resize weight are used to position the divider.
SplitPaneDemo2	This section	Puts a split pane within a split pane to create a three-way split.
TreeDemo	How to Use Trees (page 437)	Uses a split pane with a vertical split to separate a tree (in a scroll pane) from an editor pane (in a scroll pane). Does not use the one-touch expandable feature.
TextComponentDemo	Text Component Features (page 64)	Uses a split pane with a vertical split to separate a text pane and a text area, both in scroll panes.

Example	Where Described	Notes
TextSamplerDemo	Text Component Features (page 64)	Uses a split pane with a vertical split and resize weight of 0.5 to separate a text pane and an editor pane, both in scroll panes. The split pane is in the right half of a container that has a fairly complicated layout. Layout managers such as GridLayout and BorderLayout are used, along with the split pane's resize weight, to ensure that the components in scroll panes share all extra space.
ListSelectionDemo	How to Write a List Selection Listener (page 685)	Uses a split pane with a vertical split to separate an upper pane, containing a list and a table (both in scroll panes), from a lower pane that contains a combo box above a scroll pane. The lower pane uses a border layout to keep the combo box small and the scroll pane greedy for space.

S

Components

How to Use Tabbed Panes

With the JTabbedPane[1] class, you can have several components (usually panels) share the same space. The user chooses which component to view by selecting the tab corresponding to the desired component. If you want similar functionality without the tab interface, you might want to use a card layout instead of a tabbed pane.

To create a tabbed pane, you simply instantiate JTabbedPane, create the components you wish it to display, and then add the components to the tabbed pane using the addTab method. (See Figure 68.)

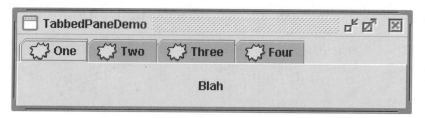

Figure 68 A picture of an application that has a tabbed pane with four tabs.

Try This:

1. Run TabbedPaneDemo using Java Web Start or compile and run the example yourself.[2]
2. Put the cursor over a tab. After a short time, you'll see the tool tip associated with the tab. As a convenience, you can specify tool tip text when you add a component to the tabbed pane.
3. Select a tab by clicking it. The tabbed pane displays the component corresponding to the tab.
4. Select a tab by entering its mnemonic. For example, in the Java look and feel you can select the tab labeled "Tab 3" by typing Alt-3.

As the TabbedPaneDemo example shows, a tab can have a tool tip and a mnemonic, and it can display both text and an image. The example shows the tabs in their default position, at

---

[1] JTabbedPane API documentation: http://java.sun.com/j2se/1.4.2/docs/api/javax/swing/ JTabbedPane.html.

[2] To run TabbedPaneDemo using Java Web Start, click the TabbedPaneDemo link on the RunExamples/ components.html page on the CD. You can find the source files here: JavaTutorial/uiswing/ components/example-1dot4/index.html#TabbedPaneDemo.

the top of the tabbed pane. You can change the tab position to be at the left, right, or bottom of the tabbed pane using the setTabPlacement method.

The following code from TabbedPaneDemo.java creates the tabbed pane in the previous example. Note that no event-handling code is necessary. The JTabbedPane object takes care of mouse and keyboard events for you.

```
JTabbedPane tabbedPane = new JTabbedPane();
ImageIcon icon = createImageIcon("images/middle.gif");

JComponent panel1 = makeTextPanel("Panel #1");
tabbedPane.addTab("Tab 1", icon, panel1,
                "Does nothing");
tabbedPane.setMnemonicAt(0, KeyEvent.VK_1);

JComponent panel2 = makeTextPanel("Panel #2");
tabbedPane.addTab("Tab 2", icon, panel2,
                "Does twice as much nothing");
tabbedPane.setMnemonicAt(1, KeyEvent.VK_2);

JComponent panel3 = makeTextPanel("Panel #3");
tabbedPane.addTab("Tab 3", icon, panel3,
                "Still does nothing");
tabbedPane.setMnemonicAt(2, KeyEvent.VK_3);

JComponent panel4 = makeTextPanel(
        "Panel #4 (has a preferred size of 410 x 50).");
panel4.setPreferredSize(new Dimension(410, 50));
tabbedPane.addTab("Tab 4", icon, panel4,
                    "Does nothing at all");
tabbedPane.setMnemonicAt(3, KeyEvent.VK_4);
```

As the previous code shows, the addTab method handles the bulk of the work in setting up a tab in a tabbed pane. The addTab method has several forms, but they all take both a string title and the component to be displayed by the tab. Optionally, you can specify an icon and tool tip string. The text or icon (or both) can be null. Another way to create a tab is to use the insertTab method, which lets you specify the index of the tab you're adding.

The setMnemonicAt method sets up a way for the user to switch to a specific tab using the keyboard. For example, setMnemonicAt(3, KeyEvent.VK_4) makes '4' the mnemonic for the fourth tab (which is at index 3, since the indices start with 0); pressing Alt-4 makes the fourth tab's component appear. Often, a mnemonic uses a character that's in the tab's title, and the character in the title is automatically underlined.

T

Components

383

Version Note: Support for mnemonics in tabbed panes was added in v1.4.

When building components to add to a tabbed pane, keep in mind that no matter which child of a tabbed pane is visible, each child gets the same amount of space in which to display itself. The preferred size of the tabbed pane is just big enough to display its tallest child at its preferred height, and its widest child at its preferred width. Similarly, the minimum size of the tabbed pane depends on the biggest minimum width and height of all its children.

In TabbedPaneDemo, the fourth panel has a preferred width and height that are larger than those of the other panels. Thus, the preferred size of the tabbed pane is just big enough to display the fourth panel at its preferred size. Every panel gets exactly the same amount of space—410 pixels wide and 50 high, assuming the tabbed pane is at its preferred size. If you don't understand how preferred size is used, please refer to How Layout Management Works (page 97) in Chapter 4.

The Tabbed Pane API

Tables 85 through 87 list the commonly used JTabbedPane constructors and methods.

Table 85: Creating and Setting up a Tabbed Pane

Method or Constructor	Purpose
JTabbedPane() JTabbedPane(int) JTabbedPane(int, int)	Create a tabbed pane. The first optional argument specifies where the tabs should appear. By default, the tabs appear at the top of the tabbed pane. You can specify these positions (defined in the SwingConstants interface, which JTabbedPane implements): TOP, BOTTOM, LEFT, RIGHT. The second optional argument specifies the tab layout policy. You can specify one of these policies (defined in JTabbedPane): WRAP_TAB_LAYOUT or SCROLL_TAB_LAYOUT. Scrollable tabs were introduced in 1.4 and, although supported, are not recommended. For more information, please see the *Java Look and Feel Design Guidelines* online at: http://java.sun.com/products/jlf/ed2/book/.

Table 85: Creating and Setting up a Tabbed Pane *(continued)*

Method or Constructor	Purpose

`addTab(String, Icon, Component, String)`
`addTab(String, Icon, Component)`
`addTab(String, Component)`
	Add a new tab to the tabbed pane. The first argument specifies the text on the tab. The optional icon argument specifies the tab's icon. The component argument specifies the component that the tabbed pane should show when the tab is selected. The fourth argument, if present, specifies the tool tip text for the tab.

`void setTabLayoutPolicy(int)` `int getTabLayoutPolicy()`	Set or get the policy that the tabbed pane uses in laying out the tabs when all the tabs do not fit within a single run. Possible values are `WRAP_TAB_LAYOUT` and `SCROLL_TAB_LAYOUT`. The default, and preferred, policy is `WRAP_TAB_LAYOUT`. Introduced in 1.4.
`void setTabPlacement(int)` `int getTabPlacement()`	Set or get where the tabs appear, relative to the content. Possible values (defined in `SwingConstants`, which is implemented by `JTabbedPane`) are `TOP`, `BOTTOM`, `LEFT`, and `RIGHT`.

Table 86: Inserting, Removing, Finding, and Selecting Tabs

Method	Purpose
`insertTab(String, Icon, Component, String, int)`	Insert a tab at the specified index, where the first tab is at index 0. The arguments are the same as for `addTab`.
`remove(Component)` `removeTabAt(int)`	Remove the tab corresponding to the specified component or index.
`removeAll()`	Remove all tabs.

`int indexOfComponent(Component)`
`int indexOfTab(String)`
`int indexOfTab(Icon)`
	Return the index of the tab that has the specified component, title, or icon.

`void setSelectedIndex(int)` `void setSelectedComponent(Component)`	Select the tab that has the specified component or index. Selecting a tab has the effect of displaying its associated component.
`int getSelectedIndex()` `Component getSelectedComponent()`	Return the index or component for the selected tab.

T Components

Table 87: Changing Tab Appearance

Method	Purpose
`void setComponentAt(int, Component)` `Component getComponentAt(int)`	Set or get which component is associated with the tab at the specified index. The first tab is at index 0.
`void setTitleAt(int, String)` `String getTitleAt(int)`	Set or get the title of the tab at the specified index.

`void setIconAt(int, Icon)`
`Icon getIconAt(int)`
`void setDisabledIconAt(int, Icon)`
`Icon getDisabledIconAt(int)`
	Set or get the icon displayed by the tab at the specified index.

`void setBackgroundAt(int, Color)`
`Color getBackgroundAt(int)`
`void setForegroundAt(int, Color)`
`Color getForegroundAt(int)`
	Set or get the background or foreground color used by the tab at the specified index. By default, a tab uses the tabbed pane's background and foreground colors. For example, if the tabbed pane's foreground is black, then each tab's title is black except for any tabs for which you specify another color using `setForegroundAt`.

`void setEnabledAt(int, boolean)` `boolean isEnabledAt(int)`	Set or get the enabled state of the tab at the specified index.
`void setMnemonicAt(int, int)` `int getMnemonicAt(int)`	Set or get the keyboard mnemonic for accessing the specified tab. Introduced in 1.4.
`void setDisplayedMnemonicIndexAt(int, int)` `int getDisplayedMnemonicIndexAt(int)`	Set or get a hint as to which character should be decorated to represent the mnemonic. This is useful when the mnemonic character appears multiple times in the tab's title and you don't want the first occurrence to be underlined. Introduced in 1.4.
`void setToolTipTextAt(int, String)` `String getToolTipTextAt(int)`	Set or get the text displayed on tool tips for the specified tab. Introduced in 1.3.

Examples That Use Tabbed Panes

This table lists examples that use `JTabbedPane` and where those examples are described.

Example	Where Described	Notes
`TabbedPaneDemo`	This section	Demonstrates a few tabbed pane features, such as tool tips, icons, and mnemonics in tabs.
`BoxAlignment-Demo`	How to Use BoxLayout (page 462)	Uses a `JTabbedPane` as the only child of a frame's content pane.

Example	Where Described	Notes
BorderDemo	How to Use Borders (page 535)	Uses its tabbed pane in a manner similar to BoxAlignmentDemo's usage.
DialogDemo	How to Make Dialogs (page 187)	Has a tabbed pane in the center of a frame's content pane, with a label below it.
DragFileDemo	How to Use Drag and Drop and Data Transfer (page 545)	Uses a tabbed pane at the bottom of the window to display the contents of one or more files. The tabbed pane isn't used until the user selects a file. The tabbed pane's state is controlled by an object of the custom type TabbedPaneController.

Components

How to Use Tables

With the JTable[1] class you can display tables of data, optionally allowing the user to edit the data. JTable doesn't contain or cache data; it's simply a view of your data. (See Figure 69.) The rest of this section tells you how to accomplish some common table-related tasks.

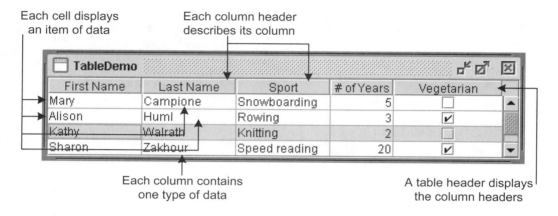

Figure 69   A typical table displayed within a scroll pane.

Creating a Simple Table

Figure 70 shows a simple table that catalogs personal tidbits about five people.

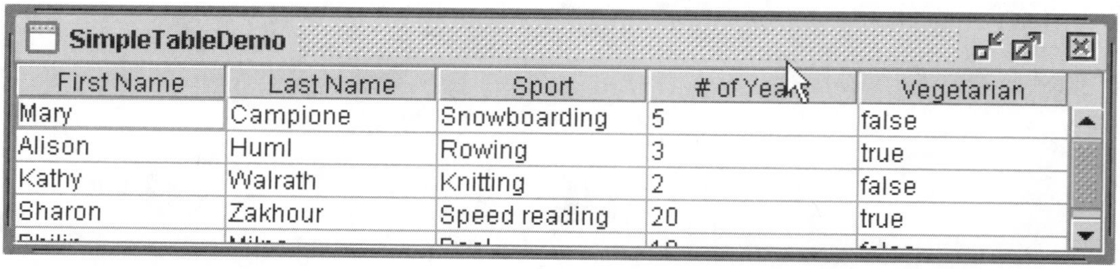

Figure 70   The SimpleTableDemo application.

---

[1] JTable   API   documentation: http://java.sun.com/j2se/1.4.2/docs/api/javax/swing/ JTable.html.

Try This:

1. Run SimpleTableDemo using Java Web Start or compile and run the example yourself.[1]

2. Click the cell that contains "Snowboarding." The entire first row is selected, indicating that you have selected Mary Campione's data. A special highlight indicates that the "Snowboarding" cell is editable. Generally, you begin editing a text cell by double-clicking it.

3. Position the cursor over "First Name." Now press the mouse button and drag to the right. As you can see, users can rearrange columns in tables.

4. Position the cursor just to the right of a column header. Now press the mouse button and drag to the right or left. The column changes size, and the other columns adjust to fill the remaining space.

5. Resize the window containing the table so that it's bigger than necessary to display the whole table. All the table cells become wider, expanding to fill the extra horizontal space.

Here's the code that implements the table in SimpleTableDemo:

```
String[] columnNames = {"First Name",
                        "Last Name",
                        "Sport",
                        "# of Years",
                        "Vegetarian"};

Object[][] data = {
    {"Mary", "Campione",
     "Snowboarding", new Integer(5), new Boolean(false)},
    {"Alison", "Huml",
     "Rowing", new Integer(3), new Boolean(true)},
    {"Kathy", "Walrath",
     "Knitting", new Integer(2), new Boolean(false)},
    {"Sharon", "Zakhour",
     "Speed reading", new Integer(20), new Boolean(true)},
    {"Philip", "Milne",
     "Pool", new Integer(10), new Boolean(false)}
};

JTable table = new JTable(data, columnNames);
```

---

[1] To run SimpleTableDemo using Java Web Start, click the SimpleTableDemo link on the RunExamples/components.html page on the CD. You can find the source files here: JavaTutorial/uiswing/components/example-1dot4/index.html#SimpleTableDemo.

T

Components

389

The `SimpleTableDemo` example uses one of two `JTable` constructors that directly accept data:

- `JTable(Object[][] rowData, Object[] columnNames)`
- `JTable(Vector rowData, Vector columnNames)`

The advantage of these constructors is that they're easy to use. However, these constructors also have disadvantages:

- They automatically make every cell editable.
- They treat all data types the same (as strings). For example, if a table column has `Boolean` data, the table can display the data in a check box. However, if you use one of the two `JTable` constructors listed previously, your `Boolean` data will be displayed as a string. You can see this difference in the last column of Figures 69 and 70.
- They require that you put all of the table's data in an array or vector, which isn't appropriate for some data. For example, if you're instantiating a set of objects from a database, you might want to query the objects directly for their values, rather than copying all their values into an array or vector.

If you want to get around these restrictions, you need to implement your own table model, as described in Creating a Table Model (page 394).

Adding a Table to a Container

It's easy to put a table in a scroll pane. You need just one or two lines of code:

```
JScrollPane scrollPane = new JScrollPane(table);
table.setPreferredScrollableViewportSize(new Dimension(500, 70));
```

The scroll pane automatically gets the table's header, which displays the column names, and puts it on top of the table. Even when the user scrolls down, the column names remain visible at the top of the viewing area. The scroll pane also tries to make its viewing area the same as the table's preferred viewing size. The previous code snippet sets the table's preferred viewing size with the `setPreferredScrollableViewportSize` method.

If you're using a table without a scroll pane, then you must get the table header component and place it yourself. For example:

```
container.setLayout(new BorderLayout());
container.add(table.getTableHeader(), BorderLayout.PAGE_START);
container.add(table, BorderLayout.CENTER);
```

Setting and Changing Column Widths

By default, all columns in a table start out with equal width, and the columns automatically fill the entire width of the table. When the table becomes wider or narrower (which might happen when the user resizes the window containing the table), all the column widths change appropriately.

When the user resizes a column by dragging its right border, then either other columns must change size or the table's size must change. By default, the table's size remains the same, and all columns to the right of the drag point resize to accommodate space added to or removed from the column to the left of the drag point. Figures 71 through 73 illustrate the default resizing behavior.

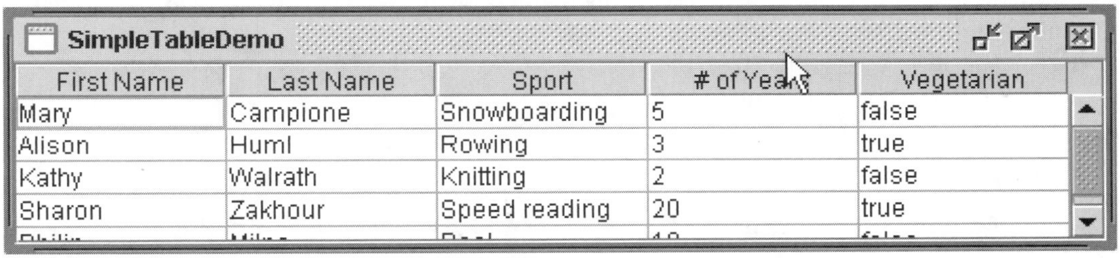

Figure 71   Initially, the columns have equal width.

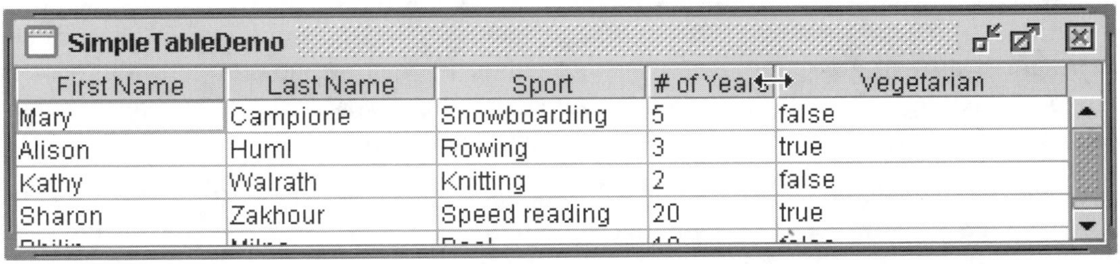

Figure 72   When the user resizes a column, some of the other columns must adjust size for the table to stay the same size.

T

Components

391

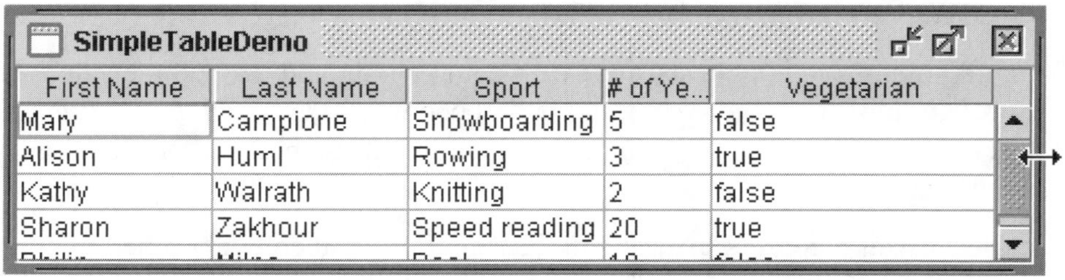

Figure 73   When the entire table is resized, all the columns are resized.

To customize initial column widths, you can invoke `setPreferredWidth` on each of your table's columns. This sets both the preferred widths of the columns and their approximate relative widths. For example, adding the following code to `SimpleTableDemo` makes its third column bigger than the other columns:

```
TableColumn column = null;
for (int i = 0; i < 5; i++) {
    column = table.getColumnModel().getColumn(i);
    if (i == 2) {
        column.setPreferredWidth(100); //sport column is bigger
    } else {
        column.setPreferredWidth(50);
    }
}
```

As the preceding code shows, each column in a table is represented by a `TableColumn`[1] object. `TableColumn` supplies getter and setter methods for the minimum, preferred, and maximum widths of a column, as well as a method for getting the current width. For an example of setting cell widths based on the actual amount of space needed to draw the cells' contents, see the `initColumnSizes` method in `TableRenderDemo.java`.[2]

When the user explicitly resizes columns, the columns' *preferred* widths are set such that the user-specified sizes become the columns' new *current* widths. However, when the table itself is resized—typically because the window has resized—the columns' preferred widths do not change. Instead, the existing preferred widths are used to calculate new column widths to fill the available space.

---

[1] TableColumn API documentation: `http://java.sun.com/j2se/1.4.2/docs/api/javax/swing/table/TableColumn.html`.

[2] You can find TableRenderDemo.java here: `JavaTutorial/uiswing/components/example-1dot4/TableRenderDemo.java`.

You can change a table's resize behavior by invoking the `setAutoResizeMode` method. The method's argument should have one of these values (defined as constants in `JTable`):

AUTO_RESIZE_SUBSEQUENT_COLUMNS
>   The default. In addition to resizing the column to the left of the drag point, adjusts the sizes of all columns to the right of the drag point.

AUTO_RESIZE_NEXT_COLUMN
>   Adjusts only the columns immediately to the left and right of the drag point.

AUTO_RESIZE_OFF
>   Adjusts the table size instead.

Detecting User Selections

The following code snippet shows how to detect when the user selects a table row. By default, a table allows the user to select multiple rows—not columns or individual cells—and the selected rows need not be next to each other. Using the `setSelectionMode` method, the following code specifies that only one row at a time can be selected.

```
table.setSelectionMode(ListSelectionModel.SINGLE_SELECTION);
...
//Ask to be notified of selection changes.
ListSelectionModel rowSM = table.getSelectionModel();
rowSM.addListSelectionListener(new ListSelectionListener() {
    public void valueChanged(ListSelectionEvent e) {
        //Ignore extra messages.
        if (e.getValueIsAdjusting()) return;

        ListSelectionModel lsm =
            (ListSelectionModel)e.getSource();
        if (lsm.isSelectionEmpty()) {
            ...//no rows are selected
        } else {
            int selectedRow = lsm.getMinSelectionIndex();
            ...//selectedRow is selected
        }
    }
});
```

T

Components

The code is from `SimpleTableSelectionDemo.java`.[1] `SimpleTableSelectionDemo` also has code (not included in the preceding snippet) that changes the table's selection orientation. By changing a couple of boolean values, you can make the table allow either column selections or individual cell selections, instead of row selections.

For more information and examples of implementing selection, see How to Write a List Selection Listener (page 685) in Chapter 10.

Creating a Table Model

As Figure 74 shows, every table gets its data from an object that implements the `TableModel`[2] interface.

Figure 74　Every table gets its data from `TableModel`.

The `JTable` constructor used by `SimpleTableDemo` creates its table model with code like this:

```
new AbstractTableModel() {
    public String getColumnName(int col) {
        return columnNames[col].toString();
    }
    public int getRowCount() { return rowData.length; }
    public int getColumnCount() { return columnNames.length; }
    public Object getValueAt(int row, int col) {
        return rowData[row][col];
    }
    public boolean isCellEditable(int row, int col)
        { return true; }
    public void setValueAt(Object value, int row, int col) {
        rowData[row][col] = value;
        fireTableCellUpdated(row, col);
    }
}
```

---

[1]　You can find `SimpleTableSelectionDemo.java` here: `JavaTutorial/uiswing/components/example-1dot4/SimpleTableSelectionDemo.java`.

[2]　`TableModel` API documentation: `http://java.sun.com/j2se/1.4.2/docs/api/javax/swing/table/TableModel.html`.

As the preceding code shows, implementing a table model can be simple. Generally, you implement your table model in a subclass of the `AbstractTableModel`[1] class.

Your model might hold its data in an array, vector, or hash map, or it might get the data from an outside source such as a database. It might even generate the data at execution time.

Figure 75 is a picture of a table implemented by `TableDemo` (which you can run using Java Web Start[2]) that has a custom table model.

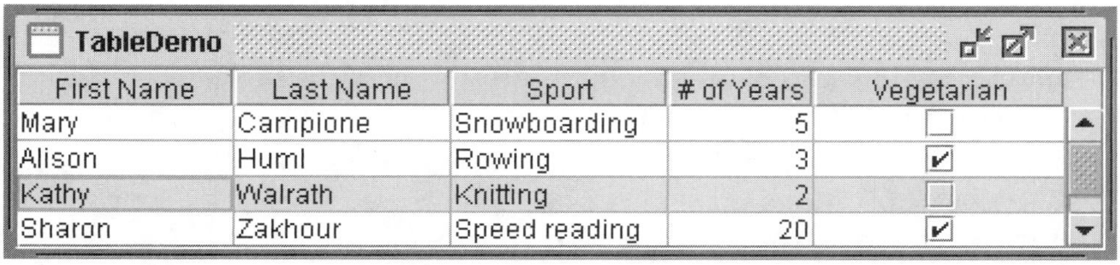

Figure 75   The table implemented by the `TableDemo` application.

This table is different from the `SimpleTableDemo` table in the following ways:

- `TableDemo`'s custom table model, even though it's simple, can easily determine the data's type, helping the `JTable` display the data in the best format. `SimpleTableDemo`'s automatically created table model, on the other hand, isn't smart enough to know that the **# of Years** column contains numbers (which should generally be right aligned and have a particular format). It also doesn't know that the **Vegetarian** column contains boolean values, which can be represented by check boxes.

- In `TableDemo`, we implemented the custom table model so that it doesn't let you edit the name columns; it does, however, let you edit the other columns. In `SimpleTable-Demo`, all cells are editable.

Below is the code from `TableDemo.java` that is different from the code in `SimpleTable-Demo.java`. Bold font indicates the code that makes this table's model different from the table model defined automatically for `SimpleTableDemo`.

```
public TableDemo() {
    ...
    JTable table = new JTable(new MyTableModel());
    ...
}
```

---

[1]   AbstractTableModel API documentation: http://java.sun.com/j2se/1.4.2/docs/api/javax/swing/table/AbstractTableModel.html.

[2]   To run TableDemo using Java Web Start, click the TableDemo link on the RunExamples/components.html page on the CD. You can find the source files here: JavaTutorial/uiswing/components/example-1dot4/index.html#TableDemo.

```
class MyTableModel extends AbstractTableModel {
    private String[] columnNames = ...//same as before...
    private Object[][] data = ...//same as before...

    public int getColumnCount() {
        return columnNames.length;
    }

    public int getRowCount() {
        return data.length;
    }

    public String getColumnName(int col) {
        return columnNames[col];
    }

    public Object getValueAt(int row, int col) {
        return data[row][col];
    }

    public Class getColumnClass(int c) {
        return getValueAt(0, c).getClass();
    }

    /*
     * Don't need to implement this method unless your table's
     * editable.
     */
    public boolean isCellEditable(int row, int col) {
        //Note that the data/cell address is constant,
        //no matter where the cell appears onscreen.
        if (col < 2) {
            return false;
        } else {
            return true;
        }
    }

    /*
     * Don't need to implement this method unless your table's
     * data can change.
     */
    public void setValueAt(Object value, int row, int col) {
        data[row][col] = value;
        fireTableCellUpdated(row, col);
    }
    ...
}
```

Detecting Data Changes

A table and its model automatically detect whenever the user edits the table's data. However, if the data changes for another reason, you must take special steps to notify the table and its model of the data change. Also, if you don't implement a table model, as in `SimpleTable-Demo`, then you must take special steps to find out when the user edits the table's data.

An example of updating a table's data without directly editing it is in the BINGO application. The BINGO application, presented in "Putting It All Together,"[1] has a table that displays some information about each user who is signed up to play the game. When a new user signs up to play BINGO, the table needs to add a new row for that user. More precisely, the table model needs to get the data for the new user, and then the table model needs to tell the table to display the new data.

To notify the table model about a new user, the BINGO application invokes the table model's `updatePlayer` method. You can see the code for that method in `PlayerInfoModel`,[2] which contains the implementation of the table model. The `updatePlayer` method records the new user's data and fires a table-model event. Because every table listens for table-model events from its model, the user-information table automatically detects the change and displays the new data.

To fire the table-model event, the model invokes the `fireTableRowsInserted` method, which is defined by the `AbstractTableModel` class. Other `fireXxxx` methods that `AbstractTableModel` defines are `fireTableCellUpdated`, `fireTableChanged`, `fireTableDataChanged`, `fireTableRowsDeleted`, `fireTableRowsInserted`, `fireTableRowsUpdated`, and `fireTableStructureChanged`.

If you have a class such as `SimpleTableDemo` that isn't a table or table model, but needs to react to changes in a table model, then you need to do something special to find out when the user edits the table's data. Specifically, you need to register a `TableModelListener`[3] on the table model. Adding the bold code in the following snippet makes `SimpleTableDemo` react to table data changes.

```
import javax.swing.event.*;
import javax.swing.table.TableModel;

public class SimpleTableDemo ... implements TableModelListener {
    ...
```

---

[1] The BINGO! game is featured in *The Java Tutorial* trail "Putting It All Together," available online and on the CD at: `JavaTutorial/together/bingo/index.html`.

[2] You can find all the code needed to play BINGO! online and on the CD at: `JavaTutorial/together/bingo/letsplay.html#download`.

[3] `TableModelListener` API documentation: `http://java.sun.com/j2se/1.4.2/docs/api/javax/swing/event/TableModelListener.html`.

```
public SimpleTableDemo() {
    ...
    table.getModel().addTableModelListener(this);
    ...
}

public void tableChanged(TableModelEvent e) {
    int row = e.getFirstRow();
    int column = e.getColumn();
    TableModel model = (TableModel)e.getSource();
    String columnName = model.getColumnName(column);
    Object data = model.getValueAt(row, column);

    ...// Do something with the data...
}
    ...
}
```

Concepts: Editors and Renderers

Before you go on to the next few tasks, you need to understand how tables draw their cells. You might expect each cell in a table to be a component. However, for performance reasons, Swing tables aren't implemented that way.

Instead, a single *cell renderer* is generally used to draw all of the cells that contain the same type of data. You can think of the renderer as a configurable ink stamp that the table uses to stamp appropriately formatted data onto each cell. When the user starts to edit a cell's data, a *cell editor* takes over the cell, controlling the cell's editing behavior.

For example, each cell in the **# of Years** column in TableDemo contains Number data—specifically, an Integer object. By default, the cell renderer for a Number-containing column uses a single JLabel instance to draw the appropriate numbers, right-aligned, on the column's cells. If the user begins editing one of the cells, the default cell editor uses a right-aligned JTextField to control the cell editing.

To choose the renderer that displays the cells in a column, a table first determines whether you specified a renderer for that particular column. (We'll tell you how to specify renderers a bit later.) If you didn't, then the table invokes the table model's getColumnClass method, which gets the data type of the column's cells. Next, the table compares the column's data type with a list of data types for which cell renderers are registered. This list is initialized by the table, but you can add to it or change it. Currently, tables put the following types of data in the list:

- Boolean—rendered with a check box.
- Number—rendered by a right-aligned label.

- Double, Float—same as Number, but the object-to-text translation is performed by a NumberFormat[1] instance (using the default number format for the current locale).
- Date[2]—rendered by a label, with the object-to-text translation performed by a Date-Format instance (using a short style for the date and time).
- ImageIcon, Icon—rendered by a centered label.
- Object—rendered by a label that displays the object's string value.

Version Note: The default renderer associations for Double, Float, and Icon were added in release 1.3.

Cell editors are chosen using a similar algorithm.

Remember that if you let a table create its own model, it uses Object as the type of every column. To specify more precise column types, the table model must define the getColumn-Class method appropriately, as demonstrated by TableDemo.java.

Keep in mind that although renderers determine how each cell or column header looks and can specify its tool tip text, renderers don't handle events. If you need to pick up the events that take place inside a table, the technique you use varies by the sort of event you're interested in.

Situation	How to Get Events
To detect events from a cell that's being edited	Use the cell editor (or register a listener on the cell editor).
To detect row/column/cell selections and deselections	Use a selection listener as described in Detecting User Selections (page 393).
To detect mouse events on a column header	Register the appropriate type of mouse listener on the table's JTableHeader object. (See TableSorter.java for an example.[a])
To detect other events	Register the appropriate listener on the JTable object.

   a. You can find TableSorter.java here: JavaTutorial/uiswing/components/example-1dot4/TableSorter.java.

---

[1] NumberFormat API documentation: http://java.sun.com/j2se/1.4.2/docs/api/java/text/NumberFormat.html.

[2] DateFormat API documentation: http://java.sun.com/j2se/1.4.2/docs/api/java/text/DateFormat.html.

The next few sections tell you how to customize display and editing by specifying renderers and editors. You can specify cell renderers and editors either by column or by data type.

Using a Combo Box as an Editor

Setting up a combo box as an editor is simple, as the following example shows. The bold line of code sets up the combo box as the editor for a specific column.

```
TableColumn sportColumn = table.getColumnModel().getColumn(2);
...
JComboBox comboBox = new JComboBox();
comboBox.addItem("Snowboarding");
comboBox.addItem("Rowing");
comboBox.addItem("Chasing toddlers");
comboBox.addItem("Speed reading");
comboBox.addItem("Teaching high school");
comboBox.addItem("None");
sportColumn.setCellEditor(new DefaultCellEditor(comboBox));
```

Figure 76 is a picture of the combo box editor in use.

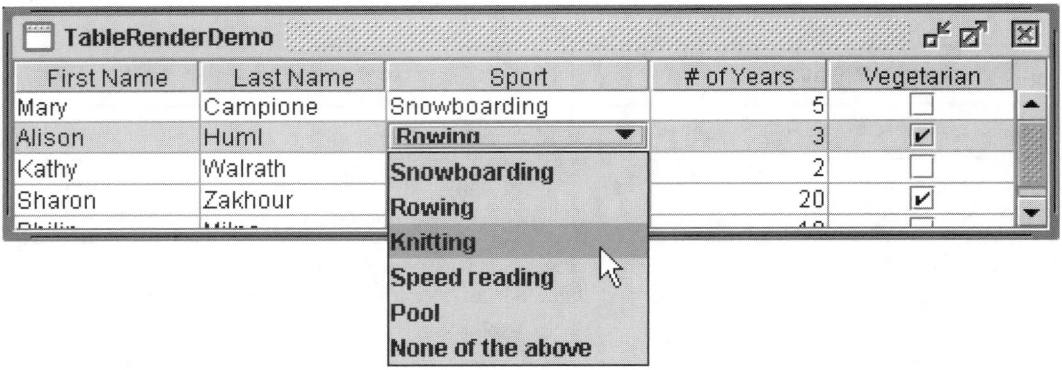

Figure 76 The TableRenderDemo application.

You can run this example, TableRenderDemo, using Java Web Start.[1]

---

[1] To run TableRenderDemo using Java Web Start, click the TableRenderDemo link on the RunExamples/ components.html page on the CD. You can find the source files here: JavaTutorial/uiswing/ components/example-1dot4/index.html#TableRenderDemo.

Using an Editor to Validate User-Entered Text

If a cell's default editor allows text entry, you get some error checking for free if the cell's type is specified as something other than String or Object. The error checking is a side effect of converting the entered text into an object of the proper type.

Version Note: Before 1.3, the default implementation did not in any way restrict the string that could be entered and didn't convert it from a String. You needed to put some ugly code in the model's setValueAt method to parse the entered string and prevent the cell's value from becoming a String.

The automatic checking of user-entered strings occurs when the default editor attempts to create a new instance of the class associated with the cell's column. The default editor creates this instance using a constructor that takes a String as an argument. For example, in a column whose cells have type Integer, when the user types in "123" the default editor creates the corresponding Integer using code equivalent to new Integer("123"). If the constructor throws an exception, the cell's outline turns red and refuses to let the focus move out of the cell. If you implement a class used as a column data type, you can use the default editor if your class supplies a constructor that takes a single argument of type String.

If you like having a text field as the editor for a cell, but want to customize it—perhaps to check user-entered text more strictly or to react differently when the text is invalid—you can change the cell editor to use a formatted text field. The formatted text field can check the value either continuously while the user is typing or after the user has indicated the end of typing (such as by pressing Enter).

You can run TableFTFEditDemo using Java Web Start.[1] The following code, taken from a demo named TableFTFEditDemo, sets up a formatted text field as an editor that limits all integer values to be between 0 and 100. It also makes the formatted text field the editor for all columns that contain data of type Integer:

```
table.setDefaultEditor(Integer.class, new IntegerEditor(0, 100));
```

The IntegerEditor class is implemented as a subclass of DefaultCellEditor[2] that uses a JFormattedTextField instead of the JTextField that DefaultCellEditor supports. It accomplishes this by first setting up a formatted text field to use an integer format and have

---

[1] To run TableFTFEditDemo using Java Web Start, click the TableFTFEditDemo link on the RunExamples/components.html page on the CD. You can find the source files here: JavaTutorial/uiswing/components/example-1dot4/index.html#TableFTFEditDemo.

[2] DefaultCellEditor API documentation: http://java.sun.com/j2se/1.4.2/docs/api/javax/swing/DefaultCellEditor.html.

the specified minimum and maximum values, using the API described in How to Use Formatted Text Fields (page 221). It then overrides the `DefaultCellEditor` implementation of the `getTableCellEditorComponent`, `getCellEditorValue`, and `stopCellEditing` methods, adding the operations that are necessary for formatted text fields.

The override of `getTableCellEditorComponent` sets the formatted text field's *value* property (and not just the *text* property it inherits from `JTextField`) before the editor is shown. The override of `getCellEditorValue` keeps the cell value as an `Integer`, rather than, say, the `Long` value that the formatted text field's parser tends to return. Finally, overriding `stopCellEditing` lets us check whether the text is valid, possibly stopping the editor from being dismissed. If the text isn't valid, our implementation of `stopCellEditing` puts up a dialog that gives the user the option of continuing to edit or reverting to the last good value. The source code is a bit too long to include here, but you can find it in `IntegerEditor.java`.[1]

Using Other Editors

Whether you're setting the editor for a single column of cells (using the `TableColumn` `setCellEditor` method) or for a specific type of data (using the `JTable` `setDefaultEditor` method), you specify the editor using an argument that adheres to the `TableCellEditor` interface. Fortunately, the `DefaultCellEditor` class implements this interface and provides constructors to let you specify an editing component that's a `JTextField`, `JCheckBox`, or `JComboBox`. You usually don't have to explicitly specify a check box as an editor, since columns with `Boolean` data automatically use a check box renderer and editor.

What if you want to specify an editor that isn't a text field, check box, or combo box? Well, because `DefaultCellEditor` doesn't support other types of components, you must do a little more work. You need to create a class that implements the `TableCellEditor`[2] interface. The `AbstractCellEditor`[3] class is a good superclass to use. It implements `TableCellEditor`'s superinterface, `CellEditor`,[4] saving you the trouble of implementing the event firing code necessary for cell editors.

Your cell editor class needs to define at least two methods—`getCellEditorValue` and `getTableCellEditorComponent`. The `getCellEditorValue` method, required by `CellEditor`,

---

[1] IntegerEditor.java is on the CD at: JavaTutorial/uiswing/components/example-1dot4/ IntegerEditor.java.

[2] TableCellEditor API documentation: http://java.sun.com/j2se/1.4.2/docs/api/javax/ swing/table/TableCellEditor.html.

[3] AbstractCellEditor API documentation: http://java.sun.com/j2se/1.4.2/docs/api/javax/ swing/AbstractCellEditor.html.

[4] CellEditor API documentation: http://java.sun.com/j2se/1.4.2/docs/api/javax/swing/ CellEditor.html.

returns the cell's current value. The `getTableCellEditorComponent` method, required by `TableCellEditor`, should configure and return the component that you want to use as the editor.

Version Note: The `AbstractCellEditor` class was added in v1.3. Before then, implementing a cell editor for a new component type was much more difficult, since you had to implement all the `CellEditor` methods yourself.

Figure 77 is a picture of a table with a dialog that serves, indirectly, as a cell editor. When the user begins editing a cell in the **Favorite Color** column, a button (the true cell editor) appears and brings up the dialog, with which the user can choose a different color.

Figure 77   The `TableDialogEditDemo` application with the "Pick a Color" dialog.

You can run `TableDialogEditDemo` using Java Web Start or compile and run it yourself.[1]
Here's the code, taken from `ColorEditor.java`, that implements the cell editor:

---

[1] To run `TableDialogEditDemo` using Java Web Start, click the `TableDialogEditDemo` link on the `RunExamples/components.html` page on the CD. You can find the source files here: `JavaTutorial/uiswing/components/example-1dot4/index.html#TableDialogEditDemo`.

```
public class ColorEditor extends AbstractCellEditor
                         implements TableCellEditor,
                                    ActionListener {
    Color currentColor;
    JButton button;
    JColorChooser colorChooser;
    JDialog dialog;
    protected static final String EDIT = "edit";

    public ColorEditor() {
        button = new JButton();
        button.setActionCommand(EDIT);
        button.addActionListener(this);
        button.setBorderPainted(false);

        //Set up the dialog that the button brings up.
        colorChooser = new JColorChooser();
        dialog = JColorChooser.createDialog(
                                button,
                                "Pick a Color",
                                true,  //modal
                                colorChooser,
                                this,  //OK button handler
                                null); //no CANCEL button handler
    }

    public void actionPerformed(ActionEvent e) {
        if (EDIT.equals(e.getActionCommand())) {
            //The user has clicked the cell, so
            //bring up the dialog.
            button.setBackground(currentColor);
            colorChooser.setColor(currentColor);
            dialog.setVisible(true);

            fireEditingStopped(); //Make the renderer reappear.

        } else { //User pressed dialog's "OK" button.
            currentColor = colorChooser.getColor();
        }
    }

    //Implement the one CellEditor method that AbstractCellEditor doesn't.
    public Object getCellEditorValue() {
        return currentColor;
    }
```

```
    //Implement the one method defined by TableCellEditor.
    public Component getTableCellEditorComponent(JTable table,
                                                 Object value,
                                                 boolean isSelected,
                                                 int row,
                                                 int column) {
        currentColor = (Color)value;
        return button;
    }
}
```

As you can see, the code is pretty simple. The only part that's a bit tricky is the call to `fire-EditingStopped` at the end of the editor button's action handler. Without this call, the editor would remain active, even though the modal dialog is no longer visible. The call to `fire-EditingStopped` lets the table know that it can deactivate the editor, letting the cell be handled by the renderer again.

Using Custom Renderers

This section tells you how to create and specify a cell renderer. You can set a type-specific cell renderer using the `JTable` method `setDefaultRenderer`. To specify that cells in a particular column should use a renderer, use the `TableColumn` method `setCellRenderer`. You can even specify a cell-specific renderer by creating a `JTable` subclass, as we'll show later.

It's easy to customize the text or image rendered by the default renderer, `DefaultTable-CellRenderer`. You just create a subclass and implement the `setValue` method so that it invokes `setText` or `setIcon` with the appropriate string or image. For example, here is how the default date renderer is implemented:

```
static class DateRenderer extends DefaultTableCellRenderer {
    DateFormat formatter;
    public DateRenderer() { super(); }

    public void setValue(Object value) {
        if (formatter==null) {
            formatter = DateFormat.getDateInstance();
        }
        setText((value == null) ? "" : formatter.format(value));
    }
}
```

If extending `DefaultTableCellRenderer` doesn't do the trick, you can build a renderer using another superclass. The easiest way is to create a subclass of an existing component, making your subclass implement the `TableCellRenderer`[1] interface. `TableCellRenderer` requires just one method: `getTableCellRendererComponent`. Your implementation of this

405

method should set up the rendering component to reflect the passed-in state, and then return the component.

In Figure 77 (page 403), TableDialogEditDemo's renderer used for **Favorite Color** cells is a subclass of JLabel called ColorRenderer. Here are excerpts from ColorRenderer.java that show how it's implemented:[1]

```
public class ColorRenderer extends JLabel
                           implements TableCellRenderer {
    ...
    public ColorRenderer(boolean isBordered) {
        this.isBordered = isBordered;
        setOpaque(true); //MUST do this for background to show up.
    }

    public Component getTableCellRendererComponent(
                        JTable table, Object color,
                        boolean isSelected, boolean hasFocus,
                        int row, int column) {
        Color newColor = (Color)color;
        setBackground(newColor);
        if (isBordered) {
            if (isSelected) {
                ...
                //selectedBorder is a solid border in the color
                //table.getSelectionBackground().
                setBorder(selectedBorder);
            } else {
                ...
                //unselectedBorder is a solid border in the color
                //table.getBackground().
                setBorder(unselectedBorder);
            }
        }

        setToolTipText(...); //Discussed in the following section
        return this;
    }
}
```

---

[1] TableCellRenderer API documentation: http://java.sun.com/j2se/1.4.2/docs/api/javax/swing/table/TableCellRenderer.html.

[1] ColorRenderer.java is on the CD at: JavaTutorial/uiswing/components/example-1dot4/ColorRenderer.java.

Here's the code from `TableDialogEditDemo.java`[1] that registers a `ColorRenderer` instance as the default renderer for all `Color` data:

```
table.setDefaultRenderer(Color.class, new ColorRenderer(true));
```

The next section shows a couple of examples of using `TableColumn`'s `setCellRenderer` method, so we'll skip that for now and show you how to specify a renderer for a particular cell. To specify a cell-specific renderer, you need to define a `JTable` subclass that overrides the `getCellRenderer` method. For example, the following code makes the first cell in the first column of the table use a custom renderer:

```
TableCellRenderer weirdRenderer = new WeirdRenderer();
table = new JTable(...) {
    public TableCellRenderer getCellRenderer(int row, int column) {
        if ((row == 0) && (column == 0)) {
            return weirdRenderer;
        }
        // else...
        return super.getCellRenderer(row, column);
    }
};
```

Specifying Tool Tips for Cells

By default, the tool tip text displayed for a table cell is determined by the cell's renderer. However, sometimes it can be simpler to specify tool tip text by overriding `JTable`'s implementation of the `getToolTipText(MouseEvent)` method. This section tells you how to use both techniques.

To add a tool tip to a cell using its renderer, you first need to get or create the cell renderer. Then, after making sure the rendering component is a `JComponent`, invoke the `setToolTipText` method on it.

An example of setting tool tips for cells is in `TableRenderDemo`, which you can run using Java Web Start or compile and run yourself.[2] It adds tool tips to the cells of the **Sport** column with the following code:

---

[1] `TableDialogEditDemo.java` on the CD at: `JavaTutorial/uiswing/components/example-1dot4/TableDialogEditDemo.java`.

[2] To run `TableRenderDemo` using Java Web Start, click the `TableRenderDemo` link on the `RunExamples/components.html` page on the CD. You can find the source files here: `JavaTutorial/uiswing/components/example-1dot4/index.html#TableRenderDemo`.

```
//Set up tool tips for the sport cells.
DefaultTableCellRenderer renderer =
        new DefaultTableCellRenderer();
renderer.setToolTipText("Click for combo box");
sportColumn.setCellRenderer(renderer);
```

Figure 78 is a picture of the resulting tool tip:

Figure 78   A tool tip for cells in the **Sport** column.

Although the tool tip text in the previous example is static, you can also implement tool tips whose text changes depending on the state of the cell or program. Here are a couple ways to do so:

- Add a bit of code to the renderer's implementation of the getTableCellRenderer-Component method.
- Override the JTable method getToolTipText(MouseEvent).

An example of adding code to a cell renderer is in TableDialogEditDemo, which you can run using Java Web Start or compile and run yourself.[1] TableDialogEditDemo uses a renderer for colors, implemented in ColorRenderer.java, that sets the tool tip text using the boldface code in the following snippet:

```
public class ColorRenderer extends JLabel
                     implements TableCellRenderer {
    ...
    public Component getTableCellRendererComponent(
                     JTable table, Object color,
                     boolean isSelected, boolean hasFocus,
                     int row, int column) {
        Color newColor = (Color)color;
        ...
        setToolTipText("RGB value: " + newColor.getRed() + ", "
                                + newColor.getGreen() + ", "
                                + newColor.getBlue());
        return this;
    }
}
```

---

[1] To run TableDialogEditDemo using Java Web Start, click the TableDialogEditDemo link on the RunExamples/components.html page on the CD. You can find the source files here: JavaTutorial/ uiswing/components/example-1dot4/index.html#TableDialogEditDemo.

Figure 79 is an example of what the tool tip looks like.

Figure 79   A tool tip showing the RGB value of the selected color.

As we mentioned before, you can specify tool tip text by overriding JTable's getToolTip-
Text(MouseEvent) method. The program TableToolTipsDemo[1] shows how. The cells with
tool tips are in the **Sport** and **Vegetarian** columns. (See Figure 80.)

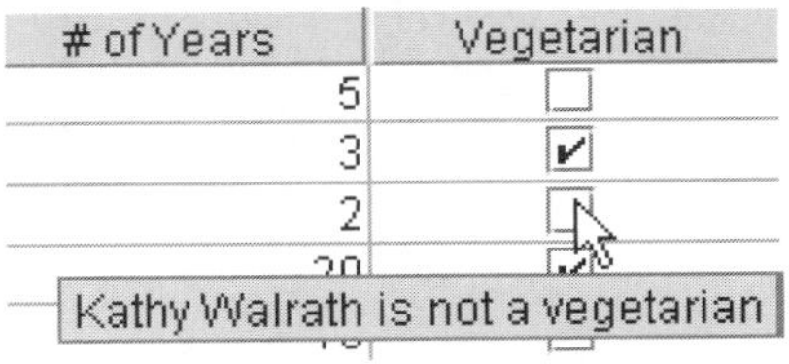

Figure 80   An example of a customized tool tip for the **Vegetarian** column.

Here's the code from TableToolTipsDemo.java that implements tool tips for cells in the
Sport and **Vegetarian** columns:

```
JTable table = new JTable(new MyTableModel()) {
    //Implement table cell tool tips.
    public String getToolTipText(MouseEvent e) {
        String tip = null;
        java.awt.Point p = e.getPoint();
        int rowIndex = rowAtPoint(p);
        int colIndex = columnAtPoint(p);
        int realColumnIndex = convertColumnIndexToModel(colIndex);

        if (realColumnIndex == 2) { //Sport column
            tip = "This person's favorite sport to "
                + "participate in is: "
                + getValueAt(rowIndex, colIndex);
```

---

[1] To run TableToolTipsDemo using Java Web Start, click the TableToolTipsDemo link on the
RunExamples/components.html page on the CD. You can find the source files here: JavaTutorial/
uiswing/components/example-1dot4/index.html#TableToolTipsDemo.

```
        } else if (realColumnIndex == 4) { //Veggie column
            TableModel model = getModel();
            String firstName = (String)model.getValueAt(rowIndex,0);
            String lastName = (String)model.getValueAt(rowIndex,1);
            Boolean veggie = (Boolean)model.getValueAt(rowIndex,4);
            if (Boolean.TRUE.equals(veggie)) {
                tip = firstName + " " + lastName
                        + " is a vegetarian";
            } else {
                tip = firstName + " " + lastName
                        + " is not a vegetarian";
            }

        } else { //another column
            //You can omit this part if you know you don't
            //have any renderers that supply their own tool
            //tips.
            tip = super.getToolTipText(e);
        }
        return tip;
    }
    ...
}
```

The code is fairly straightforward, except perhaps for the call to convertColumnIndexTo-Model, which is necessary because if the user moves the columns around, the view's index for the column doesn't match the model's index for it. For example, the user might drag the **Vegetarian** column (which the model considers to be at index 4) so that it's displayed as the first column—at view index 0. Since prepareRenderer gives us the view index, we need to translate the view index to a model index to be sure that we're dealing with the intended column.

Specifying Tool Tips for Column Headers

You can add a tool tip to a column header by setting the tool tip text for the table's JTable-Header. Often, different column headers require different tool tip text. You can change the text by overriding the table header's getToolTipText(MouseEvent) method.

An example of using the same tool tip text for all column headers is in TableSorterDemo.[1]
Here's how it sets the tool tip text:

```
table.getTableHeader().setToolTipText(
        "Click to sort; Shift-Click to sort in reverse order");
```

---

[1] To run TableSorterDemo using Java Web Start, click the TableSorterDemo link on the RunExamples/
components.html page on the CD. You can find the source files here: JavaTutorial/uiswing/
components/example-1dot4/index.html#TableSorterDemo.

TableToolTipsDemo has an example of implementing column header tool tips that vary by column. If you run TableToolTipsDemo,[1] you'll see the tool tips when you mouse over any column header except for the first two (see Figure 81). We elected not to supply tool tips for the name columns since they seemed self-explanatory. (Actually, we just wanted to show you that it could be done.)

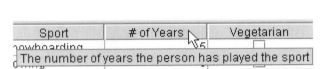

Figure 81   The column header tool tip for the **# of Years** column.

The following code implements the tool tips. Basically, it creates a subclass of JTable-Header that overrides the getToolTipText(MouseEvent) method so that it returns the text for the current column. To associate the revised table header with the table, the JTable method createDefaultTableHeader is overridden so that it returns an instance of the JTableHeader subclass.

```
protected String[] columnToolTips = {
    null,
    null,
    "The person's favorite sport to participate in",
    "The number of years the person has played the sport",
    "If checked, the person eats no meat"};
...

JTable table = new JTable(new MyTableModel()) {
    ...

    //Implement table header tool tips.
    protected JTableHeader createDefaultTableHeader() {
        return new JTableHeader(columnModel) {
            public String getToolTipText(MouseEvent e) {
                String tip = null;
                java.awt.Point p = e.getPoint();
```

---

[1] To run TableToolTipsDemo using Java Web Start, click the TableToolTipsDemo link on the RunExamples/components.html page on the CD. You can find the source files here: JavaTutorial/ uiswing/components/example-1dot4/index.html#TableToolTipsDemo.

```
                int index = columnModel.getColumnIndexAtX(p.x);
                int realIndex =
                        columnModel.getColumn(index).getModelIndex();
                return columnToolTips[realIndex];
            }
        };
    }
};
```

Version Note: Before 1.3, each column had its own header renderer, and you could use the value returned by the TableColumn method getHeaderRenderer to set a tool tip for a specific column header. For performance reasons, the default behavior is now to use a single renderer for all column headers, and getHeaderRenderer returns null. The default header renderer used for all columns is returned by the TableHeader method getDefaultRenderer, which was added in 1.3.

Sorting and Otherwise Manipulating Data

One way to perform data manipulation such as sorting is to use one or more specialized table models (*data manipulators*), in addition to the table model that provides the data (the data model). The data manipulators should sit between the table and the data model, as Figure 82 shows.

Figure 82   Data manipulators sit between the table and the data model.

If you decide to implement a data manipulator, take a look at TableMap.java and Table-Sorter.java.[1] The TableMap class implements TableModel and serves as a superclass for data manipulators. TableSorter is a TableMap subclass that sorts the data provided by another table model. You can either change these classes, using them as a basis for writing your own data manipulator, or use the classes as is to provide sorting functionality.

To implement sorting with TableSorter, you need just three lines of code. The following listing shows the differences between TableDemo and its sorting cousin, TableSorterDemo.[2]

---

[1] TableMap.java and TableSorter.java are on the CD at: JavaTutorial/uiswing/components/example-1dot4/TableSorterDemo.java.

[2] TableMap.java and TableSorterDemo.java are on the CD at: JavaTutorial/uiswing/components/example-1dot4/index.html#TableSorterDemo.

```
TableSorter sorter = new TableSorter(new MyTableModel()); //ADDED THIS
//JTable table = new JTable(new MyTableModel());          //OLD
JTable table = new JTable(sorter);                //NEW
sorter.addMouseListenerToHeaderInTable(table); //ADDED THIS
```

The addMouseListenerToHeaderInTable method adds a mouse listener that detects clicks over the column headers. When the listener detects a click, it sorts the rows based on the clicked column. As Figure 83 shows, when you click "Last Name," the rows are reordered so that "Campione" is in the first row and "Zakhour" is in the last. When you Shift-click a column header, the rows are sorted in reverse order.

First Name	Last Name	Sport	# of Years	Vegetarian
Mary	Campione	Snowboarding	5	☐
Alison	Huml	Rowing	3	☑
Philip	Milne	Pool	10	☐
Kathy	Walrath	Knitting	2	☐
Sharon	Zakhour	Speed reading	20	☑

Figure 83   The TableSorterDemo application with the **Last Name** column sorted alphabetically.

The Table API

Tables 88 through 92 cover just part of the table API. For more information about the table API, see the API documentation for JTable[1] and for the various classes and interfaces in the table package.[2] Also see The JComponent Class (page 53), which describes the API that JTable inherits from JComponent.

Table 88: Table-Related Classes and Interfaces

Class or Interface	Purpose
JTable	The component that presents the table to the user.
JTableHeader	The component that presents the column names to the user. By default, the table generates this component automatically.

---

[1] JTable   API   documentation: `http://java.sun.com/j2se/1.4.2/docs/api/javax/swing/JTable.html`.

[2] Table package API documentation: `http://java.sun.com/j2se/1.4.2/docs/api/javax/swing/table/package-summary.html`.

Table 88: Table-Related Classes and Interfaces *(continued)*

Class or Interface	Purpose
TableModel AbstractTableModel	Respectively, the interface that a table model must implement and the usual superclass for table model implementations.
TableCellRenderer DefaultTableCellRenderer	Respectively, the interface that a table cell renderer must implement and the usual implementation used.
TableCellEditor DefaultCellEditor AbstractCellEditor	Respectively, the interface that a table cell editor must implement, the usual implementation used, and the usual superclass for table cell editor implementations.
TableColumnModel DefaultTableColumnModel	Respectively, the interface that a table column model must implement and the usual implementation used. You don't usually need to deal with the table column model directly unless you need to get the column selection model, or get a column index or object.
TableColumn	Controls all the attributes of a table column, including resizability; minimum, preferred, current, and maximum widths; and an optional column-specific renderer/editor.
DefaultTableModel	A Vector-based table model used by JTable when you construct a table specifying no data model and no data.
TableModelListener	The interface that an object must implement to be notified of changes to the TableModel.
ListSelectionListener	The interface that an object must implement to be notified of changes to the table's selection.

Table 89: Creating and Setting up a Table

Constructor or Method	Purpose

JTable(TableModel)
JTable(TableModel, TableColumnModel)
JTable(TableModel,
    TableColumnModel,
    ListSelectionModel)
JTable()
JTable(int, int)
JTable(Object[][], Object[])
JTable(Vector, Vector)
	Create a table. The optional TableModel argument specifies the model that provides the data to the table. The optional TableColumnModel and ListSelectionModel arguments let you specify the table column model and the row selection model. As an alternative to specifying a table model, you can supply data and column names, using arrays or vectors. Another option is to specify no data, optionally specifying the number of rows and columns (both integers) to be in the table.

void setPreferredScrollableViewportSize(Dimension)	Set the size of the visible part of the table when it's viewed within a scroll pane.
JTableHeader getTableHeader()	Get the component that displays the column names.

Table 90: Manipulating Columns

Constructor or Method	Purpose
`TableColumnModel getColumnModel()` *(in* `JTable`*)*	Get the table's column model.

`TableColumn getColumn(int)`
 `Enumeration getColumns()`
 (in `TableColumnModel`*)*
	Get one or all of the `TableColumn` objects for the table.

`void setMinWidth(int)`
 `void setPreferredWidth(int)`
 `void setMaxWidth(int)`
 (in `TableColumn`*)*
	Set the minimum, preferred, or maximum width of the column.

`int getMinWidth()`
 `int getPreferredWidth()`
 `int getMaxWidth()`
 `int getWidth()`
 (in `TableColumn`*)*
	Get the minimum, preferred, maximum, or current width of the column.

Table 91: Using Editors and Renderers

Method	Purpose

`void setDefaultRenderer(Class,`
 `        TableCellRenderer)`
 `void setDefaultEditor(Class,`
 `        TableCellEditor)`
 (in `JTable`*)*
	Set the renderer or editor used, by default, for all cells in all columns that return objects of the specified type.

`void setCellRenderer(TableCellRenderer)`
 `void setCellEditor(TableCellEditor)`
 (in `TableColumn`*)*
	Set the renderer or editor used for all cells in this column.

`TableCellRenderer getHeaderRenderer()` *(in* `TableColumn`*)*	Get the header renderer for this column. **Version Note:** As of 1.3, this method returns null if the column uses the default renderer. You generally use the `TableHeader` method `getDefaultRenderer` instead.
`TableCellRenderer getDefaultRenderer()` *(in* `JTableHeader`*)*	Get the header renderer used when none is defined by a table column. Introduced in 1.3.

T

Components

Table 92: Implementing Selection

Method	Purpose
`void setSelectionMode(int)`	Set the selection intervals allowed in the table. Valid values are defined in `ListSelection-Model` as `SINGLE_SELECTION`, `SINGLE_INTERVAL_SELECTION`, and `MULTIPLE_INTERVAL_SELECTION` (the default).
`void setSelectionModel(ListSelectionModel)` `ListSelectionModel getSelectionModel()`	Set or get the model used to control row selections.

`void setRowSelectionAllowed(boolean)`
`void setColumnSelectionAllowed(boolean)`
`void setCellSelectionEnabled(boolean)`
	Set the table's selection orientation. The boolean argument specifies whether that particular type of selection is allowed. By default, row selection is allowed, and column and cell selection are not.

Examples That Use Tables

This table lists examples that use `JTable` and where those examples are described.

Example	Where Described	Notes
`SimpleTableDemo`	Creating a Simple Table (page 388)	A basic table with *no* custom model. Does not include code to specify column widths or detect user editing.
`SimpleTableSelectionDemo`	Detecting User Selections (page 393)	Adds single selection and selection detection to `SimpleTableDemo`. By modifying the program's `ALLOW_COLUMN_SELECTION` and `ALLOW_ROW_SELECTION` constants, you can experiment with alternatives to the table default of allowing only rows to be selected.
`TableDemo`	Creating a Table Model (page 394)	A basic table with a custom model.
`TableFTFEditDemo`	Using an Editor to Validate User-Entered Text (page 401)	Modifies `TableDemo` to use a custom editor (a formatted text field variant) for all `Integer` data.

Example	Where Described	Notes
TableRenderDemo	Using a Combo Box as an Editor (page 400)	Modifies TableDemo to use a custom editor (a combo box) for all data in the Sport column. Also intelligently picks column sizes. Uses renderers to display tool tips for the Sport cells.
TableDialogEditDemo	Using Other Editors (page 402)	Modifies TableDemo to have a cell renderer and editor that display a color and let you choose a new one, using a color chooser dialog.
TableToolTipsDemo	Specifying Tool Tips for Cells (page 407), Specifying Tool Tips for Column Headers (page 410)	Demonstrates how to use several techniques to set tool tip text for cells and column headers.
TableSorterDemo	Sorting and Otherwise Manipulating Data (page 412)	Sorts column data by interposing a data-manipulating table model between the data model and the table. Detects user clicks on column headers.
ListSelectionDemo	How to Write a List Selection Listener (page 685)	Shows how to use all list selection modes, using a list selection listener that's shared between a table and list.
SharedModelDemo	Using Models (page 50)	Builds on ListSelectionDemo, making the data model be shared between the table and list. If you edit an item in the first column of the table, the new value is reflected in the list.
TreeTable TreeTable II	"Creating TreeTables in Swing" (Parts 1, 2 and 3) in *The Swing Connection*, online at: http://java. sun.com/products/ jfc/tsc/articles/ treetable1/ index.html.	Examples that combine a tree and table to show detailed information about a hierarchy such as a file system. The tree is a renderer for the table.

T

Components

How to Use Text Areas

The JTextArea[1] class provides a component that displays multiple lines of text, optionally allowing the user to edit the text. If you need to obtain only one line of input from the user, you should use a text field instead. If you want the text area to display its text using multiple fonts or other styles, you should use an editor pane or text pane instead. If the displayed text has a limited length and is never edited by the user, consider using a label instead.

Many of this book's examples use uneditable text areas to display program output. Figure 84 is a picture of one that lets you enter text using a text field (at the top) and then appends the entered text to a text area (underneath).

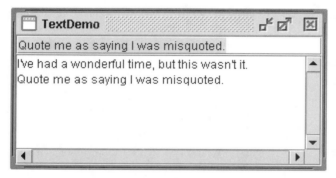

Figure 84   The TextDemo application with two Groucho Marx quotations.

You can run TextDemo using Java Web Start or compile and run the example yourself.[2] Here's the code from TextDemo.java that creates and initializes the text area:

```
textArea = new JTextArea(5, 20);
JScrollPane scrollPane = new JScrollPane(textArea,
                  JScrollPane.VERTICAL_SCROLLBAR_ALWAYS,
                  JScrollPane.HORIZONTAL_SCROLLBAR_ALWAYS);
textArea.setEditable(false);
```

The two arguments to the JTextArea constructor are hints as to the number of rows and columns, respectively, the text area should display. The scroll pane that contains the text area pays attention to these hints when determining how big the scroll pane should be.

---

[1] JTextArea API documentation: http://java.sun.com/j2se/1.4.2/docs/api/javax/swing/ JTextArea.html.

[2] To run TextDemo using Java Web Start, click the TextDemo link on the RunExamples/components.html page on the CD. You can find the source files here: JavaTutorial/uiswing/components/ example-1dot4/index.html#TextDemo.

Without the creation of the scroll pane, the text area would not automatically scroll. The `JScrollPane` constructor shown in the preceding snippet sets up the text area for viewing in a scroll pane and specifies that the scroll pane's scroll bars should both always be visible. See How to Use Scroll Panes (page 325) if you want further information.

By default, text areas are editable. The code `setEditable(false)` makes the text area uneditable. It is still selectable and the user can copy data from it, but the user can't change the text area's contents directly.

The following code adds text to the text area. Note that the text system uses the \n character internally to represent newlines; for details, see the API documentation for `Default-EditorKit`.[1]

```
private final static String newline = "\n";
...
textArea.append(text + newline);
```

Unless the user has moved the caret (insertion point) by clicking or dragging in the text area, the text area automatically scrolls so that the appended text is visible. You can force the text area to scroll to the bottom by moving the caret to the end of the text area, like this, after the call to append:

```
textArea.setCaretPosition(textArea.getDocument().getLength());
```

Customizing Text Areas

You can customize text areas in several ways. For example, although a given text area can display text in only one font and color, you can (as for any component) set which font and color it uses. You can also determine how the text area wraps lines and the number of characters per tab. Finally, you can use the methods `JTextArea` inherits from `JTextComponent` to set properties such as the caret, support for dragging, selection color, and so on.

The following code, taken from `TextSamplerDemo.java`,[2] demonstrates initializing an editable text area. The text area uses the specified italic font and wraps lines between words.

```
JTextArea textArea = new JTextArea(
    "This is an editable JTextArea. " +
    "A text area is a \"plain\" text component, " +
    "which means that although it can display text " +
    "in any font, all of the text is in the same font."
);
```

---

[1] `DefaultEditorKit` API documentation: `http://java.sun.com/j2se/1.4.2/docs/api/javax/swing/text/DefaultEditorKit.html`.

[2] `TextSamplerDemo.java` is on the CD at: `JavaTutorial/uiswing/components/example-1dot4/TextSamplerDemo.java`.

```
textArea.setFont(new Font("Serif", Font.ITALIC, 16));
textArea.setLineWrap(true);
textArea.setWrapStyleWord(true);
```

By default, a text area doesn't wrap lines that are too long for the display area. Instead it uses one line for all the text between newline characters and—if the text area is within a scroll pane—allows itself to be scrolled horizontally. This example turns line wrapping on with a call to `setLineWrap` and then calls `setWrapStyleWord` to indicate that the text area should wrap lines at word boundaries rather than at character boundaries.

To provide scrolling capability, the example puts the text area in a scroll pane.

```
JScrollPane areaScrollPane = new JScrollPane(textArea);
areaScrollPane.setVerticalScrollBarPolicy(
                JScrollPane.VERTICAL_SCROLLBAR_ALWAYS);
areaScrollPane.setPreferredSize(new Dimension(250, 250));
```

You might have noticed that the `JTextArea` constructor used in this example does not specify the number of rows or columns. Instead, the code limits the size of the text area by setting the scroll pane's preferred size.

The Text Area API

Tables 93 through 95 list the commonly used `JTextArea` constructors and methods. Other methods you are likely to call are defined in `JTextComponent` and listed in The Text Component API (page 77). You should also refer to the `JTextArea` API documentation at: `http://java.sun.com/j2se/1.4.2/docs/api/javax/swing/JTextArea.html`.

You might also invoke methods on a text area that it inherits from its other ancestors, such as `setPreferredSize`, `setForeground`, `setBackground`, `setFont`, and so on. See The JComponent Class (page 53) for tables of commonly used inherited methods.

Table 93: Setting or Getting Contents

Method or Constructor	Purpose

`JTextArea()`
`JTextArea(String)`
`JTextArea(String, int, int)`
`JTextArea(int, int)`
	Create a text area. When present, the `String` argument contains the initial text. The `int` arguments specify the desired width in columns and height in rows, respectively.

`void setText(String)`
`String getText()`
(defined in `JTextComponent`*)*
	Set or get the text displayed by the text area.

Table 94: Fine-Tuning the Text Area's Appearance

Method	Purpose

`void setEditable(boolean)`
`boolean isEditable()`
(defined in JTextComponent*)*
	Set or get whether the user can edit the text in the text area.

`void setColumns(int);` `int getColumns()`	Set or get the number of columns displayed by the text area. This is really just a hint for computing the area's preferred width.
`void setRows(int);` `int getRows()`	Set or get the number of rows displayed by the text area. This is a hint for computing the area's preferred width.
`int setTabSize(int)`	Set the number of characters a tab is equivalent to.
`int setLineWrap(boolean)`	Set whether lines are wrapped if they are too long to fit within the allocated width. By default, this property is false and lines are not wrapped.
`int setWrapStyleWord(boolean)`	Set whether lines can be wrapped at white space (word boundaries) or at any character. By default, this property is false, and lines can be wrapped (if line wrapping is turned on) at any character.

Table 95: Implementing the Text Area's Functionality

Method	Purpose
`void selectAll()` *(defined in* JTextComponent*)*	Select all characters in the text area.
`void append(String)`	Add the specified text to the end of the text area.
`void insert(String, int)`	Insert the specified text at the specified position.
`void replaceRange(String, int, int)`	Replace the text between the indicated positions with the specified string.

`int getLineCount()`
`int getLineOfOffset(int)`
`int getLineStartOffset(int)`
`int getLineEndOffset(int)`
	Utilities for finding a line number or the position of the beginning or end of the specified line.

T

Components

421

Examples That Use Text Areas

Many of this book's examples use JTextArea, typically to provide an area where events are logged. Here's a partial list of the demos that use text areas.

Example	Where Described	Notes
TextDemo	This section	An application that appends user-entered text to a text area.
TextSamplerDemo	Using Text Components (page 60)	Uses one of each of Swing's text components.
HtmlDemo	Using HTML in Swing Components (page 43)	A text area lets the user enter HTML code to be displayed in a label.
BasicDnD	How to Use Drag and Drop and Data Transfer (page 545)	Demonstrates built-in drag-and-drop functionality of several Swing components, including text areas.
ExtendedDnDDemo	How to Use Drag and Drop and Data Transfer (page 545)	Demonstrates dragging and dropping text between a text area, a list, and a table.
DragFileDemo	How to Use Drag and Drop and Data Transfer (page 545)	Demonstrates dragging file contents from a file chooser into a text area. A tabbed pane lets you easily switch between files.
FocusConceptsDemo	How to Use the Focus Subsystem (page 583)	Demonstrates how focus works, using a few components that include a text area.

How to Use Text Fields

A text field is a basic text control that lets the user enter a small amount of text. When the user indicates that text entry is complete (usually by pressing Enter), the text field fires an action event. If you need to obtain more than one line of input from the user, you should use a text area instead.

The Swing API provides several classes for components that are either varieties of text fields or that include text fields.

JTextField[a]	What this section covers: basic text fields.
JFormattedTextField	A JTextField subclass that allows you to specify the legal set of characters the user can enter. See How to Use Formatted Text Fields (page 221).
JPasswordField	A JTextField subclass that doesn't show the characters the user types. See How to Use Password Fields (page 297).
JComboBox	Can be editable, and provides a menu of strings to choose from. See How to Use Combo Boxes (page 176).
JSpinner	Combines a formatted text field with several small buttons that let the user choose the previous or next available value. See How to Use Spinners (page 357).

a. See the JTextField API documentation at: http://java.sun.com/j2se/1.4.2/docs/api/javax/swing/JTextField.html.

Figure 85 displays a basic text field and a text area. The text field is editable; the text area isn't. When the user presses Enter in the text field, the program copies the text field's contents to the text area and then selects all the text in the text field.

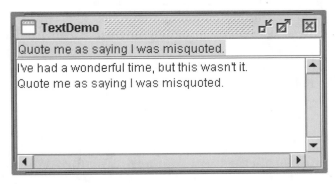

Figure 85   The TextDemo application with two Groucho Marx quotations.

T
Components

423

You can run `TextDemo` using Java Web Start or compile and run the example yourself.[1] Here's the code from `TextDemo.java` that creates and sets up the text field:

```
textField = new JTextField(20);
textField.addActionListener(this);
```

The integer argument passed to the `JTextField` constructor, `20` in the example, indicates the number of columns in the field. This number is used along with metrics provided by the field's current font to calculate the field's preferred width. It does not limit the number of characters the user can enter. To do that, you can use either a formatted text field or a document listener, as described in Text Component Features (page 64) in Chapter 3.

Note: We encourage you to specify the number of columns for each text field. If you don't specify the number of columns or a preferred size, then the field's preferred size changes whenever the text changes, which can result in unwanted layout updates.

The next line of code registers a `TextDemo` object as an action listener for the text field. Here's the `actionPerformed` method that handles action events from the text field:

```
private final static String newline = "\n";
...
public void actionPerformed(ActionEvent evt) {
    String text = textField.getText();
    textArea.append(text + newline);
    textField.selectAll();
}
```

Notice the use of `JTextField`'s `getText` method to retrieve the text currently contained by the text field. The text returned by this method does *not* include a newline character for the Enter key that fired the action event.

You've seen how a basic text field can be used. Because `JTextField` inherits from `JText-Component`, it's very flexible and can be customized almost any way you like. For example, you can add a document listener or document filter to be notified when the text changes and (in the filter case) modify the text field accordingly. Information on text components is in Text Component Features (page 64). Before customizing a `JTextField`, however, make sure that one of the other components based on text fields won't do the job for you.

---

[1]   To run `TextDemo` using Java Web Start, click the `TextDemo` link on the `RunExamples/components.html` page on the CD. You can find the source files here: `JavaTutorial/uiswing/components/example-1dot4/index.html#TextDemo`.

Often, text fields are paired with labels that describe the text fields. See Examples That Use Text Fields (page 426) for pointers to examples of creating these pairs.

The Text Field API

Tables 96 through 98 list the commonly used `JTextField` constructors and methods. Other methods you are likely to call are defined in `JTextComponent` and listed in The Text Component API (page 77). Also refer to the `JTextField` API documentation at: `http://java.sun.com/j2se/1.4.2/docs/api/javax/swing/JTextField.html`.

You might also invoke methods on a text field that it inherits from its other ancestors, such as `setPreferredSize`, `setForeground`, `setBackground`, `setFont`, and so on. See The JComponent Class (page 53) in Chapter 3 for tables of commonly used inherited methods.

Table 96: Setting or Getting the Field's Contents

Method or Constructor	Purpose

`JTextField()`
`JTextField(String)`
`JTextField(String, int)`
`JTextField(int)`
	Create a text field. When present, the `int` argument specifies the desired width in columns. The `String` argument contains the field's initial text.

`void setText(String)`
`String getText()`
(defined in `JTextComponent`*)*
	Set or get the text displayed by the text field.

Table 97: Fine-Tuning the Field's Appearance

Method	Purpose

`void setEditable(boolean)`
`boolean isEditable()`
(defined in `JTextComponent`*)*
	Set or get whether the user can edit the text in the text field.

`void setColumns(int);` `int getColumns()`	Set or get the number of columns displayed by the text field. This is really just a hint for computing the field's preferred width.
`void setHorizontalAlignment(int);` `int getHorizontalAlignment()`	Set or get how the text is aligned horizontally within its area. You can use `JTextField.LEADING`, `JTextField.CENTER`, and `JTextField.TRAILING` for arguments.

T

Components

Table 98: Implementing the Field's Functionality

Method	Purpose
`void addActionListener(ActionListener)` `void removeActionListener(ActionListener)`	Add or remove an action listener.
`void selectAll()` *(defined in* `JTextComponent`*)*	Select all characters in the text field.

Examples That Use Text Fields

This table shows a few of the examples that use `JTextField` and where those examples are described. For examples of code that's similar among all varieties of text fields, such as dealing with layout, also look at the example lists for related components such as formatted text fields and spinners.

Example	Where Described	Notes
TextDemo	This section	An application that uses a basic text field with an action listener.
DialogDemo	How to Make Dialogs (page 187)	`CustomDialog.java` includes a text field whose value is checked. You can bring up the dialog by clicking the More Dialogs tab, selecting the Input-validating dialog radio button, and then clicking the Show it! buton.

TextSamplerDemo	Using Text Components (page 60)	Lays out label-text field pairs using a `GridBagLayout` and a convenience method:
		
		`addLabelTextRows(JLabel[] labels,`
		`                 JTextField[] textFields,`
		`                 GridBagLayout gridbag,`
		`                 Container container)`

TextInputDemo	How to Use Formatted Text Fields (page 221)	Lays out label-text field pairs using a `SpringLayout` and a `SpringUtilities` convenience method:
		
		`makeCompactGrid(Container parent,`
		`                int rows, int cols,`
		`                int initialX, int initialY,`
		`                int xPad, int yPad)`

How to Use Tool Bars

A JToolBar[1] is a container that groups several components—usually buttons with icons—into a row or column. Often, tool bars provide easy access to functionality that is also in menus. How to Use Actions (page 513) in Chapter 9 describes how to provide the same functionality in menu items and tool bar buttons.

Figure 86 shows an application named ToolBarDemo that contains a tool bar above a text area. You can run ToolBarDemo using Java Web Start or compile and run it yourself.[2]

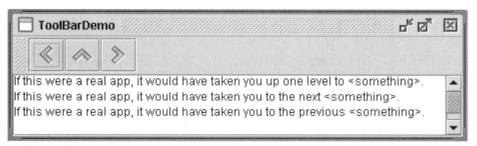

Figure 86   The ToolBarDemo application.

By default, the user can drag the tool bar to a different edge of its container or out into a window of its own. Figure 87 shows how the application looks after the user has dragged the tool bar to the right edge of its container.

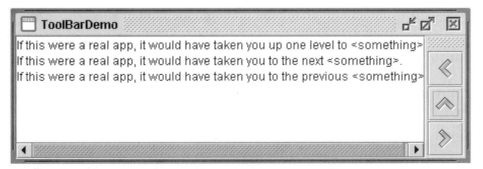

Figure 87   The ToolBarDemo application with the tool bar on the right side.

---

[1]   JToolBar API documentation: http://java.sun.com/j2se/1.4.2/docs/api/javax/swing/ JToolBar.html.

[2]   To run ToolBarDemo using Java Web Start, click the ToolBarDemo link on the RunExamples/ components.html page on the CD. You can find the source files here: JavaTutorial/uiswing/ components/example-1dot4/index.html#ToolBarDemo.

For the drag-out behavior to work correctly, the tool bar must be in a container that uses BorderLayout. The component that the tool bar affects is generally in the center of the container. The tool bar must be the only other component in the container, and it must not be in the center.

Figure 88 shows how the application looks after the user has dragged the tool bar outside its window.

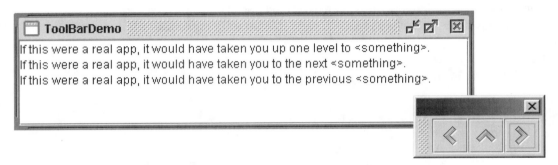

Figure 88   The ToolBarDemo application after the user has dragged the tool bar outside its window.

The following code creates the tool bar and adds it to a container.

```
public class ToolBarDemo extends JPanel
                         implements ActionListener {
    ...
    public ToolBarDemo() {
        super(new BorderLayout());
        ...
        JToolBar toolBar = new JToolBar("Still draggable");
        addButtons(toolBar);
        ...
        setPreferredSize(new Dimension(450, 130));
        add(toolBar, BorderLayout.PAGE_START);
        add(scrollPane, BorderLayout.CENTER);
    }
    ...
}
```

The code positions the tool bar above the scroll pane by placing both components in a panel controlled by a border layout, with the tool bar in the PAGE_START position and the scroll pane in the CENTER position. Because the scroll pane is in the center and no other components except the tool bar are in the container, the tool bar is automatically draggable to other edges of the container. The tool bar can also be dragged out into its own window, in which case the window may, depending on the look and feel, have the title Still draggable, as specified with the JToolBar constructor.

Note: The tool bar's window is a JDialog. This demo would normally use JDialog.set-DefaultLookAndFeelDecorated(true) to make the window's decorations be painted by the look and feel, which by default is the Java look and feel. Unfortunately, bug #4820659 prevents the user from using the mouse to close dialogs decorated by the Java look and feel. You might consider not using dialog decorations from the Java look and feel until the fix for this bug is released, which we expect will happen in v1.5. You can track this bug online at: http://developer.java.sun.com/developer/bugParade/bugs/4820659.html. Another bug to keep an eye on is # 4793741, which proposes that the tool bar's window get the default LookAndFeelDecorated setting from JFrame. You can track this bug online at: http://developer.java.sun.com/developer/bugParade/bugs/4793741.html.

Creating Tool-Bar Buttons

The buttons in the tool bar are ordinary JButtons that use images from the Java look and feel Graphics Repository. We encourage you to consider using images from the repository if your tool bar uses the Java look and feel.

Each image in the repository comes in 16x16 and 24x24 versions, provided in a file named jlfgr-1_0.jar. You can download this JAR file from the "Java look and feel Graphics Repository" page.[1] That page shows all the images and has links to pages that describe each image, including its intended use and location within the JAR file.

Here's the code that creates the buttons and adds them to the tool bar.

```
protected void addButtons(JToolBar toolBar) {
    JButton button = null;

    //first button
    button = makeNavigationButton("Back24", PREVIOUS,
                                  "Back to previous something-or-other",
                                  "Previous");
    toolBar.add(button);

    //second button
    button = makeNavigationButton("Up24", UP,
                                  "Up to something-or-other",
                                  "Up");
```

---

[1] The repository is online at: http://developer.java.sun.com/developer/techDocs/hi/repository/index.html.

T Components

```
        toolBar.add(button);
        ...//similar code for creating and adding the third button...
    }

    protected JButton makeNavigationButton(String imageName,
                                           String actionCommand,
                                           String toolTipText,
                                           String altText) {
        //Look for the image.
        String imgLocation = "toolbarButtonGraphics/navigation/"
                           + imageName
                           + ".gif";
        URL imageURL = ToolBarDemo.class.getResource(imgLocation);

        //Create and initialize the button.
        JButton button = new JButton();
        button.setActionCommand(actionCommand);
        button.setToolTipText(toolTipText);
        button.addActionListener(this);

        if (imageURL != null) {                      //image found
            button.setIcon(new ImageIcon(imageURL, altText));
        } else {                                     //no image found
            button.setText(altText);
            System.err.println("Resource not found: " + imgLocation);
        }

        return button;
    }
```

The first call to makeNavigationButton creates the image for the first button, using the 24x24 "Back" navigation image in the graphics repository. We found the image by looking at the Java look and feel Graphics Repository page, which shows the navigation images (among others) and has a link to the navigation graphics page at: http://developer. java.sun.com/developer/techDocs/hi/repository/TBG_Navigation.html. That page describes the navigation images and informs us that the 24x24 Back image is located at toolbarButtonGraphics/navigation/Back24.gif. The makeNavigationButton method gets the image from the repository's JAR file (assuming the JAR file is in the example's code base) using the getResource method.

Besides finding the image for the button, the makeNavigationButton method also creates the button, sets the strings for its action command and tool tip text, and adds the action listener for the button. If the image is missing, the method prints an error message and puts text on the button, so that the button is still usable.

Note: If any buttons in your tool bar duplicate functionality of other components, such as menu items, you should probably create and add the tool bar buttons as described in How to Use Actions (page 513) in Chapter 9.

Customizing Tool Bars

By adding a few lines of code to the preceding example, we can demonstrate some more tool bar features:

- Using `setFloatable(false)` to make a tool bar immovable.
- Using `setRollover(true)` to make the edges of the tool bar's buttons invisible except for the button (if any) that the mouse pointer is over.
- Adding a separator to a tool bar.
- Adding a non-button component to a tool bar.

Figure 89 shows a picture of the new UI. You can run `ToolBarDemo2` using Java Web Start or compile and run the example yourself.[1]

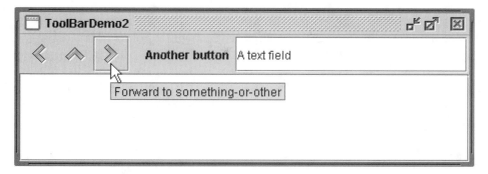

Figure 89   The `ToolBarDemo2` application.

Because the tool bar can no longer be dragged, it no longer has bumps at its left edge in the Java look and feel. Here's the code that turns off dragging:

```
toolBar.setFloatable(false);
```

---

[1] To run `ToolBarDemo2` using Java Web Start, click the `ToolBarDemo2` link on the `RunExamples/components.html` page on the CD. You can find the source files here: `JavaTutorial/uiswing/components/example-1dot4/index.html#ToolBarDemo2`.

The tool bar is in rollover mode, so only the button under the cursor has a border. Here's the code that sets rollover mode:

```
toolBar.setRollover(true);
```

Another visible difference is that the tool bar contains two new components, which are preceded by a blank space—a separator. Here's the code that adds the separator:

```
toolBar.addSeparator();
```

Here's the code that adds the new components:

```
//fourth button
button = new JButton("Another button");
...
toolBar.add(button);

//fifth component is NOT a button!
JTextField textField = new JTextField("A text field");
...
toolBar.add(textField);
```

You can easily make the components in a tool bar be aligned along their tops or bottoms, instead of centered, by invoking the setAlignmentY method. For example, to align the tops of all the components in a tool bar, invoke setAlignmentY(TOP_ALIGNMENT) on each component. Similarly, you can use the setAlignmentX method to specify the alignment of components when the tool bar is vertical. This flexibility of layout is possible because tool bars use BoxLayout to position their components. For more information, see How to Use Box-Layout (page 462) in Chapter 8.

The Tool Bar API

Table 99 lists the commonly used JToolBar constructors and methods. Other methods you might call are listed in the API tables in The JComponent Class (page 53) in Chapter 3. Also refer to the JToolBar API documentation at: http://java.sun.com/j2se/1.4.2/docs/api/javax/swing/JToolBar.html.

Table 99: JToolBar Constructors and Methods

Method or Constructor	Purpose
JToolBar() JToolBar(int) JToolBar(String) JToolBar(String, int)	Create a tool bar. The optional int parameter lets you specify the orientation; the default is HORIZONTAL. The optional String parameter, introduced in 1.3, allows you to specify the title displayed for the undocked tool bar's window.
Component add(Component)	Add a component to the tool bar. **Version Note:** Before 1.3, the only way to associate an Action with a tool bar button was to use JToolBar's add(Action) method to create the button and add it to the tool bar. As of 1.3, that method is no longer recommended. You can instead associate a button with an Action using the setAction(Action) method defined by Abstract-Button.
void addSeparator()	Add a separator to the end of the tool bar.
void setFloatable(boolean) boolean isFloatable()	The floatable property is true by default, to indicate that the user can drag the tool bar out into a separate window. To turn off tool bar dragging, use toolBar.setFloatable(false). Some look and feels might ignore this property.
void setRollover(boolean) boolean isRollover()	The rollover property is false by default. Set it to true to request that every button in the tool bar have no borders until the user passes the cursor over the button. Some look and feels might ignore this property. Introduced in 1.4.

Examples That Use Tool Bars

This table lists examples that use JToolBar and where those examples are described.

Example	Where Described	Notes
ToolBarDemo	This section	A basic tool bar with icon-only buttons.
ToolBarDemo2	This section	Demonstrates a nonfloatable tool bar in rollover mode that contains a separator and a non-button component.
ActionDemo	How to Use Actions (page 513)	Implements a tool bar using Action objects.

T

Components

433

How to Use Tool Tips

Creating a tool tip for any `JComponent` is easy. You just use the `setToolTipText` method to set up a tool tip for the component. For example, to add tool tips to three buttons, you add only three lines of code:

```
b1.setToolTipText("Click this button to disable the middle button.");
b2.setToolTipText("This middle button does nothing when you click it.");
b3.setToolTipText("Click this button to enable the middle button.");
```

When the user of the program pauses with the cursor over any of the program's buttons, the tool tip for the button comes up. (See Figure 90.) You can see this by running the `Button-Demo` example, which is explained in How to Use Buttons (page 156) and shown in Figure 90.

Figure 90   A tool tip appears when the cursor pauses over any button in `ButtonDemo`.

For components such as tabbed panes that have multiple parts, it often makes sense to vary the tool-tip text to reflect the part of the component under the cursor. For example, a tabbed pane might use this feature to explain what will happen when you click the tab under the cursor. When you implement a tabbed pane, you can specify the tab-specific tool-tip text in an argument to the `addTab` or `setToolTipTextAt` method.

Even in components that have no API for setting part-specific tool-tip text, you can generally do the job yourself. If the component supports renderers, then you can set the tool tip text on a custom renderer. You can find examples of doing this in the table and tree sections. An alternative that works for all `JComponents` is creating a subclass of the component and overriding its `getToolTipText(MouseEvent)` method.

The Tool-Tip API

Most of the API you need to set up tool tips is in the JComponent class, and thus is inherited by most Swing components. More tool-tip API is in individual classes such as JTabbedPane. In general, those APIs are sufficient for specifying and displaying tool tips; you usually don't need to deal directly with the implementing classes, JToolTip[1] and ToolTipManager.[2]

Table 100 lists the JComponent tool tip API. For information on individual components' support for tool tips, see the how-to section for the component in question.

Table 100: Tool-Tip API in JComponent

Method	Purpose
setToolTipText(String)	If the specified string is non-null, then register the component as having a tool tip and makes the tool tip (when displayed) have the specified text. If the argument is null, then this method turns off tool tips for this component.
String getToolTipText()	Return the string that was previously specified with set-ToolTipText.
String getToolTipText(MouseEvent)	By default, return the same value returned by getToolTip-Text(). Multi-part components such as JTabbedPane, JTable, and JTree override this method to return a string associated with the mouse event location. For example, each tab in a tabbed pane can have different tool-tip text.
Point getToolTipLocation(MouseEvent)	Get the location (in the receiving component's coordinate system) where the upper left corner of the component's tool tip will appear. The argument is the event that caused the tool tip to be shown. The default return value is null, which tells the Swing system to choose a location.

---

[1]   JToolTip API documentation: `http://java.sun.com/j2se/1.4.2/docs/api/javax/swing/JToolTip.html`.

[2]   ToolTipManager API documentation: `http://java.sun.com/j2se/1.4.2/docs/api/javax/swing/ToolTipManager.html`.

T

Components

Examples That Use Tool Tips

This table shows some examples that use tool tips and where those examples are described.

Example	Where Described	Notes
ButtonDemo	This section and How to Use Buttons (page 156)	Uses a tool tip to provide instructions for a button.
IconDemoApplet	How to Use Icons (page 603)	Uses a tool tip in a label to provide name and size information for an image.
TabbedPaneDemo	How to Use Tabbed Panes (page 382)	Uses an argument to the addTab method to specify tool tip text for each tab.
DragFileDemo	How to Use Drag and Drop and Data Transfer (page 545)	Uses an argument to the addTab method to specify tool tip text for each tab—the name of the file the tab's component displays.
TableRenderDemo	Specifying Tool Tips for Cells (page 407)	Adds tool tip text to a table using a renderer.
TableToolTipsDemo	Specifying Tool Tips for Cells (page 407) , Specifying Tool Tips for Column Headers (page 410)	Adds tool tips to a table using various techniques.
TreeIconDemo2	Customizing a Tree's Display (page 442)	Adds tool tips to a tree using a custom renderer.
ActionDemo	How to Use Actions (page 513)	Adds tool tips to buttons created using Actions.

How to Use Trees

With the JTree[1] class, you can display hierarchical data. A JTree object doesn't actually contain your data; it simply provides a view of the data. Like any nontrivial Swing component, the tree gets data by querying its data model. Figure 91 is a picture of a tree.

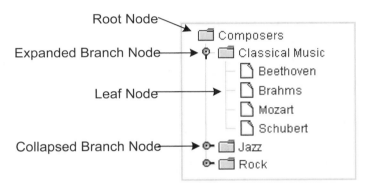

Figure 91   A tree in the Java look and feel.

As the figure shows, JTree displays its data vertically. Each row displayed by the tree contains exactly one item of data, which is called a *node*. Every tree has a *root* node from which all nodes descend. By default, the tree displays the root node, but you can decree otherwise. A node can either have children or not. We refer to nodes that can have children—whether or not they currently *have* children—as *branch* nodes. Nodes that can't have children are *leaf* nodes.

Branch nodes can have any number of children. Typically, the user can expand and collapse branch nodes—making their children visible or invisible—by clicking them. By default, all branch nodes except the root node start out collapsed. A program can detect changes in branch nodes' expansion state by listening for tree expansion or tree-will-expand events, as described in How to Write a Tree Expansion Listener (page 710) and How to Write a Tree-Will-Expand Listener (page 718) in Chapter 10.

---

[1]   JTree API documentation: http://java.sun.com/j2se/1.4.2/docs/api/javax/swing/JTree.html.

Creating a Tree

Figure 92 is a picture of an application, the top half of which displays a tree in a scroll pane.

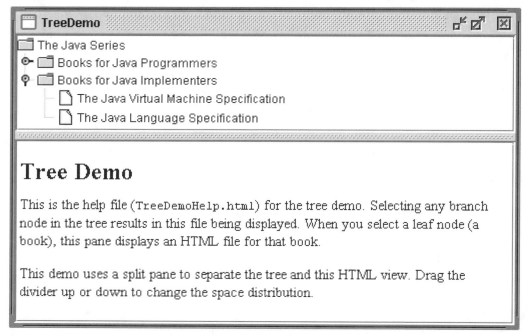

Figure 92   The TreeDemo application.

Try This:

1. Run TreeDemo using Java Web Start or compile and run the example yourself.[1]
2. Expand one or more nodes. You can do this by clicking the circle to the left of the item.
3. Collapse a node. You do this by clicking the circle to the left of an expanded node.

The following code, taken from TreeDemo.java, creates the JTree object and puts it in a scroll pane:

```
//Where instance variables are declared:
private JTree tree;
...
```

---

[1]   To run TreeDemo using Java Web Start, click the TreeDemo link on the RunExamples/components.html
page on the CD. You can find the source files here: JavaTutorial/uiswing/components/example-
1dot4/index.html#TreeDemo.

```
public TreeDemo() {
    ...
    DefaultMutableTreeNode top =
        new DefaultMutableTreeNode("The Java Series");
    createNodes(top);
    tree = new JTree(top);
    ...
    JScrollPane treeView = new JScrollPane(tree);
    ...
}
```

The code creates an instance of DefaultMutableTreeNode[1] to serve as the root node for the tree. It then creates the rest of the nodes in the tree. After that, it creates the tree, specifying the root node as an argument to the JTree constructor. Finally, it puts the tree in a scroll pane, a common tactic because showing the full, expanded tree would otherwise require too much space.

Here's the code that creates the nodes under the root node:

```
private void createNodes(DefaultMutableTreeNode top) {
    DefaultMutableTreeNode category = null;
    DefaultMutableTreeNode book = null;

    category = new DefaultMutableTreeNode("Books for Java Programmers");
    top.add(category);

    //original Tutorial
    book = new DefaultMutableTreeNode(new BookInfo
        ("The Java Tutorial: A Short Course on the Basics",
        "tutorial.html"));
    category.add(book);

    //Tutorial Continued
    book = new DefaultMutableTreeNode(new BookInfo
        ("The Java Tutorial Continued: The Rest of the JDK",
        "tutorialcont.html"));
    category.add(book);

    //JFC Swing Tutorial
    book = new DefaultMutableTreeNode(new BookInfo
        ("The JFC Swing Tutorial: A Guide to Constructing GUIs",
        "swingtutorial.html"));
    category.add(book);
```

---

[1] DefaultMutableTreeNode API documentation: http://java.sun.com/j2se/1.4.2/docs/api/javax/swing/tree/DefaultMutableTreeNode.html.

439

```
    //...add more books for programmers...

    category = new DefaultMutableTreeNode(
                        "Books for Java Implementers");
    top.add(category);

    //VM
    book = new DefaultMutableTreeNode(new BookInfo
        ("The Java Virtual Machine Specification",
         "vm.html"));
    category.add(book);

    //Language Spec
    book = new DefaultMutableTreeNode(new BookInfo
        ("The Java Language Specification",
         "jls.html"));
    category.add(book);
}
```

The argument to the `DefaultMutableTreeNode` constructor is the *user object*—an object that contains or points to the data associated with the tree node. The user object can be a string, or it can be a custom object. If you implement a custom object, you should implement its `toString` method so that it returns the string to be displayed for that node.

For example, the `BookInfo` class used in the previous code snippet is a custom class that holds two pieces of data: the name of a book and the URL for an HTML file describing the book. The `toString` method is implemented to return the book name. Thus, each node associated with a `BookInfo` object displays a book name.

Note: You can specify text formatting in a tree node by putting HTML tags in the string for the node. See Using HTML in Swing Components (page 43) in Chapter 3 for details.

To summarize, you can create a tree by invoking the `JTree` constructor, specifying the root node as an argument. You should probably put the tree inside a scroll pane so that it won't take up too much space. You don't have to do anything to make the tree nodes expand and collapse in response to user clicks. However, you do have to add some code to make the tree respond when the user selects a node—by clicking the node, for example.

Responding to Node Selection

Responding to tree node selections is simple. You implement a tree selection listener and register it on the tree. Here's the selection-related code from the `TreeDemo` program:

```
//Where the tree is initialized:
    tree.getSelectionModel().setSelectionMode
            (TreeSelectionModel.SINGLE_TREE_SELECTION);

    //Listen for when the selection changes.
    tree.addTreeSelectionListener(this);
...

public void valueChanged(TreeSelectionEvent e) {
    DefaultMutableTreeNode node = (DefaultMutableTreeNode)
                        tree.getLastSelectedPathComponent();

    if (node == null) return;

    Object nodeInfo = node.getUserObject();
    if (node.isLeaf()) {
        BookInfo book = (BookInfo)nodeInfo;
        displayURL(book.bookURL);
    } else {
        displayURL(helpURL);
    }
}
```

The preceding code performs these tasks:

- Gets the default `TreeSelectionModel`[1] for the tree and then sets it up so that at most one tree node at a time can be selected.
- Registers an event handler on the tree. The event handler is an object that implements the `TreeSelectionListener`[2] interface.
- In the event handler, determines which node is selected by invoking the tree's `get-LastSelectedPathComponent` method.
- Uses the `getUserObject` method to get the data associated with the node.

For more details about handling tree selection events, see How to Write a Tree Selection Listener (page 715) in Chapter 10.

---

[1] `TreeSelectionModel` API documentation: `http://java.sun.com/j2se/1.4.2/docs/api/javax/swing/tree/TreeSelectionModel.html`.

[2] `TreeSelectionListener` API documentation: `http://java.sun.com/j2se/1.4.2/docs/api/javax/swing/event/TreeSelectionListener.html`.

T

Components

Customizing a Tree's Display

Figure 93 is a picture of some tree nodes, as drawn by the Java, Windows, and GTK+ look and feel implementations.

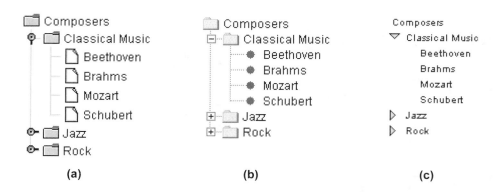

| (a) | (b) | (c) |

Figure 93   Tree nodes with the (a) Java, (b) Windows, and (c) GTK+ look-and-feel implementations.

A tree conventionally displays an icon and some text for each node. You can customize these, as we'll show shortly. A tree typically also performs some look-and-feel-specific painting to indicate relationships between nodes. You can customize this painting in a limited way. First, you can use `tree.setRootVisible(true)` to show the root node or `tree.setRootVisible(false)` to hide it. Second, you can use `tree.setShowsRoot-Handles(true)` to request that a tree's top-level nodes—the root node (if it's visible) or its children (if not)—have handles that let them be expanded or collapsed. Third, if you're using the Java look and feel, you can customize whether lines are drawn to show relationships between tree nodes.

By default, the Java look and feel draws angled lines between nodes. By setting the `JTree.lineStyle` client property of a tree, you can specify a different convention. For example, to request that the Java look and feel use only horizontal lines to group nodes, use the following code:

```
tree.putClientProperty("JTree.lineStyle", "Horizontal");
```

To specify that the Java look and feel should draw no lines, use this code:

```
tree.putClientProperty("JTree.lineStyle", "None");
```

The snapshots in Figure 94 show the results of setting the JTree.lineStyle property when using the Java look and feel.

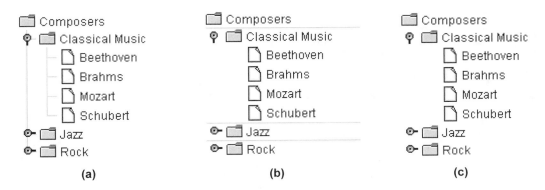

(a)   (b)   (c)

Figure 94 The JTree.lineStyle property can be set to (a) Angled (default), (b) Horizontal, and (c) None.

No matter what the look and feel, the default icon displayed by a node is determined by whether the node is a leaf and, if not, whether it's expanded. For example, in the Windows and Motif look-and-feel implementations, the default icon for each leaf node is a dot; in the Java look and feel, the default leaf icon is a paper-like symbol. In all the look-and-feel implementations we've shown, branch nodes are marked with folder-like symbols. Some look and feels might have different icons for expanded branches versus collapsed branches.

You can easily change the default icon used for leaf, expanded branch, or collapsed branch nodes. To do so, first create an instance of DefaultTreeCellRenderer.[1] Next, specify the icons to use by invoking one or more of these renderer methods: setLeafIcon (for leaf nodes), setOpenIcon (for expanded branch nodes), setClosedIcon (for collapsed branch nodes). If you want the tree to display no icon for a type of node, then specify null for the icon. Once you've set up the icons, use the tree's setCellRenderer method to specify that the DefaultTreeCellRenderer paint its nodes. Here's an example, taken from an application called TreeIconDemo:

```
ImageIcon leafIcon = createImageIcon("images/middle.gif");
if (leafIcon != null) {
    DefaultTreeCellRenderer renderer =
        new DefaultTreeCellRenderer();
    renderer.setLeafIcon(leafIcon);
    tree.setCellRenderer(renderer);
}
```

---

[1] DefaultTreeCellRenderer API documentation: http://java.sun.com/j2se/1.4.2/docs/api/javax/swing/tree/DefaultTreeCellRenderer.html.

You can run TreeIconDemo using Java Web Start or compile and run the example yourself.[1]
The resulting UI looks like Figure 95.

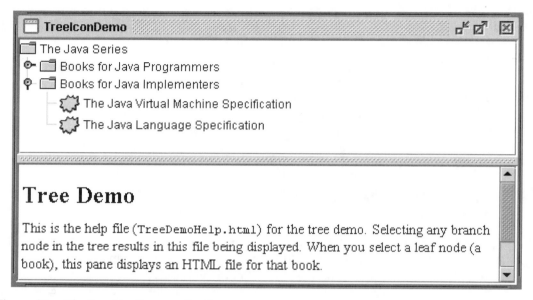

Figure 95 The TreeIconDemo application.

If you want finer control over the node icons or you want to provide tool tips, you can do so by creating a subclass of DefaultTreeCellRenderer and overriding the getTreeCellRendererComponent method. Because DefaultTreeCellRenderer is a subclass of JLabel, you can use any JLabel method—such as setIcon—to customize the DefaultTreeCellRenderer.

The following code, from TreeIconDemo2.java, creates a cell renderer that varies the leaf icon depending on whether the word "Tutorial" is in the node's text data. The renderer also specifies tool tip text, as the bold lines show. You can run TreeIconDemo2 using Java Web Start or compile and run the example yourself.[2]

---

[1] To run TreeIconDemo using Java Web Start, click the TreeIconDemo link on the RunExamples/ components.html page on the CD. You can find the source files here: JavaTutorial/uiswing/ components/example-1dot4/index.html#TreeIconDemo.

[2] To run TreeIconDemo2 using Java Web Start, click the TreeIconDemo2 link on the RunExamples/ components.html page on the CD. You can find the source files here: JavaTutorial/uiswing/ components/example-1dot4/index.html#TreeIconDemo2.

```
//...where the tree is initialized:
    //Enable tool tips.
    ToolTipManager.sharedInstance().registerComponent(tree);

    ImageIcon tutorialIcon = createImageIcon("images/middle.gif");
    if (tutorialIcon != null) {
        tree.setCellRenderer(new MyRenderer(tutorialIcon));
    }
...
class MyRenderer extends DefaultTreeCellRenderer {
    Icon tutorialIcon;

    public MyRenderer(Icon icon) {
        tutorialIcon = icon;
    }

    public Component getTreeCellRendererComponent(
                    JTree tree,
                    Object value,
                    boolean sel,
                    boolean expanded,
                    boolean leaf,
                    int row,
                    boolean hasFocus) {

        super.getTreeCellRendererComponent(
                    tree, value, sel,
                    expanded, leaf, row,
                    hasFocus);
        if (leaf && isTutorialBook(value)) {
            setIcon(tutorialIcon);
            setToolTipText("This book is in the Tutorial series.");
        } else {
            setToolTipText(null); //no tool tip
        }
        return this;
    }

    protected boolean isTutorialBook(Object value) {
        DefaultMutableTreeNode node = (DefaultMutableTreeNode)value;
        BookInfo nodeInfo = (BookInfo)(node.getUserObject());
        String title = nodeInfo.bookName;
        if (title.indexOf("Tutorial") >= 0) {
            return true;
        }

        return false;
    }
}
```

T

Components

445

The result is as shown in Figure 96.

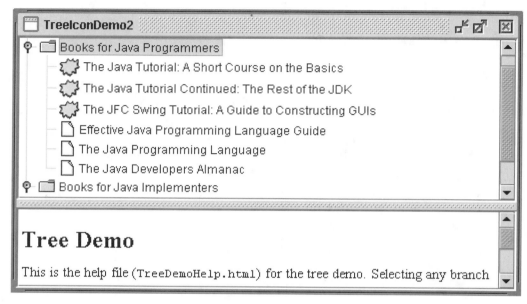

Figure 96   The `TreeIconDemo2` application.

You might be wondering how a cell renderer works. When a tree paints each node, neither the `JTree` nor its look-and-feel-specific implementation actually contains the code that paints the node. Instead, the tree uses the cell renderer's painting code to paint the node. For example, to paint a leaf node that has the string "The Java Programming Language," the tree asks its cell renderer to return a component that can paint a leaf node with that string. If the cell renderer is a `DefaultTreeCellRenderer`, then it returns a label that paints the default leaf icon followed by the string.

A cell renderer only paints; it cannot handle events. If you want to add event handling to a tree, you need to register your handler on either the tree or, if the handling occurs only when a node is selected, the tree's *cell editor*. For information about cell editors, see Concepts: Editors and Renderers (page 398). That section discusses table cell editors and renderers, which are similar to tree cell editors and renderers.

Dynamically Changing a Tree

Figure 97 shows an application called DynamicTreeDemo that lets you add nodes to and remove nodes from a visible tree. You can also edit the text in each node.

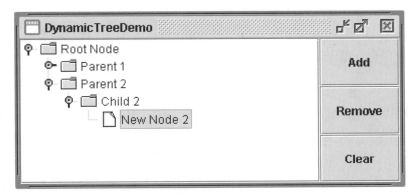

Figure 97 The DynamicTreeDemo application.

The application is based on an example provided by Tutorial reader Richard Stanford. You can run DynamicTreeDemo using Java Web Start or compile and run the example yourself.[1] Here's the code that initializes the tree:

```
rootNode = new DefaultMutableTreeNode("Root Node");
treeModel = new DefaultTreeModel(rootNode);
treeModel.addTreeModelListener(new MyTreeModelListener());

tree = new JTree(treeModel);
tree.setEditable(true);
tree.getSelectionModel().setSelectionMode
        (TreeSelectionModel.SINGLE_TREE_SELECTION);
tree.setShowsRootHandles(true);
```

By explicitly creating the tree's model, the code guarantees that it is an instance of Default-TreeModel.[2] That way, we know all the methods that the tree model supports. For example, we know that we can invoke the model's insertNodeInto method, even though that method is not required by the TreeModel[3] interface.

---

[1] To run DynamicTreeDemo using Java Web Start, click the DynamicTreeDemo link on the RunExamples/ components.html page on the CD. You can find the source files here: JavaTutorial/uiswing/ components/example-1dot4/index.html#DynamicTreeDemo.

[2] DefaultTreeModel API documentation: http://java.sun.com/j2se/1.4.2/docs/api/javax/ swing/tree/DefaultTreeModel.html.

[3] TreeModel API documentation: http://java.sun.com/j2se/1.4.2/docs/api/javax/swing/ tree/TreeModel.html.

T

Components

To make the text in the tree's nodes editable, we invoke setEditable(true) on the tree. When the user has finished editing a node, the model generates a tree model event that tells any listeners—including the JTree—that tree nodes have changed. Note that although DefaultMutableTreeNode has methods for changing a node's content, changes should go through the DefaultTreeModel cover methods. Otherwise, the tree model events won't be generated, and listeners such as the tree won't know about the updates.

To be notified of node changes, we can implement a TreeModelListener.[1] Here's an example of a tree model listener that detects when the user has typed in a new name for a tree node:

```java
class MyTreeModelListener implements TreeModelListener {
    public void treeNodesChanged(TreeModelEvent e) {
        DefaultMutableTreeNode node;
        node = (DefaultMutableTreeNode)
                (e.getTreePath().getLastPathComponent());

        /*
         * If the event lists children, then the changed
         * node is the child of the node we've already
         * gotten.  Otherwise, the changed node and the
         * specified node are the same.
         */
        try {
            int index = e.getChildIndices()[0];
            node = (DefaultMutableTreeNode)
                    (node.getChildAt(index));
        } catch (NullPointerException exc) {}

        System.out.println("The user has finished editing the node.");
        System.out.println("New value: " + node.getUserObject());
    }

    public void treeNodesInserted(TreeModelEvent e) {
    }

    public void treeNodesRemoved(TreeModelEvent e) {
    }

    public void treeStructureChanged(TreeModelEvent e) {
    }
}
```

---

[1] TreeModelListener API documentation: http://java.sun.com/j2se/1.4.2/docs/api/javax/swing/event/TreeModelListener.html.

Here's the code that the **Add** button's event handler uses to add a new node to the tree:

```
treePanel.addObject("New Node " + newNodeSuffix++);
...
public DefaultMutableTreeNode addObject(Object child) {
    DefaultMutableTreeNode parentNode = null;
    TreePath parentPath = tree.getSelectionPath();

    if (parentPath == null) {
        //There's no selection. Default to the root node.
        parentNode = rootNode;
    } else {
        parentNode = (DefaultMutableTreeNode)
                    (parentPath.getLastPathComponent());
    }

    return addObject(parentNode, child, true);
}
...
public DefaultMutableTreeNode addObject(DefaultMutableTreeNode parent,
                                        Object child,
                                        boolean shouldBeVisible) {
    DefaultMutableTreeNode childNode =
            new DefaultMutableTreeNode(child);
    ...
    treeModel.insertNodeInto(childNode, parent,
                        parent.getChildCount());

    //Make sure the user can see the lovely new node.
    if (shouldBeVisible) {
        tree.scrollPathToVisible(new TreePath(childNode.getPath()));
    }
    return childNode;
}
```

The code creates a node, inserts it into the tree model, and then, if appropriate, requests that the nodes above it be expanded and the tree scrolled so that the new node is visible. To insert the node into the model, the code uses the `insertNodeInto` method provided by the `DefaultTreeModel` class.

Creating a Data Model

If `DefaultTreeModel` doesn't suit your needs, then you'll need to write a custom data model. Your data model must implement the `TreeModel` interface. `TreeModel` specifies methods for getting a particular node of the tree, getting the number of children of a particular node, determining whether a node is a leaf, notifying the model of a change in the tree, and adding and removing tree model listeners.

Interestingly, the TreeModel interface accepts any kind of object as a tree node. It doesn't require that nodes be represented by DefaultMutableTreeNode objects, or even that nodes implement the TreeNode[1] interface. Thus, if the TreeNode interface isn't suitable for your tree model, feel free to devise your own representation for tree nodes. For example, if you have a pre-existing hierarchical data structure, you don't need to duplicate it or force it into the TreeNode mold. You just need to implement your tree model so that it uses the information in the existing data structure.

Figure 98 shows an application called GenealogyExample that displays the descendents or ancestors of a particular person. (Thanks to Tutorial reader Olivier Berlanger for providing this example.) You can run GenealogyExample using Java Web Start or compile and run the example yourself.[2]

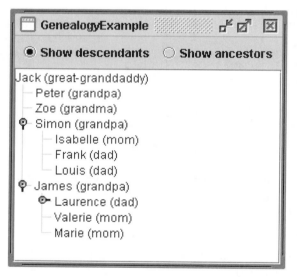

Figure 98   The GenealogyExample application.

---

[1] TreeNode API documentation: http://java.sun.com/j2se/1.4.2/docs/api/javax/swing/tree/TreeNode.html.

[2] To run GenealogyExample using Java Web Start, click the GenealogyExample link on the RunExamples/components.html page on the CD. You can find the source files here: JavaTutorial/uiswing/components/example-1dot4/index.html#GenealogyExample.

You can find the custom tree model implementation in GenealogyModel.java. Because the model is implemented as an Object subclass instead of, say, a subclass of DefaultTree-Model, it must implement the TreeModel interface directly. This requires implementing methods for getting information about nodes, such as which is the root and what are the children of a particular node. In the case of GenealogyModel, each node is represented by an object of type Person, a custom class that doesn't implement TreeNode.

A tree model must also implement methods for adding and removing tree model listeners and must fire TreeModelEvents to those listeners when the tree's structure or data changes. For example, when the user instructs GenealogyExample to switch from showing ancestors to showing descendants, the tree model makes the change and then fires an event to inform its listeners (such as the tree component).

The Tree API

The tree API is quite extensive. Tables 101 through 104 list just a bit of the API. For more information about the tree API, see the API documentation for JTree[1] and for the various classes and interfaces in the tree package.[2] Also refer to The JComponent Class (page 53) in Chapter 3 for information on the API that JTree inherits from its superclass.

Table 101: Tree-Related Classes and Interfaces

Class or Interface	Purpose
JTree	The component that presents the tree to the user.
TreePath	Represents a path to a node.
TreeNode MutableTreeNode DefaultMutableTreeNode	The interfaces that the default tree model expects its tree nodes to implement, and the implementation used by the default tree model.
TreeModel DefaultTreeModel	Respectively, the interface that a tree model must implement and the usual implementation used.
TreeCellRenderer DefaultTreeCellRenderer	Respectively, the interface that a tree cell renderer must implement and the usual implementation used.
TreeCellEditor DefaultTreeCellEditor	Respectively, the interface that a tree cell editor must implement and the usual implementation used.

---

[1] JTree API documentation: http://java.sun.com/j2se/1.4.2/docs/api/javax/swing/JTree.html.

[2] Tree package API documentation: http://java.sun.com/j2se/1.4.2/docs/api/javax/swing/tree/package-summary.html.

Table 101: Tree-Related Classes and Interfaces *(continued)*

Class or Interface	Purpose
TreeSelectionModel DefaultTreeSelectionModel	Respectively, the interface that the tree's selection model must implement and the usual implementation used.
TreeSelectionListener TreeSelectionEvent	The interface and event type used for detecting tree selection changes. For more information, see How to Write a Tree Selection Listener (page 715).
TreeModelListener TreeModelEvent	The interface and event type used for detecting tree model changes. For more information, see How to Write a Tree Model Listener (page 713).
TreeExpansionListener TreeWillExpandListener TreeExpansionEvent	The interfaces and event type used for detecting tree expansion and collapse. For more information, see How to Write a Tree Expansion Listener (page 710) and How to Write a Tree-Will-Expand Listener (page 718).
ExpandVetoException	An exception that a TreeWillExpandListener can throw to indicate that the impending expansion/collapse should not happen. For more information, see How to Write a Tree-Will-Expand Listener (page 718).

Table 102: Creating and Setting up a Tree

Constructor or Method	Purpose
JTree(TreeNode) JTree(TreeNode, boolean) JTree(TreeModel) JTree() JTree(Hashtable) JTree(Object[]) JTree(Vector)	Create a tree. The TreeNode argument specifies the root node to be managed by the default tree model. The TreeModel argument specifies the model that provides the data to the table. The no-argument version of this constructor is for use in builders; it creates a tree that contains some sample data. If you specify a Hashtable, array of objects, or Vector as an argument, then the argument is treated as a list of nodes under the root node (which is not displayed), and a model and tree nodes are constructed accordingly. The boolean argument, if present, specifies how the tree should determine whether a node should be displayed as a leaf. If the argument is false (the default), any node without children is diaplayed as a leaf. If the argument is true, a node is a leaf only if its getAllowsChildren method returns false.
void setCellRenderer(TreeCellRenderer)	Set the renderer that draws each node.
void setEditable(boolean) void setCellEditor(TreeCellEditor)	The first method sets whether the user can edit tree nodes. By default, tree nodes are not editable. The second sets which customized editor to use.

Table 102: Creating and Setting up a Tree *(continued)*

Constructor or Method	Purpose
`void setRootVisible(boolean)`	Set whether the tree shows the root node. The default value is false if the tree is created using one of the constructors that takes a data structure, and true otherwise.
`void setShowsRootHandles(boolean)`	Set whether the tree shows handles for its leftmost nodes, letting you expand and collapse the nodes. The default is false. If the tree doesn't show the root node, then you should invoke `setShowsRootHandles(true)`.
`void setDragEnabled(boolean)` `boolean getDragEnabled()`	Set or get the *dragEnabled* property, which must be true to enable drag handling on this component. The default value is false. See How to Use Drag and Drop and Data Transfer (page 545) for more details. Introduced in 1.4.

Table 103: Implementing Selection

Method	Purpose
`void addTreeSelectionListener(TreeSelectionListener)`	Register a listener to detect when the a node is selected or deselected.
`void setSelectionModel(TreeSelectionModel)` `TreeSelectionModel getSelectionModel()`	Set or get the model used to control node selections. You can turn off node selection completely using `setSelectionModel(null)`.

`void setSelectionMode(int)`
`int getSelectionMode()`
(in TreeSelectionModel)
	Set or get the selection mode. The value can be `CONTIGUOUS_TREE_SELECTION`, `DISCONTIGUOUS_TREE_SELECTION`, or `SINGLE_TREE_SELECTION` (all defined in `TreeSelectionModel`).

`Object getLastSelectedPathComponent()`	Get the object representing the currently selected node. This is equivalent to invoking `getLastPathComponent` on the value returned by `tree.getSelectionPath()`.
`void setSelectionPath(TreePath)` `TreePath getSelectionPath()`	Set or get the path to the currently selected node.
`void setSelectionPaths(TreePath[])` `TreePath[] getSelectionPaths()`	Set or get the paths to the currently selected nodes.
`void setSelectionPath(TreePath)` `TreePath getSelectionPath()`	Set or get the path to the currently selected node.

T

Components

453

Table 104: Showing and Hiding Nodes

Method	Purpose

`void addTreeExpansionListener(`
`        TreeExpansionListener)`
`void addTreeWillExpandListener(`
`        TreeWillExpandListener)`
	Register a listener to detect when the tree nodes *have* expanded or collapsed, or *will* expand or collapse, respectively. To veto an impending expansion or collapse, a `TreeWillExpandListener` can throw a `ExpandVeto-Exception`.

`void expandPath(TreePath)` `void collapsePath(TreePath)`	Expand or collapse the specified tree path.
`void scrollPathToVisible(TreePath)`	Ensure that the node specified by the path is visible—that the path leading up to it is expanded and the node is in the scroll pane's viewing area.
`void makeVisible(TreePath)`	Ensure that the node specified by the path is viewable—that the path leading up to it is expanded. The node might not end up within the viewing area.
`void setScrollsOnExpand(boolean)` `boolean getScrollsOnExpand()`	Set or get whether the tree attempts to scroll to show previous hidden nodes. The default value is true.
`void setToggleClickCount(int)` `int getToggleClickCount()`	Set or get the number of mouse clicks before a node will expand or close. The default is two. Introduced in 1.3.

`TreePath getNextMatch(String,`
`                int,`
`                Position.Bias)`
	Return the `TreePath` to the next tree element that begins with the specific prefix. Introduced in 1.4.

Examples That Use Trees

This table lists examples that use `JTree` and where those examples are described.

Example	Where Described	Notes
TreeDemo	Creating a Tree (page 438), Responding to Node Selection (page 440), Customizing a Tree's Display (page 442)	Creates a tree that responds to user selections. It also has code for customizing the line style for the Java look and feel.
TreeIconDemo	Customizing a Tree's Display (page 442)	Adds a custom leaf icon to `TreeDemo`.
TreeIconDemo2	Customizing a Tree's Display (page 442)	Customizes certain leaf icons and also provides tool tips for certain tree nodes.

Example	Where Described	Notes
DynamicTreeDemo	Dynamically Changing a Tree (page 447)	Illustrates adding and removing nodes from a tree. Also allows editing of node text.
GenealogyExample	Creating a Data Model (page 449)	Implements a custom tree model and custom node type.
TreeExpandEventDemo	How to Write a Tree Expansion Listener (page 710)	Shows how to detect node expansions and collapses.
TreeExpandEventDemo2	How to Write a Tree-Will-Expand Listener (page 718)	Shows how to veto node expansions.
TreeTable, TreeTable II, Editable JTreeTable	Creating a Tree (page 438) Examples in *The Swing Connection*, available on the CD and online at: `http://java.sun.com/products/jfc/tsc/articles/`	Combine a tree and table to show detailed information about a hierarchy such as a file system. The tree is a renderer for the table.

T

Components

Layout Manager
Reference

Eᴀᴄʜ of the following how-to sections describes how to use a particular layout manager—an object that controls the size and position of components in a container. These sections are organized alphabetically for quick reference. To see pictures of typical uses of each layout manager, you can refer to A Visual Guide to Layout Managers (page 88) in Chapter 4.

All of these sections assume that you're familiar with layout management concepts. These prerequisites are covered in Chapter 4, Laying Out Components within a Container (page 87). Chapter 4 also includes instructions on how to use absolute positioning (no layout manager) and an example of writing a custom layout manager. If you have any difficulties, be sure to refer to Solving Common Layout Problems (page 738) in the Appendix.

You can find source files for all the examples in this chapter on the CD and online:

```
JavaTutorial/uiswing/layout/example-1dot4/index.html
```

```
http://java.sun.com/docs/books/tutorial/uiswing/layout/
example-1dot4/index.html
```

The preceding URLs take you to an example index that has links to the files required by each example. You can go directly to the entry for a particular example by adding *#ExampleName* to the URL. Most examples have a "Run" link in the index which executes the example using Java Web Start technology.

B

How to Use BorderLayout

As Figure 1 shows, a BorderLayout[1] has five areas. These areas are specified by the BorderLayout constants PAGE_START, PAGE_END, LINE_START, LINE_END, and CENTER.

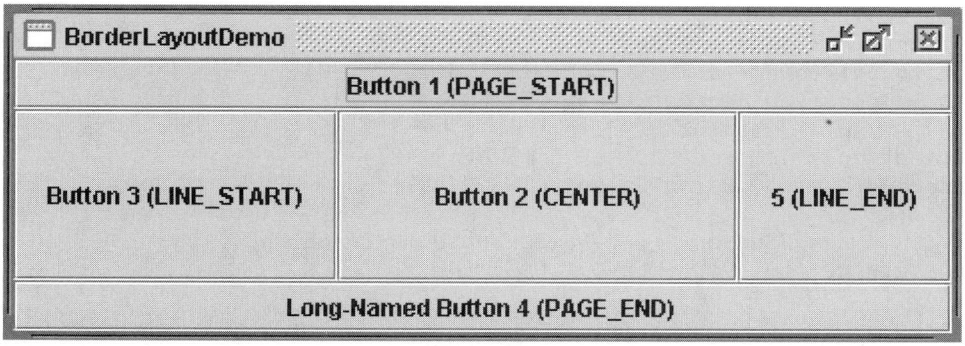

Button 1 (PAGE_START)		
Button 3 (LINE_START)	Button 2 (CENTER)	5 (LINE_END)
Long-Named Button 4 (PAGE_END)		

Figure 1 BorderLayoutDemo, an application that uses BorderLayout.

You can run BorderLayoutDemo using Java Web Start or compile and run the example yourself.[2]

Version Note: Before v1.4, the preferred names for the various areas were different, ranging from points of the compass (for example, BorderLayout.NORTH for the top area) to wordier versions of the constants we use in our examples. The constants used in our examples are preferred because they're standard and enable programs to adjust to languages that have different orientations.

If you enlarge a container that uses BorderLayout, the center area gets as much of the available space as possible. The other areas expand only as much as necessary to fill all available space. Often a container uses only one or two of the areas of the BorderLayout—say just the center or the center and the bottom.

---

[1] BorderLayout API documentation: http://java.sun.com/j2se/1.4.2/docs/api/java/awt/BorderLayout.html.

[2] To run BorderLayoutDemo using Java Web Start, click the BorderLayoutDemo link on the Run-Examples/layout.html page on the CD. You can find the source files here: JavaTutorial/uiswing/layout/example-1dot4/index.html#BorderLayoutDemo.

Layout Managers

The following code adds components to a frame's content pane. Because content panes use BorderLayout by default, the code doesn't need to set the layout manager.

```
.../Container pane = aFrame.getContentPane()...
JButton button = new JButton("Button 1 (PAGE_START)");
pane.add(button, BorderLayout.PAGE_START);

//Make the center component big, since that's the
//typical usage of BorderLayout.
button = new JButton("Button 2 (CENTER)");
button.setPreferredSize(new Dimension(200, 100));
pane.add(button, BorderLayout.CENTER);

button = new JButton("Button 3 (LINE_START)");
pane.add(button, BorderLayout.LINE_START);

button = new JButton("Long-Named Button 4 (PAGE_END)");
pane.add(button, BorderLayout.PAGE_END);

button = new JButton("5 (LINE_END)");
pane.add(button, BorderLayout.LINE_END);
```

We strongly recommend that you specify the component's location (for example, Border-Layout.LINE_END) as one of the arguments to the add method. If you leave it out, the component will be added to the center but your code will be much less clear. If you find that a component is missing from a container controlled by BorderLayout, make sure that you have specified the component's location and that you didn't put another component in the same location.

All of our examples that use BorderLayout specify the component as the first argument to the add method. For example:

```
add(component, BorderLayout.CENTER)  //preferred
```

However, you might see code in other programs that specifies the component second. Here are two alternate ways of writing the preceding code:

```
add(BorderLayout.CENTER, component)  //valid but old-fashioned
add("Center", component)             //valid but error prone
```

The BorderLayout API

Table 1 describes a couple of `BorderLayout` constructors and some methods for adding space between components. You can find the `BorderLayout` API documentation online at: `http://java.sun.com/j2se/1.4.2/docs/api/java/awt/BorderLayout.html`.

Table 1: Adding Space around Components

Constructor or Method	Purpose
`BorderLayout(int horizontalGap,` `              int verticalGap)`	Specify gaps (in pixels). By default, `BorderLayout` puts no extra space around the components it manages.
`void setHgap(int)` `void setVgap(int)`	Set the horizontal and vertical gaps.

Examples That Use BorderLayout

The following table shows a few of the many examples that use `BorderLayout`.

Example	Where Described	Notes
`BorderLayoutDemo`	This section	Puts a component in each of the five possible locations.
`TabbedPaneDemo`	How to Use Tabbed Panes (page 382)	Puts a single component in the center of a content pane so that it is as large as possible.
`CheckBoxDemo`	How to Use Check Boxes (page 163)	Creates a `JPanel` that uses `BorderLayout`. Puts components in the left (actually, `LINE_START`) and center locations.

How to Use BoxLayout

The Swing packages include a general-purpose layout manager named BoxLayout.[1] Box-Layout either stacks its components on top of each other (see Figure 2) or places them in a row—your choice. You might think of it as a full-featured version of FlowLayout.

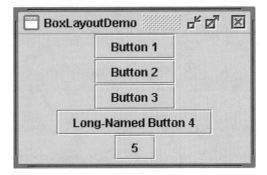

Figure 2   An application that demonstrates using BoxLayout to display a centered column of components.

You can run BoxLayoutDemo using Java Web Start or compile and run the example yourself.[2]

By creating one or more lightweight containers that use BoxLayout, you can achieve some layouts for which the more complex GridBagLayout is often used. BoxLayout is also useful in situations where you might consider using GridLayout or BorderLayout. One big difference between BoxLayout and many earlier layout managers is that it respects each component's maximum size and X and Y alignment. We'll discuss that later.

Figure 3 shows a GUI that uses two instances of BoxLayout. In the upper part, a top-to-bottom box layout places a label above a scroll pane. In the lower part, a left-to-right box layout places two buttons next to each other. BorderLayout combines the two parts of the GUI and ensures that any excess space is given to the scroll pane.

---

[1] BoxLayout API documentation: http://java.sun.com/j2se/1.4.2/docs/api/java/awt/Box-Layout.html.

[2] To run BoxLayoutDemo using Java Web Start, click the BoxLayoutDemo link on the RunExamples/layout.html page on the CD. You can find the source files here: JavaTutorial/uiswing/layout/example-1dot4/index.html#BoxLayoutDemo.

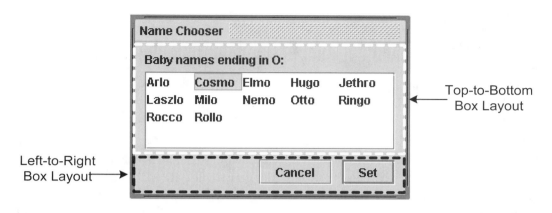

Figure 3   ListDialog uses two instances of BoxLayout, indicated by the dashed lines.

You can try out a ListDialog by running the ListDialogRunner application using Java Web Start or compile and run the example yourself.[1]

The following code, taken from ListDialog.java, lays out the GUI. It's in the constructor for the dialog, which is implemented as a JDialog subclass. The bold lines of code set up the box layouts and add components to them.

```
JScrollPane listScroller = new JScrollPane(list);
listScroller.setPreferredSize(new Dimension(250, 80));
listScroller.setMinimumSize(new Dimension(250, 80));
listScroller.setAlignmentX(LEFT_ALIGNMENT);
...
//Lay out the label and scroll pane from top to bottom.
JPanel listPane = new JPanel();
listPane.setLayout(new BoxLayout(listPane, BoxLayout.PAGE_AXIS));
JLabel label = new JLabel(labelText);
listPane.add(label);
listPane.add(Box.createRigidArea(new Dimension(0,5)));
listPane.add(listScroller);
listPane.setBorder(BorderFactory.createEmptyBorder(10,10,10,10));

//Lay out the buttons from left to right.
JPanel buttonPane = new JPanel();
buttonPane.setLayout(new BoxLayout(buttonPane, BoxLayout.LINE_AXIS));
buttonPane.setBorder(BorderFactory.createEmptyBorder(0, 10, 10, 10));
```

---

[1] To run ListDialogRunner using Java Web Start, click the ListDialog link on the RunExamples/ components.html page on the CD. You can find the source files here: JavaTutorial/uiswing/ components/example-1dot4/index.html#ListDialog.

```
buttonPane.add(Box.createHorizontalGlue());
buttonPane.add(cancelButton);
buttonPane.add(Box.createRigidArea(new Dimension(10, 0)));
buttonPane.add(setButton);

//Put everything together using the content pane's BorderLayout.
Container contentPane = getContentPane();
contentPane.add(listPane, BorderLayout.CENTER);
contentPane.add(buttonPane, BorderLayout.SOUTH);
```

The first bold line creates a top-to-bottom box layout and sets it up as the layout manager for listPane. The two arguments to the BoxLayout constructor are the container that it manages and the axis along which the components will be laid out. The next three bold lines add the label and the scroll pane to the container, separating them with a *rigid area*—that is, an invisible lightweight component used to add space between other components. In this case, the rigid area has no width and puts exactly 5 pixels between the label and the scroll pane. Rigid areas are discussed later, in Using Invisible Components as Filler (page 468).

The next chunk of bold code creates a left-to-right box layout and sets it up for the button-Pane container. Then it adds two buttons to the container, using a rigid area to put 10 pixels between them. To place the buttons at the right side of their container, the first component added to the container is *glue*. This glue is an invisible, lightweight component that grows as necessary to absorb any extra container space. Glue is discussed in Using Invisible Components as Filler (page 468).

As an alternative to invisible components, you can sometimes use empty borders to create space around components. For example, the preceding code snippet uses empty borders to put 10 pixels between all sides of the dialog and its contents and between the two parts of the contents. Borders are completely independent of layout managers. They're simply how Swing components draw their edges. See How to Use Borders (page 535) in Chapter 9 for more information.

Don't let the length of the BoxLayout discussion scare you. You can probably use BoxLayout with the information you already have. If you run into trouble or if you want to take advantage of BoxLayout's power, read on.

BoxLayout Features

As we said before, BoxLayout arranges components either on top of each other or in a row. As it arranges components, it takes their alignments and minimum, preferred, and maximum sizes into account. This section discusses top-to-bottom layout. The same concepts apply to left-to-right or right-to-left layout, simply substituting X for Y, height for width, and so on.

Version Note: Before v1.4, no constants existed for specifying the box layout's axis in a local-izable way. Instead, you specified X_AXIS (left to right) or Y_AXIS (top to bottom). Our examples use the constants LINE_AXIS and PAGE_AXIS, which are preferred because they enable programs to adjust to languages that have different orientations. In the default left-to-right orientation, LINE_AXIS specifies left-to-right layout and PAGE_AXIS specifies top-to-bottom layout.

When BoxLayout lays out components from top to bottom, it tries to size each one at its pre-ferred height. If the amount of vertical space isn't ideal, the BoxLayout tries to adjust indi-vidual components' height so that they fill the available space. However, the components might not fit exactly, since BoxLayout respects each component's requested minimum and maximum heights. Any extra space appears at the bottom of the container.

A top-to-bottom BoxLayout tries to make all of its container's components equal in width—as wide as the largest preferred width. If the container is forced to be wider than that, BoxLayout tries to make all of the components as wide as the container as well. If the com-ponents aren't all the same width (because of restricted maximum size or any of them have a strict left or right alignment), then X alignment comes into play.

The X alignments affect not only the components' positions relative to each other but also their location (as a group) within their container. Figures 4 through 6 illustrate alignment of components that have restricted maximum widths.

As shown in Figure 4, all three components have an X alignment of 0.0 (Component. LEFT_ALIGNMENT). This means that their left sides should be aligned. Furthermore, it means that all three components are positioned as far left in their container as possible.

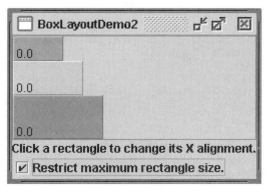

Figure 4 Left alignment with a restricted maximum width.

In Figure 5, all three components have an X alignment of 0.5 (`Component.CENTER_ALIGNMENT`). This means that their centers should be aligned and that they should be positioned in the horizontal center of their container.

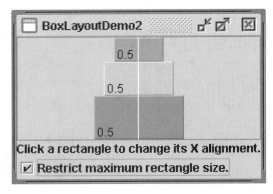

Figure 5   Center alignment with a restricted maximum width.

In Figure 6, the components have an X alignment of 1.0 (`Component.RIGHT_ALIGNMENT`). You can guess what that means for the components' alignment and position relative to their container.

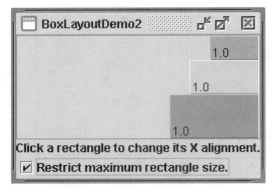

Figure 6   Right alignment with a restricted maximum width.

You might be wondering what happens when the components have both restricted maximum sizes and different X alignments. Figure 7 is an example.

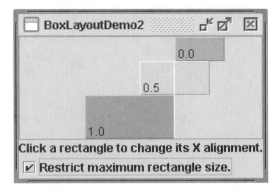

Figure 7   The components have restricted maximum sizes and different X alignments.

As you can see, the left side of the component that has an X alignment of 0.0 (`Component.LEFT_ALIGNMENT`) is aligned with the center of the component that has the 0.5 X alignment (`Component.CENTER_ALIGNMENT`), which is aligned with the right side of the component that has an X alignment of 1.0 (`Component.RIGHT_ALIGNMENT`). Mixed alignments like this are discussed in the section Fixing Alignment Problems (page 471).

What if none of the components has a maximum width? If all of them have identical X alignments, then they're all made as wide as their container. If the X alignments are different, then any component with an X alignment of 0.0 (left) or 1.0 (right) is smaller. All components with an intermediate X alignment (such as center) will be as wide as their container.

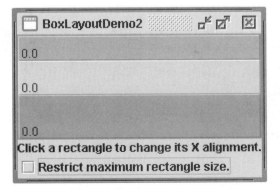 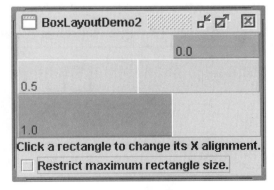

Figure 8   Two examples in which the components do not have set maximum widths.

To get to know BoxLayout better, you can run your own experiments with BoxLayoutDemo2.

Try This:

1. Run BoxLayoutDemo2 using Java Web Start or compile and run the example yourself.[1] You'll see a window like the ones in Figure 8 that contains three rectangles. Each rectangle is an instance of BLDComponent, which is a JComponent subclass.

2. Click inside one of the rectangles. This is how you change the rectangle's X alignment.

3. Click the check box at the bottom of the window. This turns off restricted sizing for all of the rectangles.

4. Make the window taller. This makes the rectangles' container larger than the sum of their preferred sizes. The container, JPanel, has a red outline so that you can tell where its edges are.

Using Invisible Components as Filler

Each component controlled by a box layout butts up against its neighboring components. If you want space between components, you can either add an empty border to one or both or insert invisible components to provide the space. You can create invisible components with the Box class.[2]

The Box class defines a nested class, Box.Filler,[3] that provides invisible components. The Box class also has convenience methods to help you create common types of filler. Table 2 gives details about creating invisible components with Box and Box.Filler.

Table 2: Creating Invisible Components with Box and Box.Filler

Type	Size Constraints	How to Create
Rigid area	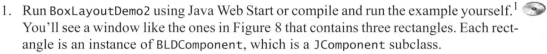	Box.createRigidArea(size)

---

[1] To run BoxLayoutDemo2 using Java Web Start, click the BoxLayoutDemo2 link on the RunExamples/layout.html page on the CD. You can find the source files here: JavaTutorial/uiswing/layout/example-1dot4/index.html#BoxLayoutDemo2.

[2] Box API documentation: http://java.sun.com/j2se/1.4.2/docs/api/javax/swing/Box.html.

[3] Box.Filler API documentation: http://java.sun.com/j2se/1.4.2/docs/api/javax/swing/Box.Filler.html.

**Table 2: Creating Invisible Components with
Box and Box.Filler** *(continued)*

Type	Size Constraints	How to Create
Glue	◀—●—▶	`Box.createHorizontalGlue()`
	↕	`Box.createVerticalGlue()`
Custom `Box.Filler`	As specified	`new Box.Filler(minSize, prefSize, maxSize)`

Here's how you generally use each filler type:

Rigid Area

Use this when you want a fixed-size space between two components (see Figure 9). For example, to put five pixels between two components in a left-to-right box, use this code:

```
container.add(firstComponent);
container.add(Box.createRigidArea(new Dimension(5,0)));
container.add(secondComponent);
```

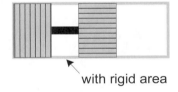
with rigid area

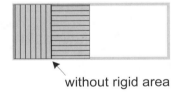
without rigid area

Figure 9   With and without a rigid area.

Note: The Box class provides another kind of filler for putting fixed space between components: a vertical or horizontal strut. Unfortunately, struts have unlimited maximum heights and widths (for horizontal and vertical struts, respectively). This means that a horizontal box within a vertical box, for example, can sometimes be too tall. For this reason, we recommend that you use rigid areas instead of struts.

Glue

Use this to specify where excess space in a layout should go. Think of it as a semi-wet adhesive—stretchy and expandable yet taking up no space unless you pull apart the components it's joining. For example, by putting horizontal glue between two components in a left-to-right box, you make any extra space go between them instead of to the right of them. Figure 10 is an example of making the space in a left-to-right box go between two components instead of to their right.

```
container.add(firstComponent);
container.add(Box.createHorizontalGlue());
container.add(secondComponent);
```

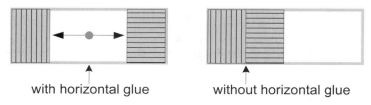

with horizontal glue   without horizontal glue

Figure 10   With and without horizontal glue.

Custom `Box.Filler`

Use this to specify a component with whatever minimum, preferred, and maximum sizes you want. For example, to create some filler in a left-to-right layout that puts at least 5 pixels between two components and ensures a minimum container height of 100 pixels, you could use this code:

```
container.add(firstComponent);
Dimension minSize = new Dimension(5, 100);
Dimension prefSize = new Dimension(5, 100);
Dimension maxSize = new Dimension(Short.MAX_VALUE, 100);
container.add(new Box.Filler(minSize, prefSize, maxSize));
container.add(secondComponent);
```

Figure 11 illustrates a layout with and without a custom filler.

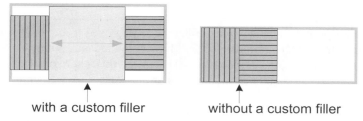

with a custom filler   without a custom filler

Figure 11   With and without a custom filler.

Fixing Alignment Problems

Two types of alignment problems sometimes occur with BoxLayout. In one group of components all have the same alignment but you want to change that to make them look better. Instead of having the centers of a group of left-to-right buttons all in a line, you might want to align them at their bottoms. Figure 12 shows an example.

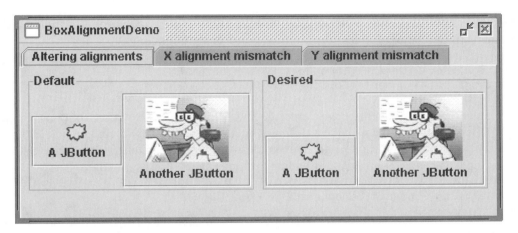

Figure 12   You can alter the default alignment of components.

Two or more components controlled by BoxLayout have different default alignments, which causes them to be misaligned. As Figure 13 shows, if a label and a panel are in a top-to-bottom box layout, the label's left edge is, by default, aligned with the panel center.

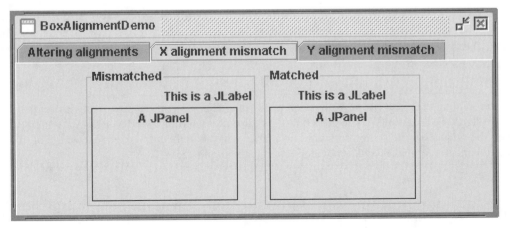

Figure 13   Misalignment can occur when two or more components controlled by BoxLayout have different default alignments.

471

In general, all components controlled by a top-to-bottom BoxLayout object should have the same X alignment. Similarly, all components controlled by a left-to-right BoxLayout should have the same Y alignment. You can set a JComponent's X alignment by invoking its setAlignmentX method. An alternative available to all components is overriding the getAlignmentX method in a custom subclass of the component class. You set the Y alignment of a component by invoking the setAlignmentY method or by overriding getAlignmentY.

Here's an example, taken from an application called BoxAlignmentDemo,[1] of changing the Y alignments of two buttons so that the buttons' bottoms are aligned:

```
button1.setAlignmentY(Component.BOTTOM_ALIGNMENT);
button2.setAlignmentY(Component.BOTTOM_ALIGNMENT);
```

By default, most components have center X and Y alignment. However, buttons, combo boxes, labels, and menu items have a different default X alignment value: LEFT_ALIGNMENT. The BoxAlignmentDemo program gives examples of fixing mismatched alignment. Usually, it's as simple as center-aligning an offending button or label. For example:

```
label.setAlignmentX(Component.CENTER_ALIGNMENT);
```

Specifying Component Sizes

As we mentioned before, BoxLayout pays attention to a component's requested minimum, preferred, and maximum sizes. You might need to adjust these sizes while you're fine-tuning the layout. Sometimes the need to adjust size is obvious. For example, a button's maximum size is generally the same as its preferred size. If you want the button to be wider when additional space is available, you need to change its maximum size.

At other times, however, the need to adjust size is not so obvious. You might be getting unexpected results with a box layout and might not know why. In this case, it's usually best to treat the problem as one of alignment first. If adjusting the alignments doesn't help, you might have a size problem. We'll discuss this further a bit later.

Note: Although BoxLayout pays attention to a component's maximum size, many layout managers don't. For example, if you put a button in the bottom part of a BorderLayout, it will probably be wider than its preferred width, no matter what its maximum size. BoxLayout, on the other hand, never makes a button wider than its maximum size.

---

[1] You can find the source files for BoxAlignmentDemo online and on the CD at: JavaTutorial/uiswing/layout/example-1dot4/index.html#BoxAlignmentDemo.

You can change the minimum, preferred, and maximum sizes in two ways:

- By invoking the appropriate set*Xxx*Size method (defined by the JComponent class):

```
comp.setMinimumSize(new Dimension(50, 25));
comp.setPreferredSize(new Dimension(50, 25));
comp.setMaximumSize(new Dimension(Short.MAX_VALUE,
                                  Short.MAX_VALUE));
```

- By overriding the appropriate get*Xxx*Size method.

```
...//in a subclass of a component class:
public Dimension getMaximumSize() {
    size = getPreferredSize();
    size.width = Short.MAX_VALUE;
    return size;
}
```

If you're running into trouble with a box layout and you've ruled out alignment, the problem might well be size-related. For example, if the container controlled by the box layout is taking up too much space, one or more of the components in the container probably needs to have its maximum size restricted.

Two techniques track down size trouble in a box layout:

- Add a garish line border to the outside of the Swing components in question. This lets you see what size they really are:

```
comp.setBorder(BorderFactory.createCompoundBorder(
                     BorderFactory.createLineBorder(Color.red),
                     comp.getBorder()));
```

- Use good old System.out.println to print the components' minimum, preferred, and maximum sizes and perhaps their bounds.

The Box Layout API

Tables 3 through 5 list the commonly used BoxLayout and Box constructors and methods. You can find the BoxLayout API documentation online at: http://java.sun.com/j2se/1.4.2/docs/api/javax/swing/BoxLayout.html.

Table 3: Creating BoxLayout Objects

Constructor or Method	Purpose
`BoxLayout(Container, int)`	Create a `BoxLayout` instance that controls the specified `Container`. The integer argument specifies the axis along which the container's components should be laid out. When the container has the default component orientation, `Box-Layout.LINE_AXIS` specifies left to right and `BoxLayout.PAGE_AXIS` specifies top to bottom.
`Box(int)`	Create a `Box`—a lightweight container that uses `BoxLayout` with the specified axis. (As of release 1.3, `Box` extends `JComponent`; before that it was implemented as a subclass of `Container`.)
`static Box createHorizontalBox()` (*in* Box)	Create a `Box` that lays out its components left to right.
`static Box createVerticalBox()` (*in* Box)	Create a `Box` that lays out its components top to bottom.

Table 4: Creating Space Fillers

Constructor or Method[a]	Purpose
`Component createRigidArea(Dimension)`	Create a rigid lightweight component.

`Component createHorizontalGlue()`
`Component createVerticalGlue()`
`Component createGlue()`
	Create a glue lightweight component.

`Component createHorizontalStrut()` `Component createVerticalStrut()`	Create a "strut" lightweight component.

`Box.Filler(Dimension,`
` Dimension,`
` Dimension)`
	Create a lightweight component with the specified minimum, preferred, and maximum sizes (with the arguments specified in that order).

a.   These methods are defined in the Box class.

Table 5: Other Useful Methods

Method	Purpose

`void changeShape(Dimension,`
` Dimension,`
` Dimension)`
(*in* Box.Filler)
	Change the minimum, preferred, and maximum sizes of the recipient `Box.Filler` object.

Examples That Use Box Layouts

The following table lists some of the many examples that use box layouts.

Example	Where Described	Notes
BoxLayoutDemo2	This section	Uses a box layout to create a centered column of components.
BoxAlignmentDemo	This section	Demonstrates how to fix common alignment problems.
BoxLayoutDemo	This section	Lets you play with alignments and maximum sizes.
ListDialog	This section	Illustrates using both a top-to-bottom and a left-to-right box layout. Uses horizontal glue, rigid areas, and empty borders; also sets a component's X alignment.
InternalFrameEvent-Demo	How to Write an Internal Frame Listener (page 670)	Uses a top-to-bottom layout to center buttons and a scroll pane in an internal frame.
MenuGlueDemo	Customizing Menu Layout (page 285)	Shows how to right-align a menu in the menu bar using a glue component.
MenuLayoutDemo	Customizing Menu Layout (page 285)	Customizes a menu layout by changing the menu bar to top-to-bottom and the popup menu to left-to-right.
ConversionPanel.java (*in* Converter example)	How to Use Panels (page 292)	Aligns two components in different box-layout-controlled containers by setting their widths to be the same and their containers' widths to be the same.

How to Use CardLayout

Here's a snapshot of an application that uses a CardLayout[1] to switch between two panels.

Figure 14   Two simple GUIs that use CardLayout.

You can run CardLayoutDemo using Java Web Start or compile and run the example yourself.[2]

The CardLayout class helps you manage two or more components (usually JPanel instances) that share the same display space. When using it, you need to provide a way for the user to choose between the components. CardLayoutDemo uses a combo box for this purpose. An easier but less flexible way to accomplish the same task is to use a tabbed pane instead.[3] Figure 15 is a picture of a tabbed pane version of Figure 14.

Figure 15   The GUI reworked to use a tabbed pane instead of CardLayout.

Because a tabbed pane provides its own GUI, it's simpler to use than CardLayout. For example, reimplementing CardLayoutDemo to use a tabbed pane results in a program with

---

[1] CardLayout API documentation: http://java.sun.com/j2se/1.4.2/docs/api/java/awt/Card-Layout.html.

[2] To run CardLayoutDemo using Java Web Start, click the CardLayoutDemo link on the RunExamples/layout.html page on the CD. You can find the source files here: JavaTutorial/uiswing/layout/example-1dot4/index.html#CardLayoutDemo.

[3] See How to Use Tabbed Panes (page 382) for more information.

several fewer lines of code. You can run the revised example, TabDemo, using Java Web Start or compile and run the example yourself.[1]

Conceptually, each component a CardLayout manages is like a playing card in a deck, where only the top card is visible at any time. You can choose the card that's showing in any of the following ways:

- By asking for either the first or last card, in the order it was added to the container.
- By flipping through the deck backward or forward.
- By specifying a card with a specific name (the scheme CardLayoutDemo uses).

The following code from CardLayoutDemo.java creates the CardLayout and the components it manages.

```
//Where instance variables are declared:
JPanel cards;
final static String BUTTONPANEL = "JPanel with JButtons";
final static String TEXTPANEL = "JPanel with JTextField";

//Where the components controlled by the CardLayout are initialized:
//Create the "cards".
JPanel card1 = new JPanel();
...
JPanel card2 = new JPanel();
...

//Create the panel that contains the "cards".
cards = new JPanel(new CardLayout());
cards.add(card1, BUTTONPANEL);
cards.add(card2, TEXTPANEL);
```

When you add a component to a container that CardLayout manages, you must specify a string that identifies it. For example, in the preceding code the first panel has the string "JPanel with JButtons" and the second has the string "JPanel with JTextField". In CardLayoutDemo, those strings are also used in the combo box.

To choose which component a CardLayout shows, you need some additional code. The following shows how the example program does this:

---

[1] To run TabDemo using Java Web Start, click the TabDemo link on the RunExamples/layout.html page on the CD. You can find the source files here: JavaTutorial/uiswing/layout/example-1dot4/ index.html#TabDemo.

```
//Where the GUI is assembled:
//Put the JComboBox in a JPanel to get a nicer look.
JPanel comboBoxPane = new JPanel(); //use FlowLayout
String comboBoxItems[] = { BUTTONPANEL, TEXTPANEL };
JComboBox cb = new JComboBox(comboBoxItems);
cb.setEditable(false);
cb.addItemListener(this);
comboBoxPane.add(cb);
...
pane.add(comboBoxPane, BorderLayout.PAGE_START);
pane.add(cards, BorderLayout.CENTER);
...
public void itemStateChanged(ItemEvent evt) {
    CardLayout cl = (CardLayout)(cards.getLayout());
    cl.show(cards, (String)evt.getItem());
}
```

The code demonstrates that you can use the CardLayout show method to set the currently showing component. The first argument to show is the container CardLayout controls—that is, the container of the components CardLayout manages. The second argument is the string that identifies the component to show. This is the same string used when adding the component to the container.

The CardLayout API

Table 6 lists the commonly used CardLayout methods that let you choose a component. You can find the CardLayout API documentation online at: http://java.sun.com/j2se/1.4.2/docs/api/java/awt/CardLayout.html.

Table 6: CardLayout Methods

Method	Purpose
void first(Container) void next(Container) void previous(Container) void last(Container) void show(Container, String)	Lets you choose a component. For each method, the first argument is the container for which CardLayout is the layout manager (the container of the cards that CardLayout controls).

Examples That Use CardLayout

Only one example in this book uses CardLayout: CardLayoutDemo. Generally, our examples use tabbed panes instead of CardLayout, since they conveniently provide a nice GUI for the same functionality.

How to Use FlowLayout

The FlowLayout[1] class provides a very simple layout manager that is used, by default, by JPanels. Figure 16 shows an example.

Figure 16 A simple GUI that uses FlowLayout.

You can run FlowLayoutDemo using Java Web Start or compile and run the example yourself.[2]

FlowLayout puts components in a row, at their preferred size. If the horizontal space in the container is too small to put all of the components in one row, FlowLayout uses multiple rows. If the container is wider than necessary for a row of components, the row is, by default, centered horizontally within it. You can specify that it stick to the left or right side instead by using a FlowLayout constructor that takes an alignment argument. You can also specify how much vertical or horizontal padding is put around the components.

Note: FlowLayout never requests more height than is required for one row. For this reason, we don't recommend using FlowLayout if, for some reason, the FlowLayout's container might start out with less horizontal space than it needs to fit all of the components in a single row.

The following code from FlowLayoutDemo.java creates the FlowLayout and the components it manages:

```
contentPane.setLayout(new FlowLayout());
contentPane.add(new JButton("Button 1"));
contentPane.add(new JButton("Button 2"));
contentPane.add(new JButton("Button 3"));
contentPane.add(new JButton("Long-Named Button 4"));
contentPane.add(new JButton("5"));
```

---

[1] FlowLayout API documentation: http://java.sun.com/j2se/1.4.2/docs/api/java/awt/Flow-Layout.html.

[2] To run FlowLayoutDemo using Java Web Start, click the FlowLayoutDemo link in the RunExamples/layout.html page on the CD. You can find the source files here: JavaTutorial/uiswing/layout/example-1dot4/index.html#FlowLayoutDemo.

The FlowLayout API

Table 7 lists the three constructors of the the FlowLayout class. You can find the Flow-Layout API documentation online at: http://java.sun.com/j2se/1.4.2/docs/api/java/awt/FlowLayout.html.

Table 7: FlowLayout Constructors

Constructor	Purpose

public FlowLayout()
public FlowLayout(int alignment)
public FlowLayout(int alignment,
                 int horizontalGap,
                 int verticalGap)
	Create a FlowLayout instance. The *alignment* argument can be FlowLayout.LEADING, FlowLayout.CENTER, or FlowLayout.TRAILING. When FlowLayout controls a container with a left-to-right component orientation (the default), LEADING specifies left alignment and TRAILING specifies right alignment. The horizontalGap and verticalGap arguments specify the number of pixels between components. (The default gap value is 5.)

Examples That Use FlowLayout

The following table lists some of the examples that use FlowLayout.

Example	Where Described	Notes
FlowLayoutDemo	This section	Sets up a content pane to use FlowLayout. If you set the RIGHT_TO_LEFT constant to true and recompile, you can see how FlowLayout handles a container that has a right-to-left component orientation.
CardLayoutDemo	How to Use CardLayout (page 476)	Centers a component in the top part of a BorderLayout, by putting the component in a JPanel that uses a Flow-Layout.
ButtonDemo	How to Use Buttons (page 156)	Uses the default FlowLayout of a JPanel.
TextInputDemo	How to Use Formatted Text Fields (page 221)	Uses a panel with right-aligned FlowLayout to present two buttons.

How to Use GridBagLayout

Here's a picture of an example that uses `GridBagLayout`.[1]

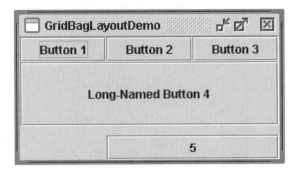

Figure 17   A simple GUI that uses `GridBagLayout`.

You can run `GridBagLayoutDemo` using Java Web Start or compile and run the example yourself.[2]

`GridBagLayout` is one of the most flexible—and complex—layout managers the Java platform provides. It places components in a grid of rows and columns, allowing specified components to span multiple rows or columns. Not all rows necessarily have the same height, and not all columns necessarily have the same width. Essentially, `GridBagLayout` places components in rectangles (cells) in a grid and then uses their preferred sizes to determine how big the cells should be.

Figure 18 shows the grid for the preceding example, `GridBagLayoutDemo`. As you can see, the grid has three rows and three columns. The button in the second row spans all the columns; the button in the third row spans the two right columns. If you enlarge the window, you'll notice that the bottom row, which contains button 5, gets all of the new vertical space; the new horizontal space is split evenly among all columns. This resizing behavior is based on weights the program assigns to individual components in `GridBagLayout`. Also notice that each component takes up all of the available horizontal space—but not (as you can see

---

[1] `GridBagLayout` API documentation: `http://java.sun.com/j2se/1.4.2/docs/api/java/awt/ GridBagLayout.html`.

[2] To run `GridBagLayoutDemo` using Java Web Start, click the `GridBagLayoutDemo` link on the Run-Examples/`layout.html` page on the CD. You can find the source files here: `JavaTutorial/uiswing/ layout/example-1dot4/index.html#GridBagLayoutDemo`.

with button 5) all of the available vertical space. This behavior is also specified by the program.

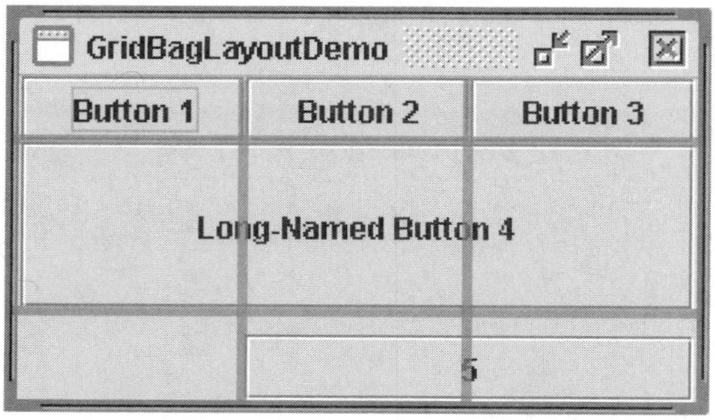

Figure 18   The GridBagLayout application with the three rows and three columns highlighted.

The program specifies the size and position of its components by specifying *constraints* for each one. To specify constraints, you set instance variables in a GridBagConstraints object and tell GridBagLayout (either with the setConstraints method or when adding the component to its container) to associate the constraints with the component.

The sections that follow explain the constraints you can set and provide examples.

Specifying Constraints

The following code is typical of what goes in a container that uses GridBagLayout. You'll see a more detailed example in the next section.

```
JPanel pane = new JPanel(new GridBagLayout());
GridBagConstraints c = new GridBagConstraints();

//For each component to be added to this container:
//...Create the component...
//...Set instance variables in the GridBagConstraints instance...
pane.add(theComponent, c);
```

You can reuse the same GridBagConstraints instance for multiple components, even if the components have different constraints. GridBagLayout extracts the constraint values and doesn't use the GridBagConstraints instance again. Be careful, however, to reset the GridBagConstraints instance variables to their default values when necessary.

Note: The following discussion assumes that GridBagLayout controls a container that has a left-to-right component orientation. A right-to-left orientation causes the GridBagLayout to adjust cell locations and spacing accordingly.

You can set the following GridBagConstraints instance variables:

gridx, gridy

Specifies the row and column at the upper left of the component. The leftmost column has address gridx=0 and the top row has address gridy=0. Use the default value GridBagConstraints.RELATIVE to specify that the component be placed just to the right of (for gridx) or just below (for gridy) the component that was added to the container just before this one was added. We recommend specifying the gridx and gridy values for each component; this tends to result in more predictable layouts.

gridwidth, gridheight

Specifies the number of columns (for gridwidth) or rows (for gridheight) in the component's display area. These constraints specify the number of cells the component uses, *not* the number of pixels. The default value is 1. Use GridBagConstraints.REMAINDER to make the component be the last one in its row (for gridwidth) or column (for gridheight). Use GridBagConstraints.RELATIVE to make the component the next-to-last one in its row (for gridwidth) or column (for gridheight).

Note: GridBagLayout doesn't allow a component to span multiple rows unless the component is in the leftmost column or you've specified positive gridx and gridy values for it.

---

fill

Used when the component's display area is larger than its requested size to determine whether and how to resize it. Valid values (defined as GridBagConstraints constants) are NONE (the default), HORIZONTAL (make the component wide enough to fill its display area horizontally, but don't change its height), VERTICAL (make the component tall enough to fill its display area vertically, but don't change its width), and BOTH (make the component fill its display area entirely).

ipadx, ipady

Specifies the internal padding, that is, how much to add to the minimum size of the component. The default value is 0. The width will be at least the component's minimum width plus ipadx*2 pixels, since the padding applies to both sides of the component. Similarly, the height will be at least the component's minimum height plus ipady*2 pixels.

insets

Specifies the external padding of the component—the minimum amount of space between it and the edges of its display area. The value is an `Insets` object. By default, a component has no external padding.

anchor

Used to determine where (within a component's display area) to place the component when it is smaller than the area. Valid values (defined as `GridBagConstraints` constants) are `CENTER` (the default), `PAGE_START`, `PAGE_END`, `LINE_START`, `LINE_END`, `FIRST_LINE_START`, `FIRST_LINE_END`, `LAST_LINE_END`, and `LAST_LINE_START`. (See Figure 19.)

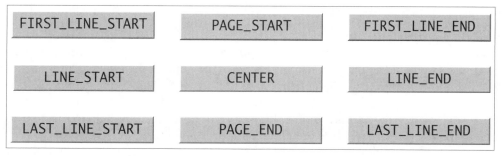

Figure 19 Interpretation of the `GridBagConstraints` anchor constants in a container that has the default left-to-right component orientation.

Version Note: The `PAGE_*` and `*LINE_*` constants were introduced in v1.4. Previous releases required values named after points of the compass—for example, `NORTHEAST` for the top-right of the display area. We recommend using the new constants since they enable easier localization.

---

weightx, **weighty**

Specifies weights used to distribute space among columns (`weightx`) and among rows (`weighty`); this is important for specifying resizing behavior. Unless you specify at least one nonzero value for `weightx` or `weighty`, all of the components clump together in the center of their container. This is because a weight of 0.0 (the default) puts any extra space between the container's grid of cells and its edges.

Generally weights are specified with 0.0 and 1.0 as the extremes, with the numbers in between used as necessary. Larger numbers indicate that the component's row or column should get more space. For each column, the weight is related to the highest component weightx specified within it, with each multicolumn component's weight split between the columns. Similarly, each row's weight is related to the highest weighty specified for a component within that row. Extra space tends to go toward the rightmost column and bottom row.

The next section discusses constraints in the context of the example program.

The Example Explained

Figure 20 is another picture of the GridBagLayoutDemo application.

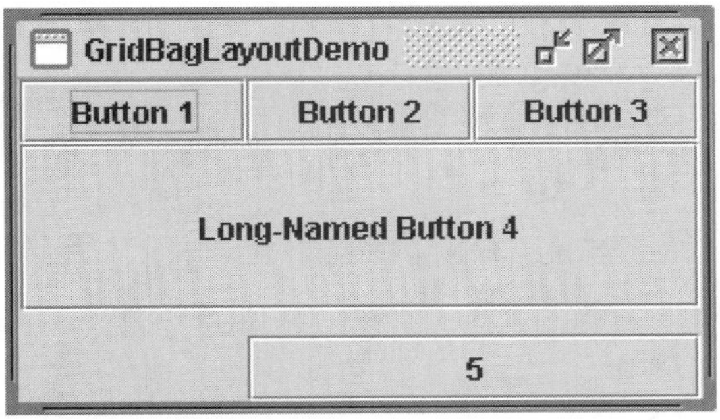

Figure 20   A simple GUI that uses GridBagLayout.

The following code creates the GridBagLayout and the components it manages. You can find the entire source file in GridBagLayoutDemo.java.[1]

```
JButton button;
pane.setLayout(new GridBagLayout());
GridBagConstraints c = new GridBagConstraints();
c.fill = GridBagConstraints.HORIZONTAL;

button = new JButton("Button 1");
c.weightx = 0.5;
c.gridx = 0;
c.gridy = 0;
pane.add(button, c);

button = new JButton("Button 2");
c.gridx = 1;
c.gridy = 0;
```

---

[1] You can find the source file here: JavaTutorial/uiswing/layout/example-1dot4/index.html #GridBagLayoutDemo.

```
pane.add(button, c);
button = new JButton("Button 3");
c.gridx = 2;
c.gridy = 0;
pane.add(button, c);

button = new JButton("Long-Named Button 4");
c.ipady = 40;        //make this component tall
c.weightx = 0.0;
c.gridwidth = 3;
c.gridx = 0;
c.gridy = 1;
pane.add(button, c);

button = new JButton("5");
c.ipady = 0;         //reset to default
c.weighty = 1.0;     //request any extra vertical space
c.anchor = GridBagConstraints.PAGE_END; //bottom of space
c.insets = new Insets(10,0,0,0);   //top padding
c.gridx = 1;         //aligned with button 2
c.gridwidth = 2;     //2 columns wide
c.gridy = 2;         //third row
pane.add(button, c);
```

The preceding example uses one GridBagConstraints instance for all of the components the GridBagLayout manages. Just before each component is added to the container, the code sets (or resets to default values) the appropriate instance variables in the GridBag-Constraints object. It then adds the component to its container, specifying the GridBag-Constraints object as the second argument to the add method.

For instance, to make button 4 extra tall, the example has this code:

```
c.ipady = 40;
```

Note: *The Java Tutorial*'s examples used to specify the constraints object differently. Rather than specifying the constraints with the add method, our examples used to invoke the set-Constraints method on the GridBagLayout object, as shown here:

```
GridBagLayout gridbag = new GridBagLayout();
pane.setLayout(gridbag);
...
gridbag.setConstraints(button, c);
pane.add(button);
```

Before setting the constraints of the next component, the code resets the value of ipady to the default:

```
c.ipady = 0;
```

Table 8 shows all of the constraints for each component in GridBagLayoutDemo's content pane. Values that aren't the default are in **bold**, values that are different from those in the previous table entry are in *italics*.

Table 8: Constraints for Components Handled by GridBagLayout

Component	Constraints
All components	```ipadx = 0``` **```fill = GridBagConstraints.HORIZONTAL```**

Button 1	```ipady = 0```
	 ```weightx = 0.5```
	 ```weighty = 0.0```
	 ```gridwidth = 1```
	 ```anchor = GridBagConstraints.CENTER```
	 ```insets = new Insets(0,0,0,0)```
	 ```gridx = 0```
	 ```gridy = 0```

Button 2	**```weightx = 0.5```** ***```gridx = 1```*** **```gridy = 0```**
Button 3	**```weightx = 0.5```** ***```gridx = 2```*** **```gridy = 0```**
Button 4	***```ipady = 40```*** *```weightx = 0.0```* ***```gridwidth = 3```*** ***```gridx = 0```*** ***```gridy = 1```***
Button 5	*```ipady = 0```* ```weightx = 0.0``` **```weighty = 1.0```** ***```anchor = GridBagConstraints.SOUTH```*** ***```insets = new Insets(10,0,0,0)```*** ***```gridwidth = 2```*** ***```gridx = 1```*** ***```gridy = 2```***

GridBagLayoutDemo has two components that span multiple columns (buttons 4 and 5). To make button 4 tall, we gave it internal padding (ipady). To put space between buttons 4 and 5, we used Insets to add a minimum of 10 pixels above button 5, which we made hug the south edge of its cell.

All of the components in the pane container are as wide as possible, given the cells they occupy. The program accomplishes this by setting the GridBagConstraints fill instance variable to GridBagConstraints.HORIZONTAL, leaving it at that setting for all of the components. If the program didn't specify the fill, the buttons would be at their natural width, as shown in Figure 21.

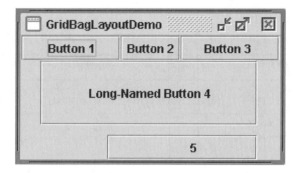

Figure 21 The GridBagLayout application without the fill specified.

When you enlarge GridBagLayoutDemo's window, the columns grow proportionately. This is because components in the first row, where each component is one column wide, have weightx = 1.0. The actual value of the components' weightx is unimportant. What matters is that all components, and consequently all columns, have an equal weight greater than 0. If no components managed by GridBagLayout had weightx set, then, when their container was made wider, they would stay clumped together as in Figure 22.

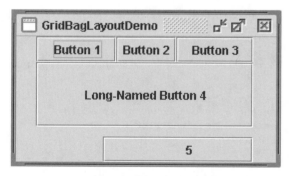

Figure 22 None of the components in this example has weightx specified.

Note that, if you enlarge the window, the last row is the only one that gets taller. This is because only button 5 has weighty greater than 0.

The GridBagLayout API

Table 9 lists the constructors of the `GridBagLayout` and `GridBagConstraints` classes. Each of these classes has only one constructor, with no arguments. You can find the relevant API documentation online at: `http://java.sun.com/j2se/1.4.2/docs/api/java/awt/GridBagConstraints.html`.

Table 9: GridBagConstraints and GridBagLayout Constructors

Constructor	Purpose
`public GridBagConstraints()`	Create an instance of `GridBagConstraints`. Instead of invoking methods on a `GridBagConstraints` object, you manipulate its instance variables, as described in Specifying Constraints (page 482).
`public GridBagLayout()`	Create an instance of `GridBagLayout`. Generally, the only method you might invoke on a `GridBagLayout` object is `setConstraints`, as demonstrated in the Note on page 486.

Examples That Use GridBagLayout

You can find examples of `GridBagLayout` throughout this book's examples. The following table lists a few.

Example	Where Described	Notes
`GridBagLayoutDemo`	This section	Uses many features—weights, insets, internal padding, horizontal fill, exact cell positioning, multi-column cells, and anchoring (component positioning within a cell).
`TextSamplerDemo`	Using Text Components (page 60)	Aligns two pairs of labels and text fields, and adds a label across the full width of the container.
`ContainerEventDemo`	How to Write a Container Listener (page 658)	Positions five components within a container using weights, fill, and relative positioning.

G

Layout Managers

How to Use GridLayout

Here's a snapshot of an application that uses a GridLayout.[1]

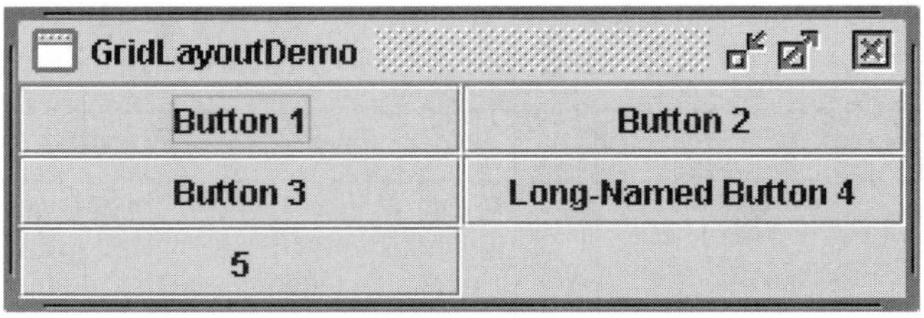

Figure 23 A simple GUI that uses GridLayout.

You can run GridLayoutDemo using Java Web Start or compile and run the example yourself.[2]

GridLayout places components in a grid of cells. Each component takes all of the available space within its cell, and each cell is exactly the same size. If you resize the GridLayout-Demo window, you'll see that GridLayout changes the cell size so that the cells are as large as possible, given the space in the container.

Here's the code that creates the GridLayout object and the components it manages. You can find the whole program in GridLayoutDemo.java.

```
pane.setLayout(new GridLayout(0,2));

pane.add(new JButton("Button 1"));
pane.add(new JButton("Button 2"));
pane.add(new JButton("Button 3"));
pane.add(new JButton("Long-Named Button 4"));
pane.add(new JButton("5"));
```

The constructor tells the GridLayout class to create an instance that has two columns and as many rows as necessary.

---

[1] GridLayout API documentation: http://java.sun.com/j2se/1.4.2/docs/api/java/awt/Grid-Layout.html.

[2] To run GridLayoutDemo using Java Web Start, click the GridLayoutDemo link on the RunExamples/layout.html page on the CD. You can find the source files here: JavaTutorial/uiswing/layout/example-1dot4/index.html#GridLayoutDemo.

The GridLayout API

Table 10 lists the constructors available in the GridLayout API. You can find the relevant API documentation online at: `http://java.sun.com/j2se/1.4.2/docs/api/java/awt/GridLayout.html`.

Table 10: GridLayout Constructors

Constructor	Purpose

`public GridLayout(int rows,`
`              int columns)`
`public GridLayout(int rows,`
`              int columns,`
`              int horizontalGap,`
`              int verticalGap)`
	Create a GridLayout instance. At least one of the rows and columns arguments must be nonzero; rows has precedence over columns. The horizontalGap and verticalGap arguments to the second constructor allow you to specify the number of pixels between cells. If you don't specify gaps, their values default to zero.

Examples That Use GridLayout

The following table lists some GridLayout examples.

Example	Where Described	Notes
GridLayoutDemo	This section	Uses a 2-column grid.
ComboBoxDemo2	How to Use Combo Boxes (page 176)	Uses a 1-x-1 grid to make a component as large as possible.
LabelDemo	How to Use Labels (page 253)	Uses a 3-row grid.
DragPictureDemo	How to Use Drag and Drop and Data Transfer (page 545)	Uses a 4-row grid to present 12 components that display photographs.

G

Layout Managers

491

How to Use SpringLayout

The SpringLayout[1] class was added in v1.4 to support layout in GUI builders. Spring-Layout is very flexible and can emulate many of the features of other layout managers.

This section starts with a simple example showing all of the things you need to create your first spring layout—and what happens when you forget them! Later it presents utility methods that let you lay out components in a couple of different grid types. Figures 24 through 26 show the SpringBox, SpringForm, and SpringCompactGrid examples, which illustrate three possible uses of SpringLayout.

Figure 24   The SpringBox application uses SpringLayout to produce a layout similar to what BoxLayout or FlowLayout would produce.

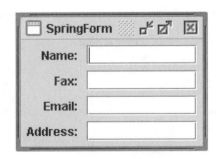

Figure 25   The SpringForm application has five rows of label–text field pairs.

---

[1] SpringLayout API documentation: http://java.sun.com/j2se/1.4.2/docs/api/javax/swing/SpringLayout.html.

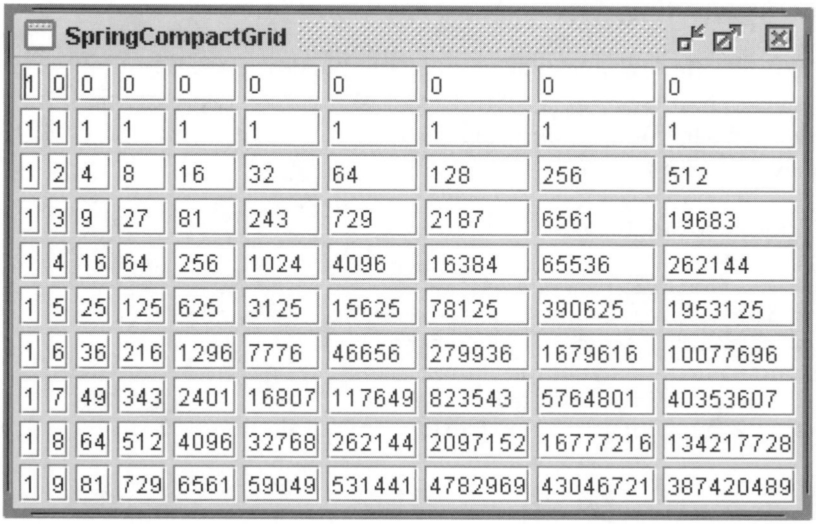

Figure 26 SpringCompactGrid presents components in a grid without forcing all of them to be the same size.

How Spring Layouts Work

Spring layouts do their job by defining relationships between the edges of components. For example, you might define the left edge of one component as a fixed distance (5 pixels, say) from the right edge of another one. By default, SpringLayout defines the width and height of a component (the distance between its left and right edges and between its top and bottom edges) as somewhere between its minimum and maximum sizes—if possible, at its preferred size.

Distances between edges are represented by Spring[1] objects. Each spring has four properties—its *minimum*, *preferred*, and *maximum* values and its actual (current) *value*. The springs associated with each component are collected in a SpringLayout.Constraints[2] object, which is like a java.awt.Rectangle except that its values are Spring objects rather than integers.

---

[1] SpringLayout API documentation: http://java.sun.com/j2se/1.4.2/docs/api/javax/swing/Spring.html.

[2] SpringLayout.Constraints API documentation: http://java.sun.com/j2se/1.4.2/docs/api/javax/swing/SpringLayout.Constraints.html.

Example: SpringDemo

Now we'll take you through the typical steps of specifying the constraints for a Spring-
Layout container. The first example, SpringDemo1.java,[1] is an extremely simple applica-
tion that features a label and a text field in a content pane controlled by SpringLayout.
Here's the relevant code:

```
public class SpringDemo1 {
    ...
    //Where the GUI is created:
    Container contentPane = frame.getContentPane()
    SpringLayout layout = new SpringLayout();
    contentPane.setLayout(layout);
    contentPane.add(new JLabel("Label: "));
    contentPane.add(new JTextField("Text field", 15));
    ...
    frame.pack();
    frame.setVisible(true);
}
```

Figure 27 shows what the GUI looks like when it first comes up.

Figure 27   SpringDemo1—the GUI starts out so small because the parent has no initial size.

Figure 28 shows what it looks like when it's resized to be bigger.

Figure 28   SpringDemo1 after it has been resized—the components overlap because all are at (0,0).

Obviously, we have some problems. Not only does the frame come up too small, but even
when it's resized the components are all located at (0,0). This happens because we didn't set

---

[1] You can find the source files for SpringDemo1 here: JavaTutorial/uiswing/layout/example-
1dot4/index.html#SpringDemo1.

any springs specifying the components' positions and the width of the container. One small consolation is that the components are at their preferred sizes—we get that for free from the default springs created by SpringLayout for each component.

Our next example, SpringDemo2,[1] improves the situation a bit by specifying locations for each component so that the components appear in a single row with 5 pixels between them. The following code specifies the location of the label:

```
//Adjust constraints for the label so it's at (5,5).
layout.putConstraint(SpringLayout.WEST, label,
                     5,
                     SpringLayout.WEST, contentPane);
layout.putConstraint(SpringLayout.NORTH, label,
                     5,
                     SpringLayout.NORTH, contentPane);
```

The first putConstraint call specifies that the label's west (left) edge should be 5 pixels from its container's west edge. This translates to an x coordinate of 5. The second putConstraint call sets up a similar relationship between the north (top) edges of the label and its container, resulting in a y coordinate of 5.

Here's the code that sets up the location of the text field:

```
//Adjust constraints for the text field so it's at
//(<label's right edge> + 5, 5).
layout.putConstraint(SpringLayout.WEST, textField,
                     5,
                     SpringLayout.EAST, label);
layout.putConstraint(SpringLayout.NORTH, textField,
                     5,
                     SpringLayout.NORTH, contentPane);
```

The first putConstraint call puts the text field's west (left) edge 5 pixels away from the label's east (right) edge. The second putConstraint call is just like the code that set the label's y coordinate, and it has the same effect for the text field.

---

[1] You can find the source files for SpringDemo2 here: JavaTutorial/uiswing/layout/example-1dot4/index.html#SpringDemo2.

We still have the problem of the container coming up too small. But when we resize the window, the components are in the right place, as seen in Figure 29.

Figure 29   SpringDemo2, an improved application with all of the components in their correct positions.

To make the container initially appear at the right size, we need to set the springs that define the east (right) and south (bottom) edges of the container itself. SpringDemo3 shows how to do this. You can run SpringDemo3 using Java Web Start or compile and run the example yourself.[1]

Here's the code that sets the container's springs:

```
layout.putConstraint(SpringLayout.EAST, contentPane,
                     5,
                     SpringLayout.EAST, textField);
layout.putConstraint(SpringLayout.SOUTH, contentPane,
                     5,
                     SpringLayout.SOUTH, textField);
```

The first putConstraint call puts the container's right edge 5 pixels to the right of the text field's right edge. The second one puts its bottom edge 5 pixels beyond the bottom edge of the tallest component (which, for simplicity's sake, we've assumed is the text field).

Finally, the window comes up at the right size (see Figure 30).

Figure 30   SpringDemo3 with the window (or "container") now at the correct initial size.

---

[1]   To run SpringDemo3 using Java Web Start, click the SpringDemo3 link on the RunExamples/ layout.html page on the CD. You can find the source files here: JavaTutorial/uiswing/layout/ example-1dot4/index.html#SpringDemo3.

When we make the window larger, we can see the spring layout in action, distributing the extra space between the available components (Figure 31). In this case, the spring layout has given all of the extra space to the text field.

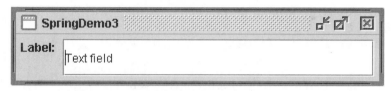

Figure 31   A screenshot of SpringDemo3 after it has been enlarged.

Although it seems like it treats labels and text fields differently, SpringLayout has no special knowledge of any Swing or AWT components. Instead, it relies on the values of a component's minimum, preferred, and maximum size properties. The next section discusses how SpringLayout uses these properties and why they can cause uneven space distribution.

Springs and Component Size

A SpringLayout object automatically installs springs for the height and width of each component it controls. These springs are essentially covers for the component's getMinimumSize, getPreferredSize, and getMaximumSize methods. By "covers" we mean not only that the springs are *initialized* with the appropriate values from these methods but also that they *track* those values. For example, the Spring object that represents the width of a component is a special kind of spring that simply delegates its implementation to the component's relevant size methods. That way it stays in sync with the size methods as the characteristics of the component change.

When a component's getMaximumSize and getPreferredSize methods return the same value, SpringLayout interprets this as that the component shouldn't be stretched. JLabel and JButton are examples of components implemented this way, which is why the label in SpringDemo3 doesn't stretch.

The getMaximumSize method of some components, such as JTextField, returns the value Integer.MAX_VALUE for the width and height of its maximum size, indicating that the component can grow to any size. For this reason, when the SpringDemo3 window is enlarged, SpringLayout distributes all of the extra space to the only springs that can grow—those determining the size of the text field.

Alternative Expressions

The SpringDemo examples used the SpringLayout method putConstraint to set the springs associated with each component. putConstraint is a convenience method that lets you modify springs without using the full SpringLayout API. Here, again, is the code from SpringDemo2 that sets the location of the label:

```
layout.putConstraint(SpringLayout.WEST, label,
                     5,
                     SpringLayout.WEST, contentPane);
layout.putConstraint(SpringLayout.NORTH, label,
                     5,
                     SpringLayout.NORTH, contentPane);
```

Here's equivalent code that uses the SpringLayout.Constraints and Spring classes directly:

```
SpringLayout.Constraints labelCons = layout.getConstraints(label);
labelCons.setX(Spring.constant(5));
labelCons.setY(Spring.constant(5));
```

To see the entire SpringDemo3 demo converted to use this API, look at SpringDemo4.java.[1] That file also includes a general-purpose method called setContainerSize, which you can use to make sure a container controlled by SpringLayout has enough space for all of its components.

As the preceding code snippets imply, SpringLayout and SpringLayout.Constraints tend to use different conventions for describing springs. The SpringLayout API uses edges, which are specified by these constants:

- SpringLayout.NORTH (top edge)
- SpringLayout.SOUTH (bottom edge)
- SpringLayout.EAST (right edge)
- SpringLayout.WEST (left edge)

The SpringLayout.Constraints class knows about edges, but only has Spring objects for the following properties:

---

[1] You can find the SpringDemo4 source file and a link that lets you run it using Java Web Start here:
JavaTutorial/uiswing/layout/example-1dot4/index.html#SpringDemo4.

- *x*
- *y*
- width
- height

Each Constraints object maintains the following relationships between its springs and the edges they represent:

```
 west = x
north = y
 east = x + width
south = y + height
```

If you're confused, don't worry. The next section presents utility methods you can use to accomplish some common layout tasks without knowing anything about the SpringLayout API.

Utility Methods for Grids

Because the SpringLayout class was created for GUI builders, setting up individual springs for a layout can be cumbersome to code by hand. This section presents a couple of methods you can use to install all of the springs needed to lay out a group of components in a grid. These methods emulate some of the features of the GridLayout, GradBagLayout, and Box-Layout classes.

The two methods—makeGrid and makeCompactGrid—are defined in SpringUtilities. java.[1] Both work by grouping components into rows and columns and by using the Spring.max method to make a width or height spring that enlarges a row or column enough to fit all components in it. In the makeCompactGrid method, the same width or height spring is used for all components in a particular column or row, respectively. By contrast, in the makeGrid method, the width and height springs are shared by all components, forcing them to be all the same size.

---

[1] You can find SpringUtilities.java here: JavaTutorial/uiswing/layout/example-1dot4/ SpringUtilities.java.

You can run `SpringGrid` using Java Web Start or compile and run the example yourself.[1]
This first example displays several numbers in text fields. The center text field is much
wider than the others. Just as with `GridLayout`, having one large cell forces all cells to be
equally large (see Figure 32).

SpringGrid		
0		1	2
3	This one is extra long.	5
6	7	8

Figure 32 The `SpringGrid` GUI.

Here's the code that creates and lays out the text fields in `SpringGrid`:

```
JPanel panel = new JPanel(new SpringLayout());
...
for (int i = 0; i < 9; i++) {
    JTextField textField = new JTextField(Integer.toString(i));
    ...//when i==4, put long text in the text field...
    panel.add(textField);
}
...
SpringUtilities.makeGrid(panel,
                         3, 3, //rows, cols
                         5, 5, //initialX, initialY
                         5, 5);//xPad, yPad
```

Now let's look at an example, in the source file `SpringCompactGrid.java`, that uses the
`makeCompactGrid` method instead of `makeGrid` (see Figure 33). This example displays lots
of numbers to show off `SpringLayout`'s ability to minimize the space required.

---

[1] To run `SpringGrid` using Java Web Start, click the `SpringGrid` link on the `RunExamples/layout.html`
page on the CD. You can find the source files here: `JavaTutorial/uiswing/layout/example-1dot4/`
`index.html#SpringGrid`.

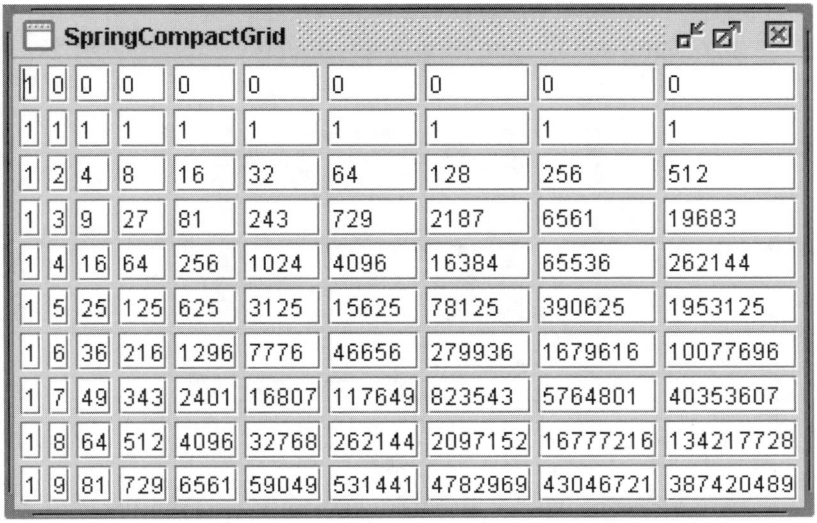

Figure 33   The SpringCompactGrid GUI.

You can run SpringCompactGrid using Java Web Start or compile and run the example yourself.[1] Here's the code that creates and lays out the text fields in SpringCompactGrid:

```
JPanel panel = new JPanel(new SpringLayout());

int rows = 10;
int cols = 10;
for (int r = 0; r < rows; r++) {
    for (int c = 0; c < cols; c++) {
        int anInt = (int) Math.pow(r, c);
        JTextField textField =
                new JTextField(Integer.toString(anInt));
        panel.add(textField);
    }
}

//Lay out the panel.
SpringUtilities.makeCompactGrid(panel, //parent
                               rows, cols,
                               3, 3,  //initX, initY
                               3, 3); //xPad, yPad
```

---

[1] To run SpringCompactGrid using Java Web Start, click the SpringCompactGrid link on the Run-Examples/layout.html page on the CD. You can find the source files here: JavaTutorial/uiswing/layout/example-1dot4/index.html#SpringCompactGrid.

One of the handiest uses for makeCompactGrid is associating labels with components, where the labels are in one column and the components are in another (see Figure 34).

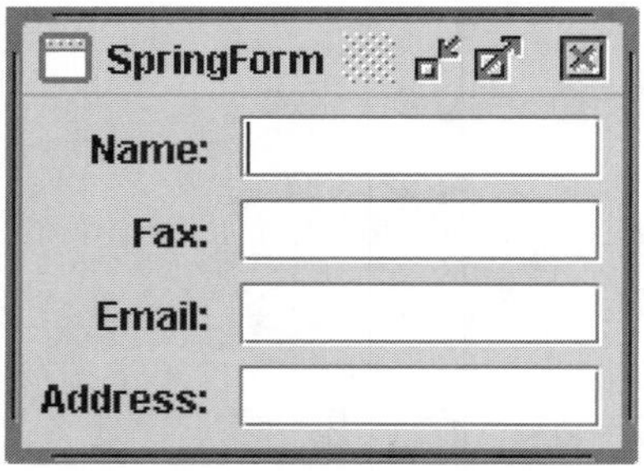

Figure 34 SpringForm uses the makeCompactGrid method to associate labels with components.

You can run SpringForm using Java Web Start or compile and run the example yourself.[1] Here's the code that creates and lays out the label–text field pairs in SpringForm:

```
String[] labels = {"Name: ", "Fax: ", "Email: ", "Address: "};
int numPairs = labels.length;

//Create and populate the panel.
JPanel p = new JPanel(new SpringLayout());
for (int i = 0; i < numPairs; i++) {
    JLabel l = new JLabel(labels[i], JLabel.TRAILING);
    p.add(l);
    JTextField textField = new JTextField(10);
    l.setLabelFor(textField);
    p.add(textField);
}

//Lay out the panel.
SpringUtilities.makeCompactGrid(p,
                                numPairs, 2, //rows, cols
                                6, 6,        //initX, initY
                                6, 6);       //xPad, yPad
```

Because we're using a real layout manager instead of absolute positioning, the layout manager responds dynamically to changes in the components involved. For example, if the names of the labels are localized, the SpringLayout produces a configuration that gives the

---

[1] To run SpringForm using Java Web Start, click the SpringForm link on the RunExamples/layout.html page on the CD. You can find the source files here: JavaTutorial/uiswing/layout/example-1dot4/index.html#SpringForm.

first column more or less room as needed. And, as Figure 35 shows, when the window is resized the flexibly sized components—the text fields—take all the excess space while the labels stick to what they need.

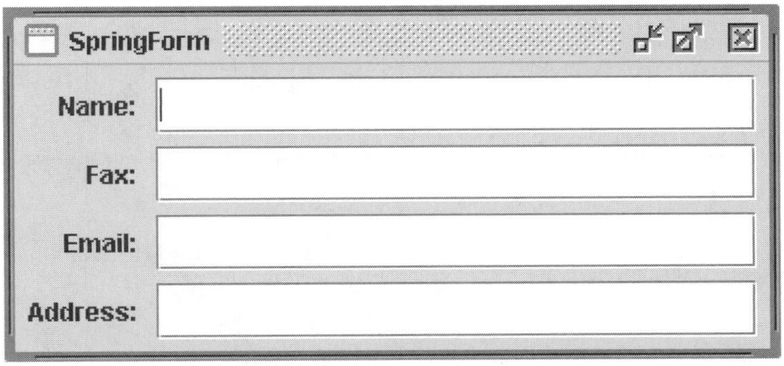

Figure 35   SpringForm after it has been enlarged.

Our last example of the makeCompactGrid method, in SpringBox.java, shows some buttons configured to be laid out in a single row (see Figure 36).

Figure 36   The SpringBox application.

You can run SpringBox using Java Web Start or compile and run the example yourself.[1]

Note that the behavior is almost identical to that of BoxLayout in the case of a single row. Not only are the components laid out as BoxLayout would arrange them but the minimum, preferred, and maximum sizes of the container that uses SpringLayout return the same results that BoxLayout would. The following is the call to makeCompactGrid that produces this layout:

---

[1]   To run SpringBox using Java Web Start, click the SpringBox link on the RunExamples/layout.html page on the CD. You can find the source files here: JavaTutorial/uiswing/layout/example-1dot4/index.html#SpringBox.

```
//Lay out the buttons in one row and as many columns
//as necessary, with 6 pixels of padding all around.
SpringUtilities.makeCompactGrid(contentPane, 1,
                          contentPane.getComponentCount(),
                          6, 6, 6, 6);
```

Let's look at what happens when we resize this window (see Figure 37). This is an odd special case that's worth noting, as you may run into it by accident in your first layouts.

Figure 37 SpringBox after it has been enlarged.

Nothing moved! That's because none of the components (buttons) or the spacing between them was defined to be stretchable. In this case, the SpringLayout calculates a maximum size for the parent container that's equal to its preferred size, meaning that the parent container itself isn't stretchable. It might be less confusing if the AWT refused to resize a window that wasn't stretchable, but it doesn't. Maximum and minimum sizes for windows are "recommendations" that the AWT defies when given suitable user input. The layout manager can't do anything sensible here, because none of the components take up the required space. Instead of crashing, it just does nothing, leaving all of the components as they were.

The SpringLayout API

The API for SpringLayout is larger than that for most layout managers. It's spread across three classes. Table 11 lists the constructors and methods for the SpringLayout class; Table 12, for the SpringLayout.Constraints class; and Table 13, for the Spring class. Also consult the API documentation:

```
http://java.sun.com/j2se/1.4.2/docs/api/javax/swing/SpringLayout.html
http://java.sun.com/j2se/1.4.2/docs/api/javax/swing/
        SpringLayout.Constraints.html
http://java.sun.com/j2se/1.4.2/docs/api/javax/swing/Spring.html
```

Table 11: SpringLayout Constructors and Methods

Constructor or Method	Purpose
`SpringLayout()`	Create a `SpringLayout` instance.
`SpringLayout.Constraints getConstraints(Component)`	Get the constraints (set of springs) associated with the specified component.
`Spring getConstraint(String, Component)`	Get the spring for an edge of a component. The first argument specifies the edge and must be one of the `SpringLayout` constants: NORTH, SOUTH, EAST, or WEST.
`void putConstraint(String, Component, int, String, Component)` `void putConstraint(String, Component, Spring, String, Component)`	Defines relationships between the edges of two components. The first two arguments specify the first component and its affected edge; the last two, the second component and its affected edge. The third argument specifies the spring that determines the distance between the two. When the third argument is an integer, a constant spring is created to provide a fixed distance between the component edges.

Table 12: SpringLayout.Constraints Constructors and Methods

Constructor or Method	Purpose
`SpringLayout.Constraints()` `SpringLayout.Constraints(Spring, Spring)` `SpringLayout.Constraints(Spring, Spring, Spring, Spring)`	Create a `SpringLayout.Constraints` instance. The first two arguments, if present, specify the X and Y springs, respectively; the second two, height and width springs, respectively. Omitting an argument causes the corresponding spring to be null, which `SpringLayout` generally replaces with suitable defaults.
`Spring getConstraint(String)` `Spring getHeight()` `Spring getWidth()` `Spring getX()` `Spring getY()` `void setConstraint(String, Spring)` `void setHeight(Spring)` `void setWidth(Spring)` `void setX(Spring)` `void setY(Spring)`	Get or set the specified spring. The string argument to the `getConstraint` and `setConstraint` methods specifies an edge name and must be one of the `SpringLayout` constants NORTH, SOUTH, EAST, or WEST.

S

Layout Managers

Table 13: Spring Methods

Method	Purpose

`static Spring constant(int)`
`static Spring constant(int,`
`                   int,`
`                   int)`
	Create a spring that doesn't track a component's sizes. The three-argument version creates a spring with its minimum, preferred, and maximum values set to the specified values, in that order. The one-argument version creates a spring with its minimum, preferred, and maximum values all set to the specified integer.

`static Spring sum(Spring,`
`                Spring)`
`static Spring max(Spring,`
`                Spring)`
`static Spring minus(Spring)`
	Create a spring that is the result of some mathematical manipulation. The `sum` method adds two springs. The `max` method returns a spring whose value is always greater than or equal to the values of the two arguments. The `minus` method returns a spring running in the opposite direction of the argument. The `minus` method can be used to create an argument to the `sum` method, letting you get the difference between two springs.

`int getMinimumValue()`
`int getPreferredValue()`
`int getMaximumValue()`
	Gets the corresponding value from the spring. For a `SpringLayout`-created spring that automatically tracks a component, these methods result in calls to the component's corresponding get*Xxx*Size method.

`setValue(int)`	Sets the spring's current value.

Examples That Use SpringLayout

The following table lists some examples that use spring layout.

Example	Where Described	Notes
`SpringDemo3`	This section	Uses `SpringLayout` to create a row of evenly spaced, natural-size components.
`SpringGrid`	This section	Uses `SpringLayout` and the `makeGrid` utility method to create a layout where all components are the same size.
`SpringCompactGrid`	This section	Uses `SpringLayout` and the `makeCompactGrid` utility method to create a layout where all of the components in a row have the same height and all of the components in a column have the same width.

Example	Where Described	Notes
`SpringForm`	This section	Uses `SpringLayout` and `makeCompactGrid` to align label–text field pairs.
`SpringBox`	This section	Uses `SpringLayout` and `makeCompactGrid` to demonstrate laying out a single row of components and what happens when no springs can grow.
`SpinnerDemo`	How to Use Spinners (page 357)	Uses `SpringLayout` and `makeCompactGrid` to lay out rows of label–spinner pairs.
`TextInputDemo`	How to Use Formatted Text Fields (page 221)	Uses `SpringLayout` and `makeCompactGrid` to lay out rows of labeled components. The components are a mix of text fields, formatted text fields, and spinners.

S

Layout Managers

9

Other Swing Features
Reference

T<small>HIS</small> chapter contains a collection of how-tos to help you use miscellaneous Swing features. You can find source files for all of this chapter's examples on the CD and online:

```
JavaTutorial/uiswing/misc/example-1dot4/index.html
```

```
http://java.sun.com/docs/books/tutorial/uiswing/misc/example-1dot4/
index.html
```

The preceding URLs take you to an example index that has links to the files required by each example. To go directly to the entry for a particular example add *#ExampleName* to the URL. Most examples have a "Run" link in the index which executes the example using Java Web Start technology.

Here are short summaries of the how-to sections in this chapter:

- How to Use Actions—With `Action` objects, you can coordinate the state and event handling of two or more components that generate action events. For example, you can use a single `Action` to create and coordinate a tool-bar button and a menu item that perform the same function.
- How to Support Assistive Technologies—Swing components have built-in support for assistive technologies. Your program can provide even better support by following a few rules.

- How to Use Borders—Bopaintingrders are very handy for painting lines, titles, and empty space around the edges of components. This section tells you how to add a border to any `JComponent`.

- How to Use Drag and Drop and Data Transfer—Most applications can benefit from the ability to transfer information between components using drag and drop or cut, copy, and paste. This section tells you how to implement these features in your program.

- How to Use the Focus Subsystem—Some programs need to manipulate focus; for example, to validate input or change the tab order of components. This section describes some techniques you can use to customize focus in your program.

- How to Use Icons—Many Swing components can display icons. Usually, icons are implemented as instances of the `ImageIcon` class.

- How to Use Key Bindings—With key bindings, you can specify how components react to a user's input.

- How to Set the Look and Feel—You can specify the look and feel of Swing components.

- How to Use Threads—Read this section to learn about using threads properly in programs that use the Swing components. This section talks about the event-dispatching thread and explains how to use methods, such as `invokeLater`, and classes, such as `SwingWorker`. It also tells you when you might want to use the `Timer` class.

- How to Use Timers—With the Swing `Timer` class, you can implement a thread that performs an action after a delay and optionally continues to repeat the action. The action executes in the event-dispatching thread.

If you encounter any problems in this chapter, you may find the solutions in Solving Common Problems Using Other Swing Features (page 743) in the Appendix.

How to Use Actions

If you have two or more components that perform the same function, consider using an Action[1] object to implement the function. An Action object is an action listener[2] that provides not only action-event handling but also centralized handling of the state of action-event-firing components such as tool-bar buttons, menu items, common buttons, and text fields. The states that an action can handle include text, icon, mnemonic, and enabled status.

You typically attach an action to a component using the setAction method. Here's what happens when setAction is invoked on a component:

- The component's state is updated to match the state of the Action. For example, if the Action's text and icon values were set, the component's text and icon are set to match them.
- The Action object is registered as an action listener on the component.
- If the state of the Action changes, the component's state is updated to match it. For example, if you change the enabled status of the action, all components it's attached to change their enabled states to match.

Here's an example of creating a tool-bar button and menu item that perform the same function:

```
Action leftAction = new LeftAction(); //LeftAction code is shown later
...
button = new JButton(leftAction)
...
menuItem = new JMenuItem(leftAction);
```

Version Note: Prior to the v1.3 release of the Java 2 platform, the only way for a button or menu item to get the full benefit of an Action was to create the component using the add(Action) method of JToolBar, JMenu, or JPopupMenu. This was because the pre-1.3 releases had no API except addActionListener(ActionListener) to connect an Action to an already existing component. Although you could use addActionListener to add an Action object as an action listener to any button, for example, the button wouldn't be notified when the action was disabled.

---

[1] Action API documentation: http://java.sun.com/j2se/1.4.2/docs/api/javax/swing/Action.html.

[2] See also How to Write an Action Listener (page 646) in Chapter 10.

To create an `Action` object, you generally create a subclass of `AbstractAction`[1] and instantiate it. In your subclass, you must implement the `actionPerformed` method to react appropriately when the action event occurs.

Here's an example of creating and instantiating an `AbstractAction` subclass:

```
leftAction = new LeftAction("Go left", anIcon,
            "This is the left button.",
            new Integer(KeyEvent.VK_L));
...

class LeftAction extends AbstractAction {
    public LeftAction(String text,
                      ImageIcon icon,
                      String desc,
                      Integer mnemonic) {
        super(text, icon);
        putValue(SHORT_DESCRIPTION, desc);
        putValue(MNEMONIC_KEY, mnemonic);
    }

    public void actionPerformed(ActionEvent e) {
        displayResult("Action for first button/menu item", e);
    }
}
```

When the action created by this code is attached to a button and a menu item, the button and menu item display the text and icon associated with the action. The L character is used for mnemonics on the button and menu item, and their tool-tip text is set to the `SHORT_DESCRIPTION` string followed by a representation of the mnemonic key.

We've provided a simple example, `ActionDemo`, which defines three actions, each attached to a button and a menu item. (See Figure 1.) Thanks to the mnemonic values set for each button's action, the key sequence Alt-L activates the left button, Alt-M the middle button, and Alt-R the right button. The tool tip for the left button displays "This is the left button. Alt-L." All of this configuration occurs automatically, without the program having to make explicit calls to set the mnemonic or the tool-tip text. As we'll show later, the program *does* make calls to set the button text, but only to avoid using the values already set by the actions.

---

[1] AbstractAction API documentation: `http://java.sun.com/j2se/1.4.2/docs/api/javax/swing/AbstractAction.html`.

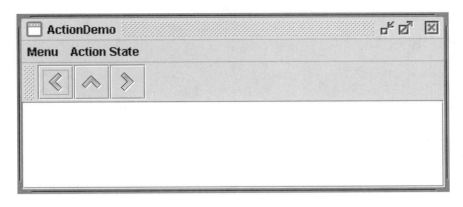

Figure 1   A screenshot of the ActionDemo example.

Try This:

1. Run ActionDemo using Java Web Start or compile and run the example yourself.[1]

2. Choose the top item from the left menu (Menu > Go left). The text area displays some text identifying both the event source and the action listener that received the event.

3. Click the leftmost button in the tool bar. The text area again displays information about the event. Note that, although the source of the events is different, both events were detected by the same action listener: the Action object attached to the components.

4. Choose the top item from the **Action State** menu. This disables the Go left Action object, which in turn disables its associated menu item and button. (See Figure 2.)

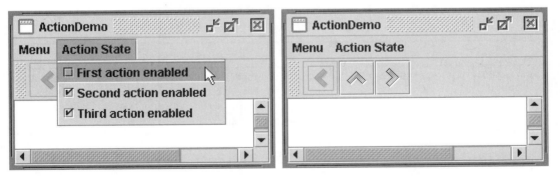

Figure 2   Two screenshots of what the user sees as the Go left Action is disabled.

---

[1] To run ActionDemo using Java Web Start, click the ActionDemo link on the RunExamples/misc.html page on the CD. You can find the source files here: JavaTutorial/uiswing/misc/example-1dot4/index.html#ActionDemo.

Here's the code that disables the Go left action:

```
boolean selected = .../true if the action should be enabled;
                        //false, otherwise
leftAction.setEnabled(selected);
```

After you create components using an Action, you might need to customize them. For example, you might want to customize the appearance of one of the components by adding or deleting the icon or text. ActionDemo has no icons in its menus and no text in its buttons. Here's the code that accomplishes this:

```
menuItem = new JMenuItem();
menuItem.setAction(leftAction);
menuItem.setIcon(null); //arbitrarily chose not to use icon in menu
...
button = new JButton();
button.setAction(leftAction);
button.setText(""); //an icon-only button
```

We chose to create an icon-only button and a text-only menu item from the same action by setting the icon property to null and the text to an empty string. However, if a property of the Action changes, the widget may try again to reset the icon and text from the Action.

The Action API

Tables 1 and 2 list the commonly used Action constructors and methods. You can find the Action API documentation online at: http://java.sun.com/j2se/1.4.2/docs/api/ javax/swing/Action.html.

Table 1: Components That Support set/getAction

Class	Purpose
AbstractButton JComboBox JTextField	As of release 1.3, these components and their subclasses may have an action directly assigned to them via setAction. For further information about components that are often associated with actions, see the sections on tool-bar buttons, menu items, common buttons, and text fields.

Table 2: Creating and Using an AbstractAction

Constructor or Method	Purpose
AbstractAction() AbstractAction(String) AbstractAction(String, Icon)	Create an Action object. Through arguments, you can specify the text and icon to be used in the components that the action controls.
void setEnabled(boolean) boolean isEnabled()	Set or get whether the components the action controls are enabled. Invoking setEnabled(false) disables all of the components that the action controls. Similarly, invoking setEnabled(true) enables the action's components.
void putValue(String, Object) Object getValue(String)	Set or get an object associated with a specified key. Used for setting and getting properties associated with an action.

Table 3 defines the properties that can be set on an action. The second column lists which components automatically use the properties (the method specifically called). For example, setting the ACCELERATOR_KEY on an action that is then attached to a menu item means that JMenuItem.setAccelerator(KeyStroke) is called automatically.

Table 3: Action Properties

Property	Auto-Applied to: Class *(Method Called)*	Purpose
ACCELERATOR_KEY	JMenuItem (*setAccelerator*)	The KeyStroke to be used as the accelerator for the action. For a discussion of accelerators versus mnemonics, see Enabling Keyboard Operation (page 282). Introduced in 1.3.
ACTION_COMMAND_KEY	AbstractButton, JCheckBox, JRadioButton (*setActionCommand*)	The command string associated with the ActionEvent.
LONG_DESCRIPTION	None	The longer description for the action. Can be used for context-sensitive help.
MNEMONIC_KEY	AbstractButton, JMenuItem, JCheckBox, JRadioButton (*setMnemonic*)	The mnemonic for the action. For a discussion of accelerators versus mnemonics, see Enabling Keyboard Operation (page 282). Introduced in 1.3.
NAME	AbstractButton, JMenuItem, JCheckBox, JRadioButton (*setText*)	The name of the action. You can set this property when creating the action using the AbstractAction(String) or Abstract-Action(String, Icon) constructors.

Table 3: Action Properties *(continued)*

Property	Auto-Applied to: Class *(Method Called)*	Purpose
SHORT_DESCRIPTION	AbstractButton, JCheckBox, JRadioButton (*setToolTipText*)	The short description of the action.
SMALL_ICON	AbstractButton, JMenuItem (*setIcon*)	The icon for the action used in the tool bar or on a button. You can set this property when creating the action using the Abstract-Action(name, icon) constructor.

Examples That Use Actions

The following examples use Action objects.

Example	Where Described	Notes
ActionDemo	This section	Uses actions to bind buttons and menu items to the same function.
TextComponentDemo	Using Text Components (page 60)	Uses text actions to create menu items for text editing commands, such as cut, copy, and paste, and to bind keystrokes to caret movement. Also implements custom AbstractAction subclasses to implement undo and redo. The text action discussion begins in Concepts: About Editor Kits (page 76) in Chapter 3.

How to Support Assistive Technologies

You might be wondering what assistive technologies are and why you should care. Primarily, assistive technologies enable people with disabilities to use the computer. Say you get carpal tunnel syndrome. You can use assistive technologies to accomplish your work without using your hands.

Assistive technologies—voice interfaces, screen readers, alternate input devices, and so on—are useful not only for people with disabilities but also for people using computers in non-office environments. For example, you might use assistive technology to check your email when you're stuck in a traffic jam, using only voice input and output. The information that enables assistive technologies can be used for other tools as well, such as automated GUI testers and input devices like touchscreens. Assistive technologies get information from components using the Accessibility API, which is defined in the `javax.accessibility` package.[1]

Because support for the Accessibility API is built into the Swing components, your Swing program will probably work just fine with assistive technologies, even if you do nothing special. For example, assistive technologies can automatically get the text information that's set by the following lines of code:

```
JButton button = new JButton("I'm a Swing button!");
label = new JLabel(labelPrefix + "0     ");
label.setText(labelPrefix + numClicks);
JFrame frame = new JFrame("SwingApplication");
```

They can also grab the tool-tip text (if any) associated with a component and use it to describe the component to the user.

Making your program function smoothly with assistive technologies is easy and in the United States may be required by federal law. For more information, see *Global Legal Resources for IT Related Accessibility Issues* at: `http://www.sun.com/access/background/laws.html`.

---

[1] `javax.accessibility` API documentation: `http://java.sun.com/j2se/1.4.2/docs/api/javax/accessibility/package-summary.html`.

Rules for Supporting Accessibility

Here are a few things you can do to make your program work as well as possible with assistive technologies:

- If a component doesn't display a short string (which serves as its default name), specify a name with the `setAccessibleName` method. You might want to do this for image-only buttons, panels that provide logical groupings, text areas, and so on.

- Set tool-tip text for components whenever it makes sense to do so. For example:

```
aJComponent.setToolTipText(
    "Clicking this component causes XYZ to happen.");
```

- If you don't want to provide a tool tip for a component, use the `setAccessible-Description` method to provide a description that assistive technologies can show the user. For example:

```
aJComponent.getAccessibleContext().
    setAccessibleDescription(
    "Clicking this component causes XYZ to happen.");
```

- Specify keyboard alternatives wherever possible. Make sure you can use your program with the keyboard only. Try hiding your mouse! If the focus is in an editable text component, you can use Shift-Tab to move it to the next component. Support for keyboard alternatives varies by component. Buttons support them with the `setMnemonic` method. Menus inherit the button mnemonics support and also support accelerators, as described in Enabling Keyboard Operation (page 282). Other components can use key bindings[1] to associate user typing with program actions.

- Assign a textual description to all `ImageIcon` objects in your program. You can set this property by either the `setDescription` method or one of the `String` forms of the `ImageIcon` constructors.

- If some components form a logical group, try to put them into one container. For example, use a `JPanel` to contain all of the radio buttons in a radio button group.

- Whenever you have a label that describes another component, use the `setLabelFor` method so that assistive technologies can find the component associated with that label. This is especially important when the label displays a mnemonic for another component (such as a text field).

- If you create a custom component, make sure it supports accessibility. In particular, be aware that subclasses of `JComponent` are not automatically accessible. Custom components that are descendants of other Swing components should override inherited accessibility information as necessary. For more information, see How Accessibility Works (page 528) and Making Custom Components Accessible (page 529).

---

[1] See also How to Use Key Bindings (page 623).

- Use the examples provided with the accessibility utilities to test your program. Although the primary purpose of these examples is to show programmers how to use the Accessibility API when implementing assistive technologies, they are also quite useful for testing application programs for accessibility. The following section, Testing for Accessibility, shows ScrollDemo running with Monkey—one of the accessibility utilities examples. Monkey shows the tree of accessible components in a program and lets you interact with those components.

- Finally, don't break what you get for free! If your GUI has an inaccessible container— for example, your own subclass of Container or JComponent or any other container that doesn't implement the Accessible interface—any components inside that container become inaccessible.

Testing for Accessibility

The examples that come with the accessibility utilities can give you an idea of how accessible your program is. For instructions on getting these utilities, see the JFC Assistive Technologies home page at http://java.sun.com/products/jfc/accessibility/. Follow the instructions in the documentation for setting up the Java Virtual Machine (VM) to run one or more of the utilities automatically.

Let's use an accessibility utility to compare the original version of one of our demos to a version in which the rules for supporting accessibility have been applied. Figure 3 is a picture of a program called ScrollDemo.

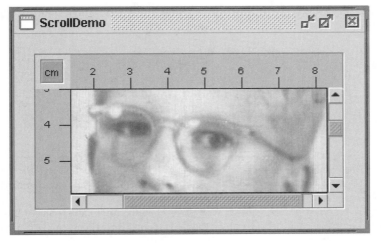

Figure 3   A screenshot of the ScrollDemo example.

Try This:

1. Run `ScrollDemo` using Java Web Start or compile and run the example yourself.[1]

2. Run `AccessibleScrollDemo` using Java Web Start or compile and run the example 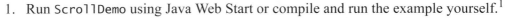 yourself.[2]

3. Compare the two versions side by side. The only noticeable difference is that the **cm** toggle button and the photograph have tool tips in the accessible version.

4. Run the two versions under the accessibility utility called Monkey. Note when the accessibility tools have been downloaded and configured in the `accessibility.` `properties` file, that the Monkey window automatically comes up when you click on the "Run `ScrollDemo`" and "Run `AccessibleScrollDemo`" links (in steps 1 and 2).

   If the Monkey window doesn't appear on startup, the problem may be that the `accessibility.properties` file isn't present in the version of the VM being used by Java Web Start. You can change the VM by running the Java Web Start Application Manager and selecting File > Preferences > Java.

5. When the Monkey window comes up, you need to select File > Refresh Trees to see information appear under `Accessible Tree`. You can then expand the tree by successively clicking on the horizontal icons displayed by each folder icon. When the tree has been expanded, you can see detailed information for the various components. The custom components (rules and corners) that weren't accessible in the original version are accessible in the modified version. This can make quite a difference to assistive technologies.

Figure 4 shows Monkey running on `ScrollDemo`. The left side of the split pane shows the actual component hierarchy for the program. The right side shows the accessible components in the hierarchy, which is what interests us.

---

[1] To run `ScrollDemo` using Java Web Start, click the `ScrollDemo` link on the `RunExamples/` `components.html` page on the CD. You can find the source files here: `JavaTutorial/uiswing/` `components/example-1dot4/index.html#ScrollDemo`.

[2] To run `AccessibleScrollDemo` using Java Web Start, click the `AccessibleScrollDemo` link on the `RunExamples/misc.html` page on the CD. You can find the source files here: `JavaTutorial/uiswing/` `misc/example-1dot4/index.html#AccessibleScrollDemo`.

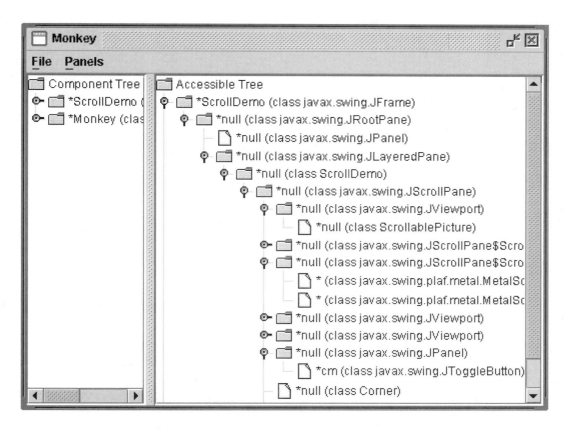

Figure 4   Monkey running on an inaccessible version of ScrollDemo.

The first thing to notice is that, even with no explicit support in ScrollDemo, Monkey is able to discover a lot of information about the various components in the example. Most of the components and their children appear in the tree. However, the names for most of them are empty (null), which is rather unhelpful. The descriptions are also empty.

Further trouble comes with the program's custom components. The two rulers are inaccessible, so they aren't included in the accessible tree. The viewports that contain the rulers are displayed as leaf nodes because they have no accessible children. The custom corners are also missing from the accessible tree.

Figure 5 shows the Monkey window for `AccessibleScrollDemo`.

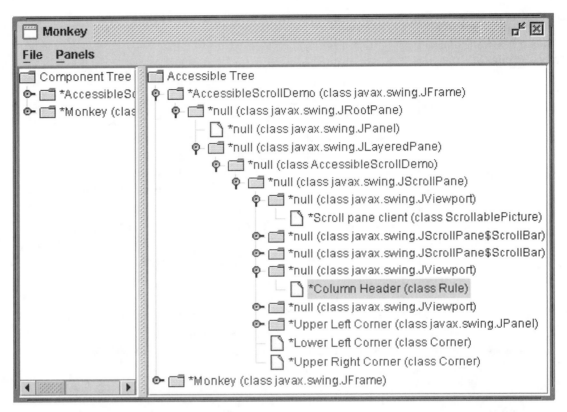

Figure 5   Monkey running on an accessible version of `ScrollDemo`.

The rules are now listed as children of the viewports, and the corners are listed as children of the scroll pane. Furthermore, many of the components now have non-null names.

In Figure 5, the Column Header item is selected. Monkey highlights the corresponding component in the `ScrollDemo` program.

When an item is selected, you can use Monkey's Panels menu to bring up one of four different panels that let you interact with the selected component. Choosing Panels > Accessibility API panel brings up a panel like the one that is shown in Figure 6. This panel displays information available through methods defined in the `AccessibleContext` base class and the `AccessibleComponent` interface.

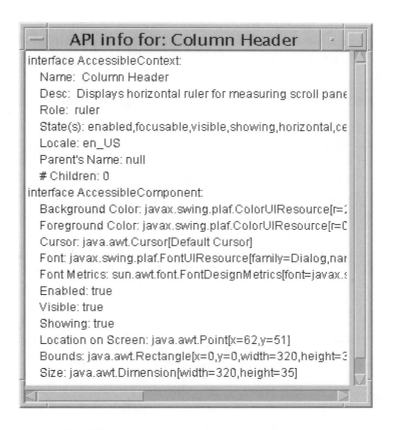

Figure 6 An Accessibility API panel.

Monkey has three other panels:

- **AccessibleAction** shows the actions supported by an accessible component and lets you invoke the action. It works only with an accessible component whose context implements the `AccessibleAction` interface.

- **AccessibleSelection** shows the current selection of an accessible component and lets you manipulate the selection. It works only with an accessible component whose context implements the `AccessibleSelection` interface.

- **AccessibleHypertext** shows any hyperlinks contained within an accessible component and lets you traverse them. It works only with an accessible component whose context implements the `AccessibleHypertext` interface.

The accessibility utilities examples are handy as testing tools and can give you an idea of how accessible the components in your program are. However, even if your components behave well in Monkey or the other examples, they still might not be completely accessible because Monkey and the other examples exercise only certain portions of the Accessibility API. The only true test of accessibility is to run your programs with real-world assistive technologies.

Setting Accessible Names and Descriptions on Components

Giving your program's components accessible names and descriptions is one of the easiest and most important steps in making your program itself accessible. Following is a complete listing of the AccessibleScrollDemo constructor that creates the scroll pane and the custom components it uses. The boldface statements give component names and descriptions that assistive technologies can use.

```
public AccessibleScrollDemo() {
    // Get the image to use.
    ImageIcon david = createImageIcon("images/youngdad.jpeg",
                        "Photograph of David McNabb in his youth.");

    // Create the row and column headers.
    columnView = new Rule(Rule.HORIZONTAL, true);
    if (david != null) {
        columnView.setPreferredWidth(david.getIconWidth());
    } else {
        columnView.setPreferredWidth(320);
    }
    columnView.getAccessibleContext().
            setAccessibleName("Column Header");
    columnView.getAccessibleContext().
            setAccessibleDescription("Displays horizontal ruler for " +
                                    "measuring scroll pane client.");
    rowView = new Rule(Rule.VERTICAL, true);
    if (david != null) {
        rowView.setPreferredHeight(david.getIconHeight());
    } else {
        rowView.setPreferredHeight(480);
    }
    rowView.getAccessibleContext().setAccessibleName("Row Header");
    rowView.getAccessibleContext().
            setAccessibleDescription("Displays vertical ruler for " +
                                    "measuring scroll pane client.");

    // Create the corners.
    JPanel buttonCorner = new JPanel();
    isMetric = new JToggleButton("cm", true);
    isMetric.setFont(new Font("SansSerif", Font.PLAIN, 11));
    isMetric.setMargin(new Insets(2,2,2,2));
    isMetric.addItemListener(this);
    isMetric.setToolTipText("Toggles rulers' unit of measure " +
                            "between inches and centimeters.");
```

```
buttonCorner.add(isMetric); //Use the default FlowLayout
buttonCorner.getAccessibleContext().
            setAccessibleName("Upper Left Corner");

String desc = "Fills the corner of a scroll pane " +
                "with color for aesthetic reasons.";
Corner lowerLeft = new Corner();
lowerLeft.getAccessibleContext().
        setAccessibleName("Lower Left Corner");
lowerLeft.getAccessibleContext().setAccessibleDescription(desc);

Corner upperRight = new Corner();
upperRight.getAccessibleContext().
            setAccessibleName("Upper Right Corner");
upperRight.getAccessibleContext().setAccessibleDescription(desc);

// Set up the scroll pane.
picture = new ScrollablePicture(david,
                                columnView.getIncrement());
picture.setToolTipText(david.getDescription());
picture.getAccessibleContext().setAccessibleName(
                                "Scroll pane client");

JScrollPane pictureScrollPane = new JScrollPane(picture);
pictureScrollPane.setPreferredSize(new Dimension(300, 250));
pictureScrollPane.setViewportBorder(
        BorderFactory.createLineBorder(Color.black));
pictureScrollPane.setColumnHeaderView(columnView);
pictureScrollPane.setRowHeaderView(rowView);

// In theory, to support internationalization you would change
// UPPER_LEFT_CORNER to UPPER_LEADING_CORNER,
// LOWER_LEFT_CORNER to LOWER_LEADING_CORNER, and
// UPPER_RIGHT_CORNER to UPPER_TRAILING_CORNER.  In practice,
// bug #4467063 makes that impossible (at least in 1.4.0).
pictureScrollPane.setCorner(JScrollPane.UPPER_LEFT_CORNER,
                            buttonCorner);
pictureScrollPane.setCorner(JScrollPane.LOWER_LEFT_CORNER,
                            lowerLeft);
pictureScrollPane.setCorner(JScrollPane.UPPER_RIGHT_CORNER,
                            upperRight);

// Put it in this panel.
setLayout(new BoxLayout(this, BoxLayout.LINE_AXIS));
add(pictureScrollPane);
setBorder(BorderFactory.createEmptyBorder(20,20,20,20));
}
```

Often the program sets a component's name and description directly through the component's accessible context. Other times, it sets an accessible description indirectly with tool tips. In the case of the **cm** toggle button, the description is set automatically to the text on the button.

How Accessibility Works

An object is accessible if it implements the `Accessible`[1] interface. The `Accessible` interface defines just one method, `getAccessibleContext`, which returns an `Accessible-Context`[2] object (see Figure 7). This object is an intermediary that contains the accessible information for an accessible object.

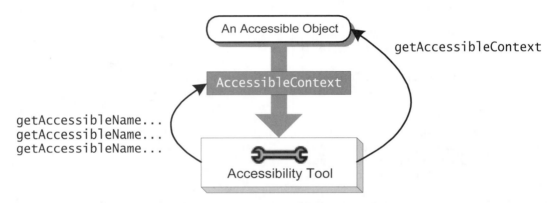

Figure 7   This figure shows how assistive technologies get the accessible context from an accessible object and query it for information.

`AccessibleContext` is an abstract class that defines the minimum information an accessible object must provide about itself. That minimum includes name, description, role, state set, and so on. To identify its accessible object as having particular capabilities, an accessible context can implement one or more of the interfaces as shown in Table 6, "Accessible Interfaces," on page 533. For example, `JButton` implements `AccessibleAction`, `Accessible-Value`, `AccessibleText`, and `AccessibleExtendedComponent`. It isn't necessary for `JButton` to implement `AccessibleIcon`, which is implemented by the `ImageIcon` attached to the button.

---

[1] Accessible   API   documentation: `http://java.sun.com/j2se/1.4.2/docs/api/javax/accessibility/Accessible.html`.

[2] `AccessibleContext` API documentation: `http://java.sun.com/j2se/1.4.2/docs/api/javax/accessibility/AccessibleContext.html`.

Because the JComponent class itself doesn't implement the Accessible interface, instances of its direct subclasses aren't accessible. If you write a custom component that inherits directly from JComponent, you need to explicitly make it implement the Accessible interface. JComponent does have an accessible context, called AccessibleJComponent, that implements the AccessibleComponent interface and provides a minimal amount of accessible information. You can provide an accessible context for your custom components by creating a subclass of AccessibleJComponent and overriding important methods. The next section, Making Custom Components Accessible, shows two examples of doing this.

All of the other standard Swing components implement the Accessible interface and have an accessible context that implements one or more of the preceding interfaces as appropriate. The accessible contexts for Swing components are implemented as inner classes and have names of this style:

> *Component*.Accessible*Component*

If you create a subclass of a standard Swing component and your subclass is substantially different from its superclass, you should provide a custom accessible context for it. The easiest way is to create a subclass of the superclass's accessible context class and override methods as necessary. For example, if you create a JLabel subclass substantially different from JLabel, your subclass should contain an inner class that extends AccessibleJLabel. The next section shows how to do this using examples in which JComponent subclasses extend AccessibleJComponent.

Making Custom Components Accessible

The ScrollDemo program uses three custom component classes. ScrollablePicture is a subclass of JLabel, and Corner and Rule are both subclasses of JComponent.

The ScrollablePicture class relies completely on accessibility inherited from JLabel through JLabel.AccessibleJLabel.[1] The code that creates an instance of Scrollable-Picture sets the tool-tip text for the scrollable picture. The tool-tip text is used by the context as the component's accessible description. This behavior is provided by AccessibleJLabel.

The accessible version of the Corner class contains just enough code to make its instances accessible. We implemented accessibility support by adding the code shown in bold to the original version of Corner in the following.

---

[1] JLabel.AccessibleJLabel API documentation: http://java.sun.com/j2se/1.4.2/docs/api/ javax/swing/JLabel.AccessibleJLabel.html.

```
public class Corner extends JComponent implements Accessible {

    public void paintComponent(Graphics g) {
        //Fill me with dirty brown/orange.
        g.setColor(new Color(230, 163, 4));
        g.fillRect(0, 0, getWidth(), getHeight());
    }

    public AccessibleContext getAccessibleContext() {
        if (accessibleContext == null) {
            accessibleContext = new AccessibleCorner();
        }
        return accessibleContext;
    }

    protected class AccessibleCorner extends AccessibleJComponent {
        //Inherit everything, override nothing.
    }
}
```

All of the accessibility provided by this class is inherited from AccessibleJComponent,[1] which is fine for Corner because AccessibleJComponent provides a reasonable amount of default accessibility information and because corners are uninteresting—they exist only to take up a little bit of space onscreen. Other classes, such as Rule, need to provide customized information.

Rule provides an accessible context for itself in the same manner as Corner, but the context overrides two methods to provide details about the component's role and state:

```
protected class AccessibleRuler extends AccessibleJComponent {

    public AccessibleRole getAccessibleRole() {
        return AccessibleRuleRole.RULER;
    }

    public AccessibleStateSet getAccessibleStateSet() {
        AccessibleStateSet states = super.getAccessibleStateSet();
        if (orientation == VERTICAL) {
            states.add(AccessibleState.VERTICAL);
        } else {
            states.add(AccessibleState.HORIZONTAL);
        }
        if (isMetric) {
            states.add(AccessibleRulerState.CENTIMETERS);
```

---

[1] AccessibleJComponent API documentation: http://java.sun.com/j2se/1.4.2/docs/api/ javax/swing/JComponent.AccessibleJComponent.html.

```
        } else {
            states.add(AccessibleRulerState.INCHES);
        }
        return states;
    }
}
```

AccessibleRole[1] is an enumeration of objects that identify the roles that Swing components can play. It contains predefined roles such as label and button. The rulers in our example don't fit well into any of the predefined roles, so the program invents a new ruler in a subclass of AccessibleRole:

```
class AccessibleRuleRole extends AccessibleRole {
    public static final AccessibleRuleRole RULER
        = new AccessibleRuleRole("ruler");

    protected AccessibleRuleRole(String key) {
        super(key);
    }

    //Should really provide localizable versions of these names.
    public String toDisplayString(String resourceBundleName,
                                  Locale locale) {
        return key;
    }
}
```

Any component that has state can provide state information to assistive technologies by overriding the getAccessibleStateSet method. A rule has two sets of states: Its orientation can be either vertical or horizontal, and its units of measure can be either centimeters or inches. AccessibleState[2] is an enumeration of predefined states. This program uses its predefined states for vertical and horizontal orientation. Because AccessibleState contains nothing for centimeters and inches, the program makes a subclass to provide appropriate states:

```
class AccessibleRulerState extends AccessibleState {
    public static final AccessibleRulerState INCHES
                = new AccessibleRulerState("inches");
    public static final AccessibleRulerState CENTIMETERS
                = new AccessibleRulerState("centimeters");
```

---

[1] AccessibleRole API documentation: http://java.sun.com/j2se/1.4.2/docs/api/javax/accessibility/AccessibleRole.html.
[2] AccessibleState API documentation: http://java.sun.com/j2se/1.4.2/docs/api/javax/accessibility/AccessibleState.html.

```
    protected AccessibleRulerState(String key) {
        super(key);
    }

    //Should really provide localizable versions of these names.
    public String toDisplayString(String resourceBundleName,
                                  Locale locale) {
        return key;
    }
}
```

You've seen how to implement accessibility for two simple components, which exist only to paint themselves onscreen. Components that do more, such as respond to mouse or keyboard events, need to provide more elaborate accessible contexts. You can find examples of implementing accessible contexts by delving into the source code for the Swing components.

The Accessibility API

Tables 4 through 6 cover just part of the accessibility API. For more information, see the API documentation for the classes and packages in the accessibility package. Also, refer to the API documentation for the accessible contexts for individual Swing components. You can find the `javax.accessibility` API documentation online at: `http://java.sun.com/j2se/1.4.2/docs/api/javax/swing/accessibility/package-summary.html`.

Table 4: Naming and Linking Components

Method	Purpose

`getAccessibleContext().`
`  setAccessibleName(String)`
`getAccessibleContext().`
`  setAccessibleDescription(String)`
(*on a* JComponent *or* Accessible *object*)
	Provide a name or description for an accessible object.

`void setToolTipText(String)` (*in* JComponent)	Set a component's tool tip. If you don't set the description, many accessible contexts use the tool-tip text as the accessible description.
`void setLabelFor(Component)` (*in* JLabel)	Associate a label with a component. This tells assistive technologies that a label describes another component.
`void setDescription(String)` (*in* ImageIcon)	Provide a description for an image icon.

Table 5: Making a Custom Component Accessible

Interface or Class	Purpose
`Accessible` (*an interface*)	Components that implement this interface are accessible. Subclasses of `JComponent` must implement it explicitly.

`AccessibleContext`
`JComponent.AccessibleJComponent`
(*an abstract class and its subclasses*)
	`AccessibleContext` defines the minimal set of information required of accessible objects. The accessible context for each Swing component is a subclass of this and named as shown. For example, the accessible context for `JTree` is `JTree.AccessibleJTree`. To provide custom accessible contexts, custom components should contain an inner class that is a subclass of `AccessibleContext`. For more information, see Making Custom Components Accessible (page 529).

`AccessibleRole`
`AccessibleStateSet`
(*classes*)
	Define the objects returned by an `AccessibleContext` object's `getAccessibleRole` and `getAccessibleStateSet` methods, respectively.

`AccessibleRelation`
`AccessibleRelationSet`
(*classes introduced in 1.3*)
	Define the relations between components that implement this interface and one or more other objects.

Table 6: Accessible Interfaces

Interface	Purpose
`AccessibleAction`	Indicate that the object can perform actions. By implementing this interface, the accessible context can give information about what actions the accessible object can perform and can tell the accessible object to perform them.
`AccessibleComponent`	Indicate that the accessible object has an onscreen presence. Through this interface, an accessible object can provide information about its size, position, visibility, and so on. The accessible contexts for all standard Swing components implement this interface, directly or indirectly. The accessible contexts for your custom components should do the same. As of v1.4, `AccessibleExtendedComponent` is preferred.
`AccessibleEditableText` (*introduced in 1.4*)	Indicate that the accessible object displays editable text. In addition to the information available from its superinterface, `AccessibleText`, methods are provided for cutting, pasting, deleting, selecting, and inserting text.
`AccessibleExtendedComponent` (*introduced in 1.4*)	In addition to the information available from its superinterface, `AccessibleComponent`, methods are provided for obtaining key bindings, border text, and tool-tip text.
`AccessibleExtendedTable` (*introduced in 1.4*)	In addition to the information available from its superinterface, `AccessibleTable`, methods are provided to convert between an index and its row or column.

Table 6: Accessible Interfaces *(continued)*

Interface	Purpose
AccessibleHypertext	Indicate that the accessible object contains hyperlinks. Through this interface, an accessible object can provide information about its links and allow them to be traversed.
AccessibleIcon *(introduced in 1.3)*	Indicate that the accessible object has an associated icon. Methods are provided that return information about the icon, such as size and description.
AccessibleKeyBinding *(introduced in 1.4)*	Indicate that the accessible object supports one or more keyboard shortcuts that can be used to select the object. Methods are provided that return the key bindings for a given object.
AccessibleSelection	Indicate that the accessible object can contain a selection. Accessible contexts that implement this interface can report information about the current selection and can modify the selection.
AccessibleTable *(introduced in 1.3)*	Indicate that the accessible object presents data in a two-dimensional data object. Through this interface information about the table, such as table caption, row and column size, description, and name, are provided. As of v1.4, AccessibleExtendedTable is preferred.
AccessibleText	Indicate that the accessible object displays text. This interface provides methods for returning all or part of the text, attributes applied to it, and other information about the text such as its length.
AccessibleValue	Indicate that the object has a numeric value. Through this interface an accessible object provides information about its current value and its minimum and maximum values.

Examples That Use the Accessibility API

The following table lists some examples that have good support for assistive technologies.

Example	Where Described	Notes
AccessibleScrollDemo	This section	Contains two custom components that implement the Accessible interface. To see a less accessible version of this program refer to How to Use Scroll Panes (page 325).
ButtonDemo	How to Use the Common Button API (page 157)	Uses three buttons. Supports accessibility through button text, mnemonics, and tool tips.

How to Use Borders

Every `JComponent` can have one or more borders. Borders are incredibly useful objects. While not themselves components, they know how to paint the edges of Swing components. They are useful not only for painting lines and fancy edges but also for providing titles and empty space around components.

> **Note:** Our examples set borders on `JPanel`s, `JLabel`s, and custom subclasses of `JComponent`. Although technically you can set the border on any object that inherits from `JComponent`, the look-and-feel implementation of many standard Swing components doesn't work well with user-set borders. In general, when you want to set a border on a standard Swing component other than `JPanel` or `JLabel`, put the component in a `JPanel` and set the border on the `JPanel`. The GTK+ look and feel handles borders differently than do other look and feels. Please refer to the v1.4.2 release notes for details: `http://java.sun.com/j2se/1.4.2/relnotes.html`.

To put a border around a `JComponent`, use its `setBorder` method. You can use the `Border-Factory`[1] class to create most of the borders that Swing provides. If you need a reference to a border—say because you want to use it in multiple components—save it in a variable of type `Border`.[2] Here's an example of code that creates a bordered container:

```
JPanel pane = new JPanel();
pane.setBorder(BorderFactory.createLineBorder(Color.black));
```

Figure 8 is a picture of the container that contains a label component. The black line drawn by the border marks the edge of the container.

line border

Figure 8   A simple line border on a label.

---

[1] BorderFactory API documentation: `http://java.sun.com/j2se/1.4.2/docs/api/javax/swing/BorderFactory.html`.

[2] Border API documentation: `http://java.sun.com/j2se/1.4.2/docs/api/javax/swing/Border.html`.

The BorderDemo Example

Figures 9 through 12 show an application called BorderDemo that displays the borders Swing provides. Figure 9 illustrates the simple border types. The code for creating these borders is provided in Using the Borders Provided by Swing (page 539).

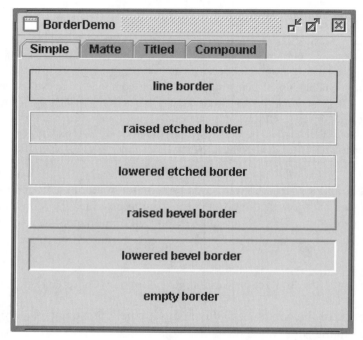

Figure 9   A screenshot of several simple borders shown on the Simple tab of BorderDemo.

You can run BorderDemo using Java Web Start or compile and run the example yourself.[1]

Figure 10 shows some matte borders. When creating a matte border, you specify how many pixels it occupies at the top, left, bottom, and right of a component. You then specify either a color or an icon for the border to paint. Be careful when choosing the icon and determining

---

[1] To run BorderDemo using Java Web Start, click the BorderDemo link on the RunExamples/misc.html page on the CD. You can find the source files here: JavaTutorial/uiswing/misc/example-1dot4/index.html#BorderDemo.

your component's size; otherwise, the icon might get chopped off or be mismatched at the component's corners.

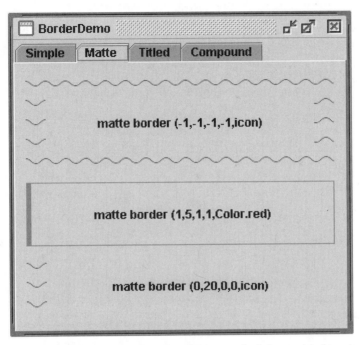

Figure 10   A screenshot of several matte borders shown on the Matte tab of BorderDemo.

Figure 11 shows titled borders.A titled border displays a text description. If you don't specify a border, a look-and-feel-specific border is used. For example, the default titled border in the Java look and feel is a gray line whereas the default titled border in the Windows look and feel is etched. By default, the title straddles the upper left of the border, as shown at the top of Figure 11.

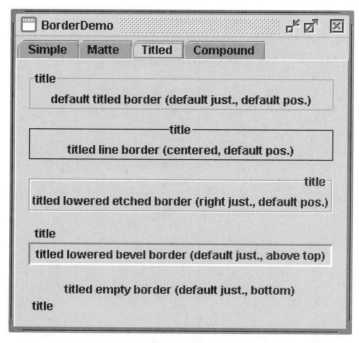

Figure 11   A screenshot of several titled borders shown on the Titled tab of BorderDemo.

Figure 12 shows compound borders. With these, you can combine any two borders, which can themselves be compound borders.

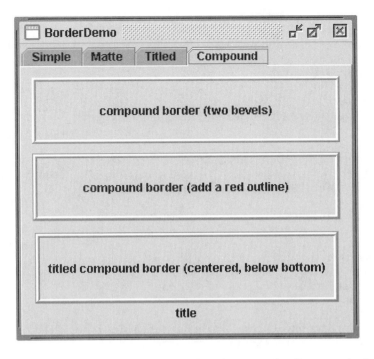

Figure 12 A screenshot of several compound borders shown on the Compound tab
of BorderDemo.

Using the Borders Provided by Swing

The code that follows shows how to create and set the borders that you saw in the preceding
figures.

```
//Keep references to the next few borders,
//for use in titles and compound borders.
Border blackline, raisedetched, loweredetched,
        raisedbevel, loweredbevel, empty;

blackline = BorderFactory.createLineBorder(Color.black);
raisedetched = BorderFactory.createEtchedBorder(EtchedBorder.RAISED);
loweredetched = BorderFactory.createEtchedBorder(EtchedBorder.LOWERED);
raisedbevel = BorderFactory.createRaisedBevelBorder();
loweredbevel = BorderFactory.createLoweredBevelBorder();
empty = BorderFactory.createEmptyBorder();
```

B

Other Features

```
//Simple borders
jComp1.setBorder(blackline);
jComp2.setBorder(raisedbevel);
jComp3.setBorder(loweredbevel);
jComp4.setBorder(empty);

//Matte borders
ImageIcon icon = createImageIcon("images/wavy.gif",
                        "wavy-line border icon"); //20x22

jComp5.setBorder(BorderFactory.createMatteBorder(
                        -1, -1, -1, -1, icon));
jComp6.setBorder(BorderFactory.createMatteBorder(
                        1, 5, 1, 1, Color.red));
jComp7.setBorder(BorderFactory.createMatteBorder(
                        0, 20, 0, 0, icon));

//Titled borders
TitledBorder title;
title = BorderFactory.createTitledBorder("title");
jComp8.setBorder(title);

title = BorderFactory.createTitledBorder(blackline, "title");
title.setTitleJustification(TitledBorder.CENTER);
jComp9.setBorder(title);

title = BorderFactory.createTitledBorder(loweredetched, "title");
title.setTitleJustification(TitledBorder.RIGHT);
jComp10.setBorder(title);

title = BorderFactory.createTitledBorder(loweredbevel, "title");
title.setTitlePosition(TitledBorder.ABOVE_TOP);
jComp11.setBorder(title);

title = BorderFactory.createTitledBorder(empty, "title");
title.setTitlePosition(TitledBorder.BOTTOM);
jComp12.setBorder(title);

//Compound borders
Border compound;
Border redline = BorderFactory.createLineBorder(Color.red);

//This creates a nice frame.
compound = BorderFactory.createCompoundBorder(raisedbevel,
                                        loweredbevel);
jComp13.setBorder(compound);
```

```
//Add a red outline to the frame.
compound = BorderFactory.createCompoundBorder(
                          redline, compound);
jComp14.setBorder(compound);

//Add a title to the red-outlined frame.
compound = BorderFactory.createTitledBorder(
                          compound, "title",
                          TitledBorder.CENTER,
                          TitledBorder.BELOW_BOTTOM);
jComp15.setBorder(compound);
```

As you probably noticed, the code uses the BorderFactory class to create each border. BorderFactory, which is in the javax.swing package, returns objects that implement the Border interface.

The Border interface, as well as its Swing-provided implementations, is in the package javax.swing.border.[1] You often don't need to directly use anything in the border package, except when specifying constants specific to a particular border class or when referring to the Border type.

Creating Custom Borders

If BorderFactory doesn't offer you enough control over a border's form, you might need to use the API in the border package—or even define your own border. In addition to containing the Border interface, the border package contains the classes that implement the borders in Figures 9 through 12: LineBorder, EtchedBorder, BevelBorder, EmptyBorder, MatteBorder, TitledBorder, and CompoundBorder. It also contains a class named SoftBevelBorder, which produces a result similar to BevelBorder, but with softer edges.

If none of the Swing borders is suitable, you can implement your own, generally by creating a subclass of the AbstractBorder[2] class. In your subclass, you must implement at least one constructor and the following two methods:

- paintBorder, which contains the painting code that a JComponent executes to paint the border.
- getBorderInsets, which specifies the amount of space the border needs to paint itself.

---

[1] javax.swing.border API documentation: http://java.sun.com/j2se/1.4.2/docs/api/javax/swing/border/package-summary.html.

[2] AbstractBorder API documentation: http://java.sun.com/j2se/1.4.2/docs/api/javax/swing/border/AbstractBorder.html.

For examples of implementing borders, see the source code for the classes in the `javax.swing.border` package.

The Border API

Tables 7 and 8 list the commonly used border methods. `BorderFactory` API documentation is at: `http://java.sun.com/j2se/1.4.2/docs/api/javax/swing/BorderFactory.html`. The rest of the border-related classes and interfaces are in the border package, which is documented at: `http://java.sun.com/j2se/1.4.2/docs/api/javax/swing/border/package-summary.html`.

Table 7: Creating a Border with BorderFactory

Method	Purpose
`Border createLineBorder(Color)` `Border createLineBorder(Color, int)`	Create a line border. The first argument is a `java.awt.Color` object that specifies the color of the line. The optional second argument specifies the width of the line in pixels.

`Border createEtchedBorder()`
`Border createEtchedBorder(Color,`
`                Color)`
`Border createEtchedBorder(int)`
`Border createEtchedBorder(int,`
`                Color,`
`                Color)`
	Create an etched border. The optional `Color` arguments specify the highlight and shadow colors to be used. In release 1.3, methods with `int` arguments were added that allow the border methods to be specified as either `EtchedBorder.RAISED` or `EtchedBorder.LOWERED`. The methods without the `int` arguments create a lowered etched border.

`Border createLoweredBevelBorder()`	Create a border that gives the illusion of the component being lower than the surrounding area.
`Border createRaisedBevelBorder()`	Create a border that gives the illusion of the component being higher than the surrounding area.

`Border createBevelBorder(int,`
`                Color,`
`                Color)`
`Border createBevelBorder(int,`
`                Color,`
`                Color,`
`                Color,`
`                Color)`
	Create a raised or lowered beveled border, specifying the colors to use. The integer argument can be either `BevelBorder.RAISED` or `BevelBorder.LOWERED`. With the three-argument constructor, you specify the highlight and shadow colors. With the five-argument constructor, you specify outer highlight, inner highlight, outer shadow, and inner shadow colors, in that order. The shadow inner and outer colors are switched for a lowered bevel border.

Table 7: Creating a Border with BorderFactory *(continued)*

Method	Purpose

`Border createEmptyBorder()`
`Border createEmptyBorder(int,`
`                 int,`
`                 int,`
`                 int)`
	Create an invisible border. If you specify no arguments, the border takes no space, which is useful when creating a titled border with no visible boundary. The optional arguments specify the number of pixels that the border occupies at the top, left, bottom, and right (in that order) of whatever component uses it. This method is useful for putting empty space around components.

`MatteBorder createMatteBorder(int, int,`
`                  int, int,`
`                  Color)`
`MatteBorder createMatteBorder(int, int,`
`                  int, int,`
`                  Icon)`
	Create a matte border. The integer arguments specify the number of pixels that the border occupies at the top, left, bottom, and right (in that order) of whatever component uses it. The color argument specifies the color with which the border should fill its area. The icon argument specifies the icon with which the border should tile its area.

`TitledBorder createTitledBorder(String)`
`TitledBorder createTitledBorder(Border)`
`TitledBorder createTitledBorder(`
`     Border, String)`
`TitledBorder createTitledBorder(`
`     Border, String, int, int)`
`TitledBorder createTitledBorder(`
`     Border, String, int, int, Font)`
`TitledBorder createTitledBorder(`
`     Border, String, int, int, Font,`
`     Color)`
	Create a titled border. The string argument specifies the title to be displayed. The optional font and color arguments specify the font and color to be used for the title's text. The border argument specifies the border that should be displayed along with the title. If no border is specified, a look-and-feel-specific default border is used.
	
	By default, the title straddles the top of its companion border and is left-justified. The optional integer arguments specify the title's position and justification, in that order. TitledBorder defines these possible positions: ABOVE_TOP, TOP (the default), BELOW_TOP, ABOVE_BOTTOM, BOTTOM, and BELOW_BOTTOM. You can specify the justification as LEADING (the default), CENTER, or TRAILING. In locales with Western alphabets, LEADING is equivalent to LEFT and TRAILING is equivalent to RIGHT.

`CompoundBorder` `   createCompoundBorder(Border, Border)`	Combine two borders into one. The first argument specifies the outer border; the second, the inner border.

Examples That Use Borders

Many examples in this book use borders. The following table lists a few interesting cases.

Example	Where Described	Notes
BorderDemo	This section	Shows an example of each type of border that `BorderFactory` can create. Also uses an empty border to add breathing space between each pane and its contents.
AlignmentDemo	How to Use BoxLayout (page 462)	Uses titled borders.
BoxLayoutDemo	How to Use BoxLayout (page 462)	Uses a red line to show where the edge of a container is so that you can see how the extra space in a box layout is distributed.
ComboBoxDemo2	How to Use Combo Boxes (page 176)	Uses a compound border to combine a line border with an empty border. The empty border provides space between the line and the component's innards.

How to Use Drag and Drop and Data Transfer

Most programs can benefit from the ability to transfer information between components, between Java applications, or between Java and native applications. Transferring data takes two forms:

- Drag and drop (DnD) support. (See Figure 13.)
- Clipboard transfer via cut/copy and paste. (See Figure 14.)

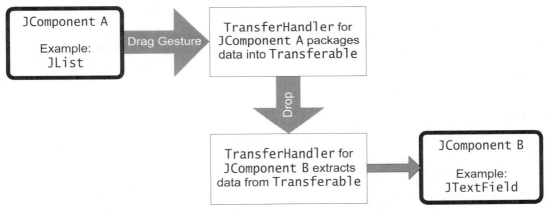

Figure 13   The Java portion of a drag-and-drop operation.

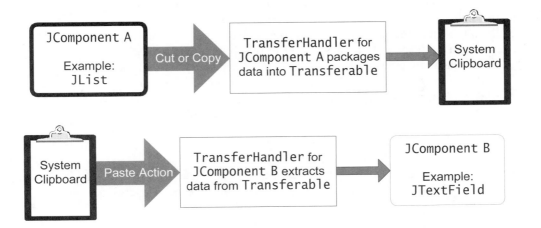

Figure 14   The Java portion of a cut/copy and a paste operation.

545

The TransferHandler object, the heart of the data transfer system, is described in more detail later. The arrows in Figures 13 and 14 show the path of the data.

Many Swing components provide out-of-the-box support for transferring data, as shown in Table 8.

Table 8: Data Transfer Support

Component	Drag Copy[a]	Drag Move[a]	Drop	Cut	Copy	Paste
JColorChooser[b]	•		•			
JEditorPane	•	•	•	•	•	•
JFileChooser[c]	•				•	
JFormattedTextField	•	•	•	•	•	•
JList	•				•	
JPasswordField	N/A	•	•	N/A	N/A	•
JTable	•				•	
JTextArea	•	•	•	•	•	•
JTextField	•	•	•	•	•	•
JTextPane	•	•	•	•	•	•
JTree	•				•	

a. Enabled by invoking component.setDragEnabled(true) on the component.

b. Imports and exports data of type java.awt.Color.

c. Exports a list of file names as java.io.File objects (preferred) and as strings for components that don't accept File objects. The File Name text field in the file chooser accepts strings; the browser in the file chooser doesn't accept data. Note that as of release 1.4, clipboard copy from a JFileChooser is broken and actually causes the file to be moved when it is pasted. You may want to track bug #4915992 online at: http://developer.java.sun.com/developer/bugParade/bugs/4915992.html.

Version Note: This section describes the drag-and-drop architecture implemented in release 1.4. Prior to 1.4, AWT support for data transfer was not well integrated into Swing components.

The data transfer mechanism is built into every JComponent. For Swing components with an empty space in Table 8, only a small amount of code is needed to customize the support. Support can easily be added to JComponents not listed in the table so that they can fully participate in data transfer.

A Visual Guide to Drag-and-Drop Cursor Icons

Before delving into drag and drop further, it's useful to take a look at the various cursor icons you may encounter when initiating a drag operation. We expect the Solaris and Linux cursor icons to change for release 1.5, but Table 9 is a guide as of release 1.4.

Table 9: Cursor Icons for Drag and Drop

Microsoft Windows	Solaris/ Linux	Description
		Copy. The component underneath accepts this type of data.
		Copy. The area underneath doesn't accept this data.
		Move. The component underneath accepts this data.
		Move. The area underneath doesn't accept this data.

On a component supporting both copy and move, a normal drag from the component performs a move and a Control-drag performs a copy. The drag behavior from a native application to a Java application is platform-dependent. If only one of the operations is supported, a normal drag performs it. For more information on the behavior of the drop action, see the class specification for DragSourceDragEvent.[1]

---

[1] DragSourceDragEvent API documentation: http://java.sun.com/j2se/1.4.2/docs/api/java/awt/dnd/DragSourceDragEvent.html.

Introduction to Data Transfer Support

The simple demo `BasicDnD` illustrates default drag and drop behavior for several Swing components. (See Figure 15.) At startup the components don't have drag turned on, but a check box allows you to enable dragging on the fly. At startup, even though drag isn't enabled, many of the components do support the cut/copy/paste of text using key bindings.

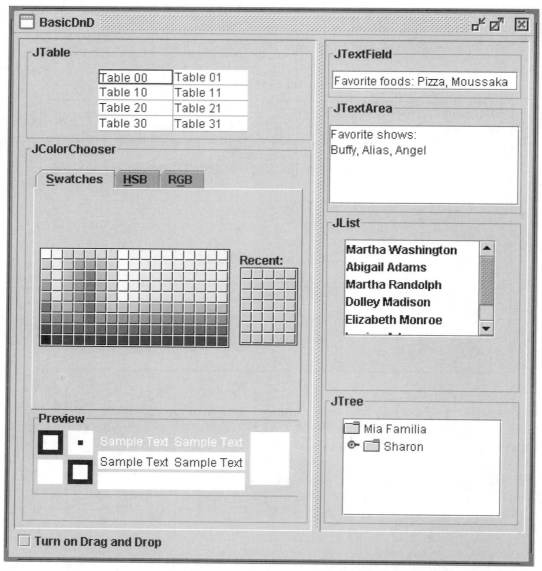

Figure 15 The `BasicDnD` example. (This image has been modified to fit the available space.)

Try This:

1. Run `BasicDnD` using Java Web Start or compile and run the example yourself.[1]

2. Select an item in the list, and then release the mouse button to highlight it.

3. Press the item again, this time holding down the mouse button, and begin to drag. Nothing happens because `setDragEnabled(true)` hasn't yet been called on the list.

4. Type Control-C. This puts the text of the selected list item onto the system clipboard.

5. Click in the text area. The caret cursor blinks, showing that this component now has the focus.

6. Type Control-V. The contents of the previously copied text are pasted at the caret location.

7. Click the **Turn on Drag and Drop** check box.

8. Once again, press the selected item in the list and begin to drag. Initially, on Microsoft Windows, you see the ⃠ cursor icon. This indicates that the area below the cursor, in this case the list itself, doesn't accept drops.

9. Drag the cursor over a text area. The cursor icon now changes to a new icon, ⌖. This text area will accept the data if you release the mouse button.

10. As you saw in the cursor icon table, Table 9 (page 547), the Copy cursor icon gives you a visual clue that it won't disturb the contents of the original component. In the case of Microsoft Windows, the clue is the small plus (+) sign.

11. Drag the selected text over a text area. The insertion point for the text is indicated by a blinking cursor.

12. Release the mouse and watch the text appear in the text area.

13. Select some text in one of the text areas.

14. Press and hold the mouse button while the cursor is over the selected text and begin to drag.

15. The icon appears, indicating that the drag is a move and will remove the text from the original component on a successful drop.

16. Release the mouse button over an area that won't accept it. The original text is undisturbed.

17. Hold the Control key down and press again on the selected text. The copy icon now appears. Move the cursor over the text area and drop. The text appears in the new location but isn't removed from the original location. The Control key can be used to change any move to a copy.

---

[1] To run `BasicDnD` using Java Web Start, click the `BasicDnD` link on the `RunExamples/misc.html` page on the CD. You can find the source files here: `JavaTutorial/uiswing/misc/example-1dot4/index.html#BasicDnD`.

18. Select a color from the color chooser. The selected color appears in the Preview panel. Press and hold the mouse button over the color in the Preview panel and drag it over the other components. None of the components accepts color by default.

19. Play with dragging and dropping between the various components and note which components accept data.

When the **Turn on Drag and Drop** check box is checked, `BasicDnD` demonstrates drag and drop behavior that becomes available to a component with the following line of code:

```
component.setDragEnabled(true);
```

Many components support text cut/copy/paste using the keyboard bindings Control-X, Control-C, and Control-V, respectively. This is because a `JTextComponent` installs the cut/copy/paste key bindings and action map when it's created. You only need to add a bit more code to create a menu with Cut, Copy, and Paste menu items and tie those items to the default text support. We show you how to do that in the `DragColorTextFieldDemo` example, which is discussed in Replacing Default Support: Color and Text (page 565). Cut/copy/paste is further discussed in Adding Cut/Copy/Paste Support (page 573).

At the heart of the data transfer mechanism is the `TransferHandler`[1] class, which provides an easy mechanism for transferring data to and from a `JComponent`. The data to be transferred is bundled into an object that implements the `Transferable`[2] interface. The components in Table 8, "Data Transfer Support" (page 546), are provided with default transfer handlers, but a transfer handler can be created and installed on any component using the `JComponent` method `setTransferHandler`:

```
component.setTransferHandler(new MyTransferHandler());
```

The default Swing transfer handlers, such as those used by text components and the color chooser, provide the support considered to be most useful for both importing and exporting of data. If you install a custom `TransferHandler` on a Swing component, the default support is replaced. For example, if you replace `JTextField`'s `TransferHandler` with a handler for colors only, you'll disable its ability to support text import and export.

This means that if you must replace a default `TransferHandler`—for example, one that handles text—you'll need to reimplement the text import and export ability. This doesn't need to be as extensive as what Swing provides; it could be as simple as supporting the `StringFlavor` data flavor, depending on your application's needs. `DragColorTextFieldDemo` gives

---

[1] TransferHandler API documentation: `http://java.sun.com/j2se/1.4.2/docs/api/javax/swing/TransferHandler.html`.
[2] Transferable API documentation: `http://java.sun.com/j2se/1.4.2/docs/api/java/awt/datatransfer/Transferable.html`.

an example of this. You might also want to watch RFE #4830695,[1] which requests the ability to add data import on top of an existing `TransferHandler`.

The remainder of this section describes how to use data transfer in a variety of ways. Here's a list of some common scenarios and where you can find more information:

How do I provide drop support for those components in Table 8 (page 546) that don't have a checkmark in the drop column?

> You need to implement a custom transfer handler to provide drop support. See Extending Default DnD Support (page 553) for an example.

I want my component to import only. How do I do that?

> You need to provide a custom transfer handler with implementations for the `canImport` and `importData` methods. The `DragColorDemo` example in Importing a New Flavor: Color (page 562) does this.

How do I create a component that can accept multiple types of data?

> A transfer handler can be created to accept more than one type of data. Replacing Default Support: Color and Text (page 565) shows the example `DragColorTextField-Demo`, which installs a custom transfer handler on a `JTextField` to import both color and text and to export text. Also, `DragFileDemo` in Importing a New Flavor: Files (page 566) installs a transfer handler on the text area/tabbed pane that imports both files and strings.

How do I create a custom transfer handler to import/export a nonstandard type of data?

> Specifying the Data Format (page 559) describes how to create a data flavor with a variety of data types. Also, the `DragListDemo` example in Data Transfer with a Custom DataFlavor (page 571) shows how to transfer data in the `ArrayList` format.

How do I make data transfer work with my custom component?

> Data Transfer with a Custom Component (page 569) discusses the requirements of making a custom component work with the data transfer system.

How do I enable the cut/copy/paste bindings?

> Adding Cut/Copy/Paste Support (page 573) describes how to enable the built-in cut/copy/paste support for text components. Implementing cut/copy/paste for nontext components is also covered.

How do I obtain the drop position in the destination component?

> You can obtain the drop location by way of the component's selection. You'll notice that the selection changes in a component as you drag over it. For lists, tables, and trees you

---

[1] You can track this bug online at: `http://developer.java.sun.com/developer/bugParade/bugs/4830695.html`.

can query the current selection at drop time to find the drop position. For text components, you can query the position of the caret. There is an example of this in `ArrayList-TransferHandler`, part of the `DragListDemo` example. You might also want to watch RFE #4468566,[1] which requests a better way of indicating (and displaying) the drop location without changing the selection.

This section has been a brief introduction to the Swing data transfer mechanism. If you want more details, see the "Swing Data Transfer" document in the release notes for your particular J2SE release.[2]

A Simple Example: Adding DnD to JLabel

By default, the `JLabel` component doesn't support drag or drop, but it's a fairly simple exercise to add this support, as the following demo shows. (See Figure 16.)

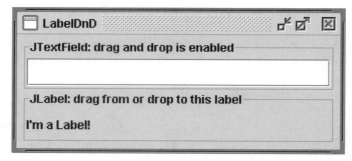

Figure 16   A screenshot of the `LabelDnD` example.

Try This:

1. Run `LabelDnD` using Java Web Start or compile and run the example yourself.[3]

2. Press and hold the mouse button while the cursor is over the label. As you begin to move the cursor, the copy cursor icon appears. Drop the text onto the text field.

---

[1] Track this bug online at: `http://developer.java.sun.com/developer/bugParade/bugs/4468566.html`.

[2] In the 1.4.2 release notes this document is at: `http://java.sun.com/j2se/1.4.2/docs/guide/swing/1.4/dnd.html`.

[3] To run `LabelDnD` using Java Web Start, click the `LabelDnD` link on the `RunExamples/misc.html` page on the CD. You can find the source files here: `JavaTutorial/uiswing/misc/example-1dot4/index.html#LabelDnD`.

3. Type text in the text field. Select and initiate the drag using the mouse. The move cursor icon appears because the default behavior for text field is move. Drop the text onto the label and note that the selected string has been removed from the original text.

4. Type more text in the text field, if necessary, and select. While holding down the Control key, drag the text. The copy cursor icon appears. Drop the text as desired.

While it's possible to extend this example to show copy and paste, JLabel doesn't have bindings for copy and paste and, by default, doesn't receive the focus that is required to support this feature.

Here's the code that creates the label and installs a transfer handler on it:

```
label = new JLabel("I'm a Label!", SwingConstants.LEADING);
label.setTransferHandler(new TransferHandler("text"));

MouseListener listener = new DragMouseAdapter();
label.addMouseListener(listener);
```

To add drag support to JLabel or any custom component, you must add the ability to detect activity on the mouse. LabelDnD implements a mouse listener for this. When the mouse is pressed, the transfer handler initiates the drag from the label by invoking exportAsDrag with the COPY argument:

```
public class DragMouseAdapter extends MouseAdapter {
    public void mousePressed(MouseEvent e) {
        JComponent c = (JComponent)e.getSource();
        TransferHandler handler = c.getTransferHandler();
        handler.exportAsDrag(c, e, TransferHandler.COPY);
    }
}
```

Specifying the Data Format (page 559) will explain what the following call does:

```
new TransferHandler("text")
```

Extending Default DnD Support

You saw in the Table 8, "Data Transfer Support," on page 546, that several components don't support drop by default. The reason for this is that there is no all-purpose way to handle a drop on them. For example, what does it mean to drop on a particular node of a JTree? Does it replace the node, insert below it, or insert as a child of that node? Also, we don't know what type of model is behind the tree—it might not be mutable. However, while Swing doesn't provide a default implementation, the framework for drop is there. All you need is to provide a custom TransferHandler that deals with the actual transfer of data.

The following example, ExtendedDnDDemo (see Figure 17), tweaks the default drag and drop behavior for two components, JList and JTable. This demo shows how to:

- Drop text onto a JList—the incoming string can be newline-delimited so that a new list item is created at each new line.
- Move data from a JList (the default Swing behavior is copy). On export, multiple list items are separated by newlines.
- Drop text onto a JTable—the incoming string can be newline- *and* comma-delimited. Strings are split into rows at newlines and into columns at commas.
- Move data from a JTable (the default Swing behavior is copy). On export, multiple table rows are separated by newlines and table columns are separated by commas.

If you've run the BasicDnD example previously, you'll see that this tweaked behavior is slightly different than the default Swing behavior, which does not use commas as a separator.

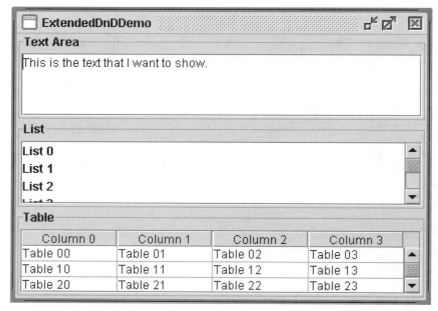

Figure 17   A screenshot of the ExtendedDnDDemo example.

Try This:

1. Run ExtendedDnDDemo using Java Web Start or compile and run the example yourself.[1]

---

[1] To run ExtendedDnDDemo using Java Web Start, click the ExtendedDnDDemo link on the RunExamples/ misc.html page on the CD. You can find the source files here: JavaTutorial/uiswing/misc/ example-1dot4/index.html#ExtendedDnDDemo.

2. Select a row in the table

3. Press the row again and drag. As you drag the cursor icon over the list, the row that is currently under the cursor highlights—the new data will be inserted after the selected row.

4. Drop the row onto the list. The row has been removed from the table and now appears in the list with commas separating the columns.

5. Select two rows from the table and drop them onto the list. Now there are two new items in the list with commas separating the columns.

6. Select one item in the list and drag it to the table. As you drag the icon over the table, the row under the cursor highlights—the new data is inserted after the selected row.

7. Drop the item onto the table. It's removed from the list and the commas are replaced by column separators.

8. Type some text into the text area, for example, "How, Now, Brown, Cow." Select the line of text and drop it into the table.

9. Select an item in the list; hold down the Control key while dragging the item to the text area and drop. The text has been copied to the new location.

The code for the example's main class is in `ExtendedDnDDemo.java`. `StringTransfer-Handler`, an abstract subclass of `TransferHandler`, defines three abstract methods for importing and exporting the strings: `exportString`, `importString`, and `cleanup`. `StringTransferHandler` also overrides the standard `TransferHandler` methods: `import-Data` and `canImport` are required to import data; `getSourceActions`, `createTransfer-able`, and `exportDone` are required for export. (`exportDone` may not be necessary if you only implement copy and therefore don't need to remove data from the source as you would for a move.) The abstract methods `importString`, `exportString`, and `cleanup` are called by the `importData`, `createTransferable`, and `exportDone` methods, respectively. Here's the code for `StringTransferHandler.java`:

```java
public abstract class StringTransferHandler extends TransferHandler {
    protected abstract String exportString(JComponent c);
    protected abstract void importString(JComponent c, String str);
    protected abstract void cleanup(JComponent c, boolean remove);

    protected Transferable createTransferable(JComponent c) {
        return new StringSelection(exportString(c));
    }

    public int getSourceActions(JComponent c) {
        return COPY_OR_MOVE;
    }
```

D

Other Features

```
    public boolean importData(JComponent c, Transferable t) {
        if (canImport(c, t.getTransferDataFlavors())) {
            try {
                String str =
                  (String)t.getTransferData(DataFlavor.stringFlavor);
                importString(c, str);
                return true;
            } catch (UnsupportedFlavorException ufe) {
            } catch (IOException ioe) {
            }
        }

        return false;
    }

    protected void exportDone(JComponent c,
                                Transferable data, int action){
        cleanup(c, action == MOVE);
    }

    public boolean canImport(JComponent c, DataFlavor[] flavors) {
        for (int i = 0; i < flavors.length; i++) {
            if (DataFlavor.stringFlavor.equals(flavors[i])) {
                return true;
            }
        }
        return false;
    }

}
```

The StringSelection[1] class implements the Transferable interface and handles the details of bundling the data for transport.

Two custom subclasses of StringTransferHandler—ListTransferHandler and Table-TransferHandler—implement the abstract importString, exportString, and cleanup methods and deal with the specifics of a list and a table, respectively. Here's the code for ListTransferHandler:

```
    public class ListTransferHandler extends StringTransferHandler {
        private int[] indices = null;
        private int addIndex = -1; //Location where items were added
        private int addCount = 0;  //Number of items added.
```

---

[1] StringSelection API documentation: http://java.sun.com/j2se/1.4.2/docs/api/java/awt/
datatransfer/StringSelection.html.

```
//Bundle up the selected items in the list
//as a single string, for export.
protected String exportString(JComponent c) {
    JList list = (JList)c;
    indices = list.getSelectedIndices();
    Object[] values = list.getSelectedValues();

    StringBuffer buff = new StringBuffer();

    for (int i = 0; i < values.length; i++) {
        Object val = values[i];
        buff.append(val == null ? "" : val.toString());
        if (i != values.length - 1) {
            buff.append("\n");
        }
    }

    return buff.toString();
}

//Take the incoming string and wherever there is a
//newline, break it into a separate item in the list.
protected void importString(JComponent c, String str) {
    JList target = (JList)c;
    DefaultListModel listModel = (DefaultListModel)target.getModel();
    int index = target.getSelectedIndex();

    //Prevent the user from dropping data back on itself.
    //For example, if the user is moving items #4,#5,#6 and #7 and
    //attempts to insert the items after item #5, this would
    //be problematic when removing the original items.
    //So this is not allowed.
    if (indices != null && index >= indices[0] - 1 &&
            index <= indices[indices.length - 1]) {
        indices = null;
        return;
    }

    int max = listModel.getSize();
    if (index < 0) {
        index = max;
    } else {
        index++;
        if (index > max) {
            index = max;
        }
    }
    addIndex = index;
    String[] values = str.split("\n");
    addCount = values.length;
```

```
            for (int i = 0; i < values.length; i++) {
                listModel.add(index++, values[i]);
            }
        }


        //If the remove argument is true, the drop has been
        //successful and it's time to remove the selected items
        //from the list. If the remove argument is false, it
        //was a Copy operation and the original list is left
        //intact.
        protected void cleanup(JComponent c, boolean remove) {
            if (remove && indices != null) {
                JList source = (JList)c;
              DefaultListModel model  = (DefaultListModel)source.getModel();
                //If we are moving items around in the same list, we
                //need to adjust the indices accordingly, since those
                //after the insertion point have moved.
                if (addCount > 0) {
                    for (int i = 0; i < indices.length; i++) {
                        if (indices[i] > addIndex) {
                            indices[i] += addCount;
                        }
                    }
                }
                for (int i = indices.length - 1; i >= 0; i--) {
                    model.remove(indices[i]);
                }
            }
            indices = null;
            addCount = 0;
            addIndex = -1;
        }
    }
```

Note that importString uses the split utility method of String to divide the incoming text so that wherever a newline occurs a new list item is created. To support moving text from a list, exportDone calls cleanup, which removes the dragged items from the original list. The cleanup method has special handling for items within the same list and data moved to a higher position in the list (with a smaller index). cleanup is called *after* the data has been inserted into the list, which changes the indices of the items to be deleted. When the indices of the original items to be moved change, they must be adjusted accordingly before they can be deleted.

The example's custom table transfer handler class, TableTransferHandler, is implemented in a similar manner, though it's slightly more complex because it has support for text that's newline- and comma-delimited.

Specifying the Data Format

Creating a `TransferHandler` can be as simple as using the constructor. For example, in the `LabelDnD` demo the label supports both importing and exporting `String`s to and from its *text* property with the following line of code:

```
label.setTransferHandler(new TransferHandler("text"));
```

When using the property name form of the constructor, there must be a `getProperty` method in the component's API to export data and a `setProperty` method to import it. The label's transfer handler works because `JLabel` has a `getText` method. This works with any property so that, if you had instead created the label's transfer handler like this:

```
label.setTransferHandler(new TransferHandler("foreground"));
```

you would be able to drag a color from the color chooser and drop it on the label; the label's text color would change because `label` has a `setForeground` method that requires a `java.awt.Color` object. We have another version of `LabelDnD`, called `LabelDnD2`, which demonstrates using the `TransferHandler` constructor, this time for the label's foreground property. (See Figure 18.)

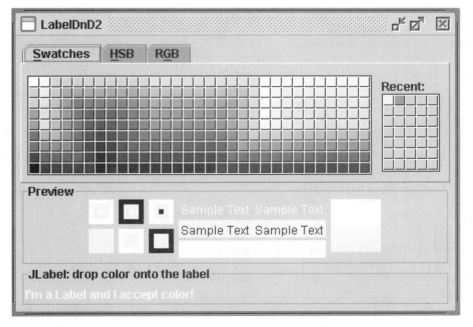

Figure 18   The `LabelDnD2` example.

Try This:

1. Run `LabelDnD2` using Java Web Start or compile and run the example yourself.[1]
2. Select a color from the palette. The selected color appears in the Preview panel.
3. Press and hold the mouse button while the cursor is over the Preview panel and begin to drag.
4. Drop the color onto the label and see the text change color.
5. Select another color from the palette so that the Preview panel now shows a new color.
6. Press on the label and begin to drag. Drop the color anywhere on the color chooser—in the palette or the Preview panel. The Preview panel now shows the label color.

If you can't use the property name form of the `TransferHandler` constructor, the `DataFlavor`[2] class allows you to specify the content-type of your data for both your `TransferHandler` and, if necessary, your `Transferable`. Three flavor types are predefined for you:

- `imageFlavor` represents data in the `java.awt.Image` format.
- `stringFlavor` represents data in the most basic form of text—`java.lang.String`.
- `javaFileListFlavor` represents `java.io.File` objects in a `java.util.List` format.

For example, a `TransferHandler` imports `String` data with this line of code:

```
String str = (String)t.getTransferData(DataFlavor.stringFlavor);
```

Or it imports a `java.awt.Image` using `imageFlavor` with this line of code:

```
Image image = (Image)t.getTransferData(DataFlavor.imageFlavor);
```

If you require a flavor other than these predefined types, you need to create your own. The format for specifying a data flavor is:

```
DataFlavor(Class representationClass, String humanPresentableName);
```

For example, to create a data flavor for the `java.util.ArrayList` class:

```
new DataFlavor(ArrayList.class, "ArrayList");
```

To create a data flavor for an integer array:

```
new DataFlavor(int[].class, "Integer Array");
```

---

[1] To run `LabelDnD2` using Java Web Start, click the `LabelDnD2` link on the `RunExamples/misc.html` page on the CD. You can find the source files here: `JavaTutorial/uiswing/misc/example-1dot4/index.html#LabelDnD2`.

[2] `DataFlavor` API documentation: `http://java.sun.com/j2se/1.4.2/docs/api/java/awt/datatransfer/DataFlavor.html`.

Transferring the data in this manner uses `Object` serialization, so the class you use to transfer the data must implement the `Serializable` interface, as must anything that is serialized with it. If not everything is `Serializable`, you'll see a `NotSerializableException` during drop or copy to the clipboard. For more information, see *The Java Tutorial*'s "Object Serialization" section[1] in the Essential Java Classes trail.

Creating a data flavor using the `DataFlavor(Class, String)` constructor allows you to transfer data between applications, including native applications. If you want to create a data flavor that transfers data only within an application, use `javaJVMLocalObjectMimeType` and the `DataFlavor(String)` constructor. For example, to specify a data flavor that transfers color from a `JColorChooser`, use this code:

```
String colorType = DataFlavor.javaJVMLocalObjectMimeType +
                   ";class=java.awt.Color";
DataFlavor colorFlavor = new DataFlavor(colorType);
```

To create a data flavor for an `ArrayList` use:

```
new DataFlavor(DataFlavor.javaJVMLocalObjectMimeType +
               ";class=java.util.ArrayList");
```

To transfer the data as an integer array use:

```
new DataFlavor(DataFlavor.javaJVMLocalObjectMimeType +
               ";class=\"" + int[].class.getName() + "\"");
```

You'll see that a MIME type containing special characters, such as **[** and **;**, must have those characters enclosed in quotes.

Finally, a `Transferable` can be implemented to support multiple flavors. For example, you can use both local and serialization flavors together, or you can use two forms of the same data together, such as the `ArrayList` and integer array flavors, or you can create a `TransferHandler` that accepts different types of data, such as color and text, as you'll see later. When you create the array of `DataFlavors` to be returned from `Transferable`'s `getTransferDataFlavors` method, the flavors should be inserted in preferred order, with the most preferred appearing at element 0 of the array. Generally the preferred order is from the richest or most complex form down to the simplest, that is, the form most likely to be understood by other objects.

See the "Components That Support DnD" table in the release notes for your particular J2SE release for which data types each component imports and exports.[2]

---

[1] The Object Serialization section is on the CD at: `JavaTutorial/essential/io/serialization.html`.

[2] In the v1.4.2 release notes the "Components That Support DnD" table is at: `http://java.sun.com/j2se/1.4.2/docs/guide/swing/1.4/dnd.html#DefaultTransferHandlerSupport`.

Importing a New Flavor: Color

The only Swing component that can, by default, import or export color is `JColorChooser`. Previously we described how you can create a transfer handler that will transfer data as specified by a named property. This is easy to do, but it has limited functionality. For example, if you specify the *foreground* property, a drop only changes the color of the text; it won't change the background color. And if your component drags and drops text by default, replacing the transfer handler in this manner causes the component to lose this default ability.

To solve this problem you need to write a custom `TransferHandler`. We show how to create one that can be installed on a component so that it can accept color on a drop. `DragColor-Demo` (see Figure 19) specifically shows how you can drop a color onto the foreground or background of a button or label.

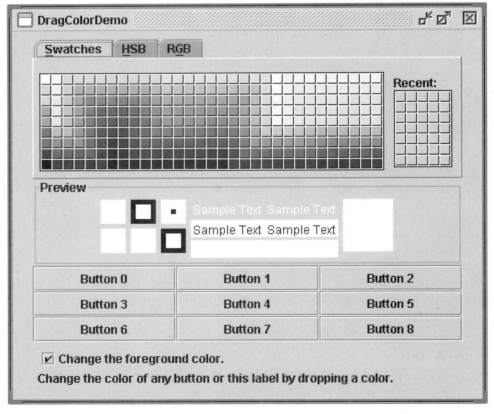

Figure 19 A screenshot of the `DragColorDemo` example.

Try This:

1. Run `DragColorDemo` using Java Web Start or compile and run the example yourself.[1]

2. Select a color from the palette. The selected color appears in the Preview panel.

3. Press and hold the mouse button while the cursor is over the Preview panel and begin to drag.

4. Drop the color onto the label. The text changes color.

5. Select another color. Drop it onto a button. The button text changes color.

6. Click the **Change the foreground color** check box so that it's no longer checked.

7. Drop another color onto a button or the label. The background changes color.

The example's main class can be found in `DragColorDemo.java`. The custom transfer handler is defined in `ColorTransferHandler.java`. In this example, we're only implementing import functionality and therefore only need to implement the methods `canImport` and `importData`. A single instance of the `ColorTransferHandler` is created and shared by all nine buttons and the label. Here's a snippet of code where the transfer handler is created and installed on the buttons:

```
colorHandler = new ColorTransferHandler();
...
for (int i = 0; i < 9; i++) {
    JButton tmp = new JButton("Button "+i);
    tmp.setTransferHandler(colorHandler);
    ....
}
```

Here's the code for `ColorTransferHandler`:

```
class ColorTransferHandler extends TransferHandler {
    //The data type exported from JColorChooser.
    String mimeType = DataFlavor.javaJVMLocalObjectMimeType +
                      ";class=java.awt.Color";
    DataFlavor colorFlavor;
    private boolean changesForegroundColor = true;

    ColorTransferHandler() {
        //Try to create a DataFlavor for color.
        try {
            colorFlavor = new DataFlavor(mimeType);
        } catch (ClassNotFoundException e) { }
    }
```

---

[1] To run `DragColorDemo` using Java Web Start, click the `DragColorDemo` link on the `RunExamples/misc.html` page on the CD. You can find the source files here: `JavaTutorial/uiswing/misc/example-1dot4/index.html#DragColorDemo`.

D

Other Features

```java
/**
 * Overridden to import a Color if it is available.
 * getChangesForegroundColor is used to determine whether
 * the foreground or the background color is changed.
 */
public boolean importData(JComponent c, Transferable t) {
    if (hasColorFlavor(t.getTransferDataFlavors())) {
        try {
            Color col = (Color)t.getTransferData(colorFlavor);
            if (getChangesForegroundColor()) {
                c.setForeground(col);
            } else {
                c.setBackground(col);
            }
            return true;
        } catch (UnsupportedFlavorException ufe) {
        } catch (IOException ioe) { }
    }
    return false;
}

/**
 * Does the flavor list have a Color flavor?
 */
protected boolean hasColorFlavor(DataFlavor[] flavors) {
    if (colorFlavor == null) {
        return false;
    }
    for (int i = 0; i < flavors.length; i++) {
        if (colorFlavor.equals(flavors[i])) {
            return true;
        }
    }
    return false;
}

/**
 * Overridden to include a check for a color flavor.
 */
public boolean canImport(JComponent c, DataFlavor[] flavors) {
    return hasColorFlavor(flavors);
}
protected void setChangesForegroundColor(boolean flag) {
    changesForegroundColor = flag;
}
protected boolean getChangesForegroundColor() {
    return changesForegroundColor;
}
}
```

The ColorTransferHandler is implemented to support JavaJVMlocalObjectMimeType with the representation class class=java.awt.Color, which is the mechanism JColor-Chooser uses to export color. For a discussion of how data is specified to the transfer mechanism, see the previous section Specifying the Data Format (page 559).

Replacing Default Support: Color and Text

The DragColorDemo example shown in the preceding section replaces the component's current transfer handler. When it installs the ColorTransferHandler on its components, it clobbers any preexisting transfer handler. This isn't so much of a problem with buttons or labels, which don't have any predefined data to transfer, but it can be a problem when you want to add the ability to import/export color on top of a component that already imports and/or exports other data, such as text. As discussed in Introduction to Data Transfer Support (page 548), if you install a custom transfer handler on a component that has a Swing-provided transfer handler, such as JTextField, you need to reimplement the Swing support. We've provided a version of DragColorDemo, called DragColorTextFieldDemo, that creates a transfer handler that accepts color and also reimplements the clobbered support for text. (See Figure 20.)

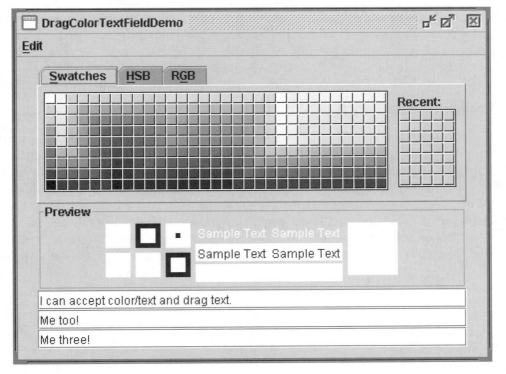

Figure 20   The DragColorTextFieldDemo.

Try This:

1. Run `DragColorTextFieldDemo` using Java Web Start or compile and run the example yourself.[1]

2. Select a color from the palette. Drag the color from the Preview panel to one of the text fields. Each text field can have its own color.

3. Select some text and drag it to another text field.

4. Hold down the Control key while dragging the text to copy to another text field.

5. Cut some text using either the menu item or the key binding: Control-X.

6. Select a location in which to paste the text and paste it, using either the menu item or the key binding: Control-V.

7. Copy some text using Control-C and paste it with Control-V.

8. Select some text, drag it to a native application, such as a text editor, and drop it. The text is inserted.

9. Select some text in the native text editor, drag it to the text area, and drop it. The text is inserted.

This transfer handler descends from `ColorTransferHandler`, which was used in the `Drag-ColorDemo` example. Since `ColorAndTextTransferHandler` must export data, it implements `createTransferable`, `getSourceActions`, and `exportDone` (in addition to the two methods it provides for import support). The code is too long to include here, but you can find the main class's source code in `DragColorTextFieldDemo.java`. The custom transfer handler can be found in `ColorAndTextTransferHandler.java`.

Importing a New Flavor: Files

The `JFileChooser` exports the `javaFileListFlavor`—a `List`[2] of `File`[3] objects discussed in Specifying the Data Format (page 559). The file chooser also exports its file names as a list of `Strings`—both in `text/plain` and `text/html` formats. Dragging a file from a drag-enabled file chooser and dropping it on a `JTextArea`, for example, causes the file name to be inserted into the text area but not the contents of the file. However, a custom transfer handler that knows about `javaFileListFlavor` can be installed to accept the file list provided by a file chooser, open the file, read the contents, and display the contents in the text area. We have provided an example that does this. Because this example reads files from your local

---

[1]   To run `DragColorTextFieldDemo` using Java Web Start, click the `DragColorTextFieldDemo` link on the `RunExamples/misc.html` page on the CD. You can find the source files here: `JavaTutorial/uiswing/misc/example-1dot4/index.html#DragColorTextFieldDemo`.

[2]   `List` API documentation: `http://java.sun.com/j2se/1.4.2/docs/api/java/util/List.html`.

[3]   `File` API documentation: `http://java.sun.com/j2se/1.4.2/docs/api/java/io/File.html`.

file system, launching the demo via Java Web Start will bring up a warning panel requiring permission before executing the application. If you prefer, you can download the application and run it locally.

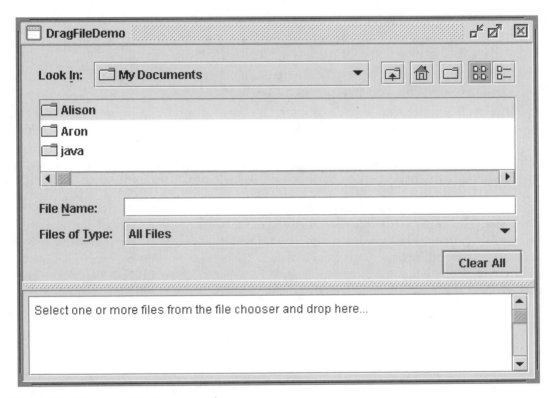

Figure 21   The DragFileDemo example.

Try This:

1. Run DragFileDemo using Java Web Start or compile and run the example yourself.[1]
2. Browse your file system and find a text file to select.
3. Drag the selected file and drop it onto the text area. The text area changes to a JTabbedPane; the file name on the tab and the contents of the file are displayed underneath.
4. Hold the cursor over the tab. The path to the file appears in the tool tip.

---

[1] To run DragFileDemo using Java Web Start, click the DragFileDemo link on the RunExamples/ misc.html page on the CD. You can find the source files here: JavaTutorial/uiswing/misc/ example-1dot4/index.html#DragFileDemo.

5. Select several files from the file chooser.

6. Drag and drop the files on the text area. Each file is put into its own tab. The current tab is set to the last file added.

7. Select text from the text area from one of the files. Drop it back on the text area. The text is moved in the expected manner for a text area.

8. Select a text file from the file chooser. Drag it to a native file explorer and drop it. The file will be copied to the location where it was dropped.

9. From the same native file explorer, select a file, drag it to the text area and drop it. The contents of the file will appear under a new tab.

10. Select a text file from the file chooser. Drag it to a native application, such as a text editor or Web browser on your system, and drop it. If that application supports drop, the text of the file should appear in that application.

11. Select the **Clear All** button. The tabbed pane is cleared and replaced by the default text area.

The code is too long to include here, but you can find the main class's source in `DragFile-Demo.java`. The custom `TransferHandler` for the text area is in `FileAndTextTransfer-Handler.java`. `DragFileDemo` doesn't do anything unusual except embed the file chooser in the main window rather than run it from a dialog. This allows the file chooser to be interactive without blocking the rest of the application. A separate class, `TabbedPaneController`, manages the `JTextArea`/`JTabbedPane` that displays the contents of the files. In the constructor for `DragFileDemo`, the tab pane controller is created and installed like this:

```
JTabbedPane tabbedPane = new JTabbedPane();
JPanel tabPanel = new JPanel(new BorderLayout());
...
tpc = new TabbedPaneController(tabbedPane, tabPanel);
```

`TabbedPaneController.java` contains the implementation for the tabbed pane controller.

The `FileandTextTransferHandler` installed on the text area imports two flavors: `java-FileListFlavor` and `stringFlavor`. As you saw before, `stringFlavor` is necessary because the new transfer handler clobbers the default behavior for the text area and this re-implements its basic behavior. In the `importData` method for the transfer handler, the code first checks to see if files are being imported. If so, the files are opened in a `BufferedReader` and the contents are appended. If the imported data isn't files, it then checks for strings.

Data Transfer with a Custom Component

We've seen how to customize data transfer for standard Swing components, but how do you add data transfer to a custom component? The simplest data transfer to implement is drag and drop:

- First determine which gesture initiates the drag. A mouse press? A press and drag? How many pixels must be traversed to define a valid drag?

- When drag conditions are met, invoke `exportAsDrag` on the component's `Transfer-Handler`.

With a bit more code, cut/copy/paste support can be added. The `DragPictureDemo` example shows how to implement full data transfer with a custom component. (See Figure 22.)

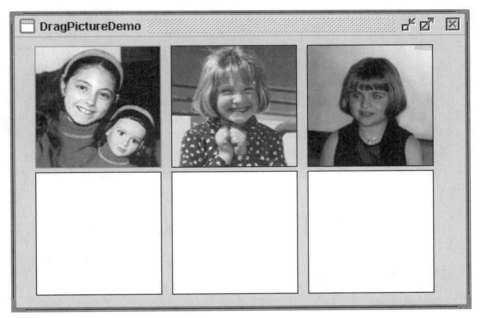

Figure 22   The `DragPictureDemo` example (modified to fit available space).

Try This:

1. Run `DragPictureDemo` using Java Web Start or compile and run the example yourself.[1]

---

[1]   To run `DragPictureDemo` using Java Web Start, click the `DragPictureDemo` link on the `RunExamples/misc.html` page on the CD. You can find the source files here: `JavaTutorial/uiswing/misc/example-1dot4/index.html#DragPictureDemo`.

2. Drag and drop the pictures using the mouse. Copy a picture by holding the Control key while dragging.

3. Cut or copy a picture using the key bindings Control-X or Control-C.

4. Paste the picture using the key binding Control-V.

5. Run this example with the keyboard only using Tab to move the focus and the Control-X, Control-C, and Control-V keys to cut, copy, and paste the pictures, respectively.

You can find the main class's source code in DragPictureDemo.java—you may recognize the basic functionality from the TrackFocusDemo example in the How to Use the Focus Subsystem (page 583) section. The custom component DTPicture is a subclass of the Picture component, modified to support data transfer. A new class is PictureTransferHandler, the custom transfer handler for DTPicture.

The custom component DTPicture enables drag and drop by implementing the Mouse-MotionListener interface. MouseMotionListener allows you to detect mouse motion by implementing the mouseDragged method. We arbitrarily chose a displacement of 5 pixels to determine whether the user is actually attempting to drag, as opposed to clicking on a picture. Once the cursor has moved a distance of 5 pixels in either direction while the mouse button is down, the transfer handler is called to initiate the drag. The mouseDragged method also checks to see if the Control button is being pushed on the keyboard—if it is, the action is a copy; otherwise, the action is a move. The mousePressed, mouseDragged, and mouse-Released methods in DTPicture look like this:

```java
MouseEvent firstMouseEvent = null;

public void mousePressed(MouseEvent e) {
    //Don't bother to drag if there is no image.
    if (image == null) return;

    firstMouseEvent = e;
    e.consume();
}

public void mouseDragged(MouseEvent e) {
    //Don't bother to drag if the component displays no image.
    if (image == null) return;

    if (firstMouseEvent != null) {
        e.consume();
```

```
            //If they are holding down the control key, COPY rather than MOVE
            int ctrlMask = InputEvent.CTRL_DOWN_MASK;
            int action = ((e.getModifiersEx() & ctrlMask) == ctrlMask) ?
                    TransferHandler.COPY : TransferHandler.MOVE;
            int dx = Math.abs(e.getX() - firstMouseEvent.getX());
            int dy = Math.abs(e.getY() - firstMouseEvent.getY());

            //Arbitrarily define a 5-pixel shift as the
            //official beginning of a drag.
            if (dx > 5 || dy > 5) {
                //This is a drag, not a click.
                JComponent c = (JComponent)e.getSource();
                //Tell the transfer handler to initiate the drag.
                TransferHandler handler = c.getTransferHandler();
                handler.exportAsDrag(c, firstMouseEvent, action);
                firstMouseEvent = null;
            }
        }
    }
}

public void mouseReleased(MouseEvent e) {
    firstMouseEvent = null;
}
}
```

The Adding Cut/Copy/Paste Support (page 573) section discusses how DragPictureDemo implements cut, copy, and paste with and without menu support.

The PictureTransferHandler class looks very much like other custom transfer handlers except that it transfers data using the built-in support for java.awt.Images—DataFlavor. imageFlavor. For more information, see Specifying the Data Format (page 559). If you're interested in more discussion on the custom Picture component, see Tracking Focus Changes to Multiple Components (page 595) in How to Use the Focus Subsystem (page 583).

Data Transfer with a Custom DataFlavor

By now you've seen several examples of transfer handlers that transfer data using conventional formats. This section takes a standard Swing object—a JList—and transfers the data using a content-type based on the java.util.ArrayList class. To achieve this, a custom Transferable is created. In order to implement a Transferable you must conform to the Transferable interface and provide implementations for the methods getTransferData, getTransferDataFlavors, and isDataFlavorSupported. The DragListDemo example (see Figure 23) shows how to implement the Transferable interface.

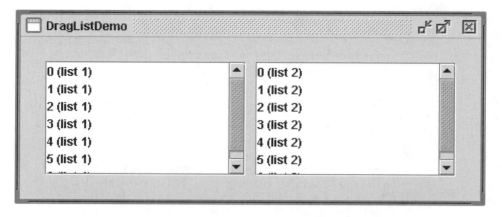

Figure 23   The DragListDemo example.

Try This:

1. Run `DragListDemo` using Java Web Start or compile and run the example yourself.[1]

2. Select one or more items from either list. To select a contiguous group of items, after selecting the first item select the last item while holding down the Shift key. All of the items in between are automatically selected.

3. As you begin to drag, the selection in the first list changes to show where a drop will occur but the items being dragged aren't affected.

4. Drop the items on either list. The data is deposited immediately after the selected item. Note that the items are removed from the first list since this was a move.

5. Repeat these steps while holding down the Control key to perform a copy.

6. Cut, copy, and paste the items using the key bindings Control-X, Control-C, and Control-V.

The `DragListDemo` class creates and displays the lists in the usual manner. Installed on each list is a shared instance of a custom transfer handler class called `ArrayListTransfer-Handler`.

---

[1] To run `DragListDemo` using Java Web Start, click the `DragListDemo` link on the `RunExamples/misc.html` page on the CD. You can find the source files here: `JavaTutorial/uiswing/misc/example-1dot4/index.html#DragListDemo`.

Adding Cut/Copy/Paste Support

So far our discussion has centered mostly around drag and drop support. However, it's an easy matter to hook up cut/copy/paste to a transfer handler. The basic steps are:

1. Make sure a transfer handler is installed on the component.
2. Create a way to invoke the `TransferHandler`'s cut/copy/paste support. Typically, this involves adding bindings to the input and action maps to have the `TransferHandler`'s cut/copy/paste actions invoked in response to particular keystrokes. You could also create menu items and/or buttons. Although this is easy to implement with text components (more later), it requires somewhat more work with other components since you need logic to determine which component to fire the action on. You can also write your own logic to call `exportToClipboard` or get the contents from the clipboard and call `importData`, but there are built-in actions for this.

The `DragColorTextFieldDemo`, in Replacing Default Support: Color and Text (page 565), shows how to use the default cut/copy/paste text support provided by `DefaultEditorKit`[1] with the custom `TransferHandler` installed on the text fields. A nice feature of the `DefaultEditorKit` methods is that they remember which component had the focus last. Here's the code that creates the Edit menu and uses the cut, copy, and paste `Action`s defined in `DefaultEditorKit` to create the menu items:

```
//Create an Edit menu to support cut/copy/paste.
public JMenuBar createMenuBar () {
    JMenuItem menuItem = null;
    JMenuBar menuBar = new JMenuBar();
    JMenu mainMenu = new JMenu("Edit");
    mainMenu.setMnemonic(KeyEvent.VK_E);

    menuItem = new JMenuItem(new DefaultEditorKit.CutAction());
    menuItem.setText("Cut");
    menuItem.setMnemonic(KeyEvent.VK_T);
    mainMenu.add(menuItem);

    menuItem = new JMenuItem(new DefaultEditorKit.CopyAction());
    menuItem.setText("Copy");
    menuItem.setMnemonic(KeyEvent.VK_C);
    mainMenu.add(menuItem);
```

---

[1] `DefaultEditorKit` is discussed in Text Component Features (page 64) in Chapter 3.

```
    menuItem = new JMenuItem(new DefaultEditorKit.PasteAction());
    menuItem.setText("Paste");
    menuItem.setMnemonic(KeyEvent.VK_P);
    mainMenu.add(menuItem);

    menuBar.add(mainMenu);
    return menuBar;
}
```

Hooking up cut/copy/paste support in this manner works with any component that descends from JTextComponent.

For any nontext component, you must manually set up the bindings in the input and action maps. The DragPictureDemo example, in Data Transfer with a Custom Component (page 569), shows how to do this. Here's a code snippet from the constructor for the DTPicture component:

```
if (installInputMapBindings) {
    InputMap imap = this.getInputMap();
    imap.put(KeyStroke.getKeyStroke("ctrl X"),
        TransferHandler.getCutAction().getValue(Action.NAME));
    imap.put(KeyStroke.getKeyStroke("ctrl C"),
        TransferHandler.getCopyAction().getValue(Action.NAME));
    imap.put(KeyStroke.getKeyStroke("ctrl V"),
        TransferHandler.getPasteAction().getValue(Action.NAME));
}

ActionMap map = this.getActionMap();
map.put(TransferHandler.getCutAction().getValue(Action.NAME),
        TransferHandler.getCutAction());
map.put(TransferHandler.getCopyAction().getValue(Action.NAME),
        TransferHandler.getCopyAction());
map.put(TransferHandler.getPasteAction().getValue(Action.NAME),
        TransferHandler.getPasteAction());
```

The boolean installInputMapBindings is true in this case and will be further discussed when we show how to add an Edit menu to support cut/copy/paste.

While you can implement cut/copy/paste to work exclusively with key bindings, it's considered good GUI design to provide menu items as well. We've provided the DragPictureDemo2 example (see Figure 24), which extends DragPictureDemo with an Edit menu.

Figure 24   A screenshot of the DragPictureDemo2 example.

Try This:

1. Run DragPictureDemo2 using Java Web Start or compile and run the example your-self.[1]

2. Cut or copy an image using the Edit > Cut or Edit > Copy menu item.

3. Select an empty square. Paste the image using the Edit > Paste menu item.

The DragPictureDemo2 example creates the Edit menu like this:

```
public JMenuBar createMenuBar() {
    JMenuItem menuItem = null;
    JMenuBar menuBar = new JMenuBar();
    JMenu mainMenu = new JMenu("Edit");
    mainMenu.setMnemonic(KeyEvent.VK_E);
    TransferActionListener actionListener =
                        new TransferActionListener();
```

---

[1] To run DragPictureDemo2 using Java Web Start, click the DragPictureDemo2 link on the RunExamples/misc.html page on the CD. You can find the source files here: JavaTutorial/uiswing/misc/example-1dot4/index.html#DragPictureDemo2.

```
menuItem = new JMenuItem("Cut");
menuItem.setActionCommand((String)TransferHandler.getCutAction().
        getValue(Action.NAME));
menuItem.addActionListener(actionListener);
menuItem.setAccelerator(
  KeyStroke.getKeyStroke(KeyEvent.VK_X, ActionEvent.CTRL_MASK));
menuItem.setMnemonic(KeyEvent.VK_T);
mainMenu.add(menuItem);

menuItem = new JMenuItem("Copy");
menuItem.setActionCommand((String)TransferHandler.getCopyAction().
        getValue(Action.NAME));
menuItem.addActionListener(actionListener);
menuItem.setAccelerator(
  KeyStroke.getKeyStroke(KeyEvent.VK_C, ActionEvent.CTRL_MASK));
menuItem.setMnemonic(KeyEvent.VK_C);
mainMenu.add(menuItem);

menuItem = new JMenuItem("Paste");
menuItem.setActionCommand((String)TransferHandler.getPasteAction().
        getValue(Action.NAME));
menuItem.addActionListener(actionListener);
menuItem.setAccelerator(
  KeyStroke.getKeyStroke(KeyEvent.VK_V, ActionEvent.CTRL_MASK));
menuItem.setMnemonic(KeyEvent.VK_P);
mainMenu.add(menuItem);

menuBar.add(mainMenu);
return menuBar;
}
```

This line ties the copy action to the menu item:

```
menuItem.setActionCommand((String)TransferHandler.getCopyAction().
                    getValue(Action.NAME));
```

This line defines Control-C as the key binding for the action:

```
menuItem.setAccelerator(
  KeyStroke.getKeyStroke(KeyEvent.VK_C, ActionEvent.CTRL_MASK));
```

The keyboard shortcuts, E (Edit), T (cuT), C (Copy), and P (Paste), are installed by calling setMnemonic. For a discussion of mnemonics versus accelerators, see Enabling Keyboard Operation (page 282) in Chapter 7.

When you register the keystroke in the input map yourself, you register it on a per-component basis—when the component has the focus and the keystroke is typed, the action is fired.

When you set a key binding on a menu, the keystroke information is added to a global input map, and the key binding is active all of the time when the window has the focus. For that reason, setting up the input maps on the components yourself is redundant when menu accelerators are used. If you're not using menu accelerators, you need to set up the input map yourself. The DTPicture class can be used by both DragPictureDemo and DragPictureDemo2 because the static property installInputMapBindings allows one demo to set the bindings on the input map and the other to skip that step. For your program, choose one approach or the other, but not both.

The final change to DragPictureDemo2 is necessary to ensure that the action goes to the correct component when the user initiates a cut, copy, or paste. The TransferActionListener class is installed as an action listener on the cut/copy/paste menu items and as a property change listener on the keyboard focus manager. Each time the focus owner changes, TransferActionListener keeps track of the new focus owner. When the user initiates a cut, copy, or paste through a menu item, TransferActionListener is notified and then fires the appropriate action on the component that has the focus. Here's the code for Transfer-ActionListener:

```java
public class TransferActionListener implements ActionListener,
                                                PropertyChangeListener {
    private JComponent focusOwner = null;

    public TransferActionListener() {
        KeyboardFocusManager manager = KeyboardFocusManager.
            getCurrentKeyboardFocusManager();
        manager.addPropertyChangeListener("permanentFocusOwner", this);
    }

    public void propertyChange(PropertyChangeEvent e) {
        Object o = e.getNewValue();
        if (o instanceof JComponent) {
            focusOwner = (JComponent)o;
        } else {
            focusOwner = null;
        }
    }

    public void actionPerformed(ActionEvent e) {
        if (focusOwner == null)
            return;
        String action = (String)e.getActionCommand();
        Action a = focusOwner.getActionMap().get(action);
        if (a != null) {
            a.actionPerformed(new ActionEvent(focusOwner,
                            ActionEvent.ACTION_PERFORMED, null));
        }
    }
}
```

The Data Transfer API

Tables 10 through 14 list the commonly used constructors and methods in data transfer. For more detailed information about the data transfer mechanism, see the "Swing Data Transfer" document in the release notes for your particular J2SE release.[1] You can find API documentation for JComponent at: `http://java.sun.com/j2se/1.4.2/docs/api/javax/swing/JComponent.html`. The documentation for the TransferHandler class is at: `http://java.sun.com/j2se/1.4.2/docs/api/javax/swing/TransferHandler.html`. The rest of the API is in the java.awt.datatransfer package, which is documented at: `http://java.sun.com/j2se/1.4.2/docs/api/java/awt/datatransfer/package-summary.html`.

Table 10: Useful JComponent Methods
(All of this API was introduced in release 1.4.)

Method	Purpose
setTransferHandler(TransferHandler) getTransferHandler()	Set or get the transfer handler. For those components that have default Swing support, the TransferHandler is installed by the ComponentUI if the value is null or marked by the presence of the UIResource interface. The default TransferHandler implementation installed by the ComponentUI is marked by the presence of the UIResource interface, enabling developers to override the default TransferHandler. Note that the same instance of a transfer handler may be shared among components.
setDragEnabled(boolean) getDragEnabled()	Set or get the *dragEnabled* property, which must be true to enable automatic drag handling. These methods are implemented on the following Swing components only: JColorChooser, JEditorPane, JFileChooser, JFormattedTextField, JList, JPasswordField, JTable, JTextArea, JTextField, JTextPane, and JTree. (Some look and feels may not support automatic drag and drop, and some components don't have default support for drop. For security reasons, JPasswordField doesn't support drag. The default value for this property is false.)

---

[1] In the v1.4.2 release notes this document is at: `http://java.sun.com/j2se/1.4.2/docs/guide/swing/1.4/dnd.html`.

Table 11: TransferHandler API

(All of this API was introduced in release 1.4.)

Constructor or Method	Purpose
`TransferHandler()` `TransferHandler(String)`	Create a transfer handler. The constructor that takes a string creates a transfer handler that can transfer a named property from one component to another. The `String` argument is the name of the property to transfer and may be null.
`canImport(JComponent, DataFlavor[])`	Return true if the specified component currently accepts data of at least one of the types specified in the list of data flavors; otherwise, returns false. If this method returns true, the data transfer system changes the cursor icon to indicate that this component will accept the data.
`protected createTransferable(` `            JComponent)`	Return a `Transferable`, encapsulating the data to be transferred.
`importData(JComponent, Transferable)`	Import the data into the component. The `Transferable` contains the actual data to import. True is returned if the import was successful; otherwise, false is returned.

`exportAsDrag(JComponent,`
`        InputEvent,`
`        int)`
	Initiate the Swing drag support. The `int` argument specifies either a COPY or a MOVE action. When this method returns, the export may not have completed. The method `exportDone` is called when the transfer is complete.

`exportToClipboard(JComponent,`
`            Clipboard,`
`            int)`
	Initiate a data transfer from the specified component to the specified clipboard. The `int` argument specifies either a COPY or a MOVE action. When this method returns, the export is completed. The method `exportDone` is called when the transfer is complete.

`protected exportDone(JComponent,`
`            Transferable,`
`            int)`
	Called after the export has completed. This method should remove the data that was transferred from the source component if the action was MOVE.

`getCutAction()`
`getCopyAction()`
`getPasteAction()`
	Return an `Action` that implements a cut, copy, or paste operation, respectively. The cut and copy actions cause `exportToClipboard` to be invoked. The paste action causes `importData` to be invoked.

D

Other Features

Table 11: TransferHandler API *(continued)*
(All of this API was introduced in release 1.4.)

Constructor or Method	Purpose
getSourceActions(JComponent)	Return the type of transfer actions supported by the component when used as the source of data transfer. It will be one of these types: COPY, COPY_OR_MOVE, MOVE, or NONE. The NONE type indicates that the component does not allow exporting of any data.
getVisualRepresentation(Transferable)	Return the Icon that establishes the look of a transfer. In v1.4, this method does nothing. For the current status of this method, track bug #4816922 online at: http://developer.java.sun.com/developer/bugParade/bugs/4816922.html.

Table 12: Transferable Classes

Class	Purpose
Transferable	An interface for classes that can be used to provide data for a transfer operation.
StringSelection	A Transferable that implements the capability required to transfer a String. Supports DataFlavor.stringFlavor and equivalent flavors.

Table 13: Transferable Interface API

Method	Purpose
getTransferData(DataFlavor)	Return an object that contains the data to be transferred.
getTransferDataFlavors()	Return an array of DataFlavors listing the flavors in which the data can be provided. The flavors are listed in preferred order, with the item at element 0 being the most preferred flavor.
isDataFlavorSupported(DataFlavor)	Return true if the requested flavor is supported for this object, otherwise return false.

Table 14: DataFlavor API

Class or Field	Purpose
DataFlavor() DataFlavor(Class, String) DataFlavor(String) DataFlavor(String, String) DataFlavor(String, String, ClassLoader)	Create a new content-type for transferring data. See Specifying the Data Format (page 559) for details on how to create new data flavors.
stringFlavor	The data flavor representing the Java Unicode java.lang.String class.
imageFlavor	The data flavor representing the java.awt.Image class.
javaFileListFlavor	The data flavor representing the java.util.List class where each element of the list must be a java.io.File.
javaJVMLocalObjectMimeType	A data flavor with this MIME type is used to transfer a reference to an arbitrary Java object using the Transferable interface within the same VM.
javaSerializedObjectMimeType	A data flavor with this MIME type represents a graph of Java objects that have been made persistent; used to transfer serialized objects.
javaRemoteObjectMimeType	A data flavor with this MIME type represents a live link to a Remote object, where the representation class of the DataFlavor represents the type of the Remote interface to be transferred.

Examples That Use Data Transfer

The following table lists examples that use data transfer.

Example	Where Described	Notes
BasicDnD	This section (page 548)	Demonstrates basic default drag-and-drop behavior.
LabelDnD	This section (page 552)	Demonstrates how to add support for dragging text from and dropping text on a JLabel.
LabelDnD2	This section (page 553)	Demonstrates how to add support for dropping color onto a JLabel.
ExtendedDnDDemo	This section (page 553)	Demonstrates how to create a custom transfer handler to extend default drag-and-drop support for JList and JTable.

Example	Where Described	Notes
DragColorDemo	This section (page 562)	Demonstrates how to drag color onto buttons and labels.
DragColorTextFieldDemo	This section (page 565)	Demonstrates how to drag color onto text fields and how to create a custom transfer handler that allows the text fields to export text. Also demonstrates cut/copy/paste using built-in text support.
DragFileDemo	This section (page 566)	Demonstrates how to implement a custom TransferHandler on a text area that accepts a list of files from a file chooser, opens those files, and appends the contents.
DragListDemo	This section (page 571)	Demonstrates how to implement a custom TransferHandler with a custom DataFlavor—java.util.ArrayList.
DragPictureDemo	This section (page 569) and (page 573)	Demonstrates how to implement a custom TransferHandler for a custom JComponent. Also implements cut/copy/paste on a custom component using keyboard accelerators.
DragPictureDemo2	This section (page 573)	Extends DragPictureDemo to support cut/copy/paste using an Edit menu.

How to Use the Focus Subsystem

Many components—even those operated primarily with the mouse, such as buttons—can be operated with the keyboard. For a key press to affect a component, the component must have the keyboard focus.

From the user's point of view, the component with the keyboard focus is generally prominent—with a dotted or black border, for example—and the window containing the component is more prominent than other windows onscreen. These visual cues tell the user to which component any typing will go. At most, one component in the window system can have the keyboard focus.

Exactly how a window gains the focus depends on the windowing system. There's no foolproof way, across all platforms, to ensure that a window gains the focus. On some systems, such as Microsoft Windows, the frontmost window becomes the focused window; in this case, the method `Window.toFront` moves the window to the front, thereby giving it the focus. However, on a system such as Solaris, some window managers choose the focused window based on cursor position; in this case, `Window.toFront` doesn't result in the same behavior.

A component generally gains the focus by the user clicking it, tabbing between components, or otherwise interacting with it. A component can also be given the focus programmatically, such as when its containing frame or dialog is made visible. This code snippet shows how to give a particular component the focus every time the window is activated:

```
//Make textField get the focus whenever frame is activated.
frame.addWindowListener(new WindowAdapter() {
    public void windowActivated(WindowEvent e) {
        textField.requestFocusInWindow();
    }
});
```

If you want to ensure that a particular component gains the focus the first time a window is activated, you can call `requestFocusInWindow` on the component after the component has been realized but before the frame is displayed. Here's some sample code showing how this can be done:

```
JFrame frame = new JFrame("Test");
JPanel = new JPanel();
```

F

Other Features

```
//...Create a variety of components here...

//Create the component that will have the initial focus.
JButton button = new JButton("I'm first");
panel.add(button);
frame.getContentPane().add(panel);  //Add it to the panel

frame.pack();  //Realize the components.

//This button will have the initial focus.
button.requestFocusInWindow();
frame.setVisible(true); //Display the window.
```

Version Note: This section describes the focus architecture implemented in release 1.4. Prior to 1.4, JComponent methods—such as setNextFocusableComponent, getNextFocusableComponent, requestDefaultFocus, and isManagingFocus—were used to manage the keyboard focus. These methods are now deprecated. Another method, requestFocus, is discouraged because it tries to give the focus to the component's window, which isn't always possible. As of v1.4, you should use requestFocusInWindow, which does not attempt to make the component's window focused and returns a boolean value indicating whether the method succeeded.

Introduction to the Focus Subsystem

The focus subsystem is designed to do the right thing as invisibly as possible. In most cases it behaves in a reasonable manner, and if it doesn't you can tweak it in various ways. Here are some common scenarios:

- The ordering is right but the first component with the focus isn't. As shown in the preceding code snippet, you can use requestFocusInWindow to set the focused component when the window becomes visible.

- The ordering is wrong. To fix this you can change the containment hierarchy, change the order in which the components are added to their containers, or create a custom focus traversal policy. For more details, see Customizing Focus Traversal (page 593).

- A component needs to be prevented from losing the focus, or you need to check a value in a component before it loses the focus. Validating Input (page 587) discusses a solution to this problem.

- A custom component isn't getting the focus. To fix this, you need to make sure that it satisfies all the requirements outlined in Making a Custom Component Focusable (page 592).

The FocusConceptsDemo example shown in Figure 25 illustrates a few concepts.

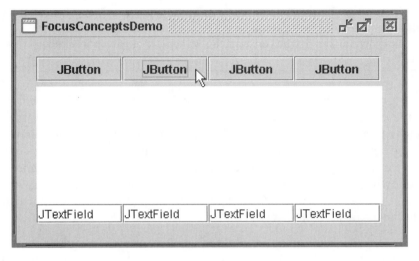

Figure 25   A screenshot of the FocusConceptsDemo example in which the second JButton has the focus.

Try This:

1. Run FocusConceptsDemo using Java Web Start or compile and run the example your-self.[1]
2. Click the window, if necessary, to give it the focus.
3. Move the focus from component to component using the Tab key. Notice that when the focus moves into the text area, it stays there.
4. Move the focus out of the text area using Control-Tab.
5. Move the focus in the opposite direction using Shift-Tab.
6. Move the focus out of the text area in the opposite direction using Control-Shift-Tab.

At the heart of the focus subsystem is the KeyboardFocusManager, which manages state and initiates changes. The keyboard manager tracks the *focus owner*—the component that receives typing from the keyboard. The *focused window* is the window that contains the focus owner.

---

[1] To run FocusConceptsDemo using Java Web Start, click the FocusConceptsDemo link on the RunExamples/misc.html page on the CD. You can find the source files here: JavaTutorial/uiswing/misc/example-1dot4/index.html#FocusConceptsDemo.

Note: If you happen to use a JWindow in your GUI, you should know that JWindow's owning frame must be visible for any components in the window to get the focus. By default, if you don't specify an owning frame for a JWindow, an invisible owning frame is created for it. The result is that components in JWindows might not be able to get the focus. The solution is to either specify a visible owning frame when creating the JWindow, or use an undecorated JFrame instead of JWindow.

A *focus cycle* (or *focus traversal cycle*) is a set of components that typically share a common ancestor in the containment hierarchy. The *focus cycle root* is the container that is the root for a particular focus traversal cycle. By default, every Window and JInternalFrame is a focus cycle root. Any Container (remember that all Swing components are containers) can be a focus cycle root as well; a focus cycle root can itself contain one or more focus cycle roots. The following Swing objects are focus cycle roots: JApplet, JDesktopPane, JDialog, JEditorPane, JFrame, JInternalFrame, and JWindow. While it might appear that JTable and JTree are focus cycle roots, they aren't.

A *focus traversal policy* determines the order in which a group of components are navigated. Swing provides the LayoutFocusTraversalPolicy[1] class, which decides the order of navigation based on layout manager-dependent factors such as size, location, and orientation of components. Within a focus cycle, components can be navigated in a forward or backward direction. In a hierarchy of focus cycle roots, upward traversal takes the focus out of the current cycle into the parent cycle.

In most look and feels, components are navigated with the Tab and Shift-Tab keys. These are the default *focus traversal keys* and can be changed programmatically. You can, for example, add Enter as a forward focus traversal key with the following four lines of code:

```
Set forwardKeys = getFocusTraversalKeys(
               KeyboardFocusManager.FORWARD_TRAVERSAL_KEYS);
Set newForwardKeys = new HashSet(forwardKeys);
newForwardKeys.add(KeyStroke.getKeyStroke(KeyEvent.VK_ENTER, 0));
setFocusTraversalKeys(KeyboardFocusManager.FORWARD_TRAVERSAL_KEYS,
               newForwardKeys);
```

Tab shifts the focus forward. Shift-Tab moves it backward. For example, in FocusConcepts-Demo the first button has the initial focus. Tabbing moves the focus through the buttons into the text area. Additional tabbing moves the cursor within the text area but not out of it because inside a text area Tab is *not* a focus traversal key. However, Control-Tab moves the

---

[1] LayoutFocusTraversalPolicy API documentation: http://java.sun.com/j2se/1.4.2/docs/api/javax/swing/LayoutFocusTraversalPolicy.html.

focus out of the text area and into the first text field. Likewise, Control-Shift-Tab moves the focus out of the text area and into the previous component. The Control key is used by convention to move the focus out of any component that treats Tab as special, such as `JTable`.

We've just given you a brief introduction to the focus architecture. If you want more details, see the specification for the Focus Subsystem at: `http://java.sun.com/j2se/1.4.2/ docs/api/java/awt/doc-files/FocusSpec.html`.

Validating Input

A common requirement of GUI design is a component that restricts the user's input—for example, a text field that allows only numeric input in decimal format (e.g., money) or a text field that allows only 5 digits for a zip code. Release 1.4 provides an easy-to-use formatted text field component that allows input to be restricted to a variety of localizable formats.[1] You can also specify a custom formatter for the text field that can perform special checking such as determining whether values are not just formatted correctly but also whether they are reasonable.

When you have a component that isn't a text field, or as an alternative to a custom formatter, you can use an input verifier. An input verifier allows you to reject specific values, such as a properly formatted but invalid zip code, or values outside of a desired range, such as a body temperature higher than 110°F. To use it, create a subclass of `InputVerifier`[2] (a class introduced in release 1.3), create an instance of your subclass, and set the instance as the input verifier for one or more components.

A component's input verifier is consulted whenever the component is about to lose the focus. If the component's value isn't acceptable, the input verifier can take appropriate action, such as refusing to yield the focus on the component or replacing the user's input with the last valid value and then allowing the focus to transfer to the next component.

Figures 26 and 27 show mortgage calculators. One uses input verification with standard text fields, and the other uses formatted text fields.

---

[1] See also How to Use Formatted Text Fields (page 221) in Chapter 7.

[2] `InputVerifier` API documentation: `http://java.sun.com/j2se/1.4.2/docs/api/javax/ swing/InputVerifier.html`.

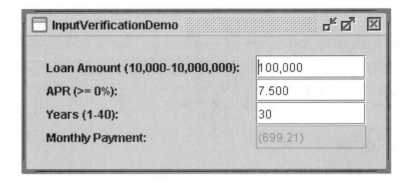

Figure 26   A screenshot of the InputVerificationDemo example.

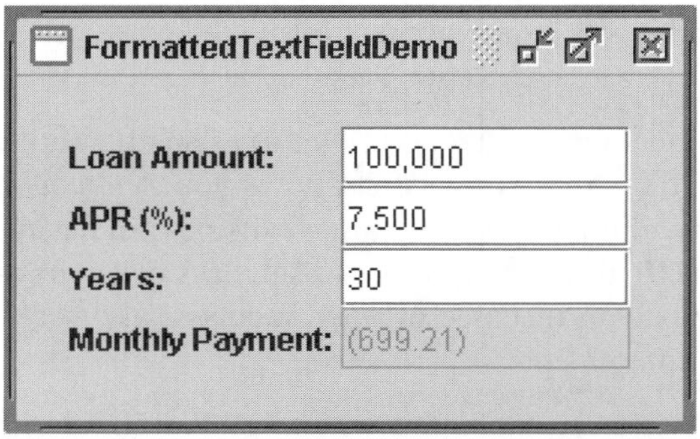

Figure 27   A screenshot of the FormattedTextFieldDemo example.

Try This:

1. Run InputVerificationDemo using Java Web Start or compile and run the example yourself.[1]

2. Run FormattedTextFieldDemo using Java Web Start or compile and run the example yourself.[2]

---

[1] To run InputVerificationDemo using Java Web Start, click the InputVerificationDemo link on the RunExamples/misc.html page on the CD. You can find the source files here: JavaTutorial/uiswing/components/example-1dot4/index.html#InputVerificationDemo.

[2] To run FormattedTextFieldDemo using Java Web Start, click the FormattedTextFieldDemo link on the RunExamples/misc.html page on the CD. You can find the source files here: JavaTutorial/uiswing/components/example-1dot4/index.html#FormattedTextFieldDemo.

3. Compare the two mortgage calculators side by side. You'll see that the input verification demo specifies valid input values in the associated label for each editable text field. Try entering badly formatted values in both examples to observe behavior. Then try entering a properly formatted but unreasonable value.

You can find the code in InputVerificationDemo.java. Here's the code for the Input-Verifier subclass, MyVerifier:

```java
class MyVerifier extends InputVerifier implements ActionListener {
    double MIN_AMOUNT = 10000.0;
    double MAX_AMOUNT = 10000000.0;
    double MIN_RATE = 0.0;
    int MIN_PERIOD = 1;
    int MAX_PERIOD = 40;

    public boolean shouldYieldFocus(JComponent input) {
        boolean inputOK = verify(input);
        makeItPretty(input);
        updatePayment();

        if (inputOK) {
            return true;
        } else {
            Toolkit.getDefaultToolkit().beep();
            return false;
        }
    }

    protected void updatePayment() {
        double amount = DEFAULT_AMOUNT;
        double rate = DEFAULT_RATE;
        int numPeriods = DEFAULT_PERIOD;
        double payment = 0.0;

        //Parse the values.
        try {
            amount = moneyFormat.parse(amountField.getText()).
                            doubleValue();
        } catch (ParseException pe) {}
        try {
            rate = percentFormat.parse(rateField.getText()).
                                doubleValue();
        } catch (ParseException pe) {}
```

```
    try {
        numPeriods =decimalFormat.parse(
                        numPeriodsField.getText()).intValue();
    } catch (ParseException pe) {}


    //Calculate the result and update the GUI.
    payment = computePayment(amount, rate, numPeriods);
    paymentField.setText(paymentFormat.format(payment));
}

//This method checks input, but should cause no side effects.
public boolean verify(JComponent input) {
    return checkField(input, false);
}

protected void makeItPretty(JComponent input) {
    checkField(input, true);
}

protected boolean checkField(JComponent input, boolean changeIt) {
    if (input == amountField) {
        return checkAmountField(changeIt);
    } else if (input == rateField) {
        return checkRateField(changeIt);
    } else if (input == numPeriodsField) {
        return checkNumPeriodsField(changeIt);
    } else {
        return true; //shouldn't happen
    }
}

//Checks that the amount field is valid.  If it is valid,
//it returns true; otherwise, returns false.  If the
//change argument is true, this method reigns in the
//value if necessary and (even if not) sets it to the
//parsed number so that it looks good--no letters,
//for example.
protected boolean checkAmountField(boolean change) {
    boolean wasValid = true;
    double amount = DEFAULT_AMOUNT;

    //Parse the value.
    try {
        amount = moneyFormat.parse(amountField.getText()).
                        doubleValue();
    } catch (ParseException pe) {
        wasValid = false;
    }
```

```
        //Value was invalid.
        if ((amount < MIN_AMOUNT) || (amount > MAX_AMOUNT)) {
            wasValid = false;
            if (change) {
                if (amount < MIN_AMOUNT) {
                    amount = MIN_AMOUNT;
                } else { // amount is greater than MAX_AMOUNT
                    amount = MAX_AMOUNT;
                }
            }
        }

        //Whether value was valid or not, format it nicely.
        if (change) {
            amountField.setText(moneyFormat.format(amount));
            amountField.selectAll();
        }

        return wasValid;
    }

    //Checks that the rate field is valid.  If it is valid,
    //it returns true; otherwise, returns false.  If the
    //change argument is true, this method reigns in the
    //value if necessary and (even if not) sets it to the
    //parsed number so that it looks good--no letters,
    //for example.
    protected boolean checkRateField(boolean change) {
        ...//Similar to checkAmountField...
    }

    //Checks that the numPeriods field is valid.  If it is valid,
    //it returns true; otherwise, returns false.  If the
    //change argument is true, this method reigns in the
    //value if necessary and (even if not) sets it to the
    //parsed number so that it looks good--no letters,
    //for example.
    protected boolean checkNumPeriodsField(boolean change) {
        ...//Similar to checkAmountField...
    }

    public void actionPerformed(ActionEvent e) {
        JTextField source = (JTextField)e.getSource();
        shouldYieldFocus(source); //ignore return value
        source.selectAll();
    }
}
```

The verify method is implemented to detect invalid values and does nothing else. It exists only to determine whether the input is valid—it should never bring up a dialog or cause any other side effects. The shouldYieldFocus method calls verify and, if the values are invalid, reigns them in. This method is allowed to cause side effects; in this case, it always formats the text field and may also change its value. In our example, shouldYieldFocus always returns true so that the transfer of the focus is never actually prevented. This is just one way verification can be implemented. We've also provided a version of this demo called InputVerificationDialogDemo[1] that puts up a dialog when user input is invalid and requires the user to enter a legal value.

The input verifier is installed using the JComponent setInputVerifier method. For example, InputVerificationDemo has this code:

```
private MyVerifier verifier = new MyVerifier();
..
amountField.setInputVerifier(verifier);
```

Making a Custom Component Focusable

To gain the focus, a component must satisfy three requirements: It must be visible, enabled, and focusable. It's also likely that you'll want to give it an input map. If you don't know what an input map is, please read How to Use Key Bindings (page 623).

The TrackFocusDemo example defines the simple component Picture. The following is its constructor:

```
public Picture(Image image) {
    this.image = image;
    setFocusable(true);
    addMouseListener(this);
    addFocusListener(this);
}
```

The call to setFocusable(true) makes the component focusable. If you explicitly give your component key bindings in its WHEN_FOCUSED input map, you don't need to call set-Focusable. To visually show changes in the focus (by painting a red border only when the component has the focus), Picture has a focus listener. To gain the focus when the user clicks on the picture, the component has a mouse listener. The listener's mouseClicked method requests that the focus be transferred to the picture. Here's the code:

---

[1] To run InputVerificationDialogDemo using Java Web Start, click the InputVerification-DialogDemo link on the RunExamples/misc.html page on the CD. You can find the source files here: JavaTutorial/uiswing/misc/example-1dot4/index.html#InputVerificationDialogDemo.

```
public void mouseClicked(MouseEvent e) {
    //Since the user clicked on us, now get the focus!
    requestFocusInWindow();
}
```

See Tracking Focus Changes to Multiple Components (page 595) for more discussion of the TrackFocusDemo[1] example.

Customizing Focus Traversal

The focus subsystem determines a default order that's used when the focus traversal keys (such as Tab) are used to navigate. A Swing application has its policy determined by LayoutFocusTraversalPolicy. You can set a focus traversal policy on any Container, though if the container isn't a focus cycle root it may have no apparent effect.

The FocusTraversalDemo example shown in Figure 28 demonstrates how to customize focus behavior.

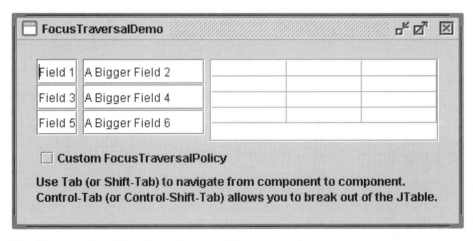

Figure 28   A screenshot of the FocusTraversalDemo example.

Try This:

1. Run FocusTraversalDemo using Java Web Start or compile and run the example yourself.[2]

---

[1] You can find the TrackFocusDemo   source files here: JavaTutorial/uiswing/misc/example-1dot4/index.html#TrackFocusDemo.

[2] To run FocusTraversalDemo using Java Web Start, click the FocusTraversalDemo link on the RunExamples/misc.html page on the CD. You can find the source files here: JavaTutorial/uiswing/misc/example-1dot4/index.html#FocusTraversalDemo.

2. Click the window, if necessary, to give it the focus.

3. Note the focus order as you tab through the components. The focus order was determined by the order that the components were added to the content pane. Note also that the check box never gets the focus; we removed it from the focus cycle.

4. To move the focus out of the table, use Control-Tab or Control-Shift-Tab.

5. Click the **Custom FocusTraversalPolicy** check box. This installs a custom focus traversal policy on the frame.

6. Try tabbing through the components again. Note that the focus order is now in numeric (left-to-right, top-down) order.

The check box was removed from the focus cycle with this line of code:

```
togglePolicy.setFocusable(false);
```

Here's the application's custom `FocusTraversalPolicy`:

```
...
JTextField tf1, tf2, tf3, tf4, tf5, tf6;
JTable table;
...
public class MyOwnFocusTraversalPolicy
            extends FocusTraversalPolicy {

    public Component getComponentAfter(Container focusCycleRoot,
                                       Component aComponent) {
        if (aComponent.equals(tf1)) {
            return tf2;
        } else if (aComponent.equals(tf2)) {
            return tf3;
        } else if (aComponent.equals(tf3)) {
            return tf4;
        } else if (aComponent.equals(tf4)) {
            return tf5;
        } else if (aComponent.equals(tf5)) {
            return tf6;
        } else if (aComponent.equals(tf6)) {
            return table;
        } else if (aComponent.equals(table)) {
            return tf1;
        }
        return tf1;
    }
```

```
public Component getComponentBefore(Container focusCycleRoot,
                                          Component aComponent) {
    if (aComponent.equals(tf1)) {
        return table;
    } else if (aComponent.equals(tf2)) {
        return tf1;
    } else if (aComponent.equals(tf3)) {
        return tf2;
    } else if (aComponent.equals(tf4)) {
        return tf3;
    } else if (aComponent.equals(tf5)) {
        return tf4;
    } else if (aComponent.equals(tf6)) {
        return tf5;
    } else if (aComponent.equals(table)) {
        return tf6;
    }
    return tf1;
}

public Component getDefaultComponent(Container focusCycleRoot) {
    return tf1;
}

public Component getLastComponent(Container focusCycleRoot) {
    return table;
}

public Component getFirstComponent(Container focusCycleRoot) {
    return tf1;
}
}
```

To use a custom `FocusTraversalPolicy`, use code like the following on any focus cycle root.

```
MyOwnFocusTraversalPolicy newPolicy = new MyOwnFocusTraversalPolicy();
frame.setFocusTraversalPolicy(newPolicy);
```

You can remove the policy by setting `FocusTraversalPolicy` to null. This restores the default policy.

Tracking Focus Changes to Multiple Components

In some situations an application may need to track which component has the focus. This information might be used to update menus or perhaps a status bar dynamically. If you need to track the focus only on specific components, it may make sense to implement a focus event listener. (See How to Write a Focus Listener (page 665) in Chapter 10.)

If a focus listener isn't appropriate, you can register a `PropertyChangeListener` on the `KeyboardFocusManager`. The property change listener is notified of every change involving the focus, including changes to the focus owner, the focused window, and the default focus traversal policy. For a complete list, see Table 17 (page 601).

Figure 29 shows `TrackFocusDemo`, which tracks the focus owner by installing a property change listener on the keyboard focus manager.

Figure 29   A screenshot of the `TrackFocusDemo` example.

Try This:

1. Run `TrackFocusDemo` using Java Web Start or compile and run the example yourself.[1]
2. Click the window, if necessary, to give it the focus.

---

[1]   To run `TrackFocusDemo` using Java Web Start, click the `TrackFocusDemo` link on the `RunExamples/misc.html` page on the CD. You can find the source files here: `JavaTutorial/uiswing/misc/example-1dot4/index.html#TrackFocusDemo`.

3. The window shows six images, each one displayed by a `Picture` component. The `Picture` that has the focus is indicated with a red border. A label at the bottom of the window describes that `Picture`.

4. Move the focus to another `Picture` by tabbing, Shift-tabbing, or clicking an image. Because a property change listener has been registered on the keyboard focus manager, the change in focus is detected and the label is updated appropriately.

You can view the demo's code in `TrackFocusDemo.java`. The custom component used for painting the images is in `Picture.java`. Here's the code that defines and installs the property change listener:

```
KeyboardFocusManager focusManager =
    KeyboardFocusManager.getCurrentKeyboardFocusManager();
focusManager.addPropertyChangeListener(
    new PropertyChangeListener() {
        public void propertyChange(PropertyChangeEvent e) {
            String prop = e.getPropertyName();
            if (("focusOwner".equals(prop)) &&
                (e.getNewValue() != null) &&
                ((e.getNewValue()) instanceof Picture)) {
                Component comp = (Component)e.getNewValue();
                String name = comp.getName();
                Integer num = new Integer(name);
                int index = num.intValue();
                if (index < 0 || index > comments.length) {
                    index = 0;
                }
                info.setText(comments[index]);
            }
        }
    }
);
```

The custom component, `Picture`, is responsible for painting the image. All six components are defined in the following manner:

```
pic1 = new Picture(createImageIcon("images/" +
            mayaString + ".gif", mayaString).getImage());
pic1.setName("1");
```

Timing Focus Transfers

Focus transfers are asynchronous, which can lead to some odd timing-related problems and assumptions, especially during automatic transfers of the focus. Imagine an application with a window containing a Start button, a Cancel button, and a text field. The components are added in this order:

1. Start button
2. Text field
3. Cancel button

When an application is launched, the `LayoutFocusTraversalPolicy` determines the focus traversal policy—in this case, it's the order in which the components were added to their container. In this example, the desired behavior is that the Start button have the initial focus; when it's clicked, it's disabled and the Cancel button gets the focus. The correct way to implement this is to add the components to the container in the desired order or to create a custom focus traversal policy. If, for some reason, this isn't possible, the way to implement this is with the following code snippet:

```
public void actionPerformed(ActionEvent e) {
    //This works.
    start.setEnabled(false);
    cancel.requestFocusInWindow();
}
```

As desired, the focus goes from the Start button to the Cancel button rather than to the text field. But a different result occurs if the same methods are called in the opposite order, like this:

```
public void actionPerformed(ActionEvent e) {
    //This doesn't work.
    cancel.requestFocusInWindow();
    start.setEnabled(false);
}
```

In this case, the focus is requested on the Cancel button before it has left the Start button. The call to `requestFocusInWindow` initiates the transfer, but doesn't immediately move the focus to the Cancel button. When the Start button is disabled, the focus is transferred to the next component (so there's always a component with the focus) and, in this case, it then moves the focus to the text field, *not* the Cancel button.

The need to make focus requests after all other changes that might affect the focus applies to

- Hiding the focus owner
- Making the focus owner nonfocusable
- Calling `removeNotify` on the focus owner

- Doing any of the above to the container of the focus owner, or causing changes to the focus policy so that the container no longer accepts the component as the focus owner
- Disposing of the top-level window that contains the focus owner

The Focus API

Tables 15 and 16 list the commonly used constructors and methods related to focus. Table 17 defines the bound properties for KeyboardFocusManager. A listener can be registered for these properties by calling addPropertyChangeListener. For more detailed information about the focus architecture, see the specification for the Focus Subsystem online at: http://java.sun.com/j2se/1.4.2/docs/api/java/awt/doc-files/FocusSpec.html. In addition, you may find How to Write a Focus Listener (page 665) in Chapter 10 useful. You should also refer to the API documentation for LayoutFocusTraversalPolicy, SortingFocusTraversalPolicy, InputVerifier, and KeyboardFocusManager at:

```
http://java.sun.com/j2se/1.4.2/docs/api/javax/swing/LayoutFocus-
      TraversalPolicy.html
http://java.sun.com/j2se/1.4.2/docs/api/javax/swing/SortingFocus-
      TraversalPolicy.html
http://java.sun.com/j2se/1.4.2/docs/api/javax/swing/InputVerifier.html
http://java.sun.com/j2se/1.4.2/docs/api/java/awt/KeyboardFocus-
      Manager.html
```

Table 15: Useful Methods for Components
(This API was introduced in release 1.4.)

Method (in Component)	Purpose
isFocusOwner()	Return true if the component is the focus owner. This method, introduced in release 1.4, makes hasFocus obsolete.
setFocusable(boolean) isFocusable()	Set or get the focusable state of the component. A component must be focusable in order to gain focus. When a component has been removed from the focus cycle with setFocusable(false), it can no longer be navigated with the keyboard. We prefer setRequestFocusEnabled so that your program can be run by users employing assistive technologies.
requestFocusInWindow()	Request that this component gets the focus. The component's window must be the current focused window. A subclass of JComponent must be visible, enabled, and focusable, and have an input map for this request to be granted. Don't assume that the component has focus until it fires a FOCUS_GAINED event. This method is preferred to requestFocus, which is platform-dependent.

Table 15: Useful Methods for Components *(continued)*
(This API was introduced in release 1.4.)

Method (in Component)	Purpose
`setFocusTraversalKeys(int, Set)` `getFocusTraversalKeys(int)` `areFocusTraversalKeysSet(int)` (*in* `java.awt.Container`)	Set or get the focus traversal keys for a particular direction or determine whether any focus traversal keys have been explicitly set on this container. If no focus traversal keys have been set, they are inherited from an ancestor or from the keyboard focus manager. Focus traversal keys can be set for these directions: `KeyboardFocusManager.FORWARD_TRAVERSAL_KEYS`, `KeyboardFocusManager.BACKWARD_TRAVERSAL_KEYS`, `KeyboardFocusManager.UP_CYCLE_TRAVERSAL_KEYS`, or `KeyboardFocusManager.DOWN_CYCLE_TRAVERSAL_KEYS`. If you set the UP_CYCLE_TRAVERSAL_KEYS or the DOWN_CYCLE_TRAVERSAL_KEYS, you must also invoke `setImplicitDown-CycleTraversal(false)` on the focus traversal policy.

Table 16: Creating and Using a Custom FocusTraversalPolicy
(This API was introduced in release 1.4. Unless otherwise specified, each method is defined in the `FocusTraversalPolicy` interface.)

Class or Method	Purpose
`LayoutFocusTraversalPolicy`	By default, determine the focus traversal policy for Swing components.
`getComponentAfter(Container, Component)`	Given the component passed in, return the component that should have the focus next.
`getComponentBefore(Container, Component)`	Given the component passed in, return the component that should have the focus before this one. This is used for backward tabbing.
`getDefaultComponent(Container)` (*in* `javax.swing.SortingFocusTraversalPolicy`)	Return the component that should have the default focus.
`getFirstComponent(Container)`	Return the first component in the traversal cycle.
`getInitialComponent(Container)`	Return the component that should receive the focus when a window is first made visible.
`getLastComponent(Container)`	Return the last component in the traversal cycle.
`setFocusTraversalPolicy(FocusTraversalPolicy)` `getFocusTraversalPolicy(FocusTraversalPolicy)` `isFocusTraversalPolicySet()` (*in* `java.awt.Container`)	Set or get the focus traversal policy or determine if one has been set. Note that setting a focus traversal policy on a container not the focus cycle root may have no apparent effect. A value of null means that a policy hasn't been explicitly set. If no policy has been set, one is inherited from the parent focus cycle root.

Table 17: KeyboardFocusManager Properties

This API was introduced in release 1.4.

Property	Purpose
focusOwner	The component that currently receives key events.
permanentFocusOwner	The component that most recently received a permanent FOCUS_GAINED event. Typically the same as focusOwner, unless a temporary focus change is currently in effect.
focusedWindow	The window that is or that contains the focus owner.
activeWindow	Always either a Frame or a Dialog. The active window is either the focused window or the first frame or dialog that is an owner of the focused window.
defaultFocusTraversalPolicy	The default focus traversal policy. Can be set by the Container setFocusTraversalPolicy method.
forwardDefaultFocusTraversalKeys	The set of default focus keys for a forward traversal. For multi-line text components, defaults to Control-Tab. For all other components, this defaults to Tab and Control-Tab.
backwardDefaultFocusTraversalKeys	The set of default focus keys for a backward traversal. For multi-line text components, defaults to Control-Shift-Tab. For all other components, defaults to Shift-Tab and Control-Shift-Tab.
upCycleDefaultFocusTraversalKeys	The set of default focus keys for an up cycle. These are null, by default, for Swing components. If you set these keys on the KeyboardFocusManager, or if you set the downCycleFocusTraversalKeys on a focus cycle root, you must also invoke setImplicitDownCycleTraversal(false) on the focus traversal policy.
downCycleDefaultFocusTraversalKeys	The set of default focus keys for a down cycle. These are null, by default, for Swing components. If you set these keys on the KeyboardFocusManager, or if you set the upCycleFocusTraversalKeys on a focus cycle root, you must also invoke setImplicitDownCycleTraversal(false) on the focus traversal policy.
currentFocusCycleRoot	The container that is the current focus cycle root.

Examples That Use Focus

The following table lists examples that manipulate the focus.

Example	Where Described	Notes
FocusConceptsDemo	This section (page 584)	Demonstrates basic default focus behavior.
FocusTraversalDemo	This section (page 593)	Demonstrates how to override the default focus order.
TrackFocusDemo	This section (page 592) and (page 595)	Demonstrates how to use a PropertyChange-Listener to track the focus owner. Also implements a custom focusable component.
InputVerificationDemo	This section (page 587)	Demonstrates how to implement an Input-Verifier to validate user input.
InputVerificationDialogDemo	This section (page 587)	Demonstrates how to implement an Input-Verifier that puts up a dialog when user input is invalid.
FocusEventDemo	How to Write a Focus Listener (page 665)	Reports all focus events that occur on several components to demonstrate the circumstances under which focus events are fired.

How to Use Icons

Many Swing components, such as labels, buttons, and tabbed panes, can be decorated with an *icon*—a fixed-sized picture. An icon is an object that adheres to the Icon[1] interface. Swing provides a particularly useful implementation of the Icon interface: ImageIcon,[2] which paints an icon from a GIF, JPEG, or PNG image.[3]

Here's a snapshot of an application with three labels (see Figure 30), two decorated with an icon:

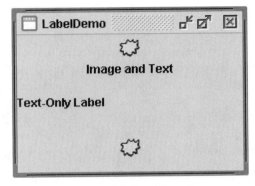

Figure 30   An application that decorates two labels with an icon.

The program uses one image icon to contain and paint the yellow splats. One statement creates the image icon and two more statements include the image icon on each of the two labels:

```
ImageIcon icon = createImageIcon("images/middle.gif",
                          "a pretty but meaningless splat");
label1 = new JLabel("Image and Text", icon, JLabel.CENTER);
...
label3 = new JLabel(icon);
```

---

[1] Icon API documentation: `http://java.sun.com/j2se/1.4.2/docs/api/javax/swing/Icon.html`.

[2] ImageIcon API documentation: `http://java.sun.com/j2se/1.4.2/docs/api/javax/swing/ImageIcon.html`.

[3] The PNG format has been supported since v1.3 of the Java platform.

Other Features

The `createImageIcon` method (used in the preceding snippet) is one we use in many of our code samples. It finds the specified file and returns an `ImageIcon` for that file, or `null` if that file couldn't be found. The following is a typical implementation:

```
/** Returns an ImageIcon, or null if the path was invalid. */
protected static ImageIcon createImageIcon(String path,
                                            String description) {
    java.net.URL imgURL = LabelDemo.class.getResource(path);
    if (imgURL != null) {
        return new ImageIcon(imgURL, description);
    } else {
        System.err.println("Couldn't find file: " + path);
        return null;
    }
}
```

If you copy `createImageIcon`, be sure to change the name of the class used for the `getResource` call; it should be the name of the class that contains the `createAppletImage-Icon` method. For example, you might change `LabelDemo.class.getResource` to *MyApp*`.class.getResource`. In the preceding snippet, the first argument to the `ImageIcon` constructor is relative to the location of the class `LabelDemo`, and will be resolved to an absolute URL. The `description` argument is a string that allows assistive technologies to help a visually impaired user understand what information the icon conveys.[1]

Generally, applications provide their own set of images used as part of the application, as is the case with the images used by many of our demos. You should use the `Class` `getResource` method to obtain the path to the image. This allows the application to verify that the image is available and to provide sensible error handling if it is not. When the image is not part of the application, `getResource` should not be used and the `ImageIcon` constructor is used directly. For example:

```
ImageIcon icon = new ImageIcon("/home/sharonz/images/middle.gif",
                               "a pretty but meaningless splat");
```

When you specify a file name or a URL to an `ImageIcon` constructor, processing is blocked until after the image data is completely loaded or the data location has proven to be invalid. If the data location is invalid (but non-null), an `ImageIcon` is still successfully created; it just has no size and, therefore, paints nothing. As we showed in the `createImageIcon` method, it's wise to first verify that the URL points to an existing file before passing it to the `Image-Icon` constructor. This allows graceful error handling when the file isn't present. If you want more information while the image is loading, you can register an observer on an image icon by calling its `setImageObserver` method.

---

[1] See How to Support Assistive Technologies (page 519) for more information.

Under the covers, each image icon uses an Image[1] object to hold the image data and a MediaTracker[2] object, which is shared by all image icons in the same program, to keep track of the image's loading status.

A More Complex Image Icon Example

Here's an applet that uses eight image icons (Figure 31). In the snapshot, you can see three of them: one displays the photograph and two decorate buttons with small arrows.

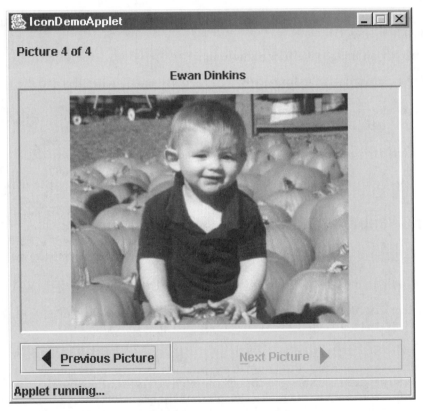

Figure 31 A screenshot of the IconDemoApplet example.

---

[1] Image API documentation: http://java.sun.com/j2se/1.4.2/docs/api/java/awt/Image.html.

[2] MediaTracker API documentation: http://java.sun.com/j2se/1.4.2/docs/api/java/awt/MediaTracker.html.

Other Features

Try This:

1. Run `IconDemoApplet` using Java Web Start, or to compile and run the example your-self, consult the example index.[1]

2. Click the **Previous Picture** and **Next Picture** buttons to view the photographs.

3. Hold the mouse over a photograph. A tool tip appears that indicates the file name of the current photograph and its width and height.

`IconDemoApplet` demonstrates icons used in the following ways:

- As a GUI element attached to a button (the left and right arrows).

- As an alternate version of the icon to be used when the button is disabled (dimmed left and right arrows).

- To display an image (the four photographs).

The following code creates the four arrow image icons and attaches them to the two buttons.

```
//Create the next and previous buttons.
ImageIcon nextIcon = createAppletImageIcon("images/right.gif",
                                            "a right arrow");
ImageIcon dimmedNextIcon = createAppletImageIcon(
                                    "imagesdimmedRight.gif",
                                    "a dimmed right arrow");
ImageIcon previousIcon = createAppletImageIcon("images/left.gif",
                                               "a left arrow");
ImageIcon dimmedPreviousIcon = createAppletImageIcon(
                                    "images/dimmedLeft.gif",
                                    "a dimmed left arrow");

nextButton = new JButton("Next Picture", nextIcon);
nextButton.setDisabledIcon(dimmedNextIcon);
nextButton.setVerticalTextPosition(AbstractButton.CENTER);
nextButton.setHorizontalTextPosition(AbstractButton.LEFT);
...

previousButton = new JButton("Previous Picture", previousIcon);
previousButton.setDisabledIcon(dimmedPreviousIcon);
previousButton.setVerticalTextPosition(AbstractButton.CENTER);
previousButton.setHorizontalTextPosition(AbstractButton.RIGHT);
```

---

[1] To run `IconDemoApplet` using Java Web Start, click the `IconDemoApplet` link on the `RunExamples/layout.html` page on the CD. You can find the source files here: `JavaTutorial/uiswing/misc/example-1dot4/index.html#IconDemoApplet`.

The action handler for the buttons initiates loading of the photographs into the image icon:

```
//User clicked either the next or the previous button.
public void actionPerformed(ActionEvent e) {
    //Show loading message.
    photographLabel.setIcon(null);
    photographLabel.setText("Loading image...");

    //Compute index of photograph to view.
    if (e.getActionCommand().equals("next")) {
        current += 1;
        if (!previousButton.isEnabled())
            previousButton.setEnabled(true);
        if (current == pictures.size() - 1)
            nextButton.setEnabled(false);
    } else {
        current -= 1;
        if (!nextButton.isEnabled())
            nextButton.setEnabled(true);
        if (current == 0)
            previousButton.setEnabled(false);
    }

    //Get the photo object.
    Photo pic = (Photo)pictures.elementAt(current);

    //Update the caption and number labels.
    captionLabel.setText(pic.caption);
    numberLabel.setText("Picture " +
                        (current+1) +
                        " of " +
                        pictures.size());

    //Update the photograph.
    ImageIcon icon = pic.getIcon();
    if (icon == null) {      //haven't viewed this photo before
        loadImage(imagedir + pic.filename, current);
    } else {
        updatePhotograph(current, pic);
    }
}
```

The photographs are loaded in a separate thread by the `loadImage` method—its code is shown a little later in this section.

Other Features

The Photo class is a simple class that manages an image icon and its properties.

```
public class Photo {
    public String filename;
    public String caption;
    public int width;
    public int height;
    public ImageIcon icon;

    public Photo(String filename, String caption, int w, int h) {
        this.filename = filename;
        if (caption == null)
            this.caption = filename;
        else
            this.caption = caption;
        width = w;
        height = h;
        icon = null;
    }

    public void setIcon(ImageIcon i) {
        icon = i;
    }

    public ImageIcon getIcon() {
        return icon;
    }
}
```

The section Loading Images into Applets (page 613) discusses how images are loaded into this applet and shows the `createAppletImageIcon` method—a version of `createImage-Icon` customized for applets that are deployed using Java Plug-in.

Loading Images Using getResource

Most often an image icon's data comes from an image file. There are a number of valid ways that your application's class and image files can be configured on your file server. You might have your class files in a JAR file, or your image files in a JAR file; they might be in the same JAR file, or they might be in different JAR files. Figures 32 through 35 illustrate a few of the ways these files can be configured. For all of the pictured configurations, you can get the URL for `myImage.gif` by invoking `getResource` with the argument `images/myImage.gif`.

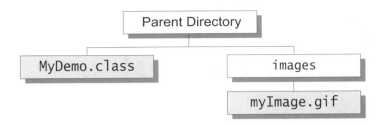

Figure 32   Class file next to an image directory containing the image file, in GIF format.

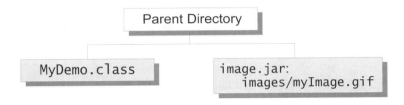

Figure 33   Class file in same directory as JAR file. The JAR file was created with all the images in an images directory.

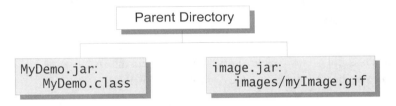

Figure 34   Class file in one JAR file and the images in another JAR file.

```
MyAppPlusImages.jar:
    MyDemo.class
    images/myImage.gif
```

Figure 35   Class and image files in the same JAR file.

If you are writing a real-world application, it is likely (and recommended) that you put your files into a package. For more information on packages, see the section "Creating and Using Packages" in *The Java Tutorial*.[1] Figures 36 through 38 show some possible configurations using a package named omega.

---

[1]   You can find "Creating and Using Packages" online and on the CD at: `JavaTutorial/java/interpack/` `packages.html`.

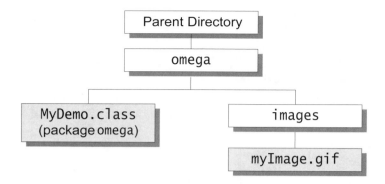

Figure 36   Class file in directory named omega; the image is in omega/images directory.

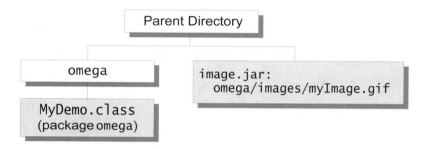

Figure 37   The class file is in omega directory; the image is in the JAR file not inside of omega directory, but created within the omega/images hierarchy.

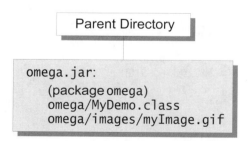

Figure 38   One big JAR file with class files under omega directory and image files under omega/images directory.

As before, you can get the URL for myImage.gif by specifying images/myImage.gif to getResource.

The following code reads the image, for any of the configurations pictured in Figures 32 through 38:

```
java.net.URL imageURL = myDemo.class.getResource("images/myImage.gif");
...
if (imageURL != null) {
    ImageIcon icon = newImageIcon(imageURL);
}
```

The getResource method causes the class loader to look through the directories and JAR files in the program's class path, returning a URL as soon as it finds the desired file. In our example, the MyDemo program attempts to load the image/myImage.gif file. The class loader looks through the directories and JAR files in the program's class path for image/myImage.gif. If the class loader finds the file, it returns the URL of the JAR file or directory that contained the file. If another JAR file or directory in the class path contains the images/myImage.gif file, the class loader returns the first instance that contains the file.

Version Note: In versions of Java Plug-in before 1.4, getResource doesn't look in JAR files. See Loading Images into Applets (page 613) for details.

Here are some ways to specify the class path:

- Using the -cp or -classpath command-line argument. For example, in the case where the images are in a JAR file named images.jar and the class file is in the current directory:

Platform	Command
Microsoft Windows	`java -cp .;image.jar MyDemo`
Unix-emulating shell on Microsoft Windows *(Note that you must quote the specified path.)*	`java -cp ".;image.jar" MyDemo`
UNIX	`java -cp .:image.jar MyDemo`

- If your image and class files are in separate JAR files, your command line will look something like (on the Microsoft Windows platform):

```
java -cp .;MyDemo.jar;image.jar MyDemo
```

- In the situation where all the files are in one JAR file,[1] you can use either of the following commands (on the Microsoft Windows platform):

```
java -jar MyAppPlusImages.jar

java -cp .;MyAppPlusImages.jar MyApp
```

- In the program's JNLP file (used by Java Web Start). For example, here is the JNLP file used by DragPictureDemo:

```
<?xml version="1.0" encoding="utf-8"?>
<!-- JNLP File for DragPictureDemo -->
<jnlp
  spec="1.0+"
  codebase="http://java.sun.com/docs/books/tutorialJWS/src/uiswing/
misc/example-1dot4"
  href="DragPictureDemo.jnlp">
  <information>
    <title>DragPictureDemo</titlhref="e>
    <vendor>The Java(tm) Tutorial: Sun Microsystems, Inc.</vendor>
    <homepage href="http://java.sun.com/docs/books/tutorial/
        uiswing/misc/example-1dot4/index.html#DragPictureDemo"/>
    <description>DragPictureDemo</description>
    <description kind="short">A demo showing how to install
        data transfer on a custom component.</description>
    <offline-allowed/>
  </information>
  <resources>
    <j2se version="1.4"/>
    <jar href="allClasses.jar"/>
    <jar href="images.jar"/>
  </resources>
  <application-desc main-class="DragPictureDemo"/>
</jnlp>
```

In this example, the class files and the images files are in separate JAR files. The JAR files are specified using the XML jar tag.

- Setting the CLASSPATH environment variable. This last approach is *not recommended*. If CLASSPATH is not set, the current directory ("."), followed by the location of the system classes shipped with the JRE, are used by default.

Most of our examples put the images in an images directory under the directory that contains the examples' class files. When we create JAR files for the examples, we keep the same relative locations, although often we put the class files in a different JAR file than the image JAR file. No matter where the class and image files are in the file system—in one JAR file,

---

[1] For more information, see *The Java Tutorial* trail "JAR Files" on the CD at: JavaTutorial/jar/index.html.

or in multiple JAR files, in a named package, or in the default package—the same code finds the image files using getResource. For more information, see "Accessing Resources in a Location-Independent Manner"[1] and the "Application Development Considerations."[2]

Loading Images into Applets

Applets generally load image data from the computer that served up the applet. There are two reasons for this. First, untrusted applets can't read from the file system on which they're running. Second, it just makes sense to put an applet's class and data files together on the server.

The IconDemoApplet program initializes each of its image icons from GIF files whose locations are specified with URLs. Because IconDemoApplet is designed to be an untrusted applet, we must place the image files under the applet's code base (the server directory containing the applet's class files). The following figure shows the locations of files for Icon-DemoApplet.

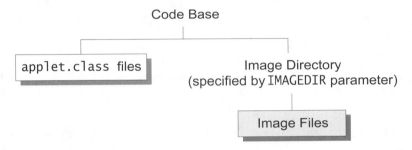

Figure 39   The image files or image directory can be deleted if the applet loads image files from a JAR file.

The APPLET tag is where you specify information about the images used in the applet. For example, here's the code for part of the tag for IconDemoApplet:

```
<applet code="IconDemoApplet.class"
        codebase="example-1dot4/"
        archive="iconAppletClasses.jar,
                 iconStartupImages.jar,
                 iconAppletImages.jar"
        width="400" height="360">
    <param name="IMAGEDIR" VALUE="images">
```

---

[1] "Accessing Resources in a Location-Independent Manner" is online at: http://java.sun.com/j2se/
1.4.2/docs/guide/resources/resources.html.

[2] "Application Development Considerations" is online at: http://java.sun.com/j2se/1.4.2/docs/
guide/jws/developersguide/development.html.

Other Features

613

```
        <param name="IMAGE0" VALUE="stickerface.gif">
        <param name="CAPTION0" VALUE="Sticker Face">
        <param name="WIDTH0" VALUE="230">
        <param name="HEIGHT0" VALUE="238">
        ...
    </applet>
```

The IMAGEDIR parameter indicates that the image files should be in a directory named images relative to the applet's code base. Applets generally use a URL that is constructed relative to the applet's code base.

As you can see from the archive attribute of the preceding APPLET tag, we have deployed IconDemoApplet using three JAR files. The classes are in one JAR file, the images required for starting up the UI (the arrow images) are in another JAR file, and the rest of the images are in a third JAR file. Separating the UI images from the other images means a quicker start-up time.[1]

When using Java Web Start to deploy an applet, you can use the same approach for loading resources as you do for applications—the getResource method. However, for applets deployed using Java Plug-in, getResourceAsStream is more efficient for loading images.

Version Note: Prior to release 1.4, when called from an applet deployed using Java Plug-in, getResource did not look in JAR files for resources, it looked only in the code base. In this situation, you must either put the images in the code base, or you must use getResourceAsStream.

Here's the code from IconDemoApplet that reads the images using getResourceAsStream:

```
    public class IconDemoApplet extends JApplet ... {
        protected String leftButtonFilename = "images/left.gif";
        ...
        public void init() {
            ...
            ImageIcon leftButtonIcon =
                    createAppletImageIcon(leftButtonFilename,
                                            "an arrow pointing left");
            ...
        }
        ...
```

---

[1] For more information on specifying JAR files with the APPLET tag, see these sections on the CD in *The Java Tutorial*: "Using the APPLET Tag" (JavaTutorial/applet/appletsonly/html.html) and the "JAR File Overview" (JavaTutorial/jar/overview.html).

```
//Returns an ImageIcon, or null if the path was invalid.
//When running an applet using Java Plug-in,
//getResourceAsStream is more efficient than getResource.
protected static ImageIcon createAppletImageIcon(String path,
                                        String description) {
    int MAX_IMAGE_SIZE = 75000; //Change this to the size of
                               //your biggest image, in bytes.
    int count = 0;
    BufferedInputStream imgStream = new BufferedInputStream(
        IconDemoApplet.class.getResourceAsStream(path));
    if (imgStream != null) {
        byte buf[] = new byte[MAX_IMAGE_SIZE];
        try {
            count = imgStream.read(buf);
        } catch (IOException ieo) {
            System.err.println("Couldn't read stream from file: "
                                + path);
        }

        try {
            imgStream.close();
        } catch (IOException ieo) {
            System.err.println("Can't close file " + path);
        }

        if (count <= 0) {
            System.err.println("Empty file: " + path);
            return null;
        }
        return new ImageIcon(Toolkit.getDefaultToolkit().
                            createImage(buf), description);
    } else {
        System.err.println("Couldn't find file: " + path);
        return null;
    }
}
...
}
```

You might want to copy the createAppletImageIcon method for use in your applet. Be sure to change the IconDemoApplet string in the call to getResourceAsStream to the name of your applet.

Improving Perceived Performance When Loading Image Icons

Because the photograph images are large, `IconDemoApplet` uses several techniques to improve the performance of the program as perceived by the user.

Providing Dimmed Icons

The applet provides dimmed versions of the arrows for the buttons (code follows):

```
imagedir = getParameter("IMAGEDIR");
if (imagedir != null)
    imagedir = imagedir + "/";
...
ImageIcon dimmedNextIcon = createAppletImageIcon(
    "images/dimmedRight.gif", "a dimmed right arrow");
ImageIcon dimmedPreviousIcon = createAppletImageIcon(
    "images/dimmedLeft.gif", "a dimmed left arrow");
...
nextButton.setDisabledIcon(dimmedNextIcon);
...
previousButton.setDisabledIcon(dimmedPreviousIcon);
```

Without this code, the dimmed versions of the arrows would be computed, which would cause a slight delay the first time each button is dimmed. Basically, this technique trades a noticeable delay when the user clicks the buttons for a smaller, less noticeable delay in the `init` method. An alternative would be to load the dimmed icons in a background thread after the GUI has been created and shown.

This applet uses four separate image files just to display arrows on two buttons. The performance impact of these little images can add up, especially if the browser in which the applet is running uses a separate HTTP connection to load each one. A faster alternative is to implement a custom `Icon` that paints the arrows. See Creating a Custom Icon Implementation (page 618) for an example.

Lazy Image Loading

The applet's initialization code loads only the first photograph. Each other photograph gets loaded when the user first requests to see it. By loading images if and when needed, the applet avoids a long initialization. The downside is that the user has to wait to see each photograph. We try to make this wait less noticeable by providing feedback about the image loading and allowing the user to use the GUI while the image is loading.

Not all programs can benefit from lazy loading. For example, the `TumbleItem.java` applet performs an animation, and all of the images in the animation are needed upfront. That applet's initialization code causes the images to be loaded in a background thread so that the applet can present a GUI (a "`Loading Images...`" label) before the images have loaded.

Background Image Loading

The applet uses a `SwingWorker`[1] to load each photograph image in a background thread. Because the image is loaded in a separate thread, the user can still click the buttons and otherwise interact with the applet while the image is loading.

Here's the code to load each image:

```
private void loadImage(final String imagePath,
                       final int index) {
    final SwingWorker worker = new SwingWorker() {
        ImageIcon icon = null;

        public Object construct() {
            icon = createAppletImageIcon(imagePath,
                                         "photo #",
                                         + index);
            return icon;  //return value not used by this program
        }

        public void finished() {
            Photo pic = (Photo)pictures.elementAt(index);
            pic.setIcon(icon);
            if (index == current)
                updatePhotograph(index, pic);
        }
    };
    worker.start();
}
```

The `construct` method, which creates the image icon for the photograph, is invoked by the thread that's created by the `SwingWorker` constructor and started by the `start` method. After the image icon is fully loaded, the `finished` method is called. The `finished` method is guaranteed to execute on the event-dispatching thread, so it can safely update the GUI to display the photograph.

Status Updates

While the image is loading in the background, the applet displays a status message:

```
photographLabel.setIcon(null);
photographLabel.setText("Loading image...");
```

This lets the user know that the program is doing something. After the image is loaded, the applet displays the photograph in the viewing area.

---

[1] See also Using the SwingWorker Class (page 636).

Other Features

Caching

After each photograph is viewed for the first time, the applet caches the image icon for later use. Thus if the user revisits a photograph, the program can use the same image icon and display the photograph quickly.

If you write a program without caching image icons, it may appear that some implicit image caching is going on within the Java platform. However, this is a side effect of the implementation and is not guaranteed. If your program uses one image in many places in its GUI, you can create the image icon once and use the same instance multiple times.

As with all performance-related issues, these techniques are applicable in some situations and not others. These are not general recommendations for all programs, but some techniques you can try to improve the user's experience. Furthermore, the techniques described here are designed to improve the program's perceived performance, but don't necessarily impact its real performance.

Creating a Custom Icon Implementation

If an image differs depending on the state of the component it's within, consider implementing a custom Icon class to paint the image. The really nice thing about a custom icon is that you can easily change the icon's appearance to reflect its host component's state.

Look-and-feel implementations often use custom icons. For example, the Java look and feel uses a single MetalCheckBoxIcon object to paint all of the check boxes in the GUI. The MetalCheckBoxIcon paints itself differently depending on whether its host component is enabled, pressed, or selected.

In this section, we'll convert a program called ButtonDemo so that it uses a custom icon to paint two arrows. You can see a picture of ButtonDemo in How to Use the Common Button API (page 157) in Chapter 7. Its source code is in ButtonDemo.java.[1] ButtonDemo uses the following code to load the arrows from GIF files and put the arrows into buttons:

```
ImageIcon leftButtonIcon = createImageIcon("images/right.gif",
                                           "an arrow pointing right");
...
ImageIcon rightButtonIcon = createImageIcon("images/left.gif",
                                            "an arrow pointing left");
```

---

[1] To run ButtonDemo using Java Web Start, click the ButtonDemo link on the RunExamples/ components.html page on the CD. You can find the source files here: JavaTutorial/uiswing/ components/example-1dot4/index.html#ButtonDemo.

```
b1 = new JButton("Disable middle button", leftButtonIcon);
...
b3 = new JButton("Enable middle button", rightButtonIcon);
```

Here's the new code, which uses a custom icon class named `ArrowIcon`. Only the bold lines have changed. You can run `CustomIconDemo` using Java Web Start or compile and run the example yourself.[1]

```
Icon leftButtonIcon = new ArrowIcon(SwingConstants.TRAILING);
...
Icon rightButtonIcon = new ArrowIcon(SwingConstants.LEADING);
b1 = new JButton("Disable middle button", leftButtonIcon);
...
b3 = new JButton("Enable middle button", rightButtonIcon);
```

You can find the implementation of the custom icon class in `ArrowIcon.java`.[2] Here are the interesting parts of its code:

```
class ArrowIcon implements Icon, SwingConstants {
    public ArrowIcon(int direction) {
        if (direction == LEADING) {
            xPoints[0] = width;
            yPoints[0] = -1;
            xPoints[1] = width;
            yPoints[1] = height;
            xPoints[2] = 0;
            yPoints[2] = height/2;
            xPoints[3] = 0;
            yPoints[3] = height/2 - 1;
        } else /* direction == TRAILING */ {
            xPoints[0] = 0;
            yPoints[0] = -1;
            xPoints[1] = 0;
            yPoints[1] = height;
            xPoints[2] = width;
            yPoints[2] = height/2;
            xPoints[3] = width;
            yPoints[3] = height/2 - 1;
        }
    }
    ...
```

---

[1] To run `CustomIconDemo` using Java Web Start, click the `CustomIconDemo` link on the `RunExamples/misc.html` page on the CD. You can find the source files here: `JavaTutorial/uiswing/misc/example-1dot4/index.html#CustomIconDemo`.

[2] You can find the `ArrowIcon` source file here: `JavaTutorial/uiswing/misc/example-1dot4/ArrowIcon.java`.

```
    public void paintIcon(Component c, Graphics g,
                          int x, int y) {
        if (c.isEnabled()) {
            g.setColor(c.setForeground());
        } else {
            g.setColor(Color.gray);
        }

        g.translate(x, y);
        g.fillPolygon(xPoints, yPoints, xPoints.length);
        g.translate(-x, -y);  //Restore Graphics object
    }
}
```

Note that the icon sets the current color. If you don't do this, then the icon's painting might not be visible. For more information about painting, see Chapter 6, Performing Custom Painting (page 129).

Using a custom icon to paint the arrows has a few implications:

- Because the icon's appearance is determined dynamically, the icon-painting code can use any information—component and application state, for example—to determine what to paint.

- Because we specified a non-ImageIcon icon for a button, the button doesn't bother to calculate the dimmed (disabled) version of the icon. Instead, the button lets the icon paint its disabled self. This can reduce computation time and save space that would otherwise be used to hold the dimmed image.

- Depending on the platform and the type of image, we might get a performance boost with custom icons, since painting simple shapes can sometimes be faster than copying images.

- Instead of loading all of the GIF files for the arrows (left and right, and perhaps dimmed left and dimmed right), we load a single class file (ArrowIcon). The performance implications of this depend on factors such as the platform, the size of the files, and the overhead for loading each type of file.

The Image Icon API

Tables 18 through 20 list the commonly used ImageIcon constructors and methods. Note that ImageIcon is not a descendent of JComponent or even of Component. You can refer to the API documentation for ImageIcon at: http://java.sun.com/j2se/1.4.2/docs/api/javax/swing/ImageIcon.html.

Table 18: Setting, Getting, and Painting the Image Icon's Image

Method or Constructor	Purpose

`ImageIcon()`
`ImageIcon(byte[])`
`ImageIcon(byte[], String)`
`ImageIcon(Image)`
`ImageIcon(Image, String)`
`ImageIcon(String)`
`ImageIcon(String, String)`
`ImageIcon(URL)`
`ImageIcon(URL, String)`
	Create an `ImageIcon` instance, initializing it to contain the specified image. The first argument indicates the source—image, byte array, file name, or URL—from which the image icon's image should be loaded. The source must be in a format supported by the `java.awt.Image` class: namely GIF or JPEG, or (as of v1.3) PNG. The second argument, when present, provides a description for the image. The description may also be set via `setDescription` and provides useful textual information for assistive technologies.

`void setImage(Image)` `Image getImage()`	Set or get the image displayed by the image icon.

`void paintIcon(Component,`
`              Graphics,`
`              int,`
`              int)`
	Paint the image icon's image in the specified graphics context. You would override this only if you're implementing a custom component that performs its own painting. The `Component` object is used as an image observer. You can rely on the default behavior provided by `Component` class and pass in any component. The two `int` argments specify the top-left corner where the icon is painted.

`URL getResource(String)` (*in* `java.lang.ClassLoader`)	Find the resource with the given name. For more information, see the section Loading Images Using getResource (page 608).

`InputStream`
`  getResourceAsStream(String)`
(*in* `java.lang.ClassLoader`)
	Find the resource with the given name and return an input stream for reading the resource. For more information, see the Loading Images into Applets (page 613) section.

Table 19: Setting or Getting Information about the Image Icon

Method	Purpose
`void setDescription(String)` `String getDescription()`	Set or get a description of the image. This description is intended for use by assistive technologies.
`int getIconWidth()` `int getIconHeight()`	Get the width or height of the image icon in pixels.

Table 20: Watching the Image Icon's Image Load

Method	Purpose
`void setImageObserver(ImageObserver)` `ImageObserver getImageObserver()`	Set or get an image observer for the image icon.
`int getImageLoadStatus()`	Get the loading status of the image icon's image. The values returned by this method are defined by `Media-Tracker`.

Other Features

Examples That Use Icons

The following table lists just a few of the many examples that use ImageIcon.

Example	Where Described	Notes
LabelDemo	This section and How to Use Labels (page 253)	Demonstrates using icons in an application's label, with and without accompanying text.
IconDemoApplet	This section	An applet. Uses a label to show large images; uses buttons that have both images and text.
CustomIconDemo	This section	Uses a custom icon class implemented by ArrowIcon.java.
TumbleItem	How to Make Applets (page 149)	Uses image icons in an animation. Shows how to use ImageIcon's paintIcon method.
ButtonDemo	How to Use Buttons (page 156)	Shows how to use icons in an application's buttons.
CheckBoxDemo	How to Use Check Boxes (page 163)	Uses multiple GIF images.
TabbedPaneDemo	How to Use Tabbed Panes (page 382)	Demonstrates adding icons to tabs in a tabbed pane.
DialogDemo	How to Make Dialogs (page 187)	Shows how to use standard icons in dialogs.
TreeIconDemo	How to Use Trees (page 437)	Shows how to change the icons displayed by a tree's nodes.
ActionDemo	How to Use Actions (page 513)	Shows how to specify the icon in a tool-bar button or menu item using an Action.
FileChooserDemo2	How to Use File Choosers (page 206)	Uses a PNG image. Shows how to implement an image previewer and an image filter in a file chooser.

How to Use Key Bindings

The JComponent class supports key bindings as a way of responding to individual keys typed by a user. Here are some examples of when key bindings are appropriate:

- You're creating a custom component and want to support keyboard access to it. For example, you might want the component to react when it has the focus and the user presses the Space bar.

- You want to override the behavior of an existing key binding. For example, if your application normally reacts to presses of the F2 key in a particular way, you might want it to perform a different action or ignore the key press.

- You want to provide a new key binding for an existing action. For example, you might feel strongly that Control-Shift-Insert should perform a paste operation.

You often don't need to use key bindings directly. They're used behind the scenes by mnemonics (supported by all buttons) and accelerators (supported by menu items). You can find coverage of mnemonics and accelerators in Enabling Keyboard Operation (page 282) in Chapter 7.

An alternative to key bindings is using key listeners.[1] Key listeners have their place as a low-level interface to keyboard input, but for responding to individual keys, key bindings are more appropriate and tend to result in more easily maintained code. Some of the advantages of key bindings are that they're somewhat self-documenting; take the containment hierarchy into account, encourage reusable chunks of code (Action objects); and allow actions to be easily removed, customized, or shared. Also, they make it easy to change the key to which an action is bound.

How Key Bindings Work

The key binding support provided by JComponent relies on the InputMap[2] and ActionMap[3] classes, which were introduced in v1.3. An input map binds keystrokes to action names, and an action map specifies the action corresponding to each action name.[4] Each JComponent has one action map and three input maps. The input maps correspond to the following focus situations:

---

[1] See also How to Write a Key Listener (page 676) in Chapter 10.
[2] InputMap API documentation: http://java.sun.com/j2se/1.4.2/docs/api/javax/swing/InputMap.html.
[3] ActionMap API documentation: http://java.sun.com/j2se/1.4.2/docs/api/javax/swing/ActionMap.html.
[4] Technically, you don't need to use action names in the maps; you can use any object as the "key" into them. By convention, however, you use a string that names an action. See also How to Use Actions (page 513).

- `JComponent.WHEN_FOCUSED`—The component has the keyboard focus. The input map `WHEN_FOCUSED` is typically used when the component has no children. For example, buttons use it to bind the Space bar.
- `JComponent.WHEN_ANCESTOR_OF_FOCUSED_COMPONENT`—The component contains or is the component that has the focus. This input map is commonly used for a composite component—one whose implementation depends on child components. For example, `JTables` make all their bindings using `WHEN_ANCESTOR_OF_FOCUSED_COMPONENT` so that, if the user is editing, the up-arrow key (for example) still changes the selected cell.
- `JComponent.WHEN_IN_FOCUSED_WINDOW`—The component's window either has the focus or contains the component that has the focus. This input map is commonly used for mnemonics or accelerators, which need to be active regardless where the focus is in the window.

Version Note: Prior to v1.3, the `JComponent` method `registerKeyboardAction` was used instead of input and action maps. `registerKeyboardAction` is now obsolete. (To ensure compatibility for older programs, `registerKeyboardAction` was reimplemented to use `InputMap` and `ActionMap`.)

When the user presses a key, the `JComponent` key event-processing code searches through one or more input maps to find a valid binding for it. When it finds a binding, it looks up the corresponding action in the action map. If the action is enabled, the binding is valid and the action is executed. If it's disabled, the search for a valid binding continues.

If more than one binding exists for the key, only the first valid one found is used. Input maps are checked in this order:

1. The focused component's `WHEN_FOCUSED` input map.
2. The focused component's `WHEN_ANCESTOR_OF_FOCUSED_COMPONENT` input map.
3. The `WHEN_ANCESTOR_OF_FOCUSED_COMPONENT` input maps of the focused component's parent, and then its parent's parent, and so on, continuing up the containment hierarchy. Input maps for disabled components are skipped.
4. The `WHEN_IN_FOCUSED_WINDOW` input maps of all of the enabled components in the focused window are searched. Because the order of searching is unpredictable, **avoid duplicate `WHEN_IN_FOCUSED_WINDOW` bindings!**

Let's consider what happens in two typical key binding cases: a button reacting to the Space bar and a frame with a default button reacting to the Enter key.

In the first case, assume that the user presses the Space bar while a `JButton` has the keyboard focus. First, the button's key listeners are notified of the event. Assuming none of the key listeners *consumes* the event (by invoking the `consume` method on the `KeyEvent`), the button's WHEN_FOCUSED input map is consulted. A binding is found because JButton uses that input map to bind Space to an action name. The action name is looked up in the button's action map, and the actionPerformed method of the action is invoked. The KeyEvent is automatically consumed, and processing stops.

In the second case, assume that the Enter key is pressed while the focus is anywhere inside a frame that has a default button (set using the JRootPane setDefaultButton method). Whatever the focused component is, its key listeners are first notified. Assuming that none of them consumes the key event, the focused component's WHEN_FOCUSED input map is consulted. If it has no binding for the key, the focused component's WHEN_ANCESTOR_ OF_FOCUSED_COMPONENT input map is consulted and then (if no binding is found) the WHEN_ANCESTOR_OF_FOCUSED_COMPONENT input maps of each of the component's ancestors in the containment hierarchy. Eventually, the root pane's WHEN_ANCESTOR_OF_FOCUSED_ COMPONENT input map is searched. Since that input map has a valid binding for Enter, the action is executed, causing the default button to be clicked.

How to Make and Remove Key Bindings

Here's an example of specifying that a component should react to the F2 key:

```
component.getInputMap().put(KeyStroke.getKeyStroke("F2"),
                            "doSomething");
component.getActionMap().put("doSomething", anAction);
//where anAction is a javax.swing.Action
```

As shown, to get a component's action map you use the getActionMap method (inherited from JComponent). To get an input map you use the getInputMap(int) method, where the integer is one of the JComponent.WHEN_*FOCUSED* constants. In the usual case where the constant is JComponent.WHEN_FOCUSED, you can just use getInputMap with no arguments.

To add an entry to one of the maps, use the put method. Specify a key using a KeyStroke object, which you get using the KeyStroke.getKeyStroke(String) method. You can find examples of creating Actions (to put in an action map) in How to Use Actions (page 513).

The following code is a slightly more complex example that specifies that a component should react to the Space bar as if the user clicked the mouse.

```
component.getInputMap().put(KeyStroke.getKeyStroke("SPACE"),
                            "pressed");
component.getInputMap().put(KeyStroke.getKeyStroke("released SPACE"),
                            "released");
component.getActionMap().put("pressed", pressedAction);
component.getActionMap().put("released", releasedAction);
//where pressedAction and releasedAction are javax.swing.Action objects
```

K

Other Features

625

To make a component ignore a key that it normally responds to, use the special action name "none." For example, the following code makes a component ignore the F2 key.

```
component.getInputMap().put(KeyStroke.getKeyStroke("F2"),
                            "none");
```

You specify the key corresponding to the action using a KeyStroke object. The preceding examples get KeyStroke objects using the KeyStroke.getKeyStroke(String) method.

Note: The preceding code doesn't prevent relevant WHEN_ANCESTOR_OF_FOCUSED_COMPONENT and WHEN_IN_FOCUSED_WINDOW input maps from being searched for an F2 key binding. To prevent this search, you must use a valid action instead of "none." For example:

```
Action doNothing = new AbstractAction() {
    public void actionPerformed(ActionEvent e) {
        //do nothing
    }
};
component.getInputMap().put(KeyStroke.getKeyStroke("F2"), "doNothing");
component.getActionMap().put("doNothing", doNothing);
```

The Key Binding API

Tables 21 and 22 list the commonly used API for key bindings. Also see the API table Table 2, "Creating and Using an AbstractAction," on page 517. You can also refer to the API documentation for InputMap, KeyStroke, and ActionMap:

```
http://java.sun.com/j2se/1.4.2/docs/api/javax/swing/InputMap.html
http://java.sun.com/j2se/1.4.2/docs/api/javax/swing/KeyStroke.html
http://java.sun.com/j2se/1.4.2/docs/api/javax/swing/ActionMap.html
```

Table 21: Getting and Using ActionMaps

Method	Purpose
ActionMap getActionMap() *(in JComponent)*	Get the object that maps names into actions for the component.
void put(Object, Action) *(in ActionMap)*	Set the action associated with the specified name. If the second argument is null, this method removes the binding for the name.

Table 22: Getting and Using InputMaps

Method	Purpose

`InputMap getInputMap()`
`InputMap getInputMap(int)`
(in `JComponent`*)*
	Get one of the input maps for the component. The arguments can be one of these `JComponent` constants: `WHEN_FOCUSED`, `WHEN_IN_FOCUSED_WINDOW`, or `WHEN_ANCESTOR_OF_FOCUSED_COMPONENT`. The no-argument method gets the `WHEN_FOCUSED` input map.

`void put(KeyStroke,`
`        Object)`
(in `InputMap`*)*
	Set the action name associated with the specified keystroke. If the second argument is null, this method removes the binding for the keystroke. To have the keystroke ignored, use "none" as the second argument.

`static KeyStroke`
`  getKeyStroke(String)`
(in `KeyStroke`*)*
	Get the object specifying a particular user keyboard activity. Typical arguments are Alt-Shift X, INSERT, and typed a. (See the `KeyStroke` API documentation for full details and for other forms of the `getKeyStroke` method at: `http://java.sun.com/j2se/1.4.2/docs/api/javax/swing/KeyStroke.html`.)

Examples That Use Icons

The following table lists just a few of the many examples that use `ImageIcon`.

Example	Where Described	Notes
`TableFTFEditDemo`	How to Use Tables (page 388)	The `IntegerEditor` class registers a key binding on a formatted text field to validate the input when the user presses the Enter key.
`SliderDemo3`	How to Use Sliders (page 348)	A key binding is registered on a text field to validate the input when the user presses the Enter key.
`TextComponentDemo`	Text Component Features (page 64)	Key bindings are registered on a text pane to navigate through the text when the user presses the Control-B, Control-F, Control-P, and Control-N keys.
`DragPictureDemo`	How to Use Drag and Drop and Data Transfer (page 545)	The `DTPicture` class registers key bindings on a custom component to cut, copy, and paste when the user presses the Control-X, Control-C, and Control-V keys.

K

Other Features

How to Set the Look and Feel

If you don't care which look and feel your program uses, you can skip this section entirely. Most of the programs in this book don't specify the look and feel, so you can easily run them with any one you prefer.

When a program doesn't set its look and feel, the Swing UI manager must figure out which one to use. It first checks whether the user has specified a preference. If so, it attempts to use that; if not, or if the user's choice isn't valid, the UI manager chooses the Java look and feel.

Version Note: Release 1.4.2 introduced two new look and feels: Microsoft Windows XP and GTK+.

You aren't limited to the look and feels supplied with the Java platform. You can use any of the ones in your program's class path. External look and feels are usually provided in one or more JAR files that you add to the class path at runtime. For example:

```
java -classpath .;C:\java\lnfdir\newlnf.jar SwingApplication
```

Once an external look and feel is in the class path, your program can use it just like any of those shipped with the Java platform.

Programmatically Setting the Look and Feel

To programmatically specify a look and feel, use the `UIManager.setLookAndFeel` method. For example, the bold code in the following snippet tells the program to use the Java look and feel:

```
try {
    UIManager.setLookAndFeel(
        UIManager.getCrossPlatformLookAndFeelClassName());
} catch (Exception e) { }

//Create and show the GUI...
```

Note: If you're going to set the look and feel, you should do it as the very first step in your application. Otherwise, you run the risk of initializing the Java look and feel regardless of what one you've requested. This can happen inadvertently when a static field references a Swing class, which causes the look and feel to be loaded. If no look and feel has yet been specified, the default Java look and feel is loaded.

The argument to `setLookAndFeel` is the fully qualified name of the appropriate subclass of `LookAndFeel`. To specify the Java look and feel, use the `getCrossPlatformLookAndFeel-ClassName` method. If you want to specify the native look and feel for whatever platform the user runs the program on, use `getSystemLookAndFeelClassName` instead. To specify a particular UI, use the actual class name. For example, if you design a program to look best with the GTK+ look and feel, you can use this code:

```
UIManager.setLookAndFeel(
          "com.sun.java.swing.plaf.gtk.GTKLookAndFeel");
```

Note: The GTK+ look and feel was released in all versions of the 1.4.2 SDK. However, it was not included in the 1.4.2 JRE release for Microsoft Windows. If you are running the 1.4.2 JRE for Windows and wish to use the GTK+ look and feel, you need to download the 1.4.2 SDK. We expect GTK+ to be shipped for all platforms in future JRE releases.

Here are some of the arguments you can use for `setLookAndFeel`:

`UIManager.getCrossPlatformLookAndFeelClassName()`
  Returns the look and feel that works on all platforms—the Java look and feel.

`UIManager.getSystemLookAndFeelClassName()`
  Specifies the look and feel for the current platform. On Microsoft Windows platforms, this specifies the Windows look and feel. On Mac OS platforms, this specifies the Mac OS look and feel. On UNIX platforms, such as Solaris, or Linux this returns the CDE/Motif look and feel.

`"com.sun.java.swing.plaf.gtk.GTKLookAndFeel"`
  Specifies the GTK+ look and feel introduced in release 1.4.2. You can specify the particular theme either using a resource file[1] or the `gtkthemefile` command-line parameter. Here's an example:

    java -Dswing.gtkthemefile=*customTheme*/gtkrc *Application*

---

[1] More information on resource files is at: `http://developer.gnome.org/doc/API/2.0/gtk/gtk-Resource-Files.html`.

Other Features

629

`"javax.swing.plaf.metal.MetalLookAndFeel"`
Specifies the Java look and feel. (The code name was *Metal*.)

`"com.sun.java.swing.plaf.windows.WindowsLookAndFeel"`
Specifies the Windows look and feel. Currently, you can use this only on Microsoft Windows systems.

Version Note: As of release 1.4.2, `WindowsLookAndFeel` has been updated to mimic the Windows XP look and feel when running on the Windows XP platform.

`"com.sun.java.swing.plaf.motif.MotifLookAndFeel"`
Specifies the CDE/Motif look and feel. This can be used on any platform.

You aren't limited to the listed arguments. You can specify the name for any look and feel in your program's class path.

Specifying the Look and Feel: Command Line

You can specify the look and feel at the command line by using the `-D` flag to set the `swing.defaultlaf` property. For example:

```
java -Dswing.defaultlaf=com.sun.java.swing.plaf.gtk.GTKLookAndFeel MyApp

java -Dswing.defaultlaf= \
    com.sun.java.swing.plaf.windows.WindowsLookAndFeel MyApp
```

Specifying the Look and Feel: swing.properties

Yet another way to specify the current look and feel is to use the `swing.properties` file to set the `swing.defaultlaf` property. This file is located in the `lib` directory of the J2SE release. If you're using the Java interpreter in *javaHomeDirectory*\bin, for example, the `swing.properties` file (if it exists) is in *javaHomeDirectory*\lib. Here's an example of the contents of a `swing.properties` file:

```
# Swing properties

swing.defaultlaf=com.sun.java.swing.plaf.windows.WindowsLookAndFeel
```

How the UI Manager Chooses the Look and Feel

Here are the look-and-feel determination steps that occur when the UI manager first initializes itself:

1. If the program sets the look and feel before any components are created, the UI manager tries to create an instance of the specified look-and-feel class. If it's successful, all components use that look and feel.

2. If the program hasn't successfully specified a look and feel, the UI manager uses the one specified by the `swing.defaultlaf` property. If the property is specified in the `swing.properties` file *and* on the command line, the command-line definition takes precedence.

3. If none of these steps has resulted in a valid look and feel, the program uses the Java look and feel.

Changing the Look and Feel after Startup

You can change the look and feel with `setLookAndFeel` even after the program's GUI is visible. To make existing components reflect the change, invoke the `SwingUtilities` `updateComponentTreeUI` method once per top-level container. Then you can resize each top-level container to reflect the new sizes of its contained components. For example:

```
UIManager.setLookAndFeel(lnfName);
SwingUtilities.updateComponentTreeUI(frame);
frame.pack();
```

Other Features

631

How to Use Threads

The information in this section assumes that you are familiar with *threads*—lightweight processes that can run concurrently. If you are unfamiliar with threads, you can read *The Java Tutorial* trail, "Threads: Doing Two or More Tasks at Once."[1]

This section discusses two aspects of thread usage. We first discuss threads as they apply to *every* Swing application—namely, why all code that paints or handles events needs to execute on a specific thread. We also discuss the invokeLater and invokeAndWait methods, which are used to ensure that events are handled on this special thread. The rest of this section applies only to those who want to use additional threads to improve performance in their application. Also included is a discussion of SwingWorker—a handy class used by many of our demos to offload time-consuming tasks.

Note: Although this section talks about Swing, the same issues apply to all Components. Specifically, AWT components are not guaranteed to be thread safe.

The Event-Dispatching Thread

Swing event-handling and painting code executes in a single thread, which is called the *event-dispatching thread*. This ensures that each event handler will finish executing before the next one executes and that painting isn't interrupted by events. To avoid the possibility of deadlock, you must take extreme care that Swing components and models are modified or queried *only* from the event-dispatching thread. As long as your program creates its GUI from the event-dispatching thread and modifies the GUI only from event handlers, it is thread safe.

You have probably noticed that most of this book's demos use a standardized main method that calls the SwingUtilities method invokeLater to ensure that the GUI is created on the event-dispatching thread. Here's an example of the main method from the FocusConcepts-Demo example. We have also included the source for createAndShowGUI—a private, static method called by each main method where the creation of the GUI is handled.

```
/**
 * Create the GUI and show it.  For thread safety,
 * this method should be invoked from the
 * event-dispatching thread.
 */
```

---

[1] This trail is on the CD and online at: http://java.sun.com/docs/books/tutorial/essential/threads/index.html.

```
private static void createAndShowGUI() {
    //Make sure we have nice window decorations.
    JFrame.setDefaultLookAndFeelDecorated(true);

    //Create and set up the window.
    frame = new JFrame("FocusConceptsDemo");
    frame.setDefaultCloseOperation(JFrame.EXIT_ON_CLOSE);

    //Create and set up the content pane.
    JComponent newContentPane = new FocusConceptsDemo();
    newContentPane.setOpaque(true); //content panes must be opaque
    frame.setContentPane(newContentPane);

    //Display the window.
    frame.pack();
    frame.setVisible(true);
}

public static void main(String[] args) {
    //Schedule a job for the event-dispatching thread:
    //creating and showing this application's GUI.
    javax.swing.SwingUtilities.invokeLater(new Runnable() {
        public void run() {
            createAndShowGUI();
        }
    });
}
```

Note: We used to say that you could create the GUI on the main thread as long as you didn't modify components that had already been realized.[1] While this worked for most applications, in certain situations it could cause problems. Out of all the demos in this book, we encountered a problem only in ComponentEventDemo. In that case, sometimes when the demo was launched, it would not come up because it would deadlock when updating the text area if the text area had not yet been realized; at other times it would come up without incident.

To avoid the possibility of thread problems, we recommend that you use invokeLater to create the GUI on the event-dispatching thread for all new applications. If you have old programs that are working fine, they are probably OK; however, you might want to convert them when it's convenient to do so.

---

[1] "Realized" means that the component has been painted onscreen, or is ready to be painted. The methods setVisible(true) and pack cause a window to be realized, which in turn causes the components it contains to be realized.

Using the invokeLater Method

You can call `invokeLater` from any thread to request the event-dispatching thread to run certain code. This code must be in the `run` method of a `Runnable` object and should specify the `Runnable` object as `invokeLater`'s argument. The `invokeLater` method returns immediately without waiting for the event-dispatching thread to execute the code.

Here's an example of using `invokeLater`:

```
Runnable updateAComponent = new Runnable() {
    public void run() { component.doSomething(); }
};
SwingUtilities.invokeLater(updateAComponent);
```

Using the invokeAndWait Method

The `invokeAndWait` method is just like `invokeLater`, except that it doesn't return until the event-dispatching thread has executed the specified code. Whenever possible, use `invokeLater` instead of `invokeAndWait`, which can cause a deadlock. If you do use `invokeAndWait`, make sure the thread that calls it doesn't hold any locks that other threads might need while the call is occurring.

Here's an example of using `invokeAndWait`:

```
void showHelloThereDialog() throws Exception {
    Runnable showModalDialog = new Runnable() {
        public void run() {
            JOptionPane.showMessageDialog(myMainFrame,
                                          "Hello There");
        }
    };
    SwingUtilities.invokeAndWait(showModalDialog);
}
```

Similarly, a thread that needs access to GUI state, such as the contents of a pair of text fields, might have the following code:

```
void printTextField() throws Exception {
    final String[] myStrings = new String[2];

    Runnable getTextFieldText = new Runnable() {
        public void run() {
            myStrings[0] = textField0.getText();
            myStrings[1] = textField1.getText();
        }
    };
```

```
    SwingUtilities.invokeAndWait(getTextFieldText);

    System.out.println(myStrings[0] + " " + myStrings[1]);
}
```

Using Threads to Improve Performance

When used properly, threads can be a powerful tool. However, you must proceed with caution when using threads in a Swing program. Despite the dangers, threads can be invaluable. You can use them to improve your program's perceived performance, and sometimes they can simplify a program's code or architecture. Here are some typical situations where threads are used:

- To move a time-consuming initialization task out of the main thread so that the GUI comes up faster. Examples of time-consuming tasks include making extensive calculations and blocking for network or disk I/O (loading images, for example).
- To move a time-consuming task out of the event-dispatching thread so that the GUI remains responsive.
- To perform an operation repeatedly, usually with some predetermined period of time between operations.
- To wait for messages from other programs.

If you need to create a thread, you can avoid some common pitfalls by implementing the thread with a utility class, such as `SwingWorker`[1] or one of the `Timer`[2] classes. A Swing-Worker object creates a thread to execute a time-consuming operation. After the operation is finished, `SwingWorker` gives you the option of executing some additional code in the event-dispatching thread. Timers are useful for performing a task either repeatedly or after a specified delay. If you need to implement your own threads, you can find information on doing so in *The Java Tutorial* trail, "Threads: Doing Two or More Tasks at Once."[3]

You can use several techniques to make multi-threaded Swing programs work well:

- If you need to update a component but your code isn't executing in an event listener, use one of the two `SwingUtilities` methods: `invokeLater` (preferred) or `invoke-AndWait`.
- If you aren't sure whether your code is executing in an event listener, then you should analyze your program's code and document which thread each method is (and can be) called from. Failing that, use the `SwingUtilities.isEventDispatchThread()`

---

[1] You can find the source code for `SwingWorker.java` online and on the CD: `JavaTutorial/uiswing/misc/example-1dot4/SwingWorker.java`.
[2] `Timers` are discussed in the next section How to Use Timers (page 639).
[3] This trail is available online and on the CD: `JavaTutorial/essential/threads/index.html`.

method, which returns true if your code is executing in the event-dispatching thread. You can safely call invokeLater from any thread, but invokeAndWait throws an exception if it's called from the event-dispatching thread.

- If you need to update a component after a delay (whether or not your code is currently executing in an event listener), use a timer.
- If you need to update a component at a regular interval, use a timer.

For information and examples of using timers, see How to Use Timers (page 639).

Using the SwingWorker Class

The SwingWorker class is implemented in SwingWorker.java,[1] which is *not* in the Swing release. To use SwingWorker, first create a subclass of it. The subclass must implement the construct method so that it contains the code to perform your lengthy operation. When you instantiate your SwingWorker subclass, the SwingWorker object creates a thread but (as of SwingWorker 3) doesn't start it. You then invoke start on your SwingWorker object to start the thread, which calls your construct method.

Note: The implementation of the SwingWorker class has been updated twice, most recently in February 2000. We recommend that you occasionally check online to see whether a new version of SwingWorker is available at: http://java.sun.com/docs/books/tutorial/uiswing/misc/threads.html#SwingWorker.

Here's an example of using a SwingWorker to move a time-consuming task from an action event listener into a background thread so that the GUI remains responsive.

```
//OLD CODE:
public void actionPerformed(ActionEvent e) {
    ...
    //...code that might take a while to execute is here...
    ...
}

//BETTER CODE:
public void actionPerformed(ActionEvent e) {
    ...
    final SwingWorker worker = new SwingWorker() {
```

---

[1] You can find the source code for SwingWorker.java online and on the CD: JavaTutorial/uiswing/misc/example-1dot4/SwingWorker.java.

```
        public Object construct() {
            //...code that might take a while to execute is here...
            return someValue;
        }
    };
    worker.start();   //required for SwingWorker 3
    ...
}
```

The value that construct returns can be any object. You get the value by invoking the get method on your SwingWorker object. Be careful with get; because it blocks, it can cause deadlock. If necessary, you can interrupt the thread (causing get to return) by invoking interrupt on the SwingWorker.

If you need to update the GUI when the time-consuming operation completes, you can either use get (which is dangerous, as we noted) or override the finished method in your Swing-Worker subclass. The finished method runs after the construct method returns. Because finished executes in the event-dispatching thread, you can safely use it to update Swing components. Of course, you shouldn't put time-consuming operations in your finished implementation.

The following example of implementing finished is taken from IconDemoApplet.java. For a full discussion of this applet, including how it improves perceived performance by using background threads to load images, see How to Use Icons (page 603).

```
public void actionPerformed(ActionEvent e) {
    ...
    if (icon == null) {       //haven't viewed this photo before
        loadImage(imagedir + pic.filename, current);
    } else {
        updatePhotograph(current, pic);
    }
}
...
//Load an image in a separate thread.
private void loadImage(final String imagePath, final int index) {
    final SwingWorker worker = new SwingWorker() {
        ImageIcon icon = null;

        public Object construct() {
            icon = new ImageIcon(getURL(imagePath));
            return icon; //return value not used by this program
        }
```

Other Features

```
        //Runs on the event-dispatching thread.
        public void finished() {
            Photo pic = (Photo)pictures.elementAt(index);
            pic.setIcon(icon);
            if (index == current)
                updatePhotograph(index, pic);
        }
    };
    worker.start();
}
```

For more examples of using SwingWorker, go to Using Progress Monitors (page 305). TumbleItem, which is discussed in How to Make Applets (page 149) in Chapter 7, uses both a SwingWorker and a Timer.

For more information on Swing thread issues, see the article index in *The Swing Connection* at: http://java.sun.com/products/jfc/tsc/articles/index.html.

How to Use Timers

A Swing timer (an instance of `javax.swing.Timer`[1]) fires one or more action events after a specified delay. Don't confuse it with the general-purpose timer facility that was added to the `java.util` package in release 1.3.[2]

In general, we recommend using Swing timers rather than general-purpose timers for GUI-related tasks because Swing timers all share the same, preexisting timer thread and the GUI-related task automatically executes on the event-dispatching thread. However, you might use a general-purpose timer if you don't plan on touching the GUI from the timer or you need to perform lengthy processing.

You can use Swing timers in two ways:

- To perform a task once, after a delay. For example, the tool tip manager uses Swing timers to determine when to show a tool tip and when to hide it.
- To perform a task repeatedly. For example, you might perform animation or update a component that displays progress toward a goal.

Swing timers are very easy to use. When you create the timer, you specify an action listener to be notified when the timer "goes off." The `actionPerformed` method in this listener should contain the code for whatever task you need carried out. You also specify the number of milliseconds between timer firings. If you want the timer to go off only once, you can invoke `setRepeats(false)` on it. To start the timer, call its `start` method. To suspend it, call `stop`.

The Swing timer's task is performed in the event-dispatching thread. This means that it can safely manipulate components, but it also means that the task should execute quickly. If it might take a while to execute, consider using a `SwingWorker` instead of or in addition to the timer. See How to Use Threads (page 632) for instructions on using the `SwingWorker` class and information on using Swing components in multi-threaded programs.

---

[1] `javax.swing.Timer` API documentation: `http://java.sun.com/j2se/1.4.2/docs/api/javax/swing/Timer.html`.

[2] This section describes only Swing timers; you can find information on general-purpose timers in "Using the Timer and TimerTask Classes" in *The Java Tutorial*, available on the CD and online: `http://java.sun.com/docs/books/tutorial/essential/threads/timer.html`.

Figure 40 is an example of using a timer to periodically update a component that displays progress toward a goal.

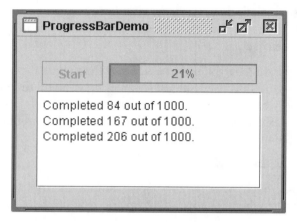

Figure 40   A screenshot of an application that uses a timer and a progress bar to display the progress of a long-running task.

Try This:

1. Run ProgressBarDemo using Java Web Start or compile and run the example your-self.[1]

2. Push the **Start** button. A timer updates the progress bar once per second as the task executes.

Here's the code from ProgressBarDemo.java that creates a timer set to go off every second. Each time the timer goes off it receives an action event. The action listener contains the code that implements the timer's task. In this case, the handler for the action event has to find out how close a thread is to completing its work and then update the progress bar accordingly. If the thread has completed its work, the action listener also stops the timer and updates the GUI to show that the thread is finished.

```
public final static int ONE_SECOND = 1000;
...
timer = new Timer(ONE_SECOND, new ActionListener() {
    public void actionPerformed(ActionEvent evt) {
        //...Update the progress bar...
```

---

[1]   To run ProgressBarDemo using Java Web Start, click the ProgressBarDemo link on the RunExamples/ components.html page on the CD. You can find the source files here: JavaTutorial/uiswing/ components/example-1dot4/index.html#ProgressBarDemo.

```
      if (/* thread is done */) {
          timer.stop();
          //...Update the GUI...
      }
    }
});
```

When the user presses the Start button, the program starts the timer:

```
    timer.start();
```

The Timer API

Tables 23 and 24 list the commonly used `javax.swing.Timer` constructors and methods. You can also refer to the API documentation for `javax.swing.Timer` at: `http://java.sun.com/j2se/1.4.2/docs/api/javax/swing/Timer.html`.

Table 23: Creating and Initializing the Timer

Method or Constructor	Purpose
`Timer(int, ActionListener)`	Create a Swing timer. The `int` argument specifies the number of milliseconds to pause between action events. Use `setDelay` to change the delay after construction. The second argument is an action listener, which the constructor registers with the timer. You can also register action listeners with `addActionListener` and remove them with `removeActionlistener`. Note that all timers share the same thread so there is no risk of Swing timers spawning more threads than the user's system can handle.
`void setDelay(int)` `int getDelay()`	Set or get the number of milliseconds between action events.
`void setInitialDelay(int)` `int getInitialDelay()`	Set or get the number of milliseconds to wait before firing the first action event. By default the initial delay is equal to the regular delay.
`void setRepeats(boolean)` `boolean isRepeats()`	Set or get whether the timer repeats. By default this value is true. Call `setRepeats(false)` to set up a timer that fires a single action event and then stops.
`void setCoalesce(boolean)` `boolean isCoalesce()`	Set or get whether the timer coalesces multiple, pending action events into a single action event. By default this value is true.
`addActionListener(listener)` `removeActionListener(listener)`	Add or remove an action listener.

Other Features

641

Table 24: Running the Timer

Method	Purpose
`void start()` `void restart()`	Turn the timer on. `restart` also cancels any pending action events.
`void stop()`	Turn the timer off.
`boolean isRunning()`	Get whether the timer is on.

Examples That Use Timers

This table shows examples that use `javax.swing.Timer` and where those examples are described.

Example	Where Described	Notes
`ProgressBarDemo`	This section and How to Use Progress Bars (page 300)	Uses a Swing timer to show periodic progress.
`SliderDemo`	How to Use Sliders (page 348)	Another animation program that uses a Swing timer. Allows the user to change the timer's delay dynamically. Also shows how to use the initial delay and `restart` to create a longer pause in an animation between certain frames.

10

Event Listeners
Reference

The following sections give details about implementing specific kinds of event listeners. While we don't have a how-to section for every single kind of event listener that you can write, we cover the listeners we think you're most likely to need. If you're interested in other listeners, you can find some information in Table 2, "Listener API Summary," on page 123 in Chapter 5.

All of these sections assume that you're familiar with event handling concepts. These prerequisites are covered in Chapter 5, Writing Event Listeners (page 107). For information about writing event listeners for specific components, refer to Chapter 7, Components Reference (page 147). Another resource is Solving Common Event-Handling Problems (page 739) in the Appendix.

You can find source files for all the examples from this chapter on the CD and online at:

```
JavaTutorial/uiswing/events/example-1dot4/index.html
```

```
http://java.sun.com/docs/books/tutorial/uiswing/events/
example-1dot4/index.html
```

The preceding URLs take you to an example index that has links to the files required by each example. You can go directly to the entry for a particular example by adding *#ExampleName* to the URL. Most examples have a "Run" link in the example index which executes the example using Java Web Start technology.

How to Write an Action Listener

Action listeners are probably the easiest—and most common—event handlers to implement. You implement an action listener to respond to the user's indication that some implementation-dependent action should occur.

When the user clicks a button, chooses a menu item, or presses Enter in a text field, an action event occurs. The result is that an `actionPerformed` message is sent to all action listeners that are registered on the relevant component.

Here's the action event handling code from an applet named `Beeper`:

```
public class Beeper ...  implements ActionListener {
    ...
    //where initialization occurs:
        button.addActionListener(this);
    ...
    public void actionPerformed(ActionEvent e) {
        Toolkit.getDefaultToolkit().beep();
    }
}
```

The `Beeper` example is described in Chapter 5's introduction to events, Some Event-Handling Examples (page 108). You can find the entire program in `Beeper.java`.[1] The other example described in that chapter, `MultiListener.java`,[2] has two action sources and two action listeners, with one listener listening to both sources and the other listening to just one.

The Action Listener API

The `ActionListener` interface[3] only has one method (see Table 1), so it does not have a corresponding adapter class. Table 2 lists the methods in the `ActionEvent` class. The `ActionListener` API documentation is online at: http://java.sun.com/j2se/1.4.2/docs/api/java/awt/event/ActionListener.html. The `ActionEvent` API documentation is online at: http://java.sun.com/j2se/1.4.2/docs/api/java/awt/event/ActionEvent.html.

---

[1] This source code is on the CD at: JavaTutorial/uiswing/events/example-1dot4/index.html#Beeper and online at: http://java.sun.com/docs/books/tutorial/uiswing/events/example-1dot4/index.html#Beeper.

[2] This source code is on the CD at: JavaTutorial/uiswing/events/example-1dot4/index.html#MultiListener and online at: http://java.sun.com/docs/books/tutorial/uiswing/events/example-1dot4/index.html#MultiListener.

[3] ActionListener API documentation: http://java.sun.com/j2se/1.4.2/docs/api/java/awt/event/ActionListener.html.

Table 1: The ActionListener Interface

Method	Purpose
`actionPerformed(actionEvent)`	Called just after the user informs the listened-to component that an action should occur.

Table 2: The ActionEvent Class

Method	Purpose
`String getActionCommand()`	Return the string associated with this action. Most objects that can fire action events support a method called `setActionCommand` that lets you set this string.

`int getModifiers()`	Return an integer representing the modifier keys the user was pressing when the action event occurred. You can use the `ActionEvent`-defined constants SHIFT_MASK, CTRL_MASK, META_MASK, and ALT_MASK to determine which keys were pressed. For example, if the user Shift-selects a menu item, then the following expression is nonzero:
	
	`actionEvent.getModifiers() &`
	`                    ActionEvent.SHIFT_MASK`

`Object getSource()` (*in* `java.util.EventObject`)	Return the object that fired the event.

Examples That Use Action Listeners

The following table lists some of the many examples that use action listeners.

Example	Where Described	Notes
`Beeper`	This section *and* Some Event-Handling Examples (page 108)	Contains one button with one action listener that beeps when you click the button.
`MultiListener`	Some Event-Handling Examples (page 108)	Registers two different action listeners on one button. Also registers the same action listener on two different buttons.
`RadioButtonDemo`	How to Use Radio Buttons (page 311)	Registers the same action listener on five radio buttons. The listener uses the `getActionCommand` method to determine which radio button fired the event.

Example	Where Described	Notes
MenuDemo	How to Use Menus (page 277)	Shows how to listen for action events on menu items.
DragPictureDemo2	How to Use Drag and Drop and Data Transfer (page 545)	Uses `setActionCommand` to attach the cut, copy, and paste actions to the menu. Then uses an action listener to forward the cut/copy/paste actions to the currently focused component.
TextDemo	How to Use Text Fields (page 423)	An applet that registers an action listener on a text field.
IconDemoApplet	How to Use Icons (page 603)	Loads an image in an action listener. Because loading an image can take a while, this program uses a `SwingWorker` to load the image in a background thread.
TableDialogEditDemo	How to Use Tables (page 388)	Registers an action listener through a factory method on the OK button of a color chooser dialog.
SliderDemo	How to Use Sliders (page 348)	Registers an action listener on a timer that controls an animation loop.

How to Write a Caret Listener

Caret events occur when the *caret*—the cursor indicating the insertion point—in a text component moves or when the selection in a text component changes (see Figure 1). The text component's document can initiate caret events when it inserts or removes text, for example.

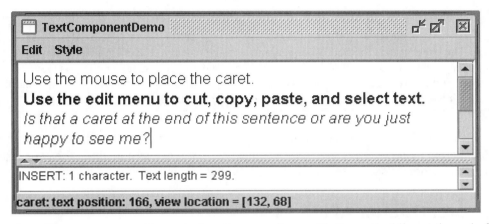

Figure 1   You can see a caret in use in TextComponentDemo—it's the vertical line at the end of the fourth line.

You can attach a caret listener to an instance of any `JTextComponent` subclass with the `addCaretListener` method.

Note: An alternate way of detecting caret changes is to attach a listener directly to the caret object itself rather than to the text component that manages the caret. A caret fires change events (not caret events), so you would need to write a change listener rather than a caret listener.

Here's the caret event-handling code from an application called `TextComponentDemo`.

```
//where initialization occurs
CaretListenerLabel caretListenerLabel =
    new CaretListenerLabel("Caret Status");
...
textPane.addActionListener(caretListenerLabel);
...
```

C

```
protected class CaretListenerLabel extends JLabel
                                implements CaretListener {
    ...
    public void caretUpdate(CaretEvent e) {
        //Get the location in the text
        int dot = e.getDot();
        int mark = e.getMark();
        ...
    }
}
```

Note: The caretUpdate method is not guaranteed to be called in the event-dispatching thread. To use any methods inside of caretUpdate that update the GUI, special handling is required to ensure that they are executed on the event-dispatching thread. You can do this by wrapping the code inside a Runnable and calling SwingUtilities.invokeLater on that Runnable.

You can find the full source code for the program and instructions for compiling and running it in Using Text Components (page 60) in Chapter 3. For a discussion about the caret listener aspect of the program see Listening for Caret and Selection Changes (page 74).

The Caret Listener API

The CaretListener interface has just one method (see Table 3), so it has no corresponding adapter class. Table 4 lists the methods in the CaretEvent class. Also see the CaretListener API documentation at: http://java.sun.com/j2se/1.4.2/docs/api/javax/swing/event/CaretListener.html. The CaretEvent API documentation is online at: http://java.sun.com/j2se/1.4.2/docs/api/javax/swing/event/CaretEvent.html.

Table 3: The CaretListener Interface

Method	Purpose
caretUpdate(CaretEvent)	Called when the caret in the listened-to component moves or when the selection in the listened-to component changes.

Table 4: The CaretEvent Class

Method	Purpose
`int getDot()`	Return the current location of the caret. If text is selected, the caret marks one end of the selection.
`int getMark()`	Return the other end of the selection. If nothing is selected, the value returned by this method is equal to the value returned by `getDot`. Note that the dot is not guaranteed to be less than the mark.
`Object getSource()` (*in* `java.util.EventObject`)	Return the object that fired the event.

Examples That Use Caret Listeners

The following examples use caret listeners.

Example	Where Described	Notes
`TextComponentDemo`	Listening for Caret and Selection Changes (page 74)	Uses a "listener label" to display caret and selection status.

How to Write a Change Listener

A change listener is similar to a property-change listener. A change listener is registered on an object—typically a component, but it could be another object, such as a model—and the listener is notified when the object has changed. The big difference from a property-change listener is that a change listener is not notified of *what* has changed, but simply that the source object *has* changed. Therefore, a change listener is most useful when it is only necessary to know when an object has changed in any way.

Three Swing components rely on change events for basic functionality—sliders, color choosers, and spinners. To learn when the value in a slider changes, you need to register a change listener. Similarly, you need to register a change listener on a color chooser to be informed when the user chooses a new color. You register a change listener on a spinner, a component introduced in release 1.4, to be notified when the spinner's value changes.

Here's an example of change event-handling code for a slider:[1]

```
//...where initialization occurs:
framesPerSecond.addChangeListener(new SliderListener());
...
class SliderListener implements ChangeListener {
    public void stateChanged(ChangeEvent e) {
        JSlider source = (JSlider)e.getSource();
        if (!source.getValueIsAdjusting()) {
            int fps = (int)source.getValue();
            ...
        }
    }
}
```

The Change Listener API

Because ChangeListener has only one method (see Table 5), it has no corresponding adapter class. Table 6 describes the method in the ChangeEvent class. Also see the Change-Listener API documentation at: http://java.sun.com/j2se/1.4.2/docs/api/javax/ swing/event/ChangeListener.html. The ChangeEvent API documentation is online at: http://java.sun.com/j2se/1.4.2/docs/api/javax/swing/event/ChangeEvent.html.

---

[1]   You can find the source file, SliderDemo.java, on the CD at: JavaTutorial/uiswing/components/ example-1dot4/index.html#SliderDemo.

Table 5: The ChangeListener Interface

Method	Purpose
stateChanged(ChangeEvent)	Called when the listened-to component changes state.

Table 6: The ChangeEvent Class

Method	Purpose
Object getSource() (*in* java.util.EventObject)	Return the object that fired the event.

Examples That Use Change Listeners

The following examples use change listeners.

Example	Where Described	Notes
SliderDemo and SliderDemo2 SliderDemo3	How to Use Sliders (page 348)	Registers a change listener on a slider that controls animation speed. The change listener ignores the change events until the user releases the slider.
ColorChooserDemo and ColorChooserDemo2	How to Use Color Choosers (page 167)	Uses a change listener on the selection model of a color chooser to learn when the user changes the current color.
SpinnerDemo3	Detecting Spinner Value Changes (page 363)	Uses a change listener on a date-field spinner to change the color of the text as the spinner's date changes.
SpinnerDemo4	Detecting Spinner Value Changes (page 363)	Uses a change listener on a spinner to cycle through the gray scale as the spinner's value changes.
ConverterRangeModel and its subclass, FollowerRangeModel	An Example: Converter (page 51)	Implements custom models for the sliders used in the Converter demo. Both models explicitly fire change events when necessary.

How to Write a Component Listener

One or more component events are fired by a Component object just after the component is hidden, made visible, moved, or resized. An example of a component listener might be in a GUI builder tool that's displaying information about the size of the currently selected component and needs to know when the component's size changes. You shouldn't need to use component events to manage basic layout and rendering.

The component-hidden and component-shown events occur only as the result of calls to a Component's setVisible method. For example, a window might be miniaturized into an icon (iconified) without a component-hidden event being fired.

Figure 2 demonstrates component events. The window contains a panel that has a label and a check box. The check box controls whether the label is visible. A text area displays a message every time the window, panel, label, or check box fires a component event.

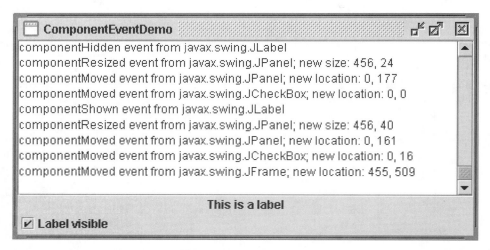

Figure 2   The ComponentEventDemo application.

Try This:

1. Run ComponentEventDemo using Java Web Start or compile and run the example.[1] When the window appears, one or more component-shown events have been fired.

---

[1] To run ComponentEventDemo using Java Web Start, click the ComponentEventDemo link on the RunExamples/events.html page on the CD. You can find the source files here: JavaTutorial/uiswing/events/example-1dot4/index.html#ComponentEventDemo.

2. Click the check box to hide the label. The label fires a component-hidden event. The panel fires component-moved and component-resized events. The check box fires a component-moved event.

3. Click the check box again to show the label. The label fires a component-shown event. The panel fires component-moved and component-resized events. The check box fires a component-moved event.

4. Iconify and then deiconify the window. You do *not* get component-hidden or -shown events. If you want to be notified of iconification events, you should use a window listener or a window state listener.

5. Resize the window. You'll see component-resized (and possibly component-moved) events from all four components—label, check box, panel, and frame. If the responsible layout managers didn't make every component as wide as possible, the panel, label, and check box wouldn't have been resized.

You can find the demo's code in ComponentEventDemo.java. Here's just the code related to handling component events:

```java
public class ComponentEventDemo ... implements ComponentListener {
    static JFrame frame;
    JLabel label;
    ...

    public ComponentEventDemo() {
        ...
        JPanel panel = new JPanel(new BorderLayout());
        label = new JLabel("This is a label", JLabel.CENTER);
        label.addComponentListener(this);
        panel.add(label, BorderLayout.CENTER);

        JCheckBox checkbox = new JCheckBox("Label visible", true);
        checkbox.addComponentListener(this);
        panel.add(checkbox, BorderLayout.PAGE_END);
        panel.addComponentListener(this);
        ...
        frame.addComponentListener(this);
    }
    ...

    public void componentHidden(ComponentEvent e) {
        displayMessage("componentHidden event from "
                    + e.getComponent().getClass().getName());
    }
```

```
    public void componentMoved(ComponentEvent e) {
        Component c = e.getComponent();
        displayMessage("componentMoved event from "
                    + c.getClass().getName()
                    + "; new location: "
                    + c.getLocation().x
                    + ", "
                    + c.getLocation().y);
    }

    public void componentResized(ComponentEvent e) {
        Component c = e.getComponent();
        displayMessage("componentResized event from "
                    + c.getClass().getName()
                    + "; new size: "
                    + c.getSize().width
                    + ", "
                    + c.getSize().height);
    }

    public void componentShown(ComponentEvent e) {
        displayMessage("componentShown event from "
                    + e.getComponent().getClass().getName());
    }

    //Where the GUI is initialized:
    JComponent newContentPane = new ComponentEventDemo();
    newContentPane.setOpaque(true); //content panes must be opaque
    frame.setContentPane(newContentPane);
    ...
}
```

The Component Listener API

Table 7 lists the methods in the ComponentListener interface and Table 8 describes the method in the ComponentEvent class. Also refer to the ComponentListener API documentation at: http://java.sun.com/j2se/1.4.2/docs/api/java/awt/event/Component-Event.html. The ComponentEvent API documentation is online at: http://java.sun.com/j2se/1.4.2/docs/api/java/awt/event/ComponentEvent.html.

Table 7: The ComponentListener Interface

(All these methods are also in the adapter class, ComponentAdapter.[a])

Method	Purpose
componentHidden(ComponentEvent)	Called after the listened-to component is hidden as the result of the setVisible method being called.
componentMoved(ComponentEvent)	Called after the listened-to component moves, relative to its container. For example, if a window is moved, the window fires a component-moved event, but the components it contains do not.
componentResized(ComponentEvent)	Called after the listened-to component's size (rectangular bounds) changes.
componentShown(ComponentEvent)	Called after the listened-to component becomes visible as the result of the setVisible method being called.

a. ComponentAdapter API documentation: http://java.sun.com/j2se/1.4.2/docs/api/java/awt/event/ComponentAdapter.html.

Table 8: The ComponentEvent Class

Method	Purpose
Component getComponent()	Return the component that fired the event. You can use this instead of the getSource method.

Examples That Use Component Listeners

The following examples use component listeners.

Example	Where Described	Notes
ComponentEventDemo	This section	Reports all component events that occur on several components to demonstrate the circumstances under which component events are fired.

How to Write a Container Listener

Container events are fired by a `Container` just after a component is added to or removed from the container. These events are for notification only—no container listener need be present for components to be successfully added or removed.

Figure 3 demonstrates container events. By clicking **Add a button** or **Remove a button**, you can add buttons to or remove them from a panel at the bottom of the window. Each time a button is added to or removed from the panel, the panel fires a container event, and the panel's container listener is notified. The listener displays descriptive messages in the text area at the top of the window.

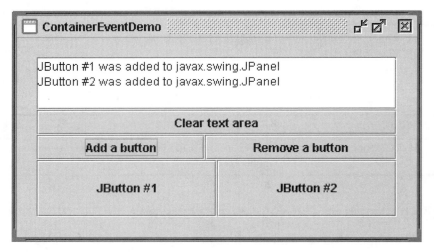

Figure 3   The `ContainerEventDemo` application.

Try This:

1. Run `ContainerEventDemo` using Java Web Start or compile and run the example yourself.[1]
2. Click the button labeled **Add a button**. You'll see a button appear near the bottom of the window. The container listener reacts to the resulting component-added event by displaying "`JButton #1 was added to javax.swing.JPanel`" at the top of the window.

---

[1]   To run `ContainerEventDemo` using Java Web Start, click the `ContainerEventDemo` link on the `RunEx-amples/events.html` page on the CD. You can find the source files here: `JavaTutorial/uiswing/events/example-1dot4/index.html#ContainerEventDemo`.

3. Click the button labeled **Remove a button**. This removes the most recently added button from the panel, causing the container listener to receive a component-removed event.

You can find the demo's code in `ContainerEventDemo.java`. Here's the demo's container event-handling code:

```
public class ContainerEventDemo ... implements ContainerListener ... {
    ...//where initialization occurs:
        buttonPanel = new JPanel(new GridLayout(1,1));
        buttonPanel.addContainerListener(this);
    ...

    public void componentAdded(ContainerEvent e) {
        displayMessage(" added to ", e);
    }

    public void componentRemoved(ContainerEvent e) {
        displayMessage(" removed from ", e);
    }

    void displayMessage(String action, ContainerEvent e) {
        display.append(((JButton)e.getChild()).getText()
                        + " was"
                        + action
                        + e.getContainer().getClass().getName()
                        + newline);
    }
    ...
}
```

The Container Listener API

Table 9 lists the methods in the `ContainerListener` interface and Table 10 describes the methods in the `ContainerEvent` class. Also refer to the API documentation for `ContainerListener` at: http://java.sun.com/j2se/1.4.2/docs/api/java/awt/event/ContainerListener.html. The API documentation for `ContainerEvent` is online at: http://java.sun.com/j2se/1.4.2/docs/api/java/awt/event/ContainerEvent.html.

C

Event Listeners

Table 9: The ContainerListener Interface

(The corresponding adapter class is ContainerAdapter.[a])

Method	Purpose
componentAdded(ContainerEvent)	Called just after a component is added to the listened-to container.
componentRemoved(ContainerEvent)	Called just after a component is removed from the listened-to container.

a. ContainerAdapter API documentation: http://java.sun.com/j2se/1.4.2/docs/api/java/awt/event/ContainerAdapter.html.

Table 10: The ContainerEvent Class

Method	Purpose
Component getChild()	Return the component whose addition or removal triggered this event.
Container getContainer()	Return the container that fired this event. You can use this instead of the getSource method.

Examples That Use Container Listeners

The following examples use container listeners.

Example	Where Described	Notes
ContainerEventDemo	This section	Reports all container events that occur on a single panel to demonstrate the circumstances under which container events are fired.

How to Write a Document Listener

A Swing text component uses a Document[1] to hold and edit its text. Document events occur when the content of a document changes in any way. You attach a document listener to a text component's document rather than to the text component itself. For more information, see Implementing a Document Filter (page 72) in Chapter 3.

Figure 4 demonstrates document events on two plain text components.

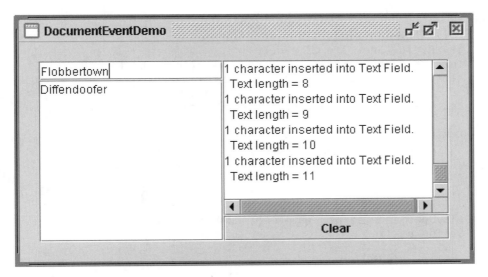

Figure 4   The DocumentEventDemo application.

Try This:

1. Run DocumentEventDemo using Java Web Start or compile and run the example yourself.[2]
2. Type in the text field at the upper left of the window or the text area beneath the text field. One document event is fired for each character typed.
3. Delete text with the backspace key. One document event is fired for each backspace key pressed.

---

[1] Document API documentation: `http://java.sun.com/j2se/1.4.2/docs/api/javax/swing/text/Document.html`.

[2] To run DocumentEventDemo using Java Web Start, click the DocumentEventDemo link on the RunExamples/events.html page on the CD. You can find the source files here: `JavaTutorial/uiswing/events/example-1dot4/index.html#DocumentEventDemo`.

4. Select text and then delete it by pressing Backspace or by using a keyboard command such as CTRL-X (cut). One document event is fired for the entire deletion.

5. Copy text from one text component into the other using keyboard commands such as CTRL-C (copy) and CTRL-V (paste). One document event is fired for the entire paste operation regardless of the length of the text pasted. If text is selected in the target text component before the paste command is issued, an additional document event is fired because the selected text is deleted first.

You can find the demo's code in `DocumentEventDemo.java`. Here's the demo's document event-handling code:

```
public class DocumentEventDemo ... {
    ...//where initialization occurs:
    textField = new JTextField(20);
    textField.addActionListener(new MyTextActionListener());
    textField.getDocument().addDocumentListener(
                                    new MyDocumentListener());
    textField.getDocument().putProperty("name", "Text Field");

    textArea = new JTextArea();
    textArea.getDocument().addDocumentListener(
                                    new MyDocumentListener());
    textArea.getDocument().putProperty("name", "Text Area");
    ...

class MyDocumentListener implements DocumentListener {
    String newline = "\n";

    public void insertUpdate(DocumentEvent e) {
        updateLog(e, "inserted into");
    }
    public void removeUpdate(DocumentEvent e) {
        updateLog(e, "removed from");
    }
    public void changedUpdate(DocumentEvent e) {
        //Plain text components don't fire these events
    }

    public void updateLog(DocumentEvent e, String action) {
        Document doc = (Document)e.getDocument();
        int changeLength = e.getLength();
        displayArea.append(
            changeLength + " character" +
            ((changeLength == 1) ? " " : "s ") +
            action + doc.getProperty("name") + "." + newline +
            "  Text length = " + doc.getLength() + newline);
    }
}
```

Document listeners shouldn't modify the contents of the document. The change is already complete by the time the listener is notified of the change. Instead, write a custom document that overrides the `insertString` or `remove` methods, or both. See Listening for Changes on a Document (page 73) in Chapter 3 for details.

The Document Listener API

Tables 9 and 10 list the methods in the `DocumentListener` and `DocumentEvent` interfaces. Also refer to the `DocumentListener` API documentation online at: `http://java.sun.com/j2se/1.4.2/docs/api/javax/swing/event/DocumentListener.html`. The Document-Event API documentation is online at: `http://java.sun.com/j2se/1.4.2/docs/api/javax/swing/event/DocumentEvent.html`.

Table 11: The DocumentListener Interface
(DocumentListener has no adapter class.)

Method	Purpose
`changedUpdate(DocumentEvent)`	Called when the style of some of the text in the listened-to document changes. This sort of event is fired only from a `StyledDocument`—a `PlainDocument` does not fire these events.
`insertUpdate(DocumentEvent)`	Called when text is inserted into the listened-to document.
`removeUpdate(DocumentEvent)`	Called when text is removed from the listened-to document.

Table 12: The DocumentEvent Interface[a]

Method	Purpose
`Document getDocument()`	Return the document that fired the event. Note that the `DocumentEvent` interface does not inherit from `EventObject`. Therefore, it does not inherit the `getSource` method.
`int getLength()`	Return the length of the change.
`int getOffset()`	Return the location within the document of the first character changed.
`ElementChange getChange(Element)`	Return details about what elements in the document have changed and how. `ElementChange` is an interface defined within the `DocumentEvent` interface.
`EventType getType()`	Return the type of change that occurred. `EventType` is a class defined within the `DocumentEvent` interface that enumerates the possible changes that can occur on a document: insert text, remove text, and change text style.

a. Each document event method is passed an object that implements the `DocumentEvent` interface. Typically, this is an instance of `DefaultDocumentEvent`, defined in `AbstractDocument`.

Examples That Use Document Listeners

The following examples use document listeners.

Example	Where Described	Notes
DocumentEventDemo	This section	Reports all document events that occur on the documents for both a text field and a text area. One listener listens to both text components and uses a client property on the document to determine which component fired the event.
TextComponentDemo	Listening for Changes on a Document (page 73)	Updates a change log every time text in the listened-to document changes.
ListDemo	How to Use Lists (page 267)	Has an event listener that implements both the DocumentListener and the ActionListener interfaces. As a document listener, it's used to disable a particular button when the text field is empty, and to enable the button when the text field contains characters.

How to Write a Focus Listener

Focus events are fired whenever a component gains or loses the keyboard focus. This is true whether the change in focus occurs through the mouse, the keyboard, or programmatically. If you're unfamiliar with basic focus concepts or want detailed information about focus, see How to Use the Focus Subsystem (page 583) in Chapter 9.

This section explains how to get focus events for a particular component by registering a FocusListener[1] on it. If you're only interested in focus events for windows, you might want to implement a WindowFocusListener instead. If you need to know the focus status of many components, consider implementing a PropertyChangeListener on the Keyboard-FocusManager, as described in Tracking Focus Changes to Multiple Components (page 595) in Chapter 9.

Figure 5 demonstrates focus events.

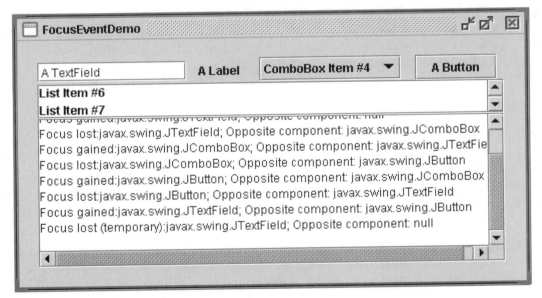

Figure 5   The FocusEventDemo application.

---

[1] FocusListener API documentation: http://java.sun.com/j2se/1.4.2/docs/api/java/awt/event/FocusListener.html.

Version Note: The focus subsystem was completely rearchitected in release 1.4. This section uses concepts and methods introduced in that release.

The window displays a variety of components. A focus listener, registered on each component, reports every focus-gained and focus-lost event. For each event, the other component involved in the focus change, the *opposite component*, is reported. For example, when the focus goes from a button to a text field, a focus-lost event is fired by the button (with the text field as the opposite component) and then a focus-gained event is fired by the text field (with the button as the opposite component). Focus-lost events can be temporary, which occurs when the window loses the focus, for example.

Try This:

1. Run FocusEventDemo using Java Web Start or compile and run the example yourself.[1]

2. You'll see a "Focus gained: JTextField" message in the text area—its opposite component is null, since it is the first component to have the focus.

3. Click the label. Nothing happens because the label, by default, can't get the focus.

4. Click the combo box. A focus-lost event is fired by the text field and a focus-gained event by the combo box. The combo box now shows that it has the focus, perhaps with a dotted line around the text—exactly how this is represented is look and feel dependent. Notice that when the focus changes from one component to another, the first component fires a focus-lost event before the second component fires a focus-gained event.

5. Select a choice from the combo box's menu. Click the combo box again. Notice that no focus event is reported. As long as the user manipulates the same component, the focus stays on that component.

6. Click the text area where the focus events are printed. Nothing happens because the text area has been rendered unclickable with setRequestFocusEnabled(false).

7. Click the text field to return the focus to the initial component.

8. Press Tab on the keyboard. The focus moves to the combo box and skips over the label.

9. Press Tab again. The focus moves to the button.

10. Click another window so that the FocusEventDemo window loses the focus. A temporary focus-lost event is generated for the button.

---

[1] To run FocusEventDemo using Java Web Start, click the FocusEventDemo link on the RunExamples/ events.html page on the CD. You can find the source files here: JavaTutorial/uiswing/events/ example-1dot4/index.html#FocusEventDemo.

11. Click the top of the FocusEventDemo window. A focus-gained event is fired by the button.

12. Press Tab on the keyboard. The focus moves to the list.

13. Press Tab again. The focus moves to the text area. Notice that even though you can't click on the text area, you can tab to it. This is so users who use assistive technologies can determine that a component is there and what it contains. The demo disables click to focus for the text area, while retaining its tab-to-focus capability, by invoking set-RequestFocusEnabled(false) on the text area. The demo could use setFocusable(false) to truly remove the text area from the focus cycle, but that would have the unfortunate effect of making the component unavailable to those who use assistive technologies.

14. Press Tab again. The focus moves from the list back to the text field. You have just completed a *focus cycle*. See the introduction in How to Use the Focus Subsystem (page 583) in Chapter 9 for a discussion of focus terminology and concepts.

You can find the demo's code in FocusEventDemo.java. Here's the code that's related to focus-event handling:

```
public class FocusEventDemo ... implements FocusListener ... {
    public FocusEventDemo() {
        ...
        JTextField textField = new JTextField("A TextField");
        textField.addFocusListener(this);

        ...
        JLabel label = new JLabel("A Label");
        label.addFocusListener(this);

        ...
        JComboBox comboBox = new JComboBox(vector);
        comboBox.addFocusListener(this);

        ...
        JButton button = new JButton("A Button");
        button.addFocusListener(this);

        ...
        JList list = new JList(listVector);
        list.setSelectedIndex(1); //It's easier to see the focus change
                                  //if an item is selected.
        list.addFocusListener(this);
        JScrollPane listScrollPane = new JScrollPane(list);
        //We want to prevent the list's scroll bars from getting the
        //focus--even with the keyboard. Note that in general we prefer
        //setRequestFocusable over setFocusable for reasons of
        //accessibility, but this is to work around bug #4866958.
        listScrollPane.getVerticalScrollBar().setFocusable(false);
        listScrollPane.getHorizontalScrollBar().setFocusable(false);
        ...
```

```
        //Set up the area that reports focus-gained and focus-lost events.
        display = new JTextArea();
        display.setEditable(false);
        //The method setRequestFocusEnabled prevents a
        //component from being clickable, but it can still
        //get the focus through the keyboard - this ensures
        //user accessibility.
        display.setRequestFocusEnabled(false);
        display.addFocusListener(this);
        JScrollPane displayScrollPane = new JScrollPane(display);

        //Work around for bug #4866958.
        displayScrollPane.getHorizontalScrollBar().setFocusable(false);
        displayScrollPane.getVerticalScrollBar().setFocusable(false);
        ...
    }
    ...
    public void focusGained(FocusEvent e) {
        displayMessage("Focus gained", e);
    }

    public void focusLost(FocusEvent e) {
        displayMessage("Focus lost", e);
    }

    void displayMessage(String prefix, FocusEvent e) {
        display.append(prefix
                + (e.isTemporary() ? " (temporary):" : ":")
                +  e.getComponent().getClass().getName()
                + "; Opposite component: "
                + (e.getOppositeComponent != null ?
                 e.getOppositeComponent().getClass().getName() : "null")
                + newline);
    }
    ...
}
```

The Focus Listener API

Table 13 lists the methods in the FocusListener interface and Table 14 describes the methods in the FocusEvent class. Also refer to the FocusListener API documentation at: http://java.sun.com/j2se/1.4.2/docs/api/java/awt/event/FocusListener.html.

The FocusEvent API documentation is online at: `http://java.sun.com/j2se/1.4.2/docs/api/java/awt/event/FocusEvent.html`.

Table 13: The FocusListener Interface

(The corresponding adapter class is FocusAdapter.[a])

Method	Purpose
`focusGained(FocusEvent)`	Called just after the listened-to component gets the focus.
`focusLost(FocusEvent)`	Called just after the listened-to component loses the focus.

a. FocusAdapter API documentation: `http://java.sun.com/j2se/1.4.2/docs/api/java/awt/event/FocusAdapter.html`.

Table 14: The FocusEvent Class

Method	Purpose
`boolean isTemporary()`	Return true if a focus-lost event is temporary. This occurs, for example, when the component's window loses the focus.
`Component getComponent()` (*in* `java.awt.event.ComponentEvent`)	Return the component that fired the focus event.
`Component getOppositeComponent()`	Return the other component involved in the focus change. For a `FOCUS_GAINED` event, this is the component that lost the focus. For a `FOCUS_LOST` event, this is the component that gained the focus. If the focus change involves a native application, a Java application in a different VM or context, or no other component, then null is returned. This method was introduced in release 1.4.

Examples That Use Focus Listeners

The following examples use focus listeners.

Example	Where Described	Notes
FocusEventDemo	This section	Reports all focus events that occur on several components to demonstrate the circumstances under which focus events are fired.
TrackFocusDemo	How to Use the Focus Subsystem (page 583)	The custom component, `Picture`, implements a focus listener to draw a red border around the component when it is the current focus owner.

How to Write an Internal Frame Listener

An InternalFrameListener[1] is similar to a WindowListener. Like the window listener, the internal frame listener listens for events that occur when the "window" has been shown for the first time, disposed of, iconified, deiconified, activated, or deactivated. Before using an internal frame listener, please familiarize yourself with the WindowListener interface in How to Write Window Listeners (page 723).

The application shown in Figure 6 demonstrates internal frame events. The application listens for internal frame events from the Event Generator frame, displaying a message that describes each event.

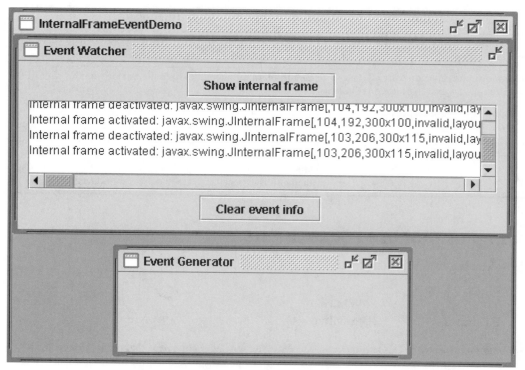

Figure 6   The InternalFrameEventDemo application.

---

[1] InternalFrameListener API documentation: http://java.sun.com/j2se/1.4.2/docs/api/javax/swing/event/InternalFrameListener.html.

Try This:

1. Run `InternalFrameEventDemo` using Java Web Start or compile and run the example yourself.[1]

2. Bring up the Event Generator internal frame by clicking the **Show internal frame** button. You should see an "`Internal frame opened`" message in the display area.

3. Try various operations to see what happens. For example, click the Event Generator so that it gets activated. Click the Event Watcher so that the Event Generator gets deactivated. Click the Event Generator's decorations to iconify, maximize, minimize, and close the window. See How to Write Window Listeners (page 723) for information on what kinds of events you'll see.

Here's the internal frame event-handling code:

```
public class InternalFrameEventDemo ...
                    implements InternalFrameListener ... {
    ...

    public void internalFrameClosing(InternalFrameEvent e) {
        displayMessage("Internal frame closing", e);
    }

    public void internalFrameClosed(InternalFrameEvent e) {
        displayMessage("Internal frame closed", e);
        listenedToWindow = null;
    }

    public void internalFrameOpened(InternalFrameEvent e) {
        displayMessage("Internal frame opened", e);
    }

    public void internalFrameIconified(InternalFrameEvent e) {
        displayMessage("Internal frame iconified", e);
    }

    public void internalFrameDeiconified(InternalFrameEvent e) {
        displayMessage("Internal frame deiconified", e);
    }

    public void internalFrameActivated(InternalFrameEvent e) {
        displayMessage("Internal frame activated", e);
    }
```

---

[1] To run `InternalFrameEventDemo` using Java Web Start, click the `InternalFrameEventDemo` link on the `RunExamples/events.html` page on the CD. You can find the source files here: `JavaTutorial/uiswing/events/example-1dot4/index.html#InternalFrameEventDemo`.

```
public void internalFrameDeactivated(InternalFrameEvent e) {
    displayMessage("Internal frame deactivated", e);
}

void displayMessage(String prefix, InternalFrameEvent e) {
    String s = prefix + ": " + e.getSource();
    display.append(s + newline);
}

public void actionPerformed(ActionEvent e) {
    if (SHOW.equals(e.getActionCommand())) {
        ...
        if (listenedToWindow == null) {
            listenedToWindow = new JInternalFrame("Event Generator",
                                      true,  //resizable
                                      true,  //closable
                                      true,  //maximizable
                                      true); //iconifiable
            //We want to reuse the internal frame, so we need to
            //make it hide (instead of being disposed of, which is
            //the default) when the user closes it.
            listenedToWindow.setDefaultCloseOperation(
                              WindowConstants.HIDE_ON_CLOSE);

            listenedToWindow.addInternalFrameListener(this);
            ...
        }
    }
    ...
}
}
```

The Internal Frame Listener API

Table 15 lists the methods in the InternalFrameListener interface; its corresponding adapter class is InternalFrameAdapter.[1] Also refer to the InternalFrameListener API documentation at: http://java.sun.com/j2se/1.4.2/docs/api/javax/swing/event/ InternalFrameListener.html.

Each internal frame event method has a single parameter: an InternalFrameEvent[2] object. The InternalFrameEvent class defines no generally useful methods. To get the internal frame that fired the event, use the getSource method, which InternalFrameEvent inherits from java.util.EventObject.

---

[1] InternalFrameAdapter API documentation: http://java.sun.com/j2se/1.4.2/docs/api/ javax/swing/event/InternalFrameAdapter.html.

[2] InternalFrameEvent API documentation: http://java.sun.com/j2se/1.4.2/docs/api/javax/ swing/event/InternalFrameEvent.html.

Table 15: The InternalFrameListener Interface

Method	Purpose
`internalFrameOpened(` `        InternalFrameEvent)`	Called just after the listened-to internal frame has been shown for the first time.
`internalFrameClosing(` `        InternalFrameEvent)`	Called in response to a user request that the listened-to internal frame be closed. By default, `JInternalFrame` hides the window when the user closes it. Use the `JInternalFrame` `setDefaultCloseOperation` method to specify another option, which must be either `DISPOSE_ON_CLOSE` or `DO_NOTHING_ON_CLOSE` (both defined in `WindowConstants`, an interface that `JInternalFrame` implements). Or by implementing an `internalFrameClosing` method in the internal frame's listener, you can add custom behavior (such as bringing up dialogs or saving data) to internal frame closing.
`internalFrameClosed(` `        InternalFrameEvent)`	Called just after the listened-to internal frame has been disposed of.

`internalFrameIconified(`
`        InternalFrameEvent)`
`internalFrameDeiconified(`
`        InternalFrameEvent)`
	Called just after the listened-to internal frame is iconified or deiconified, respectively.

`internalFrameActivated(`
`        InternalFrameEvent)`
`internalFrameDeactivated(`
`        InternalFrameEvent)`
	Called just after the listened-to internal frame is activated or deactivated, respectively.

Examples That Use Internal Frame Listeners

Just one of this book's examples uses internal frame listeners. However, internal frame listeners are similar to `WindowListeners`, which several Swing programs have.

Example	Where Described	Notes
InternalFrameEventDemo	This section	Reports all internal frame events that occur on one internal frame to demonstrate the circumstances under which internal frame events are fired.
DialogDemo	Using Text Components (page 60)	`CustomDialog.java` uses `setDefaultClose-Operation` and not a window listener to determine what action to take when a window closes.
SliderDemo	How to Use Sliders (page 348)	Listens for window iconify and deiconify events, so that it stops animation when the window isn't visible.

Event Listeners

How to Write an Item Listener

Item events are fired by components that implement the `ItemSelectable` interface.[1] Generally, `ItemSelectable` components maintain on/off state for one or more items. The Swing components that fire item events include check boxes, check box menu items, and combo boxes.

Here's some item event-handling code taken from `ComponentEventDemo.java`:[2]

```
//Where initialization occurs:
checkbox.addItemListener(this);
...

public void itemStateChanged(ItemEvent e) {
    if (e.getStateChange() == ItemEvent.SELECTED) {
        label.setVisible(true);
        ...
    } else {
        label.setVisible(false);
    }
}
```

The Item Listener API

Table 16 lists the methods in the `ItemListener` interface and Table 17 describes the methods in the `ItemEvent` class. Because `ItemListener` has only one method, it has no corresponding adapter class. Also refer to the API documentation for the `ItemListener` interface online at: http://java.sun.com/j2se/1.4.2/docs/api/java/awt/event/ItemListener.html. The API documentation for `ItemEvent` is online at: http://java.sun.com/j2se/1.4.2/docs/api/java/awt/event/ItemEvent.html.

Table 16: The ItemListener Interface

Method	Purpose
`itemStateChanged(ItemEvent)`	Called just after a state change in the listened-to component.

---

[1] `ItemSelectable` API documentation: http://java.sun.com/j2se/1.4.2/docs/api/java/awt/ItemSelectable.html.

[2] This source code is on the CD at: `JavaTutorial/uiswing/events/example-1dot4/ComponentEventDemo.java`.

Table 17: The ItemEvent Class

Method	Purpose
`Object getItem()`	Return the component-specific object associated with the item whose state changed. Often this is a `String` containing the text on the selected item.
`ItemSelectable get-ItemSelectable()`	Return the component that fired the item event. You can use this instead of the `getSource` method.
`int getStateChange()`	Return the new state of the item. The `ItemEvent` class defines two states: `SELECTED` and `DESELECTED`.

Examples That Use Item Listeners

The following table lists some examples that use item listeners.

Example	Where Described	Notes
`ComponentEventDemo`	This section and How to Write a Component Listener (page 654)	Listens for item events on a check box, which determines whether a label is visible.
`CheckBoxDemo`	How to Use Check Boxes (page 163)	Four check boxes share one item listener, which uses `getItemSelected` to determine which check box fired the event.
`MenuDemo`	How to Use Menus (page 277)	Listens for item events on a check box menu item.
`ScrollDemo`	How to Use Scroll Panes (page 325)	Listens for item events on a toggle button.

Event Listeners

How to Write a Key Listener

Key events tell you when the user is typing at the keyboard. Specifically, key events are fired by the component with the keyboard focus when the user presses or releases keyboard keys. For more information, see How to Use the Focus Subsystem (page 583) in Chapter 9.

Note: For reacting in a special way to particular keys, you usually should use key bindings instead of a key listener. See How to Use Key Bindings (page 623) in Chapter 9.

You can be notified about two basic kinds of key events: the typing of a Unicode character, and the pressing or releasing of a key on the keyboard. The first kind of event is called a *key-typed* event. The second kind is either a *key-pressed* or *key-released* event.

In general, you should try to handle only key-typed events unless you need to know when the user presses keys that don't correspond to characters. For example, if you want to know when the user types some Unicode character—whether as the result of pressing one key such as 'A' or from pressing several keys in sequence—you should handle key-typed events. On the other hand, if you want to know when the user presses the F1 key, or whether the user pressed the '3' key on the number pad, you need to handle key-pressed events.

Note: To fire keyboard events, a component *must* have the keyboard focus.

To make a component get the keyboard focus, follow these steps:

1. Make sure the component's `isFocusable` method returns `true`. This allows the component to receive the focus. For example, you can enable keyboard focus for a `JLabel` by calling `setFocusable(true)` on the label.

2. Make sure the component requests the focus when appropriate. For custom components, you'll probably need to implement a mouse listener that calls the `requestFocusInWindow` method when the component is clicked.

Version Note: This section reflects the focus API introduced in released 1.4. As of that release, the focus subsystem consumes focus traversal keys, such as Tab and Shift Tab. If you need to prevent the focus traversal keys from being consumed, you can call

    `component.setFocusTraversalKeysEnabled(false)`

on the component that is firing the key events. Your program must then handle focus traversal on its own. Alternatively, you can use a `KeyEventDispatcher` to prelisten to all key events. How to Write a Focus Listener (page 665) has detailed information on the focus subsystem.

You can obtain detailed information about a particular key-pressed event. For example, you can query a key-pressed event to determine if it was fired from an action key. Examples of action keys include Copy, Paste, Page Up, Undo, and the arrow and function keys. As of release 1.4, you can also query a key-pressed or key-released event to determine the location of the key that fired the event. Most key events are fired from the standard keyboard, but the events for some keys, such as Shift, have information on whether the user pressed the Shift key on the left or the right side of the keyboard. Likewise, the number '2' can be typed from either the standard keyboard or from the number pad.

For key-typed events you can get the key character value as well as any modifiers used.

Note: You shouldn't rely on the key character value returned from getKeyChar unless it's involved in a key-typed event.

Figure 7 demonstrates key events. It consists of a text field that you can type into, followed by a text area that displays a message every time the text field fires a key event. A button at the bottom of the window lets you clear both the text field and text area.

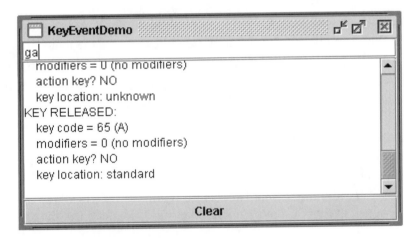

Figure 7   The KeyEventDemo application.

Try This:

1. Run KeyEventDemo using Java Web Start or compile and run the example yourself.[1]

---

[1] To run KeyEventDemo using Java Web Start, click the KeyEventDemo link on the RunExamples/events.html page on the CD. You can find the source files here: JavaTutorial/uiswing/events/example-1dot4/index.html#KeyEventDemo.

2. Type a lowercase 'a' by pressing and releasing the A key on the keyboard. The text field fires three events: a key-pressed event, a key-typed event, and a key-released event. Note that the key-typed event doesn't have key code information, and key-pressed and key-released events don't have key character information. None of the events so far are from modifier or action keys and the key location, reported on the key-pressed and key-released events, is most likely standard.

3. Press the Clear button. You might want to do this after each of the following steps.

4. Press and release the Shift key. The text field fires two events: a key pressed and a key released. The text field doesn't fire a key-typed event because Shift, by itself, doesn't correspond to any character.

5. Type an uppercase 'A' by pressing the Shift and A keys. You'll see the following events, although perhaps not in this order: key pressed (Shift), key pressed (A), key typed ('A'), key released (A), key released (Shift). Note that Shift is listed as the modifier key for the key-typed and key-pressed events.

6. Type an uppercase 'A' by pressing and releasing the Caps Lock key, and then pressing the A key. You should see these events: key pressed (Caps Lock), key pressed (A), key typed ('A'), key released (A). Note that Caps Lock is *not* listed as a modifier key.

7. Press the Tab key. No Tab key-pressed or key-released events are received by the key event listener. This is because the focus subsystem consumes focus traversal keys, such as Tab and Shift Tab. Press Tab twice more to return the focus to the text area.

8. Press a function key, such as F3. You'll see that the function key is an action key.

9. Press the left Shift key, followed by the right Shift key. The key-pressed and key-released events indicate which Shift key was typed.

10. Press the Num Lock key if your keyboard has a number pad. As for Caps Lock, there is a key-pressed event, but no key-released event.

11. Press the '2' key on the number pad. You see the key-pressed, key-typed, and key-released events for the number '2.'

12. Press the '2' key on the standard keyboard. Again, you see the three event messages. The key-typed events for both number 2 keys are identical. But the key-pressed and key-released events indicate different key codes and different key locations.

13. Press the Num Lock key again. A key-released event is fired.

You can find the example's code in `KeyEventDemo.java`. Here's the demo's key event-handling code:

```
public class KeyEventDemo ...  implements KeyListener ... {
    ...//where initialization occurs:
        typingArea = new JTextField(20);
        typingArea.addKeyListener(this);
```

```
        //Uncomment this if you wish to turn off focus traversal. The
        //focus subsystem consumes focus traversal keys, such as Tab
        //and Shift Tab. If you uncomment the following line of code,
        //this disables focus traversal and the Tab events become
        //available to this the key event listener.
        //typingArea.setFocusTraversalKeysEnabled(false);
    ...

    /** Handle the key typed event from the text field. */
    public void keyTyped(KeyEvent e) {
        displayInfo(e, "KEY TYPED: ");
    }

    /** Handle the key pressed event from the text field. */
    public void keyPressed(KeyEvent e) {
        displayInfo(e, "KEY PRESSED: ");
    }

    /** Handle the key released event from the text field. */
    public void keyReleased(KeyEvent e) {
        displayInfo(e, "KEY RELEASED: ");
    }
    ...

    protected void displayInfo(KeyEvent e, String s){
        ...
        //You should only rely on the key char if the event
        //is a key typed event.
        int id = e.getID();
        if (id == KeyEvent.KEY_TYPED) {
            char c = e.getKeyChar();
            keyString = "key character = '" + c + "'";
        } else {
            int keyCode = e.getKeyCode();
            keyString = "key code = " + keyCode
                        + " ("
                        + KeyEvent.getKeyText(keyCode)
                        + ")";
        }

        int modifiers = e.getModifiersEx();
        modString = "modifiers = " + modifiers;
        tmpString = KeyEvent.getModifiersExText(modifiers);
        if (tmpString.length() > 0) {
            modString += " (" + tmpString + ")";
        } else {
            modString += " (no modifiers)";
        }
```

```
actionString = "action key? ";
if (e.isActionKey()) {
    actionString += "YES";
} else {
    actionString += "NO";
}

locationString = "key location: ";
int location = e.getKeyLocation();
if (location == KeyEvent.KEY_LOCATION_STANDARD) {
    locationString += "standard";
} else if (location == KeyEvent.KEY_LOCATION_LEFT) {
    locationString += "left";
} else if (location == KeyEvent.KEY_LOCATION_RIGHT) {
    locationString += "right";
} else if (location == KeyEvent.KEY_LOCATION_NUMPAD) {
    locationString += "numpad";
} else { // (location == KeyEvent.KEY_LOCATION_UNKNOWN)
    locationString += "unknown";
}
.../Display information about the KeyEvent...
    }
}
```

The Key Listener API

Table 18 lists the methods in the KeyListener interface and Table 19 lists the methods in the KeyEvent class. Also refer to the KeyListener API documentation at: http://java.sun. com/j2se/1.4.2/docs/api/java/awt/event/KeyListener.html. The KeyEvent API documentation is online at: http://java.sun.com/j2se/1.4.2/docs/api/java/awt/ event/KeyEvent.html.

Table 18: The KeyListener Interface

(The corresponding adapter class is KeyAdapter.[a])

Method	Purpose
keyTyped(KeyEvent)	Called just after the user types a Unicode character into the listened-to component.
keyPressed(KeyEvent)	Called just after the user presses a key while the listened-to component has the focus.
keyReleased(KeyEvent)	Called just after the user releases a key while the listened-to component has the focus.

a. KeyAdapter API documentation: http://java.sun.com/j2se/1.4.2/docs/api/java/awt/ event/KeyAdapter.html.

Table 19: The KeyEvent Class[a]

Method	Purpose
`int getKeyChar()`	Get the Unicode character associated with this event. Only rely on this value for key-typed events.
`int getKeyCode()`	Get the key code associated with this event. The key code identifies the particular key on the keyboard that the user pressed or released. The `KeyEvent` class defines many key code constants for commonly seen keys. For example, VK_A specifies the key labeled A, and VK_ESCAPE specifies the Escape key.
`String getKeyText(int)` `String getKeyModifiersText(int)`	Return text descriptions of the event's key code and modifier keys, respectively. Note that the `InputEvent` methods `getModifiersEx` and `getModifiersExText`, introduced in release 1.4, provide more information about the key event than `getModifiers`, `getKeyText`, and `getKeyModifiersText`. For this reason, the 1.4 methods are preferred.
`boolean isActionKey()`	Return true if the key firing the event is an action key. Examples of action keys include Cut, Copy, Paste, Page Up, Caps Lock, and the arrow and function keys. This information is valid only for key-pressed and key-released events.
`int getKeyLocation()`	Return the location of the key that fired this event. This method provides a way to distinguish keys that occur more than once on a keyboard, such as the two shift keys, for example. The possible values are KEY_LOCATION_STANDARD, KEY_LOCATION_LEFT, KEY_LOCATION_RIGHT, KEY_LOCATION_NUMPAD, or KEY_LOCATION_UNKNOWN. This method always returns KEY_LOCATION_UNKNOWN for key-typed events. Introduced in release 1.4.

a. The `KeyEvent` class inherits many useful methods from the `InputEvent` class, such as `get-ModifiersEx`, and a couple useful methods from the `ComponentEvent` and `AWTEvent` classes. See Table 26, "The InputEvent Class," on page 693 for a complete list.

Examples That Use Key Listeners

The following examples use key listeners.

Example	Where Described	Notes
`KeyEventDemo`	This section	Reports all key events that occur on a text field to demonstrate the circumstances under which key events are fired.

How to Write a List Data Listener

List data events occur when the contents of a mutable list change. Since the model—not the component—fires these events, you have to register a list data listener with the list model. If you haven't explicitly created a list with a mutable list model, then your list is immutable and its model will not fire these events.

Note: Combo box models also fire list data events. However, you normally don't need to know about them unless you're creating a custom combo box model.

Figure 8 demonstrates list data events on a mutable list:

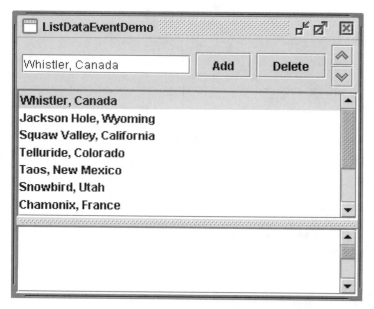

Figure 8   The ListDataEventDemo application.

Try This:

1. Run ListDataEventDemo using Java Web Start or compile and run the example your-self.[1]

---

[1] To run ListDataEventDemo using Java Web Start, click the ListDataEventDemo link on the RunExamples/events.html page on the CD. You can find the source files here: JavaTutorial/uiswing/events/example-1dot4/index.html#ListDataEventDemo.

2. Type in the name of your favorite ski resort and click the **Add** button. An `interval-Added` event is fired.

3. Select a few continguous items in the list and click the **Delete** button. An `interval-Removed` event is fired.

4. Select one item and move it up or down in the list with the arrow buttons. Two `contentsChanged` events are fired—one for the item that moved and one for the item that was displaced.

You can find the demo's code in `ListDataEventDemo.java`. Here's the code that registers a list data listener on the list model and implements the listener:

```
//...where member variables are declared...
private DefaultListModel listModel;
...
//Create and populate the list model
listModel = new DefaultListModel();
...
listModel.addListDataListener(new MyListDataListener());

class MyListDataListener implements ListDataListener {
    public void contentsChanged(ListDataEvent e) {
        log.append("contentsChanged: " + e.getIndex0() +
                   ", " + e.getIndex1() + newline);
    }
    public void intervalAdded(ListDataEvent e) {
        log.append("intervalAdded: " + e.getIndex0() +
                   ", " + e.getIndex1() + newline);
    }
    public void intervalRemoved(ListDataEvent e) {
        log.append("intervalRemoved: " + e.getIndex0() +
                   ", " + e.getIndex1() + newline);
    }
}
```

The List Data Listener API

Table 20 lists the methods in the `ListDataListener` interface and Table 21 describes the methods in the `ListDataEvent` class. Note that `ListDataListener` has no corresponding adapter class. Also refer to the `ListDataListener` API documentation at: `http://java.sun.com/j2se/1.4.2/docs/api/javax/swing/event/ListDataListener.html`. The API documentation for `ListDataEvent` is online at: `http://java.sun.com/j2se/1.4.2/docs/api/javax/swing/event/ListDataEvent.html`.

Table 20: The ListDataListener Interface

Method	Purpose
`intervalAdded(ListDataEvent)`	Called when one or more items have been added to the list.
`intervalRemoved(ListDataEvent)`	Called when one or more items have been removed from the list.
`contentsChanged(ListDataEvent)`	Called when contents of one or more items in the list have changed.

Table 21: The ListDataEvent API

Method	Purpose
`Object getSource()` (*in* `java.util.EventObject`)	Return the object that fired the event.
`int getIndex0()`	Return the index of the first item whose value has changed.
`int getIndex1()`	Return the index of the last item whose value has changed.
`int getType()`	Return the event type. The possible values are: `CONTENTS_CHANGED`, `INTERVAL_ADDED`, or `INTERVAL_REMOVED`.

Examples That Use List Data Listeners

The following examples use list data listeners.

Example	Where Described	Notes
`ListDataEventDemo`	This section	Reports all list data events that occur on a list.

How to Write a List Selection Listener

List selection events occur when the selection in a list or table is either changing or has just changed. The events are fired from an object that implements the ListSelectionModel interface.[1] To get a list or table's list selection model object, use the getSelectionModel method.

To detect list selection events, you register a listener on the appropriate list selection model object. The JList class also gives you the option of registering a listener on the list itself, rather than directly on the list selection model. This section looks at an example that shows how to listen to list selection events on a selection model. Examples That Use List Selection Listeners (page 688) lists examples that listen on the list directly.

The selection model is shared by a list and a table. Figure 9 is a picture of the example running. You can dynamically change the selection mode to any of the three supported modes:

- Single selection mode
- Single interval selection mode
- Multiple interval selection mode

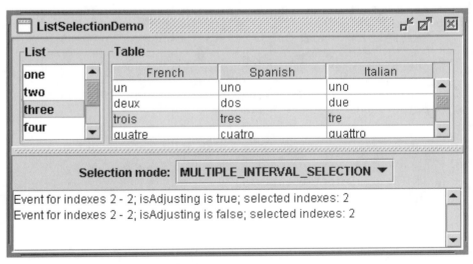

Figure 9   The ListSelectionDemo application.

---

[1] ListSelectionModel API documentation: http://java.sun.com/j2se/1.4.2/docs/api/javax/swing/ListSelectionModel.html.

Try This:

1. Run `ListSelectionEventDemo` using Java Web Start or compile and run the example yourself.[1]

2. Select and deselect items in the list and table. The mouse and keyboard commands required to select items depend on the look and feel. For the Java look and feel, click the left mouse button to begin a selection, use the Shift key to extend a selection contiguously, and use the Control key to extend a selection discontiguously. Dragging the mouse moves or extends the selection, depending on the list selection mode.

Here's the code from `ListSelectionDemo.java` that sets up the selection model and adds a listener to it:

```
...//where the member variables are defined
JList list;
JTable table;
    ...//in the init method:
    listSelectionModel = list.getSelectionModel();
    listSelectionModel.addListSelectionListener(
                        new SharedListSelectionHandler());
    ...
    table.setSelectionModel(listSelectionModel);
```

And here's the code for the listener, which works for all the possible selection modes:

```
class SharedListSelectionHandler implements ListSelectionListener {
    public void valueChanged(ListSelectionEvent e) {
        ListSelectionModel lsm = (ListSelectionModel)e.getSource();

        int firstIndex = e.getFirstIndex();
        int lastIndex = e.getLastIndex();
        boolean isAdjusting = e.getValueIsAdjusting();
        output.append("Event for indexes "
                        + firstIndex + " - " + lastIndex
                        + "; isAdjusting is " + isAdjusting
                        + "; selected indexes:");

        if (lsm.isSelectionEmpty()) {
            output.append(" <none>");
```

---

[1] To run `ListSelectionEventDemo` using Java Web Start, click the `ListSelectionEventDemo` link on the **RunExamples/events.html** page on the CD. You can find the source files here: `JavaTutorial/ uiswing/events/example-1dot4/index.html#ListSelectionEventDemo`.

```
        } else {
            // Find out which indexes are selected.
            int minIndex = lsm.getMinSelectionIndex();
            int maxIndex = lsm.getMaxSelectionIndex();
            for (int i = minIndex; i <= maxIndex; i++) {
                if (lsm.isSelectedIndex(i)) {
                    output.append(" " + i);
                }
            }
        }
        output.append(newline);
    }
}
```

This `valueChanged` method displays the first and last indices reported by the event, the value of the event's `isAdjusting` flag, and the indices currently selected.

Note that the first and last indices reported by the event indicate the inclusive range of items for which the selection has changed. If the selection mode is multiple interval selection, some items within the range might not have changed. The `isAdjusting` flag is `true` if the user is still manipulating the selection, and `false` if the user has finished changing it.

The `ListSelectionEvent`[1] object passed into `valueChanged` indicates only that the selection has changed. The event contains no information about the current selection. So, this method queries the selection model to figure out the current selection.

The List Selection Listener API

Table 22 lists the methods in the `ListSelectionListener` interface and Table 23 describes the methods in the `ListSelectionEvent` class. Note that because `ListSelectionListener` has only one method, it has no corresponding adapter class. Also refer to the List-SelectionListener API documentation at: http://java.sun.com/j2se/1.4.2/docs/api/javax/swing/event/ListSelectionListener.html. The `ListSelectionEvent` API documentation is online at: http://java.sun.com/j2se/1.4.2/docs/api/javax/swing/event/ListSelectionEvent.html.

Table 22: The ListSelectionListener Interface

Method	Purpose
valueChanged(ListSelectionEvent)	Called when the selection in the listened-to component is changing, as well as just after the selection has changed.

---

[1] `ListSelectionEvent` API documentation: http://java.sun.com/j2se/1.4.2/docs/api/javax/swing/event/ListSelectionEvent.html.

Table 23: The ListSelectionEvent API

Method	Purpose
`Object getSource()` (*in* `java.util.EventObject`)	Return the object that fired the event. If you register a list selection listener on a list directly, then the source for each event is the list. Otherwise, the source is the selection model.
`int getFirstIndex()`	Return the index of the first item whose selection value has changed. Note that for multiple interval selection, the first and last items are guaranteed to have changed but items between them might not have.
`int getLastIndex()`	Return the index of the last item whose selection value has changed. Note that for multiple interval selection, the first and last items are guaranteed to have changed but items between them might not have.
`boolean getValueIsAdjusting()`	Return true if the selection is still changing. Many list selection listeners are interested only in the final state of the selection and can ignore list selection events when this method returns true.

Examples That Use List Selection Listeners

The following examples use list selection listeners.

Example	Where Described	Notes
`ListSelectionDemo`	This section	Reports all list selection events that occur on a list and on a table. The table and the list share a list selection model, so only one listener is required. Lets the user dynamically change the selection mode.
`ListDemo`	How to Use Lists (page 267)	Listens to events on a single-selection list (not on its selection model). Enables and disables a button depending on whether any items are selected in the list.
`SplitPaneDemo`	How to Use Lists (page 267)	Listens to events on a single-selection list (not on its selection model).
`SimpleTableSelectionDemo`	How to Use Tables (page 388)	Uses two different list selection listeners on one table. One listener listens to list selection events on table columns; the other listens to list selection events on table rows.

How to Write
a Mouse Listener

Mouse events tell you when the user uses the mouse (or similar input device) to interact with a component. Mouse events occur when the cursor enters or exits a component's onscreen area and when the user presses or releases one of the mouse buttons.

Tracking the cursor's motion involves significantly more system overhead than tracking other mouse events, so mouse-motion events are separated into a separate listener type. For details, see How to Write a Mouse-Motion Listener (page 695).

To track mouse wheel events, you can register a mouse wheel listener. See How to Write a Mouse Wheel Listener (page 699) for more information.

If your program needs to detect both mouse events and mouse-motion events, you can use Swing's convenient `MouseInputAdapter`[1] class, which implements both `MouseListener`[2] and `MouseMotionListener`.[3] It does not implement the `MouseWheelListener`[4] interface.[5]

Figure 10 shows a mouse listener. At the top of the window is a blank area (implemented by a class named `BlankArea`). The mouse listener listens for events both on the `BlankArea` and on its container, an instance of `MouseEventDemo`. Each time a mouse event occurs, a descriptive message is displayed under the blank area. By moving the cursor on top of the blank area and occasionally pressing mouse buttons, you can fire mouse events.

---

[1] `MouseInputAdapter` API documentation: `http://java.sun.com/j2se/1.4.2/docs/api/javax/swing/event/MouseInputAdapter.html`.

[2] `MouseListener` API documentation: `http://java.sun.com/j2se/1.4.2/docs/api/java/awt/event/MouseListener.html`.

[3] `MouseMotionListener` API documentation: `http://java.sun.com/j2se/1.4.2/docs/api/java/awt/event/MouseMotionListener.html`.

[4] `MouseWheelListener` API documentation: `http://java.sun.com/j2se/1.4.2/docs/api/java/awt/event/MouseWheelListener.html`.

[5] `MouseInputAdapter` doesn't directly implement `MouseListener` and `MouseMotionListener`. Instead, it implements `MouseInputListener`, a convenience interface that implements `MouseListener` and `MouseMotionListener`.

M

Event Listeners

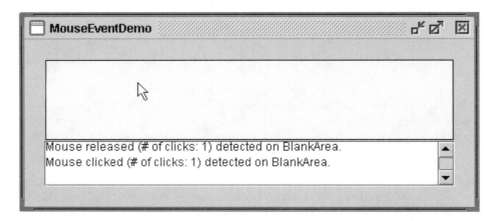

Figure 10 The `MouseEventDemo` application.

Try This:

1. Run `MouseEventDemo` using Java Web Start or compile and run the example yourself.[1]

2. Move the cursor into the yellow rectangle at the top of the window. You'll see one or more mouse-entered events.

3. Press and hold the mouse button. You'll see a mouse-pressed event. You might see some extra mouse events, such as mouse-exited and then mouse-entered.

4. Release the mouse button. You'll see a mouse-released event. If you didn't move the mouse, a mouse-clicked event will follow.

5. Press and hold the mouse button, and then drag the mouse so that the cursor ends up outside the window. Release the mouse button. You'll see a mouse-pressed event, followed by a mouse-exited event, followed by a mouse-released event. You are *not* notified of the cursor's motion. To get mouse-motion events, you need to implement a mouse-motion listener.

You can find the demo's code in `MouseEventDemo.java` and `BlankArea.java`. Here's the demo's mouse event-handling code:

```
public class MouseEventDemo ... implements MouseListener {
        //where initialization occurs:
        //Register for mouse events on blankArea and the panel.
        blankArea.addMouseListener(this);
        addMouseListener(this);
    ...
```

---

[1] To run `MouseEventDemo` using Java Web Start, click the `MouseEventDemo` link on the `RunExamples/events.html` page on the CD. You can find the source files here: `JavaTutorial/uiswing/events/example-1dot4/index.html#MouseEventDemo`.

```
    public void mousePressed(MouseEvent e) {
        saySomething("Mouse pressed; # of clicks: "
                    + e.getClickCount(), e);
    }

    public void mouseReleased(MouseEvent e) {
        saySomething("Mouse released; # of clicks: "
                    + e.getClickCount(), e);
    }

    public void mouseEntered(MouseEvent e) {
        saySomething("Mouse entered", e);
    }

    public void mouseExited(MouseEvent e) {
        saySomething("Mouse exited", e);
    }

    public void mouseClicked(MouseEvent e) {
        saySomething("Mouse clicked (# of clicks: "
                    + e.getClickCount() + ")", e);
    }

    void saySomething(String eventDescription, MouseEvent e) {
        textArea.append(eventDescription + " detected on "
                    + e.getComponent().getClass().getName()
                    + "." + newline);
    }
}
```

The Mouse Listener API

Table 24 lists the methods in the MouseListener interface and Table 25 describes the methods in the MouseEvent class. Table 26 covers the methods in MouseEvent's superclass, InputEvent. Also refer to the API documentation for MouseListener, MouseEvent, and InputEvent at:

```
http://java.sun.com/j2se/1.4.2/docs/api/java/awt/event/
        MouseListener.html
http://java.sun.com/j2se/1.4.2/docs/api/java/awt/event/MouseEvent.html
http://java.sun.com/j2se/1.4.2/docs/api/java/awt/event/InputEvent.html
```

M

Event Listeners

Table 24: The MouseListener Interface

(The corresponding adapter class is `MouseAdapter`.[a])

Method	Purpose
mouseClicked(MouseEvent)	Called just after the user clicks the listened-to component.
mouseEntered(MouseEvent)	Called just after the cursor enters the bounds of the listened-to component.
mouseExited(MouseEvent)	Called just after the cursor exits the bounds of the listened-to component.
mousePressed(MouseEvent)	Called just after the user presses a mouse button while the cursor is over the listened-to component.
mouseReleased(MouseEvent)	Called just after the user releases a mouse button after a mouse press over the listened-to component.

a. MouseAdapter API documentation: `http://java.sun.com/j2se/1.4.2/docs/api/java/awt/event/MouseAdapter.html`. You can also use the Swing adapter class, `MouseInputAdapter`, which has all the methods available from `MouseListener` and `MouseMotionListener`.

Table 25: The MouseEvent Class

Method	Purpose
int getClickCount()	Return the number of quick, consecutive clicks the user has made (including this event); for example, return 2 for a double click.
int getX() int getY() Point getPoint()	Return the (x,y) position at which the event occurred, relative to the component that fired the event.
int getButton()	Return which mouse button, if any, has changed state. One of the following constants is returned: NOBUTTON, BUTTON1, BUTTON2, or BUTTON3. Introduced in release 1.4.
boolean isPopupTrigger()	Return true if the mouse event should cause a popup menu to appear. Because popup triggers are platform-dependent, if your program uses popup menus, call `isPopupTrigger` for all mouse-pressed and mouse-released events fired by components over which the popup can appear. See Bringing up a Popup Menu (page 284) for more information about popup menus.
String getMouseModifiersText(int)	Return a `String` describing the modifier keys and mouse buttons that were active during the event, such as "Shift," or "Ctrl+Shift." These strings can be localized using the `awt.properties` file. Introduced in release 1.4.

Table 26: The InputEvent Class[a]

Method	Purpose
`int getID()` (*in* `java.awt.AWTEvent`)	Return the event type.
`Component getComponent()` (*in* `ComponentEvent`)	Return the component that fired the event. You can use this method instead of the `getSource` method.
`int getWhen()`	Return the timestamp of when this event occurred. The higher the timestamp, the more recently the event occurred.
`boolean isAltDown()` `boolean isControlDown()` `boolean isMetaDown()` `boolean isShiftDown()`	Return the state of individual modifier keys at the time the event was fired.

`int getModifiers()`	Return the state of all modifier keys and mouse buttons when the event was fired. You can use this method to determine which mouse button was pressed (or newly released) when a mouse event was fired. The `InputEvent` class defines these constants for use with the `getModifiers` method: `ALT_MASK`, `BUTTON1_MASK`, `BUTTON2_MASK`, `BUTTON3_MASK`, `CTRL_MASK`, `META_MASK`, and `SHIFT_MASK`. For example, the following expression is true if the right button was pressed:
	
	`(mouseEvent.getModifiers() & InputEvent.BUTTON3_MASK)`
	`                 == InputEvent.BUTTON3_MASK`

`int getModifiersEx()`	Return the extended modifier mask for this event. Extended modifiers represent the state of all modal keys, such as Alt, Control, Meta, and the mouse buttons just after the event occurred. You can check the status of the modifiers using one of the following predefined bitmasks: `SHIFT_DOWN_MASK`, `CTRL_DOWN_MASK`, `META_DOWN_MASK`, `ALT_DOWN_MASK`, `BUTTON1_DOWN_MASK`, `BUTTON2_DOWN_MASK`, `BUTTON3_DOWN_MASK`, or `ALT_GRAPH_DOWN_MASK`. For example, to check that button 1 is down, but that buttons 2 and 3 are up, you would use the following code snippet:
	
	`if (event.getModifiersEx() & (BUTTON1_DOWN_MASK |`
	`        BUTTON2_DOWN_MASK | BUTTON3_DOWN_MASK)`
	`    == BUTTON1_DOWN_MASK) {`
	`    ...`
	`}`
	
	Introduced in release 1.4.

`int getModifiersExText(int)`	Return a string describing the extended modifier keys and mouse buttons, such as "Shift," "Button1," or "Ctrl+Shift." These strings can be localized by changing the `awt.properties` file. Introduced in release 1.4.

a. `InputEvent` passes many useful methods to its subclass `MouseEvent`. `MouseEvent` also inherits a couple of handy methods from the `ComponentEvent` class and a couple of handy methods from the `ComponentEvent` and `AWTEvent` classes.

M

Event Listeners

Examples That Use Mouse Listeners

The following examples use mouse listeners.

Example	Where Described	Notes
MouseEventDemo	This section	Reports all mouse events that occur within a blank panel to demonstrate the circumstances under which mouse events are fired.
CoordinatesDemo	Performing Custom Painting (page 129)	An applet that draws a small circle where the user clicks the mouse. The applet also reports the x, y location of the mouse click.
SelectionDemo	Performing Custom Painting (page 129)	An applet that lets the user drag a rectangle to select a portion of an image. Uses a subclass of MouseInput-Adapter to listen to both mouse events and mouse-motion events.
GlassPaneDemo	How to Use Root Panes (page 316)	Uses a subclass of MouseInputAdapter to listen to mouse events and mouse-motion events on the root pane's glass pane. Redispatches the events to underlying components.
TableSorter	How to Use Tables (page 388)	Listens to mouse events on a table header. Sorts data in the selected column.
PopupMenuDemo	How to Use Menus (page 277)	Displays a popup menu in response to mouse clicks.
TrackFocusDemo	How to Use the Focus Subsystem (page 583)	The custom component, Picture, implements a mouse listener that requests the focus when a user clicks on the component.

How to Write a Mouse-Motion Listener

Mouse-motion events tell you when the user uses the mouse (or a similar input device) to move the onscreen cursor. For information on listening for other kinds of mouse events, such as clicks, see How to Write a Mouse Listener (page 689). For information on listening for mouse wheel events, see How to Write a Mouse Wheel Listener (page 699). If your program needs to detect both mouse events and mouse-motion events, you can use Swing's convenient `MouseInputAdapter` class, which implements both `MouseListener` and `MouseMotionListener`.

Figure 11 shows an example with a mouse-motion listener. It's exactly like the example in How to Write a Mouse Listener (page 689), except for substituting `MouseMotionListener`[1] for `MouseListener`, implementing the `mouseDragged` and `mouseMoved` methods instead of the mouse listener methods, and displaying coordinates instead of numbers of clicks.

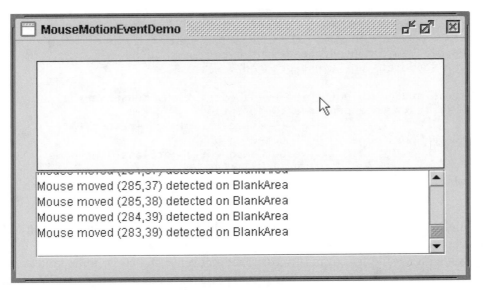

Figure 11   The `MouseMotionEventDemo` application.

---

[1]   MouseMotionListener API documentation: `http://java.sun.com/j2se/1.4.2/docs/api/java/awt/event/MouseMotionListener.html`.

M

Event Listeners

Try This:

1. Run `MouseMotionEventDemo` using Java Web Start or compile and run the example yourself.[1]

2. Move the cursor into the yellow rectangle at the top of the window. You'll see one or more mouse-moved events.

3. Press and hold the mouse button, and then move the mouse so that the cursor is outside the yellow rectangle. You'll see mouse-dragged events.

Here's the code from `MouseMotionEventDemo.java` that implements the mouse-motion event handling:

```
public class MouseMotionEventDemo extends JPanel
                                  implements MouseMotionListener {
    //...in initialization code:
        //Register for mouse events on blankArea and panel.
        blankArea.addMouseMotionListener(this);
        addMouseMotionListener(this);
        ...
    }
    public void mouseMoved(MouseEvent e) {
        saySomething("Mouse moved", e);
    }
    public void mouseDragged(MouseEvent e) {
        saySomething("Mouse dragged", e);
    }
    void saySomething(String eventDescription, MouseEvent e) {
        textArea.append(eventDescription
                        + " (" + e.getX() + "," + e.getY() + ")"
                        + " detected on "
                        + e.getComponent().getClass().getName()
                        + newline);
    }
}
```

A more interesting example is `SelectionDemo`, which is discussed in Introduction to Painting Concepts (page 134) in Chapter 6. The program draws a rectangle illustrating the user's current dragging. To do this, it must implement an event handler for three kinds of mouse events: mouse presses, mouse drags, and mouse releases. To be informed of all these events, the handler must implement both the `MouseListener` and `MouseMotionListener` interfaces, and be registered as both a mouse listener and a mouse-motion listener. To avoid having to

---

[1] To run `MouseMotionEventDemo` using Java Web Start, click the `MouseMotionEventDemo` link on the `RunExamples/events.html` page on the CD. You can find the source files here: `JavaTutorial/uiswing/events/example-1dot4/index.html#MouseMotionEventDemo`.

define empty methods, the handler doesn't implement either listener interface directly. Instead, it extends `MouseInputAdapter`, as the following code snippet shows.

```
...//where initialization occurs:
    MyListener myListener = new MyListener();
    addMouseListener(myListener);
    addMouseMotionListener(myListener);
...
private class MyListener extends MouseInputAdapter {
    public void mousePressed(MouseEvent e) {
        int x = e.getX();
        int y = e.getY();
        currentRect = new Rectangle(x, y, 0, 0);
        updateDrawableRect(getWidth(), getHeight());
        repaint();
    }

    public void mouseDragged(MouseEvent e) {
        updateSize(e);
    }

    public void mouseReleased(MouseEvent e) {
        updateSize(e);
    }
    ...

    void updateSize(MouseEvent e) {
        int x = e.getX();
        int y = e.getY();
        ...
        repaint(...);
    }
}
```

The Mouse-Motion Listener API

Table 27 lists the methods in the `MouseMotionListener`. Each mouse-motion event method has a single parameter—and it's not called `MouseMotionEvent`. Instead, each mouse-motion event method uses a `MouseEvent` argument. You can find methods defined by the `Mouse-Event` class and its superclass `InputEvent` in Table 25 (page 692) and Table 26 (page 693), respectively. Also refer to the relevant API documentation at:

```
http://java.sun.com/j2se/1.4.2/docs/api/java/awt/event/
       MouseMotionListener.html
http://java.sun.com/j2se/1.4.2/docs/api/java/awt/event/
       MouseEvent.html
http://java.sun.com/j2se/1.4.2/docs/api/java/awt/event/
       InputEvent.html
```

M

Event Listeners

Table 27: The MouseMotionListener Interface

(The corresponding adapter class is MouseMotionAdapter.[a])

Method	Purpose
mouseDragged(MouseEvent)	Called in response to the user moving the mouse while holding a mouse button down. This event is fired by the component that fired the most recent mouse-pressed event, even if the cursor is no longer over that component.
mouseMoved(MouseEvent)	Called in response to the user moving the mouse with no mouse buttons pressed. This event is fired by the component that's currently under the cursor.

a. MouseMotionAdapter API documentation: `http://java.sun.com/j2se/1.4.2/docs/api/java/awt/event/MouseMotionAdapter.html`.

Examples That Use Mouse-Motion Listeners

The following examples use mouse-motion listeners.

Example	Where Described	Notes
MouseMotionEventDemo	This section	Reports all mouse-motion events that occur within a blank panel to demonstrate the circumstances under which mouse-motion events are fired.
LayeredPaneDemo *and* LayeredPaneDemo2	How to Use Layered Panes (page 258)	Moves an image of Duke around within a layered pane in response to mouse-motion events.
SelectionDemo	Introduction to Painting Concepts (page 134)	An applet that lets the user drag a rectangle to select a portion of an image. Uses a subclass of MouseInputAdapter to listen to both mouse events and mouse-motion events.
GlassPaneDemo	How to Use Root Panes (page 316)	Uses a subclass of MouseInputAdapter to listen to mouse events and mouse-motion events on the root pane's glass pane. Redispatches the events to underlying components.
ScrollDemo	How to Use Scroll Panes (page 325)	The label subclass, ScrollablePicture, uses a mouse-motion listener to allow the user to scroll the picture even when the user drags outside the window.

How to Write a Mouse Wheel Listener

Mouse wheel events tell you when the wheel on the mouse rotates. For information on listening to other mouse events, such as clicks, see How to Write a Mouse Listener (page 689). For information on listening to mouse-dragged events, see How to Write a Mouse-Motion Listener (page 695). Not all mice have wheels and, in that case, mouse wheel events are never generated. There is no way to programmatically detect whether the mouse is equipped with a mouse wheel.

Version Note: The MouseWheelListener[1] interface was introduced in release 1.4.

You don't usually need to implement a mouse wheel listener. The mouse wheel is used primarily for scrolling, and scroll panes automatically register mouse wheel listeners that react to the mouse wheel appropriately.

However, if you create a custom component to be used inside a scroll pane you may need to customize its scrolling behavior—specifically you might need to set the unit and block increments. For a text area, for example, scrolling one unit means scrolling by one line of text. A block increment typically scrolls an entire "page," or the size of the viewport. For more information, see Implementing a Scrolling-Savvy Client (page 333) in Chapter 7.

To generate mouse wheel events the cursor must be *over* the component registered to listen for mouse wheel events. The type of scrolling that occurs, either WHEEL_UNIT_SCROLL or WHEEL_BLOCK_SCROLL, is platform dependent. The amount that the mouse wheel scrolls is also platform-dependent. Both the type and amount of scrolling may be settable via the mouse control panel for your platform.

The MouseWheelEventDemo example demonstrates mouse wheel events (see Figure 12).

---

[1] MouseWheelListener API documentation: http://java.sun.com/j2se/1.4.2/docs/api/java/awt/event/MouseWheelListener.html.

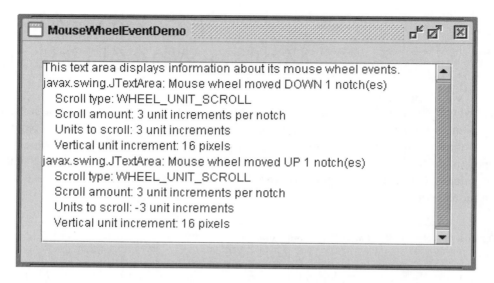

Figure 12   The `MouseWheelEventDemo` application.

Try This:

1. Run `MouseWheelEventDemo` using Java Web Start or compile and run the example yourself.[1]

2. Move the cursor over the text area.

3. Rotate the mouse wheel away from you. You will see one or more mouse wheel events in the *up* direction.

4. Rotate the mouse wheel in the opposite direction. You will see mouse wheel events in the *down* direction.

5. Try changing your mouse wheel's scrolling behavior in your system's mouse control panel to see how the output changes. You should not need to restart the demo to see the changes take effect.

The output from `MouseWheelEventDemo` for a system that uses unit increments for its mouse wheel might look like this:

```
javax.swing.JTextArea: Mouse wheel moved UP 1 notch(es)
        Scroll type: WHEEL_UNIT_SCROLL
        Scroll amount: 3 unit increments per notch
        Units to scroll: -3 unit increments
        Vertical unit increment: 16 pixels
```

---

[1] To run `MouseWheelEventDemo` using Java Web Start, click the `MouseWheelEventDemo` link on the Run-Examples/`events.html` page on the CD. You can find the source files here: `JavaTutorial/uiswing/events/example-1dot4/index.html#MouseWheelEventDemo`.

The scroll amount, returned by getScrollAmount, indicates how many units will be scrolled and is always a positive number. The units to scroll, returned by getUnitsToScroll, is positive when scrolling down and negative when scrolling up. The number of pixels for the vertical unit is obtained from the vertical scroll bar using the getUnitIncrement method. In the preceding example, rolling the mouse wheel one notch upward should result in the text area scrolling upward 48 pixels (3x16).

For a system that uses block increments for mouse wheel scrolling, for the same movement of the mouse wheel the output might look like this:

```
javax.swing.JTextArea: Mouse wheel moved UP 1 notch(es)
    Scroll type: WHEEL_BLOCK_SCROLL
    Vertical block increment: 307 pixels
```

The vertical block increment is obtained from the vertical scroll bar using the getBlock-Increment method. In this case, rolling the mouse wheel upward one notch means that the text area should scroll upward 307 pixels.

You can find the demo's code in MouseWheelEventDemo.java. Here's the code that's related to mouse wheel event handling:

```
public class MouseWheelEventDemo ... implements MouseWheelListener ... {
        //...where initialization occurs:
        //Register for mouse wheel events on the text area.
        textArea.addMouseWheelListener(this);
        ...
    }

    public void mouseWheelMoved(MouseWheelEvent e) {
        String message;
        int notches = e.getWheelRotation();
        if (notches <0) {
            message = "Mouse wheel moved UP "
                        + -notches + " notch(es)" + newline;
        } else {
            message = "Mouse wheel moved DOWN "
                        + notches + " notch(es)" + newline;
        }
        if (e.getScrollType() == MouseWheelEvent.WHEEL_UNIT_SCROLL) {
            message += "    Scroll type: WHEEL_UNIT_SCROLL" + newline;
            message += "    Scroll amount: " + e.getScrollAmount()
                    + " unit increments per notch" + newline;
            message += "    Units to scroll: " + e.getUnitsToScroll()
                    + " unit increments" + newline;
            message += "    Vertical unit increment: "
                    + scrollPane.getVerticalScrollBar().getUnitIncrement(1)
                    + " pixels" + newline;
```

```
    } else { //scroll type == MouseWheelEvent.WHEEL_BLOCK_SCROLL
        message += "    Scroll type: WHEEL_BLOCK_SCROLL" + newline;
        message += "    Vertical block increment: "
            + scrollPane.getVerticalScrollBar().getBlockIncrement(1)
            + " pixels" + newline;
    }
    saySomething(message, e);
}
...
}
```

The Mouse Wheel Listener API

Table 28 lists the methods in the MouseWheelListener interface and Table 29 describes the methods in the MouseWheelEvent class. Note that because MouseWheelListener has only one method, it has no corresponding adapter class. Also refer to the MouseWheelListener API documentation at: http://java.sun.com/j2se/1.4.2/docs/api/java/awt/event/ MouseWheelListener.html. The MouseWheelEvent API documentation is at: http:// java.sun.com/j2se/1.4.2/docs/api/java/awt/event/MouseWheelEvent.html.

Table 28: The MouseWheelListener Interface
(This API was introduced in release 1.4.)

Method	Purpose
mouseWheelMoved(MouseWheelEvent)	Called when the mouse wheel is rotated.

Table 29: The MouseWheelEvent Class
(This API was introduced in release 1.4.)

Method	Purpose
int getScrollType()	Return the type of scrolling to be used. Possible values are WHEEL_BLOCK_ SCROLL and WHEEL_UNIT_SCROLL and are determined by the native platform.
int getWheelRotation()	Return the number of notches the mouse wheel was rotated. If the mouse wheel rotated toward the user (down) the value is positive. If the mouse wheel rotated away from the user (up) the value is negative.
int getScrollAmount()	Return the number of units that should be scrolled per notch. This is always a positive number and is only valid if the scroll type is MouseWheelEvent. WHEEL_UNIT_SCROLL.
int getUnitsToScroll()	Return the positive or negative units to scroll for the current event. This is only valid when the scroll type is MouseWheelEvent.WHEEL_UNIT_SCROLL.

Examples That Use Mouse Wheel Listeners

The following examples use mouse wheel listeners.

Example	Where Described	Notes
MouseWheelEventDemo	This section	Reports all mouse wheel events that occur within a text area to demonstrate the circumstances under which mouse wheel events are fired.

How to Write a Property-Change Listener

Property-change events occur whenever the value of a *bound property* changes for a *bean*—a component that conforms to the JavaBeans™ specification.[1] All Swing components are also beans.

A `JavaBeans` property is accessed through its *get* and *set* methods. `JComponent`, for example, has the property *font* which is accessible through the `getFont` and `setFont` methods. A *bound property* fulfills the special requirement that, besides the *get* and *set* methods, it fires a property-change event when its value changes.

Some scenarios that commonly require property-change listeners include:

- You have implemented a formatted text field and need a way to detect when the user has entered a new value. You can register a property-change listener on the formatted text field to listen to changes on the *value* property. See `FormattedTextFieldDemo` in How to Use Formatted Text Fields (page 221) for an example of this.

- You have implemented a dialog and need to know when a user has clicked one of the dialog's buttons or changed a selection in the dialog. See `DialogDemo` in How to Make Dialogs (page 187) for an example of registering a property-change listener on an option pane to listen to changes to the *value* property. You can also check out `FileChooserDemo2` in How to Use File Choosers (page 206) for an example of how to register a property-change listener to listen to changes to the *directoryChanged* and *selectedFileChanged* properties.

- You need to be notified when the component that has the focus changes. You can register a property-change listener on the keyboard focus manager to listen to changes to the *focusOwner* property. See `TrackFocusDemo` and `DragPictureDemo` in How to Use the Focus Subsystem (page 583) for examples of this.

Although these are some of the more common uses for property-change listeners, you can register a property-change listener on the *bound* property of any component that conforms to the JavaBeans specification.

You can register a property-change listener in two ways. The first uses the `addPropertyChangeListener(PropertyChangeListener)` method. When you register a listener this way, you are notified of every change to every *bound* property for that object. In the

---

[1] You can find out more about beans from the "JavaBeans" trail of *The Java Tutorial*. This trail is available online and is included on the CD at `JavaTutorial/beans/index.html`.

propertyChange method, you can get the name of the property that has changed using the PropertyChangeEvent getPropertyName method, as in the following code snippet:

```
KeyboardFocusManager focusManager =
    KeyboardFocusManager.getCurrentKeyboardFocusManager();
focusManager.addPropertyChangeListener(new FocusManagerListener());
...
public FocusManagerListener() implements PropertyChangeListener {
    public void propertyChange(PropertyChangeEvent e) {
        String propertyName = e.getPropertyName();
        if ("focusOwner".equals(propertyName) {

            ...
        } else if ("focusedWindow".equals(propertyName) {
            ...
        }
    }
    ...
}
```

The second way to register a property-change listener uses the method addProperty-ChangeListener(String, PropertyChangeListener). The String argument is the name of a property. Using this method means that you only receive notification when a change occurs to that particular property. So, if you registered a property-change listener like this:

```
aComponent.addPropertyChangeListener("font", new FontListener());
```

FontListener only receives notification when the value of the component's *font* property changes. It does *not* receive notification when the value changes for *transferHandler*, *opaque*, *border*, or any other property.

The following example shows how to register a property-change listener on the *value* property of a formatted text field using the two-argument version of addPropertyChange-Listener:

```
//...where initialization occurs:
double amount;
JFormattedTextField amountField;
...
amountField.addPropertyChangeListener("value",
                                new FormattedTextFieldListener());

...
class FormattedTextFieldListener implements PropertyChangeListener {
    public void propertyChanged(PropertyChangeEvent e) {
        Object source = e.getSource();
```

```
        if (source == amountField) {
            amount = ((Number)amountField.getValue()).doubleValue();
            ...
        }
        ...//re-compute payment and update field...
    }
}
```

The Property-Change Listener API

Table 30 lists the methods for registering a `PropertyChangeListener` and Table 31 lists the methods in the `PropertyChangeListener` interface. Table 32 describes the methods in the `PropertyChangeEvent` class. Note that because `PropertyChangeListener` has only one method, it has no corresponding adapter class. Also refer to the `PropertyChangeListener` API documentation at: `http://java.sun.com/j2se/1.4.2/docs/api/java/beans/PropertyChangeListener.html`. The `PropertyChangeEvent` API documentation is at: `http://java.sun.com/j2se/1.4.2/docs/api/java/beans/PropertyChangeEvent.html`.

Table 30: Registering a PropertyChangeListener

Method	Purpose
`addPropertyChangeListener(` `        PropertyChangeListener)`	Add a property-change listener to the listener list.

`addPropertyChangeListener(`
`        String,`
`        PropertyChangeListener)`
	Add a property-change listener for a specific property. The listener is called only when there is a change to the specified property.

Table 31: The PropertyChangeListener Interface

Method	Purpose
`propertyChange(PropertyChangeEvent)`	Called when the listened-to bean changes a bound property.

Table 32: The PropertyChangeEvent Class

Method	Purpose
`Object getNewValue()` `Object getOldValue()`	Return the new, or old, value of the property, respectively.
`String getPropertyName()`	Return the name of the property that was changed.

Examples That Use Property-Change Listeners

The following examples use property-change listeners.

Example	Where Described	Notes
FormattedTextFieldDemo	How to Use Formatted Text Fields (page 221)	A property-change listener is registered on several formatted text fields to track changes to the *value* property.
DialogDemo	How to Make Dialogs (page 187)	The CustomDialog class registers a property-change listener on an option pane to listen to the *value* and *inputValue* properties.
FileChooserDemo2	How to Use File Choosers (page 206)	The ImagePreview class registers a property-change listener on the file chooser to listen to the *directoryChanged* and *selectedFileChanged* properties.
TrackFocusDemo	How to Use the Focus Subsystem (page 583)	A property-change listener is registered on the keyboard focus manager to track changes to the *focusOwner* property.

P

Event Listeners

707

How to Write a Table Model Listener

Each JTable object has a table model that holds its data. When a table model listener is registered on the table model, the listener is notified every time the table model's data changes. The JTable itself automatically uses a table model listener to make its GUI reflect the current state of the table model. You register a table model listener using the TableModel addTableModelListener method. For more information on tables, see How to Use Tables (page 388) in Chapter 7. In particular, the section Detecting Data Changes (page 397) discusses and shows an example of implementing a table model listener.

The Table Model Listener API

Table 33 lists the methods in the TableModelListener interface and Table 34 describes the methods in the TableModelEvent class. Note that TableModelListener has only one method, so it has no corresponding adapter class. Also refer to the TableModelListener API documentation online at: http://java.sun.com/j2se/1.4.2/docs/api/javax/swing/event/TableModelListener.html. The TableModelEvent API documentation is online at: http://java.sun.com/j2se/1.4.2/docs/api/javax/swing/event/TableModelEvent.html.

Table 33: The TableModelListener Interface

Method	Purpose
tableChanged(TableModelEvent)	Called when the structure of or data in the table has changed.

Table 34: The TableModelEvent API

Method	Purpose
Object getSource() (*in* java.util.EventObject)	Return the object that fired the event.
int getFirstRow()	Return the index of the first row that changed. TableModelEvent. HEADER_ROW specifies the table header.

Table 34: The TableModelEvent API   *(continued)*

Method	Purpose
`int getLastRow()`	The last row that changed. Again, HEADER_ROW is a possible value.
`int getColumn()`	Return the index of the column that changed. The constant `TableModel-Event.ALL_COLUMNS` specifies that all the columns might have changed.
`int getType()`	What happened to the changed cells. The returned value is one of the following: `TableModelEvent.INSERT`, `TableModelEvent.DELETE`, or `TableModelEvent.UPDATE`.

Examples That Use Table Model Listeners

The following examples are related to table model listeners.

Example	Where Described	Notes
`TableMap`	Sorting and Otherwise Manipulating Data (page 412)	A superclass for data-manipulating table models. It implements a table model that sits between a table data model and a JTable. The `TableMap` listens for table model events from the data model, and then simply forwards them to its table model listeners (such as the `JTable`).
`TableSorter`	Sorting and Otherwise Manipulating Data (page 412)	A sorting table model implemented as a subclass of `TableMap`. In addition to forwarding table model events, the `tableChanged` method keeps track of the number of rows.
`SharedModelDemo`	—	Does *not* implement a table model listener. Instead, it implements a combined list and table model.

T

Event Listeners

How to Write a Tree Expansion Listener

Sometimes when using a tree,[1] you might need to react when a branch becomes expanded or collapsed. For example, you might need to load or save data or you might need to prevent the user from expanding a particular node.

Two kinds of listeners report expansion and collapse occurrences: tree expansion listeners and tree-will-expand listeners. This section discusses the former. A tree expansion listener detects when an expansion or collapse has happened. In general, you should implement a tree expansion listener unless you might need to prevent an expansion or collapse from happening.

Tree-will-expand listeners are discussed in How to Write a Tree-Will-Expand Listener (page 718). A tree-will-expand listener detects when an expansion or collapse is about to happen. Figure 13 demonstrates a simple tree expansion listener. The text area at the bottom of the window displays a message every time a tree expansion event occurs. It's a straightforward, simple demo. To see a more interesting version that can veto expansions, see How to Write a Tree-Will-Expand Listener (page 718).

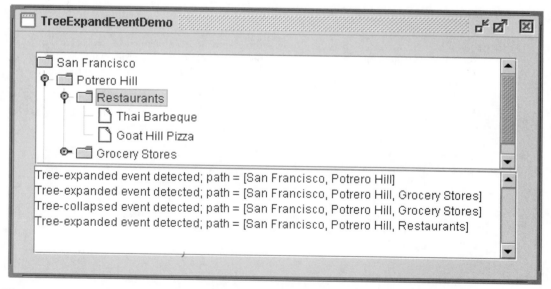

Figure 13   The TreeExpandEventDemo application.

---

[1]   See also How to Use Trees (page 437) in Chapter 7.

Try This:

1. Run TreeExpandEventDemo using Java Web Start or compile and run the example yourself.[1]
2. Expand a node. A tree-expanded event is fired.
3. Collapse the node. A tree-collapsed event is fired.

The following code shows how the program handles expansion events. You can find all the example's source code in TreeExpandEventDemo.java.

```
public class TreeExpandEventDemo ... {
    ...
    void saySomething(String eventDescription, TreeExpansionEvent e) {
        textArea.append(eventDescription + "; "
                        + "path = " + e.getPath()
                        + newline);
    }

    class DemoArea ... implements TreeExpansionListener {
        ...

        public DemoArea() {
            ...
            tree.addTreeExpansionListener(this);
            ...
        }
        ...

        // Required by TreeExpansionListener interface.
        public void treeExpanded(TreeExpansionEvent e) {
            saySomething("Tree-expanded event detected", e);
        }

        // Required by TreeExpansionListener interface.
        public void treeCollapsed(TreeExpansionEvent e) {
            saySomething("Tree-collapsed event detected", e);
        }
    }
}
```

[1] To run TreeExpandEventDemo using Java Web Start, click the TreeExpandEventDemo link on the Run-Examples/events.html page on the CD. You can find the source files here: JavaTutorial/uiswing/events/example-1dot4/index.html#TreeExpandEventDemo.

The Tree Expansion Listener API

Table 35 lists the methods in the TreeExpansionListener interface and Table 36 describes the methods in the TreeExpansionEvent class. Note that TreeExpansionListener has no adapter classes. Also refer to the TreeExpansionListener API documentation online at: http://java.sun.com/j2se/1.4.2/docs/api/javax/swing/event/TreeExpansion-Listener.html. The TreeExpansionEvent API documentation is online at: http://java.sun.com/j2se/1.4.2/docs/api/javax/swing/event/TreeExpansionEvent.html.

Table 35: The TreeExpansionListener Interface

Method	Purpose
treeCollapsed(TreeExpansionEvent)	Called just after a tree node collapses.
treeExpanded(TreeExpansionEvent)	Called just after a tree node expands.

Table 36: The TreeExpansionEvent API

Method	Purpose
Object getSource()	Return the object that fired the event.
TreePath getPath()	Return a TreePath object that identifies each node from the root of the tree to the collapsed/expanded node, inclusive.

Examples That Use Tree Expansion Listeners

The following examples use tree expansion listeners.

Example	Where Described	Notes
TreeExpandEventDemo	This section	Displays a message whenever a tree expansion event occurs.
TreeExpandEventDemo2	How to Write a Tree-Will-Expand Listener (page 718)	Adds a tree-will-expand listener to TreeExpandEventDemo.

How to Write a Tree Model Listener

By implementing a tree model listener, you can detect when the data displayed by a tree changes. You might use a tree model listener to detect when the user edits tree nodes. To see an example and a discussion, read Dynamically Changing a Tree (page 447) in Chapter 7.

The Tree Model Listener API

Table 37 lists the methods in the `TreeModelListener` interface and Table 38 describes the methods in the `TreeModelEvent` class. Note that `TreeModelListener` has no adapter class. Also refer to the `TreeModelListener` API documentation at: `http://java.sun.com/j2se/1.4.2/docs/api/javax/swing/event/TreeModelListener.html`. The `TreeModelEvent` API documentation is online at: `http://java.sun.com/j2se/1.4.2/docs/api/javax/swing/event/TreeModelEvent.html`.

Table 37: The TreeModelListener Interface

Method	Purpose
`treeNodesChanged(TreeModelEvent)`	Called when one or more sibling nodes have changed in some way.
`treeNodesInserted(TreeModelEvent)`	Called after nodes have been inserted into the tree.
`treeNodesRemoved(TreeModelEvent)`	Called after nodes have been removed from the tree.
`treeStructureChanged(TreeModelEvent)`	Called after the tree's structure has drastically changed.

Table 38: The TreeModelEvent API

Method	Purpose
`Object getSource()` (*in* `java.util.EventObject`)	Return the object that fired the event.
`int[] getChildIndices()`	For `treeNodesChanged`, `treeNodesInserted`, and `treeNodesRemoved`, return the indices of the changed, inserted, or deleted nodes, respectively. Return nothing useful for `treeStructureChanged`.
`Object[] getChildren()`	Return the objects corresponding to the child indices.
`Object[] getPath()`	Return the path to the parent of the changed, inserted, or deleted nodes. For `treeStructureChanged`, return the path to the node beneath which the structure has changed.
`TreePath getTreePath()`	Return the same thing as `getPath`, but as a `TreePath` object.

T

Event Listeners

Examples That Use Tree Model Listeners

The following examples use tree model listeners.

Example	Where Described	Notes
DynamicTreeDemo	How to Use Trees (page 437)	Implements a tree model listener to detect when the user has edited a node's data.

How to Write a Tree Selection Listener

To detect when the user selects a node in a tree, you need to register a tree selection listener. Here's an example, taken from the TreeDemo example discussed in Responding to Node Selection (page 440) in Chapter 7, of detecting node selection in a tree that can have at most one node selected at a time:

```
tree.addTreeSelectionListener(new TreeSelectionListener() {
    public void valueChanged(TreeSelectionEvent e) {
        DefaultMutableTreeNode node = (DefaultMutableTreeNode)
                        tree.getLastSelectedPathComponent();

        if (node == null) return;

        Object nodeInfo = node.getUserObject();
        ...
        /* React to the node selection. */
        ...
    }
});
```

To specify that the tree should support single selection, the program uses this code:

```
tree.getSelectionModel().setSelectionMode
        (TreeSelectionModel.SINGLE_TREE_SELECTION);
```

The TreeSelectionModel interface defines three values for the selection mode:

DISCONTIGUOUS_TREE_SELECTION
This is the default mode for the default tree selection model. With this mode, any combination of nodes can be selected.

SINGLE_TREE_SELECTION
This is the mode used by the preceding example. At most one node can be selected at a time.

CONTIGUOUS_TREE_SELECTION
With this mode, only nodes in adjoining rows can be selected.

T

Event Listeners

715

The Tree Selection Listener API

Table 39 lists the only method in the `TreeSelectionListener` interface and Table 40 describes the methods in the `TreeExpansionEvent` class. Note that `TreeSelectionListener` has no corresponding adapter class. Also refer to the `TreeSelectionListener` API documentation at: `http://java.sun.com/j2se/1.4.2/docs/api/javax/swing/event/TreeSelectionListener.html`. The `TreeExpansionEvent` API documentation is online at: `http://java.sun.com/j2se/1.4.2/docs/api/javax/swing/event/TreeExpansionEvent.html`.

Table 39: The TreeSelectionListener Interface

Method	Purpose
`valueChanged(TreeSelectionEvent)`	Called whenever the selection changes.

Table 40: The TreeExpansionEvent API

Method	Purpose
`Object getSource()` (*in* `java.util.EventObject`)	Return the object that fired the event.
`TreePath getNewLeadSelectionPath()`	Return the current lead path.
`TreePath getOldLeadSelectionPath()`	Return the path that was previously the lead path.
`TreePath getPath()`	Return the first path element.
`TreePath[] getPaths()`	Return the paths that have been added or removed from the selection.
`boolean isAddedPath()`	Return true if the first path element has been added to the selection. Return false if the first path has been removed from the selection.
`boolean isAddedPath(int)`	Return true if the path specified by the index was added to the selection.
`boolean isAddedPath(TreePath)`	Return true if the specified path was added to the selection.
`Object getLastSelectedPathComponent()`	Return the last path component in the first node of the current selection.
`TreePath getLeadSelectionPath()` (*in* `JTree`)	Return the current lead path.

Examples That Use Tree Selection Listeners

The following examples use tree selection listeners.

Example	Where Described	Notes
TreeDemo	How to Use Trees (page 437)	The tree listener responds to node clicks by showing the appropriate HTML document.

How to Write a Tree-Will-Expand Listener

As explained in How to Write a Tree Expansion Listener (page 710), you can use a tree-will-expand listener to prevent a tree node from expanding or collapsing. To be notified just *after* an expansion or collapse occurs, you should use a tree expansion listener instead.

TreeExpandEventDemo2, shown in Figure 14, adds a tree-will-expand listener to the TreeExpandEventDemo example. The new code demonstrates the ability of tree-will-expand listeners to veto node expansions and collapses: It asks for confirmation each time you try to expand a node.

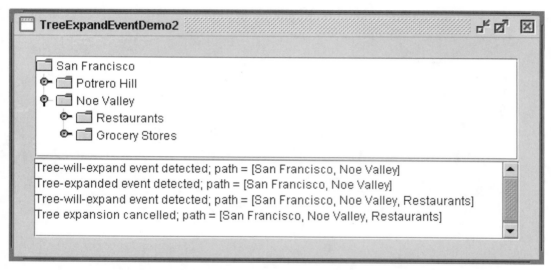

Figure 14   The TreeExpandEventDemo2 application.

Try This:

1. Run TreeExpandEventDemo2 using Java Web Start or compile and run the example yourself.[1]

---

[1] To run TreeExpandEventDemo2 using Java Web Start, click the TreeExpandEventDemo2 link on the RunExamples/events.html page on the CD. You can find the source files here: JavaTutorial/uiswing/events/example-1dot4/index.html#TreeExpandEventDemo2.

2. Click the graphic to the left of the Potrero Hill node. This tells the tree you want to expand the node. A dialog appears asking you if you really want to expand the node.

3. Click "Expand" or dismiss the dialog. Messages in the text area tell you that both a tree-will-expand event and a tree-expanded event have occurred. At the end of each message is the path to the expanded node.

4. Try to expand another node, but this time press the Cancel Expansion button in the dialog. The node does not expand. Messages in the text area tell you that a tree-will-expand event occurred, and that you cancelled a tree expansion.

5. Collapse the Potrero Hill node. The node collapses without a dialog appearing because the event handler's `treeWillCollapse` method lets the collapse occur uncontested.

The following snippet shows the code that this program adds to TreeExpandEventDemo. The bold line prevents the tree expansion from happening. You can find all the demo's source code in `TreeExpandEventDemo2.java`.

```
public class TreeExpandEventDemo2 ... {
    ...
    class DemoArea ... implements ... TreeWillExpandListener {
        ...
        public DemoArea() {
            ...
            tree.addTreeWillExpandListener(this);
            ...
        }
        ...
        //Required by TreeWillExpandListener interface.
        public void treeWillExpand(TreeExpansionEvent e)
                    throws ExpandVetoException {
            saySomething("Tree-will-expand event detected", e);
            //...show a dialog...
            if (/* user said to cancel the expansion */) {
                //Cancel expansion.
                saySomething("Tree expansion cancelled", e);
                throw new ExpandVetoException(e);
            }
        }

        //Required by TreeWillExpandListener interface.
        public void treeWillCollapse(TreeExpansionEvent e) {
            saySomething("Tree-will-collapse event detected", e);
        }
        ...
    }
}
```

The Tree-Will-Expand Listener API

Table 41 lists the methods in the TreeWillExpandListener interface. Note that this interface has no adapter class. Also refer to the TreeWillExpandListener API documentation online at: `http://java.sun.com/j2se/1.4.2/docs/api/javax/swing/event/Tree-WillExpandListener.html`.

Table 41: The TreeWillExpandListener Interface

Method	Purpose
treeWillCollapse(TreeExpansionEvent)	Called just before a tree node collapses. To prevent the collapse from occurring, your implementation of this method should throw a ExpandVetoException event.
treeWillExpand(TreeExpansionEvent)	Called just before a tree node expands. To prevent the expansion from occurring, your implementation of this method should throw a ExpandVetoException event.

See Table 36, "The TreeExpansionEvent API," on page 712 for information about the TreeExpansionEvent argument for the preceding methods.

Examples That Use Tree-Will-Expand Listeners

The following examples use tree-will-expand listeners.

Example	Where Described	Notes
TreeExpandEventDemo2	This section	Displays a confirmation dialog whenever a tree expansion event occurs.

How to Write an Undoable Edit Listener

Undoable edit events occur when an operation that can be undone occurs on a component. Currently only text components fire undoable edit events, and then only indirectly. The text component's document fires the events. For text components, undoable operations include inserting characters, deleting characters, and modifying the style of text. Programs typically listen to undoable edit events to assist in the implementation of undo and redo commands.

Here's the undoable edit event handling code from an application called TextComponent-Demo.[1]

```
...
//where initialization occurs
document.addUndoableEditListener(new MyUndoableEditListener());
...
protected class MyUndoableEditListener implements UndoableEditListener {
    public void undoableEditHappened(UndoableEditEvent e) {
        //Remember the edit and update the menus
        undo.addEdit(e.getEdit());
        undoAction.updateUndoState();
        redoAction.updateRedoState();
    }
}
```

For a discussion about the undoable edit listener aspect of the program see Implementing Undo and Redo (page 68) in Chapter 3.

The Undoable Edit Listener API

Table 42 lists the only method in the UndoableEditListener interface and Table 43 describes the methods in the UndoableEditEvent class. Note that UndoableEditListener has no corresponding adapter class. Also refer to the UndoableEditListener API documentation at: http://java.sun.com/j2se/1.4.2/docs/api/javax/swing/event/Undoable-

U

Event Listeners

---

[1] The source code, TextComponentDemo.java, is on the CD at: JavaTutorial/uiswing/components/example-1dot4/TextComponentDemo.java.

EditListener.html. The UndoableEditEvent API documentation is online at: http://java.sun.com/j2se/1.4.2/docs/api/javax/swing/event/UndoableEditEvent.html.

Table 42: The UndoableEditListener Interface

Method	Purpose
undoableEditHappened(UndoableEditEvent)	Called when an undoable event occurs on the listened-to component.

Table 43: The UndoableEditEvent Class

Method	Purpose
Object getSource() (*in* java.util.EventObject)	Return the object that fired the event.
UndoableEdit getEdit()	Return an UndoableEdit object that represents the edit that occurred and contains information about and commands for undoing or redoing the edit.

Examples That Use Undoable Edit Listeners

The following table lists the example that uses undoable edit listeners.

Example	Where Described	Notes
TextComponentDemo	Implementing Undo and Redo (page 68)	Implements undo and redo on a text pane with help from an undoable edit listener.

How to Write Window Listeners

This section explains how to implement three kinds of window-related event handlers: `WindowListener`, `WindowFocusListener`, and `WindowStateListener`. All three handle `WindowEvents`. The methods in all three event handlers are implemented by the abstract `WindowAdapter` class.

When the appropriate listener has been registered on a window (such as a frame or dialog), window events are fired just after the window is opened, closed, iconified, deiconified, activated, deactivated, maximized, or restored to normal, or gains or loses the focus. *Opening* a window means showing it for the first time; *closing* it means removing the window from the screen. *Iconifying* it means substituting a small icon on the desktop for the window; *deiconifying* means the opposite. A window is *activated* if it is a frame or a dialog that either is the focused window, or owns the focused window; *deactivation* is the opposite. *Maximizing* the window means increasing its size to the maximum allowable, in either the vertical direction, the horizontal direction, or both.

The `WindowListener` interface defines methods to handle most window events, such as the events for opening and closing the window, activation and deactivation of the window, and iconification and deiconification of the window.

The other two window listener interfaces, `WindowFocusListener` and `WindowStateListener`, were introduced in release 1.4. `WindowFocusListener` contains methods to detect when the window has gained or lost the focus. `WindowStateListener` has a single method to detect a change to the state of the window, such as when the window is iconified, deiconified, maximized, or restored to normal.

Version Note: Prior to release 1.4, focus-gained and focus-lost events were inferred by using the `WindowListener` methods `windowActivated` and `windowDeactivated`. This approach did not work with windows that were not frames or dialogs, because such windows never received those events. To determine a window's iconification, the `ComponentListener` methods `componentHidden` and `componentShown` were used. As of release 1.4, the methods defined in `WindowFocusListener` and `WindowStateListener` are preferred.

While you can use the `WindowListener` methods to detect some window state, such as iconification, there are a couple reasons why a `WindowStateListener` might be preferable: It has only one method for you to implement, and it provides support for maximization.

Note: Not all window managers support all window states. The 1.4 `java.awt.Toolkit` method `isFrameStateSupported(int)`[1] can be used to determine whether a particular window state is supported by a particular window manager. The `WindowEventDemo` example, described later in this section, shows how this method can be used.

A common use of window listeners is implementing custom window-closing behavior. For example, you might use a window listener to save data before closing the window, or to exit the program when the last window closes.

You don't necessarily need to implement a window listener to specify what a window should do when the user closes it. By default, when the user closes a window the window becomes invisible. You can specify different behavior—disposing of the window, for example—using the `JFrame` or `JDialog` `setDefaultCloseOperation` method. If you decide to implement a window-closing handler, then you might want to use `setDefaultCloseOperation(Window-Constants.DO_NOTHING_ON_CLOSE)` to specify that your window listener takes care of all window-closing duties. See How to Make Frames (Main Windows) (page 236) in Chapter 7 for details on how to use `setDefaultCloseOperation`.

Version Note: As of release 1.4, when the last displayable window within the Java Virtual Machine (VM) is disposed of, the VM may terminate. In previous releases, such as 1.3, the VM remained running even if all windows were disposed of. Note, however, that there can be a delay before the program exits automatically, and that under some circumstances the program might keep running. It is quicker and safer to explicitly exit the program using `System.exit(int)`. For more information, see "AWT Threading Issues" online at: `http://java.sun.com/j2se/1.4.2/docs/api/java/awt/doc-files/AWTThreadIssues.html`.

Another common use of window listeners is to stop threads and release resources when a window is iconified, and to start up again when the window is deiconified. This way, you can avoid unnecessarily using the processor or other resources. For example, when a window that contains animation is iconified, it should stop its animation thread and free any large buffers. When the window is deiconified, it can start the thread again and recreate the buffers.

Figure 15 demonstrates window events. A noneditable text area reports all window events that are fired by its window. This demo implements all methods in the `WindowListener`, `WindowFocusListener`, and `WindowStateListener` interfaces. You can find the demo's code in `WindowEventDemo.java`.

---

[1] `isFrameStateSupported(int)` API documentation: `http://java.sun.com/j2se/1.4.2/docs/api/java/awt/Toolkit.html#isFrameStateSupported(int)`.

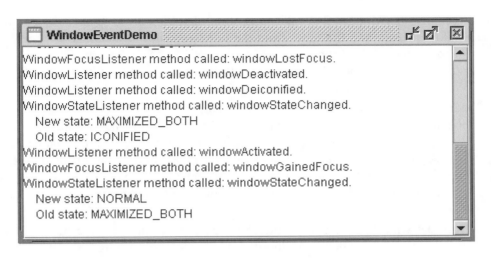

Figure 15 The WindowEventDemo application.

Try This:

1. Run WindowEventDemo using Java Web Start or compile and run the example your-self.[1]

2. When the window appears, several messages are already displayed. One line reports whether your window manager supports MAXIMIZED_BOTH. If your window manager does not support other window states, this is also reported. Next, several lines are displayed reporting that the window's window listener has received window-opened, activated, and gained-focus events. All the messages displayed in the window are also sent to standard output.

3. Click another window. You'll see windowLostFocus and windowDeactivated messages. If this window were not a frame or a dialog, it wouldn't receive the activated or deactivated events.

4. Click the WindowEventDemo window. You'll see windowActivated and window-GainedFocus messages.

5. Iconify the window, using the window controls. Two iconification messages are displayed, one from the window listener and the other from the window state listener, though you won't see them until you deiconify the window, unless looking at standard output. Window-deactivation and window-lost-focus events are also reported.

---

[1] To run WindowEventDemo using Java Web Start, click the WindowEventDemo link on the RunExamples/ events.html page on the CD. You can find the source files here: JavaTutorial/uiswing/events/ example-1dot4/index.html#WindowEventDemo.

W

Event Listeners

6. Deiconify the window. Two deiconification messages are displayed, one from the window listener and the other from the window state listener. The `windowState-Changed` method in `WindowStateListener` gives the same information that you get using the `windowIconified` and `windowDeiconified` methods in `WindowListener`. Window-activation and window-gained-focus events are also reported.

7. Maximize the window, if your look and feel provides a way to do this. Note that some look and feels running on some window managers, such as the Java look and feel on `dtwm`, provide a way to maximize the window, but no events are reported. This is because `dtwm` mimics maximization by resizing the window, but it is not a true maximization event. Some look and feels provide a way to maximize the window in the vertical or horizontal direction *only*. Experiment with your window controls to see what options are available.

8. Close the window, using the window controls. A window-closing message is displayed. Once the window has closed, a window-closed message is sent to standard output.

Here's the demo's window event-handling code:

```
public class WindowEventDemo ... implements WindowListener,
                                             WindowFocusListener,
                                             WindowStateListener {
    static JFrame frame;
    JTextArea display;

    public WindowEventDemo() {
        ...
        frame.addWindowListener(this);
        frame.addWindowFocusListener(this);
        frame.addWindowStateListener(this);

        checkWM();
    }

    //Some window managers don't support all window states.
    //For example, dtwm doesn't support true maximization,
    //but mimics it by resizing the window to be the size
    //of the screen.  In this case the window does not fire
    //the MAXIMIZED_ constants on the window's state listener.
    //Microsoft Windows supports MAXIMIZED_BOTH, but not
    //MAXIMIZED_VERT or MAXIMIZED_HORIZ.
    public void checkWM() {
        Toolkit tk = frame.getToolkit();
        if (!(tk.isFrameStateSupported(Frame.ICONIFIED))) {
            displayMessage(
                "Your window manager doesn't support ICONIFIED.");
        }
```

```java
        if (!(tk.isFrameStateSupported(Frame.MAXIMIZED_VERT))) {
            displayMessage(
                "Your window manager doesn't support MAXIMIZED_VERT.");
        }
        if (!(tk.isFrameStateSupported(Frame.MAXIMIZED_HORIZ))) {
            displayMessage(
                "Your window manager doesn't support MAXIMIZED_HORIZ.");
        }
        if (!(tk.isFrameStateSupported(Frame.MAXIMIZED_BOTH))) {
            displayMessage(
                "Your window manager doesn't support MAXIMIZED_BOTH.");
        } else {
            displayMessage(
                "Your window manager supports MAXIMIZED_BOTH.");
        }
    }

    public void windowClosing(WindowEvent e) {
        displayMessage("WindowListener method called: windowClosing.");

        //A pause so user can see the message before
        //the window actually closes.
        ActionListener task = new ActionListener() {
            boolean alreadyDisposed = false;
            public void actionPerformed(ActionEvent e) {
                if (!alreadyDisposed) {
                    alreadyDisposed = true;
                    frame.dispose();
                } else { //make sure the program exits
                    System.exit(0);
                }
            }
        };
        Timer timer = new Timer(500, task); //fire every half second
        timer.setInitialDelay(2000);        //first delay 2 seconds
        timer.start();
    }

    public void windowClosed(WindowEvent e) {
        //This will only be seen on standard output.
        displayMessage("WindowListener method called: windowClosed.");
    }

    public void windowOpened(WindowEvent e) {
        displayMessage("WindowListener method called: windowOpened.");
    }

    public void windowIconified(WindowEvent e) {
        displayMessage("WindowListener method called: windowIconified.");
    }
```

```
public void windowDeiconified(WindowEvent e) {
    displayMessage("WindowListener method called: " +
                    "windowDeiconified.");
}

public void windowActivated(WindowEvent e) {
    displayMessage("WindowListener method called: windowActivated.");
}

public void windowDeactivated(WindowEvent e) {
    displayMessage("WindowListener method called: " +
                    "windowDeactivated.");
}

public void windowGainedFocus(WindowEvent e) {
    displayMessage("WindowFocusListener method called: " +
                    "windowGainedFocus.");
}

public void windowLostFocus(WindowEvent e) {
    displayMessage("WindowFocusListener method called: " +
                    "windowLostFocus.");
}

public void windowStateChanged(WindowEvent e) {
    displayStateMessage(
        "WindowStateListener method called: windowStateChanged.", e);
}

void displayMessage(String msg) {
    display.append(msg + newline);
    System.out.println(msg);
}

void displayStateMessage(String prefix, WindowEvent e) {
    int state = e.getNewState();
    int oldState = e.getOldState();
    String msg = prefix
                + newline + space
                + "New state: "
                + convertStateToString(state)
                + newline + space
                + "Old state: "
                + convertStateToString(oldState);
    display.append(msg + newline);
    System.out.println(msg);
}
```

```
    String convertStateToString(int state) {
        if (state == Frame.NORMAL) {
            return "NORMAL";
        }
        if ((state & Frame.ICONIFIED) != 0) {
            return "ICONIFIED";
        }
        //MAXIMIZED_BOTH is a concatenation of two bits, so
        //we need to test for an exact match.
        if ((state & Frame.MAXIMIZED_BOTH) == Frame.MAXIMIZED_BOTH) {
            return "MAXIMIZED_BOTH";
        }
        if ((state & Frame.MAXIMIZED_VERT) != 0) {
            return "MAXIMIZED_VERT";
        }
        if ((state & Frame.MAXIMIZED_HORIZ) != 0) {
            return "MAXIMIZED_HORIZ";
        }
        return "UNKNOWN";
    }

    //Where the GUI is initialized:
    ...
    //Create and set up the window.
    frame = new JFrame("WindowEventDemo");
    frame.setDefaultCloseOperation(JFrame.DO_NOTHING_ON_CLOSE);
    ...
}
```

The Window Listener API

Tables 44 through 47 list the methods in the three window listener interfaces and the methods in the WindowEvent class. The methods from all three interfaces are available through the WindowAdapter class. Also refer to the API documentation for these interfaces and class online at:

```
http://java.sun.com/j2se/1.4.2/docs/api/java/awt/event/
        WindowListener.html
http://java.sun.com/j2se/1.4.2/docs/api/java/awt/event/WindowFocus-
        Listener.html
http://java.sun.com/j2se/1.4.2/docs/api/java/awt/event/WindowState-
        Listener.html
http://java.sun.com/j2se/1.4.2/docs/api/java/awt/event/WindowEvent.html
```

Table 44: The WindowListener Interface

Method	Purpose
`windowOpened(WindowEvent)`	Called just after the listened-to window has been shown for the first time.
`windowClosing(WindowEvent)`	Called in response to a user request that the listened-to window be closed. To actually close the window, the listener should invoke the window's `dispose` or `setVisible(false)` method.
`windowClosed(WindowEvent)`	Called just after the listened-to window has closed.
`windowIconified(WindowEvent)` `windowDeiconified(WindowEvent)`	Called just after the listened-to window is iconified or deiconified, respectively.
`windowActivated(WindowEvent)` `windowDeactivated(WindowEvent)`	Called just after the listened-to window is activated or deactivated, respectively. These methods are not sent to windows that are not frames or dialogs. For this reason, we prefer the v1.4 `windowGainedFocus` and `windowLostFocus` methods to determine when a window gains or loses the focus.

Table 45: The WindowFocusListener Interface
(This interface was introduced in release 1.4.)

Method	Purpose
`windowGainedFocus(WindowEvent)` `windowLostFocus(WindowEvent)`	Called just after the listened-to window gains or loses the focus, respectively.

Table 46: The WindowStateListener Interface
(This interface was introduced in release 1.4.)

Method	Purpose
`windowStateChanged(WindowEvent)`	Called just after the listened-to window's state is changed by being iconified, deiconified, maximized, or returned to normal. The state is available through the `WindowEvent` as a bitwise mask. The possible values, defined in `java.awt.Frame`, are: NORMAL: Indicates that no state bits are set. ICONIFIED MAXIMIZED_HORIZ MAXIMIZED_VERT MAXIMIZED_BOTH: Concatenates MAXIMIZED_HORIZ and MAXIMIZED_VERT. A window manager may support MAXIMIZED_BOTH, while not supporting MAXIMIZED_HORIZ or MAXIMIZED_VERT. The `java.awt.Toolkit` method `isFrameStateSupported(int)` can be used to determine what states are supported by the window manager.

Table 47: The WindowEvent Class

Method	Purpose
`Window getWindow()`	Return the window that fired the event. You can use this instead of the `getSource` method.
`Window getOppositeWindow()`	Return the other window involved in this focus or activation change. For a `WINDOW_ACTIVATED` or `WINDOW_GAINED_FOCUS` event, this returns the window that lost activation or the focus. For a `WINDOW_DEACTIVATED` or `WINDOW_LOST_FOCUS` event, this returns the window that gained activation or the focus. For any other type of `WindowEvent` with a Java application in a different VM or context, or with no other window, null is returned. This method was introduced in release 1.4.
`int getOldState()` `int getNewState()`	For `WINDOW_STATE_CHANGED` events these methods return the previous or new state of the window as a bitwise mask. These methods were introduced in release 1.4.

W

Event Listeners

Examples That Use Window Listeners

The following examples use window listeners.

Example	Where Described	Notes
WindowEventDemo	This section	Reports all window events that occur on one window to demonstrate the circumstances under which window events are fired.
SliderDemo	How to Use Sliders (page 348)	Listens for window iconify and deiconify events, so that it can stop the animation when the window isn't visible.
InternalFrameEventDemo	How to Write an Internal Frame Listener (page 670)	Reports all internal frame events that occur on one internal frame to demonstrate the circumstances under which internal frame events are fired. Internal frame events are similar to window events.
DialogDemo	Using Text Components (page 60)	CustomDialog.java uses setDefault-CloseOperation instead of a window listener to determine what action to take when the user closes the window.
Framework	—	A demo that allows multiple windows to be created and destroyed.

APPENDIX

Troubleshooting Reference

THIS appendix contains six troubleshooting references to help you solve common problems.

Java Web Start Troubleshooting

This section discusses problems that you might encounter while using Java Web Start technology. If you don't find the answer to your question or problem here, you might find it in the Java Web Start documentation online at:

```
http://java.sun.com/products/javawebstart/index.html
```

You should also refer to the Java Web Start FAQ. In addition to addressing general questions about installation, licensing, security, and how it works, there's also a troubleshooting section:

```
http://java.sun.com/products/javawebstart/faq.html
```

For the most up-to-date version of *The Java Tutorial*'s Java Web Start troubleshooting section, see:

```
http://java.sun.com/docs/books/tutorial/information/javawebstart.html
```

Problem: My browser seems to find the JNLP file, but Java Web Start says it can't find it.

Solution: This situation usually happens when your browser and your copy of Java Web Start have different proxy settings. To fix this problem:

1. Launch the Java Web Start Application Manager.[1]
2. Choose the File > Preferences menu item.
3. Choose the **General** tab from the window that appears.
4. Set the proxy to a better value. For example, if you're behind a firewall and **Use Browser** is selected, try selecting **Manual** and entering an HTTP proxy server and port (often 8080). If you aren't behind a firewall, try selecting **None**. Or, if **Use Browser** is initially deselected, try selecting it.

Problem: What should I do when Java Web Start reports that the installation is bad?

Solution: The installation is faulty when Java Web Start can't find or launch the Java runtime environment (JRE). The simplest way to fix this problem is to reinstall Java Web Start.

Problem: When I start Java Web Start nothing happens except for a splash screen.

Solution 1: The likely cause of this problem is that you're using a Beta release of JRE 1.3.0 with Java Web Start. You can check what JRE you are using by selecting the **Java** tab on the **Preference** panel (select File > Preferences to open from the Application Manager.) In this case, your best solution is to reinstall a current version.

Solution 2: The cache may be corrupted. You can clear the cache from the **Preferences** panel. Choose the **Advanced** tab and click the **Clear Folder** button.

Problem: Why does my browser show the JNLP file as plain text?

Solution: Most likely your Web server is unaware of the proper MIME type for JNLP files. You must create an association between the file extension, `jnlp`, and the mime type, `application/x-java-jnlp-file`, on your server. The steps for doing this depend on which Web server you're using; you should contact your system administrator for help. In addition, if your network uses proxy servers, ensure that up-to-date versions of files are being returned.

---

[1] You can launch the Application Manager either directly by double-clicking the Java Web Start icon on your computer's desktop or by using your browser to visit a special JNLP file such as the one at: `http://java.sun.com/docs/books/tutorial/information/player.jnlp`.

Problem: What does the "Warning: Failed to verify the authenticity of this certificate. No assertions can be made of the origin or validity of the code." mean?

Solution: A certificate can only be trusted if you trust the certificate authority (CA) that created it. Java Web Start ships with a set of trusted root certificates from the most common CAs. If you sign your application with a certificate that is authorized by someone and is not in the set of trusted root certificates, you will see this warning message; for example this will happen if you use a self-signed certificate. You can see the list of trusted root certificates by choosing the **Root Certificates** tab on the **Preferences** panel. (In the Application Manager, select File > Preferences to open the **Preferences** panel.)

Problem: I cannot seem to access my local system as "localhost" to download resources.

Solution: If you are running in an environment with a proxy server, your system will fail to load the resource. To work around this problem you can either:

- Remove your proxy settings. In the Application Manager, select File > Preferences and choose the **General** tab. Select the Manual proxy and clear both the HTTP proxy and HTTP port settings.
- Use the exact IP address or name of the host: instead of "localhost," for example, `64.124.140.199`.

Problem: How do I trace `System.out` and `System.err` to debug my application?

Solution: In the Application Manager, select File > Preferences and choose the **Advanced** tab. Select the **Show Java Console** option to display all application output to `System.out` and `System.err`. You can also select the **Log Output** option and specify a log file to record the messages.

Solving Common Component Problems

This section discusses problems that you might encounter while using components.

Problem: I'm having trouble implementing a model (or some other code that's similar to something already in Java 2 Platform, Standard Edition).

Solution: Look at the J2SE source code. It's distributed with the J2SE SDK, and it's a great resource for finding code examples of implementing models, firing events, and the like.

Problem: Whenever the text in my text field updates, the text field's size changes.

Solution: You should specify the preferred width of the text field by specifying the number of columns it should have room to display. To do this, you can use either an `int` argument to the `JTextField` constructor or the `setColumns` method.

Problem: Certain areas of the content pane look weird when they're repainted.

Solution 1: If you set the content pane, make sure it's opaque. You can do this by invoking `setOpaque(true)` on your content pane. Note that although `JPanel`s are opaque in most look and feels, that's not true in the GTK+ look and feel, which was introduced in 1.4.2. See Adding Components to the Content Pane (page 48) in Chapter 3 for details.

Solution 2: If one or more of your components perform custom painting, make sure you implemented it correctly. See Solving Common Painting Problems (page 740) for help.

Solution 3: You might have a thread safety problem. See the next problem.

Problem: My program is exhibiting weird symptoms that sometimes seem to be related to timing.

Solution: Make sure your code is thread-safe. See How to Use Threads (page 632) in Chapter 9 for details.

Problem: My modal dialog gets lost behind other windows.

Solution: If the dialog has a null parent component, try setting it to a valid frame or component when you create it. See bug #4255200 for a possible workaround online at: `http://developer.java.sun.com/developer/bugParade/bugs/4255200.html`.

Problem: The scroll bar policies don't seem to be working as advertised.

Solution 1: Some Swing releases contain bugs in the implementations for the `VERTICAL_SCROLLBAR_AS_NEEDED` and the `HORIZONTAL_SCROLLBAR_AS_NEEDED` policies. If feasible for your project, use the most recent release of Swing.

Solution 2: If the scroll pane's client can change size dynamically, the program should set the client's preferred size and then call `revalidate` on the client.

Solution 3: Make sure you specified the policy you intended for the orientation you intended.

Problem: My scroll pane has no scroll bars.

Solution 1: If you want a scroll bar to appear all the time, specify either `VERTICAL_SCROLLBAR_ALWAYS` or `HORIZONTAL_SCROLLBAR_ALWAYS` for the scroll bar policy as appropriate.

Solution 2: If you want the scroll bars to appear as needed, and you want to force the scroll bars to be needed when the scroll pane is created, you have two choices: Either set the preferred size of the scroll pane or its container, or implement a scroll-savvy class and return a value smaller than the component's standard preferred size from the `get-PreferredScrollableViewportSize` method. For more information, refer to Sizing a Scroll Pane (page 336) in Chapter 7.

Problem: The divider in my split pane doesn't move!

Solution: You need to set the minimum size of at least one of the components in the split pane. Refer to Positioning the Divider and Restricting Its Range (page 371) in Chapter 7 for information.

Problem: The setDividerLocation method of JSplitPane doesn't work.

Solution: The setDividerLocation(double) method has no effect if the split pane has no size (typically true if it isn't onscreen yet). You can either use setDividerLocation(int) or specify the preferred sizes of the split pane's contained components and the split pane's resize weight instead. Refer to Positioning the Divider and Restricting Its Range (page 371) in Chapter 7 for information.

Problem: The borders on nested split panes look too wide.

Solution: If you nest split panes, the borders accumulate—the border of the inner split pane displays next to the border of the outer split pane, causing borders that look extra wide. The problem is particularly noticeable when nesting many split panes. The workaround is to set the border to null on any split pane that is placed within another split pane. For information, see bug #4131528 online at: http://developer.java.sun.com/developer/bugParade/bugs/4131528.html.

Problem: The buttons in my tool bar are too big.

Solution: Try reducing the margin for the buttons. For example:

```
button.setMargin(new Insets(0,0,0,0));
```

Problem: The components in my layered pane aren't layered correctly. In fact, the layers seem to be inversed—the lower the depth, the higher the component.

Solution: This can happen if you use an int instead of an Integer when adding components to a layered pane. To see what happens, make the following change to Layered-PaneDemo:

Change this . . .	to this . . .
layeredPane.add(label, new Integer(i));	layeredPane.add(label, i);

Problem: The method call *colorChooser*.setPreviewPanel(null) does not remove the color chooser's preview panel as expected.

Solution: A null argument specifies the default preview panel. To remove the preview panel, specify a standard panel with no size, like this:

```
colorChooser.setPreviewPanel(new JPanel());
```

Problem: I can't make HTML tags work in my labels, buttons, etc.

Solution: Make sure your program is running in a release that supports HTML text in the desired component. See Table 1.

Table 1: Releases That Support HTML in Specific Components

Java 2 Release	Corresponding JFC 1.1 Release	Status of HTML support
J2SE v1.2, v1.2.1	JFC 1.1 (with Swing 1.1)	HTML supported in styled text components only.
J2SE v1.2.2	JFC 1.1 (with Swing 1.1.1)	HTML support added for JButton, JLabel, JMenuItem, JMenu, JCheckBox-MenuItem, JRadioButtonMenuItem, JTabbedPane, and JToolTip. Because table cells and tree nodes use labels to render strings, tables and trees automatically support HTML as well.
J2SE v1.3	None	HTML support added for JToggleButton, JCheckBox, and JRadioButton.

If you can't guarantee that your program will be executed only with a release that supports HTML text in the desired component, *don't use that feature!* See Using HTML in Swing Components (page 43) in Chapter 3 for further details.

Solving Common Layout Problems

Problem: How do I specify a component's exact size?

Solution: First make sure that you really need to set it. Each Swing component has a different preferred size depending on the font it uses and the look and feel. For this reason, it often doesn't make sense to specify a component's exact size.

If the component isn't controlled by a layout manager, you can set its size by invoking the setSize or setBounds method on it. Otherwise, you need to provide size hints and then make sure you're using a layout manager that respects them.

If you extend a Swing component class, you can give size hints by overriding the component's getMinimumSize, getPreferredSize, and getMaximumSize methods. What's nice about this approach is that each get*Xxxx*Size method can get the component's default size hints by invoking super.get*Xxxx*Size(). Then it can adjust the size, if necessary, before returning it.

Another way to give size hints is to invoke a Swing component's setMinimumSize, set-PreferredSize, and setMaximumSize methods.

Note: No matter how you specify your component's size, be sure that its container uses a layout manager that respects the requested size. The FlowLayout, GridBagLayout, and Spring-Layout managers use the component's preferred size (the latter two depending on the constraints you set), but BorderLayout and GridLayout usually don't. The BoxLayout manager generally uses a component's preferred size (although components can be larger) and is one of the few layout managers that respect the component's maximum size. If you specify new size hints for a component that's already visible, you need to invoke the revalidate method on it to make sure that its containment hierarchy is laid out again. Then invoke the repaint method.

Problem: My custom component is being sized too small.

Solution: Does the component implement the getPreferredSize and getMinimumSize methods? If so, do they return the right values? Can your layout manager use as much space as is available? See the section How Layout Management Works (page 97) in Chapter 4 for some tips on choosing a layout manager and specifying that it use the maximum available space for a particular component.

If you don't see your problem in this list, refer to Solving Common Component Problems (page 735).

Solving Common Event-Handling Problems

This section discusses problems that you might encounter while handling events.

Problem: I'm trying to handle certain events from a component, but the component isn't generating the events it should.

Solution 1: First make sure you registered the right kind of listener to detect the events. See whether another kind of listener might detect the kind of events you need.

Solution 2: Make sure you registered the listener on the right object.

Solution 3: Did you implement the event handler correctly? For example, if you extended an adapter class, then make sure you used the right method signature. Check that each event-handling method is `public void`, with the name spelled correctly, and the argument is of the right type.

If you still think that the component isn't generating the events it should, refer to the Java Developer Connection to check whether this is a known bug online at: `http://developer.java.sun.com/developer/bugParade/`.

Problem: My combo box isn't generating low-level events such as focus events.

Solution: Combo boxes are compound components—components implemented using multiple components. For this reason combo boxes don't fire the low-level events that simple components fire. For more information, see How to Use Combo Boxes (page 176) in Chapter 7.

Problem: The document for an editor pane (or text pane) isn't firing document events.

Solution: The `Document` instance for an editor pane or text pane might change when loading text from a URL. Thus, your listeners might be listening for events on an unused document. For example, if you load HTML into an editor pane or text pane that was previously loaded with plain text, the document will change to an `HTMLDocument` instance. If your program dynamically loads text into an editor pane or text pane, make sure the code adjusts for possible changes to the document (reregister document listeners on the new document, and so on).

If you don't see your problem in this list, refer to Solving Common Component Problems (page 735).

Solving Common Painting Problems

Problem: I don't know where to put my painting code.

Solution: Custom painting code usually belongs in the `paintComponent` method of any component descended from `JComponent`. See How Swing Components Are Displayed (page 130) in Chapter 6 for details.

Problem: The stuff I paint doesn't show up.

Solution 1: Check whether your component is showing up at all. Solving Common Component Problems (page 735) should help you with this.

Solution 2: Check whether `repaint` is invoked on your component whenever its appearance needs to be updated.

Problem: The background of my applet shows up, but the foreground stuff doesn't show up.

Solution: Did you make the mistake of performing painting directly in a `JApplet` subclass? If so, then your contents will be covered by the content pane that is automatically created for every `JApplet` instance. Instead, create another class that performs the painting and then add that class to the `JApplet`'s content pane. See Chapter 6, Performing Custom Painting (page 129), for more information on how painting in Swing works.

Problem: My component's foreground shows up, but its background is invisible. The result is that one or more components directly behind my component are unexpectedly visible.

Solution 1: Make sure your component is opaque. `JPanel`s, for example, are opaque by default in many but not all look and feels. To make components such as `JLabel`s and GTK+ `JPanel`s opaque, you must invoke `setOpaque(true)` on them.

Solution 2: If your custom component extends `JPanel` or a more specialized `JComponent` descendant, then you can paint the background by invoking `super.paintComponent` before painting the contents of your component.

Solution 3: You can paint the background yourself using this code at the top of a custom component's `paintComponent` method:

```
g.setColor(getBackground());
g.fillRect(0, 0, getWidth(), getHeight());
g.setColor(getForeground());
```

Problem: I used `setBackground` to set my component's background color, but it seemed to have no effect.

Solution: Most likely, your component isn't painting its background, either because it's not opaque or because your custom painting code doesn't paint the background. If you set the background color for a `JLabel`, for example, you must also invoke `setOpaque(true)` on the label to make the label's background be painted. For more help, see the preceding problem.

Problem: I'm using the exact same code as in a tutorial example, but it doesn't work. Why?

Solution: Is the code executed in the exact same method as in the tutorial example? For example, if the tutorial example has the code in the its `paintComponent` method, then this method might be the only place where the code is guaranteed to work.

Problem: How do I paint thick lines or patterns?

Solution: The Java 2D API provides extensive support for implementing line widths and styles, as well as patterns for use in filling and stroking shapes. For more information on using the Java 2D API, see *The Java Tutorial*'s "2D Graphics" trail on the CD at: `JavaTutorial/2d/index.html`.

Problem: The edges of a particular component look odd.

Solution 1: Did you set the border on a standard component? Because components often update their borders to reflect component state, you generally should avoid invoking setBorder except on JPanels and custom subclasses of JComponent.

Solution 2: Is the component painted by a look and feel such as GTK+ or Windows XP that uses UI-painted borders instead of Border objects? If so, don't invoke setBorder on the component.

Solution 3: Does the component have custom painting code? If so, does the painting code take the component's insets into account?

Problem: Visual artifacts appear in my GUI.

Solution 1: If you set the background color of a component, be sure the color has no transparency if the component is supposed to be opaque.

Solution 2: Use the setOpaque method to set component opacity if necessary. For example, the content pane must be opaque, but components with transparent backgrounds must not be opaque.

Solution 3: Make sure your custom component fills its painting area completely if it's opaque.

Problem: The performance of my custom painting code is poor.

Solution 1: If you can paint part of your component, use the getClip or getClipBounds method of Graphics to determine which area you need to paint. The less you paint, the faster it will be.

Solution 2: If only part of your component needs to be updated, make paint requests using a version of repaint that specifies the painting region. An example of doing this is in the updateSize method in SelectionDemo.[1]

Solution 3: For help on choosing efficient painting techniques, look for the word "performance" in the Java 2D API home page online at: http://java.sun.com/products/java-media/2D/index.html.

---

[1] To run SelectionDemo using Java Web Start, click the SelectionDemo link on the RunExamples/14painting.html page on the CD. You can find the source files here: JavaTutorial/uiswing/14painting/example-1dot4/index.html#SelectionDemo.

Problem: The same transforms applied to seemingly identical `Graphics` objects sometimes have slightly different effects.

Solution: Because the Swing painting code sets the transform (using the `Graphics` method `translate`) before invoking `paintComponent`, any transforms that you apply have a cumulative effect. This doesn't matter when doing a simple translation, but a more complex `AffineTransform`, for example, might have unexpected results.

If you don't see your problem in this list, refer to Solving Common Component Problems (page 735) and Solving Common Layout Problems (page 738).

Solving Common Problems Using Other Swing Features

Problem: My application isn't showing the look and feel that I have requested via `UIManager.setLookAndFeel`.

Solution: You probably either set an invalid look and feel or set your look and feel after the UI manager loaded the default. If you're sure that your look and feel is valid and setting it is the first thing your program does (at the top of its `main` method, for example), check whether you have a static field that references a Swing class. This reference can cause the default look and feel to be loaded if none has been specified. For more information, including how to set a look and feel after the GUI has been created, see the How to Set the Look and Feel (page 628) in Chapter 9.

Problem: Why isn't my component getting the focus?

Solution 1: Is it a custom component (for example, a direct subclass of `JComponent`) that you created? If so, you may need to give it an input map and mouse listener. See Making a Custom Component Focusable (page 592) in Chapter 9 for more information and a demo.

Solution 2: Is the component inside of `JWindow`? The focus system requires a `JWindow`'s owning frame to be visible for any components in the `JWindow` to get the focus. By default, if you don't specify an owning frame for a `JWindow`, an invisible one is created. The solution is either to specify a visible owning frame when creating the `JWindow` or to use a `JDialog` or `JFrame` instead.

Problem: Why can't my dialog receive the event generated when the user presses the Escape key? This worked until I ported to release 1.4.

Solution 1: If your dialog contains a text field, it may be consuming the event. (Prior to release 1.4.0, the text field didn't get the focus.)

Solution 2: If you want to get the Escape event regardless of whether a component consumes it, you should use a `KeyEventDispatcher`.

Solution 3: If you want to get the Escape event only if a component hasn't consumed it, then register a key binding on any `JComponent` in the `JDialog`, using the `WHEN_IN_FOCUSED_WINDOW` input map. For more information, see How to Use Key Bindings (page 623) in Chapter 9.

If you don't find your problem in this section, consult Solving Common Component Problems (page 735).

Index

The JFC Swing Tutorial CD

THE *JFC Swing Tutorial* CD that accompanies this book is loaded with the latest Java™ 2 Software Development Kit, example, and documentation—including the content and code of this book.

Development Kit	Version
Java 2 Platform, Standard Edition *For multiple platforms:* Solaris, Windows, and Linux.	Standard Edition, v1.4.2

Documentation	Version(s)
The Java Tutorial	HTML
The Java Tutorial Examples	—
Java Programming Language API Documentation	v1.4.2
The Swing Connection	PDF

The `README.html` file on the CD is the central HTML page that links you to all of its contents. To view this page, select File > Open (or its equivalent) in your Internet browser. On some platforms, you can simply double click on the HTML file to launch it in your browser.

You can check out the latest Sun Microsystems' Java technology product releases at: `http://java.sun.com/products/index.html`. You can receive free, early access to such products, including the latest Java platform release, if you sign up for the Java Developer Connection at `http://developer.java.sun.com/`.

See this book's Web page at: `http://java.sun.com/docs/books/tutorial/uiswing/index.html` for pointers to the latest versions of this content.

The Java™ Series

 ISBN 0-201-63456-2

 ISBN 0-201-70433-1

 ISBN 0-201-31005-8

 ISBN 0-201-79168-4

 ISBN 0-201-70393-9

 ISBN 0-201-48558-3

 ISBN 0-201-74622-0

 ISBN 0-201-75280-8

 ISBN 0-201-76810-0

 ISBN 0-201-31002-3

 ISBN 0-201-31003-1

 ISBN 0-201-48552-4

 ISBN 0-201-71102-8

 ISBN 0-201-70329-7

 ISBN 0-201-30955-6

 ISBN 0-201-31008-2

 ISBN 0-201-78472-6

 ISBN 0-201-78791-1

 ISBN 0-201-31009-0

 ISBN 0-201-70502-8

 ISBN 0-201-32577-2

 ISBN 0-201-43294-3

 ISBN 0-201-91466-2

 ISBN 0-321-19801-8

 ISBN 0-201-74627-1

 ISBN 0-201-70456-0

 ISBN 0-201-77580-8

 ISBN 0-201-78790-3

 ISBN 0-201-71041-2

 ISBN 0-201-77582-4

 ISBN 0-201-91467-0

 ISBN 0-201-70969-4

 ISBN 0-321-17384-8

Visit www.awprofessional.com/javaseries for more information on these titles.

Register
Your Book

at www.awprofessional.com/register

You may be eligible to receive:

- Advance notice of forthcoming editions of the book
- Related book recommendations
- Chapter excerpts and supplements of forthcoming titles
- Information about special contests and promotions throughout the year
- Notices and reminders about author appearances, tradeshows, and online chats with special guests

Contact us

If you are interested in writing a book or reviewing manuscripts prior to publication, please write to us at:

Editorial Department
Addison-Wesley Professional
75 Arlington Street, Suite 300
Boston, MA 02116 USA
Email: AWPro@aw.com

Visit us on the Web: http://www.awprofessional.com

CD-ROM Warranty

ADDISON-WESLEY warrants the enclosed CD-ROM to be free of defects in materials and faulty workmanship under normal use for a period of ninety days after purchase (when purchased new). If a defect is discovered in the CD-ROM during this warranty period, a replacement CD-ROM can be obtained at no charge by sending the defective CD-ROM, postage prepaid, with proof of purchase to:

> Disc Exchange
> Addison-Wesley Professional
> Pearson Technology Group
> 75 Arlington Street, Suite 300
> Boston, MA 02116
> Email: AWPro@aw.com

Addison-Wesley makes no warranty or representation, either expressed or implied, with respect to this software, its quality, performance, merchantability, or fitness for a particular purpose. In no event will Addison-Wesley, its distributors, or dealers be liable for direct, indirect, special, incidental, or consequential damages arising out of the use or inability to use the software. The exclusion of implied warranties is not permitted in some states. Therefore, the above exclusion may not apply to you. This warranty provides you with specific legal rights. There may be other rights that you may have that vary from state to state. The contents of this CD-ROM are intended for personal use only.

More information and updates are available at:

> http://www.awprofessional.com/